ASHGATE
RESEARCH
COMPANION

THE ASHGATE RESEARCH COMPANION TO POPULAR CULTURE IN EARLY MODERN ENGLAND

ASHGATE
RESEARCH
COMPANION

The *Ashgate Research Companions* are designed to offer scholars and graduate students a comprehensive and authoritative state-of-the-art review of current research in a particular area. The companions' editors bring together a team of respected and experienced experts to write chapters on the key issues in their speciality, providing a comprehensive reference to the field.

The Ashgate Research Companion to Popular Culture in Early Modern England

Edited by

ANDREW HADFIELD
University of Sussex, UK

MATTHEW DIMMOCK
University of Sussex, UK

ABIGAIL SHINN
University of Leeds, UK

ASHGATE

Published by
Ashgate Publishing Limited
Wey Court East
Union Road
Farnham
Surrey, GU9 7PT
England

Ashgate Publishing Company
110 Cherry Street
Suite 3-1
Burlington, VT 05401-3818
USA

www.ashgate.com

British Library Cataloguing in Publication Data
A catalogue record for this book is available from the British Library

Library of Congress Cataloging-in-Publication Data
The Ashgate research companion to popular culture in early modern England / edited by Andrew Hadfield, Matthew Dimmock and Abigail Shinn.
    pages cm
 Includes bibliographical references and index.
 ISBN 978-1-4094-3684-3 (hardcover) – ISBN 978-1-4094-3685-0 (ebook) –
ISBN 978-1-4724-0578-4 (epub) 1. Popular culture–England–History–17th century.
2. England–Social life and customs–17th century. 3. Social classes–England–History–
17th century. 4. Literature and society–England–History–17th century.
I. Hadfield, Andrew. II. Dimmock, Matthew. III. Shinn, Abigail. IV. Title:
Research companion to popular culture in early modern England.
 DA380.A785 2014
 306.094209'03–dc23

2013045830

ISBN 9781409436843 (hbk)
ISBN 9781409436850 (ebk – PDF)
ISBN 9781472405784 (ebk - ePUB)

Printed in the United Kingdom by Henry Ling Limited, at the Dorset Press, Dorchester, DT1 1HD

Contents

List of Figures		*vii*
Notes on Contributors		*ix*
Acknowledgements		*xiii*

Introduction: Thinking About Popular Culture In Early Modern England   1
Matthew Dimmock, Andrew Hadfield and Abigail Shinn

PART I: KEY ISSUES

1	Recovering Speech Acts	13
	Arnold Hunt	
2	Youth Culture	31
	Edel Lamb	
3	Festivals	43
	Tracey Hill	
4	Popular Reading and Writing	59
	Femke Molekamp	
5	Visual Culture	75
	Tara Hamling	
6	Myth and Legend	103
	Angus Vine	
7	Religious Belief	119
	Mike Rodman Jones	

PART II: EVERYDAY LIFE

8	Courtship, Sex and Marriage	133
	Ian Frederick Moulton	
9	Food and Drink	149
	Phil Withington	

10	Work	163
	Mark Netzloff	

11	Gendered Labour	177
	Helen Smith	

12	Crime	193
	Duncan Salkeld	

13	Popular Xenophobia	207
	Matthew Birchwood and Matthew Dimmock	

14	Games	221
	Joachim Frenk	

15	Cultures of Mending	235
	Abigail Shinn	

PART III: THE EXPERIENCE OF THE WORLD

16	Politics	253
	Andrew Hadfield	

17	Riot and Rebellion	267
	Elizabeth Sauer	

18	Time	283
	Neil Rhodes	

19	Property	295
	Ceri Sullivan	

20	Popular Medicine	309
	Margaret Healy	

21	Superstition and Witchcraft	323
	Simon Davies	

22	Military Culture	337
	Rory Rapple	

23	London and Urban Popular Culture	357
	Lawrence Manley	

Index	373

List of Figures

5.1   The Dacre Beasts, *c.* 1525. © Victoria and Albert Museum, London.   80

5.2   Purse, embroidered with heraldic shields, *c.* 1540. © Victoria and Albert Museum, London.   82

5.3   Plasterwork overmantel with the arms of Queen Elizabeth I, formerly in 229 High Street, Exeter, now installed in St Nicholas Priory, Exeter. Author's photograph   84

5.4   View of the interior of ground-floor room in the 'Old Merchants House', Great Yarmouth Row Houses, Norfolk. © English Heritage.   85

5.5   Plasterwork overmantel, late sixteenth century, in first-floor room of 'Harvard House', Stratford-upon-Avon. Author's photograph reproduced by kind permission of The Shakespeare Birthplace Trust.   86

5.6   Plasterwork overmantel formerly in 35 High Street in Stratford-upon-Avon, now installed at Packwood House, Warwickshire. Author's photograph reproduced with permission of National Trust Images.   87

5.7   Illustrations from Randle Holme, *The Academy of Armory* (1688), Book 1, Chapter 6, fol. 55 and Book 2, Chapter 1, fol. 2. These items are reproduced by permission of The Huntington Library, San Marino, California, RB 140916.   89

5.8   Henry Denham's device and imprint (1582). © The British Library Board, E3:1(146) and Titlepage from John King, *Lectures upon Jonas* (1599). This item is reproduced by permission of The Huntington Library, San Marino, California, RB 20866.   90

5.9   Allegorical designs. British Library, Stowe 309, ff. 1v-2. Accessible through the British Library's Catalogue of Illuminated Manuscripts website: http://www.bl.uk/catalogues/illuminatedmanuscripts.   91

5.10   The Lenard Fireback, dated 1636. Anne of Cleves House Museum, Lewes. Reproduced by kind permission of the Sussex Archaeological Society, Barbican House.   93

5.11   Plasterwork overmantel with a scene of the Judgement of Solomon, Barrington Court, Somerset. © National Trust Images.   96

5.12   The Blewett family pew, All Saint's Church, Holcombe Rogus, Devon. Author's photograph.   97

5.13   Moses, Aaron and Hur during the battle against the Amalekites, detail of one of the biblical scenes depicted in the Blewett family pew, All Saint's Church, Holcombe Rogus, Devon. Author's photograph.   97

5.14   Carved exterior of 'Bishop Lloyd's House' in Chester. Author's
        photograph.   98
5.15   Detail of carved exterior of 'Bishop Lloyd's House', Chester.
        Author's photograph.   99

11.1   Anon., *A womans work is never done* (London: for John Andrews, 1660?).
        BL Roxburghe 1.534–535. © The British Library Board.   178
11.2   The Wise and Foolish Virgins, carved alabaster chimneypiece in
        the great hall at Burton Agnes Hall, c. 1610. © The author.   180
11.3   Anon., *Cries of London*, C17th. British Museum 1843, 0311.279.
        © Trustees of the British Museum.   188
11.4   After Marcellus Laroon II, 'Buy any Wax or Wafers', from
        The Cryes of the City of London Drawne after the Life (London:
        Pierce Tempest, 1688). British Museum 1972, U.370.11.
        © Trustees of the British Museum.   189

14.1   Pieter Breugel the Elder's *Children's Games* (1560). By permission
        of the Kunsthistorisches Museum, Vienna.   222

15.1   John Taylor, *The Needles Excellency* (4th ed., London, 1640).
        © The British Library Board. C.31.h.30 (frontispiece).   236

Notes on Contributors

Matthew Birchwood is Senior Lecturer in English Literature at Kingston University, London. His research interests lie in the role of Islam and the East in the literary-political discourses of the seventeenth century. He is author of *Staging Islam in England: Drama and Culture 1640–1685* (2007) and is currently working on a study of toleration and drama in the early Enlightenment.

Simon Davies recently completed a doctorate at the University of Sussex and is currently finishing a monograph on the production and reception of the literature of witchcraft in early modern England. His research interests include witchcraft, the history of the book, the history of reading and seventeenth-century lyric poetry.

Matthew Dimmock is Professor of Early Modern Studies at the University of Sussex. His work focuses on the field of cultural encounter and amongst other publications he is author of *New Turkes: Dramatizing Islam and the Ottomans in Early Modern England* (2005) and *Mythologies of Muhammad in Early Modern English Culture* (2013) and editor of *William Percy's* Mahomet and His Heaven: *A Critical Edition* (2006).

Joachim Frenk is Professor of British Literary and Cultural Studies at the Universität des Saarlandes in Germany. He is co-editor of the *Jahrbuch* of the Deutsche Shakespeare-Gesellschaft, and has published, for example, on early modern authorship, Shakespeare, Jonson, Middleton and Nashe. Other research interests include nineteenth-century literature and culture and the cultural impact of James Bond. His latest book is *Textualised Objects: Material Culture in Early Modern English Literature* (2012).

Andrew Hadfield is Professor of English at the University of Sussex, Visiting Professor at the University of Granada and Vice-Chair of the Society for Renaissance Studies. He is the author of a number of books on the literature and culture of Early Modern England including *Edmund Spenser: A Life* (2012), *Shakespeare and Republicanism* (2005) and *Literature, Travel and Colonial Writing, 1540–1620* (1998). He is also the editor of the *Oxford Handbook to Early Modern Prose, 1500–1640* (2013).

Tara Hamling is Senior Lecturer in the History Department, University of Birmingham. Her research focuses on the visual arts and material culture of early modern Britain, especially in a domestic context. She is author of *Decorating the Godly Household: Religious Art in Post-Reformation Britain* (2010) and editor (with Catherine Richardson) of *Everyday Objects: Medieval and Early Modern Material Culture* (2010) and (with Richard L. Williams) *Art Re-formed: Reassessing the Impact of the Reformation on the Visual Arts* (2007). Her next book, *A Day at Home in Early Modern England: The Materiality of Domestic Life* (co-authored with Catherine Richardson) is forthcoming with Yale University Press.

Margaret Healy is Professor of English at the University of Sussex. She teaches many aspects of Renaissance literature, and is particularly interested in the cultural history of the body and the interfaces among literature, medicine and science. She is the author of *Shakespeare, Alchemy and the Creative Imagination:* The Sonnets *and* A Lover's Complaint (2011); *Fictions of Disease in Early Modern England: Bodies, Plague and Politics* (2001); *Richard II* (1998); and the co-editor of *Renaissance Transformations: The Making of English Writing 1500–1650* (2009). She is literary editor of the British Medical Journal *Medical Humanities.*

Tracey Hill is Head of English & Cultural Studies at Bath Spa University. She is the author of two books: *Pageantry and Power: A Cultural History of the Early Modern Lord Mayor's Show, 1585–1639* (2010), which won the David Bevington Award for the Best Book in Early Drama Studies in 2011, and *Anthony Munday and Civic Culture* (2004). She has also written a number of articles and essays on civic pageantry and early modern drama. Her current research focuses on modes of spectatorship in early modern London.

Arnold Hunt is a Curator of Historical Manuscripts at the British Library, and a Senior Research Fellow at King's College London. His book *The Art of Hearing: English Preachers and Their Audiences 1590–1640* was published by Cambridge University Press in 2010, and his current research focuses on religion and gesture in early modern England.

Mike Rodman Jones is a lecturer in the School of English at the University of Nottingham. He is the author of *Radical Pastoral, 1381–1594: Appropriation and the Writing of Religious Controversy* (2011) and has published a number of articles on later medieval and Tudor writing. He is currently working on a project about literature and medievalism in the sixteenth century.

Edel Lamb is Lecturer in Renaissance Literature at Queen's University Belfast. She previously held an Australian Research Council Fellow at the University of Sydney and an Irish Research Council Fellowship at University College Dublin. She is the author of *Performing Childhood in the Early Modern Theatre: The Children's Playing Companies (1599–1613)* (Palgrave Macmillan, 2008) and of various essays on early modern drama. She is currently writing a monograph on early modern books for children, *Reading Children in Early Modern Culture.*

Lawrence Manley, William R. Kenan, Jr Professor of English at Yale University, is the author of *Convention, 1500–1750* (1980) and *Literature and Culture in Early Modern England* (1995). He has edited *London in the Age of Shakespeare: An Anthology* (1986) and *The Cambridge Companion to the Literature of London* (2010). His most recent book, with Sally-Beth MacLean, is *Lord Strange's Men and Their Plays* (2014).

Femke Molekamp is Global Research Fellow at the Institute of Advanced Study, University of Warwick. She is author of the book *Women and the Bible: Religious Reading and Writing in Early Modern England* (Oxford University Press, 2013) and of essays on the writing and devotional practice of early modern women; and on the history of reading and of the book, especially the Bible. She is currently working on emotion in early modern literature.

Ian Frederick Moulton, Professor of English in Arizona State University's School of Letters and Sciences, is a cultural historian and literary scholar who has published widely on the representation of gender and sexuality in early modern European literature. He is the author of *Before Pornography: Erotic Writing in Early Modern England* (Oxford, 2000), and editor and translator of Antonio Vignali's *La Cazzaria*, an erotic and political dialogue from Renaissance

Italy (Routledge, 2003). He is currently writing a book on the cultural dissemination of notions of romantic love through the book market in sixteenth-century Europe.

Mark Netzloff is an Associate Professor of English at the University of Wisconsin-Milwaukee. He is the author of *England's Internal Colonies: Class, Capital, and the Literature of Early Modern English Colonialism* and the editor of *John Norden's The Surveyor's Dialogue: A Critical Edition*. He is currently finishing a book monograph on the writings of English state agents in early modern Europe.

Rory Rapple is an Assistant Professor in the Department of History at the University of Notre Dame. He is the author of *Martial Power and Elizabethan Political Culture: Military Men in England and Ireland 1558–1594* (2009). He is currently working on a biography of Sir Humphrey Gilbert as well as other topics to do with English political thinking in the sixteenth century.

Neil Rhodes is Professor of English at the University of St Andrews and Visiting Professor at the University of Granada. He is co-general editor of the MHRA *Tudor and Stuart Translations* with Andrew Hadfield and his most recent publication is *English Renaissance Translation Theory* (2013), which appears in that series. He is currently working on a book entitled *Common: The Development of Literary Culture in Sixteenth-Century England.*

Duncan Salkeld is Reader in Shakespeare Studies at the University of Chichester. He is author of *Madness and Drama in the Age of Shakespeare* (Manchester University Press, 1993), *Shakespeare among the Courtesans: Prostitution, Literature and Drama 1500–1650* (Ashgate, 2012) and numerous chapters and articles on Shakespeare and Renaissance drama. He is assistant editor for the New Varorium edition of *Twelfth Night* and writing a book on *Shakespeare and London* for Oxford University Press.

Elizabeth Sauer is Professor of English at Brock University, Canada and winner of a Killam Research Fellowship from the Canada Council for the Arts. Recent publications include *Milton, Toleration, and Nationhood* (2014), *The New Milton Criticism*, co-ed. (2012), *Reading the Nation in English Literature*, co-ed. (2010), *Milton and Toleration*, co-ed. (2007; Milton Society of America book award), *Milton and the Climates of Reading*, ed. (2006; a CHOICE Outstanding Academic Title of the Year); *'Paper-Contestations' and Textual Communities in England* (2005) and *Reading Early Modern Women*, co-ed. (2004), winner of the Society for the Study of Early Modern Women Best Collaborative Work.

Abigail Shinn is currently a teaching fellow in the English department at the University of Leeds. She has previously published on Edmund Spenser and popular culture, most recently in *The Elizabethan Top Ten: Defining Print Popularity in Early Modern England* ed. by Andy Kesson and Emma Smith. Her current monograph project is *Tales of Turning: Conversion Narratives in Early Modern England.*

Helen Smith is Reader in Renaissance Literature at the University of York. She is author of *Grossly Material Things: Women and Book Production in Early Modern England* (Oxford University Press, 2012), winner of the 2013 DeLong SHARP Book Prize and co-editor (with Louise Wilson) of *Renaissance Paratexts* (Cambridge University Press, 2013). Helen was CI on the AHRC-funded project 'Conversion Narratives in Early Modern Europe', and is PI on the AHRC Research Network, 'Imagining Jerusalem, 1099 to the Present Day'. She is currently working on a book-length project on early modern matter and materiality.

Ceri Sullivan is Reader in the School of English, Communication and Philosophy, Cardiff University. Her principal area of interest is in how rhetoric, exchange and prayer produce a micro-politics of resistance to centralised authority in the early modern period. Her latest book is *Literature in the Public Service: Sublime Bureaucracy* (2013).

Angus Vine is Lecturer in Early Modern Literature at the University of Stirling. His research interests include manuscript and textual culture, the works of Francis Bacon and early modern history writing. He is the author of *In Defiance of Time: Antiquarian Writing in Early Modern England* (2010) and the co-editor of Volume 3 of *The Oxford Francis Bacon*, and is also editing Thomas Traherne's student notebook for the new Oxford Texts edition of *Traherne*.

Phil Withington is Professor of History at the University of Sheffield and has published extensively on the social and cultural history of early modern England. Favourite subjects include urbanisation, popular citizenship, militarism and the social history of language. Current projects include an ESRC funded project on 'Intoxicants and Early Modernity' and a social history of the Renaissance.

Acknowledgements

The editors would like to thank Ashgate for inviting us to work on this volume and for making it such a pleasant process: in particular Beatrice Beaup and Lianne Sherlock. The School of English at the University of Sussex very generously paid for the cover image. We are also grateful to our contributors for being such models of professionalism and courtesy. Ashgate's anonymous reader made some very helpful suggestions which improved the quality of the volume.

Introduction:
Thinking About Popular Culture In Early Modern England

Matthew Dimmock, Andrew Hadfield and Abigail Shinn

Literature always gets there first. As Perry Meisel has argued in *The Myth of Popular Culture* any study of popular culture 'should really begin with Dante. Literary history, much earlier than scientific history, invents all the categories for the origins of low and high as ideas'.[1] It may well be the case that distinctions between high and low (popular) culture are exacerbated in the twentieth century, with the advent of mass popular culture produced for and consumed by a working class that had more leisure time than they had had previously, but the division pre-dated the explosion of popular cultural forms of relatively recent times. We do not need the music hall, comic books, Elvis Presley, television, the World Series, blue jeans or internet pornography to enable us to find distinctions between the lofty and the quotidian.

In the early modern period, popular culture was everyone's culture, in Peter Burke's elegant but rather over-used formula.[2] In many ways this was true and it shows how different the early modern world was from its modern counterpart, when highbrow and lowbrow cultures were firmly prised apart. But we might find rather more connections between the early modern and the postmodern world, one in which more educated people enjoy Bob Dylan, wine, Picasso and *The Sopranos*, than high Modernists did Marie Lloyd, Tin Pan Alley and horse racing, as T.S. Eliot rather provocatively acknowledged.[3] The essays included in this *Companion* demonstrate that many exalted people in early modern England appreciated culture also appreciated by those far lower down the social scale. Queen Elizabeth was not alone in enjoying the earthy bodily humour and trickster narratives contained in jest books; bear-baiting, cock-fighting and other sports we now find unspeakably cruel attracted significant audiences in London; many people enjoyed royal pageantry in a variety of ways (as they do today); and women who gathered together to perform everyday tasks, whether the sophisticated embroidery and needlepoint that Mary Queen of Scots and Bess of Hardwick produced, or the more mundane work of village women, developed their own ways of passing the time together. Moreover, the common culture of the church and the shared language of the *Book of Common Prayer* helped to unite and define the language the English spoke and

---

[1]   Perry Meisel, *The Myth of Popular Culture: From Dante to Dylan* (Oxford: Wiley-Blackwell, 2010), p. 10.

[2]   Peter Burke, *Popular Culture in Early Modern Europe* (3rd revised ed., Farnham: Ashgate, 2009), p. 28.

[3]   T.S. Eliot, 'Marie Lloyd', from *Notes towards a Definition of Culture* in *Selected Prose of T.S. Eliot*, ed. Frank Kermode (London: Faber, 1975), pp. 172–4, 292–305.

wrote.[4] And, of course, everyone experienced the same ceremonies of birth, marriage and death even if the substance of their lives were markedly different.[5] Collective rituals were joined by everyday practices such as eating, drinking, speaking, socialising, etc., which were shared by all people, albeit in different forms. This common ground provides the critic with what Fernand Braudel calls 'parahistoric languages', those frequently overlooked aspects of everyday life which not only illuminate our understanding of the past but allow us to find points of continuity with our own experience of the world.[6] Crucially, however, the shared impulses behind such everyday forms of behaviour are complicated by the variety of ways in which they were acted upon. From the differences between eating in an alehouse and being waited upon by servants, to the contrast between the colloquial vernacular and the language of courtly address, it is clear that the everyday is a site of complex variation. Nonetheless, the everyday provides us with a tantalising glimpse of the neutral space where human experiences are held in common, a backdrop which serves to highlight the diverse ways in which culture was produced, developed and appropriated.

The ways in which such neutral spaces might be constructed and idealised can be seen in the choice of cover image for this volume: Joris Hoefnagel's celebrated *Fete at Bermondsey* of around 1570, now in the possession of the Marquis of Salisbury at Hatfield House. Born in Antwerp, Hoefnagel's career took him to Mechlin and Munich before he became court painter to Emperor Rudolf II in Prague and Vienna, and his surviving output demonstrates how adept professional artists in the early modern period needed to be in negotiating changing fashions and the demands of patrons while moving between the different but interconnected marketplaces of high art and of print. The sheer variety of his work demonstrates how skillfully Hoefnagel chartered this terrain, as well as his success in appealing to patrons and finding gainful employment: engraving for cartography, natural history and calligraphy as well as topographical drawings, painted mythological scenes and miniature work.[7]

Even in such a varied body of work, the *Fete at Bermondsey* is unusual. Although some of Hoefnagel's other English work indicates an interest in English landscape and architecture – most prominently his famous depiction of Elizabeth I in an elaborate coach accompanied by guards, courtiers and hounds across a bucolic landscape on their way to Nonsuch Palace – his concern in this painting with the rituals and rites of what are often termed the 'middling sort' and the 'peasantry' rather than the nobility has given this painting a particular status among depictions of Elizabethan England.[8] It is an important source for historians of costume and of food, for instance, and has in the past been treated as an icon of a lost 'merrie England' – arguably the most significant myth of national popular culture that has at times bewitched scholars into eulogising this painting's apparently utopian panorama of class harmony. In contrast, others have insisted that it can only have been commissioned to celebrate an elite which has led them to identify Queen Elizabeth herself in the picture (as

---

[4]   *The Book of Common Prayer*, ed. B.A. Cummings (Oxford: Oxford University Press, 2011).

[5]   David Cressy, *Birth, Marriage & Death: Ritual, Religion, and the Life Cycle in Tudor and Stuart England* (Oxford: Oxford University Press, 1997).

[6]   Fernand Braudel, *The Structures of Everyday Life: The Limits of the Possible, Civilization and Capitalism 15th–18th Century*, trans. Siân Reynolds (London: William Collins, 1981), p. 27.

[7]   Roy Strong, *The English Icon: Elizabethan and Jacobean Portraiture* (London: Routledge & Kegan Paul, 1969), pp. 147–9.

[8]   The Nonsuch image has been most recently discussed in the context of Elizabeth I's gift of a similar coach with Sir Thomas Smith's embassy to the Russian Tsar Boris Godunov in 1604 in Julian Munby, 'The Moscow Coach: A Rich Chariot, One Parcell of the Great Present', in Olga Dmitrieva and Tessa Murdoch eds, *Treasures of the Royal Courts: Tudors, Stuarts & the Russian Tsars* (London: V & A Publishing, 2013), pp. 159–65.

the bride on the right), or, equally implausibly, to suggest that the wedding of Henry VIII and Anne Boleyn is represented.[9]

Accordingly, the multi-layered national mythology into which Hoefnagel's painting has been co-opted is itself a fascinating concoction of high and low cultural elements, resulting from myriad factors including the development of a literary canon around an early modern core; governmental stricture (the place of Shakespeare in the National Curriculum); a nostalgic celebration of naval supremacy and the location of the origins of the British imperium in this period; and an undimmed appetite for popular dramatisation that ranges from televisual reconstruction to 'bodice-ripping' fiction (sometimes both together – witness the popularity of *The Tudors*). However, a careful reading of the painting suggests a different kind of elite/ popular alignment. Rather than the 'fete' of the retrospectively imposed title, most scholars now agree that Hoefnagel presents the moments following a wedding but preceding its accompanying feast, and that it is a bridal party that emerges from the church of St Mary's on the right, led by four huge bride-cakes, two fiddlers and an official cup-bearer carrying a giant spray of rosemary tied with bride-knots and bride-laces in a golden ewer, suggesting that it might be more productively read alongside contemporary European depictions of marriage feasts, such as Pieter Bruegel the Elder's 'The Peasant Wedding' (1567).[10] Many of Hoefnagel's party carry the traditional wedding gift of scented white gloves. As they emerge they pass a table set for the feast and beyond it an open kitchen in which considerable cuts of meat are roasted and ovens are emptied of their contents by serving-men and women; as they process they are greeted by a large group of foregrounded figures, presumably guests for the feast.[11] The detail and colours of the clothing of this group and their specific postures delineate social status far more precisely for an early modern observer than for a twenty-first-century one, and although all are in their 'Sunday best', some are clearly household servants while others – most notably the cloaked and high-hatted man in the mid-foreground, and the cluster of finely dressed figures standing before a hawk-carrying rider behind, and those to the far left – bear the accoutrements of at least minor gentry.

The suggestion that Hoefnagel's painting represents an undifferentiated group festivity in which popular and elite intermingle through a shared ritual language of cakes, rosemary and ribbons is a fiction: unlike, for example, Breugel's *Children's Games* (1560) discussed by Joachim Frenk in this volume, social hierarchies are very deliberately delineated. The ordering of the scene is even more pronounced as the viewer's eye moves from the foreground to the rear of the image. The primary group are minutely detailed and bathed in light while others are blurred and darkened; there are those excluded from celebrating but who look on, such as the two figures who gaze from the upstairs windows of the feast-hall, the man who watches from the stocks, or those who carry platters stacked with food; and there are those further back who are apparently oblivious to the wedding, some who carry goods, another who leads a team of horses drawing a waggon, others who practise archery (required of all able-bodied men by law every Sunday) and finally those engaged in boatbuilding in the far background. These anonymised figures are not merely decorative. The labour through which they are defined supports the vision of prosperous order that the painting celebrates, a vision framed and authorised by the presence of state and church

9   As described by F.M. Kelly in 'A Horselydown Wedding', in *The Burlington Magazine* no. 174, vol. 31 (September 1917), 89–91.

10   For further context, see also Ian Moulton's chapter later in this volume on 'Courtship, Sex and Marriage', pp. 133–48.

11   The food and associated ritual elements of the painting have been closely analysed by Ivan Day chapter's 'Bridecup and Cake: The Ceremonial Food and Drink of the Bridal Procession', in Laura Mason ed., *Food and the Rites of Passage* (Totnes: Prospect Books, 2002), pp. 33–61. But see also Phil Withington's chapter later in this volume on 'Food and Drink', pp. 149–62.

embodied in the Tower of London and St Mary's church in the background on left and right. This is all the more striking given that English society was undergoing a 'crisis of labour' in this period, as Mark Netzloff observes in Chapter 10, and the role of these labourers is reinforced by the harnessing of potentially disruptive energies – in the modesty of the women present (even in the wetnurse swaddling an infant in luxurious red cloth), the chivalry of the central soldier, the absence of alcohol or drunkenness, the constraint of the three dogs, the role of the stocks and in the work of everyone else. Hoefnagel's Bermondsey painting – no doubt bought, if not commissioned, by a wealthy individual given its likely cost and current location – in this way uses the fiction of the everyday to allow popular culture to be inhabited, or at least co-opted, by elements of an English elite.

Hoefnagel's image gives us a particularly good idea of a festival or holiday, the celebratory events that punctuated people's hard-working lives in an era before leisure and travel transformed the nature of the holiday.[12] Prominent in the bottom right of the painting are two red-coated fiddlers whose playing accompanies the festivities and the entry of the wedding party (there are two more positioned before the feast in the background). Such forms of musical entertainment would have been part of everyday life throughout the year, with musical skills and popular tunes passed between individuals and generations, and rooted in local communities. Ballads provide particularly good evidence of music practices. It is clear that many different ballads borrowed the same tune, indicating that the music was at least as important a popular form as the printed words.[13] Furthermore, such literature was never class specific. As Tessa Watt points out, 'scores of contemporary references in plays, diaries, and polemical tracts indicate the ubiquity of the ballad at all social levels'.[14] Different social groups may have not always listened to the same music, but the enjoyment of popular music and dance united as well as separated classes, as the relevant sections in the chapters by Rory Rapple, Lawrence Manley and Tracey Hill demonstrate.[15]

As this complex image shows, and as the earlier example of women's work further indicates, culture could often be divisive. It is unlikely that the court music of Thomas Tallis, William Byrd and John Taverner was heard and appreciated by the masses who enjoyed singing together, nor that courtly dance fashions were precisely imitated at the numerous festivals and holidays that defined the year even after the Reformation restricted many of them. Literacy was undoubtedly more widespread than was once thought, which suggests that books were more widely disseminated, even if not actually owned, and reading practices were more routinely shared.[16] But, while many had a shared interest in jest books, romance and other modes of popular culture, the common belief, which persisted until the seventeenth century, that plays were inferior forms of writing shows that distinctions between high and low culture were certainly in operation. If we turn to the divergent forms of political culture the assumptions are more pronounced still, with the upper classes envisaging political culture in terms of pageantry and diplomacy: those further down the scale co-opting cultural forms, such as the figure of Piers the Plowman, to articulate

---

[12]   On early modern conceptions of the holiday and its subversive potential see Alison A. Chapman, 'Whose Saint Crispin's Day Is It? Shoemaking, Holiday Making, and the Politics of Memory in Early Modern England', *Renaissance Quarterly* 54:4 (2001), 1467–94.

[13]   Sandra Clark, *Women and Crime in the Street Literature of Early Modern England* (Basingstoke: Palgrave, 2003), p. 73.

[14]   Tessa Watt, *Cheap Print and Popular Piety, 1550–1640* (Cambridge: Cambridge University Press, 1991), p. 12.

[15]   See below, pages 337–56; 357–71; and 43–58 respectively.

[16]   See Watt, *Cheap Print* and Lori Humphrey Newcomb, 'What Is a Chapbook?', in Matthew Dimmock and Andrew Hadfield eds, *Literature and Popular Culture in Early Modern England* (Farnham: Ashgate, 2009), pp. 57–72.

opposition to the prevailing hegemony.[17] If culture were so obviously united then there would surely have been no need to turn the world upside down and suspend the prevailing order for the performance of the carnival, whether we think that was designed to contain or co-opt the potential opposition of the dispossessed.[18]

It should not surprise us that culture was divided then as now, nor that there were various forms of culture wars. All periods have an uneasy balance of shared and antagonistic forms of cultural production, as well as divided modes of reading and consuming culture. The problem is finding, retrieving and interpreting the evidence in order to produce a balanced and accurate picture. It was once thought that ballads were the authentic expression of a wider popular culture that had then been collected by disinterested observers in the eighteenth century. But it was then realised that many ballads were, in fact, the product of more established writers, even if they were responding to original popular forms. The evidence was unclear, contaminated and misleading. As René Wellek and Austin Warren put it, 'Though this is a view that would have shocked the Romantic believers in the creativity of the folk and the remote antiquity of folk art, nevertheless popular ballads, fairy tales, and legends as we know them are frequently of late origin and upper-class derivation'.[19] Research into the origins of the fairy tales collected by the Grimm brothers discovered that many were not gathered during field trips to remote provinces of Germany, but narrated by servants in wealthy households, another sign that the testimony of the past might lead us to rather less authentic voices than had been realised. The resulting nervousness about the ephemeral nature of popular culture – a quarry which always seems to recede into the distance – has brought into question the validity and usefulness of the term. It has subsequently been argued, particularly in relation to print culture, that the creation of the 'popular' as a category began in the early modern period as an ideologically inflected act of classification, and that it is impossible to escape the mediation of the elite when searching for its contents.[20] It is, however, the very slipperiness of the 'popular', and the frequently problematic nature of its evidence which renders it a subject of intense curiosity and scrutiny. Moreover, scepticism about the authenticity of recovered popular forms has led to fruitful discussion as to the relationship between the consumption and production of popular culture. For Roger Chartier this results in a reading of popular culture as a 'specific relation with cultural objects', and he argues that instead of identifying and distinguishing 'cultural sets' we should look to how common material was productively consumed, creating 'ways of using that cannot be limited to the intentions of those who produce'.[21] It is to this nuanced approach to cultural consumption and production that Helen Smith looks in her chapter on

---

[17]   Ethan Shagan, *Popular Politics and the English Reformation* (Cambridge: Cambridge University Press, 2003); Andy Wood, *The 1549 Rebellions and the Making of Early Modern England* (Cambridge: Cambridge University Press, 2007); Tim Harris ed., *The Politics of the Excluded, c.1500–1850* (Basingstoke: Palgrave, 2001).

[18]   Mikhail Bakhtin, *Rabelais and His World*, trans. Hélène Iswolsky (Bloomington: Indiana University Press, 1984); Christopher Hill, 'The Many-Headed Monster in Late Tudor and Early Stuart Political Thinking', in Charles H. Carter ed., *From Renaissance to the Counter-Reformation: Essays in Honour of Garrett Mattingly* (New York: Random House, 1965), pp. 296–324.

[19]   René Wellek and Austin Warren, *Theory of Literature* (3rd ed., Harmondsworth: Penguin, 1978, rpt. of 1963), p. 47.

[20]   Garrett Sullivan and Linda Woodbridge, 'Popular Culture in Print', in Arthur F. Kinney ed., *The Cambridge Companion to English Literature, 1500–1600* (Cambridge: Cambridge University Press, 2000), pp. 265–86.

[21]   Roger Chartier, 'Culture as Appropriation: Popular Cultural Uses in Early Modern France', in Steven Kaplan ed., *Understanding Popular Culture: Europe from the Middle ages to the Nineteenth Century* (New York: Mouton Publishers, 1984), pp. 229–53, at p. 234.

women's work when she argues that ballad culture not only reflects attitudes to women's labour but also the labour that goes into the making of popular culture's objects.[22]

These, at least, are cases in which the nature of the evidence can be analysed and considered, even if the surviving objects are found wanting as expressions of a *volksgeist*. The more serious problem with popular culture is that, in times when so many people were unable to sign their names, even if they were not without some ability to read, very little remains of many popular cultural forms and acts. As Arnold Hunt notes in his chapter on speech acts, early modern culture was an oral culture which we have no choice but to try and excavate from written sources. To return to an earlier example, it is frustrating that so little survives of the popular culture created by women working together, leaving critics reliant upon elite sources for evidence, as is exampled by Abigail Shinn's use of the Tudor comedy *Gammer Gurton's Needle* as a starting point for her chapter on mending. The same can be said of so many forms of music, dance, festivals and carnivals, and sports and games. When something does survive, such as the ballad *Pardonnez moi, je vous en prie*, analysed by Rory Rapple in his chapter on military culture, we have to construct its meaning through an understanding of its possible context, something that often has to be constructed from a very small sample of evidence, sometimes just the item of popular culture itself. Here, through a piece of startling ingenuity, Professor Rapple tries to recreate the aggressive and confrontational nature of the apparently polite French address, which survives only in a song by the composer, Thomas Ravenscroft, who places the words in the mouths of demobbed soldiers forcing companions and strangers to stand them drinks.[23] The example is especially interesting for a number of reasons. First, it shows how potent the threat from soldiers was, even in cities, and brings home to us the constant fear that early modern people had of underpaid, over-armed soldiers who felt – with some justification – that they were owed a living.[24] Second, we understand that things cannot be taken at face value and we need to read the ways in which evidence survives with scrupulous care if we are to make any sense of its significance in reconstructing early modern life. Third, we realise how delicate and problematic evidence is, and that there will always be a danger of over, under or misreading what has survived. Tara Hamling's chapter on visual culture raises similar issues: can we reconstruct the interior of the ordinary early modern house with any degree of accuracy? What do the remains of material culture tell us? And what can we assume about the objects chosen and where they were placed? Furthermore, can we infer how objects and environments produced different forms of sociability?[25] Again, scholars have to be on their guard, imaginative and sceptical at the same time. Reading popular culture is a demanding task and an invigorating challenge, one that cannot be ignored if we wish to make sense of the world in which our ancestors lived.

The chapters in this *Companion* have been selected in order to reflect these challenges. The aim has been to build up a series of studies which rather than shying away from the elusive nature of the 'popular', embrace the complexity and richness of critical debate in the field. As Natalie Zemon Davis has argued, unresolved critical arguments are just as

---

[22]   See also Tara Hamling and Catherine Richardson eds, *Everyday Objects: Medieval and Early Modern Material and Its Meanings* (Farnham: Ashgate, 2010) and Joachim Frenk, *Textualised Objects: Material Culture in Early Modern English Literature* (Heidelberg: Winter, 2012).

[23]   See below p. 337.

[24]   See A.L. Beier, *Masterless Men: The Vagrancy Problem in England, 1560–1640* (London: Methuen, 1985).

[25]   See also Tara Hamling, *Decorating the 'Godly' Household: Religious Art in Post-Reformation Britain* (New Haven: Yale University Press, 2010) and Hazel Forsyth with Geoff Egan eds, *Toys, Trifles & Trinkets: Base-Metal Miniatures from London 1200–1800* (London: Unicorn Press, 2005).

important as consensus when identifying 'patterns of meaning' in cultural forms.[26] The result is a collection which not only looks at the variety of practices, behaviours and experiences which can be claimed as 'popular', but proposes new ways of approaching popular culture as a category for analysis.

The *Companion* has been divided into three sections, Key Issues, Everyday Life and The Experience of the World. Key Issues aims to explore themes which are central to our understanding of early modern culture which are also hotly contested sites for the excavation of the 'popular'. In order to offer a broad but integrated approach the chapters span a range of issues, from speech acts, reading and writing, youth culture and religious belief, to festivals, myths and visual culture. This section challenges prevailing assumptions about how we approach fundamental aspects of popular culture, while simultaneously providing a useful overview of the current historiography in the field. Furthermore, by asking important questions about methodology, particularly the ways in which we categorise cultural objects, the chapters in Key Issues complicate our use of historical sources and highlight problems of cultural transmission. This includes discussions about the difficulty of assessing different forms and levels of literacy, the problems inherent in tracing the parameters of religious belief and the pitfalls involved in any attempt at recovering the spoken word. The sources used by the writers in this section include the records of Stuart parliaments, sermons, Bibles, chapbooks, pamphlets, heraldry, classical myths, saints' lives, Biblical imagery and drama. The breadth and scope of these sources testifies to the discursive nature of cultural forms while also highlighting the multifaceted approach demanded by any study of popular culture.

The section Everyday Life looks to the variety of behaviours which make up the routines and practices of quotidian experience. In uncovering attitudes towards the processes of day-to-day life as experienced by the majority of early modern people, this section brings to the fore the shared concerns and preoccupations of bodies-in-the-world. These include the rituals and practices associated with courtship, sex and marriage, attitudes towards work and gendered labour, the social importance of food and drink, the impact and management of crime, the language of xenophobia, the sociability promoted by games and the necessary and ubiquitous tools of mending. Given the ephemeral nature of these processes this section highlights the creative and unusual methods which can be employed by researchers when trying to locate evidence for the everyday. The resulting studies include an exploration of the economic and social implications of an argument over herring in an alehouse; an examination of a fictional labourer's despair at the loss of a needle as an indicator of attitudes towards the manufacture and dissemination of haberdashery items; a discussion of English attitudes towards foreigners which looks to the varying lexical registers applied to descriptions of Inuit tribes people; and an account of the organised violence of football games which highlights the links between leisure pursuits and military activity. In many cases arguments have to be made for the significance of silences in the historical record, for example the lack of any acknowledgement of particular sexual practices in early modern literature, the difficulty in locating a language of difference in an unstable and constantly shifting cultural environment and the absence of surviving textiles which show evidence of darning and patching.

The section Experience of the World looks at the importance of prevailing cultural structures and apparatus to the early modern understanding of the world, with the aim of exploring how people engaged with, and questioned, shared social constructs and attitudes at a popular level. These include studies of politics, time, property ownership,

---

[26]   Natalie Zemon Davis, 'Towards Mixtures and Margins', *American Historical Review* 97 (1992), 1409–16, at p. 1415.

medicine, riot and rebellion, superstition and witchcraft, urban life and military culture. These chapters explore accounts of shared practices and behaviours in order to analyse how people experienced the world in which they lived. These include the dominance of the figure of the ploughman in popular political discourse; the relationship of paper-based conflicts to acts of rebellion; the widespread and surprisingly mundane practices associated with witchcraft; and the importance of the changing seasons for people's relationship with the calendar year – not least because it can be difficult finding your way home in the dark. A particular focus is placed upon how people both challenged and accepted prevailing norms and hierarchies through a variety of means. For example the circulation of petitions and satirical ballads and resistance to changes in the calendar and ritual year.

This *Companion* embraces popular culture as a contested, complex, frustratingly elusive, but nonetheless essential, topic of study. Without searching for its structures and objects we would be left with a dangerously incomplete picture of how people lived. While this picture will always remain indistinct, our attempts to fill in the gaps illuminate our understanding of early modern England as a world in which cultural forms were incredibly mobile and sensitive to circumstances. In proffering a rich body of evidence for cultural practices and behaviours we have endeavoured to demonstrate that popular culture can be explored in interesting and surprising ways, and that the difficulties inherent in our use of the historical record in fact strengthen the intellectual premises behind our pursuit for the less tangible aspects of the past.

Select Bibliography

Bakhtin, Mikhail, *Rabelais and His World*, trans. Hélène Iswolsky. Bloomington: Indiana University Press, 1984.

Book of Common Prayer, ed. B.A. Cummings. Oxford: Oxford University Press, 2011.

Braudel, Fernand, *Civilization and Capitalism 15th–18th Century*, trans. Siân Reynolds. 3 vols. London: William Collins, 1981.

Burke, Peter, *Popular Culture in Early Modern Europe*. 3rd revised ed. Farnham: Ashgate, 2009.

Cressy, David, *Birth, Marriage & Death: Ritual, Religion, and the Life Cycle in Tudor and Stuart England*. Oxford: Oxford University Press, 1997.

Davis, Natalie Zemon, 'Towards Mixtures and Margins', *American Historical Review* 97 (1992), 1409–16.

Dimmock, Matthew, and Andrew Hadfield eds, *Literature and Popular Culture in Early Modern England*. Farnham: Ashgate, 2009.

Forsyth, Hazel, with Geoff Egan eds, *Toys, Trifles & Trinkets: Base-Metal Miniatures from London 1200–1800*. London: Unicorn Press, 2005.

Frenk, Joachim, *Textualised Objects: Material Culture in Early Modern English Literature*. Heidelberg: Winter, 2012.

Hamling, Tara, *Decorating the 'Godly' Household: Religious Art in Post-Reformation Britain*. New Haven: Yale University Press, 2010.

Hamling, Tara, and Catherine Richardson eds, *Everyday Objects: Medieval and Early Modern Material and Its Meanings*. Farnham: Ashgate, 2010.

Kaplan, Steven ed., *Understanding Popular Culture: Europe from the Middle Ages to the Nineteenth Century*. New York: Mouton Publishers, 1984.

Meisel, Perry, *The Myth of Popular Culture: From Dante to Dylan*. Oxford: Wiley-Blackwell, 2010.

Sullivan, Garrett, and Linda Woodbridge, 'Popular Culture in Print', in Arthur F. Kinney ed., *The Cambridge Companion to English Literature, 1500–1600*, Cambridge: Cambridge University Press, 2000, pp. 265–86.

Watt, Tessa, *Cheap Print and Popular Piety, 1550–1640*. Cambridge: Cambridge University Press, 1991.

PART I
Key Issues

Recovering Speech Acts

Arnold Hunt

In the beginning was the word – that is, the spoken word. In the early modern period, anyone with even the most basic familiarity with the Bible knew that the world had been brought into being by an act of speech: 'God said, Let there be light: and there was light' (Genesis 1:3). In one of the most famous textual emendations of the Renaissance, Erasmus had translated the Greek word *logos* (John 1:1) into Latin as 'sermo' rather than 'verbum' in order to emphasise that the divine Word was a spoken utterance, not merely a tacit concept in the mind of God.[1] Even the written word of scripture was perceived in oral terms as a form of divine speech: thus John Donne could declare in a sermon that 'the Scriptures are God's Voyce; the Church is his Eccho; a redoubling, a repeating of some particular syllables, and accents of the same voice'.[2] In that sense God's *sermo*, his original speech act, had never died away but was constantly repeated whenever the scriptures were read or preached.

At its intellectual heart, therefore, early modern culture was an oral culture. This had repercussions well beyond theology. To early modern political theorists, it was speech that distinguished man from the animals and made human society possible. Man was a social creature, wrote the Dutch philosopher Hugo Grotius, and it was to gratify this innate desire for society that 'he alone among animals possesses a special instrument, speech' (*sermo*, the same word that Erasmus had used).[3] Thomas Hobbes extolled speech as:

> the most noble and profitable invention of all other ... whereby men register their
> Thoughts; recall them when they are past; and also declare them one to another
> for mutuall utility and conversation; without which, there had been amongst men,
> neither Common-wealth, nor Society, nor Contract, nor Peace, no more than amongst
> Lyons, Bears, and Wolves.[4]

All social and political relationships were, fundamentally, speech relationships, forming what was called 'civil conversation' (the term 'conversation' in this period having a broader application than it does today, referring not just to verbal exchanges but to the whole sphere

---

[1]   Among many discussions, see especially Marjorie O'Rourke Boyle, *Erasmus on Language and Method in Theology* (Toronto: University of Toronto Press, 1977), pp. 3–31, and Terence Cave, *The Cornucopian Text: Problems of Writing in the French Renaissance* (Oxford: Clarendon Press, 1979), p. 86.

[2]   Sermon on Matthew 19:17, preached at Whitehall, 4 March 1624–5: Donne, *Sermons*, ed. George Potter and Evelyn Simpson (Berkeley and Los Angeles: University of California Press, 1953–62), VI.223.

[3]   Hugo Grotius, *On the Law of War and Peace*, ed. Stephen C. Neff (Cambridge: Cambridge University Press, 2012), p. 3.

[4]   Thomas Hobbes, *Leviathan*, ed. Richard Tuck (Cambridge: Cambridge University Press, 1996), p. 24 ('Of Speech').

of social interaction and behaviour), and could again be seen as echoes of God's original speech act, as Hobbes made clear in the opening pages of *Leviathan* when he likened the pacts and covenants that comprised the body politic to 'that *Fiat*, or the *Let us make man*, pronounced by God in the Creation'.[5]

We are still profoundly, if unconsciously, influenced by these ideas: for example, we tend to assume that speech is primary, writing secondary (this, famously, being one of the 'phonocentric' or 'logocentric' assumptions that Derrida sought to deconstruct). At the same time we no longer live in such an intensely speech-dominated world, and the early modern tendency to think of the world in oral terms, or through oral metaphors, no longer comes so naturally to us. It is telling that Grotius's Victorian editor William Whewell translated 'sermo' as 'language', missing the particular emphasis on *spoken* language.[6] In short, we think of language where the early modern period thought of speech: and there is now a substantial body of scholarship which seeks to explain how the spoken word, heard with the ear rather than read with the eye, lost its distinctive place in the early modern sensorium. This profound cultural change, conveniently symbolised by the invention of printing and the spread of literacy, was expounded by Marshall McLuhan in *The Gutenberg Galaxy* (1962) and, less oracularly, by McLuhan's pupil Walter Ong in *Orality and Literacy* (1982).[7] Briefly put, Ong's argument was that 'writing restructures consciousness' by transferring speech from the oral/aural into the new sensory world of vision. Oral discourse requires the presence of a speaker and a listener, whereas written words can be detached from their context. Speech unites people in groups, whereas reading and writing are solitary and introspective activities. Oral recitation is capable of endless variation and enlargement, whereas written texts are stable and permanent, fixed in visual space and giving the impression (or illusion) of closure and completeness.

It is hard to tell this story of the transition from orality to literacy except as a story of loss and absence. For the cultural theorist Michel de Certeau it was a story of the death of God, experienced as the inability to hear God's voice speaking in the Scriptures:

> Before the 'modern' period, that is, until the sixteenth or seventeenth century, this writing (Holy Scripture) speaks. The sacred text is a voice ... For reasons analyzed elsewhere, the modern age is formed by discovering little by little that this Spoken Word is no longer heard ... The voice that today we consider altered or extinguished is above all that great cosmological Spoken Word that we notice no longer reaches us: it does not cross the centuries separating us from it. There is a disappearance of the places established by a spoken word, a loss of the identities that people believed they received from a spoken word.[8]

---

[5]   Hobbes, *Leviathan*, p. 10. On civil conversation, see Phil Withington, *The Politics of Commonwealth: Citizens and Freemen in Early Modern England* (Cambridge: Cambridge University Press, 2005).

[6]   Hugo Grotius, *De Jure Belli et Pacis*, ed. William Whewell (Cambridge: Cambridge University Press, 1853), vol. 1, p. xliii.

[7]   Marshall McLuhan, *The Gutenberg Galaxy* (Toronto: University of Toronto Press, 1962); Walter J. Ong, *Orality and Literacy: The Technologizing of the Word* (London: Methuen, 1982; reprinted London: Routledge, 1988).

[8]   Michel de Certeau, 'The Scriptural Economy', in *The Practice of Everyday Life*, trans. Steven Rendall (Berkeley and Los Angeles: University of California Press, 1984), p. 137. See also Leigh Eric Schmidt, *Hearing Things: Religion, Illusion, and the American Enlightenment* (Cambridge, MA: Harvard University Press, 2000), pp. 28–9.

The study of the past thus becomes an act of aural recovery, summed up in Stephen Greenblatt's ringing declaration: 'I began with the desire to speak with the dead.'[9] This has particular resonance for the study of popular culture, because of the way that the world of 'the people' has so often been associated with oral culture and tradition, in contrast to the literate culture of the élite. From the nineteenth-century antiquarians who sought to salvage a disappearing tradition of folksongs and folktales to the twentieth-century historians who sought to write 'history from below' by recovering the silenced voices of ordinary people, much of the impetus for the study of popular culture has come from a powerful sense of the world we have lost.

Yet the cultural divide between orality and literacy no longer commands universal assent. The idea of the 'great divide' may be applicable to oral cultures encountering written texts for the first time, but makes less sense when applied to early modern societies where orality and literacy co-existed. It cannot easily accommodate the practice of reading aloud, a crucial means for the illiterate to gain access to written and printed texts but one which, as Joyce Coleman points out, has tended to be neglected because it occupies a 'historical and conceptual middle space' between the two poles of orality and literacy.[10] Ong is careful to qualify suggestions of a 'great divide' by stressing that the transition from orality to literacy was a gradual process occurring over centuries, but there is a deep-seated problem with his characterisation of the oral elements of early modern rhetoric and prose style as an 'oral residue' carried over into an otherwise literate culture. Oral and literate culture were so inseparably joined together in this period that it makes little sense to think of one as a diminishing residue inside the other. In many respects oral culture was actually strengthened by literate culture, as in the case of ballad-singing, which seems to have been reinvigorated in the later sixteenth century by the wider circulation of written and printed ballad texts. The still more schematic idea that an 'age of the ear' gave way to an 'age of the eye' has been challenged by numerous studies showing the continuing importance of the spoken word and suggesting, as Daniel Woolf has argued, that early modern culture was perfectly capable of maintaining a 'perceptual equilibrium' between sight and hearing.[11] Indeed, many contemporaries rated hearing as the more discriminating of the two senses: early modern playwrights, for example, preferred to think of themselves as writing for an educated 'audience' rather than mere 'spectators'.[12]

It was not uncommon in early modern England for social differences to be expressed in terms of speech differences: witness the distinction drawn by William Harrison in his *Description of England* between the 'great silence' at the tables of the gentry and the 'babbling' among their social inferiors.[13] Reconstructing the evidence of popular speech can therefore be a helpful way to approach the concept of popular culture. In order to make sense of this evidence, however, we need to abandon the binary opposition between the old (pre-modern) world of orality and the new (modern) world of literacy. It is perfectly

---

[9]   Stephen Greenblatt, *Shakespearean Negotiations* (Berkeley and Los Angeles: University of California Press, 1988), p. 1.

[10]   Joyce Coleman, *Public Reading and the Reading Public in Late Medieval England and France* (Cambridge: Cambridge University Press, 1996), p. 2.

[11]   D.R. Woolf, 'Speech, Text, and Time: The Sense of Hearing and the Sense of the Past in Renaissance England', *Albion* 18:2 (1986), 159–93, reprinted (slightly abridged) as 'Hearing Renaissance England', in Mark M. Smith ed., *Hearing History: A Reader* (Athens, GA: University of Georgia Press, 2004), pp. 112–35.

[12]   Andrew Gurr, *Playgoing in Shakespeare's London* (2nd ed., Cambridge: Cambridge University Press, 1996), pp. 86–98.

[13]   William Harrison, *The Description of England*, ed. George Edelen (Ithaca, NY: Folger Shakespeare Library, 1968), p. 132.

true that by the early modern period, the written and printed word had penetrated to every level of English society, so that it is virtually impossible to identify a pure oral tradition untouched by print. But this does not mean that the spoken word was in irreversible decline. The most extensive and authoritative treatment of the subject has concluded that oral and literate culture were joined together in a dynamic and reciprocal relationship, 'each feeding in and out of the other to the development and nourishment of both'.[14] This requires us to think about oral culture in a radically different way. What might a history of oral culture and popular speech look like if we rid ourselves of the pervasive influence of the world we have lost, and stopped thinking of the spoken word as a faint echo that can only be recovered by reading between the lines of the written sources? This chapter is an attempt to answer that question.

Studying the Oral through the Written

'How does one study speech acts some two to four hundred years after the event?' asks Peter Burke, rightly describing this as a somewhat presumptuous task. 'It is clear that historians with this kind of interest must resign themselves not only to studying the oral through the written, but also to investigating the language of ordinary people via records made, for the most part, by members of the cultural élite.'[15] As Burke points out, this is a particular problem for historians of popular culture, because of the partial and selective reporting of popular speech in written and printed sources. But it is a problem that confronts historians in studying any text that purports to be a transcript of the spoken word. In many cases there are grounds for suspecting that the text has either been garbled in transmission (as in the case of the 'bad quartos' of Shakespeare, widely thought to have been reconstructed from memory) or been revised for scribal or print publication, and in either case may be very different from what was originally said. In any case there are aspects of oral delivery such as gesture and tone of voice (*actio* and *pronunciatio* in early modern rhetoric) that simply cannot be captured in a written transcript.

The records of the early Stuart Parliaments are a case in point. These are fuller and more detailed than the records of any other representative assembly before the late eighteenth century. MPs knew they were discussing issues of major political and constitutional importance, and took pains to keep a careful record, with the result that the official *Commons Journal* can be supplemented by a large number of private diaries kept by individual members. We should therefore be in a very good position to reconstruct what was said in the course of debate. In practice, however, these different accounts frequently disagree among themselves. When Sir Robert Phelips stood up in the House of Commons on 25 March 1628 to speak 'upon the point of liberty', the *Commons Journal* records him as saying that 'liberty is the stamp of a free man', but another report has him saying that 'convenient liberty is the only mark of a true Englishman', while a third report renders his words less pithily, but possibly more accurately, as: 'The condition of a free man is to live where there is not *dominium regale*, but *dominium regale politicum*, and this is the state of England.'[16] While note-takers might have their attention caught by a memorable turn of phrase, they did not usually

---

[14] Adam Fox, *Oral and Literate Culture in England 1500–1700* (Oxford: Clarendon Press, 2000), p. 50.

[15] Peter Burke, *The Historical Anthropology of Early Modern Italy: Essays on Perception and Communication* (Cambridge: Cambridge University Press, 1987), p. 79.

[16] *Commons Debates 1628*, ed. Robert C. Johnson and Maija Jansson Cole (New Haven: Yale University Press, 1977), vol. II, pp. 99, 106, 109.

attempt a verbatim record of proceedings and should not be regarded as a seventeenth-century equivalent of Hansard. The copies of speeches that circulated as manuscript 'separates' are also an unreliable guide to what was said in the House, as MPs did not speak from a prepared script and may well have revised their speeches after delivery, to record what they would have liked to have said rather than what they actually did.[17]

Historians have learned to be cautious in using these sources. J.H. Hexter has commented on 'the asymmetries we keep encountering when we try to treat the record of spoken discourse as analogous to that of written discourse' and argued that the scholarly conventions used to record written texts, such as quotation marks, ellipses and brackets, are inappropriate for orally based texts because they give a misleading impression of verbal exactness.[18] John Morrill has recommended that parliamentary speeches and debates should be paraphrased, preferably from multiple sources, rather than directly quoted from a single source.[19] The modern scholarly editions of *Proceedings in Parliament* published by the Yale Center for Parliamentary History, in which all the available sources are laid out alongside each other for comparison, have made this task a great deal easier. But even if we could be certain that we had an accurate record of what was said in Parliament, some aspects of the oral event would still elude our grasp. Chris Kyle has recently drawn attention to the importance of non-verbal speech acts in early modern Commons debates, such as murmurs of agreement or shouts of acclamation to register approval of a good speech, coughing, hissing and shuffling of feet to register disapproval of a bad one, or dead silence as a 'deliberate signifier of shock and protest'. These and other aspects of the debate were deliberately omitted from the sanitised version in the Commons Journal. Robert Bowyer, the Jacobean Clerk of the Parliaments, commented that in transcribing his rough notes into the Journal book, the clerk 'doth in discretion forbear to enter many things spoken, though memorable, yet not necessary nor fit to be registered and left to posterity to record'.[20]

Like parliamentary speeches, sermons survive in great numbers and offer the tantalising prospect of being able to 'hear' what was said from the pulpits of early modern England. But again there are potential hazards in taking written or printed texts as a guide to what was spoken. In accordance with classical rhetoric, sermons were intended not only to teach (*docere*) but also to move (*movere*), and by the early seventeenth century some puritan ministers had developed a highly emotive preaching style designed to bring their audience to their knees in repentance for their sins before raising them up again with comfort and consolation. 'If ever we mean to doe any good,' declared the Ipswich minister Samuel Ward, 'wee must exhort and reproove, with all vehemency and authority, lifting up our voyce as a trumpet, as the sonnes of thunder, piercing their eares, witnessing, striving and contending, according to our gift whatsoever it bee, to manifest our affections, that we may worke upon the people'. Ward was emphatic that this style of preaching could not be reproduced in print, because 'onely zeale at the heart will naturally produce it'.[21] In revising their sermons for publication, preachers therefore tended to concentrate on doctrinal instruction, without

---

[17] See A.D.T. Cromartie, 'The Printing of Parliamentary Speeches, November 1640–July 1642', *Historical Journal* 33:1 (1990), 23–44, esp. p. 24.

[18] J.H. Hexter, 'Quoting the Commons, 1604–1642', in DeLloyd J. Guth and John W. McKenna eds, *Tudor Rule and Revolution: Essays for G.R. Elton* (Cambridge: Cambridge University Press, 1982), pp. 369–91, at p. 383.

[19] John Morrill, 'Review Article: Reconstructing the History of Early Stuart Parliaments', *Archives* 21 (1994), 67–72, and 'Getting over D'Ewes', *Parliamentary History* 15:2 (1996), 221–30.

[20] Chris R. Kyle, *Theater of State: Parliament and Political Culture in Early Stuart England* (Stanford: Stanford University Press, 2012), pp. 36–55, 63.

[21] Samuel Ward, *A Coal from the Altar, to kindle the holy fire of Zeale* (London, 1615), F3r at p. 69.

making much effort to stir up an emotional response. As a result, the experience of reading an early modern sermon on the page is, very often, only a shadow of what its first audience would have experienced in hearing it delivered from the pulpit.[22]

One consequence of this is that the type of sermon known to contemporaries as 'plain preaching' ('plain' meaning homely and popular, but also direct and plain-spoken) is poorly represented in print. One of the great exponents of the plain style was the Civil War preacher Stephen Marshall, who was said to be 'acquainted with all the Vulgar Proverbs, and old Country Phrases, and By-words which he would sprinkle and down in his Sermon; which captivated the People at a strange rate'.[23] A sermon preached by Marshall in his Essex parish of Finchingfield is preserved in manuscript notes taken by one of his hearers, and shows his engagingly direct mode of address: 'oh! my brethren, this is the strongest Parable in all the Gospell'; 'now, my brethren, what saith your soules to this?'[24] But this is not carried over into his printed sermons, which are generally preached on major public occasions and adopt a more formal, less colloquial style. Another of his sermons, also surviving in manuscript, is salted with short and punchy proverbs and familiar phrases ('never let the water pass by any byways from the mill'; 'multitudes there are that see not the wood for the trees') that were replaced by more elaborate similes ('to lay them up in our treasurie, not as some do their bundles of old writings in their counting-house, never looking on them in seven yeers') when Marshall revised the sermon for publication.[25] It was the oral performance that made Marshall's sermons so distinctive: his biographer justly observed that 'in his Sermons penn'd, there was nothing extraordinary; yet he had such a kind of Delivery, that he carried away the credit from all'.[26]

It is likely that printed sermons also screen out an older tradition of comic or jesting preaching going back to the medieval period. William Glibery, the Elizabethan vicar of Halsted in Essex (only a few miles away from Marshall's parish of Finchingfield), was locally famous for the racy language of his sermons, which earned him a complaint from some of his parishioners and a cameo role in the Marprelate Tracts.[27] It was reported that 'when he would perswade the people of the trueth of some poynte in his sermon, he useth many tymes to say, If this be not trew accompte me for as veary a knave as any is in Halsted', and that he had once told his congregation, in a sermon on repentance, that 'he would not have them dye as the desperat dicks of this world doe, that is take them oute of the fryeinge pan and caste them into the fyre, but he would have them repent in a mery meane, not too high for the pye nor too lowe for the crowe'. He had mocked his puritan opponents as 'my gospoylers and goosebillers' (a pun on 'gospellers'), 'my pratling stances, and such as doe bepisse and becacke the gospel', and declared that 'in callinge one another to the sermon, they were lyke to the olde proverbe, laye the puddinge in the fire, call in, call in, who shall

---

[22] This is discussed at greater length in Arnold Hunt, *The Art of Hearing: English Preachers and Their Audiences, 1590–1640* (Cambridge: Cambridge University Press, 2010), pp. 117–63.

[23] *The Life and Death of Stephen Marshal* (London, 1680), B3r at p. 7.

[24] 'Mr Marshall his Sermon dwelling at Finchingfield in Essex': Gloucestershire Record Office, D149 F15.

[25] 'Mr Marshall Sept 7th 1641 at Lincolns Inn': Cambridge University Library, Add MS 51, ff. 212–19; compared with the printed version, *A Peace-Offering to God* (London, 1641).

[26] *The Life and Death of Stephen Marshal*, B3r at p. 7.

[27] On Glibery, see Joseph L. Black ed., *The Martin Marprelate Tracts: A Modernized and Annotated Edition* (Cambridge: Cambridge University Press, 2008), p. 108, and John Craig, 'Sermon Reception', in Peter McCullough, Hugh Adlington and Emma Rhatigan eds, *The Oxford Handbook of the Early Modern Sermon* (Oxford: Oxford University Press, 2011), pp. 178–97, refs to Glibery pp. 178–9.

I call in, thy good fellowes and myne a'.[28] It would be easy to dismiss these as the antics of an eccentric pulpit comedian, but they are not so far removed from the advice of Thomas Wilson, in his *Arte of Rhetorique* (1560), that even the gravest preachers 'must now and then plaie the fooles in the pulpite, to serve the tickle eares of their fleetyng audience'.[29] If Glibery appears to us to be an isolated figure, it may simply be because this type of preaching so rarely survives in print.

These examples underline the difficulty of studying the oral through the written. They also show why this matters for an understanding of popular culture. Not only do printed sermons give us a limited view of oral preaching, they are at their most limited at the very point where preaching intersected most closely with popular, vernacular speech. If this leads us to the pessimistic conclusion that we can never expect to 'hear' the spoken voices of the early modern period, we should also bear two further points in mind. First, while we may not be able to reconstruct precisely what was said, we may still be able to reconstruct what early modern listeners thought they heard. Reports of sermons and speeches tell us what the note-takers thought was worth recording, which may be of interest in its own right: as, for example, in showing the importance of proverbs, similes and commonplaces, both as memory aids and as tools to think with. Secondly, while written notes may be partial and inaccurate, they still give us an approximation of the spoken word which should not be dismissed out of hand. As Laurie Maguire has pointed out, the defects in the early texts of Shakespeare's plays do not necessarily mean that early modern actors, scribes and printers were habitually careless; they may simply mean that they did not share the fetish of modern editors and critics for precise textual accuracy.[30] John Morrill's study of parliamentary speeches and debates leads him to a similar position of modest optimism: 'Time and again the similarity of the accounts to one another (if rarely the precise replication of words and sentences) allows us to be confident that we are getting the gist of what was spoken.'[31]

And in a few cases we may get more than just the gist. The art of shorthand, which first began to be used widely in England in the late sixteenth century, offered the possibility of reproducing the spoken word with a degree of fidelity otherwise impossible before the era of the phonograph and the tape recorder. The earliest systems of shorthand were difficult to learn and cumbersome to use, but by the mid-seventeenth century the technology had greatly improved, and shorthand became established, in Frances Henderson's words, as 'the newly fashionable accomplishment of the educated man'. It is thanks to the popularity of shorthand that we have a record of the Putney debates of 1647, which are preserved in a fair copy written up by the army secretary William Clarke from his shorthand notes. Henderson rightly cautions against treating the manuscript as though it were a transcript of a tape recording, but finds that Clarke's record of the debates is 'surprisingly complete', probably because he was working as one of a team of shorthand writers who compared their notes for greater accuracy.[32] The famous words attributed to Colonel Thomas Rainborough, 'really I think that the poorest hee that is in England hath a life to live as the greatest hee', may thus

---

[28]   'Certeyne notes of untrew, unreverent, scoffinge and blasphemous speeches, which Mr Glybery hath of late uttered from tyme to tyme in his sermons', 1583: National Archives, Kew, SP 12/159/85.

[29]   Thomas Wilson, *The Arte of Rhetorique* (London: R.Grafton, 1553), f. 2v.

[30]   Laurie Maguire, *Shakespearian Suspect Texts: The 'Bad' Quartos and Their Contexts* (Cambridge: Cambridge University Press, 1996), pp. 147–8. As Maguire observes, this concern with textual fidelity is characteristic of a print-based rather than an oral or scribal culture.

[31]   Morrill, 'Reconstructing the History of Early Stuart Parliaments', p. 70.

[32]   Frances Henderson, 'Reading, and Writing, the Text of the Putney Debates', in Michael Mendle ed., *The Putney Debates of 1647: The Army, the Levellers and the English State* (Cambridge: Cambridge University Press, 2001), pp. 36–50, at pp. 40, 46.

be reasonably close to what Rainborough actually said – a conclusion which should give us grounds for optimism about the possibility of reconstructing early modern speech.[33]

Studying the Popular through the Élite

Peter Burke makes the further point that historians of popular culture must come to terms with 'investigating the language of ordinary people via records made, for the most part, by members of the cultural élite'.[34] He may have been thinking particularly of the collections of ballads and folklore made by industrious antiquarians in the eighteenth and nineteenth centuries, but his warning also applies, with especial force, to the depositions preserved in the records of the early modern law courts. These are a uniquely rich source for the history of popular speech. As Malcolm Gaskill has commented, they are 'unusual among early modern sources as a whole for the extent to which they reflect the thoughts, beliefs, attitudes and emotions of mostly uneducated people, expressed in their own words'.[35] Laura Gowing describes them as 'arguably our best access to the worlds of ordinary women and men: servants, labourers, traders, farmers, housewives, midwives'. She also points out that they 'excelled in recording speech' because it was very often vital to reconstruct the exact words spoken, as for example in cases involving slanderous or seditious remarks, verbal marriage promises or deathbed bequests.[36] At the same time we need to retain a healthy scepticism about their reliability, given that they are mediated to us through the legal procedures of the courts and the scribal and archival practices of early modern clerks and notaries.

Even the most sceptical historian, however, may find it difficult to resist the allure of early modern depositions. What other sources are there, after all, that allow us to eavesdrop on a neighbourhood dispute from seventeenth-century London, as recounted by a witness in the archdeaconry court? Rowland Hubbersted, the parish constable, greeted Mrs Avery with the words: 'how now Landlady, what hath Nan Hoskins taken the pricke and is she with childe, and has her master Bryan fuckt her and gotten her with childe', to which she replied: 'how doe I know, you may as well doe it as he for ought that I doe knowe'. At this point they were interrupted by Ellen Nicholson, who told Hubbersted 'that he was fitter for a shrove tuesday boy than a Constable' (or, according to another witness, 'I marvell Mr Hubbersteed that you being a master of a family and an officer of the parishe should use such wordes as to say that my husband hath begott Anne Hoskins with childe'), to which he 'in a malitious manner told her that she might goe runn away with a butcher again'.[37] While this is clearly filtered through the recollections of the witnesses, there is little reason to doubt that it gives us the language of the street in a relatively raw and uncensored form. By contrast, the language of the theatre moved further away from everyday life after 1606, when the Act to Restrain Abuses of Players outlawed profanities such as 'zounds' (God's

---

[33]   Admittedly, the shorthand writers seem to have had particular difficulty in taking down Rainborough's speeches, perhaps because he spoke quickly or with an unfamiliar accent (Henderson, 'Reading, and Writing', p. 48).

[34]   Burke, *Historical Anthropology of Early Modern Italy*, p. 79.

[35]   Malcolm Gaskill, 'Reporting Murder: Fiction in the Archives in Early Modern England', *Social History* 23:1 (1998), 1–30, at p. 2.

[36]   Laura Gowing, *Common Bodies: Women, Touch and Power in Seventeenth-Century England* (New Haven: Yale University Press, 2003), p. 13.

[37]   London archdeaconry court, deposition book 1632–38: London Metropolitan Archives (formerly Guildhall Library), MS 9057/1, ff. 46–9.

wounds), 'sblood' (God's blood) and even relatively mild oaths like 'O God', so it is to legal records that we must turn if we want to get closer to the actual voices of the past.[38]

Rowland Hubbersted's case is typical of the lawsuits that came before the courts, particularly the church courts, centring on allegations of defamatory words. The broad pattern of these cases is fairly clear. A high proportion involved women suing other women, very often for using the word 'whore', as this constituted an accusation of sexual immorality which came within the jurisdiction of the church courts. In some cases one can almost hear the insults being hurled at the victim like a handful of stones: thus Alice Rochester told Jane Lilham, 'thou art a whore and an arrant whore and a common carted whore and thou art my husbands whore', while Barbara Hunter of Newcastle, in a similar tirade of abuse, called Elizabeth Allanson 'a fleminges whoore, the clocke makers whoore, and that she was all mens whoore, and went to the fields to plaie the whoore with men, and that Mr Maior was to whipp her out of the towne for whooredome'.[39] In such cases the language suggests that this was not just a private quarrel but a public shaming ritual acted out before an audience. There was no precise male equivalent to the term 'whore', but the commonest terms of abuse were 'rogue' and 'knave', which also appear regularly in defamation cases, though their lack of precision made them less actionable at law. These also had connotations of sexual immorality but tended to be applied more broadly and vaguely to criminality and low life, as one defendant explained to the vice-chancellor's court at Cambridge: 'these words Rogue, knave and base knave doe signifie a man of dishonest lyfe and conversation and one that is a vagabonde'.[40]

Defamation cases demonstrate the importance of speech in establishing credit and reputation in the early modern period. As Gowing aptly remarks, 'early modern England was a society in which spoken words still wielded enormous power'.[41] The decline of these cases in the mid-eighteenth century has likewise been linked to 'a broader cultural transformation in which the power and significance of the spoken insult was undermined'.[42] As the differing connotations of 'whore' and 'rogue' suggest, defamatory language was also highly gendered: to put the matter in a nutshell, a woman's reputation was defined by her sexual behaviour, whereas a man's reputation was defined by his social standing. Alexandra Shepard puts this slightly differently by suggesting that women were chiefly responsible for policing moral hierarchies, whereas men were chiefly responsible for policing social hierarchies; and while this is arguably an over-simplification, Gowing is undoubtedly correct when she argues that women had a crucial role as 'the brokers of oral reputation'.[43] There was also considerable interchange between the language spoken outside and inside the courtroom. Paul Griffiths has shown how the governors of Bridewell, who dealt with petty crime in London, labelled

---

[38]   On the Act of 1606, and its effect on printed playtexts, see Gary Taylor, 'Swounds Revisited: Theatrical, Editorial and Literary Expurgation', in Gary Taylor and John Jowett eds, *Shakespeare Reshaped 1606–1623* (Oxford: Clarendon Press, 1993), pp. 51–106.

[39]   Laura Gowing, 'Gender and the Language of Insult in Early Modern London', *History Workshop Journal* 35 (1993), 1–21, at p. 14. Northumberland archdeaconry court, office act book 1619–22: Durham University Library, DDR/A/ACN/1/1, f. 15v.

[40]   Alexandra Shepard, *Meanings of Manhood in Early Modern England* (Oxford: Oxford University Press, 2003), p. 175. On the meaning of 'rogue' and 'knave', see also Martin Ingram, 'Law, Litigants and the Construction of "Honour": Slander Suits in Early Modern England', in Peter Coss ed., *The Moral World of the Law* (Cambridge: Cambridge University Press, 2000), pp. 134–60, esp. pp. 156–7.

[41]   Laura Gowing, *Domestic Dangers: Women, Words, and Sex in Early Modern London* (Oxford: Oxford University Press, 1996), p. 111.

[42]   Robert Shoemaker, 'The Decline of Public Insult in London 1660–1800', *Past & Present* 169 (2000), 97–131, at p. 118.

[43]   Shepard, *Meanings of Manhood*, p. 183; Gowing, *Domestic Dangers*, p. 123.

the offenders brought before them with terms drawn from the language of defamation, such as 'rogue', 'slut' and 'vagrant'. In this way, Griffiths argues, 'street speech was absorbed into legal cultures, vocabularies, and laws'.[44] The law of defamation was simultaneously absorbed back into street speech, giving rise to a whole genre of insults that were carefully worded to minimise the risk of legal action: 'Thou art a rascally huswife, I would not call you a rascally quean.'[45]

A fuller understanding of depositions, however, requires us to think not just about insults and labelling but also about narratives and story-telling. One of the most influential works in this field is Natalie Zemon Davis's *Fiction in the Archives* (1987), a study of sixteenth-century letters of remission in which individuals convicted of capital crimes petitioned the king for pardon. By studying these documents as narrative fictions, shaped by the conventions of oral storytelling, Davis argues that it is possible to hear the spoken voices of the deponents emerging through the written texts. She admits that the royal notaries who copied the documents may have edited them to make them conform more closely to a standard legal formula, in the process removing some of the more pungent colloquial language, so that 'prick', for example, is replaced by 'virile and shameful member' (*membre virile et honteux*). But she finds that the documents have a variety about them which can only be attributed to the supplicants speaking in their own words, making these 'one of the best sources of relatively uninterrupted narrative from the lips of the lower orders'.[46] To suggest otherwise would be to underestimate the ability of ordinary people, even without formal rhetorical training, to speak eloquently and compellingly in their own defence.

On the other hand, depositions were generated as part of a formal legal process in which the speakers did not necessarily have control over the framing of their own narrative. The novelist Ronan Bennett has described how, as a Belfast teenager in 1974, he was charged with the murder of a police officer and put under pressure to sign a confession. Bennett knew nothing of the killing, but, with hindsight, imagines how easily he could have been made to confess to a murder he never committed:

> There would have been no problem about my lack of first-hand knowledge. The confession would have contained details known only to the guilty party. A detective would have asked: 'Did you meet so-and-so the morning before the robbery?' I nod. 'Did you tell him we had a job on?' Another nod or perhaps a weak yes. 'And did you go the next day in the blue four-door saloon to the bank? Was the car stolen earlier in the New Lodge area? Were you carrying the sub-machine-gun and so-and-so the pistol? Did you shoot the officer when he ambushed you on emerging from the bank?' Yes to the first question, yes to the last. Yes to all of it. And in its statement form my confession would have read: 'I met so-and-so in the morning and told him we had a job on the next day. The car we got was a blue four-door saloon which had been stolen earlier in the New Lodge area. I carried the sub-machine-gun and so-and-so had the pistol ...' And the prosecution would have adduced this statement in court as formidable and conclusive evidence against me, convincing because why else would I have confessed (in the absence of any evidence of intimidation), and because

[44]   Paul Griffiths, *Lost Londons: Change, Crime, and Control in the Capital City, 1550–1660* (Cambridge: Cambridge University Press, 2008), pp. 192–9, at p. 198.

[45]   Bernard Capp, *When Gossips Meet: Women, Family and Neighbourhood in Early Modern England* (Oxford: Oxford University Press, 2003), p. 199.

[46]   Natalie Zemon Davis, *Fiction in the Archives: Pardon Tales and Their Tellers in Sixteenth-Century France* (Stanford: Stanford University Press, 1987), p. 5.

> it contained details which could only have been known by someone who had been
> involved. And, of course, by the detectives investigating the case.[47]

This passage should be pinned up over the desk of anyone working on early modern history, as a reminder that written depositions are not always what they appear to be. It is true that English magistrates did not regard themselves as inquisitors constructing a prosecution case, and may therefore have been more inclined to let deponents speak in their own words.[48] But we do not need to suppose that early modern legal records are full of fabricated confessions in order to agree with Laura Gowing that they are 'the imperfect transcript of an exchange laden with imbalances of power, secrets, hidden agendas and meanings we can only partly recover'.[49]

The interpretative problems this creates for the historian are illustrated particularly clearly by the depositions in rape cases. Miranda Chaytor, in a pioneering study of rape narratives in seventeenth-century assize records, argued that when women came forward to lay information against their attackers, the magistrate or assize clerk would have written down their testimony precisely as dictated, 'changing nothing and omitting nothing'. This enabled her to read the depositions as direct transcripts of speech, and to apply a close psychoanalytic reading to 'slips of the tongue, the moments in a narrative when the syntax is disordered and coherence is lost, the metaphors through which meanings are compressed and displaced' as windows on the unconscious.[50] Chaytor's article is admirable in its attention to textual detail, but makes some questionable assumptions about the legal process, particularly in asserting that female plaintiffs were largely ignorant of the law and therefore did not construct their testimony with a view to securing a conviction. Garthine Walker has argued more persuasively that rape depositions have to be understood as stories told to an audience, reflecting the presence of the male officials who listened to the complainant and took down her evidence.[51] Both Chaytor and Walker are struck by the way that many depositions gloss over the details of the sexual act, but whereas Chaytor argues that this is because the women had repressed the memory of the rape and penetration, Walker argues that it is because they had no way of describing it without appearing to be complicit, and therefore had to depict the rape as an act of violence rather than sex.

What little we know about the making of depositions certainly suggests that they were shaped to a large extent by the rules of legal procedure. The mediating role of the clerk can be seen most clearly in the insertion of stock phrases such as 'he this deponent saith' and the recasting of the narrative as reported speech. However, there are occasional signs of more radical editorial intervention. Holger Syme's study of magistrates' notebooks shows that oral statements were very often reworked and paraphrased in the course of being written down.[52] Joanne Bailey's analysis of lawyer/client correspondence in the eighteenth-century church courts shows that lawyers played a major part in drafting the pre-trial narrative:

---

[47]   Ronan Bennett, 'Criminal Justice', *London Review of Books*, 24 June 1993.

[48]   Gaskill, 'Reporting Murder', p. 3. On the other hand, Andy Wood has pointed to instances of confessions extracted by torture: see Wood, *The 1549 Rebellions and the Making of Early Modern England* (Cambridge: Cambridge University Press, 2007), p. 106.

[49]   Gowing, *Common Bodies*, p. 14.

[50]   Miranda Chaytor, 'Husband(ry): Narratives of Rape in the Seventeenth Century', *Gender & History* 7:3 (1995), 378–407, at p. 394.

[51]   Garthine Walker, 'Rereading Rape and Sexual Violence in Early Modern England', *Gender & History* 10:1 (1998), 1–25.

[52]   Holger Schott Syme, *Theatre and Testimony in Shakespeare's England* (Cambridge: Cambridge University Press, 2012), pp. 46–52.

for example, she describes one case of marital rape where the plaintiff's initial statement made no mention of any sexual act, and it was left to the lawyer to supply the conventional formula, 'he then by force and compulsion had carnal knowledge of her body'.[53] If we are trying to hear the spoken voice in the written text, this is both good and bad news. On the one hand, it suggests that written depositions may be quite far removed from the original speech act and may even, as Sir Matthew Hale warned, have been revised by a clerk or lawyer 'to make a Witness speak what he never truly meant, by dressing of it up in his own Terms, Phrases and Expressions'.[54] On the other hand, it suggests that they are consciously crafted narratives drawing on a repertoire of themes, characters and plots that might already have been familiar from ballads, romances and oral storytelling.[55]

The Old Bailey *Proceedings* deserve special mention here, not just because they have been described as 'probably the best accounts we shall ever have of what transpired in ordinary English criminal courts before the later eighteenth century' but because their online publication has made them more widely accessible than ever before.[56] For many London criminal trials the *Proceedings* purport to give a verbatim account of what went on in court, even down to the stammerings and hesitations of witnesses, as in this example from a 1726 rape trial:

> They drove me along as far as Spittle-fields-Market, and there they threw me down, and two of them held me while the Prisoner, – Laud bless me, – what shall I say now, – must I speak plain, – plain English? – and before all these Gentlemen? – I vow I am quite a-sham'd, – I don't know how to speak such a Word, – but if I must, I must, – they held me while the Prisoner ravish'd me.[57]

The shorthand notes of Sir Dudley Ryder, an Old Bailey trial judge in the 1750s, provide an independent check on the accuracy of the *Proceedings*. On the whole the results are encouraging: Ryder's notes never contradict the *Proceedings*, though they sometimes contain additional details of the trial procedure. This suggests that although the editors of the *Proceedings* were selective in what they chose to include, they did not resort to outright fictionalisation.[58] Like modern tabloid journalists, however, they were chiefly interested in scandal and sensation, and where they give an exact transcription of oral testimony this is usually done for a reason, as in the example above, where the aim is clearly to titillate the reader by showing a female witness forced to describe intimate sexual details. This does not necessarily undermine their accuracy, but again it requires us to read the *Proceedings* as a form of storytelling – and as Esther Snell has commented, 'in making these stories available to the public the *Proceedings* was contributing to a popular discourse on rape and sexual behaviour that, in turn, may have influenced the very testimonies given in court'.[59]

---

[53] Joanne Bailey, 'Voices in Court: Lawyers' or Litigants'?', *Historical Research* 74 (2001), 392–408.

[54] Quoted by D.F. McKenzie, 'Speech–Manuscript–Print', in D.F. McKenzie, *Making Meaning: 'Printers of the Mind' and Other Essays* (Amherst: University of Massachusetts Press, 2002), p. 243.

[55] Gowing, *Common Bodies*, p. 14.

[56] John H. Langbein, 'Shaping the Eighteenth-Century Criminal Trial: A View from the Ryder Sources', *University of Chicago Law Review* 50:1 (1983), 1–136, at p. 3. The *Proceedings* are online at www.oldbaileyonline.org.

[57] Quoted in Esther Snell, 'Trials in Print: Narratives of Rape Trials in the Proceedings of the Old Bailey', in David Lemmings ed., *Crime, Courtrooms and the Public Sphere in Britain, 1700–1850* (Farnham: Ashgate, 2012), pp. 23–41, at p. 31.

[58] Langbein, 'Shaping the Eighteenth-Century Criminal Trial', pp. 25–6.

[59] Snell, 'Trials in Print', p. 25.

In using depositions, we must therefore be careful not to lose sight of the interventions of lawyers, clerks and trial reporters. Chaytor and Walker edit their source material by stripping out standard legal phraseology and putting the narratives into the first person singular, so that where the original deposition might read 'she the said Elizabeth cried out but he the said John stopped her mouth', the edited version reads: 'I cried out but he stopped my mouth'.[60] This reflects an understandable desire to recover the silenced voices of the victims, and an equally understandable desire to render the narratives more vivid and immediate by removing them from the courtroom or the magistrate's parlour and returning them to their original setting. But it comes at the cost of obliterating the complex and collaborative process by which these records were generated. For all the work that has been done on early modern court records, there is still much that remains unclear about the making of these records; and yet this was the point at which the testimony of ordinary people came into contact with the mechanisms of the law, which should be a focal point for investigation if we are interested in the relationship between the popular and the élite. There is a risk that in screening out the mediating role of the courts we may inadvertently be screening out the power dynamics and cultural exchanges that make these records significant.

Conclusion

In an essay of 1989, Robert Scribner posed the question, 'Is a history of popular culture possible?' and argued that in some cases it was not. Scribner was particularly sceptical of attempts to reconstruct popular mentalities on the basis of material supposedly drawn from oral culture, commenting that 'such apparently "oral" forms can place the historian at some considerable distance from the people who allegedly used them'. The ballads and folktales that appear to represent a pure oral tradition may in fact have been rewritten by the folklorists who collected and edited them; the proverbs that appear to embody an unmediated peasant wisdom may in fact have been appropriated for didactic purposes by the educated élite. 'We may recognise that all sources distort, and attempt to make allowance for it, but we must also ask whether there are unacceptable levels of distortion which defy making any allowance, where there is so much "noise" that it will drown out any "popular" voice.'[61]

I have suggested in this chapter that this is not a completely hopeless task, and that it is possible to recover at least some traces of the spoken voice from the era before modern sound recording. The difficulty lies not so much in recovering speech acts themselves as in reconstructing their context. Where spoken words were recorded, it was often because they were uttered at moments of public controversy or personal confrontation, or thought by their hearers to be seditious, slanderous or in some way deserving of censure. This is no bad thing if we are interested in language as a marker of conflict, or in speech acts as performative utterances (a notion that was already familiar in the early modern period, when lawyers and theologians were fascinated by the way that particular forms of speech, such as oaths, contracts and sacraments, could enact what they signified).[62] But it may mislead us into treating these exceptional episodes of conflict as typical of early modern culture as a whole. This is the case, for example, with Lawrence Stone's notorious assertion

---

[60]   Walker, 'Rereading Rape and Sexual Violence', p. 15.

[61]   R.W. Scribner, 'Is a History of Popular Culture Possible?', in R.W. Scribner, *Religion and Culture in Germany (1400–1800)*, ed. Lyndal Roper (Leiden: Brill, 2001), pp. 29–51, at pp. 33–4.

[62]   For a helpful introduction to the concept of performativity, see James Loxley, *Performativity* (London: Routledge, 2007).

that 'the Elizabethan village was a place filled with malice and hatred', Stone having mistakenly interpreted the records of the early modern church courts as evidence of normal social relations, rather than the breakdown of normal social relations.[63] As Scribner reminds us, it is the manner in which the words were used, rather than their mere existence, which provides access to popular mentalities.

Take the example of anticlericalism. It is not difficult to find instances in church court records of parishioners abusing their ministers as 'knaves', 'rascals' or 'scurvy priests'.[64] In some cases this clearly relates to specific disagreements over doctrine; in other cases the abuse is more generic in character, singling out clergy for their distinctive style of dress, as when a disgruntled parishioner in London was presented in 1615 for saying that 'Mr Cheshires lyfe was not according to his preaching and that he would make Mr Cheshires dealing known to all the blacke coted fellowes in the towne and sayd he was but a paltrie blacke coate'.[65] But putting this evidence together does not necessarily help us to draw out its meaning and significance. Are these isolated cases, or indicative of a more general attitude of contempt for the ministry? Do they offer glimpses of what James Scott would call the 'hidden transcript' of popular resistance, lurking behind the public transcript of deference and obedience?[66] Was this a genuinely popular discourse of anticlericalism that could be activated at moments of political conflict, as in the petitions to Parliament against 'scandalous' and 'malignant' clergy in 1641? Or was it an élite attempt to reform popular culture by labelling certain forms of speech as anticlerical and pursuing them through the church courts? Recent scholarship on 'dangerous talk' in early modern England has been highly successful in reconstructing popular speech but arguably less successful in interpreting it.[67]

Several approaches have been proposed to get around this problem. Steve Hindle has suggested reading 'against the grain', using the records generated by criminal cases and personal disputes to reconstruct the social settings that lay behind them. In sifting through the records of a murder in the town of Nantwich in 1572, for example, Hindle is less interested in the whodunit aspects of the case than in the accidental glimpses of normal urban life revealed in the depositions: 'When heard in this register, the milkmaids, weavers, salt-boilers and blacksmiths of Nantwich inadvertently disclose to us the rhythms and routines of their everyday existence, a world of industry, traffic and conversation in which their contemporary interrogators were largely uninterested.'[68] This approach has a lot in common with the German tradition of *Alltagsgeschichte*, or the study of everyday life, and has proved attractive to social historians because it focuses on precisely those types of speech that, as Scribner remarks, 'we would dearly like to find in our sources, such as private

---

[63]   Lawrence Stone, *The Family, Sex and Marriage in England 1500–1800* (London: Weidenfeld & Nicolson, 1977), p. 98.

[64]   Christopher Haigh, 'Anticlericalism and Clericalism, 1580–1640', in Nigel Aston and Matthew Cragoe eds, *Anticlericalism in Britain c. 1500–1914* (Stroud: Sutton Publishing, 2001), pp. 18–41.

[65]   London consistory court, office act book 1615–17: London Metropolitan Archives, DL/C/313, p. 139.

[66]   James C. Scott, *Domination and the Arts of Resistance: Hidden Transcripts* (New Haven: Yale University Press, 1990), esp. pp. 160–2 on oral culture.

[67]   I am thinking particularly here of David Cressy, *Dangerous Talk: Scandalous, Seditious and Treasonable Speech in Pre-Modern England* (Oxford: Oxford University Press, 2010), which comes to no clear conclusion except that 'almost everything is political', at p. 271.

[68]   Steve Hindle, '"Bleedinge Afreshe"? The Affray and Murder at Nantwich, 19 December 1572', in Angela McShane and Garthine Walker eds, *The Extraordinary and the Everyday in Early Modern England: Essays in Celebration of the Work of Bernard Capp* (Basingstoke: Palgrave Macmillan, 2010), pp. 224–45, at p. 238.

conversations, street corner discussions, pub gossip and marketsquare rumours'.[69] As Hindle points out, however, this is not just about listening for words, it is also about listening for the silences between the words: 'By studying the actions or words which contemporaries found abhorrent, upsetting or antisocial, historians might reconstruct through their unspoken assumptions the more positive attitudes and values to which they aspired.'[70]

One of the advantages of this approach is that, as well as recovering particular speech acts, it supplies an interpretative framework for them by situating them in the context of wider speech cultures (news, rumour, gossip) and characteristic spatial locations (the street, the alehouse, the coffeehouse) which together can be said to constitute an early modern public sphere. The disadvantage is that it tends to take these speech cultures as a given fact of early modern life, without being fully attentive to the value judgements involved in labelling particular speech acts as 'news', 'rumour' and so forth. These could be highly loaded terms. In April 1626, for example, the House of Commons spent a whole day debating whether 'common fame' was a sufficient legal basis for proceeding with the accusations against the Duke of Buckingham. One MP was reported as saying that common fame was stronger than mere rumour, as it was the 'general voice', or 'the voice of many men', rather than the words of one man alone.[71] Labelling speech as rumour or gossip could thus be a way of casting doubt on its reliability, and there is a risk that historians trying to reconstruct networks of rumour and gossip may unwittingly reproduce these assumptions. For an illustration of this we need look no further than the way that news and gossip have been placed in separate compartments, with news circulating primarily among the educated male élite whereas gossip spreads via 'female gossip networks' located in 'female social space'.[72] More work still needs to be done on how different speech cultures intersected with each other.[73]

A contrasting approach is offered by Andy Wood, who argues that we can do more than merely pick up the crumbs of everyday life from between the cracks of legal records. In stressing the ubiquity of the popular voice in Tudor England, Wood offers a provocative challenge to the idea that speech acts are elusive and fugitive:

> *The main problem for the historian of popular political speech arises not from an absence of material, but from its excess: an excess of contexts (so much reported speech, presenting the voices of so many individuals; so many possible motives that might underwrite that documentation); an excess of archives (so many documents, so difficult to collate and assess); and an excess of meaning (so many possible interpretations of reported words).*[74]

Wood, too, is interested in reconstructing a particular speech culture, but one in which the representation of speech is as important as the spoken words themselves. As he shows, popular protest in early modern England was very often conceptualised in oral terms, as

---

[69]   Scribner, 'Is a History of Popular Culture Possible?' p. 33.

[70]   Hindle, '"Bleedinge Afreshe"', p. 238.

[71]   *Proceedings in Parliament 1626*, ed. William B. Bidwell and Maija Jansson (New Haven: Yale University Press, 1991–96), vol. III, pp. 46, 49.

[72]   For the former, see, for example, Richard Cust, 'News and Politics in Early Seventeenth-Century England', *Past & Present* 112 (1986), 60–90; for the latter, see Steve Hindle, 'The Shaming of Margaret Knowsley: Gossip, Gender and the Experience of Authority in Early Modern England', *Continuity and Change* 9:3 (1994), 391–419, esp. pp. 406–9.

[73]   I discuss the interaction between preaching, news and rumour in 'Sermons and the Succession in Late Elizabethan England', in Susan Doran and Paulina Kewes eds, *Difficult and Dangerous: The Question of Succession in Late Elizabethan England* (Manchester: Manchester University Press, forthcoming).

[74]   Wood, *The 1549 Rebellions*, p. 104.

a 'muttering', 'murmuring' or 'grumbling', which allowed élites to dismiss it as the noise of an undifferentiated mob, but also had certain strategic advantages for protesters in enabling them to hide behind a 'common voice'. This makes it impossible to disentangle the speech acts from the way they are recorded and represented. John Walter has suggested that grumbling, 'the easiest and probably the first weapon of the weak', may have been a common form of popular protest, but one that only becomes visible in the written records when it is labelled as sedition.[75]

We cannot expect archival documents to give us the same level of insight into the early modern period that oral history interviews have given us into the twentieth century. G. M. Young famously advised historians to 'go on reading until you can hear people talking', but we have to accept that the voices of the past can only be heard indirectly through a series of distorting filters.[76] Nevertheless, it is possible to turn the limitations of the sources to our advantage. As David Sabean has written of early modern Germany, 'there is irony in the fact that because we cannot get to the peasant except through the lord, our evidence is often a good starting point for considering the relationships which we want to examine'.[77] One fruitful way into the sources may therefore be to look for the social interactions captured in the recording of speech. This is not simply a restoration exercise in which we can strip away the distortions of the written evidence to reveal a hidden culture of popular speech. Rather, we should expect to find the untidy mixture of élite and popular, oral and written, that Sabean has characterised as 'the bits and pieces of a continuing discourse in which relations between people were framed in this or that set of terms, metaphors or images' – and for all its untidiness this may ultimately give us a better model for understanding popular culture. Recovering speech acts is not just about hearing speech in the act of being uttered; it is also about seeing speech in the act of being written down.

Select Bibliography

Capp, Bernard, *When Gossips Meet: Women, Family and Neighbourhood in Early Modern England*. Oxford: Oxford University Press, 2003.

Cressy, David, *Dangerous Talk: Scandalous, Seditious and Treasonable Speech in Pre-Modern England*. Oxford: Oxford University Press, 2010.

Davis, Natalie Zemon, *Fiction in the Archives: Pardon Tales and Their Tellers in Sixteenth-Century France*. Stanford: Stanford University Press, 1987.

Farge, Arlette, *The Allure of the Archives*, trans. Thomas Scott-Railton. New Haven: Yale University Press, 2013.

Fox, Adam, *Oral and Literate Culture in England 1500–1700*. Oxford: Clarendon Press, 2000.

Gowing, Laura, 'Gender and the Language of Insult in Early Modern London', *History Workshop Journal* 35 (1993), 1–21.

---

[75] John Walter, 'Public Transcripts, Popular Agency and the Politics of Subsistence in Early Modern England', in Michael J. Braddick and John Walter eds, *Negotiating Power in Early Modern Society: Order, Hierarchy and Subordination in Britain and Ireland* (Cambridge: Cambridge University Press, 2001), pp. 123–48, at p. 129.

[76] Quoted by W.D. Handcock in his introduction to G.M. Young, *Victorian Essays* (Oxford: Oxford University Press, 1962), p. 11. On the limits of the sources, see Brad S. Gregory, 'Is Small Beautiful? Microhistory and the History of Everyday Life', *History & Theory* 38:1 (1999), 100–11, esp. p. 107. On oral history, see Paul Thompson, *The Voice of the Past: Oral History* (Oxford: Oxford University Press, 1978).

[77] David Warren Sabean, *Power in the Blood: Popular Culture and Village Discourse in Early Modern Germany* (Cambridge: Cambridge University Press, 1984), p. 3.

Gowing, Laura, *Domestic Dangers: Women, Words and Sex in Early Modern London*. Oxford: Clarendon Press, 1996.

Hindle, Steve, 'The Shaming of Margaret Knowsley: Gossip, Gender and the Experience of Authority in Early Modern England', *Continuity and Change* 9:3 (1994), 391–419.

Hunt, Arnold, *The Art of Hearing: English Preachers and Their Audiences 1590–1640*. Cambridge: Cambridge University Press, 2010.

Ingram, Martin, 'Law, Litigants and the Construction of "Honour": Slander Suits in Early Modern England', in Peter Coss ed., *The Moral World of the Law*. Cambridge: Cambridge University Press, 2000, pp. 134–60.

Kamensky, Jane, *Governing the Tongue: The Politics of Speech in Early New England*. New York: Oxford University Press, 1997.

McKenzie, D.F., 'Speech – Manuscript – Print', in McKenzie, *Making Meaning: 'Printers of the Mind' and Other Essays*, ed. Peter D. McDonald and Michael F. Suarez. Amherst: University of Massachusetts Press, 2002, pp. 237–58.

Ong, Walter J., *Orality and Literacy: The Technologizing of the Word*. London: Methuen, 1982; reprinted London: Routledge, 1988.

Sabean, David Warren, *Power in the Blood: Popular Culture and Village Discourse in Early Modern Germany*. Cambridge: Cambridge University Press, 1984.

Schmidt, Leigh Eric, *Hearing Things: Religion, Illusion, and the American Enlightenment*. Cambridge, MA: Harvard University Press, 2000.

Sharpe, J.A., *Defamation and Sexual Slander in Early Modern England: The Church Courts at York*. York: Borthwick Institute, 1980.

Shoemaker, Robert, 'The Decline of Public Insult in London 1660–1800', *Past & Present* 169 (2000), 97–131.

Stretton, Tim, 'Social Historians and the Records of Litigation', in Solvi Sogner ed., *Fact, Fiction and Forensic Evidence: The Potential of Judicial Sources for Historical Research in the Early Modern Period*. Oslo: University of Oslo, 1997, pp. 15–34.

Syme, Holger Schott, *Theatre and Testimony in Shakespeare's England: A Culture of Mediation*. Cambridge: Cambridge University Press, 2012.

Thompson, Paul, *The Voice of the Past: Oral History*. Oxford: Oxford University Press, 1978.

Walter, John, 'Public Transcripts, Popular Agency and the Politics of Subsistence in Early Modern England', in Michael J. Braddick and John Walter eds, *Negotiating Power in Early Modern Society: Order, Hierarchy and Subordination in Britain and Ireland*. Cambridge: Cambridge University Press, 2001, pp. 123–48.

Wood, Andy, *The 1549 Rebellions and the Making of Early Modern England*. Cambridge: Cambridge University Press, 2007.

Woolf, D.R., 'Speech, Text, and Time: The Sense of Hearing and the Sense of the Past in Renaissance England', *Albion* 18:2 (1986), 159–93.

Youth Culture

Edel Lamb

Francis Beaumont's *The Knight of the Burning Pestle* depicts a number of the elements of what might arguably be described as early modern English youth culture. Performed *c.* 1607 by the Children of the Revels, one of the early seventeenth-century London-based companies consisting of youthful boy players, this play represents the fantasies of a young apprentice who is promoted to perform the role of the grocer in the drama's play-within-a-play. In act one he appears on stage reading *Palmerin of England*, which he draws on, along with other early modern romance fiction including *Amadis de Gaule*, to fashion his identity throughout the play. He becomes the 'said knight'; embarks on 'the quest of this fair lady', Mistress Merrythought; rescues his fellow knights from the 'huge giant Barboroso', the barber-surgeon; seeks the love of Susan, 'my lady dear / The cobbler's maid in Milk Street'; participates in London's May Day celebrations; and finally calls 'all the youths together in battleray, with drums, and guns, and flags' to march to 'Mile End in pompous fashion'.[1] Thus even in his role as grocer-knight Rafe is depicted as the typical early modern youth. He is portrayed via contemporary stereotypes of the youth who is dangerously influenced by romance fiction and stories of apprentices rising to power, who embarks in courtship, who participates in ritual celebrations that permitted juvenile misbehaviour and who instigates a communal youthful protest, mimicking the violent raids against brothels led by youths on Shrove Tuesday in early modern London. As Mark Burnett suggests, *The Knight of the Burning Pestle* simultaneously flatters apprentice tastes and ironises youthful aspirations.[2] Although it mocks youthful behaviour it demonstrates the possibility that the young might draw on the cultures in which they engage to assert their developing social and aged identities. This depiction of Rafe 'call[ing] all the youths together' on the early modern stage points to a pervasive image of youthful behaviour. It indicates the existence of a youth culture, characterised by excessive reading of what has widely been termed 'popular' literature and lustful, riotous and disruptive activities. To a certain extent, this concept of youths and their cultural role is, as Paul Griffiths points out is often the case, a 'social construct of a dominant adult society'.[3] Yet it also raises the potential for youths to forge their own communities

---

[1]   Francis Beaumont, *The Knight of the Burning Pestle* (London: Benn, 1998), 1.259; 2.125; 3.255; 3.313–314; Interlude 4; 5.57–58.

[2]   Mark Burnett, *Masters and Servants in English Renaissance Drama and Culture* (Basingstoke: Palgrave, 1997), p. 37.

[3]   Paul Griffiths, *Youth and Authority: Formative Experiences in England, 1560–1640* (Oxford: Oxford University Press, 1996), p. 18.

and indulge their desires. In this representation of the youthful apprentice who is an avid consumer of romance fiction, *The Knight of the Burning Pestle* presents one non-elite and subordinate figure, the boy actor, performing the role of another such figure, Rafe, participating in an unofficial and potentially dissident subculture. The play conceptualises the young and their activities in relation to and in similar terms to popular culture.[4] This is common to a number of textual representations of youth in the period.

This chapter will focus on textual representations of youth to explore the connections between youth culture and popular culture in early modern England. It will suggest that youth is commonly defined via elements of the popular, particularly through an association with literature commonly deemed as 'popular' in the period, both because of its 'cheap' and 'low' status but also because of such associations with marginal groups, including youths, the less literate and those of lower social status. Critics generally agree that there is a pervasive idea of youth in the period and many propose that this idea is articulated most clearly in popular literary forms, including chivalric tales, romances and ballads. Yet they continue to debate whether or not there is a corresponding concept of youth culture. For the most part, these debates have focused on youth involvement in moments of civic carnival and misrule, particularly the Shrove Tuesday riots instigated by apprentices annually in the seventeenth century.[5] Other elements of a potential youth culture, such as their participation in literary cultures, have largely been overlooked or dismissed as not being distinct to the young. Early modern youth culture, like popular culture, continues to be difficult to define and theorise. This chapter will explore these conceptual similarities. It will begin by outlining the pervasive tropes of youth in early modern texts to evaluate the ways in which youth is defined. It will then examine the popular cheap texts produced for the young and raise questions about how they were used by the young to consider if this constitutes evidence of a youth culture. It will suggest that youth is commonly defined in relation to popular literature and that such texts were a crucial element in creating a popular youth culture.

Textual Representations of Youth

It has long been recognised that the young comprised a substantial portion of early modern English society.[6] However, whether a stage in the life cycle was perceived to be a period of youth continues to be interrogated. While some scholars have argued for an immediate transition from childhood to adulthood that elides a period of youth or adolescence, others have persuasively demonstrated that early modern society acknowledged a transitional stage of youth and through institutions such as service, apprenticeship, the guilds, schools, universities and Inns of Court defined, and even extended, this stage of life.[7] As Matthew Harkins has argued, '"Youth" as a concept was remarkably elastic in early modern England,

---

[4]   See Peter Burke, *Popular Culture in Early Modern Europe* (Aldershot: Ashgate, 1994), p. i.

[5]   See Bernard Capp, 'English Youth Groups and *The Pinder of Wakefield*', *Past and Present* 76 (1977), 127–33; Ilana Krausman Ben-Amos, *Adolescence and Youth in Early Modern England* (New Haven: Yale University Press, 1994); Griffiths, *Youth and Authority*; Alexandra Shepard, *Meanings of Manhood in Early Modern England* (Oxford: Oxford University Press, 2003); Steven Smith, 'The London Apprentices as Seventeenth-Century Adolescents', *Past and Present* 61 (1973), 149–61; Anne Yarbrough, 'Apprentices as Adolescents in Sixteenth-Century Bristol', *Journal of Social History* 13:1 (1979), 67–81.

[6]   Griffiths, *Youth and Authority*, pp. 1, 5.

[7]   Ben-Amos, *Adolescence and Youth*, pp. 1–9; Keith Thomas, 'Age and Authority in Early Modern England', *Proceedings of the British Academy* 62 (1976), 205–48.

with regularly shifting boundaries.'[8] It generally referred to the period between the onset of puberty and the achievement of full adult status in the 20s. In Shakespeare's *The Winter's Tale* the Old Shepherd terms the period between 10 and 23 as youth when he bemoans, 'I would there were no age between ten and three-and-twenty, or that youth would sleep out the rest; for there is nothing in the between but getting wenches with child, wronging the ancientry, stealing, fighting.'[9] The Shepherd's complaint against the youths who have scared off his sheep during hunting not only defines this group according to their age but implies a common experience of youth dependent on shared attitudes and values, manifested through illicit behaviour in opposition to that of the older generation. Others, such as John Ferne in *The Blazon of Gentry*, saw youth as extending over a much longer period, terming 14 to 20 as the 'Yong age of adolescentia' and from 20 to 30 years as 'Lusty green youth'.[10] Like the Shepherd, age is not the only determining factor. For Ferne, it is also defined by shared characteristics. In this case, the traits of lustiness and greenness.

This is a recurrent image in depictions of youth in the period. It forms one dimension of Rafe's characterisation as a youth in *The Knight of the Burning Pestle* as he pursues his own maid and rescues his peers ridden with sexual disease from the barber-surgeon. As one of the seven stages in the life cycle, youth was commonly defined in early modern texts through its associations with Venus and excessive sensuality. Shakespeare's famous version of the seven ages of man, for example, characterises the stage after school boyhood as that of the lover 'Sighing like furnace, with a woeful ballad / Made to his mistress' eyebrow'.[11] This defining feature of youth was common across genres. Conduct manuals and moral advice books also highlighted the tendency of youths to engage in lustful behaviour. Richard Turner, for instance, writes 'Tis hee, or she, that Venus shrine adores, / That's in the teenes, and not come to the scores' before proceeding to warn the young against 'thousand of such lust-full variations' in *Youth Know Thyself* (1624).[12] It also commonly formed the topic of ballads directed at the young, such as *An Excellent Ditty, Both Merry and Witty, Expressing the Love of the Youthes of the City* (1624). A number of books were directed specifically at youths to assist them in their courtships, ranging from *Cupids Schoole: Wherein, Young Men and Maids May Learne Diverse Sorts of Complements* in 1632 to *Delights for Young Men and Maids* in 1725. These combined instructions in how to court, with sample sayings and verses to use in this situation, as well as riddles, jests and puzzles for general merriment.

In a number of early modern depictions of youth, the tendency to sexual desire was linked directly to the habit of the young to read material that indulged these inclinations. Francis Lenton's comic verse condemnation of the sins of youth, *The Young Gallants Whirligigg; or Youths Reakes* (1629) highlights the common fear of early modern pedagogues and moralists in an image of the youth reading Ovid. This youth does not read Ovid in an educational context, as many did, but instead reads it in disruptive ways: 'against his fathers minde' to 'Finde pleasant studies of another kinde'.[13] Lenton's extended portrait of youth offers further insight into the ways in which this stage of life was commonly defined in early modern England. In the verse describing the young man's entry into youth and move to London to study law, Lenton outlines the true nature of the youth's studies:

---

[8]   Matthew Harkins, '"Forward Youth" and Marvell's "An Horation Ode"', *Criticism* 45:3 (2003), 343–58, at p. 344.

[9]   William Shakespeare, *The Winter's Tale*, in *The Norton Shakespeare*, ed. Stephen Greenblatt et al. (London: Norton, 1997), 3.3.58–61.

[10]   John Ferne, *The Blazon of Gentrie* (London, 1586), p. 169.

[11]   William Shakespeare, *As You Like It*, in *The Norton Shakespeare*, ed. Stephen Greenblatt et al., 2.7.144–48.

[12]   Richard Turner, *Youth Know Thyself* (London, 1624), A3v.

[13]   Francis Lenton, *The Young Gallants Whirligig, or Youths Reakes* (London, 1629), p. 4.

> Now here the mine of Youth begins,
> For when the Country cannot find out sinnes
> To fit his humour, London doth invent
> Millions of vices that are incident
> To his aspiring minde; for now one yeare
> Doth elevate him to a higher sphere;
> And makes him thinke he hath achieved more,
> Then all his fathers auncestors before.
> Now thinkes his father, here's a godly Sonne,
> That hath approached unto Littleton,
> But never lookt on't; for instead of that
> Perhaps hee's playing of a game at Cat.
> No, no, good man, hee reades not Littleton,
> But Don Quix Zot, or els The Knight o'th Sun:
> And if you chance unto him put a Case,
> Hee'll say perhaps you offer him disgrace,
> Or else upon a little further pawse,
> Will sweare hee never could abide the Lawes:
> That they are harsh, confus'd: and to be plaine,
> Transcend the limits of his shallow braine.
> Instead of Perkins pedlers French, he says
> He better loves Ben Johnsons booke of Playes,
> But that therein of wit he findes such plenty,
> That he scarce understands a Jest of twenty[14]

Youth is here humorously marked by an ongoing immersion in sin. Lenton's youth avoids his studies by seizing the opportunities that the city and this move away from the home provides. As Ilana Ben-Amos argues the common lists of youthful sins in the period included anything a young man or woman was likely to do for leisure, including drinking wine, spending money or participating in sports, games and other recreations.[15] In this instance, the youth's disruptive behaviour largely takes the form of reading romances, chivalric tales, plays and jests, as well as Ovid. Although Lenton's subject is socially distant from Beaumont's apprentice-player, both youths are characterised in similar ways. The law student, like the apprentice, indulges in games and in his own reading tastes that, like Rafe's, include popular romance. His reading of *Don Quixote* and *The Mirror of Knighthood* replace his study of Littleton's legal treatise. Instead of learning French, he reads Jonson's plays. Lenton's youth is depicted through his reading of popular literature and his mode of reading – reading against his father's wishes. In similar terms to *The Winter's Tale* youth is depicted through generational differences and illicit and disruptive behaviour. However, it is primarily defined through an immersion in popular literary cultures.

Early modern youths are portrayed via this taste for popular literature throughout the seventeenth century. Francis Kirkman remembers reading *Amadis de Gaule*, *Palmerin of England* and other Iberian romances as a schoolboy in his autobiography, *The Unlucky Citizen* (1673), and describes how he shared these books with his peers.[16] In his criminal biography of the notorious Mary Carleton he notes that she 'took much pleasure in reading, especially Love Books, and those that treated of Knight Errantry' in her youth, 'believing all she read

---

[14] Lenton, *Young Gallants*, pp. 3–4.
[15] Ben-Amos, *Adolescence and Youth*, p. 13.
[16] Francis Kirkman, *The Unlucky Citizen* (London, 1673), pp. 10–11.

to be true'.[17] In another fictional representation of a law student in William Wycherley's *The Plain Dealer* (1677), Jerry Blackacre, 'under age and his mother's government', conveys his literary tastes in visits to the bookstalls at Westminster Hall with his mother.[18] His request for '*St George for Christendom; or, the Seven Champions of England*' or a 'play' is denied by his mother who wants him to read, as preparation for the law, Sir Richard Hutton's *The Young Clerk's Guide*, first printed in 1649.[19] Richard Norwood offers a similar list of youthful reading material in his diary in 1639, recalling his 'great delight in reading in vain and corrupt books as *Palmerin de Olivia, The Seven Champions* and others like'.[20] Similarly John Bunyan describes the youth of the damned rich man in 1658 as spent reading various forms of small books and cheap print, including news books, ballads, chapbooks of the English heroes, Saint George and Bevis of Southampton, books of magic and fables, instead of the scriptures.[21] This representation of youthful tastes serves a specific function as moral exemplar in this spiritual narrative of conversion, and is repeated in other spiritual narratives, including those of Vasavour Powell and Richard Baxter who recall delighting in 'Hystorical or Poetical Books, Romances' and 'romances, fables and old tales' above scripture before being converted by reading Richard Sibbes' biblical exegesis, *The Bruised Reed* (1631).[22] Nonetheless, this pervasive trope of youth desiring popular tales aligns the young with this textual culture in early modern England.

Scholars interrogating the existence of youth culture in early modern England have located elements of this in these fables, ballads, chivalric tales, romances and cheap print. Although Ilana Ben-Amos concludes that there is no distinct culture for youths in her seminal study *Adolescence and Youth in Early Modern England* (1994), she suggests that popular chivalric romances are a primary source embodying 'ideas about what constituted the age of youth'.[23] She proposes that the descriptions of young heroes in traditional texts such as *Bevis of Southampton, St George* and *The Famous History of Guy Earl of Warwick* and in newly invented heroes based on this model including *Aurelius, the Valiant London Prentice, Dick Whittington, The Most Pleasant History of Tom-a-Lincoln* and Thomas Deloney's *Jack of Newberry* and *The Gentle Craft* would have 'led readers to identify the hero's qualities with the age of youth'.[24] Yet Ben-Amos points out that although these characters embark on adventures during their teens and early 20s, they were not necessarily representative of the age group to which they belonged. Instead, she argues, 'they served to stimulate the fantasy and imagination of the reader and the hero's adventures unfolded as a corollary less of his age than of his social background'.[25] For Ben-Amos class supersedes age in defining the shared identity potentially forged in these texts and by their readers.

The common social background and apprentice status of many of these heroes have been taken by other scholars as indicative of an apprentice subculture. In his persuasive study of seventeenth-century London apprentices as adolescents, Steven Smith suggests that 'the heroic tradition in the literature for apprentices was part of the search for identity

---

[17]   Francis Kirkman, *The Counterfeit Lady Unveiled* (London, 1673), pp. 9–10.
[18]   William Wycherley, *The Plain Dealer*, in *The Country Wife and Other Plays*, ed. Peter Dixon (Oxford: Oxford University Press, 1996), p. 289.
[19]   Wycherley, *The Plain Dealer*, 3.1.305–15.
[20]   Wesley Craven and Walter Hayward eds, *The Journal of Richard Norwood* (New York: Bermuda Historical Monuments Trust, 1945), p. 17.
[21]   John Bunyan, *A Few Sighs from Hell* (London, 1658), p. 157.
[22]   Edward Bagshaw, *The Life and Death of Mr Vavasour Powell* (London, 1671), p. 2; N. H. Keeble ed., *The Autobiography of Richard Baxter* (New York: Rowman and Littlefield, 1974), pp. 4–6.
[23]   Ben-Amos, *Adolescence and Youth*, p. 25.
[24]   Ibid., p. 25.
[25]   Ibid., p. 24.

as well as an attempt to endow the subculture with a tradition of its own'.[26] He contends that the body of literature for and about youth indicates that apprentices thought of themselves and were thought of as a separate order and that these texts were an integral part of the shared experiences of apprenticeship and adolescence, and constituted a form of subculture. Margaret Spufford also claims that apprentices were a 'group with their own culture' who had 'their own chapbooks'.[27] Spufford notes that texts presenting the apprentice as hero did not only involve fantasies of heroic adventures and of social climbing, but also catered for specifically sexual adolescent fantasies. In *John and His Mistress*, for instance, the handsome apprentice hero seduces his master's wife and in *Tom Stitch the Tailor* the apprentice hero goes further in cuckolding his master, blackmailing his mistress and deserting 16 pregnant servant girls and a rich widow. If, as Anthony Fletcher suggests, popular literature fed the fantasy lives of youths, particularly young men, by developing notions of youth as adventurous, vigorous and courageous, it also indulged sexual and social fantasies.[28] Many contemporary moralists deemed this youthful indulgence in literary fantasy, which seemed to hold a particular appeal to this age group, dangerous as it not only constituted wasteful sin in youth but was also a formative influence on a group of readers unable to distinguish between fantasy and reality. This fear is one of the many objects of satire in *The Knight of the Burning Pestle* when Rafe plays out his fantasies shaped by the chivalric romances that he has read on stage.

In one sense, it is perhaps unsurprising that youth are represented in this way in adult representations. In the gerontocratic society of early modern England, youth are a subordinate and potentially disruptive group requiring control.[29] However, as this play indicates in its dual flattery and ironisation of youthful apprentice culture, this immersion in popular literature is not straightforwardly ridiculous or dangerous. It simultaneously permits youth to forge these shared experiences with their peers. Yet this assumes independent deployment by the young of their reading experiences and the existence of communities of youths in early modern society. I would suggest that this might be located by considering texts produced for youths.

Popular Texts and the Construction of Youth Culture

Many of the chivalric tales featuring youthful heroes and early modern appropriations of this motif were adapted in cheap and abbreviated formats such as ballads and chapbook texts throughout the seventeenth century. This potentially indicates a market for these texts amongst young and apprentice readers.[30] This was accompanied by a proliferation of books directly addressing a youthful readership. In addition to the ballads and courtship manuals such as *An Excellent Ditty* and *Cupids School*, mentioned above, a series of advice books were printed for the young advising on their behaviour, their morals and, for apprentices and

---

[26]   Smith, 'London Apprentices', p. 159.
[27]   Margaret Spufford, *Small Books and Pleasant Histories: Popular Fiction and Its Readership in Seventeenth-Century England* (Cambridge: Cambridge University Press, 1985), p. 55.
[28]   Anthony Fletcher, *Gender, Sex and Subordination in England 1500–1800* (New Haven: Yale University Press, 1995), pp. 88–9.
[29]   On early modern society as gerontocratic, see Thomas, 'Age and Authority'.
[30]   On cheap print versions and their readers, see Spufford *Small Books*, and Tessa Watt, *Cheap Print and Popular Piety 1550–1640* (Cambridge: Cambridge University Press, 1991).

servants, on how to carry out their duties.[31] These manuals also circulated as fictional dialogues and verses, for example, T. S.'s *Youths Tragedy* (1671) and Turner's *Youth Know Thyself* (1624), and in ballad form, including *Youths Warning-Piece* [*sic*] (1685). Nathaniel Crouch, operating under the pseudonyms Robert or Richard Burton, adapted a number of genres for the young in his prolific plagiarising, reprinting and remarketing of late seventeenth-century texts, including versions of Samuel Crossman's *The Young Man's Monitor* (first published in 1664) as *The Young Man's Calling* (first published in 1685), *Remarks upon the Lives of Several Excellent Young Persons of Both Sexes* (1678) and *Youth's Divine Pastime* (1691).[32] Crouch also published a companion specifically for apprentices, *The Apprentices Companion* (1681). However, although a number of books specifically identified the youthful, and often male, apprentice as the intended reader thus forging a sense of a separate apprentice subculture, this was not the only type of youth identified as reader in seventeenth-century print culture. Many claimed simply to be for young men and maids, such as *Delights for Young Men and Maids*, mentioned above. Other publications separately identified the male and female youth. The French advice book, *Youths Behaviour, or Decency in Conversation amongst Men*, was translated into English in 1646 by the eight-year-old Francis Hawkins and was extended in 1664 to *The Second Part of Youths Behaviour, or Decency in Conversation amongst Women*. Female servants could be guided apart from their male counterparts by *The Compleat Servant-Maid; or, The Young Maidens Tutor* (1677), which was 'composed for the great benefit and advantage of all young Maidens'.[33] However, there were significantly more texts for and about male youth than female youth.

One text printed for youths clearly imagines a communal identity among this age group erasing distinctions of gender and social status. The title page woodcut of *Youth's Treasury, or, A Store-House of Wit and Mirth*, printed in 1688, depicts a carnivalesque gathering of young men and women dancing with joined hands and no clothing under the supervision of a pedagogue figure, also naked and a youth but differentiated by the fact that he holds the symbolic objects of the teacher, a birch rod and book. This humorously imagines an alternative group of youths forging their own subversive culture replacing the typical books of the pedagogue with this treasury. The text itself is an anthology of the 'Choicest and Newest Songs', love letters, 'Pleasant Tales, Witty Jests and Merry Riddles' thus indicating the range of genres adapted and brought together under the aegis of being a collection for youths.[34] It combines abbreviated versions of songs from contemporary broadside ballads, playhouse songs, comic tales (including one on the follies of old age), jests, riddles and some model compliments or 'protestations of love'. Evolving from earlier seventeenth-century miscellanies or drolleries and registering a culture of mirth and leisure against Puritan models of reading for profit, this book is more a politicised comment on religious and social attitudes to leisure than it is an indication of the traits of different age groups in the period.[35] Yet it simultaneously positions this culture of mirth under the ownership of youth via its opening illustration and its emphasis throughout on the material as being presented 'new' for the young.

Another late seventeenth-century text repackages popular genres for the young. J. M.'s *Sports and Pastimes: Or, Sport for the City, and Pastime for the Country*, printed in 1676, offers

---

[31]   Louis Wright, 'Handbook Learning of the Renaissance Middle Class', *Studies in Philology* 28:1 (1931), 58–86; Burnett, *Masters and Servants*, p. 8.

[32]   See Robert Mayer, 'Nathaniel Crouch, Bookseller and Historian: Popular Historiography and Cultural Power in Late Seventeenth-Century England', *Eighteenth-Century Studies* 27:3 (1994), 391–419.

[33]   Anon., *The Compleat Servant-Maid* (London, 1677), title page.

[34]   Anon., *Youth's Treasury: Or, A Store-House of Wit and Mirth* (London, 1688), title page.

[35]   See Adam Smyth, *Profit and Delight: Printed Miscellanies in England, 1640–1682* (Detroit: Wayne State University Press, 2004), pp. 1–31.

instruction in the arts of tricks and magic, claiming on its title page to be a 'touch of Hocus Pocus, or Leger-demain. Fitted for the delight and recreation of Youth'.[36] It specifically highlights the young male reader in the address to the reader when it states, 'The design of this was for the recreation of Youth, especially School-boys, whose wits are generally sharpned on such Whetstones'.[37] Like *Youth's Treasury*, it draws on a range of popular texts and reprints these genres in a form that it claims to be suited for the young. It adapts miscellanies such as John Cotgrave's *Wits Interpreter, or the English Parnassus* (first published in 1655) and the anonymous *Hocus Pocus Junior* (first published in 1634), which combined tricks using eggs, balls, strings, cups and coins and a discussion of the art of witchcraft, science and 'other curiosities' with witty sayings, short poems, anecdotes and letters or statements for imitation. *Sports and Pastimes* acknowledges its debt to this tradition in 'The Epistle to the Reader', which notes that tricks have been omitted that 'were in Print before' and directs the reader to '*English Parnassus, Hocus Pocus Junior,* &c.'.[38] It deliberately omits the more serious discussion of the art of magic contained in other books of tricks, claiming 'There's no Hobgoblins here for to affright ye, / But innocence and mirth that will delight ye'.[39] It only includes tricks that youths might carry out to impress others, such as appearing to turn water into wine, making two coins into one, making invisible ink, getting revenge on maids, and making 'one laugh until the tears stand in his eyes'.[40] It instructs the individual reader on how to carry out these tricks but like *Youths Treasury* it imagines a wider usage of the text among a shared culture of youths. For example, one trick 'To make sport in company' offers detailed instruction on what to do and say 'when you are shewing tricks' and another 'When you are in company and intend mirth'.[41] Another one is to be used 'If you are drinking in company'.[42] This book imagines an engaged and active form of reading. It provides delight to the individual youth by offering instruction in this trick but in implying that this must be enacted to peers it forges a community among the reader/performer and his audience.

Establishing the existence of structured groupings of youths has been at the centre of scholarship on early modern youth culture. Following Natalie Zemon Davis' seminal work on the youth abbeys and their festivities of misrule of early modern France as giving formal structure to the stage of life now known as adolescence, scholars have struggled to locate equivalent institutions in England in this period.[43] While some have turned to institutions populated by the young, such as the schools, universities, Inns of Court, guilds and theatres, or to instances of civic carnival and misrule, the strongest identifiable point of comparison has been the late sixteenth- and early seventeenth-century apprentice riots, the most famous of which was the annual Shrove Tuesday raid against the brothels.[44] Evolving from annual festivals in which juvenile misbehaviour was sanctioned, the seventeenth-century Shrove Tuesday riots shared the deployment of public ridicule and misrule against deviant behaviour with the French youth groups. Yet, although they were instigated by groups of youths, they lacked the formal organisation of the French example. As a result, early modern England has been widely perceived to lack the formal youth culture of other nations at this

---

[36]   J. M., *Sports and Pastimes* (London, 1676), title page.
[37]   Ibid.
[38]   Ibid., A3r.
[39]   Ibid., A3r.
[40]   Ibid., p. 7.
[41]   Ibid., pp. 15; 27.
[42]   Ibid., p. 3.
[43]   Natalie Zemon Davis, 'The Reasons of Misrule: Youth Groups and Charivaris in Sixteenth-Century France', *Past and Present* 50 (1971), 41–75.
[44]   See Capp, 'English Youth Groups'; Keith Thomas, 'Children in Early Modern England', in Gillian Avery and Julia Briggs eds, *Children and Their Books: A Celebration of the Work of Iona and Peter Opie* (Oxford: Oxford University Press, 1989), pp. 45–77.

time. However, instances of youthful misrule, including these raids, are just one instance of the shared culture among youth, whether or not this was associated with a formal institution. The imagined reading and performance of what the youth has read among his or her peers indicates another way in which the young forged a shared space to participate in their distinct popular culture. Whether or not books such as *Sports and Pastimes* and *Youth's Treasury* were bought by the young or read by them at all, this text constructs a culture of the young by representing them as consumers of a particular type of text and as engaging with these texts in certain ways. Mark Burnett contends that texts identifying apprentice readers played a 'key part in creating a servant culture, and spaces within which particular preoccupations and projects could be highlighted'.[45] I would suggest that books identifying this wider community of youths similarly forge a youth culture, creating not only a textual space in which pertinent preoccupations might be addressed but also facilitating an imaginative space through which youths might come together to share this culture textually and orally.

The material space in which youths participated in this culture varied. Youths consumed and purveyed popular culture in some impromptu settings. Ballads might be read but could also be heard or passed on by illiterate youths orally. One 1613 version of the story of Dick Whittington reaches out to a group of young listeners, beginning with the lines 'Brave *London* 'Prentices, come listen to my Song'.[46] In 1621, Robert Burton claims that 'boys and prentices, when a new song is published with us, go singing that new tune still in the streets'.[47] Apprentices came together at playhouses, such as the group of apprentices who met at the theatre in 1592 to plan the rescue of one of their fellow apprentices from prison.[48] The number of plays presenting apprentice heroes, including Thomas Heywood's *The Four Prentices of London* (c. 1594) and George Chapman, Ben Jonson and John Marston's *Eastward Ho* (c. 1605) as well as Beaumont's *The Knight of the Burning Pestle*, implies that apprentices frequented the theatres to enjoy the plays too.

The tavern also seems to be a common place for the young to come together for trickery, misrule and the sharing of popular tales and jests. *Sports and Pastimes* imagines youths 'drinking in company'.[49] In Richard Head and Francis Kirkman's *The English* Rogue (1665), fictional apprentices recount how apprentices meet in taverns to scheme on how to cheat their masters.[50] A seventeenth-century chapbook, *The Pinder of Wakefield* (1632), further describes youths sharing jests, riddles, songs and stories orally as a group at the tavern. Based on the story of George a Greene, widely disseminated in the period through dramatic, romance and ballad versions of the tale, this version is similar in structure to *Youths Treasury*. The story of the youthful George who organises his 'companions' into a group to meet at the tavern every Monday morning to plan opportunities to punish improper social behaviour, in a manner similar to Zemon Davis' French youth groups, is interrupted repeatedly by the tales, 'Jests, Catches and Songs and Riddles' which the youths share at the tavern 'to make our selves merry withall'.[51] This includes sections such as 'A ready witty answer a Maid', providing material that youths might draw on in their own experiences.[52] This text thus combines an account of a fictional youth group with a selection of short tales, songs and jests that youths might share among themselves in such a manner.

---

[45] Burnett, *Masters and Servants*, p. 9.
[46] Cited in Burnett, *Masters and Servants*, p. 17.
[47] Cited in Adam Fox, *Oral and Literate Culture in England 1500–1700* (Oxford: Oxford University Press, 2000), p. 206.
[48] Burnett, *Masters and Servants*, p. 21.
[49] J. M., *Sports and Pastimes*, p. 3.
[50] Cited in Smith, 'London Apprentices', p. 153.
[51] Capp, 'English Youth Groups', p. 132.
[52] Anon., *The Pinder of Wakefield* (London, 1632), C1v.

A mid-seventeenth-century chapbook version of *The Canterbury Tales* also combines 'a choice of Banquet of delightful Tales, pleasant Stories, witty Jests and merry Songs to divert the young Men and Maids when they come to the Bake house, Forge, or Mill'. This recurrent collecting of popular genres and representing it anew through this identification of a youthful readership suggests a particular appeal of these forms to the young. However, in contrast to *The Pinder of Wakefield* and *Youth's Treasury*, this text does not present the sharing of these tales at the instigation of the youths. Instead it is dedicated to 'Bakers, Smiths and Millers' so that they might divert the young, hence attracting them to their shops and increasing their trade. This strange method of trade depends on the fact that such tales are primarily composed for 'the Entertainment of All Ingenious Young Men and Maids'. Furthermore, it is interesting to note that this age-specific group gather together frequently. The epistle states it is intended for 'their merry Meetings, upon Christmas, Easter, Witsuntide, or any other time'.[53] Youths, male and female, gather together to listen to, read and perhaps even pass on tales, songs and jests on holidays and at places of trade with enough frequency to make it worth marketing texts directly for this purpose.

Youth Culture as Popular Culture

Youths were commonly represented via their participation in diverse elements of popular culture. They were frequently defined in terms of their reading tastes and were both humoured and condoned for what was seen as an age-related desire to indulge in popular romances and chivalric tales. These forms often presented young heroes, thus refracting the aspirations and fantasies of youth and providing a narrative for their self-definition. Popular literary cultures, therefore, were evoked to characterise youthful behaviour, and also actively participated in shaping the experience of youth in this period.

It seems that youths also came together in diverse ways and locations to participate in a range of cultural activities widely defined as popular in the period. As scholarship has noted, apprentices and youths participated in festivals of misrule and even instigated their own acts of misrule, particularly on festive days of the annual calendar. However, they also gathered frequently to share plays, tales, romances, fables, songs and ballads, jests and riddles. They encountered these forms in texts, which encouraged the youthful reader to share examples suited to the occasion. Youths also encountered these forms aurally as they were passed on by their peers and by their social and aged superiors. The association of the young with popular forms of culture is established further by the range of cheap texts that explicitly identified youth as the primary market. It is perhaps unsurprising that as a subordinate group in this gerontocratic society, youth were commonly associated with elements of popular culture. These genres would have been economically more accessible to this portion of society and texts since deemed 'low' were also open to, and made suitable for, appropriation for their own cultural activities in diverse spaces from the street to the tavern. Youths, it seems, were significant consumers and purveyors of multiple aspects of popular culture.

Yet, does this constitute youth culture in the period? The main reason that scholars have argued against the existence of youth culture in spite of this evidence is because it does not comprise a distinct culture for youth, separate from that of other age groups.[54] For instance, the youthful tastes for popular chivalric romances foregrounded in Beaumont's play, Lenton's verse and numerous autobiographies are not unique to youth. These texts

---

53 Cited in Spufford, *Small Books*, p. 67.
54 For example, Ben-Amos, *Adolescence and Youth*, p. 183.

were also enjoyed by readers from a range of social and aged backgrounds.[55] Although some of these books reprint existing material and identify the young as the intended readers on title pages and prefaces, this material in the very nature of being reprinted, albeit in new selections and formats, is clearly not distinctive to youth. Moreover, even if these texts identify youth as the primary users, the contents were open to circulation in printed and oral forms to other audiences. However, Alexandra Shepard's formulation on the rituals of youth is useful here. These materials and the modes of reading may not be age-specific but they are presented in early modern discourse as age-related via the common trope of youthful reading.[56] Furthermore although youths may gather to share this culture in material locations inhabited and often controlled by non-youths, this method of shared participation forges a community among youths and an imaginative space in which they can explore their own preoccupations via these popular forms. Even if the culture of youth in the texts about and for them is largely one of a trope of misrule, misbehaviour, merriment and fantastical adventure constructed from the perspective of adults, we can begin to uncover a set of shared attitudes and experiences determined by the young by considering the ways in which youth appropriated these ideas and participated in this culture.

As this volume makes clear, these approaches have been carefully worked out in relation to popular culture since the publication of Peter Burke's *Popular Culture in Early Modern Europe* in 1978.[57] It is, I would suggest, by approaching the study of youth culture through the conceptual frameworks used in studying popular culture that we can move beyond a simplistic understanding of early modern youth culture being determined by a distinct set of practices, texts, objects or institutions unique to the young. If a study of youth culture includes an examination of texts and objects about and for youth, of the usage of these texts and objects by youths and also by others, and of a set of shared attitudes and experiences and the ways that these might be appropriated beyond the youth group, then a more complex understanding of the multiple manifestations of what we might term 'youth culture' in early modern England emerges. Youth culture, therefore, is not only aligned with elements of popular culture in early modern England, the study of it might usefully be extended by bringing the methodological approaches ofpopular culture studies to bear upon it.

Select Bibliography

Ben-Amos, Ilana Krausman, *Adolescence and Youth in Early Modern England*. New Haven: Yale University Press, 1994.

Burke, Peter, *Popular Culture in Early Modern Europe*. Aldershot: Ashgate, 1994.

Burnett, Mark, *Masters and Servants in English Renaissance Drama and Culture*. Basingstoke: Palgrave, 1997.

Capp, Bernard, 'English Youth Groups and *The Pinder of Wakefield*', *Past and Present* 76 (1977), 127–33.

Fletcher, Anthony, *Gender, Sex and Subordination in England 1500–1800*. New Haven: Yale University Press, 1995.

---

[55] For instance, see Spufford, *Small Books*, p. 75 on examples of elite readers of chapbooks.

[56] Shepard, *Meanings of Manhood*, p. 101.

[57] See also Burke, 'Introduction to the Revised Edition', *Popular Culture*, pp. xiv–xxvii; Sue Wiseman, '"Popular Culture": A Category for Analysis', in Matthew Dimmock and Andrew Hadfield eds, *Literature and Popular Culture in Early Modern England* (Aldershot: Ashgate, 2009), pp. 15–28.

Fox, Adam, *Oral and Literate Culture in England 1500–1700*. Oxford: Oxford University Press, 2000.

Griffiths, Paul, *Youth and Authority: Formative Experiences in England, 1560–1640*. Oxford: Oxford University Press, 1996.

Shepard, Alexandra, *Meanings of Manhood in Early Modern England*. Oxford: Oxford University Press, 2003.

Smith, Steven, 'The London Apprentices as Seventeenth-Century Adolescents', *Past and Present* 61 (1973), 149–61.

Smyth, Adam, *Profit and Delight: Printed Miscellanies in England, 1640–1682*. Detroit: Wayne State University Press, 2004.

Thomas, Keith, 'Age and Authority in Early Modern England', *Proceedings of the British Academy* 62 (1976), 205–48.

Thomas, Keith, 'Children in Early Modern England', in Gillian Avery and Julia Briggs eds, *Children and Their Books: A Celebration of the Work of Iona and Peter Opie*. Oxford: Oxford University Press, 1989, pp. 45–77.

Yarbrough, Anne, 'Apprentices as Adolescents in Sixteenth-Century Bristol', *Journal of Social History* 13:1 (1979), 67–81.

Zemon Davis, Natalie, 'The Reasons of Misrule: Youth Groups and Charivaris in Sixteenth-Century France', *Past and Present* 50 (1971), 41–75.

Festivals

Tracey Hill

Defining the Genre

Early modern festivals foreground issues central to the study of popular culture. They raise the important questions to do with audience, participation and agency which in themselves define what constitutes popular culture in this period. The distinction between popular and elite culture is not a simple matter to resolve; as Matthew Dimmock and Andrew Hadfield have argued, 'popular culture is a complex phenomenon … What might seem popular may really be elite and what appears to be elite may really be popular.'[1] I discuss below a couple of 'case studies' which bear out their view and which demonstrate the characteristic interplay between what one might call 'top–down' and 'bottom–up' elements of festive culture. Indeed, these instances bring into question the very nature of the genre: what was an early modern festival? Who produced it and who consumed it? Whose interests did it serve? As we will see in more detail below, crucial questions about participation and spectatorship as well as issues to do with passivity versus active involvement are involved in the analysis of popular festive culture. It is worth pointing out from the outset that the focus here is not on festivity as a *mode* within, for example, drama (à la C.L. Barber) but on actual instances of early modern festive culture.[2] This chapter therefore draws on tangible and material as well as textual evidence. In the two examples I have chosen to illustrate this topic, we will see how popular engagement with forms of festivity played out in practice.

In the sixteenth and early seventeenth centuries festivals of various kinds were still numerous, and they punctuated the lives of early modern people in ways that are now largely lost to us. Games, plays, feasts and other kinds of entertainment dominated popular festivity. This chapter does not attempt a comprehensive genealogy of early modern festivals. It is worth noting, though, that like so much of early modern culture, festivals can be traced back to the medieval period; indeed, as Lawrence Clopper and Anne Lancashire have shown, ostensibly 'medieval' festive culture continued well into the sixteenth century.[3] In the earlier periods, by and large, festivals (or at least the organised ones, an important distinction to which I will return) were associated with the religious calendar. In London and the larger provincial towns the year was regularly punctuated by quasi-theatrical events based on biblical stories and allegories, which were used to mark notable religious dates

---

[1]   Matthew Dimmock and Andrew Hadfield, 'Introduction', in Matthew Dimmock and Andrew Hadfield eds, *Literature and Popular Culture in Early Modern England* (Aldershot: Ashgate, 2009), p. 7.

[2]   C.L. Barber, *Shakespeare's Festive Comedy: A Study of Dramatic Form and Its Relation to Social Custom* (Princeton: Princeton University Press, 1972).

[3]   Lawrence Clopper, *Drama, Play, and Game: English Festive Culture in the Medieval and Early Modern Period* (London: University of Chicago Press, 2001); Anne Lancashire, *London Civic Theatre* (Cambridge: Cambridge University Press, 2002).

such as Corpus Christi and Whitsun as well as various saints' days. A particular continuity with the medieval period is the use of allegory, which retained an important presence into the sixteenth and seventeenth centuries. In urban settings such festivities were often organised by guilds and other civic bodies, as we will see further below.

London was the venue for some of the most important ceremonial and celebratory occasions, but festivals in early modern England took place in a range of civic, courtly and regional locations. As befits forms of celebration with their roots in feast days, they were primarily date-specific (my examples are 29 October 1617 and 5 October 1623) as well as space-specific. The majority were instances of cyclical ritual culture, taking place on a set date every year.[4] At the same time, Clifford Davidson reminds us that 'the ritual year was not celebrated in the same way by towns and parishes as by university, the court, or aristocratic households'.[5] Diversity was a perennial feature of festive culture and by the early modern period, as David Cressy argues in his seminal account of English festivity, *Bonfires and Bells*, 'several calendrical schemes operated together … combining economic, ecclesiastical, dynastic and patriotic seasons and dates'.[6] Tradition, continuity and innovation, as is so often the case in this period, operated simultaneously. Although the religious calendar was not entirely expunged by the Reformation, the sixteenth century saw the development of what Cressy calls 'a new national, secular and dynastic calendar', fit for newly Protestant England.[7] Accession Day, celebrated on 17 November to mark the anniversary of the start of Elizabeth's reign is an example of a post-Reformation feast day. Nevertheless, Shrovetide and Maytide and other such longstanding calendrical events were still occasions for popular festive celebration which drew on antique roots and often exceeded the bounds of behaviour deemed acceptable by the authorities. Drunkenness was a constant feature of popular festivity, as were impromptu bonfires; even the ubiquitous bell-ringing stood as an implicit rejection of the workaday responsibilities of 'normal' time.

The celebration of London's mayoral inauguration is a good example of an 'organised' festival that combined ecclesiastical and civic traditions. One of the chief predecessors of the Lord Mayor's Show was the Midsummer Watch (which itself probably dated back to the mid-thirteenth century), held overnight on the eve of St John the Baptist's Day, 23–24 June, and St Peter and St Paul's Day, 28–29 June.[8] Pageantry, from which emerged the mayoral Show of the early modern period, became part of the Watch in the course of the fifteenth century, and from an early date the Watch included secular elements such as wildmen, giants and the like that were inherited by the Shows. Lord Mayor's Day itself traditionally took place on 29 October (unless that date happened to be a Sunday), the day after the feast of St Simon and St Jude, an approved feast day under Protestantism; a smaller-scale event to mark the election of the new mayor preceded this on Michaelmas Day.[9] Mayoral installations were also celebrated in the larger regional towns such as Coventry and Norwich. Other moments of festive celebration, such as my second example below, served as sometimes quite spontaneous responses to ad hoc events or series of events. The increasingly secularised

---

[4]   A useful calendar of early modern festive events can be found here: www.chsbs.cmich.edu/Kristen_McDermott/ENG235/EM_calendar.htm.

[5]   Clifford Davidson, *Festivals and Plays in Late Medieval Britain* (Aldershot: Ashgate, 2007), p. 4.

[6]   David Cressy, *Bonfires and Bells: National Memory and the Protestant Calendar in Elizabethan and Stuart England* (London: Weidenfeld and Nicholson, 1990), p. xi.

[7]   Ibid., p. xii.

[8]   For more on the connections between the Watch and mayoral Shows, see my *Pageantry and Power: A Cultural History of the Early Modern Lord Mayor's Show, 1585–1639* (Manchester: Manchester University Press, 2010), pp. 28–30 and Davidson, *Festivals and Plays*, pp. 38–42.

[9]   The Lord Mayor's Show also dates back to the thirteenth century. It has even more historically remote links with the triumphal entries and processions of classical Roman times.

festivals of the late sixteenth and seventeenth centuries – particularly those in the latter category, as I will show – at times engaged directly with contemporary politics.

Although festivals are by their very nature ephemeral in part (how easily can a permanent record exist of shouts on the street or inebriated celebrations?), from the sixteenth century onwards aspects of many were captured in print.[10] There was an increasingly busy industry in England producing texts to commemorate or disseminate the festive moment. Printed books of the Lord Mayor's Show, as I have discussed in more detail elsewhere, began to appear from the 1580s, and celebratory occasions involving domestic or visiting royalty were written up to perform a quasi-news function for the public.[11] Partly because they were more closely connected to elite celebrations, festival books produced on the Continent were more likely to attempt to reproduce the visual spectacle than English books (Stephen Harrison's drawings of James's royal entry in 1604, published in a handsome folio, is an exception).[12] English festival books, by and large, took the forms of pamphlet, ballad or broadside (with no illustrations beyond the occasional woodcut), genres that have been categorised as cheap or popular print; some accounts of festivity like verse libels did not even get the authority of print.[13] There are important consequences to this distinction that I explore in more depth below.

In addition to urban celebrations, early modern festive culture has been defined in such a way as to include royal entries, progresses and one-off events such as weddings and royal visits, as well as the court masque.[14] Royal entries were predominantly processional, with gates and triumphal arches being set up for the occasion. Like the mayoral Shows, they tended to feature sporadic tableaux set up at ceremonially significant locations, which formed an opportunity for speeches and music. Examples of ad hoc events would include the marriage of Princess Elizabeth and the Elector Palatine in 1613, the investiture of Prince Henry in 1610 and the visit of King James's brother-in-law, Christian of Denmark, in 1606.[15] Fireworks and entertainments on the Thames were consistent features of the civic celebrations of such events, as was music, in the form of instrumental play and songs.[16] As mentioned above, celebrity occasions such as these, especially the royal wedding in 1613, prompted many

---

[10]   The study of festival books as a genre has been facilitated by various online resources, many with searchable images. These include the British Library's site www.bl.uk/treasures/festivalbooks/homepage.html; a similar initiative, based on Watanabe-O'Kelly and Simon's book: http://festivals.mml.ox.ac.uk/index.php?page=home; books from the Folger Shakespeare Library: www.folger.edu/html/exhibitions/festive_renaissance/; the Warburg Institute (mostly Italian books): http://warburg.sas.ac.uk/library/links/action/festivals/; and a site dedicated to German festival books: www.hab.de/bibliothek/wdb/festkultur/index-e.htm.

[11]   For the print history of the Lord Mayor's Show, see my *Pageantry and Power*, esp. ch. 4.

[12]   Stephen Harrison, *The arch's* [*sic*] *of triumph* (London: printed by John Windet, 1604). The lavishly illustrated two-volume *Europa Triumphans* is an excellent resource for the visual dimensions of European festivals. J.R. Mulryne, Helen Watanabe-O'Kelly and Margaret Shewring, *Europa Triumphans: Court and Civic Festivals in Early Modern Europe* (2 vols, Aldershot: Ashgate, 2004).

[13]   See Joad Raymond ed., *The Oxford History of Popular Print Culture* (vol. 1, Oxford: Oxford University Press, 2011) and Tessa Watt, *Cheap Print and Popular Piety, 1550–1640* (Cambridge: Cambridge University Press, 1991).

[14]   For royal progresses, see Mary Hill Cole, *The Portable Queen: Elizabeth I and the Politics of Ceremony* (Amherst: University of Massachusetts Press, 1999) and William Leahy, *Elizabethan Triumphal Processions* (Aldershot: Ashgate, 2004).

[15]   For discussions of specific royal events on the Continent, see, for example, Stijn Bussels, *Spectacle, Rhetoric and Power: The Triumphal Entry of Prince Philip of Spain into Antwerp* (Amsterdam: Rodopi, 2012) and Mara R. Wade, *Triumphus Nuptialis Danicus: German Court Culture and Denmark: The 'Great Wedding' of 1634* (Wiesbaden: Harrossowitz, 1996).

[16]   Two of the printed Lord Mayors' Show include musical notation of some of the songs performed on the day: John Squire's 1620 *The tryumphs of peace* and Middleton's 1613 *The triumphs of truth*. In the 1620 Show the song appears to have been composed specially for the occasion.

writers to try to cash in on public interest by producing (allegedly) documentary accounts of the entertainments.[17] However, in general terms royal entertainments were less public and more exclusive in terms of audience once the Stuarts took power; festivities at the London Inns of Court and in noble households also took place in a more restricted environment. In keeping with their ideological function, royal entries and progresses in particular offered little opportunity for popular engagement beyond spectatorship; on such occasions ideals of monarchical power were imposed on the urban landscape.[18] Neither of my case studies derives from court culture, for there is, of course, an argument about whether masques and the like belong in the category of festive culture at all, which foregrounds once again the point about the role of the audience and their degree of participation in the event. Furthermore, it is not coincidental that both of my examples are taken from the late Jacobean period, when the monarchy had distanced itself from festivity to a greater extent than during Elizabeth's reign.[19]

Critical Approaches to Festival Culture: A Brief Overview

Scholarly work on early modern festival culture has deep roots. It dates back to the pioneering archival research undertaken by figures such as Robert Withington and John Nichols from the late eighteenth to the early twentieth centuries.[20] However, it has in the past been inclined to reproduce the polarity between 'popular' and 'elite' forms of entertainment outlined above. As recently as Sydney Anglo and Roy Strong's day, for example, royal entertainments were unthinkingly prioritised: Strong's statement in *Art and Power* that 'Renaissance festivals focussed on the prince' exemplifies his approach.[21] As a consequence, popular forms of festivity tended to be relegated to studies in 'folklore' and the popular tradition.[22] Many opportunities were lost for comparative and comprehensive analyses of

---

[17]   Examples of works produced on such occasions include *The most royall and honourable entertainement, of the famous and renowmed king, Christiern the fourth, King of Denmarke* (1606), Anthony Munday's *Londons loue, to the royal Prince Henrie … With a breife [sic] reporte of the water fight, and fire workes* (1610) and Taylor's *Heauens blessing, and earths ioy. Or a true relation, of the supposed sea-fights & fire-workes, as were accomplished, before the royall celebration, of the al-beloved mariage, of the two peerlesse paragons of Christendome, Fredericke & Elizabeth* (1613).

[18]   This is not to claim that active engagement invariably came from the protagonist: Archer and Knight emphasise Elizabeth's 'strategic' silence whilst on progress. Contemporary witnesses, they write, 'place great emphasis on being able to see, follow, and describe the body of the Queen'. Jayne Elisabeth Archer and Sarah Knight, 'Elizabetha Triumphans', in Jayne Elisabeth Archer, Elizabeth Goldring and Sarah Knight eds, *The Progresses, Pageants, and Entertainments of Queen Elizabeth I* (Oxford: Oxford University Press, 2007), p. 11.

[19]   In 1625, there was neither a mayoral Show in London nor the traditional accession entry for King Charles: this was partly due to plague but it set a marker for Charles's attitude towards popular festivity thereafter.

[20]   Robert Withington, *English Pageantry: An Historical Outline* (2 vols, New York: Arno Press, 1980, first published in 1918); John Nichols, *The Progresses and Public Processions of Queen Elizabeth; among which are interspersed other solemnities, public expenditures, and remarkable events during the reign of that … Princess: … with historical notes* (3 vols and vol. 4. pt 1, London: J. Nichols, 1788–1821). For more on Nichols' work, see Julian Pooley, 'A Pioneer of Renaissance Scholarship: John Nichols and *The Progresses and Public Processions of Queen Elizabeth*', in Archer et al. eds, *The Progresses, Pageants, and Entertainments of Queen Elizabeth I*, pp. 268–86.

[21]   Roy Strong, *Art and Power: Renaissance Festivals* (Woodbridge: Boydell and Brewer, 1984), p. 21.

[22]   An important quasi-anthropological study of festival culture is offered by Clifford Geertz, 'Centers, Kings and Charisma: Reflections on the Symbolics of Power', in Joseph Ben-David and Terry Nichols Clark eds, *Culture and Its Creators* (Chicago: Chicago University Press, 1977), pp. 150–71.

early modern festivals as a result. Popular festive culture was marginalised in other ways, too. It was from its earliest days fundamentally dramatic in form, and by the middle of the sixteenth century, street pageantry was the main festive mode in early modern England when it came to organised events. It is therefore unfortunate that scholars have too often treated pageantry as quite separate to theatre despite the fact that these two cultural forms share many characteristics. Indeed, the history of scholarship in the area of festivals until quite recently is largely one of fragmentation, both in terms of genre and also of nationality.

Non-British European festival research is perhaps the better-established.[23] One attempt to broach the continental and generic divide is Pierre Béhar and Helen Watanabe-O'Kelly's *Spectaculum Europaeum*, which presents brief summaries of civic and royal festivals, masques, ballets and related theatrical entertainments from across early modern and early eighteenth-century Europe.[24] Some instances of festival (such as the Lord Mayor's Show) are given very perfunctory treatment, however, and since the book's coverage is not exhaustive in any of these contexts, its value lies primarily in the pan-European juxtapositions it throws up, enabling scholars to form comparisons between, for instance, the English court masque and Polish ballet. In contrast, the voluminous *Europa Triumphans* presents more extended treatments of festival culture from France, Italy, Poland, Scandinavia, the Protestant Union and the Netherlands to early colonial Mexico and Peru.[25] Here too, though, even where the location under scrutiny is an urban one, the focus is almost exclusively on elite entertainments.

Scholars of popular culture such as Peter Burke, followed by the important contributions of Peter Stallybrass and Allon White in the 1980s, changed the picture in Britain. Equally, the revival of interest in the seminal work of Mikhail Bakhtin, together with the impact of cultural materialist approaches to early modern culture, led to a renewed attention to the carnivalesque aspects of festivity and highlighted the crucial questions of control, spontaneity, audience and participation that I engage with in this essay. Critics such as David Bergeron, R. Malcolm Smuts, Gordon Kipling, J.R. Mulryne, Jane Archer, Margaret Shewring and Elizabeth Goldring have offered more granulated and local approaches to festive culture. In general terms, scholars are now more likely to explore materiality and the lived experience of early modern culture.[26] The study of early modern festivity has also benefited from a groundswell of interest in the history and culture of sixteenth- and seventeenth-century London. In addition, festivals serve as a reminder to modern scholars of how *visual* early modern culture could be, and how central spectacle and theatre were to people's lives, especially in urban environments. Modern critical approaches to festivity are in general terms more comfortable with hybrid forms of culture than in the past. Such interdisciplinarity suits the study of early modern festivals very well, for they were inherently heterogeneous events, possessing dramatic, literary, historical and artistic elements. Scholars have accordingly explored festivals' use of music and dance and special effects such as fireworks, their architectural qualities, and their appearance in print. Ronnie Mulryne has rightly argued, then, that 'festival is pre-eminently a composite topic of study ... Music, choreography, visual design and script are as crucial to the presentation and interpretation

---

[23]   A major organisation in this field is the Society for European Festivals Research: www2.warwick. ac.uk/fac/arts/theatre_s/research/festivals_research. It is perhaps telling that no UK organisations are listed as contributing to the European PALATIUM project. See www.courtresidences.eu/index.php/home/.

[24]   Pierre Béhar and Helen Watanabe-O'Kelly eds, *Spectaculum Europaeum: Theatre and Spectacle in Europe (1580–1750)* (Wiesbaden: Harrassowitz, 1999).

[25]   Mulryne et al., *Europa Triumphans*.

[26]   A fascinating insight into the lived experience of festival is provided by the International Network for the Study of Early Modern Festival's online reconstruction of a royal entry: http://www.recreatingearlymodernfestivals.com/exhibition_laura.htm.

of festival as political intent and economic supply.'[27] The two examples I explore in more depth below demonstrate that interplay between genres and modes.

Early Modern Festival in Action

Early modern festivity was by its very nature a transient business. All the same, it is possible to reconstruct many aspects of the lived experience of those who participated in and watched festive events through the exploration of the printed books and various eyewitness accounts of festive events. The two moments given prolonged attention here are connected, not just by their shared festive qualities, but by date – both took place in October of their respective years – and, indirectly, by the figure of Thomas Middleton. Middleton co-produced the 1617 Lord Mayor's Show and he also exploited the moment of my second example at least twice: in the 1623 mayoral Show, printed as *The triumphs of integrity*, as well as, most famously, in *A game at chesse*, performed the following year and printed in 1625.[28] In both of these case studies we can perceive what Dimmock and Hadfield have called a 'potent intermingling of elite and popular culture' since both reveal a combination of authorised and unauthorised forms of celebration, demonstrating the extent to which these two modes were intertwined in the period.[29]

'These Great Uproars': Watching the Lord Mayor's Show

The 1617 mayoral Show was produced by the Grocers' Company to celebrate the inauguration of one of their members, George Bolles. The resultant book, entitled *The tryumphs of honor and industry*, was written by Middleton, who in association with his collaborators Rowland Bucket, Henry Wilde and Jacob Challoner had designed the pageantry and devised the speeches. The Show itself was composed of the by-now conventional series of emblematic tableaux commenting on some aspect of the Grocers' Company and on the requisite moral qualities for the chief governor of the City, accompanied by various sideshows, pyrotechnics, music and cannon-fire. The Show was a major event in the civic calendar and, as we will see, it attracted a very large and diverse audience. In principle, these triumphs (the preferred term in the period) presented a coherent and unified version of civic power; in practice, however, they were as prone to reveal signs of conflict and tension as any other form of mass popular culture.

The formal, admonitory aspect of the Shows, however, was always at the forefront of Middleton's mind. In this particular instance he was at pains to stress that the festivities were not simply 'an idle Relish' produced for empty, extravagant display, but that they had a serious purpose, which was to put on an 'imitation of Vertue and Noblenesse'.[30] 'A Company of Indians' formed the centre-piece of the first pageant, enabling references to the Grocers' trade in exotic spices such as pepper and nutmeg. The personage of India, 'the Seate

---

[27]   'Introduction', in J.R. Mulryne and Elizabeth Goldring eds, *Court Festivals of the European Renaissance* (Aldershot: Ashgate, 2002), p. 2.

[28]   I discuss the treatment of the Spanish match in the 1623 Lord Mayor's Show in more detail in my *Pageantry and Power*, pp. 298–300.

[29]   Dimmock and Hadfield, *Literature and Popular Culture*, p. 1.

[30]   *The tryumphs of honor and industry* (London: printed by Nicholas Okes, 1617), A3r-v. George Bolles was a man of quite stringent Protestant views: during his term of office he is said to have rebuked the King for progressing through the City during divine services on a Sunday.

of Merchandise', as Middleton puts it, was accompanied by emblematic figures representing the qualities of trade, 'Traffique or Merchandize' and 'Industry' (sig. A4v). To reinforce the message about the global reach of traffic and industry, the second device centred on 'the Pageant of seuerall Nations'. Here the audience were presented with speeches delivered by a Frenchman and a Spaniard, who were included, Middleton claims, because they had 'a thirst to utter their gladnesse' at the installation of the new Lord Mayor (sigs B1v–B2r). As we will see from an eyewitness account shortly, however, the onlookers' reaction to the appearance of these strangers demonstrated rather less decorum. Finally, the day concluded with 'the Castle of Fame or Honor', where notable past dignitaries of the Company were paraded.

One does not, however, have to rely exclusively on the printed book with its own specific agenda for a sense of how the event transpired. Fortuitously, a very detailed account of the 1617 Show was drawn up for an official report back to Venice by Orazio Busino, the Venetian ambassador's chaplain.[31] Our eyewitness appears to have had a particular interest in entertainments, for he recorded his impressions of a court masque and a play at the Fortune theatre as well as the 1617 Show. Eyewitness accounts such as these are especially valuable in capturing the most ephemeral, impromptu aspects of popular festive celebrations. They offer a space for contingency and interaction with audience and participants that the printed books could not accommodate. Busino's first-hand account of the latter event also provides an outsider's perspective, and since he is unlikely to have been able to understand the songs and speeches (he confesses to having been 'bewildered' by what he was seeing), his recollections focus on the spectacle and, importantly, the behaviour of the audience. The title of his report states that the Show was a 'Public Solemnity performed for the satisfaction of the populace', and accordingly he describes the vast audience as 'a fine medley' of young and old, rich and poor, male and female, English and 'alien'. The official part of the day was not neglected. Busino witnessed the water show as well as the show on land and he provides a colourful description of the lavish formal festivities:

> The ships were beautifully decorated with balustrades and various paintings. They carried immense banners and countless pennons [pennants]. Salutes were fired, and a number of persons bravely attired played on trumpets, fifes and other instruments … We also saw highly ornamented stages with various devices which subsequently served for the land pageant.

This description bears out the 'no expense spared' approach one gleans from the records of the Grocers' Company, whose members funded the Show. Busino also notes accompanying music – the City Waits with their trumpets, flutes and fifes were usually employed to play on the barges and on Cheapside – and the use of cannon-fire to punctuate the proceedings. Indeed, the musical instruments – trumpets, drums and fifes – were those conventionally used for processions; they were chosen to produce the loudest and most robust sound possible.[32]

At the same time, Busino's attention was often drawn to incidents that had little to do with the actual Show but which evidently provided an enjoyable spectacle on the sidelines. Those who watched the Lord Mayor's Show, it appears, were willing to participate as well as spectate. *The tryumphs of honor and industry* includes a speech in Spanish to accompany 'the

---

[31]   Ambassadors often attended the Lord Mayor's Show. All quotations from Busino are taken from *CSP Venetian*, vol. XV, pp. 62–3: www.british-history.ac.uk/report.aspx?compid=88665.

[32]   See also Jane Palmer, 'Music in the Barges at the Lord Mayor's Triumphs in the Seventeenth Century', in Kenneth Nicholls Palmer, *Ceremonial Barges on the River Thames* (London: Unicorn Press, 1997), pp. 171–4. Less noisy musical interludes were provided by the child singers often employed on these occasions (indeed, Anthony Munday was chastised in 1609 by the Ironmongers' Company because 'the Musick and singinge weare wanting' (GH MS 16,967/2, fol. 66b)).

Pageant of the Nations'. In performance on the day, the man playing the Spaniard – who, Busino writes, 'imitated the gestures of that nation perfectly' – took advantage of the presence of recognisable overseas spectators (the Spanish wore distinctive costume) to extemporise.[33] Busino writes that the actor 'kept kissing his hands, right and left, but especially to the Spanish ambassador, who was a short distance from us, in such wise as to elicit roars of laughter from the multitude'.[34] Clearly, regardless of the probable intention of the pageant to present unity within the various nations, the actor was appealing to the longstanding popular animus against Spain which was such a central feature of my second example below.[35] Busino, who admits to anti-Spanish 'prejudice', never passes up an opportunity to record the indignities suffered by Spaniards. He goes on to describe how

> some of our party saw a wicked woman in a rage with an individual supposed to belong to the Spanish embassy. She urged the crowd to mob him, setting the example by belabouring him herself with a cabbage stalk and calling him a Spanish rogue, and although in very brave array his garments were foully smeared with a sort of soft and very stinking mud ... Had not the don saved himself in a shop they would assuredly have torn his eyes out.

The degree of coverage given in the report to the treatment of Spaniards, real and pretended, indicates that Busino was struck by the unruly behaviour of the crowd at least as much as he was by the formal celebrations. He remarked less sympathetically that 'the insolence of the mob is extreme'; certain individuals, he wrote, 'cling behind the coaches and should the coachman use his whip, they jump down and pelt him with mud. In this way we saw them bedaub the smart livery of one coachman, who was obliged to put up with it.' 'In these great uproars', he concludes, 'everything ends in kicks, fisty cuffs and muddy faces'.

Although Middleton's printed text strives to confer decorum and formality upon the proceedings, as befitting the nature of a day of 'solemnity', it is clear that the assembled crowd had ideas of their own about how the festivities should be enjoyed. For many present on the day, the boundary between onlooker and participant was there to be transgressed. 'An incessant shower of squibs and crackers' were thrown down into the streets from the windows above, Busino records, and although (as was the usual practice) 'a number of lusty youths and men armed with long fencing swords', as well as 'men masked as wild giants who by means of fireballs and wheels hurled sparks in the faces of the mob' attempted to clear the way and control the crowds, the impression is one of barely controlled chaos. Documentary records bear out what Busino says, with drunkenness and misbehaviour being a regular aspect to the civic festivities. In November 1629, for example, Benjamin Norton, a Clothworker, appeared before the Court of Aldermen after having been 'arrested for throwing squibbs into the streete upon the Lord Maiors Day past' in precisely the way outlined by Busino above.[36]

---

[33] To make a convincing Spaniard, 'he wore small black moustachios and a hat and cape in the Spanish fashion with a ruff round his neck and others about his wrists, nine inches deep'.

[34] Busino also mentions 'two ugly Spanish women ... ill dressed, lean and vivid with deep set eye balls [who were] perfect hobgoblins'.

[35] Cressy argues that in this period 'popular opinion, in as far as it can be reconstructed, was vehemently, almost pathologically, anti-Spanish'. Cressy, *Bonfires and Bells*, p. 96.

[36] Court of Alderman Repertories, vol. 44, fol. 2r.

Bonfires, Bells and Booze: Celebrating the Return of Prince Charles

The crowd were given even greater freedom to produce their own version of festival on another October day just six years later. Prince Charles, the Duke of Buckingham and their entourage arrived back in England from the failed marriage negotiations in Madrid on 5 October 1623, three weeks before that year's mayoral Show. Celebrations of their safe arrival at Portsmouth – or rather, celebrations of the perceived failure of the Spanish match thinly disguised as joy at their safe arrival – were widespread, and they extended, reports claimed, to Scotland and Ireland.[37] Indeed, as with 5 November, 5 October 1623 became a date to commemorate for years to come.[38] The festivities had every appearance of spontaneity, too. Various contemporary witnesses testify that the delight expressed 'by all sorts of people' was unprecedented in the Jacobean period; powerful figures including Archbishop Laud expressed their astonishment at the popular response to the prince's return from Spain.[39] Although there undoubtedly were on this occasion aspects of what Cressy calls 'stage-management', as he remarks, 'authenticity and manipulation are not ... necessarily exclusive [and] a truly popular celebration can be fuelled or fostered by official prompts'.[40]

There are accordingly many and diverse sources of evidence for the popular celebrations of Charles's salvation from the twin perils of a perilous sea voyage and a Catholic bride. Letters flew back and forth across the country to spread the news, and the event prompted the publication of a number of broadsides, ballads and pamphlets and the circulation of illicit verse 'libels'. All these printed books and manuscript texts focused on the numerous outbreaks of apparently spontaneous street festivities, and the fact that these were testified to in very similar terms in both public and private media confers a degree of accuracy upon the varying accounts. Interestingly, a more straightforwardly 'elite' treatment of the return of the prince, Jonson's masque *Neptune's triumph for the returne of Albion*, designed to be performed during the Christmas festivities at court, never actually took place although it was printed.[41] The field was left, then, to other voices to convey their feelings about the events.

A lively sense of popular celebration is conveyed by one of the anonymous broadsides produced to exploit the joyous occasion, *The high and mighty Prince Charles ... his happy returne, and hearty welcome ... the fifth of October, 1623*. 'No tongue can halfe expresse / The rauisht Countries wondrous ioyfulnesse', the writer begins, although he or she then proceeds to try. The whole country was given over to raucous celebration, it would appear:

> *The Peoples clamour, Trumpets clangor, sound*
> *Of Drums, Fifes, Violls, Lutes, these did abound;*
> *Loud Cannons thundring from the Castels, Towers,*
> *And Ships, shooke Ayre and Earth ...*

---

[37] A highly ideological version of the reaction to events in the English plantations in Ireland is presented in Stephen Jerome, *Irelands iubilee, or ioyes Io-paean, for Prince Charles his welcome home* (Dublin: printed by the Society of Stationers, 1624).

[38] Thomas Cogswell writes that 'for the rest of the decade the return of the prince remained popular material for literary treatment ... [A]t St Margaret's, Westminster, church bells continued to toll on [5 October] until the outbreak of the Civil War'. Thomas Cogswell, *The Blessed Revolution: English Politics and the Coming of War, 1621–1624* (Cambridge: Cambridge University Press, 1989), pp. 10–11.

[39] Ibid., pp. 10–11.

[40] Cressy, *Bonfires and Bells*, p. 101.

[41] Ben Jonson, *Neptune's triumph for the returne of Albion* ([London: s.n.], 1624). The title page nevertheless claims that it was 'celebrated ... at the Court on the Twelfth night'. In fact, the masque was first postponed to Shrovetide and then cancelled entirely due to irreconcilable political pressures from the Spanish and French ambassadors. See Ian Donaldson, *Ben Jonson: A Life* (Oxford: Oxford University Press, 2011), pp. 393–4.

To accompany the racket, the traditional devices of popular festivity were employed: 'all to their powers', we are told, 'Pourde healths of wine for welcome; Bels were rung, / Bonefires [*sic*] were kindled, fire-workes each-where flung'.[42] Indeed, Cressy argues that the usual elements of festivity, 'fire, noise, alcohol, and crowds', achieved an unparalleled 'intensity' on this occasion.[43]

John Taylor, who managed to be on the spot at both Portsmouth and London, produced a longer and more detailed work on the subject.[44] His equally hyperbolic account, *Prince Charles his welcome from Spaine*, claims that on hearing that the Prince had merely arrived at port to *depart* from Spain, the celebrations commenced immediately: 'the great Ordnance thundered and filled the earth and skies with loud reioycings, the trumpets clangor pierced the welkin, the beaten drummes ratled [*sic*] triumphantly [and] all manner of Instruments sounded melodiously'.[45] Again, the celebrations must have been very noisy, with trumpets, drums and 'all manner of Instruments' (probably not played as 'melodiously' as Taylor claims) adding to the din. As one might expect, this was just a taster of what was to come. Taylor, as a de facto Londoner of some 30 years' standing, singles out the City of London as the location of the most extensive celebrations of the Prince's return. He concedes that 'the whole Kingdome' experienced 'excessive ioy'; however, as with mayoral inaugurations, the City 'spared for no cost' and showed the rest of the country how to party.[46] Taylor summarises the festivities in London thus:

> The Bels proclaim'd aloud in euery steeple,
> The ioyfull acclamations of the people.
> The Ordnance thundred with so high a straine,
> As if great Mars they meant to entertaine.
> The Bonfires blazing, infinit almost,
> Gaue such a heat as if the world did roast.
> True mirth and gladnesse was in euery face,
> And healths ran brauely round in euery place. (B1r)

From his urban vantage point Taylor was able to provide an apparently first-person description of the forms of celebration in London with equivalent detail to that of Busino's

---

[42] Anon., *The high and mighty Prince Charles, Prince of Wales, &c. the manner of his arriuall at the Spanish Court, the magnificence of his royall entertainement there: his happy returne, and hearty welcome both to the king and kingdome of England, the fifth of October, 1623* ([London: s.n.], 1623). To underscore its authenticity as a documentary record, the text includes footnotes 'for the better explayning some of the Verses, and Story'.

[43] Cressy, *Bonfires and Bells*, p. 104.

[44] 'At Portsmouth [Taylor and some friends] were welcomed aboard the flagship of the fleet waiting to fetch Prince Charles home from Spain' (Bernard Capp, *ODNB*). Taylor's pamphlet about Charles's return was rushed to the press, being registered with the Stationers' Company only a day after the London celebrations. By this date Taylor, who held both strong Protestant and royalist sympathies, had established a productive sideline in pamphlets about events concerning the royal family: he published verses on the death of Prince Henry in 1612 and a celebratory work about the marriage of Princess Elizabeth to the Elector Palatine in 1613. For more on Taylor's involvement in the 1623 moment, see Clare Wikeley, 'Honour Conceal'd; Strangely Reveal'd': The Fool and the Water-Poet', in Alexander Samson ed., *The Spanish Match: Prince Charles's Journey to Madrid, 1623* (Aldershot: Ashgate, 2006), 189–208.

[45] John Taylor, *Prince Charles his welcome from Spaine* (London: printed by G[eorge] E[ld] for John Wright, 1623), A4r. Further references to this work are given in the body of the essay.

[46] Cogswell described the reception Charles received in the capital as 'pandemonium'. Cogswell, *The Blessed Revolution*, p. 6.

treatment of the 1617 Show.[47] He provides anecdotes replete with local colour: 'I heard it credibly reported', he states, 'that there was one Bonefire made at the Guildhall … which cost one hundred pounds (belike it was some Logwood which was prohibited or unlawful to be used by Dyers, and being forfeited it was ordained to be burnt in triumph)' (B1v). Alastair Bellany and Andrew McRae write that 'the festivities for the return of Prince Charles – church bells, bonfires in the streets, drums and cannon salutes – were part of the early modern English "vocabulary of celebration" … and were thus similar to those used at the installation of Lord Mayors of London'.[48] The correspondences with the Lord Mayor's Show are indeed numerous. For one thing, Taylor (who was to write a mayoral Show himself a decade later) calls the celebrations of Charles's return 'triumphs', the usual term for mayoral Shows in this period, and like Busino he focuses on the behaviour of 'all estates' of the people. Further echoing Busino, he invokes a 'most merry and ioyfull confusion' of celebration involving 'people of all degrees, from the highest to the lowest, both rich and poore' (B1v, B2v). As in Busino's account of the 'incessant shower of squibs and crackers' being thrown around during the 1617 Show, Taylor recounts that there were 'Cressit lights, and most excellent fireworkes, with squibs, crackers [and] racketts, which most delightfully flew euery way' (B2v–B3r).[49] The sheer din of the celebrations also resembles that of the Lord Mayor's Show, featuring what Taylor calls 'the reioycing noyses of Instruments, Ordnance, Muskets, Bels, Drums, & Trumpets' (B1v).

One of the major differences between the festivities in October 1623 and those of the mayoral Show, however, was that the person who was being celebrated, Prince Charles, was virtually absent on the former occasion. In the context of that absence, what comes across particularly vividly from Taylor's pamphlet as well as from other contemporary witnesses is the degree of unfettered agency on show. As with popular festival since time immemorial, the City's population treated the occasion as a holiday. 'No shops were opened', Taylor writes, and 'no manner of worke was done from morning till night' apart from building the ubiquitous bonfires and, of course, the 'filling and emptying of pots' (B1v). Although, Cogswell writes, 'the Lord Mayor had ordered the constables to prepare the customary demonstrations of joy … [t]he citizens … had already anticipated the command and were in the midst of celebration'.[50] Indeed, according to Simonds D'Ewes, a student in London at the time, ''Twas pretty to observe the difference between the bonfires made by command … [and those] that were made upon the matter voluntarily, the first being thin and poor, [the latter] many and great.'[51] On this day of revelry Londoners were en fête – free to drink vast quantities, to feast from communal tables, to set off muskets and cannons and set fire to anything that came to hand, from logs and baskets to hogsheads and barrels (the latter no doubt emptied specially). One contemporary observer, John Woolley, wrote to William Trumbull (an overseas diplomat) that 'the people for joy and gladness ran up and down like madde men and none of what condition soever would work upon that day'.[52]

---

[47]   Other printed works, such as William Hockham's broadsheet *Prince Charles his welcome to the Court* (London: printed by Edward Allde for John Wright, 1623), are much vaguer than Taylor about the festivities, suggesting the use of second-hand sources.

[48]   'Early Stuart Libels: An Edition of Poetry from Manuscript Sources', ed. Alastair Bellany and Andrew McRae, *Early Modern Literary Studies Text Series* I (2005): http://purl.oclc.org/emls/texts/libels/, Nv18, note 10 (further references to this collection are abbreviated to 'Early Stuart Libels').

[49]   Cressets were metal holders or baskets for torches. They were purchased in large numbers for mayoral Shows since part of the day's entertainment would have taken place in autumnal darkness.

[50]   Cogswell, *The Blessed Revolution*, p. 6.

[51]   Cited in Cressy, *Bonfires and Bells*, p. 94. D'Ewes is referring to when Londoners responded 'grudgingly' to orders to light bonfires on Charles's arrival at Madrid some seven months earlier. Ibid., p. 96.

[52]   Trumbull MSS, XLVIII/104; cited in Cogswell, *The Blessed Revolution*, p. 8.

Unlike the Lord Mayor's Show or the royal entry, as Cressy suggests, 'there was no centrepiece to the celebration, no contrived court ceremony [and] no triumphant procession'.[53] There was instead a literally intoxicating and doubtless quite perilous juxtaposition of booze and bonfires. As Cressy notes, 'Taylor was inspired by the vast and varied drinking of the day.'[54] The latter indeed evokes a bacchanalian picture: 'Whole pintes, quarts, pottles, and gallons, were made into Bonefires of Sacke and Claret', he writes, and in turn 'good fellowes like louing Salamanders swallowed those liquid fires most sweetly and affectionately' (B2r). Danger was present throughout the day: George Calvert, the Secretary of State, observed that the bonfires 'might have hazarded the burning of the streets, had they not been allayed with London liquor'.[55] The sheer number of impromptu conflagrations did cause some problems, ironically enough, for the man whose return was being celebrated. The coach bearing Prince Charles himself was prevented from travelling through the City due to the vast numbers of bonfires blocking the thoroughfares.[56]

One therefore gains a sense of the *materiality* of popular festive culture in the period. According to Taylor, households were ransaked for items to burn, with items including 'mouse-traps' and 'old graters and stooles' being added to the various conflagrations. Local knowledge is also brought into play. As we have already seen, place names add to the authority of the text. Taylor notes that 'the very Vintners burnt their bushes in Fleetstreet and other places' (B2r) and as a high-profile member of the Watermen's Company he could not resist the addendum, 'it is to be remembered, that two Watermen at the Tower Wharfe burnt both their Boats in a Bonefire most merrily' (C3r). Similarly to the Shows, which were pre-eminently street entertainments, Taylor's text reveals the extensive use of outside locations as the venues for festivity. 'Streets, lanes, courts, and corners' all had their bonfires; indeed, according to Taylor, 'betwixt Paules Church yard & London-bridge … there were at least 108 Bonefires', not including those set up in 'the Strand, Westminster, and Holborn' as well as 'hundreds of places which [Taylor] saw not' (B3r).[57] Paul's Churchyard, the traditional location of one of the mayoral pageants, was the site for 'two mighty bonfires', along with 'a crosse of wood … extended into foure branches'; Paul's Cross itself was adorned with 'as many burning Linkes as the Prince his Highnesse was years old' (B2v).

Corroboration of these various accounts is provided by a series of contemporary anonymous 'libels'. These illicit texts arguably offer an even more 'popular' and certainly more irreverent voice than the two printed works discussed above. Expressions of joy remain indisputable; what remains at issue, as Cressy reminds us, are 'the ambiguous issues of spontaneity and control, and the haunting question of who was saying what to whom'.[58] At some levels, the libels reiterate the messages put across in printed works. Thus 5 October will remain 'for eternitie / A day of rest and sport', states the libel entitled 'Oh for an Ovid or a Homer now'.[59] Another, 'Of Prince Charles his voyage into Spayne' (otherwise known as 'The fift of August, and the fift') notes the common ground with the mayoral Show. On hearing bells and cannon-fire one might presume that celebrations of a mayoral installation were underway; however, on this occasion, 'It is not for a Mayor, or such a toye; / The melancholy drums do beate'. The same festive features highlighted in the printed sources

---

[53]   Cressy, *Bonfires and Bells*, p. 101.
[54]   Ibid., p. 99.
[55]   *CSPD*, 1623–5, p. 89; cited in Cressy, *Bonfires and Bells*, p. 96.
[56]   See Cogswell, *The Blessed Revolution*, p. 7.
[57]   Simonds D'Ewes's diary records '335 [bonfires] between Whitehall and Temple Bar'. Cited in Cressy, *Bonfires and Bells*, p. 94.
[58]   Cressy, *Bonfires and Bells*, p. 93.
[59]   'Early Stuart Libels', Nv16, lines 80–81.

re-occur: 'the bonefires all are in a sweate', 'the belles ring' and 'gunnes sing'; moreover, it 'shalbee treason to bee sober / On the fift day of October'.[60]

One significant difference between these libels and printed texts, however, is the overt treatment of religious politics. Lighting so many fires on a day of constant rain and in the context of a wood shortage stood not just for 'community and joy', Cressy argues, but also 'defiance'. The ceaseless bell-ringing, too, can be seen to have acted as what Cressy calls 'a communal exorcism of the Spanish threat'.[61] England is celebrating, the second libel asserts, not solely because the Prince is safely returned, but because there is no longer the prospect that 'the pope / Could make here a Romish plantation'. Another libel, 'The Prince is now come out of Spayne' (which features a scurrilous reference to 'the Cunninge of old Gundamore'),[62] puts forward the same point in even more explicit terms:

> They tolde us twenty thousand lyes,
> To feede the peoples fantasies;
> And put them in great feare.
> But when the Prince to England came,
> And brought not home the Spanish Dame,
> The Papists hung their eares.[63]

This work also presents a more sceptical take on popular festivity than is evident in the other texts under discussion.[64] Here the celebrations are evidence of political naivety rather than righteous elation. A man rejoicing at the Prince's deliverance is for this writer just 'some Maudlinn drunke' (line 34), and in place of Taylor's scene of spontaneous comradeship a sourer note is struck: 'So to the taverne all they went, / And every foole his verdict spent, / And then the bells did ring' (lines 40–42). This anonymous writer offers a dispassionate contemporary view on Cressy's observation that 'princes were supposed to be greeted with enthusiasm, and a genre had developed to describe it'.[65] More troublingly for James's 'pacific' rule, the searing religious politics of the period are foregrounded here. The bonfires so widely cited simply as evidence of unmitigated joy in the other accounts of the 1623 festivities serve in this instance as what Bellany and McRae call a 'mordant' reminder of the fires that consumed Protestant 'martyrs' in the mid-sixteenth century: 'It's thought that since Queene Maries days / There was no such a fyre', observes the poet.[66]

The 'great excess and drunkenness' that D'Ewes lamented in 1623 resulted in a virtually carnivalesque scene that day: as Cressy argues, 'conventional respect for property and commodities was inverted, private possessions became public property, wood carts

---

[60]   'Early Stuart Libels', Nv18, lines 31–5, 4–5.

[61]   Cressy, *Bonfires and Bells*, pp. 104–5.

[62]   'Gundamore' is Count Gondomar, the notorious Spanish ambassador, who played a central role in the marriage negotiations and who was extensively mocked in *A game at chesse* the following year.

[63]   'Early Stuart Libels', Nv17, lines 7–12.

[64]   A different perspective is presented by a work by Andrés Almansa y Mendoza, *The ioyfull returne, of the most illustrious prince* (London: printed by Edward Allde for Nathaniell Butter and Henry Seile, 1623). As one might expect of a text apparently 'translated out of the Spanish Copie', Charles's safe arrival back at Portsmouth is here described as a cause for the 'unspeakable Ioy of *both* Nations' (A1r, my emphasis). The text resembles the English versions, however, by referring to bells, bonfires and ordnance being set off on Charles's arrival. See also Henry Ettinghausen, 'The Greatest News Story since the Resurrection? Andrés de Almansa y Mendoza's Coverage of Prince Charles's Spanish Trip', in Samson, *The Spanish Match*, pp. 75–89.

[65]   Cressy, *Bonfires and Bells*, p. 100.

[66]   'Early Stuart Libels', Nv17, lines 29–30.

[normally protected by law] were commandeered, and valuable items were consigned to the flames'.[67] Furthermore, the events that took place in October 1623 reveal the potentially dangerous interconnections between popular festivity and domestic and foreign affairs in early Stuart England. The popular celebrations of Charles's return, with their double-edged reference to the failed marriage negotiations, had the potential to highlight, even to challenge, the precarious balance being struck by Jacobean state policy. King James would have been left in no doubt about the weight of popular feeling against closer links with Spain. In this respect the October festivities form a link with more trenchant commentators like Thomas Scott, whose fervently anti-Catholic and anti-Spanish tracts such as *Vox populi* were the chief sources for Middleton's final word on the events of 1623, *A game at chesse*, which itself received unprecedented popular acclaim.

Early modern festive culture was therefore embedded in what Cressy calls 'a cycle of cultural and political collisions' and it manifested both elite and popular traditions and concerns.[68] As historians of popular culture and disorder such as Steve Hindle, Paul Griffiths and Keith Wrightson have shown, festive culture could at times spill over from exuberance into genuine disorder.[69] Festivals reveal the impact of social, political and (especially) religious change on the mass of the population. They acted as a means by which ancient traditions and rituals could be both memoralised and adapted, and they serve as a reminder to future generations that elite, canonical cultural practices cannot tell the full story of the lived experience of early modern popular culture.

Select Bibliography

Anglo, Sydney, *Spectacle, Pageantry, and Early Tudor Policy*. Oxford: The Clarendon Press, 1969.

Archer, Jayne Elisabeth, Elizabeth Goldring and Sarah Knight eds, *The Progresses, Pageants, and Entertainments of Queen Elizabeth I*. Oxford: Oxford University Press, 2007.

Béhar, Pierre, and Helen Watanabe-O'Kelly eds, *Spectaculum Europaeum: Theatre and Spectacle in Europe (1580–1750)*. Wiesbaden: Harrassowitz, 1999.

Bergeron, David, *English Civic Pageantry 1558–1642*. Revised ed. Medieval and Renaissance Texts and Studies vol. 267. Arizona: University of Arizona, 2003.

Cannadine, David, and Simon Price eds, *Rituals of Royalty: Power and Ceremonial in Traditional Societies*. Cambridge: Cambridge University Press, 1987.

Clopper, Lawrence, *Drama, Play, and Game: English Festive Culture in the Medieval and Early Modern Period*. London: University of Chicago Press, 2001.

Cressy, David, *Bonfires and Bells: National Memory and the Protestant Calendar in Elizabethan and Stuart England*. London: Weidenfeld and Nicholson, 1990.

Davidson, Clifford, *Festivals and Plays in Late Medieval Britain*. Aldershot: Ashgate, 2007.

Dimmock, Matthew, and Andrew Hadfield eds, *Literature and Popular Culture in Early Modern England*. Aldershot: Ashgate, 2009.

Hanawalt, Barbara A., and Kathryn L. Reyerson eds, *City and Spectacle in Medieval Europe*. Minneapolis: University of Minnesota Press, 1994.

Heal, Felicity, *Hospitality in Early Modern England*. Oxford: Clarendon Press, 1990.

---

[67]   Cressy, *Bonfires and Bells*, p. 105.
[68]   Ibid., p. xiv.
[69]   See, for example, Steve Hindle, 'Custom, Festival and Protest in Early Modern England: The Little Budworth Wakes, St Peter's Day, 1596', *Rural History* 6:2 (1995), 155–78.

Heaton, Gabriel, *Reading and Writing Royal Entertainments*. Oxford: Oxford University Press, 2010.

Hill, Tracey, *Pageantry and Power: A Cultural History of the Early Modern Lord Mayor's Show, 1585–1639*. Manchester: Manchester University Press, 2010.

Howe, Nicholas ed., *Ceremonial Culture in Pre-Modern Europe*. Notre Dame: University of Notre Dame Press, 2007.

Hutton, Ronald, *The Rise and Fall of Merry England: The Ritual Year 1400–1700*. Oxford: Oxford University Press, 1996.

Johnston, Alexandra F., and Wim Hüsken eds, *Civic Ritual and Drama*. Amsterdam: Rodopi 1997.

Kipling, Gordon, *Enter the King: Theatre, Liturgy, and Ritual in the Medieval Civic Triumph*. Oxford: Clarendon Press, 1998.

Klausner, David N., and Karen Sawyer Marsalek eds, *'Bring Furth the Pagants': Essays in Early English Drama Presented to Alexandra F. Johnston*. Toronto: University of Toronto Press, 2007.

Lancashire, Anne, *London Civic Theatre*. Cambridge: Cambridge University Press, 2002.

Leahy, William, *Elizabethan Triumphal Processions*. Aldershot: Ashgate, 2004.

McGee, C.E., and John C. Meagher, 'Preliminary Checklist of Tudor and Stuart Entertainments: 1588–1603', *Research Opportunities in Renaissance Drama* 24 (1981), 51–155.

Middleton, David, and Derek Edwards eds, *Collective Remembering*. London: Sage, 1990.

Mulryne, J.R., and Elizabeth Goldring eds, *Court Festivals of the European Renaissance*. Aldershot: Ashgate, 2002.

Mulryne, J.R., Helen Watanabe-O'Kelly and Margaret Shewring eds, *Europa Triumphans: Court and Civic Festivals in Early Modern Europe*. 2 vols. Aldershot: Ashgate, 2004.

Lancashire, Anne, *London Civic Theatre*. Cambridge: Cambridge University Press, 2002.

Palmer, Daryl W., *Hospitable Performances: Dramatic Genre and Cultural Practices in Early Modern England*. West Lafayette, IN: Purdue University Press, 1992.

Strong, Roy, *Art and Power: Renaissance Festivals*. Woodbridge: Boydell and Brewer, 1984.

Watanabe-O'Kelly, Helen, and Anne Simon, *Festivals and Ceremonies: A Bibliography of Works Relating to Court, Civic and Religious Festivals in Europe 1500–1800*. London: Mansell, 2000.

Withington, Robert, *English Pageantry: An Historical Outline*. 2 vols. New York: Arno Press, 1980.

Popular Reading and Writing

Femke Molekamp

Forms of popular reading and writing in Early Modern England hang together in a dense patchwork made up of vast numbers of varied publications and practices. Everyday writing practices ranged from interpretative annotations in books, to records of family births, deaths and other anniversaries (often written into the blank leaves of bibles), accounts, culinary and medical recipes, letters, prayers, sermon notes and graffiti. The history of such practices is undoubtedly a material history that is centred on the household as a locus of popular textual production as well as a receptacle for text that might be painted on the walls, embroidered onto samplers, graffitied onto furniture or inscribed onto implements.[1] In their heterogeneity, these popular writing practices broadly associated with the household are matched, and perhaps surpassed, by the ever-increasing variety of cheap publications that were offered by the expanding printing press.

Bestselling cheap books, to name a few, included bibles and godly books as well as ballads (from the godly to the scurrilous), abridged romances such as *Guy of Warwick* or *Bevis of Hampton*, almanacs, cony-catching tracts and the vast array of 'news' publications that ranged from sensationalist accounts of wonders, prodigies and gruesome murders to evolving newsbooks containing political and military news (and editorial comment) from home and abroad. A chapman in seventeenth-century England would have a number of bibles and these cheap, popular books in his bag of wares as he travelled door to door. Books of this kind could also be found on market stalls in London and in rural market towns, as well as on the shelves of book shops and as a handful of bestsellers in unspecialised country shops.[2] With the exception of bibles, broadsides and almanacs, these cheap publications have often been described by scholars as 'pamphlets' or 'chapbooks', although there has been no scholarly consensus as to how these categories can be distinguished from each other in either format or content. Joad Raymond specifies that pamphlets were books smaller than a folio of a short-length, usually costing a few pennies only, and Jason Peacey points out that the rough stitching of the pages 'effectively defined the genre, the resulting pamphlets being

---

[1] On embroidering text in early modern England see Susan Frye, *Pens and Needles: Women's Textualities in Early Modern England* (Philadelphia: University of Pennsylvania Press, 2010); and on graffiti and inscriptions onto objects see Juliet Fleming, *Graffiti and the Writing Arts of Early Modern England* (Philadelphia: University of Pennsylvania Press, 2001).

[2] On the distributors of such books see Margaret Spufford, *Small Books and Pleasant Histories: Popular Fiction and Its Readership in Seventeenth-Century England* (Cambridge: Cambridge University Press, 1985), pp. 111–28; Tessa Watt, *Cheap Print and Popular Piety 1550–1640* (Cambridge: Cambridge University Press, 1991), pp. 26–9, 267; and on female roles in distribution: Helen Smith, *Grossly Material Things: Women and Book Production in Early Modern England* (Oxford: Oxford University Press, 2012), pp. 135–74.

sold unbound, and probably with their pages uncut'.[3] Sometimes they were sold bundled together, although this was a more common practice in France and Germany than in England.[4] Exploring the question of what a 'chapbook' is, Lori Humphrey Newcomb reminds us that the term is anachronistic, although the term 'chapmen' is not, as it was used in early modern England to describe itinerant tradesmen selling, among other possible goods, cheap books. Newcomb points out that although scholars have adopted the term 'chapbook' as a heuristic tool, there has been little consensus as to what it actually designates.[5] Definitions and usages have often focused on the cheapness of the publications termed 'chapbooks', and the related low-quality of the paper, type and woodcuts used for them, although one scholar sees the term as purely bibliographical designating 'a half sheet duodecimo'.[6] It is often not clear how chapbooks differ from pamphlets – bibliographical designations in terms of format are very similar – although there has been an occasional emphasis on the heightened social/political topicality of pamphlets.[7] 'Pamphlet', unlike 'chapbook' was a term used in medieval and early modern England. Raymond traces its shifting meanings, and notes that it was often used pejoratively in the Elizabethan period, while in the seventeenth century it is closely associated with controversy. Raymond remarks that 'during the sixteenth and seventeenth centuries "pamphlet" became a useful and meaningful word, but without a firm definition'.[8]

As Newcomb rightly elaborates, the lack of consensus over what, exactly, a chapbook (and arguably a 'pamphlet') is mirrors a wider difficulty in defining popular culture as a category.[9] Acknowledging this perennial problem, which has been examined from an array of theoretical perspectives too numerous to recount here, I want to move to an analogous lack of unity in 'popular' reading and writing practices in early modern England. I want to suggest particularly that the remarkable variety in cheap print publications (and in early modern textual culture more widely) leads to hybridity: early modern popular print culture appears to be a forum in which a host of different genres and reading practices mingle, blend and cross over. Cheap early modern publications, whether we want to call them chapbooks or pamphlets, were often resistant to the boundaries of genre as they frequently displayed generic hybridity, eliciting a multiplicity of reading styles or practices within a single short publication. This essay will explore this hybridity through focusing on a number of different kinds of popular publication, and examine especially, as case studies, a handful of printed reports of miraculously starving maidens produced over almost a century in early modern England.

---

[3]   Joad Raymond, *Pamphlets and Pamphleteering in Early Modern Britain* (Cambridge: Cambridge University Press, 2003), p. 5; Jason Peacey, 'Pamphlets', in Joad Raymond ed., *The Oxford History of Print Culture: Volume I: Cheap Print in Britain and Ireland to 1660* (Oxford: Oxford University Press, 2011), p. 454.

[4]   Andrew Pettegree, *The Book in the Renaissance* (New Haven: Yale University Press, 2010), pp. 149; 4–5.

[5]   Lori Humphrey Newcomb, 'What Is a Chapbook?', in Matthew Dimmock and Andrew Hadfield eds, *Literature and Popular Culture in Early Modern England* (Farnham: Ashgate, 2009), pp. 57–71.

[6]   John Feather, *A Dictionary of Book History* (London: Croom Helm, 1986), p. 63; quoted in Newcomb, 'What Is a Chapbook?', p. 61.

[7]   See, for instance, Peter Lake with Michael Questier, *The Antichrist's Lewd Hat: Protestants, Papists and Players in Post-Reformation England* (New Haven: Yale University Press, 2002); Raymond, *Pamphlets and Pamphleteering*, pp. 6–7; Susan Wiseman, *Conspiracy and Virtue: Women, Writing and Politics in Seventeenth-Century England* (Oxford: Oxford University Press, 2006), pp. 143–79.

[8]   Raymond, *Pamphlets and Pamphleteering*, p. 7.

[9]   Newcomb, 'What Is a Chapbook?',pp. 57–8.

Literacy

Cheap publications varied quite considerably in the density and complexity of their texts: the simplest cheap publications were predominately pictorial broadsides with the inclusion of a simple ditty, while we might count masques and political tracts among the more sophisticated cheap publications of the period. Print could be short and cheap and yet high-brow. As paper was the most expensive commodity in the making of a book, it was the length of a book, rather than its literary sophistication, which exerted the greatest influence over its price. The range in sophistication of cheap print connects, not surprisingly, with the great variety in literacy among the populace, even within the book-buying market. The initial stages of literacy in English were most commonly achieved using the catechism, Psalter and Bible, alongside the ABC, and it should be remembered that these books, including prayer books, were bestsellers.[10] As Margaret Ferguson and Adam Fox have emphasised, it is necessary to treat literacy in early modern England as plural: reading was taught before writing and some individuals who could not write may well have been able to read.[11] Those with the benefits of a good humanist education would have been taught to read and write from a young age, and carefully instructed in grammar and rhetoric. Students engaged in a humanist education programme usually began Latin and writing at seven. Reading was taught before writing and so it may be assumed that those with a lesser education, either at school or at home, may have learnt to read but not to write.[12]

The Protestant mother was exhorted to teach her child to read, and as devotional life fell increasingly into the sphere of the home, mothers became more responsible for their children's education. However much we can contest literacy figures, it is clear that literacy rates for women were consistently lower than for men. Cressy observes that 'more than two thirds of the men and nine tenths of the women were so illiterate at the time of the civil war that they could not even write their own names'.[13] Furthermore, we can deduce from the restricted possibilities for the education of women that the female population struggled to achieve the same literacy rates as the male.[14] In many cases, therefore, where a mother was in a position to teach her children at all, she may only have been able to pass on partial literacy skills.

Outside cities, in communities centred on agriculture, there would have been less of a drive to literacy: 'many people lived on the margins of literacy and were either not convinced of its value or had little opportunity to test it'.[15] In a country of such stratified literacy skills it would have been usual for the literate to assist those who could not read by reading texts aloud. This might occur in the public places where proclamations and statutes were posted; it would also have entailed reading the Bible and other devotional material to those who could not read it for themselves. The influence of print culture in early modern England was such that few could eschew the written word, however, and so many of those who could not write may still have acquired some basic reading skills, and consumed publications such as

---

[10]   Keith Thomas, 'The Meaning of Literacy in Early Modern England', in Gerd Baumann ed., *The Written Word: Literacy in Transition, Wolfson College Lectures 1985* (Oxford: Clarendon Press, 1986), p. 99.

[11]   Margaret Ferguson, *Dido's Daughters: Literacy, Gender and Empire in Early Modern England* (Chicago: University of Chicago Press, 2003), pp. 3–4; Adam Fox, *Oral and Literate Culture in England 1500–1700* (Oxford: Oxford University Press, 2000), p. 47.

[12]   Spufford, *Small Books*, p. 26.

[13]   David Cressy, *Literacy and the Social Order: Reading and Writing in Tudor and Stuart England* (Cambridge: Cambridge University Press, 1980), p. 2.

[14]   Eve Sanders, *Gender and Literacy on Stage in Early Modern Europe* (Cambridge: Cambridge University Press, 1998), p. 170.

[15]   Cressy, *Literacy and the Social Order*, p. 17.

pictorial broadsides with a verse of scripture and a large woodcut or engraved illustration. Versions of this combination of religious text and image were also encountered as wall paintings in the early modern domestic interior, and even on the walls of alehouses.[16]

Popular Print and Strategic Variety in Sophistication

The expanding field of the history of reading has stimulated an interest in tracing not just what was read in early modern England but in *how* it was read. The work of Anthony Grafton, Lisa Jardine and William Sherman first emphasised the 'goal-orientated' or 'active' reading styles of Renaissance scholars such as Gabriel Harvey and John Dee.[17] Stephen Dobranski has shown that active reading in the early modern period involved collaboration between writers (or editors) and readers, in which 'blank spaces' in the text invite readerly intervention.[18] Reading transactions also took place through the act of copying passages into commonplace books, under systematic headings. Recently, scholars have attended to the materiality of reading through studies of what readers wrote, drew or pasted into their books.[19]

The ephemeral nature of so much popular print from this period means that only a small proportion of it is extant. Reading practices associated with much of this material are likewise difficult to capture using measures such as annotation, since so much of the material is lost, and given that annotation of pamphlets was probably not a usual practice; ephemeral material did not lend itself as much to commonplacing, either.[20] Evidences of reading are more visible in the contents of the pamphlets themselves; these publications often responded to each other through reproducing or challenging material expressed in other pamphlets. Pamphlets might, for example, pick up on popular news items reported elsewhere, or they might spar with or further opinions expressed in other tracts. This sometimes lead to a proliferation of pamphlets on a certain topic as a means of generating debate, as in the famous Marprelate controversy, when polemical puritan pamphlets were produced in 1558–9 under the pseudonym 'Martin Marprelate', prompting a tide of responses.

Using collecting practices as evidence of reading habits, some scholars have taken an interest in the fact that a number of bibliophiles such as Anthony Wood, Sir William Clarke, George Thomason, John Egerton, Second Earl of Bridgewater and Samuel Pepys saw fit to

---

[16] See Watt's chapter 'Stories for Walls', in *Cheap Print*, pp. 178–216. Tara Hamling has also written on iconography drawn from print found on the walls of early modern homes: 'Guides to Godliness: From Print to Plaster', in Michael Hunter ed., *British Printed Images: Essays in Interpretation* (Farnham: Ashgate, 2010), pp. 65–85; and *Decorating the Godly Household: Religious Art in Post-Reformation Britain* (New Haven: Yale University Press, 2010).

[17] See Lisa Jardine and Anthony Grafton, '"Studied for Action": How Gabriel Harvey Read His Livy', *Past and Present* 129 (1990), 30–78; and William H. Sherman, *John Dee: The Politics of Reading and Writing in the English Renaissance* (Amherst: University of Massachusetts Press, 1995).

[18] Stephen Dobranski, *Readers and Authorship in Early Modern England* (Cambridge: Cambridge University Press, 2005), p. 22.

[19] See, for instance, Heidi Brayman Hackel, *Reading Material in Early Modern England: Print, Gender and Literacy* (Cambridge: Cambridge University Press, 2005); Femke Molekamp, '"Of the Incomparable Treasure of the Holy Scriptures": The Geneva Bible in the Early Modern Household', in Dimmock and Hadfield eds, Literature and Popular Culture, pp. 121–36; William Sherman, *Used Books: Marking Readers in Renaissance England* (Philadelphia: University of Pennsylvania Press, 2008).

[20] My assertion is that cheap print, by nature of its ephemerality, was less likely to be copied into a commonplace book. Anna Bayman reminds that there are a few examples, however: see Anna Bayman, 'Printing, Learning, and the Unlearned', in Raymond ed., *Oxford History of Print Culture: Volume I*, pp. 76–7.

collect large numbers of pamphlets and chapbooks.[21] This practice was the exception rather than the rule, however. As Andrew Pettegree aptly observes, early modern 'books and pamphlets were torn up for wrapping, for stuffing bindings (and later furniture) and for use in the toilet', and therefore small popular publications were far more likely to meet with an undignified end than to enter a catalogue or a library.[22] The activities of these gentlemen do however serve as an important reminder that popular print was not consumed exclusively by lower social classes, even though, as Spufford and Tessa Watt have pointed out, the average price of 2*d* for a pamphlet in seventeenth-century England meant that a manual labourer could afford to buy this kind of material, if he chose.[23] The market for popular print in early modern England drew together readers from a range of socio-economic classes, arguably challenging normative class boundaries in fostering the development of a 'reading class' with a burgeoning variety of new kinds of reading material available for consumption.[24]

Popular print aptly responded to the considerable variety in literacy and education of the reading public in the range of its publications. Interestingly, the exceptionally popular Geneva Bible also achieved this variety across its editions. We may not automatically think of bibles as 'popular' or 'cheap' print, but the Geneva Bible was , 'in all likelihood, the most widely distributed book in the English Renaissance', selling more than half a million copies by the end of the sixteenth century.[25] It was published in over 140 editions between 1560 and the 1640s. Its popularity depended on the fact that it was produced in smaller formats and therefore cheap, and that it was packed with marginal notes, summaries, diagrams, tables and maps to aid the reader. It was designed to make the scriptures accessible for the purposes of private reading. Prior to its publication, English printed bibles were mostly produced as large folios, lacking the extensive range of reading aids supplied in the Geneva Bible, and more suited to the lectern than to portable reading. The Bishops' Bible folios were considerably more expensive than the popular Geneva quarto. The most sumptuous Bishops' folio edition sold in 1571 for the considerable sum of 27*s*. 8*d*. By contrast, unbound quarto bibles cost between 6 and 7*s*. in the early seventeenth century, and octavo bibles were priced at 3*s*. 4*d* at the end of the century.[26] The Geneva Bible was responsible for popularising these affordable, smaller formats, in which Authorised Versions of the Bible were then also produced.

The Geneva Bible was by no means a single book, fixed in its form, however. It was produced in many different editions, some in roman type and some in black letter, and there are notable differences between the quartos of each typeface. Black letter is a typeface that tended to be used for popular literature such as early chapbooks and ballads; it was also used for children's hornbooks, as well as for catechisms, the Prayer Book and Psalter, which were some of the most commonly read books of the period constituting the standard

---

[21] See especially Michael Mendle, 'Preserving the Ephemeral: Reading, Collecting, and the Pamphlet Culture of Seventeenth-Century England', in Jennifer Andersen and Elizabeth Sauer eds, *Books and Readers in Early Modern England: Material Studies* (Philadelphia: University of Pennsylvania Press, 2002), pp. 201–16.

[22] Pettegree, *The Book in the Renaissance*, p. 334. Spufford also notes that 'chapbooks, with the rest of cheap print, had a secondary function of supplying the very real social need for lavatory paper', *Small Books*, p. 48.

[23] Spufford, *Small Books*, p. 48; Watt, *Cheap Print*, pp. 262–3.

[24] Naomi Conn Liebler, 'Introduction', in Naomi Conn Liebler ed., *Early Modern Prose Fiction: The Cultural Politics of Reading* (New York: Routledge, 2007), p. 6.

[25] Sherman, *Used Books*, p. 72. These figures are taken from Gerald Hammond, 'Translations of the Bible', in Michael Hattaway ed., *A Companion to English Renaissance Literature and Culture* (Oxford: Blackwell, 2000), p. 166.

[26] Ian Green, *Print and Protestantism in Early Modern England* (Oxford: Oxford University Press, 2000), p. 60.

complement of texts for learning to read.[27] Roman type, by contrast, had associations with humanist reading material. While roman type began to overtake black letter during the seventeenth century and is far easier on a modern eye, black letter would have been easier to read for a semi-literate Elizabethan and Jacobean society, who was more used to it.[28] Accordingly, the black letter editions (published from 1578) contained an easy-to-use catechism offering 'Certain questions and answers concerning predestination'; they also provide a short explanation of 'The summe of the whole Scripture of the bookes of the olde and Newe Testament' and a 'Glossary of strange names' which is an index of 'all the English wordes, conducting vnto most of the necessariest and profitable doctrines, sentences and instructions, which are to be found in the olde and newe Testament'. The glossary, in other words, serves as a tool to enhance literacy, as well as to aid bible-reading. In 1587 and 1599 the Roman quartos, but not the black letter, were updated with new translations and notes (by Laurence Tomson and Franciscus Junius, respectively) for the New Testament, even though the black letter quartos continued to be printed until 1616. It appears that the reader of the roman quarto was being offered the latest in continental biblical scholarship, while the reader of the black letter quarto was being schooled in literacy and the basics of bible-reading and theology.[29] The Geneva Bible, the most popular bible of the sixteenth century, had something to offer all kinds of readers who might possess varying degrees of education.

Strategic variety in sophistication of texts also existed in the broad market of news publications in early modern England, catering for an array of different literacies and levels of education. We could count at the more basic end of the spectrum ballads reporting an event using a short, simple text set to a tune, with an accompanying woodcut picture. This is not to say that ballads were designed exclusively for less educated readers, as it is important to bear in mind that 'popular print culture ... was in large part produced, and rapaciously consumed, by the elite', as Anna Bayman remarks.[30] However, ballads might be thought of as potentially reaching a particularly wide array of readers. Printed ballads connect strongly with oral culture too, as they were sung as well as read; they might be heard in the streets since hawkers sung them as a marketing ploy.[31] A pamphlet reporting an event would typically consist of approximately four to 12 pages of text, and sometimes require a higher level of literacy, although some longer ballads containing a longer, more detailed narrative, required the same proficiency of reading (if read rather than heard) as a pamphlet, and so the division between ballads and pamphlets in terms of the requisite reading proficiency cannot be sharply made. Sometimes a reported event would be captured in both a ballad and a pamphlet as the reading public was offered the choice to read about an event through the medium of various different kinds of publication, each drawing on different reading practices.

---

[27] Thomas, 'Meaning of Literacy', p. 99.

[28] For a discussion of trends in typeface during this period see Joseph Loewenstein, '*Idem*: Italics and the Genetics of Authorship', *Journal of Medieval and Renaissance Studies* 20 (1990), 205–24.

[29] For a more detailed discussion of these differences see Femke Molekamp, 'The Geneva and the King James Bible: Legacies of Reading Practices', *Bunyan Studies: A Journal of Reformation and Nonconformist Culture* 15 (2011), 11–17.

[30] Anna Bayman, 'Printing: Learning and the Unlearned', in Raymond ed., *Oxford History of Popular Print Culture: Volume I*, pp. 76–87.

[31] Joshua B. Fisher, '"He Is Turned a Ballad-Maker": Broadside Appropriations in Early Modern England', *Early Modern Literary Studies* 9 (2003), 3.2, http://purl.oclc.org/emls/09-2/fishball.html (accessed 10 October 2012).

Popular Reports of Miraculously Fasting Maidens

Interesting case studies of the appeal to multiple kinds of reading practices in the reporting of a single case can be drawn from a handful of publications reporting the miraculous fasting of virgins that appeared between the late sixteenth and late seventeenth centuries. These young women were alleged to have gone without food for years, surviving, in some cases, on a few drops of liquid, or, in one case, on the scent of a 'pleasant smelling flower'.[32] The common important inference in these reports is that these (Protestant) maidens are ultimately living through faith alone. Such reports take their place within the popular market for accounts of prodigies such as comets and apparitions in the clouds, and marvels such as monstrous births and oddly shaped fish and animals, and miracles.

Although there is only a relatively small number of news reports of miraculously fasting maidens, interest in particular cases saw a proliferation of different kinds of publication reporting on the fasting maiden in question. This suggests the appeal of these stories to the popular imagination. The story of Eve Fliegen, an impoverished 'Dutch maiden' from the town of Meurs who, in 1611 had apparently 'neither eate nor drunke, any manner of Sustenance, by the space of 14 yeares' circulated in England in both a printed pamphlet and a ballad in the Shirburn manuscript, which was almost certainly copied from a lost printed broadside.[33] The manuscript contains 80 ballads copied from printed broadsides mostly dating between *c.* 1585 and 1616.[34] The copying of these cheap forms of print into manuscript itself raises interesting questions about the cultural value of printed ballads, aside from interest in the particular narrative concerning Fliegen.

The news of Fliegen's miraculous fast inspired such interest in her that her image was also memorialised in a woodcut portrait of her that was circulated, and 'apparently a wax figure of her body was displayed in a Madame Tussaud-like museum in Amsterdam'.[35] Fliegen's fasting was also included in George Hakewill's *An Apologie or Declaration of the Power or Providence of God* (1635) as one of a number of examples of 'wonderfull works of God', and included later in the century in a number of encyclopaedic works such as John Reynolds' *A Discourse upon Prodigious Abstinence* (London, 1669) and Nathaniel Wanley's, *The Wonders of the Little World* (London, 1673). A report of a woman from Derbyshire named Martha Taylor, who 'hath lived above forty weeks without tasting any manner of mortal food' was also transmitted in several different forms. It was published in three different pamphlets between 1668 and 1669; it was also included, like Fliegen's story, in Reynolds' *Discourse*, and referenced in a 1669 pamphlet report of another fasting maiden, Jane Stretton of Hertfordshire, and in William Winstanley's popular compendium of knowledge and news which blended 'pleasant astrological, astronomical, philosophical, grammatical, physical, chyrurgical, historical, moral, and poetical questions and answers'.[36] As I have discussed,

---

[32] 'Of a maiden nowe dwelling at the towne of meurs in dutchland, that hath not taken any foode this 16 years, and is not yet neither hungry nor thirsty; that which maide hath lately beene presented to the lady elizabeth, the king's daughter of England. This song was mde by the maide her selfe, and now translated into English', in Andrew Clarke ed., *Shirburn Ballads 1585–1616* (Oxford: Clarendon Press, 1907), p. 56.

[33] *The protestants and Iesuites vp in armes in Gulicke-land. Also, a true and wonderfull relation of a Dutch maiden (called Eue Fliegen on Meurs in the county of Meurs) who being now (this present yeare) 36 yeares of age, hath fasted for the space of 14 yeares, confirmed by the testimony of persons, both honourable and worshipfull, (as well English, as Dutch)* (London, 1611), p. 2.

[34] Clarke, *Shirburn Ballads*, p. 2.

[35] Nancy Gutierrez, *'Shall She Famish Then?': Female Food Refusal in Early Modern England* (Burlington: Ashgate, 2003), p. 84.

[36] Thomas Robins, *News from Darby-shire. Or The wonder of all wonders* (London, 1668), p. 5. This is Robins' first pamphlet concerning Martha Taylor, the second is, *The Wonder of the World; Being a*

it is difficult to ascertain the patterns of reading of ephemeral print, but the transmigration of this story, and others like it, to different forms of writing and print tell us something about its reception, or at least that such stories appeared to be well circulated and to find an enduring place in popular imagination.

Hybrid Reading Practices in the Report of Eve Fliegen: News, Politics and Proofs

The English pamphlet reporting Eve Fliegen's miraculous fasting is translated from the Dutch, and itself is notably hybrid in the forms of writing it contains. Imitating the epistolary form adopted by many early modern news publications, the translated report of Eve Fliegen is embedded within a letter that frames the report at the start and finish. The opening letter proclaims that the translator wished 'to haue my Countreymen in England acquainted with so miraculous a power of Gods worke on so weake a creature, therby the more to magnifie his glory'. In this way, the letter stresses the religio-political significance of the 'news'. The letter urges that: 'If the newes of this be not as yet come to London, I wish you to send it to the Presse.' Like many newsbooks, this pamphlet stresses the currency of the report: 'it is not to be doubted but that a relation so fresh and vn-common, wil be acceptable to our Nation … The report is new and lately published.'[37] The closing letter completes the epistolary frame for the report. Addressed anonymously to 'Beloued Brother' it performs a series of rhetorical gestures to plead for the verisimilitude of the report, urging,

> *if you call to remembrance my former letters (written vnto you about the beginning of September 1605) you shall find in them, a report of this Maiden of Meurs, who at ye time had fasted but eight yeares: which report I know you very sleightly entertained, and as I thinke, thought it fabulous and vntrue: But before that time, and euer since, her manner of liuing hath bene so narrowly looked into, that I am now my selfe thoroughly perswaded to beleeue it, because not onely I, but thousands besides, haue seene her, & can testify with mee.*[38]

Reports of wonders, as well as of crimes, in early modern England frequently incorporate names of witnesses to lend authority to the report, a textual practice that is also adopted by

---

perfect Relation of a young Maid about eighteen years of age, which hath not tasted of any food this two and fifty week (London, 1669). The third pamphlet is H. A., *Mirabile Pecci; or the Non-such Wonder of the Peak in Darbyshire, discover'd in a full, tho' succinct narrative of the more than ordinary parts, piety, and preservation of Martha Taylor, one that hath been supported in time above a year, beyond the ordinary course of nature, without meat or drink* (London, 1669). She is referenced also in M. Y., *The Hartford-shire wonder. Or, Strange news from vvare being an exact and true relation of one Jane Stretton the danghter [sic] of Thomas Stretton, of ware in the county of Hartford, who hath been visited in a strange kind of manner by extraordinary and unusual fits, her abstaining from sustenance for the space of 9 months, being haunted by imps or devils in the form of several creatures here described the parties adjudged of all by whom she was thus tormented and the occasion thereof with many other remarkable things taken from her own mouth and confirmed by many credible witnesses* (London, 1669), p. 1; and in William Winstanley, *The new help to discourse or, Wit, mirth, and jollity intermixt with more serious matters consisting of pleasant astrological, astronomical, philosophical, grammatical, physical, chyrurgical, historical, moral, and poetical questions and answers. As also histories, poems, songs, epitaphs, epigrams, anagrams, acrosticks, riddles, jests, poesies, complements, &c. With several other varieties intermixt; together with The countrey-man's guide; containing directions for the true knowledge of several matters concerning astronomy and husbandry, in a more plain and easie method than any yet extant* (London, 1680).

[37] *The protestants and Iesuites,* p. 1.
[38] Ibid., p. 8.

communications relating to natural philosophical experiments. In the seventeenth century, a scientific culture that had managed to 'purge the body of philosophy' by abandoning reliance upon textual authorities, replaced citation to ancient and modern writers with citation to empirical witnesses of experiments or of reported events (such as monstrous births, comets, tides, etc.).[39] Testimony was no longer sought in ancient textual authorities, but via reputable people who had witnessed 'things', who were thus analogous to witnesses in legal trials.[40] This is matched in the use of eyewitnesses in popular news publications, especially those pertaining to prodigies and wonders. After the Reformation, Protestants generally insisted that the age of miracles had ended. During the seventeenth century, however, the proliferation of Protestant sects, alongside the persistence of Catholicism, led to competing truth-claims within Christianity. Subsequently we see the emergence of propositional, rationalised discourses of religion comparing the religions, and undertaking surveys of 'evidences' of the Christian religion. This is a forensic approach, consonant with that undertaken by experimental science. Peter Harrison has argued that miracles became attached to this evidentiary purpose.[41]

The report of Fliegen draws together the epistolary style of foreign news publications with the forensic style of witnessing found in many other popular news reports. It presents itself as a middle-brow publication aimed at readers with a moderate to high level of literacy in its identification with foreign political news. For this more educated readership the report includes some lines of Latin appearing 'ouer the picture of the maiden in the Dutch Coppy', along with an English translation of the verse, catering also for readers without training in Latin. The textual hybridity of this pamphlet is furthered in the inclusion, interestingly, in four stanzas of ballad verse advertising a similar report concerning another miraculous fasting maiden named Jone Balam from France. The final stanzas attest that:

> Full strange it was to see, her belly was so flat,
> The passages were shut, no entrance there was found,
> She voided nothing forth, nothing at all she ate,
> Her priuy parts were cleane, thence nothing fel to ground
> But yet she speakes, she sighs, she grones, she feels I know,
> Mine eies are witnes sure, here of you need not doubt:
> Which wondrous work doth teach, that nature here below
> By God alone is rul'd, who gouernes all about.

The verse furnishes the possibility for another set of reading practices to come into use for readers who are familiar with or fond of ballads. The lines closely resonate with the story of Fliegen and encapsulate several of the dominant hermeneutic practices found across the pamphlet reports of fasting maidens: a quasi-medical index of the maiden's bodily condition, an eye-witness testimony and a reading of the girl's fasting body as a sign of God's glorious providential work on earth. Despite the religious context, there is also often a voyeuristic quality to these reports, which emerges in the anatomical descriptions, and

---

[39]   Abraham Cowley, 'Ode to the Royal Society', in Thomas Sprat, *History of the Royal Society* (London, 1667), sig. B3ᵛ.

[40]   On comparisons of the Royal Society's methods of testimony and the legal arena see Barbara J. Shapiro, *A Culture of Fact: England 1550–1720* (London: Cornell University Press, 2000), pp. 8–34; and on the importance of the respectability and reputation of witnesses to knowledge-acquisition see Steven Shapin, *A Social History of Truth: Civility and Science in Early Modern England* (Chicago: University of Chicago Press, 1994), pp. 3–42.

[41]   Peter Harrison, 'Miracles, Early Modern Science, and Rational Religion', *Church History* 75 (2006), 493–511.

more pruriently, perhaps, in the double register of the 'sighs and grones' uttered forth by maidens such as Jone Balam.

Implicit or explicit providential readings of maidens' miraculous fasts were often politically inflected in the pamphlet reports. Indeed, sensational news of miracles and prodigies tended to be read within political contexts in Early Modern Europe. They were frequently interpreted with either anxiety or hope as signs of God's' judgement upon contemporary religious and political states of affairs, and during periods of considerable political upheaval they resonated with millenarian hopes. In the 1640s and 1650s, a glut of reports concerning prodigies emerged to serve polemical religio-political agendas on both republican and royalist sides. The early 1660s saw the publication of the *Mirabilis Annus* tracts by opponents of the Restoration, collecting together contemporary prodigies and wonders as signs of 'divine indignation' that 'fore-signifie some remarkable changes and revolutions which bring with them very sad calamities and distresses to the generality of the people'.[42] These polemical collections were produced as instalments in order to keep their price down so that they could be targeted at a popular readership.[43]

The pamphlet report of Fliegen is published together with a political report entitled, *The Protestants vp in Armes in Gulicke-land*, describing the uprising of Protestants against Catholic rule in the Duchy of Jülich situated in the Holy Roman Empire, a conflict which formed part of the 80 years war for Dutch Independence. The Protestant-ruled Palatinate (which became an important international centre of Calvinism) supported Calvinist rebellions in both the Low Countries and France. Although the story of Fliegen appears first in sequence in the pamphlet, the general pamphlet title places news of the Protestant uprising before that of Fliegen: *The protestants and Iesuites vp in armes in Gulicke land. Also a true and wonderfull relation of a Dutch maiden (called Eue Fliegen of Meurs in the county of Meurs) ...*' The structure of the title encourages a politically inflected reading of the miracle of Fliegen, while also of course implicitly furnishing a providential interpretation of the Protestant revolt.

Katerin Cooper and Martha Taylor: Reading Fact and Fiction

Fliegen was not the only maiden living in the Holy Roman Empire who was reported to be the subject of a miraculous fast. Katerin Cooper was another such wonder, described in a pamphlet entitled *A notable and prodigious Historie of a Mayden, who for sundry yeeres neither eateth, drinketh nor sleepeth, nor voydeth any excrements, and yet liueth* (London, 1589). Quite a different set of generic conventions are deployed in this report, which combines the format of a legal inquest or proclamation with extensive medical description of the maiden: numbered items are used to describe the results of an 'inquest' including an examination of Katerin's body, from her face, to her arms, chest, stomach, legs and womb. This anatomical index is used to establish the veracity of the report, and is an early example of a medical interest in fasting women, which increases in the second half of the seventeenth century.[44] Again, the

---

[42]   *Mirabilis annus secundus: or, The second part of the second years prodigies. Being a true additional collection of many strange signs and apparitions, which have this last year been seen in the heavens, and in the earth, and in the waters* (London, 1661), sig. A3ʳ, A3ᵛ.

[43]   Chris Durston, 'Signs and Wonders and the English Civil War', *History Today* 37:10, www.historytoday.com/chris-durston/signs-and-wonders-and-english-civil-war (accessed 12 October 2012).

[44]   On the increasing medical interest in fasting women see Jane Shaw, 'Fasting Women: The Significance of Gender and Bodies in Radical Religion and Politics, 1650–1813', in Tim Morton and Nigel Smith eds, *Radicalism in British Literary Culture, 1650–1813* (Cambridge: Cambridge University Press, 2002), pp. 101–17, 101, 108.

linguistic display of the body of the fasting maiden additionally serves to offer a voyeuristic experience to the reader. The medical inquiry into Cooper's condition is combined with comment on her background, piety and faith, signalling the religio-political interests of the publication. Like Fliegen, Katerin is of a humble Protestant family: her father is a cooper (a maker of wooden vessels such as casks, tubs, buckets, churns, etc.). The report gains an overtly political dimension when it claims that she lost her speech for a while, but that it was miraculously restored by the prayers of a Protestant minister. Here there is further generic diversity as the narrative modulates briefly into the style of romance, describing a pastoral setting and a fabulous event, as it recounts the stealing of a mysterious man into the bucolic setting of Katerin's home:

> *While her father ... as a man of occupation was making of planckes in the forest, and her mother had gone to him ... there came a man into the roome in a Ministers apparel, and drawing neere the bed, lifted her vp vnder the left elbowe, & walking vp and downe with her began to question to with her wither she could pray well whereat she ... could make him no answer, for she was yet dombe. Then he began to pray vnto her (as she termeth it) Gods ten commaundements after the Lutheran manner, and then after such sort as her Minister and Pastor had taught her them, together with the Articles of the faith, the Lordes praier, and the Institution of Baptisme and the Lords Supper, repeating all the premises vnto her, exhorting to her patience, consolation, and assurance that she should shortly receiue her speech, and so he departed suddainly from her.*[45]

Following this recitation of Lutheran liturgy, Katerin does indeed regain her speech, and while the report purports to be a true and literal account of events, there is no doubt a metaphoric value to this example of Lutheran prayer and liturgy restoring a voice at a time when Lutheran (as well as Calvinist) reform had taken hold in the Holy Roman Empire. Likewise the miraculous body of the starving Protestant girl appears, implicitly, to be a providential sign that God will maintain his faithful in the most difficult circumstances.

Published almost a century later, the first of Thomas Robins' two different reports of Martha Taylor shares with Cooper's report an appeal both to fact and to fable that is embedded within a reading of Taylor's body as an edifying sign of God's providential work. The extended title of the report itself conveys the intersection of these various modes of reading:

> *News from Darby-shire. Or The wonder of all wonders That ever yet was printed, being a perfect and true relation of the handy work of almighty God shown upon the body of one Martha Taylor now living about a mile or something more from Backwell in Darby shire, hard by a pasture commonly called Hadin pasture, this maid as it hath pleased the Lord, she hath fasted forty weeks and more, which may very well be called a wonder of all wonders, though most people wh[i]ch hear this may censure this to be some fable, yet if they please but to take the pains to read over the book, I hope that they will be better satisfied and have some faith to believe. This maid is still alive and hath a watch set over her by order of the Earl of Devon-shire. Written by me T. Robins. B. of D. a well wisher to the gospel of Iesus Christ. Oct.13.1668*

Robins stresses here, and in the report itself, that this account deals in the realm of facts and witnesses (including the Earl of Devonshire), and is not a 'fable', and yet it repeatedly

---

[45]   *A notable and prodigious Historie of a Mayden, who for sundry yeeres neither eateth, drinketh nor sleepeth, nor voydeth any excrements, and yet liueth* (London, 1589), pp. 6–7.

deploys the conventions of prose fiction. As a 'wonder of all wonders' existing in the pastoral setting of 'Hadin pasture', Martha sounds here like a character from a pastoral romance. The report itself tells us, in a style redolent of fictional storytelling, that 'near to a Pasture commonly called *Hadin* Pastury in a little house hard by the Mill, there liveth a Damsel called *Martha Taylor*'.[46] Following the usual forensic conventions in these reports, there are witnesses to Martha's fasting, but the description of these witnesses, and the scene they witness, also has a fabulous aspect:

> there was twenty Maids chosen and they did wait with her every one her turn, and has satisfied for very truth that she doth not receive any kind of food into her body, but all that is done unto her, her mother anointeth her lips with a feather and spring water, by reason of the hotness of her breath[47]

Interestingly, as a counterpoint to this fictional style of writing, Robins immediately protests,

> I ... wou'd have you to understand that my belief is that I should be worse then an infidel, if I should set out any such a miraculous thing as this if it were a fable, and being so bold to joyn it with Gods word, no, far be it from me so to do: for I know it to be true by the evidence of her neighbours, and divers persons and men of quality which hath been with her, and doth affirm it to be true[48]

The blend of conventions drawn from prose fiction, and from news (which itself draws upon the convention of offering proofs that is found in legal and scientific writing) simultaneously proffers two different reading styles. The reader is seduced and entertained through the storytelling motifs, and yet asked to read the document as an accurate report that apparently has real, and not simply symbolic, meaning. It effectively 'mediates distinctions among different kinds of narrative agency', to use Amelia Zurcher's observation on the conventions of roman a clef romance.[49] Interestingly, the genre of romance in the seventeenth century, like news, is concerned with the value of both fact (in the form of social realism) and fiction in the act of storytelling.[50] Madeleine de Scudéry emphasises, in her preface to *Ibrahim*, the importance of the rule of *vraisemblance* to her handling of romance:

> To give a more true resemblance to things, I have made the foundations of my work Historical, my principal personages such as are marked out in the true history for illustrious persons, and the wars effective ... for when as falshood and truth are confounded by a dexterous hand, wit hath much adoe to disentangle them, and is not easily carried to destroy that which pleaseth it; contrarily whenas invention doth not make use of this artifice, and that falshood is produced openly, this gross untruth makes no impression in the soul, nor gives any delight.[51]

Fictionality has a more obvious, explicit role in romance than in news; while Thomas Robins claims that he is not writing a fable, de Scudéry writes of her endeavour, 'I am

---

[46]   Robbins, *News from Darby-shire*, p. 2.
[47]   Ibid., p. 3.
[48]   Ibid., pp. 3–4.
[49]   Amelia Zurcher, *Seventeenth Century English Romance: Allegory, Ethics and Politics* (Basingstoke: Palgrave Macmillan, 2007), p. 9.
[50]   My thanks to Alice Eardley for sharing thoughts on these aspects of early modern romance.
[51]   Madeleine de Scudéry, *Ibrahim, or, The illustrious bassa the whole work, in four parts*, trans. Henry Cogan (London, 1674), sig. A2ᵛ.

inventing a fable, not writing a history.'[52] Seventeenth-century romance does, however, demonstrate an interest in the threshold that lies between fact and fiction, which has led Leonard Davis to comment that this 'state of ambivalence … constituted a kind of norm in reading narrative, and narrative as such seems to have been indifferent to the extremes of fact and fiction, preferring to rest in the grey area between'.[53] I want to suggest that a similar 'norm in reading narrative' appears to present itself in some of the pamphlet reports of fasting maidens, and more widely in popular news publications. In 'corantos' (newsbooks reporting overseas news in the 1620s) fable and news reporting were juxtaposed, but more clearly differentiated, usually placing an introductory homiletic fable before the news report. Across the spectrum of news print we can see that literary conventions of storytelling shape or frame reportage.

Hagiography and Reports of Fasting Maidens

Some narrative conventions in the reports of fasting maidens (and other human wonders) are drawn, additionally, from hagiography. The hagiographical dimension of the accounts of the miracle maidens connects particularly with the patterns of self-starvation that occurred in the lives of medieval female saints such as Catherine of Siena, Clare of Assisi, and Bridget of Sweden, and in England of the mystics Margery Kempe and Julian of Norwich. Such practices tended to form part of a model of affective piety. A thirteenth-century chronicler, James of Vitry, describes women in a semi-monastic 'Beguine' community, who

> *dissolved with such a particular and marvellous love toward God that they languished with desire and for years had rarely been able to rise from their beds. They had no other infirmity save that their souls were melted with desire of him, and sweetly resting with the Lord, as they were comforted in spirit they were weakened in body … The cheeks of one were seen to waste away, while her soul was liquefied with the greatness of her love.*[54]

The description has something in common with that of the fasting maidens of the sixteenth and seventeenth centuries, whose bodies have wasted away, while their minds and souls remain fixed upon heaven. In 1668, Thomas Robbins describes how Martha Taylor's body 'is worn away so bare that she hath very smal left on her but skin and bone, she hath no belly to be seen, for her intrails are dried up insomuch that you may see her back bone through the skin of her belly', but 'she is fed with Angels food and the powers of Heaven is with her', and she 'has a great delight to talk and discourse in the Scripture with any Scholar'.[55] Eve Fliegen's fasting, we are told, 'hath brought her body to a weaknes, and her face to an exceeding palenes', and yet she enjoys a visionary experience of heavenly light and taste:

> *She saith that euery second day an exceeding cleere light shineth about her body: the common light or brightnes of the day, being nothing comparable to it: which light*

---

[52]   Madeleine de Scudéry, *Artamene ou Le Grand Cyrus* (Paris, 1664), 4; quoted in Lennard J. Davis, *Factual Fictions: The Origins of the English Novel* (Philadelphia: University of Pennsylvania Press, 1997), p. 28.

[53]   Davis, *Factual Fictions*, p. 30.

[54]   Quoted in Caroline Walker Bynum, *Holy Feast and Holy Fast: The Significance of Food to Medieval Women* (Berkeley and Los Angeles: University of California Press, 1987), p. 13.

[55]   Robbins, *News from Darby-shire*, pp. 4, 6.

> *when she beholdeth and (as she saith) feeleth shining vpon her, she hath likewise a*
> *feeling on her tongue of a strange and extraordinary delicate sweeteness, the moisture*
> *of which strengthens her (to her seeming) for her eies can behold no other thing but*
> *only that perfect and vnusuall light.*[56]

There is a strong connection between asceticism and affectivity in the reports of Taylor and Fliegen: the body in its usual corporeality is dispensed with, to be replaced with heavenly sensuality. This ecstatic dimension of late medieval piety, frequently identified with various saints as mentioned above, is mobilised by the pamphlet writers reporting on miraculous maidens in the late sixteenth, and seventeenth century, who are mostly exponents of experimental Protestantism. The language of desire that we find is still focused on the body, however, as in the description of Fliegen's heavenly 'feeling on her tongue of a strange and extraordinary delicate sweeteness'. These popular publications certainly invested in presenting titillating accounts of the holy maidens they describe, and are not afraid of a tension between a spiritual and prurient register.

Hagiography is, of course, a political form of writing, and in early modern England it is closely connected with martyrology, especially through the immensely popular work, Foxe's *Booke of Martyrs*. There appears to be a kind of syncretism at work in the reports of fasting maidens: these miraculously fasting Protestant women of the pamphlets elicit associations with medieval visionaries that are overlain with associations with Protestant martyrology. Most of the fasting maidens of the reports are handled as exempla of reformist piety, often existing in a locality where political threats are posed to their religion. These publications use the idea of the damaged body, but intact spirituality, of the Protestant in order to champion Protestant fortitude and resistance in times of political adversity. It is not clear what Martha Taylor's religious affiliation was, and so the religio-political agenda is hard to reconstruct, although writing in the 1660s Robbins (who appears to have been a Royalist through the civil war period) may be implicitly appropriating Taylor as a sign of God's pleasure at the Restoration of the monarchy. What is clear, as in other reports of starving maidens, is that her miraculously fasting body is to be read as a glorious sign of divine intervention and sustenance.

I have pointed to the hybridity of genres present in these publications, which, like so many kinds of cheap print, call upon a variety of different reading practices. This hybridity, found also in the conventions of early modern prose fiction, elicits multiple modes of reading. Like prose fiction, popular news publications made these genres and modes of reading 'available to a wider reader audience of "middling classes"'.[57] In the reports of miraculously fasting maidens a forensic narrative approach is frequently coupled with styles and forms drawn from fable, romance, foreign political news, ballad, and hagiography. The variety of different reading and writing styles deployed in these reports may also be seen as an assemblage of a multitude of tools to inculcate a specific political reading, given that these reports of starving pious women were often serving definite religio-political agendas. Popular print publications of various kinds were so often a vehicle for political commentary or propaganda in the seventeenth century, which saw a considerable increase in pamphlet publication. The interesting medley of literary kinds in the reports of miraculous maidens, and other forms of early modern news publication (from ballads to corantos), is well designed to catch the interest of a readership which is itself not only characterised by socio-economic heterogeneity, but also by highly varied tastes in reading in an age in which the printing press offered an ever-expanding choice of reading material.

---

[56] *The protestants and Iesuites*, p. 5.
[57] Liebler, 'Introduction', in *Early Modern Prose Fiction*, p. 2.

Select Bibliography

Cressy, David, *Literacy and the Social Order: Reading and Writing in Tudor and Stuart England*. Cambridge: Cambridge University Press, 1980.

Dimmock, Matthew, and Andrew Hadfield eds, *Literature and Popular Culture in Early Modern England*. Farnham: Ashgate, 2009.

Dobranski, Stephen, *Readers and Authorship in Early Modern England*. Cambridge: Cambridge University Press, 2005.

Ferguson, Margaret, *Dido's Daughters: Literacy, Gender and Empire in Early Modern England*. Chicago: University of Chicago Press, 2003.

Fleming, Juliet, *Graffiti and the Writing Arts of Early Modern England*. Philadelphia: University of Pennsylvania Press, 2001.

Fox, Adam, *Oral and Literate Culture in England 1500–1700*. Oxford: Oxford University Press, 2000.

Green, Ian, *Print & Protestantism in Early Modern England*. Oxford: Oxford University Press, 2000.

Halasz, Alexandra, *The Marketplace of Print: Pamphlets and the Public Sphere in Early Modern England*. Cambridge: Cambridge University Press, 1997.

Hamling, Tara, 'Guides to Godliness: From Print to Plaster', in Michael Hunter ed., *British Printed Images: Essays in Interpretation*. Farnham: Ashgate, 2010, pp. 65–85.

Jucker, Andreas ed., *Early Modern English News Discourse: Newspapers, Pamphlets and Scientific News Discourse*. Amsterdam: John Benjamins, 2009.

Newcomb, Lori Humphrey, *Reading Popular Romance in Early Modern England*. New York: Columbia University Press, 2002.

Pettegree, Andrew, *The Book in the Renaissance*. New Haven: Yale University Press, 2010.

Raymond, Joad, *Pamphlets and Pamphleteering in Early Modern Britain*. Cambridge: Cambridge University Press, 2003.

Raymond, Joad ed., *The Oxford History of Print Culture: Volume I: Cheap Print in Britain and Ireland to 1660*. Oxford: Oxford University Press, 2011.

Richards, Jennifer, and Fred Schurink eds, 'The Textuality and Materiality of Reading in Early Modern England', Special Issue of *Huntington Library Quarterly* 73:3 (2010).

Sherman, William, *Used Books: Marking Readers in Renaissance England*. Philadelphia: University of Pennsylvania Press, 2008.

Spufford, Margaret, *Small Books and Pleasant Histories: Popular Fiction and Its Readership in Seventeenth-Century England*. Cambridge: Cambridge University Press, 1985.

Watt, Tessa, *Cheap Print & Popular Piety 1550–1640*. Cambridge: Cambridge University Press, 1991.

Visual Culture

Tara Hamling[1]

Just a few decades ago a chapter dedicated to 'visual culture' in a volume on the popular culture of early modern England would have been considered a redundant exercise. The standard line found in most traditional accounts of the period is that the culture of early modern England was determinedly anti-visual. Its cultural achievements are generally described in terms of a flowering of literature which, it is implied, overshadowed the limited and inelegant artistic output of (mainly) émigré artists at the royal court. Meanwhile the demise of a vibrant medieval tradition of devotional art and ascendency of an 'iconophobic' Protestant faith created an austere and barren culture of the Word and a population inherently hostile to imagery in all its forms. The inclusion, therefore, of this chapter as a key issue represents a significant sea change in thinking about the nature of visual expression and experience in early modern England.

The standard narrative resulted from biases and omissions in the art historical canon. Traditionally preoccupied with the history of 'great' works of art in grand settings, art historical scholarship has focused overwhelmingly on the achievements of Renaissance Europe. Early modern England, by comparison, has generally been cast as a backward nation on the artistic front with a dependence on the imported knowledge and skills of foreign artists and craftsmen for innovation and progression beyond the residual gothic forms and style of the medieval past. This rather dismal account of the visual arts of early modern England has been amplified by a wider interdisciplinary historiography, with two parallel strands reflecting dominant narratives in literary scholarship and historical disciplines. Firstly, that the cultural developments of the period took the form of poetry and drama centred on London and the court so that there was limited opportunity for access or exposure to the arts elsewhere in provincial England. For example, under the entry for 'art' *The Oxford Companion to Shakespeare* explains:

> *The comparative paucity of references to the visual arts in Shakespeare's works – largely confined to figurative tapestries (such as those which decorate Innogen's bedchamber, Cymbeline 2.4.68–76) and to portraits (most famously those of King Hamlet and Claudius, Hamlet 3.4.52–66) – accurately reflects the poverty and inaccessibility of the visual arts in Shakespeare's England.[2]*

---

[1]   I gratefully acknowledge the generous support provided by a Philip Leverhulme Prize, which allowed me the time to write this chapter and supported the costs involved in reproducing images.
[2]   Michael Dobson and Stanley Wells eds, *The Oxford Companion to Shakespeare* (Oxford: Oxford University Press, 2005), p. 22.

The second strand to conventional wisdom is that the process of religious reform and establishment of Protestantism resulted in a widespread rejection of visual art in favour of a bible-centric culture dominated by oral and written forms of communication. In a highly influential account of the cultural impact of the English Reformation, the religious historian Patrick Collinson described how the secondary thrust of Protestantism 'gathering momentum around 1580 came close to dispensing with images and the mimetic altogether, while disparaging the tastes and capacities of the illiterate, the mass of the people'.[3] Collinson described this 'creeping disappearance of pictorial art' as 'iconophobia', a catchy label that has been picked up and applied indiscriminately to the whole culture in much subsequent writing, with little regard to the careful caveats in Collinson's own formulation of the term.

The first wave of scholarship to take seriously the visual arts of early modern England focused almost exclusively on court culture and elite patronage[4] but more recent scholarship published from the late 1980s onwards has begun to flesh out a wider visual culture and identify a broader range of consumers. It is not feasible to offer a comprehensive survey of this growing body of literature here but it is possible to identify significant interdisciplinary research trajectories for the study of, for example, print;[5] funeral monuments and commemorative culture more generally;[6] buildings;[7] clothing[8] and portraiture.[9] These studies have responded to a broader methodological turn in the humanities concerned with situating cultural products within their historical context and there has been a particular interest in the role of visual art in representing and constructing identity, including my own work on the functions of religious imagery in domestic decoration.[10] A number of museum

---

[3]   Patrick Collinson, 'From Iconoclasm to Iconophobia: The Cultural Impact of the Second English Reformation', first published as *The Stenton Lecture* (Reading, 1985) reprinted in Peter Marshall ed., *The Impact of the English Reformation 1500–1640* (London: Arnold, 1997), pp. 279–308, at p. 297.

[4]   Such as the seminal work on Tudor and Jacobean portraiture by Erna Auerbach, *Tudor Artists* (London: Athlone Press, 1954) and Roy Strong, *Portraits of Queen Elizabeth I* (Oxford: Oxford University Press, 1963) and *The English Icon* (London: Routledge & Kegan Paul, 1969). A notable exception is Eric Mercer's *English Art 1553–1625* (Oxford: Clarendon Press, 1962), which is admirably comprehensive.

[5]   Tessa Watt, *Cheap Print and Popular Piety, 1550–1640* (Cambridge: Cambridge University Press, 1991); Sheila O'Connell, *The Popular Print in England 1550–1850* (London: British Museum Press, 1999); Helen Pierce, *Unseemly Pictures: Graphic Satire and Politics in Early Modern England* (New Haven: Yale University Press, 2009); Malcolm Jones, *The Print in Early Modern England: An Historical Oversight* (New Haven: Yale University Press, 2010); Michael Hunter ed., *Printed Images in Early Modern Britain* (Aldershot: Ashgate, 2010). See also the Arts and Humanities Research Council funded 'British Printed Images to 1700' on-line database: www.bpi1700.org.uk/index.html.

[6]   Nigel Llewellyn, *The Art of Death: Visual Culture in the English Death Ritual c.1500–c.1800* (London: Reaktion, 1991) and *Funeral Monuments in Post-Reformation England* (Cambridge: Cambridge University Press, 2000); Peter Sherlock, *Monuments and Memory in Early Modern England* (Aldershot: Ashgate, 2008); Andrew Gordon and Thomas Rist eds, *The Arts of Remembrance in Early Modern England* (Aldershot: Ashgate, 2013).

[7]   Nicholas Cooper, *Houses of the Gentry, 1480–1680* (New Haven: Yale University Press, 1999); Maurice Howard, *The Building of Elizabethan and Jacobean England* (New Haven: Yale University Press, 2007); Matthew Johnson, *English Houses 1300–1800: Vernacular Architecture, Social Life* (Harlow: Longman, 2010).

[8]   Ann Rosalind Jones and Peter Stallybrass, *Renaissance Clothing and the Materials of Memory* (Cambridge: Cambridge University Press, 2001); Catherine Richardson ed., *Clothing Culture, 1350–1650* (Aldershot: Ashgate, 2004); Robert I. Lublin, *Costuming the Shakespearean Stage: Visual Modes of Representation in Early Modern Theatre and Culture* (Aldershot: Ashgate, 2011).

[9]   Robert Tittler, *The Face of the City: Civic Portraiture and Civic Identity in Early Modern England* (Manchester: Manchester University Press, 2007) and *Portraits, Painters and Publics in Provincial England, 1540–1640* (Oxford: Oxford University Press, 2012); Tarnya Cooper, *Citizen Portrait: Portrait Painting and the Urban Elite of Tudor and Jacobean England and Wales* (New Haven: Yale University Press, 2012).

[10]   Tara Hamling, *Decorating the Godly Household: Religious Art in Post-Reformation England* (New Haven: Yale University Press, 2010).

department catalogues have also in recent years paid greater attention to the social and cultural context of objects alongside more conventional descriptions of technique and levels of skill in the crafting of specific materials.[11]

Yet because single-author publications tend to focus attention on specific categories of building (such as churches, town halls, country houses) or media (whether portraits, ceramics, embroidery, tomb monuments or plasterwork) this growing body of new work on the visual arts of early modern England is rather fragmented and there are still traces of some of the more dominant assumptions and prejudices inherited from the older tradition of scholarship. It can be hard to break free, for example, from the conventional language of connoisseurial judgement based on standards of assessment formalised in the eighteenth century in describing the appearance of vernacular English art from this earlier period. There is still a tendency to focus on patrons and artists at the upper end of the social spectrum and on works of art considered to be technically or historically exceptional. In moving away from a focus on style or technical skill new approaches tend to adopt a linguistic model for interpretation so that works of art are said to have been 'read like a text'. This text-based model assumes a particular kind of engagement with imagery requiring static, close-hand, focused and sustained viewing which in turn restricts the number of individuals able to view effectively at any given time. These various aspects to conventional approaches for studying the architecture and visual arts of early modern England militate against bringing the wider visual culture into view.

This chapter adopts a broad but integrated approach to visual culture in order to acknowledge the permeability between various spheres of experience in early modern England and the role of shared visual forms and motifs in creating connections between them. I am less concerned here with the producers of visual art than with how images operated within culture, that is, in identifying the kinds of imagery on view to a general public and attempting to understand how people below the ranks of the gentry experienced and assimilated the visual messages to which they were exposed. This switch of focus from patrons and artists to the reception of imagery involves paying attention to the contexts and locations in which imagery was seen as well as the physical conditions for viewing. Imagery was not always situated at convenient eye-level for perusal by people at leisure, so that practical constraints on viewing because of the physical position of an image (for example, high up on the exterior of a building) or the interruptions and distractions associated with viewing in environments associated with other activities (domestic, commercial, religious) might determine the form and appearance of art works as well as influencing how viewers looked and assimilated what they saw. Finally, and linked to this interest in the implications of the physical contexts and circumstances for viewing, the chapter responds to Michael Baxandall's concept of the 'period eye' which acknowledges that cultural factors influence the visual characteristics that are considered attractive at any particular time.[12] Following Baxandall, researchers in visual culture differentiate the physiology of sight (vision) from modes of viewing that are culturally determined and conditioned by social values (visuality).[13] Putting emphasis on the visuality – rather than the visual arts – of early modern

---

[11]   To point towards just a few examples: Michael Archer, *Delftware, the Tin-Glazed Earthenware of the British Isles: A Catalogue of the Collection in the Victoria and Albert Museum* (London: Victoria and Albert Museum, 1997); Mary Brooks, *English Embroideries of the Sixteenth and Seventeenth Centuries (Ashmolean Handbooks)* (Oxford: Oxford University Press, 2004); Andrew Morrall and Melinda Watt eds, *English Embroidery from the Metropolitan Museum of Art, 1580–1700* (New Haven: Yale University Press, 2008).

[12]   Michael Baxandall, *Painting and Experience in Fifteenth Century Italy: A Primer in the Social History of Pictorial Style* (Oxford: Oxford University Press, 1974).

[13]   This distinction was first formulated in Hal Foster ed., *Vision and Visuality* (Seattle: New Press, 1988). A working definition of the term 'visuality' is provided in John A. Walker and Sarah

England allows us to investigate ways of seeing and thinking that have been obscured by the imposition of later aesthetic values and artificial hierarchies of 'high' and 'low' culture.

The discussion that follows examines two ubiquitous aspects of the visual culture of early modern England; heraldic and biblical imagery. Sustained discussion of these two iconographic categories might seem surprising as part of this volume's concern with popular culture because they are conventionally associated with the interests and patronage of the social elite on the one hand and ecclesiastical authorities on the other. Yet in early modern England there was considerable mobility and intermingling of iconographies in and across various contexts. This circulation of a common stock of visual motifs is evident in the replication of imagery in and from print. The same woodcut images, for example, were used and reused for a variety of different broadside ballads possibly as a sort of familiar brand to launch new texts to an existing market.[14] The copying of imagery was not confined to printed wares; as Anthony Wells-Cole has shown, prints imported from the continent provided essential sources of design and iconography for a wide range of vernacular crafts.[15] This chapter focuses, however, not on print but on the role of ornament – defined here as applied decoration used in architecture, interior furnishings and other crafted objects – in the transmission of a common visual vocabulary throughout society. As Matthew Rampley points out, many studies of visual culture equate it with the study of the image but this is too narrow a focus because 'the generation of visual meaning involves complex interactions between images and material artefacts, and ... the various practices of visual culture frequently rely on such interactions'.[16] Ornament epitomises this concept of visual culture as an amalgamation of imagery and materiality, with its meanings and functions situated somewhere in the coming together of these two aspects of a crafted art work. The study of decoration has, however, been neglected within the wider turn towards understanding art in its social and cultural context although this oversight is starting to be addressed and new ways of approaching ornament are emerging.[17] For early modern England, ornament was arguably the most significant vehicle for the display and transmission of visual messages and represents an important intersection between the spheres of elite and popular culture. During this period the middling-sort in society increasingly participated in the self-fashioning of identities through investment in their built environment, possessions and clothing so that decoration of these belongings was a key ingredient in the construction of social position, civility and piety. Heraldry and biblical imagery were routinely depicted and often united within the decorative arts of early modern England yet the visual messages and cultural meanings of these forms of imagery are rarely questioned or probed beyond simple identification. It is suggested that these iconographic categories were indissolubly

---

Chaplin, *Visual Culture: An Introduction* (Manchester: Manchester University Press, 1997), p. 22.

[14]   For a brief introduction to these 'promiscuous images' see Simone Chess, 'Woodcuts: Methods and Meanings of Ballad Illustration', *English Broadside Ballad Archive*, http://ebba.english.ucsb.edu/page/woodcuts (accessed 17 December 2012).

[15]   Anthony Wells-Cole, *Art and Decoration in Elizabethan and Jacobean England: The Influence of Continental Prints, 1558–1625* (New Haven: Yale University Press, 1997).

[16]   Matthew Rampley ed., *Exploring Visual Culture: Definitions, Concepts, Contexts* (Edinburgh: Edinburgh University Press, 2005), p. 2.

[17]   Michael Snodin and Maurice Howard's *Ornament: A Social History since 1450* (New Haven: Yale University Press, 1996) was the first major survey of ornamental design in its social context. Recent approaches to early modern ornament are represented by Andrew Morrall, 'Ornament as Evidence', in Karen Harvey ed., *History and Material Culture* (Abingdon: Routledge, 2009), pp. 47–66. An excellent overview of the historiography of architectural decoration is provided in the introduction to Christine Casey and Conor Lucey eds, *Decorative Plasterwork in Ireland and Europe: Ornament and the Early Modern Interior* (Dublin: Four Courts Press, 2012).

linked in the visual and conceptual landscapes of early modern people and had a reach way beyond the 'learned' groups with which they are most often associated.

***

Heraldry was probably the most ubiquitous form of imagery in early modern England and it permeated virtually all spheres of experience. Heraldry developed from its origins in the middle ages as a striking personal emblem to visually identify members of the ruling elite, especially in military pageantry, to become a hereditary mark of distinction indicating an elite bloodline, which could also be used to identify ownership of property. In the later middle ages the system became highly developed with established conventions regulated by professional heralds, yet there was also a more popular and wide-reaching dimension to the heraldic tradition. By the later 1500s heraldic imagery had proliferated and diversified so that full coats of arms and the component parts (shields, charges, crests, supporters) as well as para-heraldic badges could be seen on the exterior of public and domestic buildings and on a range of surfaces including interior decoration, funeral monuments, portraits, clothing, print and a wide variety of crafted objects.[18] Writing between 1635 and 1641 Sir Thomas Shirley observed that:

> *Armes accompany noble families as the shadow doth the body ... They cause them to be painted in their houses, on their household stuff and on their buildings; they make them to be cut on their ringes and signettes; they carry them always aboute them to putt them in mynde of virtue at every step ...*[19]

Shirley's comment seems disingenuous, intentionally or otherwise, in claiming that such depictions of arms were principally intended to benefit the bearer and their social peers. It is clear that heraldic display was used to claim and construct status and identity in the public realm as, for example, in funeral monuments in churches. As Nigel Llewellyn has observed, some tomb programmes comprised virtually nothing but heraldry and while few knew how to decipher its complex rules, all would have recognised its power: 'Those despised by the chivalrous may not have understood its esoteric lore and complex systems of signification but they must have understood it for what it was; a species of social practice restricted to an elite and used in a corporate way by that elite to preserve its distinction.'[20] Cases brought to the Court of Chivalry between 1634 and 1640 demonstrate how heraldry was used as evidence in active competition for degrees of status within the expanding ranks of the gentry.[21] Shirley would hardly wish to draw attention to this vulgar function of heraldic display, even though his own exercises in the genre participated in this fashioning of identities as an attempt to promote the reputation of Catholic gentry.[22]

---

[18]   Heraldic badges may use elements of a coat of arms, such as a charge, crest or supporter but are sometimes a personal device entirely distinct from arms proper. The use of badges was less regulated and therefore more flexible than that of arms, which might explain their proliferation in the early modern period.

[19]   As quoted in Richard Cust, 'Catholicism, Antiquarianism and Gentry Honour', *Midland History* 23 (1998), 40–70, at p. 51. My thanks to Richard Cust for bringing this and other useful material to my attention.

[20]   Nigel Llewellyn, 'Claims to Status through Visual Codes: Heraldry on Post-Reformation Funeral Monuments', in Sydney Anglo ed., *Chivalry in the Renaissance* (Woodbridge: Boydell and Brewer, 1990), pp. 145–60, at p. 145.

[21]   R.P. Cust and A.J. Hopper eds, *Cases in the High Court of Chivalry 1634–1640* (Harleian Society, new series, 18, 2006); examples include case 123: *Constable v. Constable*, pp. 52–4 and case 339: *Kelliawe v. Cullys*, pp. 145–6. Full transcripts available on the searchable website, 'The Court of Chivalry, 1634–1640': http://arts-itsee.bham.ac.uk/AnaServer?chivalry+0+start.anv (accessed 21 November 2012).

[22]   Cust, 'Catholicism, Antiquarianism and Gentry Honour'.

The form and appearance of extant material evidence also suggests that much heraldic imagery was intended for an audience beyond a small clique of nobles. The personal and domestic contexts for display identified by Shirley are now understood to be highly public in their implications. Larger houses were populated by tens if not hundreds of people of various degrees while contemporary expectations surrounding hospitality meant that households were always, at least theoretically, open to guests and strangers. Meanwhile the capacity for clothing and other items worn on the body to demonstrate, or feign, status was recognised by legislation in the form of sumptuary laws.[23] The public function of heraldic display is indicated by the Dacre beasts in the Victoria and Albert Museum (Figure 5.1).

Figure 5.1   The Dacre Beasts, *c.* 1525.
             © Victoria and Albert Museum, London.

These are four large-scale heraldic sculptures in painted oak in the form of a white ram, red bull, black gryphon and dolphin.[24] The sculptures were commissioned by Lord Thomas Dacre around 1520 and celebrate past dynastic alliances through marriage with other leading

---

[23]   Maria Hayward, *Rich Apparel: Clothing and the Law in Henry VIII's England* (Aldershot: Ashgate, 2009).
[24]   Richard Marks and Paul Williamson eds, *Gothic: Art for England 1400–1547* (London: Victoria and Albert Museum, 2003), pp. 292–3.

noble families in the north of England by representing their supporters, that is, the creatures that appear on either side of an armorial shield. They were displayed in the newly created great hall at Naworth Castle in Cumbria and this location, together with their sheer physical scale (the figures range between 185 and 206 cm in height) suggests a desire to impress and intimate larger gatherings of people. In late medieval models of hospitality liberality and largesse were the expected attributes of powerful householders and these virtues were given physical expression in the grandeur and capacity of the great hall. The scale and vivid colour of these sculptures ensure that they capture attention in this space while contributing towards its function as a venue for spectacle and the exercise of rank. The use of supporters to identify families requires little knowledge of the subtler arts of heraldic language and so indicates a desire for notice and comprehension by a wider public. In a culture where scale signified status and power, the message of these crafted figures was unequivocal.

Another item also in the V&A provides a sense of arms being carried around, as Shirley describes, as if shadow to a body. This is an embroidered purse, dating from the 1540s, formed of four shield-shaped panels, each showing the arms of a husband (left) with those of his wife (right) (Figure 5.2). It represents four family alliances, culminating in that of Sir Henry Parker and Elizabeth Calthorpe, which united the heirs of two leading Suffolk houses. The long strings of this purse suggest that it was intended to hang from the waist, so the object is both personal and public. When this purse was worn on the body and therefore seen at some distance it would have been impossible to view the imagery in the round or in sufficient detail to decipher the individual arms. The main impression created by the form of the imagery is the sense of marshalling (the combination of several sets of arms) which signifies multiple family alliances. This in itself communicates a sense of rank because only families with a long and noble lineage could claim pedigrees with armigerous ancestry on both sides of the family. Visual complexity, therefore, like scale and colour, could operate as part of a basic level of heraldic signification when viewed at a distance or in larger groups and this is part of its power.

It is the case, however, that knowledge and use of heraldry was becoming more common outside the ranks of the nobility. The number of publications dedicated to the subject printed from the 1560s onwards indicates an increased interest in the complexities of heraldic language amongst the gentry.[25] Mastery of the rules and complexities of this language was considered desirable in a gentleman but had to be acquired through careful study. A character in Henry Peacham's 'dialogue tending to the Blazon of Arms' printed in 1612 explains his desire to be instructed in heraldry because 'the principal use I would make of this skill is, that when I come into an old decayed Church or Monastery ... or Gentelmans house, I might busie myself in viewing Armes, and matches of Houses in the windows or walls'.[26] This reflects the fashion in the later sixteenth century to adorn the main reception rooms of gentry houses with displays of family lineage and alliances in large-scale surface decoration such as painted schemes, carved chimneypieces and painted glass. This fashion was embraced enthusiastically by the newly elevated, such as Sir Edward Phelips, whose brand new mansion built *c.* 1600 at Montacute in Somerset was adorned with armorial decorations including a stained glass window in the great chamber representing the arms of the Phelips family, their neighbours and allies, which served to cement his standing in the locality. The carved chimneypiece in the great chamber of Chastleton House in Oxfordshire, which was built *c.* 1607–12 by the successful clothier Walter Jones to establish himself as a country gentleman, bears his arms with those of Pope for his wife, but there is no evidence

---

[25]   Notably, Gerard Legh, *The Accedens of Armory* (first pub. London, 1562); Sir John Ferne, *The Blazon of Gentrie* (London, 1586) and John Guillim, *A Display of Heraldrie* (first pub. 1610).

[26]   Henry Peacham, *The gentlemans exercise* (London, 1612), p. 141.

Figure 5.2   Purse, embroidered with heraldic shields, *c.* 1540.
                    © Victoria and Albert Museum, London.

that his bride, apparently the daughter of an émigré settler from the duchy of Cleves, had
any right to arms so these must be 'borrowed' or fictional. Jones had previously had to
defend his right to use an armorial bearing very similar to that borne by the Talbot earls
of Shrewsbury, a lion rampant. The Heralds decided that both parties were entitled to use
it: Walter was acknowledged to have established 'by one scienced in the antiquities and

genealogies' his own right to a coat of arms.[27] This dispute and the display of apparently bogus Pope arms in the principal reception room at Chastleton demonstrates the importance of heraldic display, even if contested or unsubstantiated, in the homes of upwardly mobile members of society.

But how might a householder lacking any right to bear arms follow this fashion? Peacham's character explains how:

> *Excellent have beene the conceipt of some Citizens, who wanting Armes, have coined themselves certaine devises as neere as may be alluding to their names, which wee call Rebus. Master Bishoppe caused to be painted in his glasse windowes the picture of a Bishop in his Rochet, his square cappe on his head, by which was written his Christen name George. One Foxe-craft caused to be painted in his Hall & Parlour a Foxe, counterfeiting himselfe dead upon the Ice, among a company of ducks and Goslings. These and a thousand the like, if you bee a diligent observer you shall finde both in City and Country, especially in Towne halls, Churchwalls, and Windowes, olde Monasteries and such places, which many a time and often I have enquired after as the best receipt against Melancholy.[28]*

Such rebus-style devices may be amusing as a visual pun, but they hardly carried the gravitas, status and honour of an achievement of arms.[29] It seems, therefore, that some householders of middling rank chose to employ a different strategy.

From 1561 the royal arms were set up in parish churches to represent the role of the monarch as head of church as well as state. Patrick Collinson viewed this development as part of a wholesale shift in the nature of experience at the parish level: 'the replacement of the rood imagery by the wholly abstract symbolism of the royal coat of arms meant that churchgoers were not required to look at different pictures but at no pictures at all'.[30] This implies not only that it is possible to distinguish between 'pictorial' and 'abstract' imagery, but that the royal arms offered little in the way of visual interest or stimulation. I would argue quite the opposite; that the new visibility of the royal arms and concentration of heraldic decoration on monuments in parish churches fostered a sense of familiarity with a particular visual aesthetic and popularised this ancient mechanism for establishing or appropriating identity within a wider community. One example serves to indicate how the royal arms occupied the most visible and privileged place in the post-Reformation parish and presented extraordinary opportunity for visual elaboration. In the church of St Margaret in Tivetshall, Norfolk, is a massive depiction of the arms of Elizabeth I dated 1587. Painted on the boarded tympanum of the chancel arch it stretches the entire width of the nave from the top of the roodscreen to the roof. A huge lion and dragon support the arms and they stand on a grassy mound set above and behind a *trompe l'oeil* architectural structure, the lower part of which contains texts including the Ten Commandments. The design also includes symbols for the other four Tudor monarchs, as well as the badge of Elizabeth's mother, Anne Boleyn. It is hard to equate this sort of exuberant and extravagant dynastic display with the absence of pictures evoked by Collinson.

---

[27]   Hilary L. Turner, 'Walter Jones of Witney, Worcester, and Chastleton: Rewriting the Past', *Oxoniensia* 73 (2008), 33–44.

[28]   Peacham, *The gentlemans exercise*, pp. 166–7.

[29]   An example of this sort of rebus in domestic decoration is described in M. Carrick, P.M. Ryan and M.C. Wadhams, 'Wall Paintings at Creswells Farm, Sible Hedingham, Essex', *Archaeological Journal* 144 (1987), 328–39.

[30]   Patrick Collinson, *The Birthpangs of Protestant England* (Basingstoke: Palgrave, 1988), pp. 118–19.

The assertive presence of royal arms in church space created a conceptual association between royal and divine authority. This is made explicit in the Tivetshall arms which includes the monogram IHS to refer to the name of Christ at the apex of the design while underneath is painted a slightly perplexing combination of texts: 'God Save Our Quene Elizabeth' and 'Let every sowle submit hym selfe unto the authority of the hyer powers, for there is no power but of God, the powers that be are ordayned by God.' This association with temporal and cosmic order and authority might explain the depiction of royal arms in relatively humble domestic settings in the sixteenth and seventeenth centuries in England. There is not the space to do justice to the nature or ramifications of this migration of the royal arms from public to domestic settings as well as down the social scale in any detail but brief consideration of just two examples serves to illustrate this wider trend. The royal arms of Elizabeth I adorned several chimneypieces at 229 High Street in Exeter, a massive townhouse largely rebuilt in 1585 by George Smith, a former mayor. One example in plasterwork was salvaged and is now in the parlour at St Nicholas Priory in Exeter (Figure 5.3).

Figure 5.3   Plasterwork overmantel with the arms of Queen Elizabeth I, formerly in 229 High Street, Exeter, now installed in St Nicholas Priory, Exeter.
Author's photograph

Smith's house was very grand but the elaborate display of the royal arms of James I in an embellished plasterwork ceiling at 'The Old Merchant's House' in Great Yarmouth seems incongruous in what was a relatively modest merchant's house, containing only two rooms on the ground floor (Figure 5.4).

This sort of heraldic display creates visual connections between so-called 'domestic' space and other spheres of experience, such as churches and civic institutions, and undermines scholarly practice which sets up artificially rigid distinctions between them. The presence in domestic rooms of the royal arms as a stamp of royal, judicial as well as spiritual authority

Figure 5.4   View of the interior of ground-floor room in the 'Old Merchants House',
Great Yarmouth Row Houses, Norfolk.
© English Heritage.

appropriates this authority for the householder, possibly as a sign of local office, which
seems especially important for the construction of identity within local communities and the
social differentiation and competition this entails. Such imagery may also reinforce the role
of householders as religious instructors; the presence of the royal arms in domestic rooms

also furnished with a bible or psalters indicates that these rooms were used for the daily devotions of the gathered family.[31]

A similar argument about the blurring of distinctions of place could be made for the depiction of para-heraldic imagery in domestic decoration. The townhouse known as 'Harvard House' in Stratford upon Avon was rebuilt in 1596 by a butcher and corn and cattle dealer called Thomas Rogers. In the best room on the first floor, overlooking the street, is a plaster overmantel displaying on shields heraldic badges associated with English royalty; the rose, lion rampant and fleur-de-lis (Figure 5.5). A very similar overmantel in Wood Street in the town has the same symbols, with the addition of an oak leaf. Another overmantel

Figure 5.5   Plasterwork overmantel, late sixteenth century, in first-floor room of 'Harvard House', Stratford-upon-Avon.
Author's photograph reproduced by kind permission of The Shakespeare Birthplace Trust.

from 35 High Street, now installed in the great hall at Packwood House, also includes a fleur-de-lis and a lion rampant with a cartouche along with the initials of the owners, John and Margaret Smith and their eldest son Ralph. These initials are also carved along the top of the fireplace with, at each end, a wine barrel as symbol of John's trade as a vintner (Figure 5.6).[32]

This sort of imagery is usually regarded as a straightforward and unsophisticated expression of loyalty to the crown. But these overmantels are not simply a representation

---

[31]   For example, an inventory of 1585 for John Semark, gent, of Canterbury records a bible, service book and three psalters in a hall decorated with a 'map of the queens arms set in wainscot'. I'm grateful to Catherine Richardson for sharing her data on Kentish probate documents and for reading and commenting on a draft of this chapter.

[32]   Robert Bearman, 'The "Stratford Fireplace" at Packwood House', *Birmingham & Warwickshire Archaeological Society Transactions* 96 (1989–90), 83–7.

Figure 5.6   Plasterwork overmantel formerly in 35 High Street in Stratford-upon-Avon, now installed at Packwood House, Warwickshire.
Author's photograph reproduced with permission of National Trust Images.

of stock heraldic motifs; the borrowing of authority in the use of specifically royal badges implies a connection with the chivalric culture of the court. Each work is distinctive, so must have been customised for each commission, but the similarities in the style and content of these overmantels create a connection between different houses in the town and thereby suggest a shared sense of taste and values between families within a community. The inclusion of initials and symbols of profession in the Packwood example combines familial, commercial and national identity and can be understood as a visual representation of the common contemporary metaphor of the individual household as a microcosm of the state.

The badges depicted in the Stratford overmantels are representative of a more general appropriation of para-heraldic imagery in domestic decoration. For example a vogue for ornate plasterwork ceilings from *c.* 1590 onwards made extensive use of heraldic badges among other symbols including various fruit, flora and fauna, birds, animals, cherubim and mermaids. These symbols formed part of a popular visual language, which operates at a fairly basic level of signification. Randle Holme provides an explanation for the evolution and operation of such symbols in his late seventeenth-century treatise *The Academy of Armoury*. He describes how armorial bearings fall into two groups; proper charges (known as ordinaries) and 'common charges'.[33] Ordinaries are bold rectilinear and geometrical shapes which could be configured in various ways so that their symbolism required a level of specialist knowledge to interpret. Common charges, on the other hand, are usually representational and transparent in meaning. Holme explains that 'by common charges may be meant all

---

[33]   Randle Holme, *The Academy of armory* (Chester, 1688), Book 1, p. 18.

things both Natural and Artificial which are used in Coats of Arms'.[34] Earlier in his treatise Holme explained that arms were first consisted of such 'things in Essence' because:

> *no doubt they were such as the Vulgar (as well as the more Skilfuller sort) did well understand, and knew, through frequent use, what they were: As being the express Portraictures either of Celestial Bodies, as Sun, Moon, Stars, &c. Or of Things Sublunary, as Fire, Water: Or else Vegetables, as Trees, Plants, Fruit, Herbs and Flowers, &c. Or else they were resemblances of Earthly and Intelligible Creatures, as Men, Beasts, Fowles, creeping Things, &c. Or else of Instruments, or Tools of familiar use, and exercise, in Mechanical Trades; which in respect of their common use, were best known to Men: And therefore served most fitly for Notes and Marks of precise differencing of each particular Person from another.*[35]

So, the straightforward pictorial language of 'express portraitures' or 'resemblances' of things observed in nature allowed ready identification and comprehension especially by the 'vulgar sort' or those otherwise unskilled in heraldic rules. Holme attempted to record all such natural and artificial things as depicted in coats of arms – no mean feat – and this has encouraged scholars to remark upon the encyclopaedic quality of his treatise, which includes numerous illustrations of common charges, ranged in geometric grids. Figure 5.7 shows two illustrations from the *Academy* with variations on one of the ordinaries on the left and some common (natural) charges representing things from the heavens on the right. These tiny representations of the Trinity, Holy Spirit, crucifixion and angels indicate how standardised religious iconographies crossed between ostensibly sacred or secular contexts. Holme understood the 'compass of Armory' to include not only the representation of heavenly beings and the natural world but also the world of commerce – his illustrations include a wide range of objects representing various trades. The next two sections of the chapter interrogate how heraldry in turn informed visual forms and systems of communication in these other contexts, starting with the imagery of commercial signs.

***

Trade signs are another neglected aspect of the visual culture of early modern England, although they have attracted the notice of some historians and literary scholars. Signs are generally understood at face value simply as navigational markers or as advertising but David Garrioch has identified significant distinctions and particularities by region, which indicate their role in expressing a sense of collective culture and identity. He also examines the processes of renewal and reinterpretation which reflect changing times and attitudes. In this way signs can 'provide rare access to the tastes, culture and mental world of early modern city dwellers – most often artisans and shopkeepers'.[36] Shop and inn signs were a significant presence in the English urban environment, displaying in prominent and eye-catching form an extensive range of imagery. Andrew Gordon has described these signboards as 'highly standardized acts of representation' forming 'a familiar repertoire of visual imagery'.[37] In order to function effectively these painted images were necessarily straightforwardly representational and recognisable, in the same manner as heraldic charges. Indeed, while the range of symbols depicted upon signboards drew from religious and classical iconography as well as heraldic badges, the incorporation and organisation

---

[34]   Holme, *Academy of armory*, Book 2, p. 1.

[35]   Holme, *Academy of armory*, Book 1, p. 15.

[36]   David Garrioch, 'House Names, Shop Signs and Social Organisation in Western European Cities, 1500–1900', *Urban History* 21:1 (1994), 20–48, at p. 27.

[37]   Andrew Gordon, '"If My Sign Could Speak": The Signboard and the Visual Culture of Early Modern London', *Early Theatre* 8:1 (2005), 35–51, at p. 36.

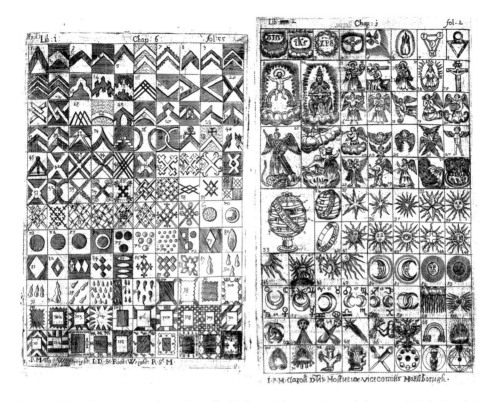

Figure 5.7   Illustrations from Randle Holme, *The Academy of Armory* (1688), Book 1,
Chapter 6, fol. 55 and Book 2, Chapter 1, fol. 2.
These items are reproduced by permission of The Huntington Library,
San Marino, California, RB 140916.

of this imagery within a heraldic schema is indicated by Randle Holme's attempt at a
comprehensive survey of heraldic charges, as described earlier.

Shops in London selling books printed between 1590 and 1620 had signs bearing royal
badges; the 'Flower de luce' and 'Rose and Crown'; a range of heraldic beasts, 'Green Dragon',
'Red Lyon' and 'Black Beare'; the more exotic 'Tygers Head' and 'Catte and Parrots' to signs
with religious associations such as the 'gilded Cuppe', 'cross keys' [for St Peter] 'S. John
Evangelist', 'Brazen Serpent', 'Angel', 'Holy lambe' and 'Holy-ghost'. The imagery depicted
in these trade signs provides one example, discussed in detail below, of the continued
presence of traditional religious iconographies during the supposedly 'iconophobic' period
of post-Reformation Protestantism. The iconic image of the holy lamb (Agnus dei) and the
representation of the Holy Spirit, probably in the form of a dove, were evidently considered
acceptable in this context. Only fanatical reformers looked to the imagery of sign boards as
a contravention of the divine command against graven images and while there are accounts
of the zealous railing against signs of Popes-heads and Triple-Crowns, this extreme position
can hardly be considered as representative of wider opinion. Nevertheless accommodations
were sometimes made – in the transformation, for example, of the Annunciation into the two

Gallants or the St Catherine and Wheel into the Cat and Wheel.[38] In 1643 the landlord of the Golden Cross in the Strand was made to take down his 'superstitious and idolatrous sign'.[39] Meanwhile the adoption of the sign of the 'Bible' by several London booksellers offered a new kind of iconic image with solid Protestant credentials.

The title page to John King's *Lectures upon Jonas* printed at Oxford in 1599 to be sold in London 'at the sygne of the Bible' or the device and imprint of Henry Denham 'dwelling ... at the signe of the Starre' may reflect the general appearance of these signs (Figure 5.8).

Figure 5.8   Henry Denham's device and imprint (1582).
© The British Library Board, E3:1(146) and
Titlepage from John King, *Lectures upon Jonas* (1599).
This item is reproduced by permission of The Huntington Library, San Marino, California, RB 20866.

But these illustrations do not do justice to the scale, colour and physical quality of the signboards as a prominent feature of the urban environment. Some signs were sculptural; an etching of 1851 in the Guildhall Museum, London, records the appearance of six carved stone street signs including the Fruiterers' Company arms featuring Adam and Eve, a Bear dated 1610, an Ape and a Unicorn, while a carved limestone pub sign dated 1667 in the Museum of London shows three Kings in relief.[40] In several works by William Hogarth

---

[38]   Catherine Dent, 'The Functions of Inn Signs and Their Place in Early Modern British History', *Reinvention: An International Journal of Undergraduate Research* 4:1 (2011), www2.warwick.ac.uk/fac/cross_fac/iatl/ejournal/issues/volume4issue1/dent (accessed 12 November 2012).

[39]   Dent, 'The Functions of Inn Signs', quoting Fritz Endell, *Old Tavern Signs; an excursion in the history of hospitality* (1916).

[40]   London Metropolitan Archives, Main Print Collection, Pr.L86.1; www.museumoflondon.org.uk/Collections-Research/Collections-online/object.aspx?objectID=object-148214&start=6&rows=1

there is a sense of the imposing physical presence of painted signboards jutting into the space above the street. In Hogarth's painting and subsequent engraving *Canvassing for Votes* (1755), the inn sign has been appropriated as a site for the display of political satire in visual form, suggesting its significance as a visual marker of place and affiliation. A manuscript drawing dated after 1628 in the British Library includes an illustration of signboards as part of two 'Allegorical Designs Relating to Political Events in the Reigns of King James I and Charles I' (Figure 5.9). Four signs are shown dominating the left-hand side of the composition; they depict an anchor and shears with the royal arms and Prince of Wales's feathers; an anchor hooking a sheep with the arms of London and of the Merchant Taylors' Company; a sun and a clock. All four signs include dates and initials. On the facing page are street scenes, a procession and what appears to be a vision of hell with the Pope and others surrounded by flames. It is unclear what this allegorical drawing is meant to convey but the prominence of these four signboards within a religio-political commentary in visual form is significant. The drawing seems to represent another manifestation of a wider cultural interest in the operation of signboards identified by Andrew Gordon in relation to early modern literature. He suggests that 'what characterises the signboard of the city for the urban inhabitant is after all its very availability to a host of different interpretive strategies'.[41] This 'superfluity of meaning' results from the essentially visual character of signboards, which transcends textual equivalents and resists linguistic models of interpretation. Gordon references W.J.T. Mitchell's call back in 1992 for a 'pictorial turn' in the humanities, to

Figure 5.9   Allegorical designs. British Library, Stowe 309, ff. 1v-2.
              Accessible through the British Library's Catalogue of Illuminated Manuscripts
              website: http://www.bl.uk/catalogues/illuminatedmanuscripts.

(accessed 12 December 2012).
    [41]   Gordon, 'If My Sign Could Speak', p. 35.

respond to a renewed interest in and prevalence of pictures and images in an increasingly extensive and diverse visual culture. Mitchell's proposed pictorial turn has generated a good deal of academic interest and enthusiasm but as yet no practicable critical framework for the study of images that acknowledges the immediacy and autonomy of visual modes of communication without recourse to textual formulae has emerged.

An heraldic style of presentation and mode of signification, then, with a basic, shared level of meaning involving identification and association with an individual or place but with the potential for additional layers of interpretation depending on knowledge or inclination (for example the Puritan zealot seeing Popish infiltration in the sign of the Golden Cross) extended beyond coats of arms and badges to inform and permeate other aspects of the wider visual culture. The impact of the heraldic tradition on artistic style has been recognised recently by Robert Tittler in his book on provincial portraiture in early modern England. He suggests that the form and character of vernacular painting was influenced by the techniques and visual characteristics of heraldry. He points towards the schematic definition of form, bold outlines, two-dimensional perspective, indifference to correct proportion and limited palette of colours in provincial portraiture which, he suggests, are distinctively heraldic footprints.[42] In other words, and to argue this point even further, these characteristics may reflect a dominant aesthetic rather than, simply, deficient artistic ability. This suggests we should be wary to dismiss the seemingly inferior, 'primitive' quality of much native English craft. Perhaps its peculiar (to our eyes) aesthetic quality should be approached on its own terms. These insights from Gordon's work on sign boards and Tittler's study of portraits can be brought to bear on an object that seemingly combines both categories; the Lenard fireback.

Cast-iron firebacks were produced in England from the first half of the sixteenth century and served to protect the back of chimneys and reflect heat back into the room. As domestic buildings increasingly incorporated chimneys these functional accessories were in demand and gradually the plain iron plates were embellished with imagery, including heraldry and biblical subject matter.[43] Among the collection of iron firebacks at Anne of Cleve's House in Lewes, Sussex, is a personalised fireback dated 1636 depicting Richard Lenard, who succeeded his father as tenant of the iron foundry at Brede in 1605 (Figure 5.10).[44] He stands in the centre of the composition with a hammer in his hand and along the top rim are the words RICHARD LENARD FOVNDER AT BRED FOURNIS. There are examples of similar trade signs representing evidence of the skills on offer. A carved wood panel depicting a joiner and turner appears to have been made by a seventeenth-century tradesman who worked in a similar shop, presumably to represent and advertise his skills.[45] And yet Lenard's fireback is not a straightforward emblem of his trade; the imagery appears to place his identity between the spheres of domestic and business interests. On the right-hand side of the panel is depicted an ornate fireplace complete with its own fireback (with his initials R. L.) and a display of drinking vessels above. A faithful dog leaps to greet his owner. On the left-hand side are the tools of Lenard's business operation; a brick furnace with a wheelbarrow above containing charcoal and, in the top left-hand corner, a shield bearing a blacksmith's hammer, bell and andiron. Lenard straddles these spheres dressed in what appears to be

---

[42] Tittler, *Portraits, Painters and Publics*, esp. pp. 117–24.

[43] Jeremy Hodgkinson, *British Cast Iron Firebacks of the 16th to mid 18th centuries* (Crawley: Hodgers Books, 2010).

[44] Several versions of this fireback design are recorded, some more degraded than others; it was copied throughout the nineteenth century. There are other versions in the V&A and the Geffrye Museum.

[45] The panel is in private ownership. It will feature in a forthcoming publication on the craft of joinery and the authors have provided a photograph with information as a preview on this website: http://pfollansbee.wordpress.com/2009/01/22/seventeenth-century-joiners-bench/.

Figure 5.10   The Lenard Fireback, dated 1636. Anne of Cleves House Museum, Lewes.
Reproduced by kind permission of the Sussex Archaeological Society,
Barbican House.

a nightgown, with its tie and lace collar – a garment worn in the evenings by those who
had access to leisure time. There is a striking incongruity in the combined accoutrements of
robe and hammer but this meeting of symbols represents Lenard's self-fashioned identity
as that of a well-to-do member of society, proud to exhibit the skills of his trade but equally
keen to signal the range of quality possessions furnished by his successful business. This
seemingly humble object, therefore, employs a common language of visual signifiers, such
as trade tools, high-status domestic objects and distinctive clothing, which were also used
in heraldry as bearings to identify the social rank and qualities of armigerous individuals
or institutions. The combination of these symbols displayed without regard to correct
perspective or proportion on the flat background of the iron plate resembles the appearance
of charges on shields, the product of using moulds but perhaps not an unwelcome feature
given its congruence with the dominant aesthetic. This pseudo-heraldic personal emblem

93

constructs a social identity for Lenard that cannot be defined as distinctively commercial or domestic in nature, but encompasses both.

The final section of this chapter carries forward these insights about the influence of the heraldic tradition on the form and appearance of vernacular visual art, and the specificity and efficiency of visual modes of communication, to inform analysis of another ubiquitous form of imagery in early modern England; biblical imagery.

**

There is no doubt that the processes of religious change and consolidation that took place from the 1530s into the second half of the seventeenth century had a dramatic effect on the wider visual culture. The removal and destruction of icons from churches which occurred under official instruction in the 1540s, 1560s and 1640s must have occasioned a radical shift in the nature of visual experience at the parish level. It is, however, possible to exaggerate the effects of religious reformation on the visual culture as a whole. While the paraphernalia associated with Roman Catholic worship was discredited and dismantled, the careful distinctions made by contemporary commentators between images that infringed the divine command against 'graven images' and those that fell outside its strictures meant that a significant amount of the visual art of the pre-Reformation past could be retained. While images in churches were at risk of being treated as the focus of worship – as idols – given the sacred function and associations of the building, most theologians within the established church agreed that there was less danger of image-worship in spaces used for matters outside the purposes of religion. This meant that many of the subjects and themes familiar from church art could legitimately be displayed in domestic houses. Indeed, during the second half of the sixteenth century and throughout the seventeenth century it was common for scenes and characters from the Bible to be depicted within the interior decoration of larger houses, including the country houses of the gentry and the town and rural houses of merchants and prosperous farmers. There was, however, an important shift in emphasis. Prior to the Reformation, saints and sacred subjects were depicted in wall paintings and hangings in domestic houses as well as in churches to help support personal devotion, but after the Protestant religious settlement of 1559 there was a move away from iconic images of sacred figures towards the representation of biblical stories. The illustration of subject matter from the Old and New Testaments was acceptable in Protestant thought as long as the imagery adhered to the scriptural account. These new religious images, often copied from iconography in print, were not merely decorative but meaningful expressions of status and belief. Exemplary stories from the Bible operated to reflect and construct a sense of identity and were possibly used to support practices of household piety, such as collective and individual bible-reading, prayer and meditation.

Certain scenes and stories from the Old Testament were particularly popular throughout the period and in various media. I have argued elsewhere that the most common iconographies in post-Reformation decorative art were chosen because of their traditional use as types, or prefigurations, of key moments in the life of Christ.[46] This tradition had been established and popularised through medieval picture bibles such as the Biblia Pauperum, *Speculum Humanae Salvationis* and books of hours. Illustrations in the printed versions of these books were copied widely for church decoration, such as stained glass and carved seating. The Sacrifice of Isaac, for example, was commonly depicted in medieval art as a type for the Crucifixion and thus represented the concepts of obedience, sacrifice and redemption. This association with the core Christian message helps to explain its popularity as a subject for representation in early modern decorative art. Other biblical episodes had also become synonymous with key doctrinal messages so that Adam and Eve's temptation and fall from

---

[46]   Hamling, *Decorating the Godly Household*, ch. 5.

grace served to represent sin. This metonymic use of specific subject matter to stand for an associated concept reflects a specifically early modern way of thinking. As Andrew Morrall has observed,

> *the themes of ornament are closely related to the early modern tendency to hypostatize abstract concepts like History or Time, or moral entities like Fortitude or Prudence, qualities that attach to people or things and by which they come to be defined. One of the values of ornament for understanding cultural attitudes and beliefs lies precisely in this function of bodying forth mental constructs and attitudes.*[47]

This point about how images make tangible such abstract concepts as moral qualities is well made in relation to Morrall's discussion of European architectural ornament and applies equally to the operation of heraldic and biblical imagery in early modern England.

This symbolic function of some biblical scenes might account for the simplified and formulaic form of the imagery, which is stripped of visual components that do not contribute to the core meaning of the episode. Such images are not narrative in a strict sense because they contain insufficient information to tell the story; rather they evoke stories that were already familiar in verbal and visual form. They can be described as 'synoptic images' in that they present a summary of the principal parts of the story and can stand as a general synopsis of the whole. As a sign system these images are not meant to be naturalistic but are more properly 'representational', like heraldic charges, in representing the essence of the story and referring the viewer efficiently to wider concepts, such as sin or sacrifice. There is a connection, therefore, between heraldry and certain kinds of biblical images popular during this period; both categories of imagery share a similar form of presentation, with the essence of the subject pared back to its core elements to aid clarity and ease in communication. They therefore cater to the same way of seeing.

Three case studies of biblical subject matter in applied decoration serve to illustrate this point and indicate the various contexts in which these synoptic images were deployed. At Barrington Court in Somerset a chimneypiece of *c.* 1625 in one of the main reception rooms on the first floor is decorated with the Judgement of Solomon. This story was relatively popular in early modern visual art and is found in a range of contexts, including a gold prayer book case of *c.* 1540–45 in the British Museum, several seventeenth-century embroidered panels and even as church decoration.[48] It was also depicted as part of the interior decoration of several domestic houses. At the house now known as The Forge in Much Hadham a detailed depiction of the story in wall painting is paired with an elaborate version of the royal arms of Elizabeth I along with the arms of the owner. This is quite a grand statement for a relatively modest town house and might have been created in hopeful anticipation of a visit from the Queen.[49] Although Barrington Court is a much larger, country, house the version of the subject depicted there is strangely unsophisticated; the image is simplified to the extreme, with the necessary components of the standard iconography condensed into a form that resembles an armorial shield with bearings (Figure 5.11). The manner of depiction can be explained by the wider meaning of this subject matter which, as with the display of royal arms or badges, served as an expression of judicial power and authority on behalf of the householder. This concept requires minimal pictorial detail to convey effectively.

That such imagery was aimed at a more public audience beyond the family is indicated by the Bluett family pew created around 1614 in the church at Holcombe Rogus in Devon.

---

[47] Morrall, 'Ornament as Evidence', pp. 48–9.
[48] For example, in wall painting *c.* 1620 at Walsoken Church, Norfolk.
[49] Discussed and illustrated, with notes, in Hamling, *Decorating the Godly Household*, pp. 100–102.

Figure 5.11   Plasterwork overmantel with a scene of the Judgement of Solomon, Barrington
              Court, Somerset.
              © National Trust Images.

The programme of biblical scenes from Genesis, Exodus and Numbers is on the exterior of
the surrounding wooden screen to face the congregation, so the family would not be able
to view these scenes whilst occupying the pew (Figure 5.12).[50] The pew can be understood
as a variation on decorated rood screens but instead of screening the holy chancel area it
partitions off the social elite of the parish from the rest of the community. Each scene is
enclosed within a series of oval frames forming an architectural embellishment along the
top of the screen. The simplicity of the iconography, with minimal pictorial detail depicted
in carved relief, is exemplified by the image of Moses, with Aaron and Hur supporting his
raised hands during the battle against the Amalekites (Exodus 17:12), another common Old
Testament type for the Crucifixion of Christ (Figure 5.13). The synoptic quality of the series of
images is presumably meant to impress upon this wider public the piety of the Bluetts while
evoking the core concepts of the Christian faith. The simplistic, formulaic representation of
biblical episodes operates effectively and efficiently at a distance to reinforce the essentials
of belief while the lack of visual complexity deters the sort of prolonged gazing associated
with discredited devotional art.

---

[50]   It is possible the pew was reconfigured at a later date but there is no indication that this would
have affected the orientation of the imagery.

Figure 5.12   The Blewett family pew, All Saint's Church, Holcombe Rogus, Devon.
Author's photograph.

Figure 5.13   Moses, Aaron and Hur during the battle against the Amalekites, detail of one
of the biblical scenes depicted in the Blewett family pew, All Saint's Church,
Holcombe Rogus, Devon.
Author's photograph.

Figure 5.14   Carved exterior of 'Bishop Lloyd's House' in Chester.
            Author's photograph.

Finally, the decorated facade of a timber-framed townhouse at 41 Watergate Street in Chester illustrates how such imagery might respond to a more superficial or preoccupied form of viewing. The building's frontage exhibits a scheme of heraldic and biblical imagery (Figure 5.14). It is thought to have been constructed for George Lloyd, who was Bishop of Chester from 1605 to 1615. On the right-hand side of the double-fronted house between the row on the ground floor and the windows above are eight recessed panels filled with imagery. The two central panels display the heraldic badge of James I, with his initials, and the arms of the Bishopric of Sodor and Man, which was George Lloyd's office before he became Bishop of Chester. On the left-hand side are scenes depicting Adam and Eve, Cain and Abel and Abraham sacrificing Isaac (Figure 5.15). This choice of scenes can be understood to represent the advent and consequences of sin and redemption through sacrifice. Two scenes on the right-hand side depict Susanna and the Elders and Lucretia stabbing herself with a dagger. These heroines from history both exemplify the virtue of chastity but in the context of the other scenes the choice of subject matter reiterates the overarching theme of sin (represented by the elder's lust) and sacrifice (Lucretia). The position and form of the imagery is significant in thinking about the meaning and function of the scheme. This sort of biblical imagery in interior decoration is generally defined as moral and didactic, used by householders to educate their family or to entertain guests. It seems highly unlikely that the owner of this house would make himself available in the street to explicate the imagery to passersby. Indeed, in its extreme simplicity and straightforwardly synoptic nature the imagery lends itself to the casual gaze of people on the move; each scene encapsulates the essence of the story with as little extraneous detail as possible.

Figure 5.15   Detail of carved exterior of 'Bishop Lloyd's House', Chester.
Author's photograph.

Further up the facade are 10 arched panels containing carvings of heraldic beasts, which extend the heraldic display of the central panels below. Heraldic motifs are repeated within the interior decoration too, with crests and roses depicted in a plasterwork ceiling. The seemingly random combination of 'secular' heraldic imagery and religious imagery on the facade of Bishop Lloyd's house suggests that there was no rigid distinction between categories of imagery in the eyes and minds of early modern people. In fact, the fusion of heraldic and biblical imagery as brought together in architectural decoration can be understood to represent the interpenetration of social and spiritual concerns. In representing symbols of rank and honour together with images expressing the core concepts of the Christian scheme of sin and salvation, the building's exterior decoration celebrates and reinforces a sense of temporal and cosmic order. For viewers on the move busy in the street below little interpretative effort is required to assimilate the message of this imagery and position themselves within its framing structure. The combination of heraldic and biblical imagery, then, is not only an assertion or appropriation of identity and authority within early modern strategies of self-fashioning but functions as an ordering mechanism to bolster the old hierarchies of the great chain of being in the face of profound religious and social change.

***

This chapter has examined a shared visual language that straddled elite and popular cultures in early modern England. The system of standardised, easily recognisable pictorial signs which 'bodied forth' and stood for abstract concepts such as moral qualities or spiritual tenets formed a common vocabulary developing from two visual traditions that had dominated the late medieval world; heraldry and devotional art.[51] By the 1500s these traditions had defined the conventions and aesthetic character best suited to communicate with clarity and ease essential information about social rank and identity on the one hand and spiritual truths on the other. The representational but simplified form of heraldic bearings or 'synoptic' biblical images served to express on sight a sense of the nature and character of an individual, family or institution, or encapsulated the metaphorical meaning of a biblical episode. These systems therefore came to inform visual representations in other contexts wherever such clarity and efficiency in communication was desirable, notably in the commercial and domestic spheres. In the sixteenth and seventeenth centuries the 'plain' language of visual symbols long associated with status and authority was appropriated and displayed by individuals in the middling ranks to represent, construct or claim identities within communities of peers and differentiate themselves from those further down the social scale. Architectural decoration and personalised emblems such as the Packwood chimneypiece or the Lenard fireback can therefore be understood to rely upon and exploit inherited visual traditions to cater to a way of seeing indissolubly linked to this cultural and social context. In this sense the kinds of imagery described here and the essential meanings conveyed visually through ornament can be understood as a fundamental part of everyone's culture in early modern England, while the additional layers of meaning and varieties of response that might be elicited from such imagery could be used to negotiate or demarcate the lines between popular and learned understanding.

---

[51] These traditions are indeed conflated in the medieval tradition of the *Arma Christi*, an iconographic device which sometimes took the form of a full 'Coat of Arms of Christ'; see Lisa H. Cooper and Andrea Denny-Brown eds, *The Arma Christi in Medieval and Early Modern Material Culture* (Aldershot: Ashgate, 2014).

Select Bibliography

Collinson, Patrick, *The Birthpangs of Protestant England*. Basingstoke: Palgrave, 1988.

Collinson, Patrick, 'From Iconoclasm to Iconophobia: The Cultural Impact of the Second English Reformation', in Peter Marshall ed., *The Impact of the English Reformation 1500–1640*. London: Arnold, 1997, pp. 279–308.

Cooper, Nicholas, *Houses of the Gentry, 1480–1680*. New Haven: Yale University Press, 1999.

Gent, Lucy ed., *Albion's Classicism: The Visual Arts in Britain 1550–1660*. New Haven: Yale University Press, 1996.

Gordon, Andrew, '"If My Sign Could Speak": The Signboard and the Visual Culture of Early Modern London', *Early Theatre* 8:1 (2005), 35–51.

Hamling, Tara, *Decorating the Godly Household: Religious Art in Post-Reformation England*. New Haven: Yale University Press, 2010.

Hamling, Tara, and Richard L. Williams eds, *Art Re-formed: Reassessing the Impact of the Reformation on the Visual Arts*. Newcastle: Cambridge Scholars Publishing, 2007.

Hodgkinson, Jeremy, *British Cast Iron Firebacks of the 16th to Mid 18th Centuries*. Crawley: Hodgers Books, 2010.

Howard, Maurice, *The Tudor Image*. London: Tate Publishing, 1996.

Hunter, Michael ed., *Printed Images in Early Modern Britain*. Aldershot: Ashgate, 2010.

Jones, Malcolm, *The Print in Early Modern England: An Historical Oversight*. New Haven: Yale University Press, 2010.

Llewellyn, Nigel, *The Art of Death: Visual Culture in the English Death Ritual c.1500–c.1800*. London: Reaktion, 1991.

Llewellyn, Nigel, *Funeral Monuments in Post-Reformation England*. Cambridge: Cambridge University Press, 2000.

Morrall, Andrew, 'Ornament as Evidence', in Karen Harvey ed., *History and Material Culture*. Abingdon: Routledge, 2009, pp. 47–66.

Tittler, Robert, *Portraits, Painters and Publics in Provincial England, 1540–1640*. Oxford: Oxford University Press, 2012.

Watt, Tessa, *Cheap Print and Popular Piety, 1550–1640*. Cambridge: Cambridge University Press, 1991.

Wells-Cole, Anthony, *Art and Decoration in Elizabethan and Jacobean England: The Influence of Continental Prints, 1558–1625*. New Haven: Yale University Press, 1997.

Myth and Legend

Angus Vine

In his *De ratione studii* of 1512, the foundation text for the curriculum at the newly established St Paul's School in London, Erasmus reminded prospective schoolmasters that they needed a proper knowledge of mythology:

> *Certainly in an exposition of the poets, who are accustomed to flavour their compositions with knowledge drawn from every quarter, you must command a good supply of mythology, and from whom is it better to seek this than Homer, the father of all myth? But the Metamorphoses and Fasti of Ovid, although written in Latin, are of no small importance.*[1]

Erasmus's assertion here is part of a larger argument about how masters should select the best models for their pupils to imitate. But it is also a more specific observation on the exposition of poetry. Classical poetry is full of mythological allusions. Masters therefore need a sufficient grasp of mythology to explain these. Later in the work, when he turns in more detail to the selection of topics for the classroom, Erasmus reiterates his point. First, he reminds masters that, when choosing material, they should 'avoid above all the common mistake of having topics vacuous in content or dull in form'; they should instead select ones that 'have a certain point or charm which is not too remote from youthful capabilities, so that while they are concentrating on something else, they will learn material relevant to higher studies'. Then, he suggests two possibilities, two fields of knowledge that do appeal precisely to those 'youthful capabilities': either the master should 'have a theme or memorable historical episode to set before the boys', or he 'should employ mythology'. Finally, he cites two examples of what he means by 'mythology': two fables from the classical world – how 'Hercules won immortality for himself by vanquishing monsters' and how 'the Muses take special delight in springs and groves and shun the smoky cities'.[2] Knowledge of mythology, in other words, was required for a practical reason as well as a pedagogical one; it was needed not only to explain otherwise arcane references in schoolroom texts, but also more fundamentally to make lessons appealing to schoolboys.

Erasmus's comments here correspond with what we know about the subsequent history of early modern education. Much of the early modern period's knowledge of classical myth did come from the classroom, and most of that came from Ovid. When pupils reached the upper forms of grammar schools, they began to read Roman poets in their entirety rather than in selections and started to learn their works by rote. Ovid occupied the foremost place

---

[1] Desiderius Erasmus, *De ratione studii*, in *Collected Works of Erasmus: Literary and Educational Writings 2*, ed. Craig R. Thompson (Toronto: University of Toronto Press, 1978), p. 673.

[2] Ibid., p. 676.

here, and the *Metamorphoses*, his collection of mythological fables about transformation, was the single most important text. School curricula from the sixteenth century almost universally required the *Metamorphoses*, and most grammar schoolboys also studied one or more of Ovid's *Fasti*, *Heroides* and *Tristia*. At Winchester, for example, the curriculum in the 1530s specified memorisation of the *Metamorphoses* to the extent of 12 lines a week in the fourth and fifth forms, and probably also in the sixth and seventh, while poetical and rhetorical exercises based on Ovid's poem began in the fifth.[3]

For the educated, then, their knowledge of myth began at school. As T.W. Baldwin put it, speaking more generally of the influence of grammar schools in the sixteenth century, '[i]t was in grammar school that every learned grammarian got his fundamental ideas, however he might later have modified them.'[4] Furthermore, the importance afforded to memorisation in that schooling may explain why classical myth continued to exert such a hold over the early modern imagination; why so many writers who were the products of a grammar school education continued to draw on a stock of mythological stories that they had learnt in their youth. Recent scholarship has paid extensive attention to this, unearthing the importance of classical mythology for both early modern literature in general and for individual writers in particular.[5] Much of this work builds on Douglas Bush's groundbreaking *Mythology and the Renaissance Tradition in English Poetry*, which remains the standard treatment of the use of classical myth in English non-dramatic poetry up to 1680.[6]

What is less familiar, and what remains imperfectly understood, is the importance of myth for early modern popular culture. This chapter is therefore an attempt to fill that gap. No doubt this unfamiliarity is in part because of the problem of identifying what popular culture actually was and the related difficulty of separating 'high' and 'low' forms of early modern cultural production. Popular culture is, as Peter Burke points out, an elusive thing, and it therefore 'has to be approached in a roundabout manner, recovered by indirect means, and interpreted by a series of analogies'.[7] This is certainly the case with myth and legend: two forms of knowledge transmitted in the early modern period through learned institutions such as the grammar schools and 'high' forms of production such as mythological handbooks, but just as influential and pervasive in more popular forms of entertainment such as pageants, progresses and the public theatre.[8] In *The Return from Parnassus, Part Two*, one of a trilogy of

---

[3]   T.W. Baldwin, *William Shakspere's Small Latine & Lesse Greeke* (2 vols, Urbana: University of Illinois Press, 1944), II, pp. 417–55; Jonathan Bate, *Shakespeare and Ovid* (Oxford: Clarendon Press, 1993), pp. 19–32.

[4]   Baldwin, *Shakespere's Small Latine & Lesse Greeke*, II, p. 422.

[5]   For useful overviews, see H. David Brumble, 'Let Us Make Gods in Our Image: Greek Myth in Medieval and Renaissance Literature', in Roger D. Woodard ed., *The Cambridge Companion to Greek Mythology* (Cambridge: Cambridge University Press, 2007), pp. 407–24; and Jane Kingsley-Smith, 'Mythology', in Michael Hattaway ed., *A New Companion to English Renaissance Literature* (Oxford: Blackwell, 2010), pp. 134–49. For a splendid account of the importance of myth for an individual writer, which also provides an invaluable account of the place of classical myth in early modern thought more generally, see Rhodri Lewis, 'Francis Bacon, Allegory and the Uses of Myth', *The Review of English Studies* 61 (2010), 360–89.

[6]   Douglas Bush, *Mythology and the Renaissance Tradition in English Poetry* (Minneapolis: University of Minnesota Press, 1932). Other classic accounts include DeWitt T. Starnes and Ernest William Talbert, *Classical Myth and Legend and Renaissance Dictionaries* (Chapel Hill: University of North Carolina Press, 1955); and Don Cameron Allen, *Mysteriously Meant: The Rediscovery of Pagan Symbolism and Allegorical Interpretation in the Renaissance* (Baltimore: Johns Hopkins University Press, 1970).

[7]   Peter Burke, *Popular Culture in Early Modern Europe* (Aldershot: Ashgate, 1994; first published 1978), p. 87.

[8]   For plays and pageants as exemplary forms of early modern popular culture, see Peter Burke, 'Popular Culture in Seventeenth-Century London', in Barry Reay ed., *Popular Culture in Seventeenth-Century England* (London: Croom Helm, 1985), pp. 31–58, at p. 31.

plays acted at St John's College, Cambridge, between 1599 and 1603, a character comments satirically on the ubiquity of classical myth in university drama: 'Few of the vniuersity pen plaies well, they smell too much of that writer *Ouid*, and that writer *Metamorphosis*, and talke too much of *Proserpina* & *Iuppiter*.'[9] But the same comment could be made about the popular stage, about plays written for audiences, part of whom, at least, we might expect to have been less familiar with the works of Ovid than students at Cambridge. An interest in myth and legend was not only the preserve of those who had had the benefit of a university or even just a grammar school education. That wider interest in myth is the focus of this essay, as it follows Burke's method and seeks to recover popular beliefs about myth and legend by tracing them indirectly through a range of literary and historical texts, from dramatic works to antiquarian collections. Together these works attest to, but also sometimes document, early modern ideas about myth and legend, and they therefore enable us to highlight not only popular conceptions of them, but also popular myths and legends themselves.

But before turning to those texts we need first to establish what the early modern period actually understood by myth and legend. For those words did not always mean the same thing as they do today. In fact, the word myth does not seem to have been used at all in the early modern period. According to the *OED*, the word was not coined until 1830 when it appeared for the first time in an essay in the *Westminster Review*. This does not, however, mean that the early moderns had no concept of myth. The fact that the word was used in Latin, as in Erasmus's *De ratione studii*, makes this clear. Furthermore, the idea of a traditional story, which embodies and provides an explanation, aetiology or justification for something, was an important part of early modern culture. But the word that the early moderns used to signify that was not myth, but mythology.[10] Thus a word that we now understand exclusively as a collection of stories or fables was used interchangeably in the early modern period to designate either a collection or an individual tale. Philemon Holland's definition of mythology in the glossary to his 1603 translation of Plutarch's *Moralia* makes this clear: '*Mythologie*, A fabulous Narration: or the delivery of matters by way of fables and tales'.[11] In addition, mythology in the early modern period could also mean the exposition of individual fables or tales, the interpretation of their allegorical, historical or physical meanings.[12] Again, Holland's translation of the *Moralia* provides an example of this. Slightly earlier in the work he speaks of the Egyptian god Osiris and his adoption of Jupiter and observes that 'the Muthology of this fable, as it evidently appeareth, accordeth covertly, with the trueth of Nature'.[13]

Furthermore, legend also had a different meaning in the early modern period. In the medieval period, legend had had a very specific sense, designating either the story of the life of a saint or, in a liturgical context, a book to be read, often containing just such a life. That sense persisted into the sixteenth century, mostly thanks to the continued popularity of the best known medieval collection of saints' lives: the *Legenda aurea* or *Golden Legend*.[14] This thirteenth-century work is a compilation from some 130 sources, put together around 1260 by Jacobus de Voragine, archbishop of Genoa, and its subject matter is the dealings of God with mankind as revealed through his agents and instruments, the saints. The *Legenda* was

---

[9]   *The Retvrne from Pernassvs: Or The Scourge of Simony* (London, 1606), sig. G3r; also cited in Bate, *Shakespeare and Ovid*, p. 43.

[10]   *OED*, *s.v.* 'myth', *n*. 1(a), and 'mythology', *n*. 2.

[11]   *The Philosophie, Commonlie Called, The Morals Written by the learned Philosopher Plutarch of Chæronea*, trans. Philemon Holland (London, 1603), sig. 5Z5r.

[12]   *OED*, *s.v.* 'mythology', *n*. 1(a) and (b).

[13]   *Philosophie, Commonlie Called, The Morals*, sig. 5R3v.

[14]   Sherry L. Reames, *The Legenda aurea: A Reexamination of Its Paradoxical History* (Madison: University of Wisconsin Press, 1985), pp. 61–2.

immensely popular and by the fifteenth century it had been widely translated. In English there were two full translations: an anonymous prose version of *c.* 1438 and William Caxton's one published some 45 years later in 1483. Caxton's translation was based partly on the previous English version and partly on a French translation printed by Peter Keyser at Paris. Caxton also added a considerable amount of material of his own, mostly lives of English or Irish saints. The book was an immediate hit with readers and a second edition appeared later in the same year. Further editions followed in 1493, 1498, 1504, 1507, 1512, 1521 and 1527.[15] In addition, in 1501, there also appeared a series of extracts from the *Legenda*, made up of biblical stories from Adam to Judith. This enthusiasm for Caxton's book ran counter to the growing scholarly consensus. By the beginning of the sixteenth century humanist scholars had started to point out the untrustworthiness of Jacobus's stories and they were almost universal in their disapproval of the book.[16] Readers, however, continued to buy the *Legenda* in droves, making it one of the most popular books of the early sixteenth century.

In his preface Caxton explains that he had two reasons for translating Jacobus's work:

> & for as moche as saynt austyn aforesayd sayth vpon a psalme that good werke ought
> not to be doon for fere of payne but for the loue of rightwysnesse & that it be of veray
> & souerayn fraunchise and by cause me semeth to be a souerayn wele to Incyte &
> exhorte men & wymmen to kepe them from slouthe and ydlenesse and to lete to be
> vnderstonden to suche peple as been not letterd the natuytees the lyues the passyons
> the myracles and the dethe of the holy sayntes & also some other notorye dedes and
> actes of tymes passed I haue submysed my self to translate in to englysshe the legende
> of sayntes Which is callyd legenda aurea in latyn that is to say the golden legende.[17]

Caxton's first reason, then, was an admonitory one: to warn his readers against idleness and sloth and to incite and exhort them to virtue through the exemplary lives contained in the work. His second reason was a more overtly didactic one: to teach 'suche peple as been not letterd' about those exemplary lives. Given what he goes on to say about translation, this presumably means people who do not read Latin. It therefore reminds us that Caxton's *Legend* was intended for a popular and probably also a lay readership. Taken together, the two reasons also remind us that, despite scholars' increasing concerns, the *Legenda* continued to be regarded as an exemplary piece of both learning and piety into the early modern period.

After 1527, however, things changed, and there was not another edition of Caxton's translation until the nineteenth century. This shift is usually explained by the Reformation. Sherry Reames, for example, asserts that the changing history of Caxton's book is 'consistent with the theory that the *Legenda* fell victim to the Reformation'.[18] The same reason can perhaps also explain a shift in meaning in the word legend itself. By the beginning of the seventeenth century, legend had begun to acquire a pejorative sense, consistent with Reformed attitudes towards hagiography and with Reformation thought more generally. In his essay 'Of Atheisme' (1612) Francis Bacon asserted that he would 'rather beleeve all

---

[15]   These editions were all printed by Wynkyn de Worde, except that of 1504, which was brought out by his fellow London printer Julian Notary. See A.W. Pollard and G.R. Redgrave, *A Short-Title Catalogue of Books Printed in England, Scotland, and Ireland and of English Books Printed Abroad 1475–1640* [hereafter *STC*], 2nd edn, rev. W.A. Jackson, F.S. Ferguson and K.F. Pantzer (3 vols, London: The Bibliographical Society, 1976–91), nos 24875–80.

[16]   Reames, *Legenda aurea*, pp. 11–13. For the reception of the *Legenda* in England more generally, see Manfred Görlach, *The Textual Tradition of the South English Legendary*, Leeds Texts and Monographs, n.s. 6 (Leeds: University of Leeds School of English, 1974), pp. 21–63.

[17]   Jacobus de Voragine, *Legenda aurea sanctorum*, trans. William Caxton (London, 1483), sig. π1v.

[18]   Reames, *The Legenda aurea*, p. 28.

the Fables in the *Legend*, and the *Talmud*, and the *Alcoran*, then that this universall Frame, is without a Minde', while just a year later Samuel Purchas used legend repeatedly as a synonym for something inauthentic or unbelievable.[19] Speaking of a tree that grows in Goa, the so-called *Arbore triste*, for example, he comments:

> And that yee may know the Indians want not their Metamorphoses and Legends, they tell that a man, named Parisatico, had a daughter, with whom the Sunne was in loue; but lightly forsaking her, he grew amorous of another: whereupon this Damosell slew her selfe, and of the ashes of her burned carcasse came this tree.[20]

By the seventeenth century, therefore, the meaning of legend had altered from the narrow liturgical sense current in the medieval period and sixteenth century to something closer to the modern sense of an unauthentic or non-historical story.

In addition to the liturgical and pejorative senses, legend also had a third meaning in the early modern period. As with the pejorative sense, this was a secular one. But, unlike that sense, it was also a broadly historical one, understanding legend as an old tale or account. Early modern lexicographers often defined the word in this way. John Bullokar explained legend as 'A story of olde matters', while Henry Cockeram defined legends as 'Tales' and a legendary as 'A booke of old histories'.[21] It was also in this sense that the word was used in the full title of Robert Chester's long and little loved narrative poem *Loves Martyr* (1601). The title page to Chester's poem announces that it is printed '[w]ith the true legend of famous King *Arthur*, the last of the nine Worthies, being the first *Essay* of a new Brytish Poet: collected out of diuerse Authenticall Records'. Chester's poem narrates the journey of Dame Nature and the Phoenix across Europe to the isle of Paphos, and this provides the occasion for a series of digressions, including the one on the history of King Arthur promised in the title.[22] Chester prefaces this digression with an epistle 'To the courteous Reader', which bristles with indignation at those writers who deny Arthur's historicity, those who '*in their erronious censures haue thought no such ma*n *euer to be liuing*'.[23] Chester reminds any readers doubtful about Arthur of the print of that king's wax seal that was to be found in Westminster Abbey. In referring to the seal, Chester was citing one of the most widely used pieces of evidence for the historicity of Arthur in the sixteenth century. John Leland afforded the same sigillographic evidence pride of place in his influential *Assertio inclytissimi Arturij Regis Britanniae* (1544), and defences based on it date back at least as far as Caxton's preface to his 1485 edition of the *Morte Darthur*.[24] Chester's poem shares the same confidence in the authenticating power of the wax seal as its more illustrious predecessors. Like them, Chester uses it to confirm the historical reality of Arthur, to confirm the 'true legend' of his title.

---

[19] Francis Bacon, 'Of Atheisme', in *The Essayes or Counsels, Civill and Morall*, ed. Michael Kiernan, *The Oxford Francis Bacon XV* (Oxford: Oxford University Press, 2000; first published 1985), p. 51 (sig. N1v).

[20] *Purchas his Pilgrimage. Or Relations of the World and the Religions Observed in All Ages And places discouered, from the Creation vnto this Present* (London, 1613), sig. 2P2v. See also, inter alia, sigs S3r, 2A2v, 2O4v, 2S4r and 3B6r.

[21] John Bullokar, *An English Expositor: Teaching the Interpretation of the hardest words vsed in our Language* (London, 1616), sig. I8v; and Henry Cockeram, *The English Dictionarie: Or, An Interpreter of hard English Words* (London, 1623), sig. G4r.

[22] Robert Chester, *Loves Martyr Or, Rosalins Complaint. Allegorically shadowing the truth of Loue, in the constant Fate of the Phœnix and Turtle* (London, 1601), sigs F2v–L3r.

[23] Ibid., sig. F2v.

[24] See John Leland, *Assertio inclytissimi Arturij Regis Britanniae* (London, 1544), sigs D4r–E2v; and Thomas Malory, *Le morte darthur* (London, 1485), sig. π2v.

Chester's poem is not the only early modern book to conjoin the words true and legend in this way. This same sense of a legend as something authentic is also at play in the title of a very different early seventeenth-century work: *The Friers Chronicle: Or, The Trve Legend of Priests and Monkes Lives* (1623). Here, however, the truth of the legend is not something to be celebrated, but something to be condemned. This anonymously published work, often attributed to the Calvinist theologian Thomas Goade, is a compendium of priestly knavery and popish trickery and is designed explicitly to reveal the treachery of the Catholic Church. The dedicatory epistle describes it as 'the Discouery of the vnswept corners of Popish Monasteries' and tells its patron, the countess of Devonshire, that in its pages she 'may reade such loathsome particulars against Papistry, that in [her] friends behalfe, [she] will doe, as wee wont to do in *England*, euen spit at the naming of the Diuell'.[25] Here, therefore, the conjunction of the words true and legend is part of the author's rhetoric and one of his strategies for revealing popish iniquities. It is also, of course, a disparaging allusion to the title of the *Golden Legend*, recasting that mainstay of Catholic devotional practice in the light of what the author repeatedly calls 'True Religion'. Early on in the book the author makes the connection with the *Golden Legend* explicit when he describes Jacobus, 'hee that writ their Golden Legend', as 'the father of Lyes'.[26]

The diverse meanings of the two words illustrate how broad what constituted myth and legend really was in the early modern period. First of all, there was, as Erasmus's stipulations make clear, the large body of classical myth. In addition to school curricula, knowledge of this reached a wide and popular readership through a variety of literary means. One of these was the emblem book tradition, which, as Jane Kingsley-Smith has pointed out, was a valuable resource for the English encounter with mythology.[27] Another means were the mythological handbooks that were published in increasingly large numbers in the sixteenth century. In Europe as a whole the best-known handbooks were the *De deis gentium* (1548) of Lilio Gregorio Giraldi, the *Mythologiae* (1567) of Natale Conti and *Le imagini ... degli dei degli antichi* (1556) of Vincenzo Cartari.[28] While none of these could be described as a work of popular culture, Cartari's handbook at least did reach a wider English readership through Richard Linche's 1599 translation *The Fovntaine of Ancient Fiction*. However, the most popular mythological handbook in England, and one that was widely used, was Thomas Cooper's 'Dictionarivm Historicum & Poeticum propria locorum & Personarum vocabula breuiter complectens'. This was appended to Cooper's massive *Thesaurus*, first published in 1565 and reissued in 1573, 1578 and 1584. Despite its Latin title, the 'Dictionarivm' is one of the more straightforward vernacular handbooks and so is particularly useful as a source for contemporary senses of different classical myths. Cooper's entries are, on the whole, simple, synthesising the knowledge of particular myths from a variety of (not always acknowledged) ancient sources under nominal headings. The following example, on the myth of Tantalus, is a case in point:

---

[25]   Thomas Goade (?), *The Friers Chronicle: Or, The Trve Legend of Priests and Monkes Lives* (London, 1623), sig. A2v.

[26]   Ibid., sig. B2v.

[27]   Jane Kingsley-Smith, 'Mythology', p. 138. For overviews of the emblem book tradition, see Peter M. Daly ed., *The English Emblem and the Continental Tradition* (New York: AMS Press, 1988); and Michael Bath, *Speaking Pictures: English Emblem Books and Renaissance Culture* (London: Longman, 1994).

[28]   See Jean Seznec, *The Survival of the Pagan Gods: The Mythological Tradition and Its Place in Renaissance Humanism and Art*, trans. Barbara F. Sessions (Princeton: Princeton University Press, 1981; first published 1953), pp. 219–56; Bush, *Mythology and the Renaissance Tradition*, pp. 31–2; and Lewis, 'Bacon, Allegory, and the Uses of Myth', pp. 370–71.

> *Tantalus, The sonne of Iupiter and Plota, kynge of Phrygia, of whome the poetes dooe wryte, that because he disclosed the counsayle of the gods, he is in hell tormented in this wyse: He standeth by a fayre ryuer, hauynge before hym a tree laden with pleasant appuls, and yet he is alwayes thursty and hungry: for as often as he stoupeth to drynke, or holdeth vp his hands to gather the appuls, bothe the water and the tree dooe withdrawe them so from hym, that he can not touche theim.*[29]

Occasionally, too, Cooper's entries are more interpretative, offering explanations for individual myths. He begins his account of the life of Hercules, for example, with an attempt to rationalise that myth: '*Hercules*, Seemeth to be a general name geuen to men excellynge in strengthe all other of their tyme.'[30] He does the same with his entry on Orpheus, where he amalgamates different accounts of the myth, and with his entry on Vesta, where he explains the connection between that goddess's virginity and her divinity.[31]

Perhaps the most important way, though, in which popular culture encountered classical myth was through the theatre. Early modern plays are full of allusions, some in passing and some more extended, to mythology. While it is unlikely that audiences would have been expected to identify the sources for these allusions – only the small educated elite would have been able to do that – the frequency with which playwrights make them suggest that they were a staple of popular entertainment. Shakespeare's plays are, of course, good examples of this, and they provide a series of excellent illustrations of the currency that classical myth could have in the early modern period. At the end of *King Henry VI, Part 2*, for instance, one of Shakespeare's earliest plays, Young Clifford draws upon two different classical myths to articulate his grief at the death of his father and his determination to revenge it:

> *Henceforth I will not have to do with pity.*
> *Meet I an infant of the house of York,*
> *Into as many gobbets will I cut it*
> *As wild Medea young Absyrtus did.*
> *In cruelty will I seek out my fame.*
> *Come, thou new ruin of old Clifford's house;*
> *As did Aeneas old Anchises bear,*
> *So bear I thee upon my manly shoulders;*
> *But then Aeneas bare a living load,*
> *Nothing so heavy as these woes of mine.*[32]

The comparisons here depend on an audience recognising Medea as a figure for cruelty and understanding Aeneas's bearing of his father upon his shoulders as an *exemplum* of piety and familial duty.[33] But the comparisons also, of course, depend on an audience recognising the differences between Young Clifford and his mythological forebears: unlike Medea, he does not seek to kill his own kin, and unlike Aeneas he bears the burden of a dead father. In a similar fashion, when Rosalind in *As You Like It* disguises herself as a man and calls

---

[29]   Thomas Cooper, 'Dictionarivm Historicum & Poeticum propria locorum & Personarum vocabula breuiter complectens', in *Thesavrvs Lingvæ Romanæ & Britannicæ* (London, 1565), sig. Q3r–v.

[30]   Ibid., sig. I5r.

[31]   Ibid., sigs N2v and R3v.

[32]   William Shakespeare, *King Henry VI, Part II*, ed. Ronald Knowles (London: Thomson Publishing, 1999), 5.2.56–65.

[33]   Shakespeare's likely source for the story of Medea killing and cutting up her younger brother Absyrtus to enable her and Jason to escape from her father is Ovid's *Tristia* (see III.ix.25–28), another stalwart of the early modern grammar school curriculum.

herself Ganymede ('I'll have no worse a name than Jove's own page, / And therefore look you call me Ganymede'), the joke, but also the subversion of gender roles here and the related homoerotic associations, depend on an audience having at least a rudimentary knowledge of that myth.[34] A third and perhaps more elaborate example of this kind of recognition occurs in *Titus Andronicus*, where the plot and Titus's vicious revenge turn on an analogy between the rape of his daughter Lavinia and 'the tragic tale of Philomel'.[35] The violated, mutilated and supposedly silenced Lavinia is still able to reveal in Act 4 Scene 1 what happened to her by pointing to a copy of Ovid's *Metamorphoses* and drawing attention to the mythological parallel.

The best evidence, though, for the currency of classical myth in the popular theatre comes from a series of five plays written by Thomas Heywood in the early seventeenth century: *The Golden Age*, *The Silver Age*, *The Brazen Age*, *The Iron Age* and *The Second Part of the Iron Age*. Heywood wrote these plays, which date from around 1609, for the most populist of the early modern playhouses, the Red Bull in Clerkenwell, where they were staged by that theatre's resident company, the Queen's Men.[36] The plays dramatise a series of classical myths, ranging from the triumph of the Olympian Gods over the Titans through to the Trojan War and its aftermath. While the plays are episodic and structurally crude, they are undoubtedly spectacular and exploit to the full the theatrical possibilities of the early modern stage. As such, they are typical of the dramatic output of the Red Bull and embody much that was popular about that theatre. *The Silver Age*, for example, calls for the presence of two snakes on stage, while in Act 2 Scene 1 of *2 The Iron Age* the Trojan Horse itself is *'discovered'*. As Aeneas comments there with surprise, 'Soft, what huge Engine's that left on the strond, / That beares the shape and figure of an Horse'.[37] The first two plays, in particular, also call for repeated descents and ascents of the gods: a theatrical device that has a parallel in Act 5 Scene 3 of Shakespeare's very different play *Cymbeline*. In both cases, the gods would have descended from the heavens thanks to a flying apparatus operated by a winch. Heywood's plays, then, were designed to impress the Red Bull's citizen audiences and, on the whole, they seem to have been successful.[38] Heywood himself attests to the theatrical success of *The Golden Age*. 'Therefore rather to keep custome, then any necessity,' he wrote in the prefatory epistle to the 1611 edition of the play, 'I haue fixt these few lines in the front of my Booke: neither to approue it, as tastfull to euery palat, nor to disgrace it, as able to relish none, onely to commit it freely to the generall censure of Readers, as it hath already past the approbation of Auditors'.[39] The fact that in a later play, *Calisto, or The Escapes*

---

[34]   William Shakespeare, *As You Like It*, ed. Juliet Dusinberre (London: Thomson Publishing, 2006), 1.3.121–22. For interpretations of the myth of Ganymede in the Renaissance, see Bruce R. Smith, *Homosexual Desire in Shakespeare's England: A Cultural Poetics* (Chicago: University of Chicago Press, 1994; first published 1991), pp. 191–201.

[35]   William Shakespeare, *Titus Andronicus*, ed. Jonathan Bate (London: Thomson Publishing, 1995), 4.1.47.

[36]   For the traditional view of the Red Bull and its populism, see G.E. Bentley, *The Jacobean and Caroline Stage* (7 vols, Oxford: Oxford University Press, 1941–68), VI, pp. 238–47. For revisionist accounts that celebrate that theatre's populism, see Andrew Gurr, *Playgoing in Shakespeare's London* (Cambridge: Cambridge University Press, 1987), pp. 189–96; and Mark Bayer, 'The Red Bull Playhouse', in Richard Dutton ed., *The Oxford Handbook of Early Modern Theatre* (Oxford: Oxford University Press, 2009), pp. 225–39.

[37]   Thomas Heywood, *The Second Part of the Iron Age*, in *The Dramatic Works of Thomas Heywood Now First Collected with Illustrative Notes and A Memoir of the Author in Six Volumes* (London, 1874), III, p. 372.

[38]   See Michel Grivelet, *Thomas Heywood et le drame domestique Élizabéthain* (Paris: Richard West, 1957), pp. 51–3.

[39]   Thomas Heywood, *The Golden Age*, in *The Dramatic Works of Thomas Heywood*, III, p. 3.

of Jupiter, Heywood returned to *The Golden Age* and *The Silver Age* and recycled large parts of them is also suggestive of their popularity and theatrical success.[40]

Heywood's *Ages* also give us a sense of how certain learned notions of classical myth were transmitted, consciously or not, to popular audiences. The first three plays, for example, are presented by Homer, who operates as a kind of chorus figure, and in whose depiction Heywood seems to take his cue, at least in part, from Erasmus. As he had done, Heywood also portrays Homer as the 'father of all myth'. In the opening lines of *The Golden Age*, Homer describes himself in precisely this way:

> *The Gods of Greece, whose deities I rais'd*
> *Out of the earth, gaue them diuinity,*
> *The attributes of Sacrifice and Prayer*
> *Haue giuen old Homer leaue to view the world*
> *And make his own presentment.*[41]

In making the argument here that Homer is the creator of the divinity of the Greek gods, Heywood was also transmitting another widespread learned belief about classical myth: that the gods were originally mortal men and historical persons, who were only later elevated to their divine status. This belief, known as euhemerism after its founder, the Sicilian mythographer Euhemerus, dated back to the fourth century BC, but it remained a powerful influence on learned conceptions of the classical gods well into the early modern period.[42] Heywood's plays convey this belief to a much wider audience and suggest that, contrary to some assumptions, popular poets could be interested in it. Euhemerism informs the vision of the gods throughout the five plays, but it is perhaps most apparent in *The Golden Age*. That play ends with the deification of Jupiter, Neptune and Pluto and with their translation from the world of men. The translation is performed through a series of dumb shows, with Homer providing an accompanying commentary. This makes clear the play's conception of the gods, as the following speech from just before the first dumb show indicates:

> *Yet to keepe promise, ere we further wade,*
> *The ground of ancient Poems you shall see:*
> *And how these (first borne mortall) Gods were made,*
> *By vertue of diuinest Poesie.*[43]

Homer's words here thus confirm the depiction of the gods that the rest of the play has suggested.

Classical myth also played an important role in other forms of early modern popular entertainment. Pageants and progresses, for example, often drew upon mythology as source material. These entertainments were open to all, elite and non-elite, learned and unlearned. The upper classes would have watched them from balconies above, while the masses would have thronged the streets.[44] In the Elizabethan period, mythological subjects

---

[40] See Grivelet, *Thomas Heywood*, p. 373.
[41] Heywood, *The Golden Age*, III, p. 5.
[42] See further Seznec, *Survival of the Pagan Gods*, pp. 11–36; Arthur B. Ferguson, *Utter Antiquity: Perceptions of Prehistory in Renaissance England* (Durham: Duke University Press, 1993), pp. 13–22; and Jane Chance, *Medieval Mythography: From Roman North Africa to The School of Chartres, A. D. 433–1177* (Gainesville: University Press of Florida, 1994), pp. 25–6.
[43] Heywood, *The Golden Age*, III, p. 78.
[44] See Burke, 'Popular Culture in Seventeenth-Century London', p. 44.

seem to have been particularly popular in the progress entertainments.[45] In August 1578, for example, on her progress through Suffolk and Norfolk, Elizabeth I was welcomed into the city of Norwich with a pageant that included a visit from Mercury in a coach. The classical god, who appeared in his full iconographic splendour, greeted the queen on behalf of the citizens.[46] The use of mythological subjects was even more popular in the Jacobean period, as the entry of James I into the city of London in March 1604 attests. This involved triumphal arches and a series of devices and entertainments that incorporated a range of figures from classical myth. The Italian merchants, for instance, erected an arch in Gracious Street on whose back there was the figure of Apollo 'with all his Ensignes and properties belonging unto him', while in Cheapside James witnessed the *Hortus Euporiae*, which included the goddesses Pomona, 'attirde in greene, a wreath of frutages circling her temples', and Ceres, 'crowned with ripened ears of Wheate'.[47] Myth was also an important part of that mainstay of civic entertainment and popular culture: the Lord Mayor's Show. The 1561 pageant for the inauguration of Sir William Harper involved Orpheus, Amphion and Arion, with each of the mythological characters appearing with his story painted about him and in traditional garb.[48] The same figures, especially the first two, recurred in many of the future mayoral pageants. Perhaps the most striking use of a mythological subject in a mayoral show occurred in 1615 in the pageant performed in honour of Sir John Jolles of the Drapers' Company. This pageant, *Metropolis Coronata, The Trivmphes of Ancient Drapery*, was based around the story of Jason and the Argonauts, with the Golden Fleece an obvious homage to the new mayor's livery company. The highlight of the pageant was an elaborate water show on the Thames, involving a boat that represented the Argo and which conveyed Jason and his companions, Hercules, Telamon, Orpheus, Castor, Pollux, Calais and Zethes, down the river.[49]

Myth and legend did not, however, just designate classical material. As the title to Chester's poem makes clear, they could equally describe the vast body of stories associated with King Arthur, and they could also allude to the matter of Britain more generally. Much of this material originated with Geoffrey of Monmouth's twelfth-century *History of the Kings of Britain*: a long and eventful account ranging from the founding of Britain by the eponymous Brutus, great-grandson of Aeneas, through to the Saxon invasions of the fifth century AD. By the early modern period Geoffrey's *History* had attracted extensive controversy in scholarly circles and its veracity was widely disputed, but it continued to exert a considerable influence on popular culture.[50] One of the most widespread of the Arthurian and Galfridian stories was the myth of Arthur as *rex quondam rexque futurus*. This popular belief held that Arthur was not in fact dead, but only sleeping, and would return in the future to conquer his enemies and liberate his people and thus herald a new Golden Age.[51] Related to this was the widely bruited tale of the discovery of Arthur's tomb during the reign of Henry II. Antiquaries from Leland to Humphrey Llwyd and even William Camden reported this tale, suggesting that it did enjoy considerable currency in the sixteenth century.[52] According to this tale,

---

[45]   David M. Bergeron, *English Civic Pageantry 1558–1642* (Columbia: University of South Carolina Press, 1971), p. 64.

[46]   Ibid., pp. 37–44; Thomas Churchyard, *A Discovrse Of The Queenes Maiesties entertainment in Suffolk and Norffolk: With a description of many things then presently seene* (London, 1578), sigs C2r–C3v.

[47]   Bergeron, *English Civic Pageantry*, pp. 82–3.

[48]   Ibid., pp. 126–8.

[49]   Ibid., pp. 152–4.

[50]   For the controversy over Geoffrey of Monmouth, see T.D. Kendrick, *British Antiquity* (London: Methuen, 1950), pp. 78–98; and Ferguson, *Utter Antiquity*, pp. 84–105.

[51]   Burke, *Popular Culture*, pp. 152–3.

[52]   Leland, *Assertio*, sigs H2r–H3v; *The historie of Cambria, now called Wales: A part of the most famous Yland of Brytaine, written in the Brytish language aboue two hundreth yeares past: translated into English by H Lhoyd Gentleman* (London, 1584), sigs R7v–R8r; and William Camden, *Britain, or A Chorographicall*

Henry had been entertained during a banquet at St Davids in Wales by a bard who sang of Arthur's mysterious burial and tomb. Shortly afterwards, on the bard's authority, that tomb was discovered at Glastonbury, and inside a greater discovery still was made: the preternaturally well-preserved bodies of Arthur and Guinevere, who did indeed appear to be sleeping rather than dead.

Arthurian stories also provided subject matter for ballads, another mainstay of early modern popular culture. An early seventeenth-century example is the anonymous *A brave warlike Song. Containing a briefe rehearsall of the deeds of Chivalry, performed by the Nine Worthies of the world*. This ballad, which was probably printed in 1626, and was sung to the tune Lusty Gallant, celebrates Arthur as one of the Nine Worthies: the figures who, in the medieval and early modern periods, were popularly believed to be the embodiment of heroic virtues. The ballad is patriotic in tone, praising Arthur and his knights for their 'many famous fights' and for making 'the foes of Brittaine / in those dayes sore to quake'. As the ballad celebrates the Nine Worthies, it also, of course, engages with classical myth. Hector, the son of Priam, is another of the Worthies, and the ballad praises him as 'the Prince and pride of Troy', who 'all his life preserued / the Citie from anoy'. Other ballads on Arthurian themes include *Saint Georges commendation to all Souldiers*, printed in 1612, and sung to the tune St George for England, and Thomas Deloney's *The Noble Acts newly found, Of Arthur of the Table Round*.[53] This ballad celebrates the knights of the Round Table and tells of Sir Lancelot's fight with Sir Tarquin and his delivery of the 'threescore Knights and four', whom that churlish knight held prisoner. Samuel Butler's 1671 *A New Ballad of King Edward and Jane Shore* also makes a passing reference to Arthur, albeit in a rather less celebratory fashion than the previous examples ('Queen Quiniver with Arthur fought singly hand to hand / In Bed, though afterward she made horns on his head to stand').

Another way in which Arthurian and Galfridian material manifested itself in popular culture was through prophecies. These, as Keith Thomas has shown, were elusive, vague or ambiguous pieces of prose or verse, usually attributed to a historical or mythological personage.[54] That personage was normally Merlin: a composite figure whose prophecies derived in part from Welsh bardic tradition and in part from the predictions that make up Book 7 of Geoffrey's *History*. While these prophecies were almost universally condemned by scholars, they continued to be popular and widely believed. They were also sometimes controversial, as the arrest of one Edward Sawford, an embroiderer from Leicester, in 1586 makes clear. Sawford had uttered a prophecy that outlined the dire consequences that would follow if Mary, Queen of Scots, were executed, and when he was interrogated, he admitted that the ultimate source for it was 'the book of King Arthur', which he described as 'a[s] pleasant book of fables as ever he read in his life'. He also described Merlin as 'a man that foretold many things to come, yea even to the world's end'.[55] These prophecies continued to be popular well into the seventeenth century. Indeed, their reception received a boost in 1641 through the publication of Heywood's *Life of Merlin, Sirnamed Ambrosivs*: a popular chronicle history from the legendary Brutus up to Charles I, which sought to show the fulfilment of Merlin's prophecies in subsequent events. It was not until the last

---

Description of the Most flourishing Kingdomes, England, Scotland, and Ireland, and the Ilands adioyning, out of the depth of Antiquitie, trans. Philemon Holland (London, 1610), sig. T5r–v.

[53] Deloney's ballad seems to have been particularly popular. The *English Broadside Ballad Archive* (http://ebba.english.uscb.edu) records three different versions that circulated in the later seventeenth century, while *STC* also records an earlier version, printed *c*. 1620 (*STC* 6558.5).

[54] Keith Thomas, *Religion and the Decline of Magic: Studies in Popular Beliefs in Sixteenth and Seventeenth Century England* (London: Weidenfeld and Nicholson, 1971), pp. 389–432; see also Burke, *Popular Culture*, pp. 273–4.

[55] Quoted in Thomas, *Religion and the Decline of Magic*, p. 407.

part of the seventeenth century, by which time the Galfridian history had lost almost all its credibility, that their popularity began to wane.

Just as with classical myth, Arthurian legends and Galfridian matter more broadly were also popular source material for the theatre. Plays on Arthurian themes include the now lost 'kynge arthore', for which Henslowe's *Diary* records payments to Richard Hathway in April 1598, and William Rowley's rumbustious *The Birth of Merlin* (c. 1622).[56] Rowley's play dramatises the dynastic struggles between the British kings Vortiger and Aurelius Ambrosius and the invasions of the Saxon brothers Hengist and Horsa, material that derives ultimately from Geoffrey. But the play also contains a comic subplot about the birth and parentage of Merlin. This concerns Merlin's mother, the aptly named Joan Goe-too't, and her desperate search for the identity of the man who made her pregnant. The dynastic struggles between Vortiger and Aurelius Ambrosius were themselves also popular theatrical subjects: Henslowe's *Diary* records 12 performances of a play called 'valteger' in 1596–7 alone.[57] Sometimes, too, plays conjoined this kind of material with classical myth: something that Geoffrey himself had done in the opening chapters of the *History* in which he describes the flight of Brutus from Troy and his arrival in Britain.[58]

Perhaps the best example of this conjunction of Galfridian material with classical myth comes in *The Lamentable Tragedy of Locrine*, an anonymous play printed in 1595, but which may have been written as much as 10 years earlier. *Locrine* combines legendary history, derived primarily from Geoffrey, with moralistic readings of classical myth and comic scenes, involving the clown Strumbo, that seem to come from contemporary London. These comic scenes, which include Strumbo's absurd courtship of his wife, cobbling episodes and drinking songs, remind us that, despite its long speeches and its echoes of academic and Senecan drama, the play was written with a popular audience in mind.[59] The legendary history concerns Brutus's division of the island of Britain between his three sons and the titular hero's ill-fated and adulterous love affair with Estrild, the wife of his Scythian foe Humber. Classical myth provides the basis for a series of dumb shows at the beginning of Acts 2, 4 and 5. These are presented by the Greek goddess Ate, and they portray in turn the kidnap of Andromeda by Phineus and a party of Ethiopians, Hercules spinning for Omphale and Medea's revenge upon Jason and Creusa. These dumb shows offer a moralistic commentary on the action of the main plot. In each case Ate draws an exact parallel between the mythological story and the conduct of Locrine, as her speech at the beginning of Act 4 illustrates:

> *Quem non Argolici mandata severa tyranni,*
> *Non potuit Juno vincere, vincit amor.*
> *Stout Hercules, the mirror of the world,*
> *Son to Alcmena and great Jupiter,*
> *After so many conquests won in field,*
> *After so many monsters quelled by force,*
> *Yielded his valiant heart to Omphale,*
> *A fearful woman, void of manly strength.*

---

[56] *Henslowe's Diary*, ed. Walter W. Greg (3 vols, London: A.H. Bullen, 1904–8), fo. 45v: 'Lent vnto the co^mpany the 12 of ap^rell 1598 to paye m^r hathwaye in fulle payment for his boocke of kynge arthore the some of fower pownde'. See also fo. 46r for a further record of payment.

[57] Ibid., fos 25v–26r.

[58] See Geoffrey of Monmouth, *The History of the Kings of Britain*, trans. Lewis Thorpe (Harmondsworth: Penguin, 1966), pp. 54–73 (i.3–i.16).

[59] Unfortunately, there are no contemporary records of performance, which might have corroborated this assumption. We do not know which company staged the play, when they staged it or where.

She took the club and ware the lion's skin;
He took the wheel and maidenly 'gan spin.
So martial Locrine, cheered with victory,
Falleth in love with Humber's concubine,
And so forgetteth peerless Guendoline.[60]

Ate's other speeches follow the same model, first of all explicating the myth and explaining what the audience has seen in dumb show, and then applying it to the legendary history of the rest of the play.

Arthurian and Galfridian material was also popular with the devisers of pageants. Here, too, it was often conjoined with classical myth. Elizabeth I's official passage through London on 14 January 1559, to give one example, culminated in a Galfridian tableau after a series of symbolic devices. When the queen reached Temple Bar, she found it 'dressed finely with two ymages of Gotmagot the Albione, and Corineus the Briton, two gyantes bigge in stature furnished accordingly'. The two giants held a pair of tablets with verses explaining the progress as a whole and with a final wish from the people to their new sovereign: 'Liue long, and as long raygne, adourning thy countrie / With vertues, and mayntayne thy peoples hope of thee'.[61] Anthony Munday's *The Triumphes of Re-United Britannia*, his mayoral show presented in honour of Sir Leonard Halliday, is another example. Munday's pageant draws upon the legendary history of Britain, and in particular the myth of Brutus, to compliment James I on behalf of the citizens of London and to offer their support for his policy of the union. The pageant figures James as 'our second *Brute*' and notes that by his 'happye comming to the Crowne, *England*, *Wales*, & *Scotland*, by our first Brute seuered and diuided, is in our second *Brute* re-vnited, and made one happy *Britania* again'.[62] Moreover, Munday's pageant also draws upon mythological figures: as well as Brutus, Locrine, Camber and Albanact, Neptune and Amphitrite make an appearance.

Of all the authors discussed in this chapter, Munday is perhaps the most obviously associated with popular culture. Indeed, given his involvement in so many forms of popular entertainment, he is in some ways the bellwether of that culture.[63] And yet his 1605 pageant is filled with abstruse historical discussion and informed by extensive antiquarian learning: material that, on the face of it, we might not associate with a popular form of cultural production. This is particularly apparent in the printed text, as Munday prefaces his description of the pageant's central device with an extended disquisition on the etymology of Britain, focusing in antiquarian fashion on both the origin of the name and the origin of its inhabitants. This apparent discrepancy between content and form thus reminds us, as Heywood's spectacular staging of classical mythology in the *Ages* also does, of how rich the interplay between 'high' and 'low' culture really was when it came to myth and legend. Popular culture's conception of myth and legend, that is to say, owed a great deal to learned culture – to antiquarian collections, mythological handbooks and school curricula. In the

---

[60]   *The Lamentable Tragedy of Locrine: A Critical Edition*, ed. Jane Lytton Gooch, Garland English Texts Number 7 (New York: Garland, 1981), IV.i.1–13.

[61]   *The Passage of our most drad soueraigne Lady Quene Elizabeth through the citie of London to westminster the daye before her coronacion* (London, 1559), sig. E1r–v; also quoted in Bergeron, *English Civic Pageantry*, p. 22.

[62]   Anthony Munday, *The Trivmphes of re-vnited Britania* (London, 1605), sig. B2r.

[63]   For a case study in Munday's appeal to popular audiences, see William D. Wolf, 'Anthony Munday as Popular Artist', *Journal of Popular Culture* 13 (1980), 659–62. For an account that makes a virtue more generally of Munday's popularity and range, see Tracey Hill, *Anthony Munday and Civic Culture: Theatre, History and Power in Early Modern London 1580–1642* (Manchester: Manchester University Press, 2004).

same way, the myths and legends dramatised in popular forms of entertainment often had their analogues in elite forms of cultural production. The plot of *Locrine*, for example, finds a parallel in John Milton's 1634 *A Masque Presented at Ludlow Castle*, written in celebration of the inauguration of John Egerton, earl of Bridgewater, as lord president of Wales.[64]

Furthermore, this traffic between learned and popular culture was not just one way. Learned culture was itself increasingly interested in myths and legends transmitted through more popular means. Oral tradition, for example, became the subject of renewed interest for scholars, with antiquaries in particular starting to pay attention to it.[65] They also started to collect examples, preserving in their papers and works myths and legends that were otherwise in danger of dying out. Camden's *Britannia*, perhaps the pre-eminent early modern antiquarian book, is full of this kind of material. Much of what Camden collects is etymological and aetiological, as he traces the derivations of certain place names and finds their origins in local myths or legends. One such example is the town of Halifax. Writing about its history, Camden notes that it was formerly known as Horton, 'as some of the Inhabitants doe report'. He also notes that the inhabitants tell a 'prety story' about 'the alteration of the name', which he proceeds to recount at some length:

> *A certaine Clerke, as they call him, was farre in loue with a maiden who when he might not haue his purpose of her, for all the faire meanes and entismentes hee could use, his loue beeing turned vnto rage (vilanous wretch that hee was) cut off the maides head: which beeing hung afterwards upon an Eughtree, the common people counted as an hallowed relique, untill it was rotten, yea and they came deuoutly to visit it, and every one gathered and carried away with him a branch or sprig of the sayd tree. But after the tree was bare and nothing left but the very stock (such was the credulity of that time) it maintained the opinion of reverence and religion still. For, the people were perswaded, that the little veines that are stretched out and spred betweene the barke and bodie of the eugh tree in manner of haires or fine threads, were the very haires in deed of the virgins head. Hereupon, they that dwelt there about repaired on pilgrimage hither, and such resort was there unto it, that Horton beeing but a little village before, grew up to a great towne, and was called by a new name Halig-Fax, or Hali-fex, that is, Holy haire.*[66]

While Camden leaves his readers in little doubt about his own opinion of the legend – his parenthetical aside about 'the credulity of that time' sees to that – he still takes great care over documenting it. What matters for him here is not the credibility of the legend, but the very fact of its existence. And the same goes for the rest of the *Britannia*, as Camden meticulously documents popular beliefs and local legends, whether he believes them or not, and thus preserves them through his own written words. Without his intervention, and without the intervention of antiquaries like him, many of these early modern legends would now be lost.

There were, of course, limits to this interplay between learned and popular culture and clear differences in the ways in which the two apprehended myth and legend. Perhaps the most important of these, as Camden's pointed aside illustrates, was the question of credibility. While sources of authority mattered for learned culture, they were much less important in popular culture. This perhaps explains why the Galfridian tradition and the

---

[64]   For a recent discussion of Milton's engagement with the Galfridian story in his masque, see Philip Schwyzer, 'Purity and Danger on the West Bank of the Severn: The Cultural Geography of *A Masque Presented at Ludlow Castle, 1634'*, *Representations* 60 (1997), 22–48.

[65]   Adam Fox and D.R. Woolf eds, *The Spoken Word: Oral Culture in Britain 1500–1850* (Manchester: Manchester University Press, 2002), p. 36.

[66]   Camden, *Britain*, sig. 3M2r–v.

Golden Legend both continued to have considerable popular currency long after scholars had thoroughly debunked them. But the common interest in myths and legends, and the sometimes surprising mythological subjects of popular entertainments, suggest that we cannot draw too absolute a distinction between the two. Peter Burke has spoken of the need 'to think … in terms of interaction between the two cultures, learned and popular, dominant and dominated'.[67] When it comes to myth and legend, that is certainly the case. When audiences saw performances of *The Golden Age* at the Red Bull, they are unlikely to have recognised that play's euhemerism, let alone have had the terminology to articulate this. But that is nonetheless what they were seeing. Learned and unlearned, scholarly and popular representations of myth and legend were inextricably linked. And those links legitimise, perhaps even necessitate, the methodology that this chapter has taken. Those links mean that, to recover the place of myth and legend in popular culture, we do have to turn sometimes to surprising sources as well as to the more familiar embodiments of popular culture. We do have to turn to handbooks and antiquarian collections as well as to ballads, images and performances.

Select Bibliography

Baldwin, T.W., *William Shakspere's Small Latine & Lesse Greeke*. 2 vols. Urbana: University of Illinois Press, 1944.

Bate, Jonathan, *Shakespeare and Ovid*. Oxford: Oxford University Press, 1993.

Bergeron, David M., *English Civic Pageantry 1558–1642*. Columbia: University of South Carolina Press, 1971.

Brumble, H. David, 'Let Us Make Gods in Our Image: Greek Myth in Medieval and Renaissance Literature', in Roger D. Woodard ed., *The Cambridge Companion to Greek Mythology*. Cambridge: Cambridge University Press, 2007, pp. 407–24.

Burke, Peter, 'Popular Culture in Seventeenth-Century London', in Barry Reay ed., *Popular Culture in Seventeenth-Century England*. London: Croom Helm, 1985, pp. 31–58.

Bush, Douglas, *Mythology and the Renaissance Tradition in English Poetry*. Minneapolis: University of Minnesota Press, 1932.

Ferguson, Arthur B., *Utter Antiquity: Perceptions of Prehistory in Renaissance England*. Durham: University of North Carolina Press, 1993.

Fox, Adam, and D.R. Woolf eds, *The Spoken Word: Oral Culture in Britain 1500–1850*. Manchester: Manchester University Press, 2002.

Görlach, Manfred, *The Textual Tradition of the South English Legendary*, Leeds Texts and Monographs, n.s. 6. Leeds: University of Leeds School of English, 1974, pp. 21–63.

Kendrick, T.D., *British Antiquity*. London: Methuen, 1950.

Lewis, Rhodri, 'Francis Bacon, Allegory and the Uses of Myth', *The Review of English Studies* 61 (2010), 360–89.

Reames, Sherry L., *The Legenda aurea: A Reexamination of Its Paradoxical History*. Madison: University of Wisconsin Press, 1985.

Seznec, Jean, *The Survival of the Pagan Gods: The Mythological Tradition and Its Place in Renaissance Humanism and Art*, trans. Barbara F. Sessions. Princeton: Princeton University Press, 1981; first published 1953.

Starnes, DeWitt T., and Ernest William Talbert, *Classical Myth and Legend and Renaissance Dictionaries*. Chapel Hill: University of North Carolina Press, 1955.

---

[67] Burke, 'Popular Culture in Seventeenth-Century London', p. 32.

Thomas, Keith, *Religion and the Decline of Magic: Studies in Popular Beliefs in Sixteenth and Seventeenth Century England*. London: Weidenfeld & Nicholson, 1971.

Religious Belief

Mike Rodman Jones

To place the terms 'religious belief' and 'popular culture' together in the early modern period is to court controversy. Few other areas of study have been so consistently marked by sharply ideological agendas, from the sixteenth century itself to the twentieth and beyond. This chapter will trace the historiography of religious belief from its earliest incarnations through the controversies and perspectives that developed over the course of the later twentieth century, and finally offer some observations and suggestions for current and future research in the area.[1]

Historiography (I): Popular Reform?

Changing popular beliefs was one of the central tenets of the early Reformations in England, notably because many of the central documents of the period are historiographically orientated. Tyndale's biblical translations were supported by a sequence of polemical works that argued that the people of Christendom had been habitually duped and deceived by the clergy for hundreds of years.[2] Similarly, the *Book of Common Prayer* (first edition 1549, with numerous later amended editions) founded its own reform of devotional practice on the grounds that the 'Godly and decent ordre of the auncient fathers, hath been so altered, broken, and neglected' over the preceding centuries.[3] The rhetorical (if nothing else) battle for the beliefs of the population of England, however, often assumed that the 'multitude' and their beliefs were actually almost unknowable: curiously positioned between the (supposedly) deceptive machinations of Roman Catholic institutions and the isolated minority of the 'godly' who liked to think of themselves fighting for their souls. In an exemplary case, the early reformer and ex-Carmelite John Bale figured 'The People' (or sometimes 'turba vulgaris') as a separate dramatic character in plays such as *King Johan* (*c.* 1536) always – like Everyman – wavering between straight and crooked paths under the influence of other figures. 'Popular religious belief' in this writing is both the central aim and

---

[1]   This essay is much indebted to excellent earlier work detailing the historiography of the English Reformations, in particular, Peter Marshall and Alec Ryrie eds, *The Beginnings of English Protestantism* (Cambridge: Cambridge University Press, 2002); Alec Ryrie ed., *Palgrave Advances in the European Reformations* (London: Palgrave, 2005); and Peter Marshall, '(Re)defining the English Reformation', *Journal of British Studies* 48 (2009), 564–86.

[2]   See, for example, the passages in G.E. Duffield ed., *The Work of William Tyndale* (London: Sutton Courtney Press, 1964), pp. 31–2.

[3]   Brian Cummings ed., *The Book of Common Prayer: The Texts of 1549, 1559, and 1662* (Oxford: Oxford University Press, 2011), p. 5.

objective, but also absent; imagined to be a malleable, indefinite substance which could be manipulated, fought over and trained by distinctly elite forces.

The most important formulation of popular religious belief across the period of the early Reformations was offered after the muddy and unstable exchanges of dynastic government and religious policy seen in the mid-century, in John Foxe's iconic *Acts and Monuments* (frequently called the *Book of Martyrs*, first edition 1563, with major revisions and additions in 1570, 1576 and 1583). According to Foxe (an astonishingly able antiquarian, historian and polemicist whose work has only been properly addressed in the last 20 years or so) the history of the Reformations, both in England and across Europe, was a powerful, deeply emotive narrative about the progressive liberation of belief from the corrupting influence of Rome.[4] This narrative introduced and subsumed the most powerful sections of Foxe's text: the quasi-historical (often documentary) accounts of martyrdoms from the fifteenth-century Wycliffites whose public executions left marks on place names which persist today (Norwich's 'Lollard's Pit'; the 'Lollards' Tower' at Lambeth Palace) to the lurid number of those burnt in Smithfield between 1553 and 1558. The polemical point of Foxe's accumulative history is that while isolated individuals in history such as Wycliffe, Jan Huss – or apparently Geoffrey Chaucer and 'Piers Plowman' – were flashes of spiritual light in a 'dark' period between apostolic and contemporary time, by the mid-sixteenth century the population of England were converted and were being brutally persecuted for it. They were also a kind of new *gens dei*, a nation not entirely dissimilar to the biblical Israelites or Bede's ninth-century vision of the English people. The discourse of national identity is clearly interwoven here with a particular kind of religious historiography, in a way which would command tacit respect and both wide and academic support for centuries. This narrative of persecution, progressive liberation and national, politico-religious destiny became one of the more precarious foundations of the enlightenment and colonial era construction now generally referred to as 'Whig History'.

Much modern work on the popularity (or not) of belief and confessional identities in the sixteenth-century has had to deal to some extent with the wider cultural heritage outlined above as it commanded – and one might say continues to command, in certain places – an authority which exists outside the academy, but the scholarship which shaped the grounds of the controversies over the last century was that of A.G. Dickens and G.R. Elton. In a sequence of books, most notably *The English Reformation* (1964, revised 1989), Dickens laid the foundations for a number of the most important flashpoints in Reformation historiography. Dickens' first book, *Lollards and Protestants in the Diocese of York, 1509–1558* (1959), made a localised case for the rise of Protestant belief, and an associated case for the continuity between English Lollardy and the early adoption of Protestantism. Later work continued this thread, arguing that the early sixteenth century produced a sea-change in popular belief so great that by the time Elizabeth acceded to the throne in 1558 the vast majority of the nation were already Protestant.

Dickens' and Elton's work remains respected (though questioned), but it is worth noting that this picture of religious and cultural change had wider ramifications for the study of the period, particularly in terms of the connections drawn by some between changing religious belief and a *longe dureé* account of early modernity. For Foxe himself, the Reformation of belief came about partly because of the divinely inspired coincidence of reformism with particular types of media: 'Preachers, Printers, & Players [...] be set up of God, as a triple bulwarke against the triple crown of the Pope'.[5] This claim became its own kind of defence for arguments

---

[4]   Work on Foxe has been transformed and enabled by the excellent John Foxe project, which has included online transcriptions of the different editions of Foxe's work. See http://www.johnfoxe.org/.

[5]   1570 edition, sig. DDDd3v. See also John N. King, 'Foxe's *Book of Martyrs* and the History of the Book', *Explorations in Renaissance Culture* 30 (2004), 171–96.

about the connections between the printing press, Protestantism and early modernity. Most influentially, Elizabeth Eisenstein's classic study *The Printing Press as an Agent of Change* (1979, revised and abridged as *The Printing Revolution in Early Modern Europe*, 1983, 1993) made a compelling case for the transformational power of changing technologies of textual reproduction, but also stated explicitly that 'Printing and Protestantism seem to go together naturally'.[6] While they were engaged in quite distinct scholarly activities, the combination of Dickens', Elton's and Eisenstein's arguments themselves might be said to 'go together naturally', creating – tacitly if not explicitly – a portrait of the early sixteenth century as energetically transformative and decisively unlike the culture of previous periods. This is a picture of a period in which it is hard to imagine popular religious belief not being caught up in the teleological and hurried rush of western culture towards something which might be called 'modernity'.

Historiography (II): Popular and Unpopular Religion

This picture of the reform of popular belief has been thoroughly questioned by a host of 'revisionist' historians who frequently take the idea of popular religion as their focus. The most influential of these have been J.J. Scarisbrick, Christopher Haigh and Eamon Duffy. Every related concept of the Reformation came under attack in this wave of counter-argument. Rather than the pre-Reformation church and laity being morose, sullen and stolid, awaiting the great enlightenment of Luther and the printing press, the later medieval church is instead an energetic, communal and engaged institution in which the vast majority of the population partake, often with enthusiasm (something, it has to be said, that most medievalists would have known already). Lollardy, for some a democratising and quasi-modern ancestor of Protestantism, becomes an eccentric and geographically specific phenomenon with few adherents and little popular support.[7] Instead, the early English Reformation becomes something decisively separate from popular belief and practice, a political event driven by monarchical and elite interests. The concept of popular religion is central to this 'revisionist' movement, because it sets out to argue that the reform of religious belief was anything *but* popular. In the introduction to *The Stripping of the Altars*, Duffy writes that:

> *much writing about late medieval and early modern religion has taken it as axiomatic that there was a wide gulf between 'popular' and 'élite' religion, that the orthodox teaching of the clergy was poorly understood and only partially practised, that paganism and superstition were rife [...] To judge by the amount of interest that has been shown in them, the English religious landscape of the late Middle Ages was peopled largely by Lollards, witches, and leisured, aristocratic ladies.*[8]

---

[6]   Elizabeth Eisenstein, *The Printing Press as an Agent of Change* (Cambridge: Cambridge University Press, 1979), pp. 43–4, 306.

[7]   See, especially, Richard Rex's *The Lollards* (London: Palgrave, 2002), the diminutive length of which is a clue to its wider argument, particularly in comparison to the still vital (and sizable) work in Ann Hudson's *The Premature Reformation: Wycliffite Texts and Lollard History* (Oxford: Oxford University Press, 1988). Earlier scholarship, such as F.M. Powicke's *The Reformation in England* (Oxford: Oxford University Press, 1941) had previously developed similar arguments to those of later revisionists.

[8]   Eamon Duffy, *The Stripping of the Altars: Traditional Religion in England, 1400–1580* (New Haven: Yale University Press, 1992), p. 2. Duffy's preface to the second edition (2005) is also a useful digest of reactions to the book, recording, for example, the traces of a vitriolic exchange between Duffy and the medievalist David Aers.

The powerful and often compelling recovery of 'traditional' religion that takes place in Duffy's work, in particular, is also a renewal of what Duffy refers to as 'the religious world-view of ordinary men and women': popular religious belief and practice.[9] This rather sharp dismissal of academic interest in niche groups (one might ask why one should not be interested in Lollards, witches or aristocratic women) is a part of a wider argument of revisionism. Famously, Christopher Haigh posed the question of whether the Reformation was something that came 'from above', or 'from below', a question that clearly intersects with the hierarchical conceptualisations which studies of popular culture more generally are still attempting to revise.[10]

While some revisionists have managed to suggest the complexity and patchiness of the progress of altered religious belief over the period with the graceful use of a plural, it is still striking that revisionism relied on the notion of popular religious belief as an argumentative counter to Whig historiography.[11] This movement, however, frequently (if not always) kept the question of popular religious culture closely bound up with confessional categories. While some of these categories (Protestant, Catholic, Puritan, Recusant, Anglican) retain an explanatory power at particular moments, and in particular communities, much of the drive of post-revisionist approaches to popular religion has been to re-categorise some of the historical phenomena – Alexandra Walsham's work on 'Church Papists' is a fine example – or even undermine the efficacy of such a nomenclature.[12] It is still worth noting that even if the majority of England's population *were* Protestant by the middle of the sixteenth century, few would have described themselves using that term.[13] More importantly, while we might want the diverse range of things that make up religious identity (theological thought, devotional practice, a communal self-consciousness, shared sensibilities and antipathies) to be coterminous, in many cases this is something that confessional historiography of any allegiance often had to assume using *a priori* labels, rather than something that necessarily existed. As Alec Ryrie has put it, more studies now try 'to move beyond a zero-sum game in which Catholic and Protestant historians each try to count their legions'.[14]

Indeed, a number of noteworthy studies of religious belief in the period have side-stepped this 'zero-sum game' by focusing not necessarily on numerical approaches to what might be considered 'popular' but by paying attention to other phenomena, such as particular places or communities, multiple conversion between confessions or the pragmatic complexities than complicate ideas of adherence to religious beliefs. One striking example is Ethan Shagan's *Popular Politics and the English Reformation* (2003). Shagan's work – based on evidence such as court proceedings rather than wills or church wardens' accounts – suggests how local and pragmatic priorities were key to a number of ways in which the

---

[9]   Duffy, *The Stripping of the Altars*, p. 2.

[10]   Christopher Haigh uses the terms a number of times, for example in 'Some Aspects of Recent Historiography of the English Reformation', *Historical Journal* 25 (1982), 995–1007, reprinted in his *The English Reformation Revised* (Cambridge: Cambridge University Press, 1992), pp. 19–33. On the problem of simplistic divisions between elite and popular see Andrew Hadfield and Matthew Dimmock eds, *Literature and Popular Culture in Early Modern England* (Farnham: Ashgate, 2009), esp. pp. 1–12.

[11]   See, for example, Christopher Haigh, *English Reformations: Religion, Politics, and Society under the Tudors* (Oxford: Clarendon, 1993). The phrase is from Brian Cummings, *The Literary Culture of the Reformation: Grammar and Grace* (Oxford: Oxford University Press, 2002), p. 13.

[12]   Alexandra Walsham, *Church Papists: Catholicism, Conformity and Confessional Polemic in Early Modern England* (Woodbridge: Boydell and Brewer, 1993).

[13]   On this particular word, see Diarmaid MacCulloch, *Tudor Church Militant: Edward VI and the Protestant Reformation* (London: Allen Lane, 1999), p. 2.

[14]   Alec Ryrie, 'Britain and Ireland', in Ryrie ed., *Palgrave Advances in the European Reformations*, p. 129. Ryrie's comment is directed specifically at geographically localised studies, but might be applied more broadly.

general population complicitly (rather than ideologically) forwarded the process of reform. As Shagan writes, the reform of popular religious belief 'was not done *to* people, it was done *with* them'.[15] Similarly, Robert Whiting's work on popular religion in the South West has a number of suggestive points to make about both the importance of locality and adherence. He notes, for example, the possibility of significant differences in religious ideology between urban and rural populations, and that the nature of religious belief was frequently neither uniform nor necessarily 'committed'.[16] Michael Questier's work on conversion both to and from Catholicism, and indeed on multiple experiences of conversion, suggests how transitory and fluid confessional adherence might have been at points.[17] Susan Brigden's monumental *London and the Reformation* (1989) traces the religious beliefs of the capital's people over the course of the sixteenth century in ways which are all the more compelling for being situated at the level of individual parishes and communities within the metropolis.[18] Tessa Watt, in a seminal work that I return to again in the section on 'Books and Belief', compellingly argues – in ways which dovetail with Shagan's and Whitings' work – that even by the early seventeenth century what 'popular religion' means might be something '"post-Reformation", but not thoroughly "Protestant"'.[19] In a number of ways, then, work on popular religious culture in the period has been working past the assumptions of 'popular' and 'elite' which were inherent in confessional arguments, towards a muddier and more complicated picture of intersections between religious identity and popular culture.

Books and Belief

Amongst the flashpoints of early controversies about religious belief was that of popular reading and literacy. Famously, Thomas More argued against the need for vernacular biblical translations on the grounds that 'farre more then fowre partes of all the whole [English population] diuided into tenne, coulde neuer reade englishe yet', even as he imagined 'a tynker or a tyler which coulde (as some there can) reade Englishe, and beying instructed and taught by some olde cunnynge weauer in Wycliffes Wyckette, & Tyndalles books, and Frythes, and frère Barns' would end up 'lurking aboute and teaching hys ghospell in corners'.[20] This vision of religious belief as being closely bound up with the idea of a democratisation of literacy (or at least scriptural literacy) was a central part of religious rhetoric in the period. Erasmus stated in 1516 that 'I would ... that the farmer sing some part of them at the plow, the weaver hum some parts of them to the movement of his shuttle'. Tyndale similarly vowed 'I will cause a boy that driveth the plough, shall know more of the scripture' than some of the

---

[15]   Ethan Shagan, *Popular Politics and the English Reformation* (Cambridge: Cambridge University Press, 2003), p. 25, emphases in original.

[16]   Robert Whiting, *The Blind Devotion of the People: Popular Religion and the English Reformation* (Cambridge: Cambridge University Press, 1989), pp. 146, 259.

[17]   Michael Questier, *Conversion, Politics, and Religion in England, 1580–1625* (Cambridge: Cambridge University Press, 1996).

[18]   Susan Brigden, *London and the Reformation* (Oxford: Clarendon, 1989). Brigden's associated work also makes some suggestive cases for religious beliefs being particularly attractive to certain demographics. See, especially, 'Youth and the English Reformation', *Past and Present* 95 (1982), 37–67.

[19]   Tessa Watt, *Cheap Print and Popular Piety, 1550–1640* (Cambridge: Cambridge University Press, 1991), p. 327.

[20]   Both are from More's *Apology* (1533), quoted from William Rastell ed., *The vvorkes of Sir Thomas More Knyght, sometyme Lorde Chauncellour of England, wrytten by him in the Englysh tonge* (London: Tottell et al., 1557), pp. 850, 924.

clergy.[21] While some of these claims are problematic (Erasmus' farmer and weaver would have had to have been rather *avant-garde* to be familiar with the editing and Greek of the *Novum Testamentum*), this argument – that the rise of Protestantism went hand-in-hand with the rises of literacy, the vernacular and democratisation – has long pervaded popular (and indeed often academic) ideas about the period.[22] The claims of Eisenstein and Foxe about the advent of print quoted above are also parts of that construction. One might wonder about important qualifications here, such as the legislative history of access to the Bible, not least the *Act for the Advancement of True Religion* (1543), which aggressively restricted readership on the grounds of conservative categories of class and gender. While some of this pervasive idea might be deeply questionable, the importance of books and literacy to popular religion across the period cannot be understated. However, rather than a broad-brush, 'cultural history' approach to this question, some of the most productive work on books and belief has sought to approach the question of popular belief through the medium of specific types of popular books. As ever, the categorisation of 'popular' is far from straightforward, but a number of approaches are worth singling out. Judith Maltby's *Prayer Book and People in Elizabethan and Early Stuart England* (1998), for example, traces the history of conformity to the reformed prayer book – and therefore also the reformed version of the liturgy it contained – between the accession of Elizabeth and the outbreak of the Civil War.[23] Maltby's conception of a whole stratum of Tudor and Stuart society as 'Prayer Book Protestants' is compelling and has proved highly influential. While avoiding the proselytising of other accounts of the Reformation, Maltby focuses on conformity to the *Book of Common Prayer*, but in doing so re-situates our sense of popular religion in the network of language and ritual which this central book contained. For generations, ultimately, one book shaped the most widespread experience of religious belief and practice, regardless of social status. In many ways, perhaps, Maltby's 'Prayer Book Protestantism' dovetails with Peter Burke's, and others', conceptions of 'popular culture' as a phenomenon – a set of ways of thinking about and experiencing religion – which was prolific and dominant enough to be part of almost all culture in the period: elite, inclusive and all.[24] The study of the *Book of Common Prayer* as both a text and a set of liturgical ritual and song has recently been enabled by the work of Brian Cummings, who has edited the texts of 1549, 1559 and 1662 for Oxford World's Classics. Cummings' introduction to the volume could be read as a case for the *Book of Common Prayer* being the single most influential document of popular culture in the period.[25] Elsewhere, books remain a vital part of discussions about religious belief in the period. Ian Green's

---

[21]   Erasmus, 'The Paraclesis', in *Christian Humanism and the Reformation: Desiderius Erasmus, Selected Writings*, ed. John C. Olin (New York: Fordham University Press, 1965), pp. 92–106, at p. 97. Tyndale's much-quoted words are possibly apocryphal, and come from Foxe, *Acts and Monuments* (London: John Day, 1563), III. 570. On the rhetoric of democratisation, see Mike Rodman Jones, *Radical Pastoral, 1381–1594: Appropriation and the Writing of Religious Controversy* (Farnham: Ashgate, 2011), pp. 85–6.

[22]   See, especially, David Daniell, *William Tyndale: A Biography* (New Haven: Yale University Press, 1994). For a strongly argued counter, see James Simpson, *Burning to Read: English Fundamentalism and Its Reformation Opponents* (Cambridge, MA: Belknap Press of Harvard University Press, 2007).

[23]   Judith Maltby, *Prayer Book and People in Elizabethan and Early Stuart England* (Cambridge: Cambridge University Press, 1998).

[24]   A useful essay on conceptions of popular culture is Sue Wiseman, '"Popular Culture": A Category for Analysis?', in Hadfield and Dimmock eds, *Literature and Popular Culture*, pp. 15–28. The forms of ritual and prayer contained in the *Book of Common Prayer* also work well with Natalie Zemon Davis' conception of popular culture as 'that which is most mobile, most exchangeable, most ready at hand in all areas of a culture', cited in Wiseman, p. 21. It is worth noting, too, that religious books – especially printed sermons and Sternhold's and Hopkins' ubiquitous metrical psalms – were amongst the most widely circulated texts in the period.

[25]   Cummings, *The Book of Common Prayer*.

monumental *Print and Protestantism in Early Modern England* (1993) has been followed by further substantial work on catechisms – again, probably one of the most pervasive ways in which large numbers of early modern people experienced religion at a basic level.[26] Another immensely influential work is Tessa Watt's *Cheap Print and Popular Piety, 1550–1640* (1991). Watt explicitly situates her study of the period's most accessible books within arguments about popular culture, including Peter Burke's study, and focuses on the 'commonplace mentalities', the 'unconscious or semi-conscious values and assumptions' produced through a reading of these volumes. Acutely aware of the dangers of implying the existence of a singular, stratified idea of 'popular piety', Watt produces a compelling portrait of a complex 'mosaic' of popular religious belief through cheap books. While not entirely new as an idea – Laura Stevenson had previously used the idea of regularly re-printed literary books as the basis for a category of 'popular culture' – Watt's work remains essential reading for those interested in the ways in which books and religious belief were connected in the period.[27]

Belief, Practice and Performance

As the centrality of books and the types of evidence historical studies depend upon might suggest, one of the difficulties with pursuing the nature of popular religious belief in the early modern period (indeed any period) is the essential privacy of 'belief' itself. Writing at the start of the twentieth century, the great philosopher of religion William James (brother of novelist Henry) described the process of religious conversion in poetic but telling terms:

> *Neither an outside observer nor the subject who undergoes the process can explain fully how particular experiences are able to change one's centre of energy so decisively, or why they so often have to bide their hour to do so. We have a thought, or we perform an act, repeatedly, but on a certain day the real meaning of the thought peels through us for the first time, or the act has suddenly turned into a moral impossibility. All we know is that there are dead feelings, dead ideas, and cold beliefs, and there are hot and live ones; and when one grows hot and alive within us, everything has to re-crystallize about it.*[28]

Amongst James' intriguing language – full of images of Church bells ('peel') and biochemical movements ('cold', 'hot', 're-crystallize') – the experience of changing belief, or perhaps even feeling the difference between a thought and a belief – remains unknowable both to 'subject' and 'outside observer', even as it becomes palpably, even centrally, important to the individual. Religious historians have found that not only are there 'complex definitional and evidential problems' with recovering religious beliefs, but that 'belief' itself can remain 'intangible and illusive'.[29] While transhistorical, even anthropological, approaches to

---

26   Ian Green, *The Christian's ABC: Catechisms and Catechizing in England, c. 1530–1740* (Oxford: Oxford University Press, 1996).
27   Watt, *Cheap Print*, p. 325 See, also, Laura Caroline Stevenson, *Praise and Paradox: Merchants and Craftsmen in Elizabethan Popular Literature* (Cambridge: Cambridge University Press, 1984). Stevenson's excellent analysis includes an appendix of popular texts, which she classifies as those which went through at least three editions in the decade after their first appearance (though she excludes bibles, textbooks and translations). The resulting list would make a fine starting point for a study of popular literature.
28   William James, *The Varieties of Religious Experience: A Study in Human Nature* (New York: Simon & Schuster, 1997), pp. 165–6.
29   Peter Marshall, *Religious Identities in Henry VIII's England* (Aldershot: Ashgate, 2006), pp. 19–42, at p. 19. Marshall is referring specifically to the phenomenon of conversion, though the comments are

popular religion remain important – Carlo Ginzberg's *The Cheese and the Worms* is often used as a touchstone here – the fact remains that historical beliefs are only recoverable through the way in which those beliefs were practised in material terms, or the way in which they are performed in or through textual records.[30] Court records, wills, Church wardens' accounts and narrative chronicles all bring their own evidentiary problems and limitations with them.

One important direction over recent years has been towards studies of religion in the period that focus less on traditional 'documentary' sources of evidence, and more on literary sources. While such 'evidence' is no less problematic, it is notable that the 'linguistic turn' in historical studies has coincided with a 'religious turn' in early modern literary studies. It is striking that a great deal of work done on religious belief over the course of the last decades has come not from scholars one might describe as religious historians but from literary critics, broadly understood. Tessa Watt's seminal *Cheap Print and Popular Piety* (1991) is an important example, as is Brian Cummings' *The Literary Culture of the Reformation: Grammar and Grace* (2002). While Cummings' book might be said to focus on elite writers (Luther and More, Tyndale and Erasmus, through Wyatt, Spenser and Donne, to Milton) it ultimately produces a rich tableau about the ways in which theological ideas and arguments thread their way through literary writing, emerging in powerful but also frequently paradoxical ways in writing whose audience is not restricted to theologians as such.

Spiritual autobiography – an increasingly important genre of writing as the period goes on – is also an area in which religious belief and literary studies coalesce. While some scholarship might turn to such texts as straightforward evidence about historical individuals, other work has increasingly emphasised just how generically framed such autobiographies are: 'an elaborate form of self-fashioning', as one scholar has put it.[31] Some important historians of later Protestantism have – for a long time – argued that religious identities were part of a hostile two-way relationship: in a sense, that religious belief and identity in the period were created through the performance of polemical ideas of difference. Patrick Collinson, the great historian of English Puritanism, has long suggested that 'Puritanism' itself was 'not a thing definable in itself but only one half of a stressful relationship'.[32] However, again, it might be more important that these texts bring us into proximity with 'popular' religious sentiment, at least amongst some of the population, because of the ubiquity and persistence of ways of thinking about religious experience in narrative terms. 'I once was blind but now I see' might remain a powerful way of recording the experience of religious belief, however many times it is repeated in different forms and in different cultures.[33] Kathleen Lynch's recent *Protestant Autobiography in the Seventeenth-*

---

more widely applicable.

[30] Carlo Ginzberg, *The Cheese and the Worms: The Cosmos of a Sixteenth-Century Miller*, trans. John and Anne Tedeschi (Baltimore: Johns Hopkins University Press, 1980). For an outline of such anthropological approaches, see P. M. Soergel, 'Popular Religion', in Ryrie ed., *Palgrave Advances in the European Reformations*, pp. 232–51.

[31] See, for example, Michael Davies, 'Shaping Grace: The Spiritual Autobiographies of John Bunyan, William Cowper, and John Newton', *Bunyan Studies: John Bunyan and His Times* 12 (2007), 36–69, and Davies' monograph, *Graceful Reading: Theology and Narrative in the Works of John Bunyan* (Oxford: Oxford University Press, 2002). The quotation is from Alexandra Walsham, 'The Godly and Popular Culture', in John Coffey and Paul C.H. Lim eds, *The Cambridge Companion to Puritanism* (Cambridge: Cambridge University Press, 2008), pp. 277–93, at p. 289.

[32] Patrick Collinson, *The Birthpangs of Protestant English* (Basingstoke: MacMillan, 1988), p. 143. On this point, see also Collinson, 'Ecclesiastical Vitriol: Religious Satire in the 1590s and the Creation of Puritanism', in John Guy ed., *The Reign of Elizabeth I: Court and Culture in the Last Decade* (Cambridge: Cambridge University Press, 1995), pp. 150–70.

[33] The phrase, and point, is borrowed from an excellent discussion of conversion narratives in Molly Murray, *The Poetics of Conversion in Early Modern English Literature: Verse and Change from Donne to Dryden* (Cambridge: Cambridge University Press, 2009), p. 27.

Century Anglophone World (2012) continues this interest, and Alexandra Walsham's work has shown that the providentialism once assumed to be an exclusive aspect of puritan belief was shared across the spectrum of sixteenth- and seventeenth-century culture, even as puritans intuitively fashioned themselves as a beleaguered minority at odds with the luke-warm beliefs of the majority.[34]

This 'literary turn' in some studies of religious belief in the period is noteworthy, because the methodological differences have also allowed the kinds of questions posed and answered to be more nuanced and less empirical. Peter Lake's work is another fine example. While still, of course, a 'historian', Lake's willingness to read narrative and dramatic texts as sources, and frequently to do so with the sophistication and acuteness of a literary critic, has produced some important arguments. For example, arguing against some revisionist historians, Lake takes issue with the idea of Protestantism as an ideology of elitism set in perpetual opposition to the 'people', a picture of religious belief centred on literacy and the much repeated 'Reformation of Manners'.[35] Instead, through a reading of a sequence of cheap 'Murder pamphlets', Lake suggests how religious belief exists in a more complex relationship with popular forms than we might expect, allowing synthesis and opportunistic overlap in genres which might be said to be *both* popular and Protestant.[36]

Another strand in recent 'literary-historical' studies of the Reformations needs to be mentioned. Enabled by some revisionist studies (especially Duffy's *The Stripping of the Altars*), a sequence of books have appeared by high-profile scholars of medieval writing who have developed an interest in diachronic studies of literary, cultural and religious change across the later Middle Ages and the usually sacrosanct barrier of the Reformation. Important examples are James Simpson's *Burning to Read: English Fundamentalism and Its Reformation Opponents* (2010) and Sarah Beckwith's *Shakespeare and the Grammar of Forgiveness* (2011).[37] These works have their own argumentative agendas, born out of a drive to interrogate the institutionalisation of cultural epochs and what both see as the misapprehension of many traditional claims about early modernity. Like earlier revisionists, much of this scholarship, and the way it is written, partakes in the combative energies of the Reformation's debates over theology, belief and practice, even as it offers a powerful critique of some of the cultural claims about the place of Protestantism in the construction of liberal traditions. They also, though, harbour a deep antipathy towards Protestantism – popular or not – imagined as a culturally impoverished, tyrannical cultural movement whose modern inheritance is not an Eisenstein-like enlightenment but a 'dark', anxious and aggressive thread in western modernity. In some ways, rather than a focus on the historical detail of specific periods, this work acts as a modern heir to Max Weber's sociological analysis of the 'Spirit' of capitalism and its connections to Calvinist thought and culture, but in a way which is strikingly hostile. As a reviewer of Beckwith's book puts it, this is an image of 'a Reformed tradition figured in [...] unremittingly negative terms [...] a dismissal of all that medieval Catholicism is

---

[34] Kathleen Lynch, *Protestant Autobiography in the Seventeenth-Century Anglophone World* (Oxford: Oxford University Press, 2012); Alexandra Walsham, *Providence in Early Modern England* (Oxford: Oxford University Press, 1999).

[35] For a discussion of the idea of the Puritan 'Reformation of Manners', see Walsham, 'The Godly and Popular Culture', pp. 279–82.

[36] Peter Lake, 'Deeds against Nature: Cheap Print, Protestantism, and Murder in Early Seventeenth-Century England', in Kevin Sharpe and Peter Lake eds, *Culture and Politics in Early Stuart England* (Stanford: Stanford University Press, 1993), pp. 257–83.

[37] Sarah Beckwith, *Shakespeare and the Grammar of Forgiveness* (Ithaca, NY: Cornell University Press, 2011).

supposed to represent: the communal, the certain, the knowable, the pastorally reassuring. For Beckwith, Protestantism is inhumanly devoid of all such humane facets'.[38]

Another important and nascent area of inquiry here is the theatrical performance of religion on the early modern stage. While the professional theatres of London are sometimes rather tendentiously viewed as sources of a newly secularised identity – particularly in Stephen Greenblatt's numerous works – others have sought to trace the ways in which religious practice was 'played'.[39] Elizabeth Williamson, for example, traces the ways in which religious objects (rosaries, books and so on) were used as symbolic objects in stage performances.[40] Other studies, particularly the work of Alison Shell and Arthur Marotti, have sought to uncover the ways in which theatrical and literary works produced a kind of popular anti-Catholicism which is ingrained also in more recent culture.[41] Peter Lake's and Michael Questier's massive *The Antichrist's Lewd Hat: Protestants, Papists and Players in Post-Reformation England* (2002) is another important study.[42] Given the way in which some early modern drama explicitly stages devotional culture and religious difference, a number of plays have not been read until recently in terms of what they reveal about popular religion only because of their comparative obscurity. Some recent work has sought to rectify this, and David Womersley's ambitious *Divinity and State* (2010) is also likely to make an important body of 'Reformation History Plays' better known by placing them in dialogue with better known Shakespearian works and their chronicle sources.[43] Much further work remains to be done on these plays, because in important ways such performances can be seen to both reflect and create widely disseminated conceptions about the nature and meaning of religion in the period, at least in England's capital. These very different approaches to the question of popular religious belief in the early modern period have opened the field to future work of even more various kinds. This variety of approach is itself a positive thing, as taken together these approaches might allow scholars to react to Tessa Watt's eloquent comments, written now over 20 years ago:

> *'Religion' cannot just be measured in terms of knowledge of particular doctrines, or attendance at Church [...] We must also look at the hazier area of images, emotions and fears; of the rules by which people ordered their lives [...] of how people placed themselves in history and the universe.*[44]

---

[38] As Davis continues: 'Yet it could easily be objected that "reformed versions of grace" are hardly without humanity, human agency, or a sense of community. Far from it, one might argue'. Michael Davis, review of Sarah Beckwith, *Shakespeare and the Grammar of Forgiveness*, *Review of English Studies* 63 (2012), 504–6, at p. 505.

[39] See, especially, Stephen Greenblatt, *Hamlet in Purgatory* (Princeton: Princeton University Press, 2002). For sharp critiques of Greenblatt's work, see David Aers, 'A Whisper in the Ear of Early Modernists; or, Reflections on Literary Critics Writing the "History of the Subject"', in David Aers ed., *Culture and History, 1350–1600: Essays on English Communities, Identities and Writing* (London: Harvester, 1992) and Sarah Beckwith, 'Stephen Greenblatt's Hamlet and the Forms of Oblivion', *Journal of Medieval and Early Modern Studies* 33 (2003), 261–80.

[40] Elizabeth Williamson, *The Materiality of Religion in Early Modern English Drama* (Farnham: Ashgate, 2009).

[41] See, especially, Alison Shell, *Catholicism, Controversy and the English Literary Imagination, 1558–1660* (Cambridge: Cambridge University Press, 1999) and Arthur F. Marotti, *Religious Ideology and Cultural Fantasy: Catholic and Anti-Catholic Discourses in Early Modern England* (Notre Dame: University of Notre Dame Press, 2005).

[42] Peter Lake with Michael Questier, *The Antichrist's Lewd Hat: Protestants, Papists and Players in Post-Reformation England* (New Haven: Yale University Press, 2002).

[43] David Womersley, *Divinity and State* (Oxford: Oxford University Press, 2010), and see also Teresa Grant and Barbara Ravelhofer eds, *English Historical Drama 1500–1660: Forms Outside the Canon* (Basingstoke: Palgrave MacMillan, 2008) and Paulina Kewes ed., *The Uses of History in Early Modern England* (San Marino: Huntington Library, 2006).

[44] Watt, *Cheap Print*, p. 327.

Select Bibliography

Aers, David ed., *Culture and History, 1350–1600: Essays on English Communities, Identities and Writing*. London: Harvester, 1992.

Cummings, Brian ed., *The Book of Common Prayer: The Texts of 1549, 1559, and 1662*. Oxford: Oxford University Press, 2011.

Duffy, Eamon, *The Stripping of the Altars: Traditional Religion in England, 1400–1580*. New Haven: Yale University Press, 1992.

Ginzberg, Carlo, *The Cheese and the Worms: The Cosmos of a Sixteenth-Century Miller*, trans. John and Anne Tedeschi. Baltimore: Johns Hopkins University Press, 1980.

Hadfield, Andrew, and Matthew Dimmock eds, *Literature and Popular Culture in Early Modern England*. Farnham: Ashgate, 2009.

Marshall, Peter, and Alec Ryrie eds, *The Beginnings of English Protestantism*. Cambridge: Cambridge University Press, 2002.

Ryrie, Alec ed., *Palgrave Advances in the European Reformations*. London: Palgrave, 2005.

Shagan, Ethan, *Popular Politics and the English Reformation*. Cambridge: Cambridge University Press, 2003.

Stevenson, Laura Caroline, *Praise and Paradox: Merchants and Craftsmen in Elizabethan Popular Literature*. Cambridge: Cambridge University Press, 1984.

Walsham, Alexandra, *Providence in Early Modern England*. Oxford: Oxford University Press, 1999.

Watt, Tessa, *Cheap Print and Popular Piety, 1550–1640*. Cambridge: Cambridge University Press, 1991.

Whiting, Robert, *The Blind Devotion of the People: Popular Religion and the English Reformation*. Cambridge: Cambridge University Press, 1989.

PART II
Everyday Life

Courtship, Sex and Marriage

Ian Frederick Moulton

Like many early modern comedies, Shakespeare's *Much Ado about Nothing* ends with the promise of multiple marriages. But in *Much Ado*, not all marriages are alike; Shakespeare famously contrasts two different models of marriage, one more traditional, the other seemingly more modern. The main plot of the play concerns the courtship of Hero by Claudio. Hero is the only daughter and sole heir of Leonato, the wealthy Governor of Messina. Claudio is a callow young nobleman in search of a wealthy and attractive wife. He begins his courtship not by talking to Hero, but by consulting with his male friends, especially his patron, the Prince of Aragon. The Prince woos on Claudio's behalf, raising the matter first with Hero, and then, having obtained her consent, with her father Leonato. Claudio is physically attracted to Hero (and she to him), but financial concerns are very much on his mind; he only proceeds once he has confirmed that Hero will inherit all of Leonato's magnificent estate.

Though Claudio and Hero are charmed by each other, they have had almost no prior contact. This makes Claudio vulnerable to the slanders of the play's villain, Don John, who has no trouble falsely convincing him that Hero is unchaste. Don John then goads Claudio into publicly renouncing Hero in the midst of their marriage ceremony. Everyone, including Hero's own father, immediately assumes Don John's baseless slander is true, and it takes a whole comedy's worth of machinations to convince Claudio that he has misjudged Hero and to reconcile the couple by the play's end.

The other couple in the play are Beatrice and Benedick, who have been unhappily involved in the past. They are both quick-witted and verbally aggressive, and spend much of their time wittily insulting each other. As part of an elaborate practical joke the other characters trick them into believing that despite their scornful words, each actually loves the other. When Beatrice and Benedick find themselves thus thrown together, they realise that their similar temperaments and intellectual abilities make them a perfect match. Beatrice is an orphan with no dowry, and Benedick a young nobleman with no visible family. It seems neither brings much money to the match, and since both are remarkably detached from traditional kinship networks, they are left to woo each other as they wish. They soon resolve to marry, despite their previous mockery of anything to do with wedlock and their deep cynicism about love and sexual attraction.

Though structurally the story of Hero and Claudio is the main plot of the play, Beatrice and Benedick inevitably steal the show. To modern audiences who believe that marriage choices are personal and that compatibility and affection are essential to marital happiness, Beatrice and Benedick's courtship seems normative and admirable, while Hero and Claudio's relationship seems shallow and artificial. But in early modern England negotiated matches like Hero and Claudio's were the norm. Claudio and Hero's courtship conforms to all four of the criteria for choosing a marriage partner identified by Ralph Houlbrooke in his study of the early modern English family: 'the advancement of the individual or the family, the ideal of parity, the character of the proposed partner, and personal affection'.[1] Beatrice and Benedick, on the other hand, ignore family concerns; their match is based solely on personal affection and similarity of character.

Such free-spirited choice was not common in early modern society, at least not at Beatrice and Benedick's social level. More common was the case of Anthony Bagot, whose 1594 courtship of a certain Mistress Lowe began with the Earl of Essex, his father's patron, who wrote a letter to Mr Weston, Mistress Lowe's kinsman, to begin serious negotiations.[2] As one might expect, brokered matches were most prevalent among the elite. As a rule of thumb, the less money and property involved, the less familial negotiation. Indeed, servants, both male and female, often lived at some distance from their parents and frequently established relationships on their own.

Still, most marriages at all social levels took at least some account of parents' wishes and a family's needs. In 1632, when Simon Johnson, a young London scissor-maker, was refused his father's permission to marry Mary Elliot, he spent more than six months trying to change his father's mind before marrying Mary in a clandestine ceremony – and the couple only took that step knowing they had the full support of Mary's family and friends. After the wedding Mary's friends and kin did all they could to reconcile Simon with his father, apparently to no avail.[3] Even though the father's opinions were disregarded, they still carried weight, and the decision to marry without his blessing entailed serious consequences.

Although *Much Ado* ends with the promise of happy weddings, there is, as often in Shakespeare, a certain ambivalence about the couples' future happiness. Benedick's concluding words include the observation that 'man is a giddy thing' (5.4.105)[4] and his encouragement for the Prince to marry is followed by a prophesy that all marriages, however joyful, will entail infidelity: 'Get thee a wife', Benedick advises, 'There is no staff more reverend than one tipped with horn' (5.4.116–17) – alluding to the mythical and apparently inescapable horns of a cuckolded husband. Marriage may be necessary to restrain and channel disorderly sexual passions, but no institution can fully repress human giddiness. *Much Ado* at once celebrates marriage and admits that it is not a simple recipe for personal happiness or fulfilment. This celebratory ambivalence is typical of much early modern discourse on marriage.

The scholarship on early modern courtship, sex and marriage is vast and growing, and a brief survey such as this can only hope to delineate some of the main areas of debate. For a variety of reasons, scholarship on sexuality has tended to develop separately from the study of marriage and courtship. The fields have differing intellectual and disciplinary roots: the study of marriage and courtship draws primarily on social history, whereas the study of sexuality developed in conjunction with gender studies and queer studies, and is greatly influenced by literary and cultural theory. The study of marriage and courtship tends to focus on social norms, while studies of sexuality have focused primarily on transgressions of those norms. In what follows, we will address the norms established by customs of courtship and marriage before turning to the various ways in which those norms could be challenged, undermined, transgressed and even ignored.

---

[1]   Ralph A. Houlbrooke, *The English Family 1450–1700* (New York: Longman, 1984), p. 73.

[2]   Folger Shakespeare Library, Ms. L.a. 473. See also David Cressy, *Birth, Marriage and Death: Ritual, Religion, and the Life-Cycle in Tudor and Stuart England* (New York: Oxford University Press, 1997), pp. 252–3.

[3]   Greater London Record Office, DL/C 319, fos 172–3; see also Cressy, *Birth, Marriage and Death*, pp. 259–60.

[4]   All references to the works of Shakespeare are to Stephen Greenblatt, Walter Cohen, Jean E. Howard and Katharine Eisaman Maus eds, *The Norton Shakespeare* (2nd ed., New York: Norton, 2008).

To start with, it is worth briefly tracing the relation between the three topics. Although courtship, sex and marriage are clearly related, for the purpose of cultural analysis they remain three very different phenomena. Sexuality might be considered a common factor linking all three. But although both courtship and marriage can be understood as social mechanisms for channelling sexual attraction, this is only one aspect of their overall significance. There are obviously many kinds of sexual activity which are not accommodated within the practices of courtship or by the institution of marriage. As is well known, early modern marriage, strictly construed, endorsed only one form of sexual activity: vaginal intercourse between husband and wife in the interests of propagating children. So although much early modern discourse on marriage, from wedding poems to marriage manuals, celebrated the sexual aspects of the relationship, it did so in a context that drastically restricted the scope of permissible sexual activity.

Indeed, from a certain perspective, it might seem that sex and early modern marriage were only tangentially related. Of course, one of the primary social functions of marriage was to produce legitimate offspring. As Benedick says, 'the world must be peopled' (2.3.213–14). But marriage also fulfilled a host of functions only marginally concerned with sexuality: it knit together communities; it united families in bonds of kinship; it allowed for a structured and orderly transmission of property and wealth from one generation to the next; it transferred legal and financial authority over women from fathers to husbands; it marked a transition from youth to adulthood for both men and women; and as a religious ritual, marriage legitimated and consecrated the couple and their offspring in the eyes of God and before the community.

Courtship of some sort almost always preceded marriage in early modern England. But the two practices are not analogous: courtship is a series of informal customs designed to bring potential couples together, whereas marriage was a social institution and religious rite that took specific ritual and legal forms. And of course, not all courtships ended in marriage.

Besides these structural differences, courtship, sex and marriage also differ in their relation to what one might term 'private life'. Early modern life did not provide much opportunity for what we now think of as privacy. In elite households, servants were ubiquitous,[5] even during what we would consider private moments, such as undressing for bed or defecation. In middle and lower class homes, space was at a premium, and bedrooms and even beds were habitually shared by multiple family members, sometimes of different genders.[6] Nonetheless, sex and much of what goes on in courtship were seen in the period as intimate acts. Early modern courtship was more public and supervised than in later periods, but courting couples often had the opportunity to walk and talk together (and sometimes more) without any other company.[7] Some scholars have suggested that 'intimate courting' was especially common among the lower classes, and that it may have served as a 'relief valve' for youthful sexual energy in a society that strongly advocated pre-marital chastity.[8] In any case, despite the realities of crowded living space, it seems most people preferred to have sex away from prying eyes if at all possible. Even in the very public festivities of the wedding night, friends and family left the couple on their own to consummate the marriage.[9]

---

[5] Lawrence Stone, *The Family, Sex and Marriage in England, 1500–1800* (New York: Harper and Row, 1977), pp. 253–4.

[6] Stone, *Family, Sex and Marriage*, p. 6. Ilana Krausman Ben-Amos, *Adolescence and Youth in Early Modern England* (New Haven: Yale University Press, 1994), p. 204.

[7] See Keith Wrightson, *English Society 1580–1680* (New Brunswick: Rutgers University Press, 1982), p. 74; Cressy, *Birth, Marriage and Death*, p. 243.

[8] Stone, *Family, Sex and Marriage*; Ben-Amos, *Adolescence and Youth*, pp. 200–205.

[9] Cressy, *Birth, Marriage and Death*, pp. 374–6.

Getting married, on the other hand, was not intimate at all; the wedding ceremony was one of the most public events in a person's life – in most cases announced in advance and witnessed by scores of people. Marriage represented a union of families and kin as well as the joining together of a couple, and like Hero and Claudio's disrupted wedding ceremony, most early modern marriage celebrations involved entire communities, not just couples or families.

Social historians have focused on marriage at least since the 1970s, when the subject was broadly defined by the publication of Lawrence Stone's magisterial study *The Family, Sex and Marriage in England, 1500–1800* (1977).[10] Stone's ambitious work remains valuable, though some aspects of his thesis have been criticised. His overarching argument is that between the sixteenth and the eighteenth centuries marriage in England became a more personal affective relationship, in which individual choice of a partner and the strength of loving affection between spouses was seen as more important than the older conception of marriage as a kinship alliance between families. This is a broad and ambitious claim, and Stone provides a lot of documentation to support it. There is little question that the transformation Stone describes occurred at some point between the medieval period and our own time;[11] the question is not whether such a change occurred, but how and why it did, and how significant a change it was.

There is little reason to doubt that both individual choice of a marital partner and spousal affection were highly valued at all social levels by the early nineteenth century,[12] although the contemporary novels of Jane Austen remind us how much such decisions could still be impacted by familial concerns, notions of propriety and the prospects of financial security and stability. But Stone tends to downplay the importance of affection and choice in earlier periods.[13] His contention that in the early modern period 'a majority of individuals ... found it very difficult to establish close emotional ties to any other person'[14] is clearly overstated. It is easily refuted by reference to personal letters, the literary representation of personal and familial relationships, and exhortations on the importance of spousal affection in popular marriage manuals. The culture that produced Ben Jonson's heartbreaking poem on the death of his son, John Donne's 'Valediction' poems to his wife and the passionate emotions represented in the plays of Shakespeare clearly did not lack strong emotional ties.

Stone is right to point out that the early modern world was generally more violent than ours, and that death was a more familiar part of daily life in the period than it is in many parts of western society today. But it does not follow that the relative brevity and uncertainty of life resulted in a general emotional coldness or callousness. Indeed, in much Elizabethan writing, beauty and love are valued all the more highly because of their evanescence. That said, Stone's data on the brevity of early modern marriages is revealing: 'Till death do us part' meant about 20 years on average; if spouses married in their mid-20s, chances were

---

[10]   Peter Laslett's study, *The World We Have Lost* (1965; 2nd ed., London: Methuen, 1971), pp. 84–112, used archival evidence to disprove the common and mistaken assumptions that early modern women married in their early teens, and that early modern households were made up of multiple related married couples living under a single roof.

[11]   Stephanie Coontz, *Marriage, a History: How Love Conquered Marriage* (New York: Penguin, 2006), a popular study of marriage from antiquity to the present day, makes the same argument. Like Stone, she locates the change primarily in the eighteenth century.

[12]   Alan Macfarlane, *Marriage and Love in England: Modes of Reproduction 1300–1840* (New York: Blackwell, 1986) argues for the autonomy of individual choice in marriage throughout the early modern period.

[13]   On the notion that spousal affection was widely seen as an essential element of a good marriage in medieval literature, see Henry Ansgar Kelly, *Love and Marriage in the Age of Chaucer* (Ithaca, NY: Cornell University Press, 1975).

[14]   Stone, *Family, Sex and Marriage*, p. 99.

one of them would be dead in their mid-40s.[15] And the practice of putting children out to apprenticeship often meant that parents and offspring lived together for a relatively short period of time in comparison to the modern family.

The second difficulty with Stone's study is its strong bias in favour of the social elite. Stone was a historian of the aristocracy, and his study focuses primarily upon the upper classes – from the squirarchy to the nobility. Such a bias is endemic to early modern social history in general, since documentation is much more plentiful for elite families than for the middling sort or the lower classes. But Stone also tends to see aristocratic practices as normative; he believes that dominant cultural practices originate in elites and then spread to the rest of the population. There is plenty of evidence for such cultural transmission in the early modern period, but cultural movements in the other direction did occur, and should not simply be discounted. Besides, many aristocratic norms and practices did not spread to other classes. To take just one example, the transgressive pleasures of libertine sexuality had little appreciable practical effect on the rural village life of the majority of English people, though libertinism marked a major transformation in the sexual culture of elite men, beginning in the late seventeenth century.[16] Indeed, Peter Burke has argued the opposite of Stone, that the early modern period saw a withdrawal of the elite from popular culture into an increasingly isolated and refined world of aristocratic taste that defined itself in part by its difference from common practices and values.[17]

A comprehensive description and overview of early modern English marriage and courtship practices may be found in David Cressy's *Birth, Marriage and Death: Ritual, Religion, and the Life-Cycle in Tudor and Stuart England* (1997). Cressy's subject is the ritual and custom surrounding all aspects of the early modern life cycle, from cradle to grave. His study is more descriptive than thesis-driven, and its findings are well documented, making it an excellent resource for factual information on period customs.[18]

Cressy demonstrates that although courtship was an informal process, it was nonetheless highly structured, and that the steps involved were similar at varying social levels and in different areas of the country: 'The ritual ... of courtship included mutual familiarization, clarification of intentions, and consideration of prospects. It usually involved the exchange of gifts or tokens, and negotiation of privileges and opportunities, before the sealing of consent.'[19] Courtship was often, in fact, the place where individual couples and families worked out the balance between family interest and individual choice that Stone identified as the main conflict associated with marriage in the early modern period. For a courtship to end successfully in marriage, the couple had to agree to the match, and the families had to agree not only that the marriage was desirable, but also that economic arrangements could be resolved to give the couple an equitable share of goods, wealth and property.[20]

Cressy makes a useful distinction between formal courtship, whose end was marriage, and flirtatious behaviour or casual wooing.[21] Although courtship could certainly involve

---

[15]   Ibid., p. 55.

[16]   On libertine culture see James Grantham Turner, *Schooling Sex: Libertine Literature and Erotic Education in Italy, France, and England, 1534–1685* (New York: Oxford University Press, 2003).

[17]   Peter Burke, *Popular Culture in Early Modern Europe* (1978; revised ed., New York: Ashgate, 1994), pp. 270–81.

[18]   For an insightful comparison of Stone and Cressy, see Lena Cowen Orlin, 'Rewriting Stone's Renaissance', *Huntington Library Quarterly* 64:1–2 (2002), 189–230.

[19]   Cressy, *Birth, Marriage and Death*, p. 234.

[20]   Diana O'Hara, *Courtship and Constraint: Rethinking the Making of Marriage in Tudor England* (New York: Manchester University Press, 2000), based on sixteenth-century records from the diocese of Canterbury, stresses the communal nature of courtship decisions. See also Houlbrooke, *The English Family*, pp. 68–73.

[21]   Cressy, *Birth, Marriage and Death*, p. 234.

romantic moments between the man and woman involved, it was a fundamentally serious process that entailed detailed practical negotiations among families and friends as well as the couple. Courtship in this sense can seem far removed from passionate romantic love or strong sexual desire – even though such feelings may have provoked the courtship in the first place. Indeed, in early modern culture, passionate love was the object of marked ambivalence. It was often considered an irrational obsession that threatened to descend into lovesickness – believed by some medical authorities to be a serious mental and physical affliction.[22] Whatever the depth of feelings a couple had for each other, courtship involved parents, friends and kin, not to mention matchmakers and, at more affluent social levels, attorneys.

While Cressy, like Stone, is constrained by the fact that most detailed accounts of courtship involve wealthier couples, he also draws on the folk wisdom of the period to explore commonly held attitudes to courtship and marriage: for example, the popular proverb, 'Like blood, like good, and like age make the happiest marriage' points to the notion that marriages were most likely to be successful if they did not cross lines of region, class or age.[23] And what data exist indicate that most early modern marriages did not transgress these bounds; most young men married young women from their own community, from families of similar occupation or income level. Men were slightly older than women at the time of marriage, but the marriages of elderly men to young girls mocked in so many contemporary fictional texts were comparatively rare.[24]

Betrothals and verbal marriage contracts represented a liminal stage between courtship and marriage, and as such they were controversial and problematic. Verbal contracts of marriage, if spoken in the present tense (*verba de presenti*), were binding and indissoluble. So were verbal contracts in the future tense (*verba de futuro*), if the couple subsequently had sexual intercourse. Thus if an English couple said to each other, 'I take you as my spouse', or words to that effect, they were considered to be married in the eyes of God, even though there had been no Church ceremony to sanctify the union.[25] Many disputes in matrimonial law arose when a woman claimed that she had made such a verbal contract with a man and he denied the claim. A verbal contract did not require parental consent to be valid and entailed no arrangements about property. It did not have to be uttered in a church or even before witnesses. Such contracts thus offered couples a way to commit to each other without the support of their kin or community and without waiting to establish the financial stability of their relationship. If not followed by a church ceremony presided over by a properly ordained clergyman, such unions were widely believed to be improper and shameful, but they were nonetheless legal.[26] They could only be invalidated if the couple were forbidden to marry either because they were blood relations or were already married to someone else. It is no surprise that the Church preferred to promote formal betrothal ceremonies, but many couples dispensed with this stage all together, and simply went straight from courtship to a church wedding.

Sexual intercourse was supposedly forbidden in the period between a contract or betrothal and the actual wedding, but many couples ignored this prohibition. Indeed, based

---

[22]   On lovesickness, see Jacques Ferrand, *A Treatise on Lovesickness*, ed. and trans. Donald A. Beecher and Massimo Ciavolella (Syracuse, NY: Syracuse University Press, 1990), and Lesel Dawson, *Lovesickness and Gender in Early Modern English Literature* (New York: Oxford University Press, 2008).

[23]   Wrightson, *English Society*, p. 87. Cressy, *Birth, Marriage and Death*, p. 255.

[24]   Vivian Brodsky, *Londoners, Migration, Kinship and Neighbourhood, 1500–1640* (New York: Oxford University Press, 1997).

[25]   Cressy, *Birth, Marriage and Death*, pp. 267–76; Stone, *Family, Sex and Marriage*, pp. 32–4.

[26]   Houlbrooke, *The English Family*, pp. 78–9; Cressy, *Birth, Marriage and Death*, p. 316. See Stone, *Family, Sex and Marriage*, pp. 33–4 on the mistaken but common perception that the blessing of a clergyman was necessary for a marriage to be valid.

on a comparison of marital dates with dates of christening, it is estimated that one-fifth of all brides, including Shakespeare's wife Anne Hathaway, were pregnant on their wedding day.[27]

Cressy, like Stone, stresses the ubiquity of marriage: '90 per cent of those reaching adulthood in the sixteenth century would marry, and more than 80 per cent in the seventeenth century.'[28] Although these numbers may seem high by modern standards, Ralph Houlbrooke points out that they are lower than the corresponding figures for the late Middle Ages.[29] Houlbrooke also demonstrates that the number of people who married fluctuated with economic circumstance and with demographics: 'the chances of marriage depended to a large extent upon the availability of suitable partners and the prospects of future employment'.[30] In London, where young men tended to outnumber young women, rates of marriage for young women were naturally higher than elsewhere.

The vast majority of weddings in early modern England were conducted according to the Church of England rite, as set down in the Book of Common Prayer and repeated in the canons of 1604. Marriage, in the eyes of the Church, served a four-fold purpose: 'the procreation of children, the perpetuation of the church, the containment of sexual desire, and the mutual assistance and comfort afforded one another by the married couple'.[31] As the Anglican Church solidified its position under Elizabeth as the established Church, one of its goals was to increase ecclesiastical control over marriage. According to Church of England practice, the impeding nuptials had to be publically announced in church on three successive Sundays – a process known as posting the banns. This was to ensure that all those who married were entitled to do so, and that any challenges to their eligibility to marry based on kinship restrictions or on prior marriages could be addressed in a timely manner. Banns could be avoided by the purchase of a 5 or 7 shilling marriage licence from the episcopal authorities.

Whether in the Church of England, or in a dissenting Church, the wedding ceremony was a highly structured and very public affair.[32] Though the Protestant churches no longer considered marriage to be a sacrament, the Anglican rite placed the ceremony firmly at the centre of the church, before the altar, as opposed to the Catholic practice of performing part of the wedding on the church porch. The Anglican ceremony was designed to be conducted before a full congregation in regular daylight hours. It involved the reading of a homily on marriage followed by a call for anyone who knew of any impediment to the marriage to come forward. If there was no objection, the ceremony then moved to an exchange of vows. The bride's father would present her to the priest, who would then prompt the couple to join hands. The groom would give the bride the ring, and the ceremony would conclude with prayers and benedictions.

Although the giving of the ring was much simplified in the Anglican ceremony, some Puritans objected to the practice, seeing it as a Catholic superstition. But as time went by, these objections grew fainter and the wedding ring came to be widely accepted as the dominant symbol and outward sign of marriage.[33]

Clandestine weddings occurred in cases where couples lacked parental consent, or were in too much of hurry to post the banns, or too poor to pay for a marriage licence. Catholics may also have favoured clandestine marriages in order to avoid Protestant rites. Cressy

---

[27]   Cressy, *Birth, Marriage and Death*, p. 374; Stone, *Family, Sex and Marriage*, p. 608. On Anne Hathaway, see Greenblatt et al. eds, *The Norton Shakespeare*, p. 46.
[28]   Cressy, *Birth, Marriage and Death*, p. 285. See also Stone, *Family, Sex and Marriage*, pp. 42–6.
[29]   Houlbrooke, *The English Family*, pp. 63–4.
[30]   Ibid., p. 67.
[31]   Wrightson, *English Society*, p. 67.
[32]   Cressy, *Birth, Marriage and Death*, pp. 336–42.
[33]   Ibid., pp. 342–6.

claims that even clandestine marriages were generally performed before a priest in a church or chapel of some kind. Weddings in private rooms, inns and prisons did occur, but were rare. Such irregular services could be legally challenged, especially if the presiding official turned out not to be a real priest. And cohabiting couples who could not prove their marriage by reference to a parish registry might be in serious trouble if their union was questioned. Single women who gave birth while travelling were a source of particular suspicion unless they could document their marriage in some way.[34]

Marriages were festive occasions, and indeed, much more energy was put into the social celebration than the religious ceremony. While the marriage service took about half-an-hour to perform, wedding feasts and celebrations of various kinds could last for several days. The service might be preceded by a wedding breakfast, and would frequently be followed by a large public celebration involving dancing, eating, drinking and singing. The newlyweds and the wedding guests wore special clothes, decorated with ribbons and wedding knots – a peasant custom followed at all levels of English society.[35] Puritan reformers often railed against the lewdness of wedding celebrations, and especially against the sexuality expressed in public dancing – particularly offensive since most weddings were celebrated on the Sabbath. But the celebrations continued unabated, even during the Interregnum.

In the evening, the newly married couple would be taken to bed by their friends, guests and family. Precise customs differed, but the process tended to be marked by lewd humour and general merriment. To put them in the right mood for the night to come, the couple might drink a special 'sack posset' of spiced wine (the 'sack and sugar' favoured by Shakespeare's Falstaff). The bride-men would pull off the bride's garters and put them on their hats. The couple would have their stockings pulled off by their attendants, who would then throw them into the bed. Only then were the couple left alone, though in many cases they would be serenaded throughout the night by drunken revellers. And the next morning, the couple would be wakened by music.[36]

What do early modern marriage customs tell us about sexual and gender relations? Though Cressy argues that the 'giving' of the bride by her father signified permission to marry rather than a transfer of ownership of the bride from father to husband,[37] this seems to be splitting hairs. You only give things that are yours to give, and men were not given in the same fashion. The patriarchal nature of early modern society is relatively self-evident, and the marriage ceremony, with its stipulation that the wife must promise to obey her husband, accurately reflects this. But while the ceremony itself stressed duty and obedience, the celebrations endorsed fertility, sexuality and sensual indulgence. They were also an occasion of carnivalesque inversion, where the husband might serve his new wife at dinner – something she was supposed to do for him for the rest of their married lives.[38]

In her 2008 study, *Marriage and Violence: The Early Modern Legacy*, Frances E. Dolan argues that marriage in contemporary American society is still caught in a logical contradiction inherent in the early modern ideology of marriage. On the one hand, Christian teaching sees the married couple as 'one flesh' created from the union of both husband and wife. On the other, husbands are supposed to rule their wives just as the head rules the body. Marriage cannot at the same time be a loving union of equals and a hierarchy in which one member is subordinate to the other. Literary and dramatic traditions that see marriage as a site of conflict for dominance between the spouses suggest that rather than being an ideal

---

[34]   Ibid., p. 331.
[35]   Ibid., p. 363.
[36]   Ibid., pp. 375–6. See also Macfarlane, *Marriage and Love in England*, pp. 312–17.
[37]   Cressy, *Birth, Marriage and Death*, p. 339.
[38]   Ibid., p. 370.

union of two into one, marriage is a battleground in which only one person can win and the other must lose. Rather than 'one flesh', Dolan argues, traditional marriage creates a 'two-headed monster'.[39]

While the logical contradiction Dolan points to seems clear enough, the institution of marriage was largely unquestioned in the early modern period itself. Although a radical like John Milton could argue that divorce should be available to a husband who found he was spiritually incompatible with his wife,[40] no one seriously questioned the existence of marriage as the foundation of the family or of society. As we have seen, the great majority of those who could marry, did. This in itself represents an ideological change from late medieval society, when Catholic doctrine stressed that holy virginity was a more honourable estate than marriage for both men and women. Not that everyone expected marriage to bring happiness. Indeed, as much of Beatrice and Benedick's banter suggests, the notion that marriage could be a miserable form of bondage for both husband and wife was proverbial. Almost everyone may have gotten married, but almost no-one assumed married life would be easy.[41]

The history of marriage and courtship is largely the study of official and widely sanctioned social practices. The history of sexuality, on the other hand, has tended to stress various forms of transgression. The study of early modern sexuality in particular has been enormously influenced by two dominant strands in early modern scholarship: women's studies and queer studies. Beginning in the 1970s and 1980s feminist scholars began to explore the role of women in early modern culture by asking the loaded question: 'Did women have a Renaissance?'[42] Given the double standards regarding education, status and opportunity, to what extent and in what ways did early modern women participate in the cultural transformations of the early modern period? The study of early modern women obviously goes far beyond issues of sexuality, exploring and analysing women's place in early modern economics, education and politics, as well as their role as producers, consumers and patrons of both high and popular culture. But from the outset, feminist scholarship necessarily engaged with issues surrounding female sexuality.[43]

At the same time, influenced above all by Michel Foucault's *History of Sexuality* (translated 1978), sexuality came increasingly to be seen not as a biologically determined set of ahistorical actions and tendencies, but rather as a fluid field of practices and desires, all contingent on changing cultural context, and thus eminently historical.[44] Works like Thomas Laqueur's *Making Sex: Body and Gender from the Greeks to Freud* (1990) stressed that sexual knowledge and even notions about anatomy and physiology were culturally constructed and changed over time.[45]

---

[39]   Frances E. Dolan, *Marriage and Violence: The Early Modern Legacy* (Philadelphia: University of Pennsylvania Press, 2008), pp. 26–66.

[40]   John Milton, *The Doctrine and Discipline of Divorce* (1643), and subsequent tracts. See John Milton, *The Complete Prose Works of John Milton. Volume 2, 1643–1648*, ed. Ernest Sirluck (New Haven: Yale University Press, 1959).

[41]   Cressy, *Birth, Marriage and Death*, p. 289.

[42]   Joan Kelly-Gadol, 'Did Women Have a Renaissance?', in Renate Bridenthal and Claudia Koonz eds, *Becoming Visible: Women in European History* (Boston: Houghton Mifflin, 1977), pp. 148–61. Ian Maclean, *The Renaissance Notion of a Woman: A Study of the Fortunes of Scholasticism and Medical Science in European Intellectual Life* (New York: Cambridge University Press, 1980) provides a useful reference to common intellectual and medical beliefs about women in the early modern period.

[43]   For example, the first chapter in Lisa Jardine's groundbreaking study *Still Harping on Daughters: Women and Drama in the Age of Shakespeare* (Sussex: Harvester, 1983) is entitled 'Female Roles and Elizabethan Eroticism', pp. 9–36.

[44]   Michel Foucault, *The History of Sexuality, Vol. 1, An Introduction*, trans. Robert Hurley (New York: Vintage, 1980).

[45]   Thomas Laqueur, *Making Sex: Body and Gender from the Greeks to Freud* (Cambridge, MA: Harvard University Press, 1990).

By the mid-1990s, the history of sexuality had shifted its focus from feminist studies as such to a more broadly based field of gender studies that studied and critiqued masculinity as well as femininity.[46] The development of gender studies was accompanied and facilitated by the rise of queer studies, and the corresponding focus on gender transgression and trans-gender practices.[47] The early modern convention of using young male actors to play women's parts in the public theatres provided a natural focus for this scholarship, as did the treatment of gender ambiguity in the plays and poetry of Shakespeare.[48]

Broadly speaking, the study of early modern sexuality has built on the following insights and premises. Not all of them are proven, provable or universally accepted, but they have structured the debate nonetheless.

- Sexual activity is more culturally constructed than biologically determined.
- Modern forms of sexual identity such as homosexual or heterosexual originate in the nineteenth century and do not apply in the early modern period.
- Early modern culture saw sexual behaviour in terms of sexual acts rather than sexual identity.
- The definition of what acts are or are not sexual is culturally determined and historically variable. Masturbation, for example, is rarely mentioned in early modern texts, and may not have been considered 'sexual' because it does not relate directly to the procreation of children.
- Homosexual activity, though decried as 'sodomy', was relatively common and in certain circumstances had a measure of acceptance.
- Gender was seen as a continuum of identities, rather than a binary opposition between the two fixed categories of masculine and feminine. One could move on the continuum by adopting behaviours and dress considered more or less masculine or feminine.
- Masculine sexuality was often defined in terms of penetration or the so-called active role, rather than whether one's partner was male or female.
- For men, 'excessive' devotion to sex with women was seen as a sign of effeminacy rather than of hyper-masculinity.
- Sexuality and pleasure were on the whole considered feminine, as opposed to the masculine sphere of violence and warfare.

Since the mid-1980s there have been a plethora of studies on early modern sexuality, but due in part to a lack of documentary evidence most of these studies have focused more on discourses of sexuality than actual practices, and on literary texts rather than cultural evidence more broadly defined. Very little is known with any certainty about the early

---

[46] See, for example, Judith Butler, *Gender Trouble: Feminism and the Subversion of Identity* (New York: Routledge, 1990).

[47] Major publications in early modern queer studies include Alan Bray's groundbreaking *Homosexuality in Renaissance England* (London: Gay Men's Press, 1982); Bruce R. Smith, *Homosexual Desire in Shakespeare's England* (Chicago: University of Chicago Press, 1991); and Valerie Traub, *The Renaissance of Lesbianism in Early Modern England* (New York: Cambridge University Press, 2002). See also Madhavi Menon, ed. *Shakesqueer: A Queer Companion to the Works of Shakespeare* (Raleigh, NC: Duke University Press, 2011).

[48] Major studies addressing gender ambiguity and cross-dressing in early modern England include Marjorie Garber, *Vested Interests: Cross-Dressing and Cultural Anxiety* (New York: Routledge, 1992); Jonathan Goldberg, *Sodometries: Renaissance Texts, Modern Sexualities* (Stanford: Stanford University Press, 1992); and Stephen Orgel, *Impersonations: The Performance of Gender in Shakespeare's England* (New York: Cambridge University Press, 1996). For a comprehensive account of homoeroticism on the early modern stage, see Mario DiGangi, *The Homoeroticism of Early Modern Drama* (New York: Cambridge, 1997).

modern sexual practices of the vast majority of the British people – those who lived away from London and had little connection to literary culture or to the public theatres. It is telling that one of the best studies of the dissemination of sexual knowledge through print culture, Roy Porter and Lesley Hall's *The Facts of Life*, begins in the mid-seventeenth century, when the written record on such matters becomes much richer due to the expansion of literacy and the book market.[49] Stone's *Family, Sex and Marriage* is largely dependent on eighteenth-century evidence for the same reason.

Most surviving explicitly erotic writing from early modern England originates in high culture rather than in popular culture: English translations of Classical erotic texts such as Ovid's *Amores*; bawdy lyrics and satires circulated by young men at Oxbridge colleges or the Inns of Court; imported erotic texts in foreign languages such as French and Italian.[50] There was no shortage of bawdy songs and ballads, but in many cases even these survive in high culture sources such as university students' manuscript miscellanies rather than popular ones like printed broadsides. It is likely that sexual culture in rural villages was expressed more through dances and flirtatious games like leap-frog than through writing of any kind. Although courting couples almost always exchanged tokens, love letters were relatively rare – much less commonly exchanged than jewellery, gloves, coins or food.[51]

Given that much popular culture was not expressed in writing, court records and other legal documents provide much of the surviving documentary evidence of social practices. There is a danger, of course, in getting the majority of one's information about a culture from records of conflict and transgression. The anomalous and the extraordinary can come to seem the norm. And indeed, the study of sexual practices tends to focus on transgressive behaviours – prostitution, homosexuality and sexual violence.

It may be that the structures of early modern society encouraged illicit sexual behaviours. In early modern England, the average age of marriage was the mid- to late 20s.[52] Given that most young men and women were sexually mature by their late teens, one must assume that for a period of several years of youthful virility and fertility most young people had no licit sexual outlet of any kind. Humoral theory endorsed the idea that young adulthood was the natural time for love and sexual attraction, but social norms dictated that sexual activity be deferred until after marriage. This gap between physiology and respectability has often been used to explain the high incidence of prostitution, as well as a culture that at times seemed to tacitly ignore homosexual dalliance in young people.

Prostitution was a constant feature of London life. In the late medieval period, brothels were located primarily in the 'Liberties' of the South Bank of the Thames – an area that fell under the nominal jurisdiction of the City of London but outside the purview of the city's law enforcement, and thus was a magnet for all sorts of socially marginal activities, including gambling, bear-baiting and in later years, the public theatre.[53] In 1546 Henry VIII ordered the licensed Bankside brothels closed, with the predictable result that prostitution

---

[49]   Roy Porter and Lesley Hall, *The Facts of Life: The Creation of Sexual Knowledge in Britain, 1650–1950* (New Haven, CT: Yale University Press, 1995).

[50]   On erotic writing in early modern England, see David O. Frantz, *Festum Voluptatis: A Study of Renaissance Erotica* (Columbus: Ohio University Press, 1989) and Ian Frederick Moulton, *Before Pornography: Erotic Writing in Early Modern England* (New York: Oxford University Press, 2000). For the seventeenth century, see Sarah Toulalan, *Imagining Sex: Pornography and Bodies in Seventeenth Century England* (New York: Oxford University Press, 2007).

[51]   O'Hara, *Courtship and Constraint*, p. 69.

[52]   Wrightson, *English Society*, p. 68; Cressy, *Birth, Marriage and Death*, p. 285. On average, women tended to be two or three years younger at marriage than men.

[53]   Stephen Mullaney, *The Place of the Stage: License, Play, and Power in Renaissance England* (Chicago: University of Chicago Press, 1988), pp. 20–24.

spread from this suburban area to the city as a whole.[54] Whores worked in brothels, but also from inns and private homes, and others simply roamed the streets.[55] London's population quadrupled from 50,000 to 200,000 in the late sixteenth century, and the ratio of men to women in the city was 113 to 100,[56] so there was no shortage of clients for prostitution, especially since many young men living in London were unmarried apprentices or foreign travellers and merchants, far from their wives and families.[57] Though it was more visible in the city, prostitution was a feature of rural life as well, and some towns near the capital were especially notorious as centres for the trade.[58]

The place of homoeroticism in early modern culture has been the subject of enormous debate and re-evaluation in recent decades. While anal intercourse between males was condemned under the amorphous category of 'sodomy',[59] which was a crime punishable by death, very few cases were actually prosecuted, and those tend to involve what we would think of as child abuse.[60] Despite the fact that James I strongly condemned sodomy in his official writings, it seems likely that he and his favourite, George Villiers, the Duke of Buckingham, were lovers.[61] As is well known, poems by Shakespeare, Marlowe and Barnfield use highly erotic language to describe relations between men. Although English records do not permit the kind of detailed study of early modern male homosexuality that Michael Rocke has conducted for Renaissance Florence,[62] it remains clear that the level of such activity was higher than previously believed, and that despite the harsh laws in place, male homoeroticism, although viciously condemned, could be tolerated in some circumstances.

In elite culture, male friendship was praised and even idealised. The modern formulation of marriage as a union of 'soul-mates' has its origin not in biblical doctrines of marriage (which prescribe one flesh, not one soul) but in early modern ideas of friendship. To what degree such intense same-sex friendships were thought of as erotic at the time is the subject of much debate.[63] Certainly the language of friendship was often quite passionate, especially to modern readers, accustomed to a certain amount of reticence in the expression of male affection. Alan Bray's 2003 study *The Friend*, controversially argues that early modern male friendship was fiercely intimate but often non-sexual, a form of relationship that has no modern equivalent.[64]

In part because records of early modern women's lives are scarcer than those of early modern men, the nature of homoerotic relations between women in the period has proved

---

[54]   For a map showing the location of brothels in Elizabethan London, see Ian Archer, *The Pursuit of Stability: Social Relations in Elizabethan London* (New York: Cambridge University Press, 1991), p. 212.

[55]   Ibid., pp. 211–15.

[56]   Laura Gowing, *Domestic Dangers: Women, Words, and Sex in Early Modern London* (New York: Oxford University Press, 1996), p. 17. See also Jean E. Howard, *Theater of a City: The Places of London Comedy, 1598–1642* (Philadelphia: Pennsylvania University Press, 2007), pp. 122–7, on the geography of prostitution in early modern London.

[57]   See Howard, *Theater of a City*, pp. 141–8, on the popular association of London brothels with foreigners.

[58]   Ibid., pp. 123–4.

[59]   On definitions of sodomy see Bray, *Homosexuality*, pp. 14–16; Gregory W. Bredbeck, *Sodomy and Interpretation: Marlowe to Milton* (Ithaca, NY: Cornell University Press, 1991), pp. 9–23, 89–96; Goldberg, *Sodometries*, pp. xv–xvi, 19, 120–4.

[60]   Smith, *Homosexual Desire*, pp. 49–53.

[61]   Ibid., p. 14.

[62]   Michael Rocke, *Forbidden Friendships: Homosexuality and Male Culture in Renaissance Florence* (New York: Oxford University Press, 1996).

[63]   See, for example, Katherine O'Donnell and Michael O'Rourke eds, *Love, Sex, Intimacy and Friendship between Men, 1550–1800* (New York: Palgrave, 2003), as well as Jeffrey Masten, *Textual Intercourse: Collaboration, Authorship and Sexualities in Renaissance Drama* (New York: Cambridge University Press, 1997), pp. 28–62; and Eve Sedgwick, *Between Men: English Literature and Male Homosocial Desire* (New York: Columbia University Press, 1985), pp. 28–48, on Shakespeare's sonnets.

[64]   Alan Bray, *The Friend* (Chicago: University of Chicago Press, 2003).

difficult to assess. For a long time, scholars tended to assume that lesbian relationships, though they presumably existed, were largely invisible in early modern texts.[65] Much of the male-authored discourse around sexuality in the early modern period focuses on what might be called an economy of sperm, in which all sexual activity is measured by whether or not sperm is appropriately 'spent' (the most common early modern verb for orgasm).[66] But as Valerie Traub's groundbreaking study *The Renaissance of Lesbianism in Early Modern England* (2002) amply demonstrates, female centred discourses of eroticism also permeated early modern culture, from Shakespearean plays like *Midsummer Night's Dream* and *Twelfth Night*, to bawdy songs sung by women like 'My Thing Is My Own', and engravings of idealised female nudes representing Justice and Prudence locked in passionate embrace.[67] Traub demonstrates that there were at least two differing cultural images of female homoeroticism in the period – the monstrous 'tribade', who was said to usurp male sexual authority by using an enlarged clitoris in place of a penis, and the more feminine figure of the 'friend', who like the idealised male friend was conceived of as a soul-mate and mirror-image of the self. Both these stereotypes had roots in Classical literature and, Traub argues, played a formative role in shaping modern notions of lesbianism. With lesbianism, as with all forms of early modern sexual activity, it is easier to discuss the discursive ways in which sex was represented and understood than to study actual practices, especially for non-elite classes or rural communities.

The study of courtship, sex and marriage in the early modern period is such a vital field of scholarship in part because the period is often seen as formative for modern practices. As the work of scholars as diverse as Lawrence Stone and Frances Dolan demonstrates, notions about marriage, the family, intimacy and sexuality formed in the early modern period have been enormously influential – for good or bad – on the ways we still think about such things today. Romantic love as a crucial component of a successful relationship; courtship as a negotiation between passionate affection and practical planning for the future; marriage as a loving union of two compatible people – all these can seem recognisably familiar when we compare early modern discourses with those of our own time. But great differences exist as well. What a marriage is, how couples establish relationships and what forms of sexuality are endorsed or condemned change over time. Despite its many forms of erotic representation, early modern culture had no concept of pornography. Despite the wealth of evidence of same-sex eroticism, it did not categorise people as homo or hetero-sexual. Love and sexual desire were seen as natural, but also thought by many to be either sinful, diseased or both. As is the case in other areas of inquiry, studies of early modern sexuality thrive on the fascination between sameness and difference, the Mirror and the Other.

Customs and norms for sexual behaviour obviously change over time, but due both to the intimate nature of sexual activity and to the broad range of sexual practices across a culture, it is difficult to speak of such changes with much precision. Changes in marriage are in some ways easier to trace. There is no question that marriage customs were transformed in the early modern England, primarily as a result of the Reformation, which established new forms of marriage ritual and encouraged new ways of thinking about marriage. Still, it is much easier to speak specifically about changes in ritual and doctrine than about the transformation of broader social attitudes.

Even in our own time, much of how sexuality works can seem mysterious or impossible to adequately explain in scholarly discourse. The sexual habits of cultures distant in time and space can seem even more baffling. No culture has a secure and widely accepted

---

[65] See, for example, Smith, *Homosexual Desire*, pp. 27–8.
[66] Moulton, *Before Pornography*, pp. 28–9.
[67] Traub, *Renaissance of Lesbianism*, pp. 56–69, 100–102, 160–63.

definition of exactly what constitutes sex. There may be relatively strict notions of what is considered appropriate sexual behaviour, but where sex begins and ends is always ambiguous. Is a foot massage sexual? Is a shared bed or bath? A kiss on the cheek? Some scholars have suggested that, since the early modern period did not use the words 'sex' or 'sexuality' to describe sexual activity, in some sense, the period pre-dates 'sex' altogether.[68] Of course, things can exist and be understood even if a culture does not name them; it would be dangerous to assume that what we call 'sex' first appeared at the moment that term was coined. But, lacking the concept of 'sex', in what ways did early modern culture structure its understanding of what we call sexuality?

One mystery out of many: for all its sexual frankness, early modern culture left almost no written mention of such seemingly common practices as masturbation or oral sex. Does this mean early modern people did not engage in these practices? Did they think they were unspeakable? Or were they seen as unremarkable, not worthy of mention? We can interpret the silence, and speculate on its meaning, but in such cases the silence remains, despite our best efforts.

Select Bibliography

Bray, Alan, *Homosexuality in Renaissance England*. London: Gay Men's Press, 1982.

Bray, Alan, *The Friend*. Chicago: University of Chicago Press, 2003.

Bredbeck, Gregory W., *Sodomy and Interpretation: Marlowe to Milton*. Ithaca, NY: Cornell University Press, 1991.

Coontz, Stephanie, *Marriage, a History: How Love Conquered Marriage*. New York: Penguin, 2006.

Cressy, David, *Birth, Marriage and Death: Ritual, Religion, and the Life-Cycle in Tudor and Stuart England*. New York: Oxford University Press, 1997.

Dawson, Lesel, *Lovesickness and Gender in Early Modern English Literature*. New York: Oxford University Press, 2008.

DiGangi, Mario, *The Homoeroticism of Early Modern Drama*. New York: Cambridge, 1997.

Dolan, Frances E., *Marriage and Violence: The Early Modern Legacy*. Philadelphia: University of Pennsylvania Press, 2008.

Foucault, Michel, *The History of Sexuality, Vol. 1, An Introduction*, trans. Robert Hurley. New York: Vintage, 1980.

Frantz, David O., *Festum Voluptatis: A Study of Renaissance Erotica*. Columbus: Ohio University Press, 1989.

Garber, Marjorie, *Vested Interests: Cross-Dressing and Cultural Anxiety*. New York: Routledge, 1992.

Goldberg, Jonathan, *Sodometries: Renaissance Texts, Modern Sexualities*. Stanford: Stanford University Press, 1992.

Gowing, Laura, *Domestic Dangers: Women, Words, and Sex in Early Modern London*. New York: Oxford University Press, 1996.

Houlbrooke, Ralph A., *The English Family 1450–1700*. New York: Longman, 1984.

Jardine, Lisa, *Still Harping on Daughters: Women and Drama in the Age of Shakespeare*. Sussex: Harvester, 1983.

Kelly, Henry Ansgar, *Love and Marriage in the Age of Chaucer*. Ithaca, NY: Cornell University Press, 1975.

---

[68] See, for example, William Stockton and James Bromley eds, *Sex before Sex* (New York: Palgrave, forthcoming).

Kelly-Gadol, Joan, 'Did Women Have a Renaissance?', in Renate Bridenthal and Claudia Koonz eds, *Becoming Visible: Women in European History*. Boston: Houghton Mifflin, 1977, pp. 148–61.

Laqueur, Thomas, *Making Sex: Body and Gender from the Greeks to Freud*. Cambridge, MA: Harvard University Press, 1990.

Macfarlane, Alan, Marriage and Love in England: Modes of Reproduction 1300–1840. New York: Blackwell, 1986.

Maclean, Ian, *The Renaissance Notion of a Woman: A Study of the Fortunes of Scholasticism and Medical Science in European Intellectual Life*. New York: Cambridge University Press, 1980.

Masten, Jeffrey, *Textual Intercourse: Collaboration, Authorship and Sexualities in Renaissance Drama*. New York: Cambridge University Press, 1997.

Menon, Madhavi ed., *Shakesqueer: A Queer Companion to the Works of Shakespeare*. Raleigh, NC: Duke University Press, 2011.

Moulton, Ian Frederick, *Before Pornography: Erotic Writing in Early Modern England*. New York: Oxford University Press, 2000.

O'Donnell, Katherine, and Michael O'Rourke eds, *Love, Sex, Intimacy and Friendship between Men, 1550–1800*. New York: Palgrave, 2003.

O'Hara, Diana, *Courtship and Constraint: Rethinking the Making of Marriage in Tudor England*. New York: Manchester University Press, 2000.

Orgel, Stephen, *Impersonations: The Performance of Gender in Shakespeare's England*. New York: Cambridge University Press, 1996.

Porter, Roy, and Lesley Hall, *The Facts of Life: The Creation of Sexual Knowledge in Britain, 1650–1950*. New Haven, CT: Yale University Press, 1995.

Rocke, Michael, *Forbidden Friendships: Homosexuality and Male Culture in Renaissance Florence*. New York: Oxford University Press, 1996.

Sedgwick, Eve, *Between Men: English Literature and Male Homosocial Desire*. New York: Columbia University Press, 1985.

Smith, Bruce R., *Homosexual Desire in Shakespeare's England*. Chicago: University of Chicago Press, 1991.

Stockton, William, and James Bromley eds, *Sex before Sex*. New York: Palgrave, forthcoming.

Stone, Lawrence, *The Family, Sex and Marriage in England, 1500–1800*. New York: Harper and Row, 1977.

Toulalan, Sarah, *Imagining Sex: Pornography and Bodies in Seventeenth Century England*. New York: Oxford University Press, 2007.

Traub, Valerie, *The Renaissance of Lesbianism in Early Modern England*. New York: Cambridge University Press, 2002.

Turner, James Grantham, *Schooling Sex: Libertine Literature and Erotic Education in Italy, France, and England, 1534–1685*. New York: Oxford University Press, 2003.

Food and Drink

Phil Withington

Towards the end of 1598 Edward Hodgson, a yeoman from York, was called as a witness to the church courts. Hodgson recalled that: 'One day in July last past or thereabouts being a workday about eleven O'clock [he] was in the new dwelling house of William Bonas situated within the parish of St Michael's together with Edward Clint, Emma Clark, and others.'[1] Bonas was a beer-brewer who had recently opened an alehouse to sell his beer. Robert Malton, a York tanner, likewise remembered that 'one day about Lamas last past' he 'went to William Bonas his house where he found Edward Clint and others drinking'. More particularly, Malton found 'Edward Clint sitting quietly with Edward Hodgson, James Denning and William Barker and Roger Deane and others'.[2] Here the accounts of Hodgson and Malton diverge slightly. Hodgson, who admitted he could not remember 'all the speeches that then passe[d] amongst them', testified that 'Edward Clint called Emma Clark whore and said to her 'Thou whore why wilt thou not bring in herring'?[3] Malton remembered the incident slightly differently. He testified that, after he sat down with Clint, 'he willed Bonas's maid [Emma Clark] to broil a herring and after she had [served him] such he thought the same was not well broiled then quoth Clint in merriment "Thou whore cans't thou not broil a herring?"' Clint's outburst prompted James Denning to ask his companion, 'Why do you call her whore? It will hold plea in our court' to which Clint replied 'I think her no harm, I laugh at her'.[4] Unfortunately for Clint neither Emma Clarke nor Elizabeth Bonas, wife of William and Emma's mistress, saw the funny side. According to Malton, when Clint tried to leave the house 'Elizabeth Bonas met the said Edward Clint and said to him "Call thou me a whore?" and hit him on the face with her fist.'[5] And as Denning predicted, Emma later sued Clint in the church courts in York ('our court') for defamation, with Elizabeth launching her own legal suit for good measure.

This chapter is about the popular culture of food and drink in early modern England; the spat over herring in the house of William and Elizabeth Bonas introduces some of its key issues and concerns. The first and most obvious of these is the absolute centrality of food and drink to the everyday lives of early modern people. This is true, of course, in the sense of basic nutritional and dietary needs. All people need enough food and drink to function in the world in which they live, though how those needs are estimated differs from culture to culture. Likewise how or even whether those needs are satisfied will vary from one social group to the next, and be dependent on a range of inter-related dynamics. One of the basic

---

[1] Borthwick Institute of Historical Research (BI), CPG 3032 (1598), deposition of Edward Hodgson.
[2] BI CPG 3041 (1598), deposition of Robert Malton.
[3] BI CPG 3032 (1598), deposition of Edward Hodgson (punctuation added).
[4] Ibid., deposition of Edward Hodgson; also deposition of James Denning.
[5] IBI CPG 3041, deposition of Robert Malton.

concerns of historians of food and drink, therefore, must be the understanding of dietary needs and wants across the social order, and also the factors which influenced the types and amounts of food and drink consumed by different social groups. It so happens that the 1590s is known to have been a decade of general scarcity in England as in Europe, one in which not only hunger but famine was a real concern, especially for poorer groups in society.[6] The means by which communities coped with these conditions in the short and medium term – how a man like Robert Malton could expect herring with his beer, for example – is an important historical question. It begs questions about the political economy of food and drink: the organisation and techniques of the fishermen, farmers and brewers who put the herring and beer on the table; the control and regulation of wholesalers and retailers (like William and Elizabeth Bonas) at the local and national levels; the place of the food and drinks trades not only within local and national economies but also Europe and, increasingly after 1570, the wider world. Herring stocks, for example, were a much contested and valued resource that was central to the economy of the North Sea fishing ports and a potential source of diplomatic tension.[7] The right to trade in herring or serve it in an alehouse was likewise subject to national legislation and local licensing laws.[8] As with most foodstuffs, a complex nexus of institutions and interests determined precisely how commodities like herring and beer were sold and consumed from one place to the next.

The social importance of food and drink can also be appreciated in terms of how their production and consumption were embedded in the rituals, institutions and temporal rhythms of everyday life.[9] In this instance Edward Clint and his companions – male artisans and yeomen in York – gravitated to the 'dwelling house' of William Bonas as the middle of their 'workday' approached. This they did to keep what they styled 'company'; drink beer or ale; and, in the case of Robert Malton at least, eat broiled herring.[10] For these men the need for sustenance was also an occasion for sociability and 'merriment' at the expense of the serving maid. For Elizabeth Bonas and Emma Clark, in contrast, food and drink was their work and closely connected to their role in the household. The only women mentioned in the depositions, they were present as the producers and providers of the beer and herring and *de facto* custodians of the 'house'. The use of this language is a reminder, in turn, of the extremely close links between the preparation and consumption of food and drink on the one hand and the institution of the household on the other hand. This was certainly the case for the 'household family', the dynamics of which were defined in large part by cooking, eating and drinking.[11] William and Elizabeth Bonas ran, of course, a commercial establishment: indeed one testimony claimed 'Edward Clint began to chide with the said Elizabeth Bonas' when they began to discuss 'the paying of his shot'.[12] The Bonas alehouse was nevertheless conceived by its patrons as an extension of the household family or 'dwelling house'. The

---

[6]   John Walter and Roger Schofield eds, *Famine, Disease and the Social Order in Early Modern Society* (Cambridge: Cambridge University Press, 1989); Peter Clark, ed. *The European Crisis of the 1590s: Essays in Comparative History* (London: Unwin, 1985); Keith Wrightson, *Earthly Necessities: Economic Lives in Early Modern Britain* (New Haven: Yale University Press, 2000), pp. 198–9.

[7]   Robert Tittler, *Townspeople and Nation: English Urban Experiences 1540–1640* (Stanford: Stanford University Press, 2001), pp. 122–4, 136.

[8]   Peter Clark, *The English Alehouse: A Social History 1200–1830* (London: Longman, 1983).

[9]   Mary Douglas ed., *Constructive Drinking: Perspectives on Drink from Anthropology* (Cambridge: Cambridge University Press, 1987); Martin Jones, *Feast: Why Humans Share Food* (Oxford: Oxford University Press, 2007).

[10]   Phil Withington, 'Company and Sociability in Early Modern England', *Social History* 32:3 (2007), 291–307.

[11]   Emma Griffiths and Jane Whittle, *Consumption and Gender in the Early Seventeenth Century Household: The World of Alice Le Strange* (Oxford: Oxford University Press, 2012).

[12]   BI CPG 3041 (1598), charge against defendant.

depositions accordingly described the intersection of two social institutions which were absolutely integral to eating and drinking in the early modern period: the (feminine) *household* where food and drink was prepared; and, in this instance, the masculine *company* which met and consumed. On this occasion, it seems, the 'merriment' of one institution grated against the honour and reputation of the other.

All of which points to third set of issues raised by the dispute, concerning questions of taste and skill. Clearly Emma Clark's efforts to prepare the herring were not to the liking of Edward Clint and his companions. This implies a sense of taste on the part of the men: they expected a kind of dish prepared and flavoured in a certain way.[13] The expectation assumes, in turn, that the women of the house possessed the requisite knowledge and techniques to prepare the herring as required. That this knowledge was lacking or misapplied was the real source of contention underlying the exchange of words. Clint's use of the word 'whore' was significant in that it enabled the women to take him to court for defamation. However, his substantive insult was that Clarke, and by extension the household, could not cook: a slur against the skills which defined a good woman, and hardly the reputation for a 'new dwelling house' to acquire. What is particularly interesting about the depositions is that they reveal what historians instinctively know but can rarely show: that tastes and skills relating to food and drink were not simply the preserve of a culinary elite, but rather characterised eating and drinking across the social spectrum.[14] Broiling fish – meaning grilling or baking – was a relatively complex procedure with attendant techniques and outcomes. The tastes and skills associated with the term may have been acquired through 'custom' and everyday habits or disseminated by the rapidly increasing number of printed cook-books in circulation; though distinguishing between the two can be an artificial exercise given the inter-penetration of literate and oral culture.[15] The provenance of John Partridge's recipe 'To bake Bream, Trout, Mullets, Pike, or any Fish', for example, is unclear; but it may well have described the kind of dish the company of Edward Clint anticipated. Published in 1588, Partridge advised his 'courteous reader' to let the fish 'be well seasoned with Cloves and Mace, Salt and Pepper, and so bake them with small Currants Verjuice and butter, great raisons and prunes'.[16] A rich dish, for sure, but one within the ken of a reasonably equipped provincial kitchen in the late sixteenth century.

The can of thematic worms opened by Edward Clint indicates that the subject of food and drink is wide and encompassing. Insofar as its 'popular' aspects are concerned, however, it is also a notoriously difficult and elusive subject. This is true in terms of theoretical frameworks. Historians of food and drink can claim a range of influences, from the Annales School in both its empiricist and cultural guises through to anthropology, literature, the history of medicine and most recently material culture.[17] Yet despite or perhaps because of this theoretical diversity it is difficult to delineate a distinctive and coherent historiography of food and drink in the

---

[13]   Massimo Montanari, *Food Is Culture* (New York: Columbia University Press, 2004); Paul Freedman ed., *Food: The History of Taste* (London: Thames & Hudson, 2009).

[14]   Joan Thirsk, *Food in Early Modern England: Phases, Fads, Fashions 1500–1760* (London: Continuum, 2007).

[15]   Wendy Wall, *Staging Domesticity: Household Work and English Identity in Early Modern Drama* (Cambridge: Cambridge University Press, 2002); Adam Fox, *Oral and Literate Culture in England, 1500–1700* (Oxford: Oxford University Press, 2000).

[16]   John Partridge, *The Widow's Treasure* (1588), sig. F7.

[17]   See, for example, Montanari, *Food Is Culture*; Freedman, *Food*; Ken Albala, *Eating Right in the Renaissance* (Berkeley and Los Angeles: University of California Press, 2002); Jordan Goodman, Paul E. Lovejoy and Andrew Sherratt eds, *Consuming Habits: Global and Historical Perspectives in How Cultures Define Drugs* (London: Routledge, 2007); Ann Tlusty, *Bacchus and Civic Order: The Culture of Drink in Early Modern Germany* (Virginia: University Press of Virginia, 2001); Sara Pennell, 'The Material Culture of Food in Early Modern England', in Sara Tarlow and Susie West eds, *Familiar Pasts? Archaeologies of Later Historical Britain 1550–1860* (London: Routledge, 1999), pp. 35–50.

manner of (for example) popular politics, crime or gender relations. Rather the field of study is inchoate and ill-defined. Indeed for many historians, food and drink, especially alcoholic drinks, are distinct phenomena to be studied separately (an ironic distinction given the holistic way in which early modern people tended to conceive of their diet). The subject's difficulties also stem from problems of evidence and interpretation. Food and drink are comestibles which, by definition, do not last; it is extraordinarily difficult to know in any detail the diets and consumption habits of ordinary people.[18] Given that biological archaeology is yet to be utilised by early modernists, we can only usually know our subject vicariously: through their material culture (for example pans and fires for cooking, plates and cups for consuming, barrels and stills for fermenting); their literary culture (for example, printed recipe and medical guides and biographical writings like letters and diaries); their administration and regulation (households accounts, for example, or licensing documentation and civic records); their visual and literary representation (in paintings, plays, drinking bowls). In the case of 'popular culture', however, each of these types of source begs important questions. Did literary precepts or public rules really inform the everyday practices and experiences of ordinary people in any meaningful way?[19] How do we reconstruct everyday behaviour and attitudes from household inventories, or drinking bowls, or a sheaf of alehouse licences?[20] And do these sources tell us anything about the lives of the large numbers of people who did not read books directly, or leave inventories or diaries?

Legal testimonies like those by Hodgson and Malton are important, therefore, because they describe everyday moments and events involving men and women potentially excluded from the kinds of evidence upon which food historians usually rely. Such descriptions were often inadvertent in the sense that the main concern of the court was always the misdemeanour alleged to have taken place. However, the business of the church courts was such that the context for the misdemeanour – whether defamatory words, immoral behaviour or marital cruelty – was often precisely those places and scenarios (public and domestic) that other kinds of evidence cannot reach. Although these descriptions were mediated, in that witnesses spoke in a court of law (with its own expectations and formulas of expression) and their words were transcribed by a clerk, the statements by Hodgson and Malton clearly contain a range of voices which can still be heard through the procedural fug. Indeed it might well be argued that when used carefully and critically these legal depositions are the closest an early modern historian can get to 'ethnographic' transcripts.[21]

In this particular instance, recollections of a dispute over broiled herring illuminate a number of avenues down which the popular history of food and drink can be coherently approached. One such road is political economy: how the production, traffic and consumption of food and drink was organised and regulated, and the consequent impact on the dietary experiences of different social groups. Another is the rituals, practices, institutions and temporalities informing the exchange, preparation and consumption of comestibles: how

---

[18]   Michel Morineau, 'Growing without Knowing Why: Production, Demographics, Diet', in Jean-Louis Flandrin and Massimo Montanari eds, *Food: A Culinary History from Antiquity to the Present* (New York: Columbia University Press, 1996), pp. 379–82; Craig Muldrew, *Food, Energy and the Creation of Industriousness: Work and Material Culture in Agrarian England, 1550–1780* (Cambridge: Cambridge University Press, 2011), pp. 115–16.

[19]   Natasha Glaisyer and Sara Pennell, *Didactic Literature in England, 1500–1800: Expertise Constructed* (Farnham: Ashgate, 2003).

[20]   The point is well made in Lorna Weatherill, 'The Meaning of Consumer Behaviour in Late Seventeenth and Early Eighteenth Century England', in John Brewer and Roy Porter eds, *Consumption and the World of Goods* (London: Routledge, 1993), pp. 206–27.

[21]   Withington, 'Company'. For the analytical potential of these sources see Keith Wrightson, *Ralph Tailor's Summer: A Scrivener, His City, and the Plague* (New Haven: Yale University Press, 2011).

food and drink was integral to the social structures, identities and relationships of everyday life and vice versa. A third and adjacent avenue is the techniques and tastes associated with different foods and drinks: the skills and meanings implicit to particular dishes and beverages, and the range of media by which and through which these aptitudes and semantics were disseminated, learned and represented. Any one of these avenues is clearly far too long for a chapter of this size and scope even to begin to explore properly. The rest of the chapter accordingly notes some of the most important developments in the political economy of the period before turning to the 'places' and 'spaces' of eating and drinking. It concludes by raising some questions about 'popular' tastes.

Political Economy

The early modern period was, almost by definition, an era of marked and formative change. According to the French food historian Jean-Louis Flandrin, 'the most striking' of these was the 'European conquest of the Seven Seas and the subsequent integration of other continents into Europe's commercial network': processes which 'had an impact on the European diet that has continued to the present day'.[22] In the most systematic extrapolation of this insight, Jan de Vries has argued that the middle classes of north-west European societies underwent an 'industrious revolution' in the century and a half after 1650 as the purchase of these newly available 'colonial groceries' (not least new comestibles) became part of coherent household strategies. In the meantime the consumption of the lower orders also increased, but at the expense of the household.[23] From the perspective of England there can be no question that colonial and commercial expansion profoundly shaped the popular culture of food and drink. Not only did new commodities like tea, sugar and potatoes become integral to the modern British diet; they were also sources of nutrition and energy which sustained the dramatic demographic increases from the second half of the eighteenth century.[24] However, it is also the case that aside from tobacco (a product which many food historians would be loath to consider as part of their subject) the mass commodification of both colonial groceries and crops successfully introduced into domestic cultivation occurred largely after 1700.[25] Although the conquests and networks of British imperialism were very much a feature of early modernity, and although new goods like coffee and chocolate played a significant part in English public life from the middle of the seventeenth century, the popular dietary consequences of this expansion and assimilation came later.[26]

As importantly, the historiographical emphasis on global commerce can mask other, equally significant developments in the political economy of food and drink which occurred closer to home. These include the intensification of European trade and imports from the middle of the sixteenth century and the concurrent impact of European production techniques

---

[22] Jean-Louis Flandrin, 'The Early Modern Period', in Flandrin and Montanari eds, *Food*, p. 349.

[23] Jan de Vries, *The Industrious Revolution: Consumer Behaviour and the Household Economy, 1650 to the Present* (Cambridge: Cambridge University Press, 2008), pp. 177–80.

[24] Sidney W. Mintz, *Sweetness and Power: The Place of Sugar in Modern History* (London: Penguin, 1986); Denys Mostyn Forrest, *Tea for the British: the Social and Economic History of a Famous Trade* (London: Chatto & Windus, 1973); Redcliffe N. Salaman, *The History and Social Influence of the Potato* (Cambridge: Cambridge University Press, 1985; first ed. 1949).

[25] S.D. Smith, 'Accounting for Taste: British Coffee Consumption in Historical Perspective', *Journal of Interdisciplinary History* 27:2 (1996), 183–214.

[26] Brian Cowan, *The Social Life of Coffee: The Emergence of the British Coffeehouse* (New Haven: Yale University Press, 2005).

on English diets. The emergence of the Levant Company as an economic force is perhaps the best indicator of the former, the amount of imported currents rising from 9,000–10,000 hundredweight a year in the 1590s to 50,000 hundredweight in the 1630s.[27] More protracted but ultimately more momentous as far as popular consumption was concerned was the adoption of Dutch techniques for brewing beer.[28] Ale and beer were a major source of nourishment and energy in the medieval and early modern eras.[29] By the end of the sixteenth century beer made with hops had eclipsed locally brewed ales (which did not keep and could not be moved over distance). The economies of scale which accompanied this switch in taste facilitated at once the wholesale commercialisation of the brewing industry and the surge in output to meet demand. Indeed transformations in the brewing industry were one of several developments which allowed the English population to not merely more than double between 1530 and 1640 but also 'slipped the shadow of famine at an early date'.[30] Like brewing, farming underwent significant commercialisation and market integration, so much so that scholars talk of an early modern 'agricultural revolution' between the sixteenth and eighteenth centuries.[31] In the meantime the institutionalisation of parochial poor relief after 1600 (first in cities and towns, more gradually in rural areas) must have done something to put bread and beer on otherwise empty tables.[32] So, too, did the proliferation of alehouses. While these might be profitable establishments – the 'new dwelling house' of William and Elizabeth Bonas was a commercial undertaking – many others were licensed to supplement the makeshift economy of poorer householders.[33] Other kinds of paternalism, both formal and informal, included price regulation, the policing of markets and fairs, rules against hoarding and profiteering and the extension of credit and charity within communities.[34] When local governors failed to maintain a community's 'moral economy' then inhabitants staged food riots to do it for them; the marked increase in food riots *after* 1740 may well have reflected the decline of economic paternalism and the concomitant rise of 'free trade' as a governing ideology.[35] Be that as it may, so reliable did the provision of food and drink become in the seventeenth century that by 1700 London had grown into the largest city in Europe, a population of 600,000 people largely dependent for their diet on European imports and the market gardens and commercial farms of south-east England.[36] And whereas European urbanisation largely faltered in the decades after 1660, in England the urban system continued to grow despite the national population stagnating.[37]

---

[27]   Wrightson, *Earthly Necessities*, p. 178.

[28]   Richard W. Unger, *Beer in the Middle Ages and the Renaissance* (Philadelphia: University of Pennsylvania Press, 2004).

[29]   Donald Woodward, *Men at Work: Labourers and Building Craftsmen in the Towns of Northern England, 1450–1750* (Cambridge: Cambridge University Press, 1997), pp. 147–57.

[30]   John Walter, 'The Social Economy of Dearth in Early Modern England', in Walter and Schofield eds, *Famine*, p. 75.

[31]   Mark Overton, *Agricultural Revolution in England: The Transformation of the Agrarian Economy 1500–1850* (Cambridge: Cambridge University Press, 1996), pp. 206–7.

[32]   Paul Slack, *Poverty and Policy in Tudor and Stuart England* (London: Longman, 1988); Steve Hindle, *On the Parish? The Micro-Politics of Poor Relief in Rural England c. 1550–1750* (Oxford: Oxford University Press, 2004).

[33]   Keith Wrightson, 'Alehouses, Order and Reformation in Rural England, 1590–1660', in Eileen Yeo and Stephen Yeo eds, *Popular Culture and Class Conflict 1590–1914: Explorations in the History of Labour and Leisure* (Brighton: Branch Line, 1981), pp. 1–23.

[34]   Walter, 'The Social Economy of Dearth', pp. 96–128.

[35]   John Bohstedt, *The Politics of Provisions: Food Riots, Moral Economy and Market Transition in England 1550–1850* (Farnham: Ashgate, 2010). Thanks to Craig Muldrew for discussing these issues.

[36]   A.E. Wrigley, 'A Simple Model of London's Importance in Changing English Society and Economy 1650 – 1750', *Past & Present* 37 (1967), 44–70.

[37]   Jan de Vries, *European Urbanization 1500–1800* (London: Routledge, 1984), pp. 38–40.

That ordinary people were not starving to death in England after the first quarter of the seventeenth century does not necessarily mean, of course, that they were not hungry, free of 'hard times' or ate especially well. Given that this is known to be an era in which high inflation and declining real wages coincided with significant increases in the number of labouring (wage-dependent) poor, it is hardly surprising that historians have assumed diets lower down the social scale were monotonous, unhealthy and meagre. Robert Fogel, for example, has calculated that as late as the 1790s the diet of the bottom 20 per cent of the English population would have yielded enough energy to do only six hours light work or 65 minutes heavy work a day.[38] More recently this view has been challenged, Michel Morineau arguing that, although there are problems 'devising statistical indices' of how much people ate, 'no matter what method is chosen, the findings are similar' for early modern Europe. He suggests that 'in normal years caloric rations were always above, and often well above, the level today regarded as adequate for a worker engaged in moderately hard physical labour (2,400 calories per day); indeed, they were close to the level required by a man engaged in hard labour (4,000 calories)'. He also argues that while more than half of 'this total caloric intake was in the form of grain', the intake of fat and protein 'did not regularly fall below minimum daily requirements'.[39] The conclusion is echoed by Craig Muldrew's recent work on English labourers' incomes and diets between the sixteenth and eighteenth centuries. Muldrew argues that 'there were enough calories to do hard work', though warns that in years of dearth 'these undoubtedly had to be rationed between individuals'. He also suggests that, insofar as calories were concerned, a significant line should be drawn between employed labourers, who needed to eat to work, and 'underemployed' labourers, who did not; and that labouring should not be straightforwardly equated with poverty.[40] Muldrew accordingly suggests that dietary options were much more varied and healthy than is often assumed; that the family earnings of labourers begin to show a surplus after 1650 'which then potentially quadrupled by 1760'; and that this increase coincided with an 'increase in energy available through calories' – by 17 per cent between 1600 and 1700 and another 41 per cent by 1770, before falling significantly thereafter.[41] Viewed in these terms – and the question, as ever, is whether it is really possible to calculate caloric percentages with such apparent certainty – England's 'industrious revolution' was caused not merely or even mainly by the middling sorts working harder to purchase colonial groceries. Rather it was due to the surprising quality and quantity of working men's and women's diets – a diet which, increasingly over time, enabled labouring households to work harder in order to improve their standards of living.

Places and Spaces

If Muldrew's revisionism is purposefully provocative then it nevertheless indicates just how integral the political economy of food and drink was to the lives and experiences of early modern people. This becomes clearer still when we turn from politics, class and calories to places, spaces and social practice. The distinction between 'place' and 'space' has been nicely made by Michel de Certeau, who characterises *place* as a 'location' with 'rules' and

---

[38] Robert Fogel, 'New Sources and Techniques for the Study of Secular Trends in Nutritional Statius, Health, Mortality, and the Process of Aging', *Historical Methods* 26 (1993), 12.

[39] Morineau, 'Growing without Knowing Why', p. 382.

[40] Muldrew, *Food*, pp. 161, 294.

[41] Ibid., pp. 116, 258, 161.

'stability' which exists in relation to other 'positions', and *space* as what happens when people occupy and use the place, bringing with them their 'vectors of direction, velocities, and time variables'.[42] Space, in effect, 'is a practiced place': 'a street geometrically defined by urban planning is transformed into a space by walkers';[43] William Bonas's alehouse becomes a space through the groups who frequent it. This simple schema is useful for thinking about eating and drinking for two reasons. On the one hand, the concept of place foregrounds the topographies of food and drink in early modern England: the locations – both institutions and physical sites – where different sorts of people were expected to prepare, serve and consume food and drink. On the other hand, the concept of space invokes the inter-personal dynamics of that production and consumption: how and by whom places were colonised and appropriated in practice.

The topographies of everyday eating and drinking in early modern England can be understood (albeit somewhat schematically) as three overlapping types: domestic; commercial; and corporate. By *domestic* is meant those places given over to eating and drinking under the auspices of the family household. This was defined by Sir Thomas Smith in 1584 'as the man, the woman, their children, their servants bond and free, their cattle, their household stuff, and all other things which are reckoned in their possession, so long as all these remain together in one'.[44] Naomi Tadmor has shown that this conception of the household-family – which encompassed not only the conjugal or 'nuclear' core but also the contracted household dependants who were gathered under the authority of the household head – remained normative for all social classes well into the eighteenth century.[45] Likewise the great bulk of food production and consumption occurred in the 'dwelling house' or 'home' and the various rooms (kitchens, parlours) and out-spaces (gardens, orchards, brew-houses) which constituted it. Given that a large percentage of ordinary people were engaged in service and apprenticeship in wealthier households at any given time – many of them preparing food and drink for their masters and mistresses, as well as themselves eating and drinking in different parts of the house – then large and more 'elite' homes must also be considered as part of this 'popular' domestic topography.[46] Indeed, the politics surrounding the domestic geography of food and drink – in terms of inclusion and exclusion, and habitual or legitimate positioning – was a fundamental feature of everyday life and experience for most people.[47] Nor was it simply the consumption of household members – whether of family and children, or servants and apprentices – which characterised domestic places. Although its story is yet to be properly told, household hospitality remained an important dimension of both rural and urban rural life throughout the period, involving neighbours, friends, kin, godparents, tenants and the like in various kinds of consumptive practice.[48]

As the language surrounding the incident in the Bonas house demonstrates, because the household family was the main institution of economic activity in the early modern period, the difference between domestic and *commercial* places of eating and drinking could seem imperceptible. The lines, physical and symbolic, were there nonetheless. Isabel Branton, a

---

[42]   Michel de Certeau, *The Practice of Everyday Life* (Berkeley and Los Angeles: University of California Press, 1988), p. 117.

[43]   Ibid.

[44]   Sir Thomas Smith, *De Republica Anglorum* (1584), p. 13.

[45]   Naomi Tadmor, 'The Concept of the Household Family in Eighteenth-Century England', *Past & Present* 151 (1996), 111–40.

[46]   Ann Kussmaul, *Servants in Husbandry in Early Modern England* (Cambridge: Cambridge University Press, 1981), pp. 11–42.

[47]   See later.

[48]   Historians have not followed up the initial inroads made by Felicity Heal, *Hospitality in Early Modern England* (Oxford: Oxford University Press, 1990).

servant to one of William Bonas's neighbours, testified to the church courts that one John Eden had told her how 'he was in William Bonas his house and [did] see Elizabeth Bonas go into a parlour of the said house and Edward Clint follow her whereupon she thrust him back with her hand saying "Why does thou follow me?"'[49] This particular parlour was clearly separate to and distinct from the rooms in the house given over to paying company.[50] The defining feature of commercial dwelling houses was that sections of the household were devoted to eating and drinking by non-household members for some kind of fiscal exchange, be it cash or credit. Because alcohol licensing was successfully institutionalised from the 1620s (so providing lists of licensees and their houses) much more is known about commercial premises selling alcohol – the famous triumvirate of alehouses, taverns and inns – than unlicensed victualling houses and other kinds of baking, broiling and cooking establishment. Likewise because coffeehouses were subsequently licensed through the same procedure as alehouses, there is the impression that it was only with the popularisation of these and other beverages in the later seventeenth century that the topography of consumption became more variegated. While there is no question that the number of alehouses, taverns and inns – and latterly coffeehouses, chocolate shops and gin houses – expanded exponentially over the period, there is no reason to assume that this was the limit of the commercial food and drink sector. As with early modern hospitality much more research is needed. But to keep with the Bonas example in York for a moment, there is no evidence that the Bonas family continued as beer-brewers, alehouse keepers, tavern holders or innkeepers after William and Elizabeth. However, what we do find is a relatively prosperous householder called Matthew Bonas making his way in the world. Matthew Bonas listed his occupation as *cook*. More, he was a named as a tobacco licensee in 1636. Although he did not run a drinking establishment (which is what the vast majority of tobacco licensees did) he did own a cook's house in which it can be inferred that people ate, socialised and by the 1630s took tobacco.[51] This hints, perhaps, at a largely undiscovered topography of everyday eating and drinking at once beyond the alehouse and prior to the post-Restoration 'urban renaissance'.[52] And given that Bonas was an unusual name in York, there is every chance that Matthew learned his trade in a kitchen which, according to Edward Clint, could not broil a herring.

The commercial topography of eating and drinking beyond the physical boundaries of the household was also extensive. However, it is much harder to map in any detail because of its itinerant and shifting nature. Important in this respect were the weekly or seasonal markets, both urban and rural, and the great annual fairs which drew traders and visitors from across England and beyond: Bartholomew in London, Stourbridge in the Fens, Beverley in Yorkshire and so on. Ben Jonson's great play famously depicted Bartholomew Fair as (among other things) one enormous opportunity for consumption – a place in which every kind of appetite could be satiated, and in which the concatenation of people in a strange environment created a festive and carnival feel.[53] This may have been something like the experience of Elizabeth Burdas on her visit to Beverley Fair. In the same year that Edward

---

[49]   BI CPG 3041 (1598), deposition of Isabel Branton.

[50]   Amanda Flather, *Gender and Space in Early Modern England* (Woodbridge: Boydell and Brewer, 2007).

[51]   The National Archives (TNA), E 178/5793.

[52]   Sara Pennell, '"Great Quantities of Gooseberry Pye and Baked Clod of Beef": Victualing and Eating Out in Early Modern London', in Paul Griffiths and Mark Jenner eds, *Londonopolis: Essays in the Cultural and Social History of Early Modern London* (Manchester: Manchester University Press, 2000), pp. 228–49; Peter Borsay, *The English Urban Renaissance: Culture and Society in the Provincial Town, 1660–1770* (Oxford: Clarendon, 1989).

[53]   Ben Jonson, *The Selected Plays of Ben Jonson, Volume II*, ed. Martin Butler (Cambridge: Cambridge University Press, 1989).

Clint complained about his herring, Burdas found herself 'lodged in an inn in Beverley in the fair time', sharing a bed with Millicent Pratt in a 'chamber' with three other men – two brothers and Thomas Watson. There is, unfortunately, no record of what she ate or drank; however, Pratt described in some detail how Burdas contrived to have sex with Thomas Watson as she listened on 't'other side of the bed'.[54] Even more elusive than these seasonal institutions were itinerant pedlars of food and drink: women like Elizabeth Simpson and Margery Wilson, 'being both sellers of sausage'.[55] There is little record of the kind of sausage they sold or their clientele. However, it does seem that in 1637 they became involved in a dispute over territory, the tailor John Trowlop deposing that he saw them 'meet in the street, near his shop' and heard Wilson say 'in angry manner … Hear'est thou, thou will never let me alone, but I will make thee let me alone, like a scurvy queen as you is'.[56]

The third alimentary topography to bear in mind – one much easier to trace in the records than markets and pedlars, but often forgotten by historians – was that associated with *corporate* institutions, buildings and activities. This included the eating and drinking of parishes (civil and ecclesiastical) and religious organisations (the episcopal establishment and, after 1640, gathered churches like the Quakers); of guilds and craft companies; of urban corporations; of trading corporations (like the Levant or East India Company); of educational institutions (schools, colleges, universities, Inns of Court); of legal courts, like quarter sessions and county Assizes; and of parliament and the bodies of the monarchical state. Corporate eating and drinking included acts of *communitas*, whereby members of the particular body confirmed their association, obligations and hierarchy to each other: the annual feasts which characterised guild and civic life, for example, or communion or churchwardens feasts in the parish. It encompassed modes of hospitality and festivity, whereby food and drink were used to entertain or appeal to the wider communities and constituencies to which the corporate body was connected or obligated: the 'entertainments' on parliamentary election days, or the Lord Mayor's Pageant in London. And it included acts of charity and payment, whereby food and drink was provided to the deserving 'poor' (whether in the neighbourhood or in hospitals and workhouses) or supplied to functionaries and office-holders of a corporate institution.

Taken in sum, these modes of eating and drinking clearly constituted a vast nexus of food production and consumption and reflected the deeply corporate nature of early modern life. Although (as with most aspects of this subject) much more research is needed, a few general points can be made here. The first concerns change over time. Although it is orthodox to bemoan the loss of corporatism following the Dissolution, there was, in fact, less a declension of associational life after 1540 and more a process of redistribution and expansion. Trade guilds, craft companies, corporations, educational establishments and trading companies all increased in number and membership during the early modern period. So too did modern kinds of society and club, from civic militia companies to gathered churched to learned societies, also become features of the social landscape.[57] The early modern era was, in short, a time of corporate fecundity; and in each instance food and drink was integral to this landscape. Second, increasing corporate consumption stimulated the commercial sector both in terms of supplying food and drink at corporate venues or spilling over into commercial sites. Inns and alehouses were as packed during the Assizes and quarter sessions as they were for markets and fairs; often parochial and borough feasting was held in a local inn. Third, the

---

[54]   BI CPH 8 1600, deposition of Millicent Pratt.
[55]   BI CPH 2161 1637, deposition of Jane Dossie.
[56]   Ibid., deposition of John Trowlop.
[57]   Phil Withington, *Society in Early Modern England: The Vernacular Origins of Some Powerful Ideas* (Cambridge: Polity, 2010).

social depth of corporate drinking and eating should not be underestimated. Historians are now well aware of the participatory extent of the English commonwealth, which depended on thousands of corporate office-holders from the parish upwards.[58] Craft companies and borough corporations were hardly crammed with genteel 'elites', after all.[59] That is not to say eating and drinking as an expression of *communitas* was not exclusionary: by its very definition it included and identified only those who were members of the corporate group. But defining purposeful association below the rank of gentry as either 'elite' or 'popular' – as opposed to patriarchal, which they almost invariably were, or perhaps oligarchical, which they often (though not invariably) became – is an arbitrary and potentially anachronistic interpretative decision. This is as true for Essex parishioners or Newcastle craftsmen as it is for Derbyshire lead-miners or Cambridge burgesses.[60]

This politics of inclusion and exclusion shifts attention away from 'place' to 'space': the manner in which, and by whom, these sites and institutions – whether domestic, commercial or corporate – were colonised and used in practice. The distinction is important for at least two reasons. It highlights the importance of social practice, and how the realities and contingencies of behaviour could be very different from the prescribed rules and roles of a place. And it moves beyond the characterisation of places in abstract and presumptive terms – as 'elite' or 'popular', for example – to the everyday moments of inclusion, exclusion and interaction by which people defined themselves in relation to others. To go back to the house of Elizabeth and William Bonas for a moment: while a certain kind of clientele and behaviour might be expected of a 1590s alehouse, it was nevertheless the *companies* of drinkers (to use the language of deponents) who met there which determined the sociology and culture of the place (in this instance as artisanal, patriarchal, 'merry'). Too often historians confuse social interaction within an institution – like the alehouse – with the institution itself.[61]

A particular household from the later seventeenth century illustrates the point. It also touches on a famous literary mystery: whether Andrew Marvell, the Restoration poet, was married. The question arose because when Marvell died unexpectedly in 1678 his erstwhile housekeeper, Mary Palmer, declared herself his widow and executor of his estate. The estate was not much in terms of possessions or credit, though it did include Marvell's papers (Mary accordingly published Marvell's poems posthumously in 1681, referring to herself as Mary Marvell in the preface). However, others suspected that amongst Marvell's papers was a bond for £500 which Marvell had been looking after for his nephew, Edmond Nelthorpe. The back story to this was that Nelthorpe was a merchant whose joint-stock company had failed catastrophically in 1676. With the partners fearing arrest Marvell and Palmer established a safe-house on Russell Street where the merchants could hide. Unfortunately

---

[58]   Mark Goldie, 'The Unacknowledged Republic: Office-Holding in Early Modern England', in Tim Harris ed., *The Politics of the Excluded, c. 1500–1850* (Basingstoke: Palgrave, 2001), pp. 153–94.

[59]   Jonathan Barry, 'Bourgeois Collectivism? Urban Association and the Middling Sort', in Jonathan Barry and Christopher Brooks eds, *The Middling Sort of People: Culture, Society and Politics in England, 1550–1800* (Basingstoke: Palgrave, 1994), pp. 84–113; Christopher Brooks, 'Apprenticeship, Social Mobility and the Middling Sort, 1550–1800', in Barry and Brooks eds, *Middling Sort of People*, pp. 52–84.

[60]   Keith Wrightson and David Levine, *Poverty and Piety in an English Village: Terling 1525–1700* (2nd ed., Oxford: Oxford University Press, 1995), 103–9; Phil Withington, *The Politics of Commonwealth: Citizens and Freemen in Early Modern England* (Cambridge: Cambridge University Press, 2005), pp. 169–80; Andy Wood, 'Custom, Identity and Resistance: English Free-Miners and Their Law c. 1550–1800', in Paul Griffiths, Steve Hindle and Adam Fox eds, *The Experience of Authority in Early Modern England* (Basingstoke: Palgrave, 1996), pp. 249–85; Phil Withington, 'Agency, Custom, and the English Corporate System', in Henry French and Jonathan Barry eds, *Identity and Agency in English Society, 1500–1800* (Basingstoke: Palgrave, 2004), pp. 200–23.

[61]   Phil Withington, 'Intoxicants and the Early Modern City', in Steve Hindle, Alex Shepard and John Walter eds, *Remaking English Society* (Woodbridge: Boydell and Brewer, 2013), pp. 135–63.

Nelthorpe died only a few months before Marvell; with Marvell now dead John Farrington, another business partner, launched a series of suits in the court of Chancery to reclaim the bond. This involved denying Mary was really the wife of Andrew Marvell in order to refute her claim to the bond (if it indeed existed) and discredit her as a legal witness.[62]

How Farrington questioned Mary's marital status says everything about the importance of eating and drinking in the household and the politics of company this involved. Farrington claimed that:

> *Although the said Mr Marvell and Mr Nelthorpe did dwell in the same house together and she the said [Mary] did also dwell therein … yet the said Mr Marvell and [Mary] did not lodge together as man and wife nor diet together that is to say that [Mary] did not sit at meals with the said Andrew Marvell and the company but eat her meals after they had done as servants use to do as [I] have seen and doubt not to prove.*[63]

This proved the general assumption:

> *that the said Andrew Marvell who was a Member if the house of Commons for many years together and a very learned man would [never] undervalue himself to intermarry with so mean a person as one the said Mary then was being the widow of a Tennis Court keeper in or near the city of Westminster who died in a mean condition.*[64]

Mary replied first to the general suspicion:

> *Although it be true that her former husband Palmer was a Tennis Court keeper and did die in a mean condition … And though it be likewise true that the said Andrew Marvell was a Parliament man and a learned man yet it doth not follow but he might marry [me] as in truth he did, and so it appears by the Register [of the church: now missing], but the difference in their conditions might be one reason why the said Mr Marvell was pleased to have the marriage kept private.*[65]

She then repudiated the specific claim:

> *it is true she did not till after his death pretend or give out she was his wife because it was contrary to what he had Engaged her But she did what she could to conceal the same and therefore she did sometimes attend upon him more like a servant than wife (which was the better to conceal their being man and wife) …*
> *And whilst the Mr Nelthorpe and [Farrington] dwelt together in the house [on Russell Street] True as it is she not always sat down with them at Meals having sometimes other Occasions But she did very often as she pleased sit down with them at Meals and Eat her meal with them.*[66]

Whether she was Mrs Marvell or not depended, in effect, on who ate meals with whom.

---

[62]   The most influential but also misleading interpretation of the surviving evidence is Fred S. Tupper, 'Mary Palmer, Alias Mrs Andrew Marvell', *Publications of the Modern Language Association* 53:2 (1938), 386–8; Withington, *Politics of Commonwealth*, pp. 222–7.

[63]   TNA C8/252/9, deposition of John Farrington.

[64]   TNA C6/242/13, deposition of John Farrington.

[65]   TNA C8/242/13, deposition of Mary Palmer.

[66]   TNA C8/242/13; C6/252/9, depositions of Mary Palmer.

Conclusion: Questions of Taste

Reconstructing not only where different sorts of people ate and drank but also how and with whom they consumed is essential to understanding how eating and drinking shaped, and was shaped by, social identities and relationships in early modern England. This is in addition to the complicated political economy of the period and the myriad factors dictating choice and diet across the social spectrum. In all of these respects it is problematic to talk meaningfully about the 'popular culture' of food and drink, at least if this refers to a simple distinction between 'elite' and 'popular' values and practices.[67] Rather eating and drinking were as socially and culturally messy as society itself; the product, first and foremost, of complex economics, quotidian habits and the politics of the everyday. That is not to say that patterns and trends are not apparent; and hopefully this chapter has established not only the importance and complexity of the subject but also some of the salient features, both synchronic and diachronic, of the period. If nothing else it suggests there is plenty of research to be done.

This is never more than with the issue of popular tastes – a subject that has encouraged generalisations as ambitious and sweeping as the evidence is limited and methodologically difficult.[68] This is less the case in terms of taste understood as physical sensation and appetite. The popularisation of new commodities – such as beer, tobacco, tea and sugar – suggests that this was an era which saw the rise of the hoppy-, nicotine-, caffeine- and (most of all) sweet-tooth. The period also saw striking continuities – the perennial popularity of beef, wine and grain – as well as those discontinuities which can be inferred from the marked decline of the medieval spice trade.[69] More problematic is when a more sociological and cultural conception of taste is considered. On these terms, the two major claims for popular tastes in the early modern period involve a major continuity and a significant change. On the one hand is the apparent importance, in printed texts at least, of humoral medicine in determining the perceived qualities and effects of particular foods and drinks; begging the question to what extent was this printed discourse shared and assimilated by ordinary men and women?[70] On the other hand is the widespread assumption (implicit or explicit) that food and drink – and eating and drinking – was integral to what Norbert Elias styled the 'civilizing process' and the rise of French style.[71] In this narrative, 'popular' preferences and manners were increasingly rescinded by the upper and middling classes, who exchanged feasts, commonalty and trenchers for cuisine, politeness and the fork.[72] Such a story raises important questions about the relationship between English and European fashions and the role of food and drink in national identities.[73] It also oversimplifies the variegated and complicated culture of the

[67]   Peter Burke, *Popular Culture in Early Modern England* (Aldershot: Ashgate, 1978). For critiques see Robert Scribner, 'Is a History of Popular Culture Possible?', *History of European Ideas* 10 (1989), 175–91 and Roger Chartier, 'Texts, Printing, Readings', in Lynn Hunt ed., *The New Cultural History* (Berkeley and Los Angeles: University of California Press, 1989), pp. 169–71.

[68]   Jack Goody, *Cooking, Cuisine and Class* (Cambridge: Cambridge University Press, 1982), esp. ch. 4; Stephen Mennell, *All Manners of Food: Eating and Taste in England and France from the Middle Ages to the Present* (Oxford: Blackwell, 1996).

[69]   Paul H. Freedman, *Out of the East: Spices and the Medieval Imagination* (New Haven: Yale University Press, 2008).

[70]   Albala, *Eating Right in the Renaissance*; Allen Grieco, 'Food and Social Classes in Late Medieval and Renaissance Italy', in Flandrin and Montanari eds, *Food*, pp. 302–12; Muldrew, *Food*, pp. 32–45.

[71]   Norbert Elias, *The Civilizing Process: The History of Manners and State Formation and Civilization* (Oxford: Blackwell, 1994); Mennell, *All Manners of Food*.

[72]   Jean-Louis Flandrin, 'From Dietetics to Gastronomy: The Liberation of the Gourmet', in Flandrin and Montanari eds, *Food*, pp. 418–32.

[73]   Mennell, *All Manners of Food*.

'better sorts', and risks caricaturing and stereotyping quotidian habits and practices. This was a culture which knew, after all, when a herring 'was not well broiled'.

Select Bibliography

Albala, Ken, *Eating Right in the Renaissance*. Berkeley and Los Angeles: University of California Press, 2002.

Clark, Peter, *The English Alehouse: A Social History 1200–1830*. London: Longman, 1983.

Cowan, Brian, *The Social Life of Coffee: The Emergence of the British Coffeehouse*. New Haven: Yale University Press, 2005.

Flandrin, Jean-Louis, and Massimo Montanari eds, *Food: A Culinary History from Antiquity to the Present*. New York: Columbia University Press, 1996.

Freedman, Paul H., *Out of the East: Spices and the Medieval Imagination*. New Haven: Yale University Press, 2008.

Freedman, Paul H. ed., *Food: The History of Taste*. London: Thames & Hudson, 2009.

Goodman, Jordan, Paul E. Lovejoy and Andrew Sherratt eds, *Consuming Habits: Global and Historical Perspectives in How Cultures Define Drugs*. London: Routledge, 2007.

Goody, Jack, *Cooking, Cuisine and Class*. Cambridge: Cambridge University Press, 1982.

Griffiths, Emma, and Jane Whittle, *Consumption and Gender in the Early Seventeenth Century Household: The World of Alice Le Strange*. Oxford: Oxford University Press, 2012.

Mennell, Stephen, *All Manners of Food: Eating and Taste in England and France from the Middle Ages to the Present*. Oxford: Blackwell, 1996.

Mintz, Sidney W., *Sweetness and Power: The Place of Sugar in Modern History*. London: Penguin, 1986.

Montanari, Massimo, *Food Is Culture*. New York: Columbia University Press, 2004.

Muldrew, Craig, *Food, Energy and the Creation of Industriousness: Work and Material Culture in Agrarian England, 1550–1780*. Cambridge: Cambridge University Press, 2011.

Overton, Mark, *Agricultural Revolution in England: The Transformation of the Agrarian Economy 1500–1850*. Cambridge: Cambridge University Press, 1996.

Thirsk, Joan, *Food in Early Modern England: Phases, Fads, Fashions 1500–1760*. London: Continuum, 2007.

Tlusty, Ann, *Bacchus and Civic Order: The Culture of Drink in Early Modern Germany*. Virginia: University Press of Virginia, 2001.

Unger, Richard W., *Beer in the Middle Ages and the Renaissance*. Philadelphia: University of Pennsylvania Press, 2004.

Walter, John, and Roger Schofield eds, *Famine, Disease and the Social Order in Early Modern Society*. Cambridge: Cambridge University Press, 1989.

Withington, Phil, 'Company and Sociability in Early Modern England', *Social History* 32:3 (2007), 291–307.

Withington, Phil, 'Intoxicants and the Early Modern City', in Steve Hindle, Alex Shepard and John Walter eds, *Remaking English Society*. Woodbridge: Boydell and Brewer, 2013, pp. 135–63.

Wrightson, Keith, 'Alehouses, Order and Reformation in Rural England, 1590–1660', in Eileen Yeo and Stephen Yeo eds, *Popular Culture and Class Conflict 1590–1914: Explorations in the History of Labour and Leisure*. Brighton: Branch Line, 1981, pp. 1–23.

Work

Mark Netzloff

Labour History and Early Modern Studies

In 1696, Gregory King compiled the first statistical analysis of the population of England. Dividing the nation according to a hierarchical list of titles and occupations, he provided estimates of the number, income and expenses of each group. As reflected in King's analysis, early modern culture was inevitably centred on *popular* culture in the sense of an emerging concern with the productive capabilities of the population itself. A discussion of the early modern period's attitudes towards work is especially pertinent because it was in this era that figures like King began to conceptualise what we would now term as the labour theory of value. As King calculated, the nation's power was contingent on the productive work of its population. 'Work' was therefore not solely confined to the actual labour of specific social groups. Even those elite segments that by definition did not engage in manual labour – temporal lords, knights and gentlemen – were included in the chart as contributing to the 'work' of the nation.[1]

King's chart offers a vivid example of the central place of labour in early modern English culture. As Tom Rutter has insightfully argued, one of the distinctive aspects of the early modern idea of work is that this category began to take on a more encompassing and theoretical aspect: it thereby represented not only one's actual work but also served as a model – of 'vocation' – that included all forms of social labour.[2] Drawing on Rutter's observation, this essay will similarly expand the purview of work so as to address the varied forms of early modern labour. While some of the analysis will be devoted to expected figures and groups, such as urban artisanal workers, servants and apprentices, it will also be extended to include two often overlooked labour contexts that contributed significantly to changing nations of work in the period: labourers in the countryside, where the disruptive effects of capitalism first appeared, and labourers in England's new colonies, which emerged as an extension of the crises of labour affecting the nation.

In addition, the essay will complicate the association of labour with class and status through an analysis of the intellectual labour of increasingly professionalised writers. The status of literary work was often contingent on its differentiation from the dominant

---

[1] King's chart is reproduced in Peter Laslett, *The World We Have Lost* (New York: Charles Scribner's Sons, 1965), pp. 32–3.

[2] Tom Rutter, *Work and Play on the Shakespearean Stage* (Cambridge: Cambridge University Press, 2008), p. 3.

artisanal model of urban labour. The fact that many forms of productive labour are seldom thought of as 'work' reflects some of the abiding legacies of this period, which witnessed an unprecedented separation of labour from capital, a process that had devastating effects on the social position of labourers in early modern society. King's chart gives shape to the logic of capital by dividing the population into 'productive' and 'unproductive' groups, responsible for either 'increasing the wealth of the kingdom' or 'decreasing the wealth of the kingdom'. His calculations conclude with the stunning pronouncement that 2,825,000 people, or 51 per cent of a population of 5.5 million, did not contribute to the common wealth of the nation. While the model of work as vocation offered a means for membership in a national community, this paradigm was at the same time one of exclusion, witnessed by the fact that King's list of unproductive labour encompasses not only the destitute poor (cottagers and paupers, gypsies and vagrants) but also day labourers, servants, mariners and soldiers. The unprecedented capital expansion of this period was predicated by more rigidly defined forms of exclusion; and for many labouring groups, the inability to gain access to capital and the erosion of many of their customary rights and protections were interconnected parts of the same process.

Even the most conservative historical assessments have emphasised the declining position of labourers and the poor in the early modern era. Given the place of the sixteenth century as a pivotal stage in the early history of capitalism, the overarching and structural erosion of the rights and protections of labour illustrates the forms of displacement attendant to an era of capital expansion. As Marxist economic historians such as Robert Brenner and Ellen Wood have recognised, critical attention to commercial expansion alone has often overlooked the class conflicts and material conditions that made possible any production of surplus.[3] The early modern period witnessed an ongoing crisis of labour. Although statistical estimates have been a matter of dispute, real wages fell by at least 28 per cent over the course of the sixteenth century, and may have declined by more than 50 per cent according to some accounts.[4] At the same time, demographic changes in population exacerbated problems of unemployment and scarcity of resources: 20 per cent of labourers comprised a surplus labour pool, a number which swelled to 50 per cent unemployment in times of crisis.[5] As I will discuss later, problems of overpopulation and unemployment were motivating factors for colonial projects, which thought of new markets not only as ways to revitalise English industries, especially the cloth trade, but also as outlets for exporting surplus labourers.

Given the labour problems that pervaded the early modern period, it is striking that the topic has garnered relatively little critical attention. Some of the groundbreaking studies of the topic date from the early twentieth century, as represented by the work of R.H. Tawney and L.C. Knights, among others.[6] Significantly, this earlier criticism was avowedly Marxist, both in methodology and in terms of the political sympathies of this generation of socialist and progressive intellectuals. One reason for the subsequent neglect of the topic was the correlation of labour history with Marxist criticism, which suffered a backlash in post-war Anglo-American academia. Eric Kerridge, for instance, began his study of the early modern

---

[3]   See especially Robert Brenner, 'The Origins of Capitalist Development: A Critique of Neo-Smithian Marxism', *New Left Review* 104 (July–August 1977), 25–92 and Ellen Meiksins Wood, *The Origin of Capitalism* (New York: Monthly Review Press, 1999).

[4]   Steve Rappaport, *Worlds within Worlds: Structures of Life in Sixteenth-Century London* (Cambridge: Cambridge University Press, 1989), pp. 150–51.

[5]   E.A. Wrigley and R.S. Schofield, *The Population History of England, 1541–1871: A Reconstruction* (Cambridge: Cambridge University Press, 1981), pp. 531–2.

[6]   R.H. Tawney, *The Agrarian Problem in the Sixteenth Century* (London: Longmans, Green and Company, 1912); L.C. Knights, *Drama and Society in the Age of Jonson* (London: Chatto & Windus, 1937).

agrarian economy, published in 1969, by dismissing Tawney's earlier study of the very same topic due to its 'harmful prejudice' against capitalism.[7]

Historical discussions of early modern labour inevitably evoke the question of whether occupational status entailed a kind of class identity. Social historians have generally resisted addressing class as a concept relevant for the early modern period. This approach argues that 'class' as we know it was solely a product of the industrial revolution, and that it is only after this point, with the creation of a landless population of wage labourers in the factory system, in which broader class categories such as that of a 'working class' began to emerge. Peter Laslett, for example, asserts that early modern England was a 'one-class system' because economic production was generally limited to the household: due to the immediacy and quasi-familial setting of labour, work denoted not so much status as function. As a result, early moderns did not think of themselves 'in terms of classes that rise, conflict and fall'.[8] Laslett's model does helpfully orient discussions of labour to the domestic setting of economic production. And while feminists have critiqued Laslett's argument, one should note that he is far from nostalgic about the social formation of domestic labour that preceded industrialisation.[9] Indeed, in recent years materialist feminist critics have expanded on aspects of Laslett's discussion, and some of the richest analyses of early modern work are those specifically dealing with domestic labour.[10]

Other social historians of Laslett's generation similarly focused their analysis on 'status' groups rather than classes. Status, seen as a more neutral and descriptive term, was thereby opposed to 'class' with its associations with Marxist histories of labour. Influenced by Max Weber, these social historians turned to status as a category through which to better understand social connections and community identifications that did not always correlate with economic position in a deterministic manner.[11] Despite the positive effects of this revisionist project, there were some key limitations to this analysis. As seen in the work of Lawrence Stone, discussions of 'status groups' were often limited to elite segments of the population.[12] While the focus on gentry and aristocratic subjects and their jockeying for social position provided a fine case study of status-based identities, it was less successful in analysing the relation of these elite populations to economic production. But as more recent criticism has addressed, even elite groups that by definition did not 'work' nonetheless served an important role in the economic developments of the period. In terms of the agrarian roots of English capitalism, it is now generally recognised that the traditional landowning class embraced these changes as much as their socially mobile tenants. In the

---

[7] Eric Kerridge, *Agrarian Problems in the Sixteenth Century and After* (London: Allen and Unwin, 1969), p. 15.

[8] Laslett, *The World We Have Lost*, p. 37.

[9] Ibid., p. 3. For a critique of Laslett, see Nancy Armstrong and Leonard Tennenhouse, 'Family History', in *The Imaginary Puritan: Literature, Intellectual Labor, and the Origins of Personal Life* (Berkeley and Los Angeles: University of California Press, 1992), pp. 69–88.

[10] Among other recent sources, see Natasha Korda, *Shakespeare's Domestic Economies* (Philadelphia: University of Pennsylvania Press, 2002) and Wendy Wall, *Staging Domesticity: Household Work and English Identity in Early Modern Drama* (Cambridge: Cambridge University Press, 2002).

[11] Max Weber, *Economy and Society: An Outline of Interpretive Sociology*, ed. Guenther Roth and Claus Wittich (New York: Bedminster, 1968), pp. 302–7. Among discussions of the advantages of classifications of 'status' over 'class', see Lawrence Stone, 'Social Mobility in England, 1500–1700', *Past and Present* 33 (1966), 16–55; Alan Everitt, 'Social Mobility in Early Modern England', *Past and Present* 33 (1966), 56–73; and Jonathan Barry, 'Introduction' to Jonathan Barry and Christopher Brooks eds, *The Middling Sort of People: Culture, Society and Politics in England, 1550–1800* (Basingstoke: Palgrave, 1994), pp. 1–27.

[12] Armstrong and Tennenhouse, 'Family History', p. 75.

context of colonialism, elite investors formed a core constituency in joint-stock companies.[13] Many of the colonial projects of this era bore this imprint in terms of their efforts to model colonial society on feudal hierarchies that were increasingly under threat in England.[14]

The work of revisionist social historians from the 1960s through the 1980s had a profound influence on the comparable neglect of labour history in New Historicist literary studies from the 1980s and 1990s, many of which similarly disavowed the intellectual legacies of Marxism. Stephen Greenblatt, for instance, implied that Marxist theory was somehow programmatic in form, an orthodoxy that limited analysis.[15] David Scott Kastan set a critical precedent by arguing that 'the language of class relations applied to the social formation of early modern England is an anachronism'.[16] Just as Kastan grounded his observation with reference to the earlier work of social historians, subsequent literary studies have often cited Kastan in similarly dismissing the relevance of class.[17] However, in his original comment Kastan actually complicates this rejection of class by acknowledging that the early modern period nonetheless showed power dynamics that produced comparable effects *as* class.[18] These social historians and literary critics preferred status to class because it offered a vocabulary for analysing questions of power, patronage and social mobility without necessary reference to labour and economic production. It is no coincidence that so much New Historicist criticism of this earlier generation focused on the court as a privileged site of literary production, for example, rather than texts produced in the context of civic or artisanal communities.

But another problem with this dismissal of class is that it loses sight of how class operates most powerfully and immediately in terms of the impact of economic forces on the consciousness and self-identification of individual subjects. This is also the most elusive register for class, due to the ubiquitous failure of subjects to recognise the shaping effects of labour and economic production. But, to draw on the phrasing of E.P. Thompson, identifying instances of 'class struggle' in the early modern period is not predicated on a stable, monolithic and anachronistically modern sense of class consciousness.[19] One of the most influential critical frameworks applied to early modern forms of 'class struggle' has been Mikhail Bakhtin's theory of the carnivalesque.[20] A particularly valuable aspect of this model is that it provides a heuristic category for focusing specifically on manifestations of popular culture in the period. Nonetheless, the carnivalesque is often relegated to a marginal position: as a licensed festive period that effectively contains social discontent, for instance, or as an anarchic principle that rarely effects social change through protest.[21] The efforts

---

13   On elite investors in colonial projects, see Theodore K. Rabb, *Enterprise and Empire: Merchant and Gentry Investment in the Expansion of England* (Cambridge, MA: Harvard University Press, 1967) and Robert Brenner, *Merchants and Revolution: Commercial Change, Political Conflict, and London's Overseas Traders, 1550–1653* (Princeton: Princeton University Press, 1993).

14   On colonial feudalism, see Mark Netzloff, 'Writing Britain from the Margins: Scottish, Welsh, and Irish Projects for American Colonization', *Prose Studies* 25 (2002), 1–24.

15   Stephen Greenblatt, 'Towards a Poetics of Culture', in *Learning to Curse: Essays in Early Modern Culture* (New York: Routledge, 1990), p. 147.

16   David Scott Kastan, *Shakespeare after Theory* (New York: Routledge, 1999), p. 149.

17   See, for example, Ronda Arab, *Manly Mechanicals on the Early Modern Stage* (Selinsgrove, PA: Susquehanna University Press, 2011), p. 20.

18   Kastan, *Shakespeare after Theory*, p. 150.

19   E.P. Thompson, 'Eighteenth-Century English Society: Class Struggle without Class?', *Social History* 3 (1978), 133–65.

20   Mikhail Bakhtin, *Rabelais and His World* (Bloomington, IN: Indiana University Press, 1984).

21   As Michelle O'Callaghan notes, viewing the carnivalesque solely as part of 'plebeian' culture also deflects attention away from the extent to which 'popular' culture traverses the boundaries of elite and subordinate social groups. '"Thomas the Scholar" versus "John the Sculler": Defining Popular Culture in the Early Seventeenth Century', in Matthew Dimmock and Andrew Hadfield eds, *Literature and Popular Culture in Early Modern England* (Farnham: Ashgate, 2009), p. 50. Peter Burke's canonical

of subordinate classes to articulate political grievances is therefore cast solely as a mode of disorder or social inversion, rather than a desperate – and at times effective – means for combating political neglect and economic deprivation.

Another context in which forms of class protest and critique have been underanalysed is in the work of social historians on early modern London. Despite the value of this impressive body of criticism, these studies have overstated the case for the seemingly remarkable stability of the city due to the rarity of wide-scale protests throughout the period.[22] What is overlooked, however, is the extent to which these political disturbances stemmed from underlying economic causes. As E.P. Thompson argued in reference to the 'moral economy' of popular uprisings, these collective efforts, however unruly in form, were provoked by specific unaddressed grievances, including dearth, lack of poor relief and the unequal effects of free trade.[23] Thompson's work on the time-discipline imposed by capitalist production provides another useful framework for analysing the relation of the carnivalesque to changing models of work.[24] The increasingly draconian work-regime mandated under such measures as the Statute of Artificers, which will be discussed shortly, rendered any non-productive activity as transgressive: festivity was therefore no longer a culturally sanctioned occasion but instead a subversive threat to the order of the disciplinary society that began to emerge in the period, one that Foucault has analysed as grounded in a correlation of docile productive workers with increasing profitability.[25]

Urban Labour

Discussions of labour in early modern England often limit their attention to the urban environment of London. For social historians, this focus is not particularly surprising, given the rapid growth of London from a small city of 50,000 at the beginning of the Tudor dynasty to a sprawling metropolis of 120,000 in 1603.[26] The most rapid expansion took place in the second half of the sixteenth century, when London's population increased from 70,000 to 150,000.[27] This period of intense urbanisation is also of central interest to literary historians, particularly those analysing the emergence of the public theatre in this period. One effect of the growth of market relations in urban London was a consequent degree of social mobility, albeit mostly among landed and mercantile elites. As Holinshed noted, merchants 'often change estate with gentlemen, as gentlemen do with them, by mutuall conversion of the one into the other'.[28]

Because many studies have concentrated solely on elite segments of urban society, other forms of urban labour have been comparatively neglected. Bruce Robbins's analysis of the role of the serving class in Victorian England set a precedent for a number of recent studies

---

analysis of popular culture similarly recognised the 'two-way traffic' between 'great' and 'little' traditions. *Popular Culture in Early Modern Europe* (1978; Farnham: Ashgate, 2009), p. 50 and *passim*.

[22] Ian Archer, *The Pursuit of Stability: Social Relations in Elizabethan London* (Cambridge: Cambridge University Press, 1991), pp. 9, 11; Rappaport, *Worlds within Worlds*, pp. 8, 19.

[23] E.P. Thompson, 'The Moral Economy of the English Crowd in the Eighteenth Century', *Past and Present* 50 (1971), 76–136.

[24] E.P. Thompson, 'Time, Work-Discipline, and Industrial Capitalism', *Past and Present* 38 (1967), 56–97.

[25] Michel Foucault, *Discipline and Punish: The Birth of the Prison* (New York: Knopf Doubleday, 1979), pp. 25, 206, 219–21.

[26] Rappaport, *Worlds within Worlds*, p. 61.

[27] Ibid., p. 64.

[28] Raphael Holinshed, *The Chronicles of England, Scotland, and Ireland* (London, 1587), p. 163.

of servants in early modern culture.[29] Servants were a given feature of domestic work, comprising part of an estimated 29 per cent of households in the period.[30] As David Evett has argued, relations of service were a prominent fixture in early modern culture due to the fact that most individuals served as a master or servant at some point in their lives.[31] Many servants – between one-quarter to one-third of the total – were born into the gentry, and their placement in extra-familial households served to cement family alliances and pave the way for future patronage and advancement.[32] Servants were typically young, with around 60 per cent of subjects between the ages of 18 to 24 placed in household service.[33] There were nonetheless some important changes affecting the profile of servants in this period. Servants were increasingly likely to be younger and female, with their placement in service stemming more from economic necessity than familial alliance or social advancement. Their terms of service tended to be shorter and more likely based on contractual bond. The rise of 'free labour' in the servant market, in other words, also rendered their position more acutely vulnerable.[34]

The role of servants reinforces Peter Laslett's emphasis on the domestic setting of much economic production in the period. Servants were often linked with apprentices as domestic dependants in households. Apprentices comprised more than 10 per cent of London's population in this period, forming 'the largest and certainly the least privileged of the livery companies' social groups'.[35] Apprenticeship served as the linchpin for the urban artisanal economy, providing the structured path for the training and recruitment into membership of London's classes of 'citizens'.[36] The number of apprentices increased along with London's overall growth in the period, rising by 27 per cent to reach an overall population of around 15,000 apprentices in the city.[37] As a result, this group suffered the same problems of economic displacement and underemployment as the rest of the population, with an estimated 60 per cent of apprentices not fully employed during the crisis years of the 1590s.[38] Journeymen artisans formed another large constituency in the urban economy. Workers who were officially members of a livery company following the completion of their apprenticeships, journeymen were defined as those who did not possess sufficient capital to set up their own shop.[39] Their prominence revealed some of the paradoxes of early modern free labour: even as workers could increasingly take on a trade other than the craft in which they were apprenticed, this was a mobility often based on necessity as they were relegated to a position of wage labour in the service of others.

As John Michael Archer has shown in his recent work, the category of the 'citizen' offers a productive framework for analysing the workings of class in early modern London.[40] A

---

[29]   Bruce Robbins, *The Servant's Hand: English Fiction from Below* (New York: Columbia University Press, 1986). Among recent studies of early modern servants, see Mark Thornton Burnett, *Masters and Servants in English Renaissance Drama and Culture: Authority and Obedience* (New York: St Martin's Press, 1997); David Evett, *Discourses of Service in Shakespeare's England* (New York: Palgrave, 2005); Judith Weil, *Service and Dependency in Shakespeare's Plays* (Cambridge: Cambridge University Press, 2005).

[30]   Burnett, *Masters and Servants*, p. 1.

[31]   Evett, *Discourses of Service*, p. 22.

[32]   Keith Wrightson, *English Society, 1580–1680* (London: Routledge, 1990), p. 12.

[33]   Ann Kussmaul, *Servants in Husbandry in Early Modern England* (Cambridge: Cambridge University Press, 1981), p. 3.

[34]   Evett, *Discourses of Service*, p. 22; Weil, *Service and Dependency*, pp. 12–13.

[35]   Rappaport, *Worlds within Worlds*, p. 232.

[36]   One-eighth of apprentices hailed from families of gentry rank, reflecting the porous boundaries between landed and mercantile wealth. Wrightson, *English Society*, p. 12.

[37]   Rappaport, *Worlds within Worlds*, pp. 11, 109.

[38]   Burnett, *Masters and Servants*, p. 16; Rappaport, *Worlds within Worlds*, p. 311.

[39]   Burnett, *Masters and Servants*, p. 54.

[40]   John Michael Archer, *Citizen Shakespeare: Freemen and Aliens in the Language of the Plays* (New York: Palgrave, 2005).

citizen was narrowly defined as someone who had completed the terms of apprenticeship, thereby becoming 'free' through membership in one of the city's traditional livery companies. Citizens comprised one of the chief constituencies of an early modern 'middling sort'. In Sir Thomas Smith's fourfold classification of English society, they formed a third category, below gentlemen and the gentry but above 'the fourth sort of men which do not rule'. Smith defined this latter group as a '*proletarii*' comprised of 'day labourers, poor husbandmen, yea merchants or retailers which have no free land, copyholders, and all artificers'. These propertyless masses, Smith concludes, 'have no voice nor authority in our commonwealth and no account is made of them, but only to be ruled and not to rule other'.[41] Smith's comment reflects the period's increasing separation of capital from labour: after all, relegation to the fourth class stemmed not from one's occupation but instead lack of property or wealth valued at 40 shillings. The precarious status of apprentices and journeymen additionally reveals the underside of the period's apparent social mobility, illustrating the ease with which the middling sort could join the ranks of the underclass. The numbers of this fourth sort swelled over the course of the seventeenth century: in Gregory King's enumeration of the nation's social groups in 1688, he estimated the number of 'labouring people and out servants' at 1,275,000; the second largest group (after rural cottagers and paupers), they comprised over 23 per cent of the entire population.[42]

In response to the instabilities of the nation's labour market, the English state began to assert its authority by mandating standard terms for service and wages. In doing so, they seized control over an economic sphere of production that traditionally had been delegated to civic institutions and individual householders. The most important development in this regard came with the passage of the Statute of Artificers (1563), a set of regulations that remained in place for 250 years.[43] The Statute of Artificers possessed such an abiding legacy because it successfully drew together and codified a disparate set of labour laws dating back to the mid-fourteenth-century Statute of Labourers. One of its chief innovations was that it enacted a centralised state control over the labour market and assumed some of the powers previously allotted to urban guilds and livery companies.[44] The reach of the Statute was nearly universal, as it affected all those between the ages of 12 to 60 who possessed property worth less than £40 and placed them collectively under forms of service. The terms mandated by the Statute reflect the generally conservative position of the English state, which attempted to mitigate the most disruptive forms of social change. The Statute therefore limited the mobility of labour, stipulating that all bonds of service must be at least four years in duration. It also levied heavy penalties for servants leaving their masters, who were to be imprisoned, 'whipped and used as a vagabunde'.[45] Similar penalties were exacted for day labourers, with any who left employment before finishing contracted work subjected to a month's imprisonment and fined the exorbitant amount of £4. Given these terms, it is only fitting that the Statute has been characterised as 'the most powerful instrument devised for degrading and impoverishing the English labourer'.[46]

---

[41] Sir Thomas Smith, *De Republica Anglorum*, ed. Mary Dewar (Cambridge: Cambridge University Press, 1982), p. 76. Smith does allot minor functions to this group, however, conceding that they could serve as jurors or church wardens.

[42] Gregory King, cited in Laslett, *The World We Have Lost*, pp. 32–3.

[43] Joan Lane, *Apprenticeship in England, 1600–1914* (London: UCL Press, 1996), p. 2; also see M.G. Davies, *The Enforcement of English Apprenticeship: A Study in Applied Mercantilism, 1563–1642* (Cambridge, MA: Harvard University Press, 1956).

[44] Lane, *Apprenticeship in England*, p. 3.

[45] *Statute of Artificers* (1563), in R.H. Tawney and Eileen Power eds, *Tudor Economic Documents* (London: Longmans, Green, 1924), vol. 1, p. 341.

[46] Quoted in Maurice Dodd, *Studies in the Development of Capitalism* (New York: International Publishers, 1947), p. 233.

One of the paradoxes of the Statute of Artificers is that in criminalising the mobility of labour, it inadvertently brought about the very conditions it attempted to forestall: because any labourer who left service or travelled to find work was placed among a criminal class of vagabonds, the number of vagrants skyrocketed as more workers were potentially subsumed under its jurisdiction; ironically, rather than keeping workers in their place, the statute turned them (in legal terms) into vagrants. Historians have often argued that the fear of vagrancy was overstated in early modern culture by pointing to the relatively small statistical size of this group.[47] But the cultural implications of vagrancy extended beyond a mere demographic base. The threat of vagrancy was that it reflected a general breakdown of a social order grounded on a hierarchical classification of work. As Richard Halpern insightfully argued, in their ability 'to mimic the quality of capital itself' through their ceaseless circulation and breakdown of traditional feudal boundaries, vagrants served as a 'nightmarishly exaggerated image of *modernity*'.[48] Contemporaries similarly thought of vagrancy as a new threat that reflected profound transformations to society. William Harrison's *Description of England* not only estimated a large population – 10,000 – but also saw vagrancy as a recent development that marked a break from a more tranquil past: 'It is not yet full threescore years since this trade began.'[49]

Vagrants additionally gained a prominence belied by their numbers due to the extent to which they generated numerous textual images, particularly in the popular genre of 'cony-catching' pamphlets. Linda Woodbridge has traced how this literary genre helped to shape cultural attitudes to the poor, perpetuating stereotypes of vagrants as a well-organised criminal class with distinct cultural mores and possessing a secretive 'cant' language.[50] The evidence found in early modern court records actively counters any argument imputing a professionalisation of crime or distinct subculture of vagrants in the period; most of those prosecuted for vagrancy were in fact merely isolated, displaced individuals travelling to mete out some form of survival. But the genre did facilitate the professionalisation of *writing*: authors such as Robert Greene and Thomas Dekker established their own careers through a pamphlet literature that offered an ambivalent, comic assessment of the social effects of the increasing urbanisation of London. The criminal games described in these texts depend upon an environment of anonymity and nearly animalistic competitive market relations. Moreover, as seen in a text like Dekker's *Lantern and Candlelight*, the erosion of old social codes and class hierarchies was linked to the blurring of boundaries of country and city, signalled by the disruptive effects of socially and geographically mobile vagrants.[51]

---

[47]   Steve Rappaport offers the lowest figure, estimating that vagrants represented less than one-fifth of 1 per cent of the general population. *Worlds within Worlds*, p. 5. In the fullest account of early modern vagrancy, A.L. Beier gives a more reliable figure of 16,000–20,000 across the nation. *Masterless Men: The Vagrancy Problem in England, 1560–1640* (London: Methuen, 1985), p. 15. Beier's estimates are close to those of early modern observers such as William Harrison.

[48]   Richard Halpern, *The Poetics of Primitive Accumulation: English Renaissance Culture and the Genealogy of Capital* (Ithaca: Cornell University Press, 1991), p. 74, emphasis in original.

[49]   William Harrison, *The Description of England* (1577), ed. Georges Edelen (Washington, DC: Dover, 1968), pp. 183–4.

[50]   Linda Woodbridge, *Vagrancy, Homelessness, and English Renaissance Literature* (Urbana: University of Illinois Press, 2001).

[51]   Thomas Dekker, *Lantern and Candlelight* (1608), ed. Viviana Comensoli (Toronto: Publications of the Barnabe Riche Society, 2007).

Rural Labour and Agrarian Capitalism

Exclusive attention to London has obscured the interrelations between the metropolis and other provincial commercial hubs and market towns throughout England. The labour market was one of the chief conduits that connected London with other regions, as the city's growth was fuelled by migration from the rest of the country, with an estimated 3,750 migrants arriving each year, mostly from distant and rural areas of England.[52] The travel of migrants to London was driven not only by new venues of opportunity in the rapidly expanding city but also by the deteriorating status of labourers in the English countryside.[53] Early modern forms of capital formation were not based solely in the expanding markets of London but rather had their foundations in structural changes to the agrarian economy.

Early modern England has often served as a case study for analysing the early, formative stages of capitalist development in the period. This tradition dates back to Marx's closing section from the first volume of *Capital* on 'the primitive accumulation of capital'.[54] Marx located capital formation in terms of changing relations of landownership, tenure, economic production and labour in the English countryside. The early modern period therefore served as a transitional period, a time of increased profitability and capital extraction predicated by a process of social stratification and displacement that created the conditions for mass industrialisation in the following two centuries. As Robert Brenner has argued, 'It was indeed, ... an agricultural revolution, based on the emergence of capitalist class relations in the countryside, which made it possible for England to become the first nation to experience industrialization.'[55]

The vast majority of tenants (around 80 per cent) possessed their lands through customary tenure.[56] But the protections allotted through customary tenure were progressively weakened over the course of the period. Landlords could increasingly raise rents, increase entry fines when land was transferred or inherited, alter boundaries through new surveys and even challenge tenants' title to the land itself. As a result, half of customary tenants, or roughly 40 per cent of those working the land, lacked security over tenure and were vulnerable to eviction.[57] It is telling that roughly the same percentage of the rural population (40 per cent) was displaced from agriculture and moved into manufacturing industries by the end of the seventeenth century.[58] Agricultural work became increasingly unsustainable for smallholding tenants, with wages for agrarian labourers declining by 50 per cent from 1450 to 1600.[59] At the same time, agriculture became a much more profitable enterprise for a class of capitalist tenants and large landowners, with the prices for agricultural goods rising by 600 per cent over the period.[60]

---

[52] Rappaport, *Worlds within Worlds*, pp. 76, 77, 81.

[53] London also drew elite and more prosperous migrants: more than 90 per cent of London merchants and 75 per cent of Lord Mayors were born outside of the city. Wrightson, *English Society*, p. 12.

[54] Karl Marx, *Capital: A Critique of Political Economy, Volume One*, trans. Ben Fowkes (Harmondsworth: Penguin, 1976), pp. 873–913.

[55] Robert Brenner, 'Agrarian Class Structure and Economic Development in Pre-Industrial Europe', in T.H. Aston and C.H.E. Philpin eds, *The Brenner Debate: Agrarian Class Structure and Economic Development in Pre-Industrial Europe* (Cambridge: Cambridge University Press, 1985), p. 54.

[56] John E. Martin, *Feudalism to Capitalism: Peasant and Landlord in English Agrarian Development* (London: Macmillan, 1983), p. 128.

[57] Ibid., p. 128.

[58] Brenner, 'Agrarian Class Structure', p. 52.

[59] See Richard Lachmann, *Capitalists in Spite of Themselves: Elite Conflict and Economic Transitions in Early Modern Europe* (Oxford: Oxford University Press, 2000), p. 191; Stephen Bending and Andrew McRae eds, *The Writing of Rural England 1500–1800* (New York: Palgrave, 2003), p. xvi.

[60] Martin, *Feudalism to Capitalism*, p. 131.

The early modern era witnessed a separation of labour from capital in the English countryside. Practices of enclosure, of converting arable land worked by tenants into enclosed pasture, served to depopulate the countryside and ensure that the most profitable holdings were the lands requiring the least amount of productive labour. Enclosure was not unique to the period, but it did occur most rapidly at this time, with nearly half (47.6 per cent) of the land enclosed after the Reformation transferred in the seventeenth century.[61] Although enclosure was the most visible marker of the changes affecting the English countryside, there were other developments that further eroded the rights traditionally held by customary tenants. In particular, the legal protections allotted tenants were increasingly undermined: because copyhold tenure was secured through entry in the legal records of individual manors, these manors began to assert their autonomy from rival authorities such as clerical courts and royal judges. Some landlords even began to boycott their own manorial courts, leaving tenants with no legal recourse for appealing changes to tenure.[62] These policies facilitated a massive concentration of wealth: by the end of the seventeenth century, English landlords controlled 70–75 per cent of cultivated land in England.[63] The process accelerated even further in the eighteenth century, with half of cultivated land owned by 5,000 families and one-quarter of all land in the possession of only 400 families.[64]

This monopoly over landownership was accomplished through an erosion of the rights and protections of customary tenants, who were consequently driven into market-based leases.[65] These changes effectively split the population of rural labourers and pitted their interests against one another: while a small number were able to expand their holdings and advance their social position, the vast majority were left susceptible to eviction and landlessness. John Norden's *The Surveyor's Dialogue* offers a vivid illustration of the social chasm that emerged among the population of smallholding tenants.[66] The text addresses a socially mobile audience of freeholding tenants, who are advised on ways to advance their position through adopting marked-based leases. Readers are also offered rudimentary instructions on techniques for land improvement as well as the increasingly professionalised and technical skills of surveying. In the text's dialogues, a tenant farmer initially resistant to these changes ultimately embraces technical and market-based innovations, even declaring an interest in becoming a surveyor himself and thereby moving from a traditional role of tenant to the mobile figure of the professionalised 'expert mediator'.[67]

The Work of Literary Professionalism

The emerging figure of the professional author exemplifies the increasing complexity of definitions of work in the early modern period. Many early modern writers steadfastly refused to see their writing in terms of 'work', instead presenting their literary pursuits as a leisurely activity conferred by their gentlemanly status. J.W. Saunders's influential

---

[61] Lachmann, *Capitalists in Spite of Themselves*, p. 174.

[62] Ibid., p. 173.

[63] Brenner, 'Agrarian Class Structure', p. 48.

[64] Raymond Williams, *The Country and the City* (New York: Oxford University Press, 1973), p. 60.

[65] Robert Brenner, 'Agrarian Roots of European Capitalism', in Aston and Philpin eds, *The Brenner Debate*, p. 214; 'Agrarian Class Structure', p. 47.

[66] *John Norden's* The Surveyor's Dialogue *(1618): A Critical Edition*, ed. Mark Netzloff (Farnham: Ashgate, 2010).

[67] This term is taken from Eric Ash, *Power, Knowledge, and Expertise in Early Modern England* (Baltimore: Johns Hopkins University Press, 2004).

argument regarding the 'stigma of print' emphasised that many writers wrote for coterie circulation rather than publication, which was associated with the market activities of social inferiors, and were often forced to distance themselves from any works that did in fact make their way into print.[68] But while this model accounts for elite figures such as Sir Philip Sidney, it ignores the impact of writers emerging from socially mobile backgrounds of commercial and artisanal families. Richard Helgerson's analysis of early modern definitions of a literary career stressed not only the classical precedents that writers appropriated as 'self-crowned laureates' but also the ways that they increasingly accommodated themselves to market forces.[69]

As Laurie Ellinghausen has argued, literary writers emphasised their lack of place within traditional structures of labour, calling attention to the materiality of their work as well as their own social dislocation and economic dispossession.[70] George Gascoigne, often held to be the first 'professional' writer in early modern England, depicts the circuitous path leading to his own literary career in similar terms in the poem 'Gascoigne's Woodmanship'. Gascoigne presents himself in the traditional role of domestic retainer, as a 'woodman' (hunter) in domestic service to his aristocratic addressee.[71] Having missed hitting a doe, he uses his errant shot as the occasion for reflecting on his missed vocational opportunities as scholar, lawyer, courtier and soldier. His ultimate career path, as writer, takes shape only as a final option when all other paths have been blocked; it is, moreover, not a recognisable vocation but instead only a hypothetical possibility, which he represents at the poem's conclusion by imagining the writing of the poem itself as enacting a belated, imaginary success in which his aim is finally true.

As Gascoigne's poem reveals, literary work fit uneasily into available categories of labour, whether the artisanal work of civic livery companies or traditional professions such as law, the church or medicine. Several recent studies have examined literary writing in connection to artisanal labour and forms of knowledge.[72] However, as illustrated most memorably in Shakespeare's representation of Bottom and the 'rude mechanicals' of *A Midsummer Night's Dream*, the professionalism of literary writing was often established by distancing this work from its artisanal roots.[73] Nonetheless, the organisation of professional players into *companies* attests to how the civic structure for organising labour had an abiding influence on literary forms of work. Many playwrights came from livery backgrounds, such as John Webster, trained in the Merchant Taylors' Company.[74] Webster's social position reflects the extent to which company members increasingly practised trades other than the occupation in which they were raised and apprenticed.[75] The correlation of writers with emergent kinds of 'free labour' is reinforced in the form of the dramatic company itself, which bore more

---

[68]   J.W. Saunders, 'The Stigma of Print: A Note on the Social Bases of English Poetry', *Essays in Criticism* 1 (1951), 139–64.

[69]   Richard Helgerson, *Self-Crowned Laureates: Spenser, Jonson, Milton, and the Literary System* (Berkeley and Los Angeles: University of California Press, 1983). For an engaging discussion of responses to the literary marketplace, see Alexandra Halasz, *The Marketplace of Print: Pamphlets and the Public Sphere in Early Modern England* (Cambridge: Cambridge University Press, 1997).

[70]   Laurie Ellinghausen, *Labor and Writing in Early Modern England, 1567–1667* (Farnham: Ashgate, 2008), pp. 7–8.

[71]   George Gascoigne, 'Gascoigne's Woodmanship', in *The Complete Works of George Gascoigne*, volume 1, ed. John W. Cunliffe (Cambridge: Cambridge University Press, 1907), pp. 348–52.

[72]   Paul Yachnin, *Stage-Wrights: Shakespeare, Jonson, Middleton, and the Making of Theatrical Value* (Philadelphia: University of Pennsylvania, 1997); Henry S. Turner, *The English Renaissance Stage: Geometry, Poetics, and the Practical Spatial Arts 1580–1630* (Oxford: Oxford University Press, 2006).

[73]   Among other discussions of the rude mechanicals, see Annabel Patterson, 'Bottom's Up: Festive Theory in *A Midsummer Night's Dream*', *Renaissance Papers* (1988), 25–39.

[74]   Michelle Dowd, 'Shakespeare and Work', *Literature Compass* 7:3 (2010), 185–94 at p. 186.

[75]   Rappaport, *Worlds within Worlds*, p. 110.

resemblance to the innovative sharing of capital and risk of the joint-stock company than London's traditional liveries. Thomas Dekker's oft-cited reference to the theatre as 'your Poets Royal Exchange' not only locates theatrical work at the nexus of London's commercial life, a space where literary workers vie for the patronage of elite and popular audiences alike, but also correlates it with the Royal Exchange, one of the new sites built (in 1571) to facilitate international commerce.[76] The theatrical marketplace is thereby linked to 'the market' and the complex financial transactions of global capital.[77]

Colonial Labour

Over the past decade, several important critical studies have examined the interconnections between the commercial marketplace of the early modern theatre and England's increasing involvement in international networks of trade.[78] However, what has been relatively absent from these studies is attention to the effects of global trade on the condition of early modern labourers. Such elisions reproduce a modern, laissez view of 'the economy' as a free-standing set of institutions that operate according to an internal and self-organising logic. But Adam Smith's model of an 'invisible hand' directing economic affairs is a concept alien to the early modern period, a context in which labour and capital were not yet seen as antithetical social forces. As the economic historian Craig Muldrew has argued, borrowing on credit was an integral component of economic activity, one that was in fact employed by all classes. The period witnessed a movement away from informal credit mechanisms, founded on interpersonal trust and embedded in local social relations and obligations, leading to the dominance of an 'increasingly abstract, calculated, artificial credit of large-scale businesses' who were dependent on 'rationally determined future profitability' as well as 'the accumulated physical or monetary capital of an enterprise'.[79] The end result of this process was that capital no longer served a more limited role, as an instrument facilitating labour, but instead was increasingly separated from labour and achieved a newfound status as the end goal of economic exchange and central object of political economy.

'Free trade', in fact, was a contentious idea in the period, a minority opinion that was asserted against a number of customary and traditional protections.[80] Foundational to the emergence of global capital was the paradoxical dependence of 'free trade' on the expansion of unfree labour.[81] The national economy and foreign markets were inextricably connected in this process. The expansion of global trade and colonial settlement was fuelled by

---

[76] Thomas Dekker, *The Guls Hornbook and the Belman of London* (London, 1905), p. 47; for discussion of the Royal Exchange, see Mark Netzloff, *England's Internal Colonies: Class, Capital, and the Literature of Early Modern English Colonialism* (New York: Palgrave 2003), pp. 36–43.

[77] Among discussions, see especially Jean-Christophe Agnew, *Worlds Apart: The Market and the Theater in Anglo-American Thought, 1550–1750* (Cambridge: Cambridge University Press, 1986) and Douglas Bruster, *Drama and the Market in the Age of Shakespeare* (Cambridge: Cambridge University Press, 1992).

[78] Particularly noteworthy on this topic are Jonathan Gil Harris, *Sick Economies: Drama, Mercantilism and Disease in Shakespeare's England* (Philadelphia: University of Pennsylvania, 2004) and Jyotsna Singh ed., *A Companion to the Global Renaissance* (Oxford: Wiley-Blackwell 2009), esp. Daniel Vitkus, 'The New Globalism: Transcultural Commerce, Global Systems Theory, and Spenser's Mammon', pp. 31–49.

[79] Craig Muldrew, 'Interpreting the Market: The Ethics of Credit and Community Relations in Early Modern England', *Social History* 18 (1993), 163–83, at pp. 181, 182.

[80] Brenner analyses overseas traders as a political opposition in *Merchants and Revolution*.

[81] See Robert J. Steinfeld, *The Invention of Free Labour: The Employment Relation in English and American Law and Culture, 1350–1870* (Chapel Hill: University of North Carolina Press, 1991).

concerns over England's growing and restive underclass, with new colonial markets posited as a means for exporting the nation's surplus labour.[82] Moreover, in a domestic context, the erosion of the rights of labour that was effected in the colonies offered a precedent that, in a sense, returned home and was adopted as a solution for domestic crises of labour. One sees this development not only institutionally, with the spread of a workhouse economy in early modern England, but also in representational terms, as reflected in Jonson's reference to the workers of Bartholomew Fair as 'civil savages' populating an area likened to the 'Bermudas' and waiting to be discovered by a Columbus or Drake.[83]

In comparing Bartholomew Fair to Bermuda, Jonson is also invoking a more contemporary reference, one that would have resonated with his original audience: the recent history of a Virginia Company fleet that was shipwrecked on Bermuda while en route to the fledgling Virginia colony in 1610, an event that precipitated a notorious mutiny among the company's population of artisanal workers, who organised a months-long protest against their terms of service and the work conditions they (correctly) anticipated in the colonies. This protest is relevant for literary history due to the account written by William Strachey, a secretary to the Virginia Company, which was reworked in dramatic form in Shakespeare's *The Tempest* and influenced the depiction of the labour issues that pervade this play.[84] The Bermuda Mutiny reflects the extent to which colonial settings made manifest the grievances of labour that were increasingly being marginalised in domestic contexts. The central role of labour in early colonial projects also stemmed from necessity, as seen in the writings of Captain John Smith, who drew on the colony's need for skilled artisans in order to fashion a new ethos of colonial labour and husbandry.[85] The history of labour in early modern England was therefore crucially a global history as well. Colonies served not only as an outlet for England's excess labour but also as a transatlantic breeding ground that produced more radical reassessments of the place of labour. One of the tragic paradoxes of this history is the extent to which expressions of colonial liberty occurred alongside the codification of institutions of slavery.[86] These ambivalent legacies reinforce the importance of the history of labour in early modern England, a site of development of so many of the keywords that continue to shape our definitions of modernity.

Select Bibliography

Archer, Ian, *The Pursuit of Stability: Social Relations in Elizabethan London*. Cambridge: Cambridge University Press, 1991.

Archer, John Michael, *Citizen Shakespeare: Freemen and Aliens in the Language of the Plays*. New York: Palgrave, 2005.

Beier, A.L., *Masterless Men: The Vagrancy Problem in England, 1560–1640*. London: Methuen, 1985.

Brenner, Robert, 'The Origins of Capitalist Development: A Critique of Neo-Smithian Marxism', *New Left Review* 104 (July–August 1977), 25–92.

---

[82] On colonial transportation, see Netzloff, *England's Internal Colonies*, pp. 91–134.

[83] Jonson, *Bartholomew Fair*, ed. G.R. Hibbard (London, 1977), 3.4.31; 2.6.70; 5.6.36.

[84] On Strachey and the labour contexts of Shakespeare's play, see Netzloff, *England's Internal Colonies*, pp. 110–11, 116–22, and 127–34.

[85] Ibid., pp. 114–21.

[86] Among other accounts, see Theodore W. Allen, *The Invention of the White Race, Volume One: Racial Oppression and Social Control* (London: Verso, 1994) and *The Invention of the White Race, Volume Two: The Origin of Racial Oppression in Anglo-America* (London: Verso, 1997).

Brenner, Robert, 'Agrarian Class Structure and Economic Development in Pre-Industrial Europe', in T.H. Aston and C.H.E. Philpin eds, *The Brenner Debate: Agrarian Class Structure and Economic Development in Pre-Industrial Europe*. Cambridge: Cambridge University Press, 1985, pp. 10–63.

Brenner, Robert, 'Agrarian Roots of European Capitalism', in T.H. Aston and C.H.E. Philpin eds, *The Brenner Debate: Agrarian Class Structure and Economic Development in Pre-Industrial Europe*. Cambridge: Cambridge University Press, 1985, pp. 213–327.

Burnett, Mark Thornton, *Masters and Servants in English Renaissance Drama and Culture: Authority and Obedience*. New York: St Martin's Press, 1997.

Ellinghausen, Laurie, *Labour and Writing in Early Modern England, 1567–1667*. Farnham: Ashgate, 2008.

Kussmaul, Ann, *Servants in Husbandry in Early Modern England*. Cambridge: Cambridge University Press, 1981.

Lachmann, Richard, *Capitalists in Spite of Themselves: Elite Conflict and Economic Transitions in Early Modern Europe*. Oxford: Oxford University Press, 2000.

Laslett, Peter, *The World We Have Lost*. New York: Charles Scribner's Sons, 1965.

Martin, John E., *Feudalism to Capitalism: Peasant and Landlord in English Agrarian Development*. London: Macmillan, 1983.

Netzloff, Mark, *England's Internal Colonies: Class, Capital, and the Literature of Early Modern English Colonialism*. New York: Palgrave, 2003.

Rappaport, Steve, *Worlds within Worlds: Structures of Life in Sixteenth-Century London*. Cambridge: Cambridge University Press, 1989.

Rutter, Tom, *Work and Play on the Shakespearean Stage*. Cambridge: Cambridge University Press, 2008.

Steinfeld, Robert J., *The Invention of Free Labour: The Employment Relation in English and American Law and Culture, 1350–1870*. Chapel Hill: University of North Carolina Press, 1991.

Thompson, E.P., 'Time, Work-Discipline, and Industrial Capitalism', *Past and Present* 38 (1967), 56–97.

Thompson, E.P., 'The Moral Economy of the English Crowd in the Eighteenth Century', *Past and Present* 50 (1971), 76–136.

Thompson, E.P., 'Eighteenth-Century English Society: Class Struggle without Class?', *Social History* 3 (1978), 133–65.

Gendered Labour

Helen Smith

In an anonymous ballad, printed around 1660, a male speaker overhears the complaint of a housewife, who recounts scenes of daily drudgery, from cleaning and making a fire to preparing breakfast, lunch and dinner, caring for her children, knitting, spinning, sewing and washing (Figure 11.1).[1] Each stanza closes with a variation on the refrain, 'A womans work is never done', altered to most obviously comic effect in a stanza describing those conjugal labours 'which I cannot shun / Yet I could wish that Work were oftner done'. The ballad presents a model of marital femininity familiar to scholars of the period: the good housewife remains at home, constantly busy and focused on the needs of the family.

By turning to the evidence of ballads – 'one of the key components of popular culture',[2] and perhaps the form which does most to draw together the fields of practice, ritual, text and orality which Stuart Gillespie and Neil Rhodes identify as the competing domains of early modern popular literature – we can uncover a rich variety of attitudes towards women's labour. Some, including *A womans work*, detail domestic practices; others represent women's agricultural work; still more position women within the service and manufacturing trades of London. Brought into dialogue with the evidence of women's varied work commitments, these sources enrich our picture of women's participation in the formal and informal economies of early modern England, whilst drawing attention to the uneasy relationship between those kinds of women's work which formed the *subject* of popular texts and traditions, and those which went into the making and dissemination of the *objects* of popular culture.

Introducing the third edition of *Popular Culture in Early Modern Europe*, Peter Burke suggests that studies of women's popular culture 'are still relatively sparse (compared with studies of women's work, for instance)', an assertion that implicitly divides 'culture'

Thanks to members of the Edinburgh English Literature Seminar, and to participants in the workshop 'Women and the Popular in Early Modern England', held at the University of York, for their questions and observations on an earlier version of this chapter. Mark Jenner and Abigail Shinn offered invaluable comments and guidance.

[1]   *A womans work is never done* (London: John Andrews, [1660?]). Michelle Dowd notes that this ballad 'portrays women's daily tasks as diverse, time-consuming, and rigorous'. *Women's Work in Early Modern English Literature and Culture* (London: Palgrave Macmillan, 2009), p. 2; whilst its refrain forms a leitmotif for Natasha Korda, *Labors Lost: Women's Work and the Early Modern English Stage* (Philadelphia: University of Pennsylvania Press, 2011).

[2]   Matthew Dimmock and Andrew Hadfield, 'Introduction' to Matthew Dimmock and Andrew Hadfield eds, *Literature and Popular Culture in Early Modern England* (Aldershot: Ashgate, 2009), pp. 1–12, at p. 10. Stuart Gillespie and Neil Rhodes, 'Introduction' to Stuart Gillespie and Neil Rhodes eds, *Shakespeare and Elizabethan Popular Culture* (London: Arden Shakespeare, 2006), pp. 1–17 at pp. 7–10. On ballads, see also Patricia Fumerton and Anita Guerrini eds, *Ballads and Broadsides in Britain, 1500–1800* (Aldershot: Ashgate, 2010).

Figure 11.1   Anon., *A womans work is never done* (London: for John Andrews, 1660?). BL
Roxburghe 1.534–535.
© The British Library Board.

from 'work'.[3] This distinction reflects a critical tendency to see popular culture as a field
of consumption rather than production. Perhaps because of an enduring fascination with
'folk' or communal creation, scholarship on popular culture tends to ignore the labour that
went into making its objects, as well as the possibility that the workplace might itself be a
locus of identity formation and cultural expression.[4] In this chapter, I want both to suggest
the varied forms of allegiance and sociability which surrounded and structured women's
work, and to argue that popular depictions of women's work must be read in parallel
with an excavation of the sometimes effaced forms of gendered labour crucial to their own
production, circulation and reception.

---

[3]   Peter Burke, *Popular Culture in Early Modern Europe* (3rd ed., Aldershot: Ashgate, 2009), p. 2. See,
however, Pamela Allen Brown, *Better a Shrew than a Sheep: Women, Drama, and the Culture of Jest in Early
Modern England* (Ithaca, NY: Cornell University Press, 2003); Pamela Allen Brown and Peter Parolin
eds, *Women Players in England, 1500–1600: Beyond the All-Male Stage* (Aldershot: Ashgate, 2008); Bernard
Capp, *When Gossips Meet: Women, the Family and Neighbourhood in Early Modern England* (Oxford: Oxford
University Press, 2004); and Laura Gowing, *Domestic Dangers: Women, Words, and Sex in Early Modern
London* (Oxford: Oxford University Press, 1996) for a variety of approaches to women and the popular.

[4]   James R. Farr suggests that Dijonnaise artisans experienced 'a form of worker solidarity' in
'the growth of journeyman brotherhoods' which offered a culture and identity rooted in work. *Hands
of Honor: Artisans and Their World in Dijon, 1550–1650* (Ithaca, NY: Cornell University Press, 1988),
pp. 75, 63. Burke argues that the idea of the texts of popular culture as emerging, unauthored, from the
people, originated in the early nineteenth-century project to recover its artefacts. *Popular Culture*, p. 24.

Women's work was not only a frequent subject of popular culture, it was central to the production of that culture's objects and traditions, and can itself be viewed as a series of subcultures structured by sociability, allegiance and the experience of labour. Patrick Joyce insists upon the 'intimacy of the link between work and mentality', suggesting that 'much of what had seemed [to historians] to lie outside the purview of work was in truth an expression of the experience of work'. Though Joyce's focus is on northern, Victorian industrialism, his contentions that 'attitudes to work mutually reinforc[ed] attitudes in the life beyond work' and that 'the sense of neighbourhood community was permeated by the presence of the workplace' are pertinent to the study of early modern culture, particularly given the insecure distinction between workplace and home, forms of work and forms of leisure in this period.[5] Thomas Dekker's *The Shoemaker's Holiday*, first performed in 1599 and published in 1600, offers an instructive example, establishing the shoemakers as a lively subculture, possessed of a distinctive language and rituals; a form of London citizenship which, John Michael Archer suggests, was constituted as 'a working form of subjectivity, and a form of subjectivity that proceeded from the selective accreditation of work itself'.[6]

In *The Usurer's Daughter*, Lorna Hutson identifies women's housebound work as essential to humanist principles of 'husbandry', derived from Xenophon's *Oeconomicus*.[7] The clergyman Stephen Gosson, in his anti-theatrical *The schoole of abuse*, urged female readers: 'if there be peace in your houses, and plentie in your Coafers, let the good precept of *Xenophon* be your exercise'.[8] The ideal of husbandry positions the man as active in the socio-economic world, expending his energies to earn the substance which his wife at home, defined by her domestic setting, manages – and even increases – with thrift and care. As instructed by the Bible, arguably the most popular text of early modern England, and one whose contents circulated orally and proverbially as well as in textual and graphic forms, 'she looketh well to the ways of her household, and eateth not the bread of idleness' (Proverbs 31.27).

Images of women's textile work proliferated in ballad woodcuts but also in depictions of biblical scenes or abstract virtues. A carved alabaster overmantel at Burton Agnes Hall in Yorkshire depicts scenes of domestic drudgery, showing the wise virgins engaged in the tasks of sewing, spinning and laundry, whilst their foolish counterparts dance and play bagpipes (Figure 11.2). Scarcely an artefact of popular culture, the overmantel nonetheless suggests how women's work could be imbued with theological meaning, and the extent to which representations of female labour formed a distinctive and widespread genre. The carving possesses a vexed relationship to the realities of women's working lives; as Tara Hamling points out, this image, with its message that industrious workers would ascend to heaven at the final judgement, was 'an appropriate instruction on behalf of the master to the servants in his household', yet the literal elevation of this scene places it at some distance from the practical experience of domestic labour.[9] So too, the piece stages a distinction between the evidently onerous, lower-status work of laundry, and the higher-status virgins clustered near a stately bed in the scene of sewing, drawing our attention to the relationship

---

[5]   Patrick Joyce, *Work, Society and Politics: The Culture of the Factory in Later Victorian England* (Brighton: Harvester Press, 1980), pp. xiv, xiii, xv, xx, xxi.

[6]   Thomas Dekker, *The shomakers holiday* (London: Valentine Sims, 1600); John Michael Archer, 'Citizens and Aliens as Working Subjects in Dekker's *The Shoemaker's Holiday*', in Michelle Dowd and Natasha Korda eds, *Working Subjects in Early Modern English Drama* (Aldershot: Ashgate, 2011), pp. 37–52, at p. 39.

[7]   Lorna Hutson, *The Usurer's Daughter: Male Friendship and Fictions of Women in Sixteenth-Century England* (London: Routledge, 1994).

[8]   Stephen Gosson, *The schoole of abuse* (London: Thomas Woodcocke, 1579), sig. F3v.

[9]   Tara Hamling, *Decorating the 'Godly' Household: Religious Art in Post-Reformation Britain* (New Haven: Yale University Press, 2010), p. 127.

between cultures of elite working and the popular counterparts which either accompanied them, established the conditions which allowed for them (creating the fabrics to be worked upon, for example) or tended to their products as they entered the household economy.

Figure 11.2   The Wise and Foolish Virgins, carved alabaster chimneypiece in the great hall at Burton Agnes Hall, c. 1610.
© The author.

In his description of *The Holy State*, reprinted at least five times between 1642 and 1663, Thomas Fuller insisted that the good wife *'keeps home if she hath not her husbands company, or leave for her patent to go abroad*: For the house is the womans centre'. Fuller links the woman's housebound state to the performance of domestic business; whilst the husband rises with the sun to go to work, the woman should get up earlier, since she 'hath her work within the house, and therefore can make the sunne rise by lighting of a candle'.[10] The divide between male mobility and female domesticity is marked within *A womans work*, in part through the husband's absence from the majority of its scenes, but also through the contrast between the protagonist's work, whose constant demands allow for a double reading of her complaint that she is 'constrain'd the house to keep', and the man's labour, which impels him from home: 'When dinner time is gone and over-past, / My Husband he runs out o'th doors in haste'.

The woman's confinement is intensified in the temporal and spatial progression of the narrative from household to bed, where, all too often, her husband decides against conjugal 'work' and 'turns [her] to the wall'. 'Debarr'd' from 'all my pleasures', as from movement, by her 'hard' labour, the wife works at home to facilitate her family's movement beyond the household. Even her children are granted greater mobility than their mother, as she 'packs' them 'away to School'. This domestic incarceration is reproduced textually and materially: the

---

[10]   Thomas Fuller, *The holy state* (Cambridge: for John Williams, 1642), sig. B1v, emphasis in first quotation in original.

housewife's voice is doubly encased within a framing device which emphasises the ambulatory freedom of the male speaker, 'wandring on the way', and a short sales verse which describes the ballad as 'a pretty conceited thing' 'for Maids to sing', contrasting unmarried women's mobility – 'Maids may sit still, go, or run' – to the Sisyphean stasis of household labours.

In reality, women's work was varied, and a site of spatial and social movement. Amy Louise Erickson concludes that for yeomanry families, 'women's work was not only essential but appears to have constituted at least half of the total household economy', and included vegetable, dairy and poultry production, as well as making cloth, clothing and linens.[11] Some forms of textile work were distinctly gendered. In 1617, Margaret Pierce, a farmer's wife from Wapping, testified that 'she spendeth her time as other women use to do in spinning and carding'.[12] Even in Proverbs, however, the virtuous woman 'maketh fine linen, and selleth it; and delivereth girdles to the merchant' (31.24), implying participation not just in textile production but in trade. Within an urban context, women were not formally excluded from the livery companies, but single women were usually effectively excluded from guild structures.[13] Nonetheless, wives worked as partners with their husbands, pursuing debts, handling customers and demonstrating a sound commercial and legal knowledge. On 18 March 1615, one book-binder, Henry Pyke, was accused of stealing 26 books from another, John Drawater. Notably, it was John's wife, Dorothy, who served as the prosecutor, suggesting her business competence.[14] In 1617, Ann Soome, wife of a London threadmaker, testified in the Consistory Court of London that 'this respondent for her part useth to make thread ... she liveth of her self by her husband's means and by her own means in the trade she useth'. Marie Cable, a butcher's wife, revealed that she 'keepeth shop for her husband's trade', a common gendering of the distinction between sale and manufacture.[15]

Some women had distinct trade identities as part of a mixed family economy. The wife of the printer and bookseller John Wolfe was recorded as a distiller in 1595, whilst Lena Cowen Orlin has recovered the separate commercial identity of Alice Barnham, a London silkwoman and wife of the prosperous merchant, Sir Francis.[16] Widows possessed particular freedoms, and sometimes inherited their husband's businesses.[17] Occasionally, single women, especially of middling status, succeeded in establishing themselves as independent

[11] Amy Louise Erickson, 'Introduction' to Alice Clark, *Working Life of Women in the Seventeenth Century* (3rd ed., London: Routledge, 1992), pp. xix, xxv.

[12] Consistory Court of London Deposition Books, cited in Patricia Crawford and Laura Gowing eds, *Women's Worlds in Seventeenth-Century England: A Sourcebook* (London: Routledge, 2000), p. 79.

[13] See Steve Rapapport, *Worlds within Worlds: Structures of Life in Sixteenth-Century London* (Cambridge: Cambridge University Press, 1989), esp. pp. 36–41.

[14] 'Sessions, 1615: 28 and 29 March', *County of Middlesex. Calendar to the sessions records: new series, volume 2: 1614–15* (1936), pp. 220–56. www.british-history.ac.uk/report.aspx?compid=82341&strquery=book.

[15] Consistory Court of London Deposition Books, cited in Crawford and Gowing eds, *Women's Worlds*, pp. 78, 79.

[16] Ian Gadd, 'Hunting Down John Wolfe for the New DNB', in Robin Myers, Michael Harris and Giles Mandelbrote eds, *Lives in Print: Biography and the Book Trade from the Middle Ages to the 21st Century* (Delaware: Oak Knoll Press, 2002), pp. 193–202, at p. 196; Lena Cowen Orlin, *Locating Privacy in Tudor London* (Oxford: Oxford University Press, 2007), esp. pp. 7–8, 287–9, 291–4.

[17] Amy Froide reminds us that widows 'had a public and independent place within the patriarchal society'. *Never Married: Singlewomen in Early Modern England* (Oxford: Oxford University Press, 2005), p. 17. All unmarried women, as *femes soles*, possessed an independent legal status that they surrendered upon marriage, when they became *femes coverts*. Married women lost the right to make contracts, own or dispose of property or sue and be sued in a court of law. These categories were, however, more flexible than has sometimes been assumed. See Amy Louise Erickson, *Women and Property in Early Modern England* (London: Routledge, 1993), pp. 24, 30, 100, 146.

traders, for example within the male-dominated Oxford millinery trade.[18] Within the informal economy, which intersected with, and did much to maintain, the formal guild and trade structures of the period, women took on a variety of roles, particularly in textile work, sales and victualling.[19] In desperate straits, women's work was demeaning and dangerous: women on poor relief were appointed as plague searchers, inspecting the corpses of those who had died within the Parish to determine the cause of death.[20]

In 1631, Thomas Powell insisted 'those Trades are of least use and benefit, which are called Huswives Trades (as *Brewer, Baker, Cooke,* and the like.) Because they be the skill of Women as well as of men, and common to both'.[21] The association of women's work with unskilled labour appears again in Powell's description of a physician, a profession which, he complained 'is growne to be a very huswiues trade, where fortune prevailes more then skill'.[22] Powell's complaint, however, writes out the variety of women's medical work in early modern England.[23] Recounting her work history in order to persuade readers of her authority, Hannah Woolley explained that she learned 'a little' medicine from her mother and sisters, before entering a noblewoman's household. The noblewoman, 'finding my genius', encouraged Woolley's medical ambitions, buying her books and allowing her to purchase ingredients for cures, and consult with physicians and surgeons, so that Woolley 'soon became a practitioner, and did begin with cut fingers, bruises, aches, agues, head-ache, bleeding at the nose, felons, whitlows on the fingers, sore eyes, drawing of blisters, burnings, tooth-ache, and any thing which is commonly incident' before proceeding to more complex conditions including 'convulsion-fits and rickets among children', 'violent fits of the stone' and 'a young maid' who 'cut her leg sorely' 'as she was cutting sticks with an axe'.[24]

Even within *A womans work*, the dynamic of wifely enclosure is not wholly secure: the woman is given a compelling voice, privileging her version of events. Bruce Smith argues that the performative and embodied nature of ballad singing means that the act of reception is particularly engaged: 'what ballads offer the singer and the listener is the possibility of becoming many subjects, by internalizing the sounds and rhythms of those subjects' voices'.[25] Within the popular culture of ballad reading and singing, performers crossed the

---

[18]   Mary Prior, 'Women and the Urban Economy: Oxford 1500–1800', in Mary Prior ed., *Women in English Society 1500–1800* (London: Methuen, 1985), pp. 93–117, at p. 112.

[19]   Froide notes that 'In London close to half (44 per cent) of the never-married women who maintained themselves by means other than service did so by making or mending clothes'. *Never Married*, p. 97.

[20]   Crawford and Gowing, *Women's Worlds*, pp. 90–91.

[21]   Thomas Powell, *Tom of all Trades* (London: B. Alsop and T. Fawcet, for Benjamin Fisher, 1631), sig. E4v.

[22]   Ibid., sig. E1v.

[23]   Doreen Evenden, *The Midwives of Seventeenth-Century London* (Cambridge: Cambridge University Press, 2000); Deborah E. Harkness, 'A View from the Streets: Women and Medical Work in Elizabethan London', and Elaine Leong, 'Making Medicines in the Early Modern Household', both in *Bulletin of the History of Medicine* 82 (2008), 52–85, 145–68; Rebecca Laroche, *Medical Authority and Englishwomen's Herbal Texts, 1550–1650* (Aldershot: Ashgate, 2010); Margaret Pelling, 'Thoroughly Resented? Older Women and the Medical Role in Early Modern London', in Lynette Hunter and Sarah Hutton eds, *Women, Science and Medicine, 1500–1700* (Stroud: Sutton, 1997), pp. 63–88; Margaret Pelling, 'Defensive Tactics: Networking by Female Medical Practitioners in Early Modern London', in Alex Shepard and Phil Withington eds, *Communities in Early Modern England: Networks, Place, Rhetoric* (Manchester: Manchester University Press, 2000), pp. 38–53.

[24]   Hannah Woolley, *A supplement to the Queen-like Closet* (London: T. R. for Richard Lowndes, 1674), sig. B5v–B7r.

[25]   Bruce Smith, *The Acoustic World of Early Modern England: Attending to the O-Factor* (Chicago: Chicago University Press, 1999), p. 201.

boundaries of gender and even species to voice a range of positions.[26] Although it is possible to imagine a satirical coding of the housewife's complaint, the sheer length of the ballad text lends the refrain a compelling force, suggesting that a male singer might physically and psychically endorse the rigours of women's domestic work. The enclosed work of the household is thus made visible – and its rhythms audible – to diverse actors and audiences.

The regularity of the ballad metre reminds us of the relationship between singing and working. A ballad of *The Countrey peoples Felicity* describes 'Mary, Bess and Nanny' engaged in the seasonal work of haymaking, and articulates in song the women's own 'singing at their labours, / with sweet and pleasant noats'.[27] Textile work and song were closely linked: a ballad of *True love exalted* tells of the upwardly mobile marriage of a maid first spied 'singing, and a Spinning, / at her poor old Fathers door'.[28] In a frequently cited attack on 'stale Ballad-newes', Richard Brathwait complained that 'every poore Milk maid can chant and chirpe it under her Cow, which she useth as an harmelesse charme to make her let downe her milk', a formulation that reveals Brathwait's adherence to stereotypes of country naivety but also suggests the intimate connection between singing and manual labour: we can assume that it is the rhythm of the ballad that regulates the work, encouraging the milk to flow.[29] Brathwait's invocation of country charms effaces the embodied or muscular knowledge central to the successful performance of women's work, and obscures the skill needed to complete a complex task.

Though the demands of the rhyme-scheme force the speaker of *A womans work* to imagine that she sits and sews 'by my self alone', reinforcing the image of women's domestic confinement, textile work was frequently a communal activity. In a poem by Thomas Middleton, a ghostly Lucrece laments a cheerful past in which 'still I said, / Sing merrily my maides, our wheeles goe round', reminding us that the twin rhythms of popular song and spinning wheels formed part of the soundscape of the noble house.[30] When Shakespeare's Duke Orsino wishes to hear an 'old and antic song', he remarks 'The spinsters and the knitters in the sun / And the free maids that weave their thread with bones / Do use to chant it' in a scene that at once stages the elite appropriation of popular culture, brings popular song into the commercial theatre, and hints at the sociability, visibility, and audibility, of women's working practices as a site of group identification and identity.[31]

Women's working song entered and informed even the textual record of elite literary culture: a poem 'Of the meane and sure estate written to Iohn Poins', collected in Tottell's miscellany, informs its addressee that 'My mothers maides when they do sowe and spinne: / They sing a song made of the feldishe mouse', a story which is appropriated to form the subject of the poem.[32] A few years later, in his University play *Ralph Roister-Doister*, Nicholas Udall mocked the popular practice of sociable textile singing: the maids Tibet Talkapace and Annot Alyface, along with Madge Mumblecrust, a former nurse, repeatedly attempt to drive forward their work with song, only to discover that their materials revolt against them. Whilst Annot proposes that 'we thrée sing a song; / So shall we pleasantly both the tyme beguile now, / And eke dispatche our workes ere we can tell how', Tibet discovers 'This

---

[26] See also Natascha Würzbach, *The Rise of the English Street Ballad, 1550–1650*, trans. Gayna Walls (Cambridge: Cambridge University Press, 1990).

[27] *The Countrey peoples Felicity* (London: for Francis Grove, [between 1641 and 1661]).

[28] *True love exalted* (London: for P. Brooksby, [1670–96]).

[29] Richard Brathwait, *Whimzies, or a new cast of characters* (London: Felix Kingston, 1631), sig. B4v.

[30] Thomas Middleton, *The ghost of Lucrece* (London: Valentine Simmes, 1600), sig. B4v.

[31] William Shakespeare, *Twelfth Night*, ed. Keir Elam, *The Arden Shakespeare* (third series, London: Cengage Learning, 2008), 2.4.3, 44–6. See also Stuart Gillespie, 'Shakespeare and Popular Song', in Gillespie and Rhodes eds, *Shakespeare*, pp. 174–92.

[32] *Songes and Sonettes* (London: Richard Tottel, 1557), sig. M1r.

sleue is not willyng to be sewed, I trowe... / eche finger is a thombe to day me thinke'.[33] Udall presents his lower-status female characters as comically bad workers, but also registers the possibility that work and its tools might possess a degree of agency which made them participants in the popular culture of household labour. Women's working song might thus be registered and reproduced within both popular and elite representations of female labour, even as those representations re-formed women's vocal practices to fit cultural expectations of semantically simple or vacant content and unsophisticated musical form.

We can read *A womans work* within a longstanding ballad tradition that contrasted male and female labours. One fifteenth-century example tells of a tyrannical ploughman, convinced his wife is idle at home. The wife offers a trenchant defence of her labours before accepting her husband's challenge to change places.[34] An eighteenth-century iteration of this theme tells of a farmer who berates his wife: 'you and your children do live at home in ease, / You little think of any work you do just as you please' and demands that she take the work 'turn about or I will break your bones, / For in the morning you shall go to plow with my man John'.[35] The wife consents, both to 'please' her husband and 'to keep the house at ease', suggesting a popular vision of women's labour as essential to the maintenance of domestic and social harmony as well as material order. The farmer soon realises the difficulty of his wife's work: the pigs break into the dairy, and when he goes into the parlour to bandage his thumb (bitten by a sow) his neglected children cry, fall over and soil themselves. Eventually, he fetches his spinning wheel, which goes up in flames when his drying 'tow' (flax or hemp) catches a spark from the fire. Vowing 'he would to plow again he would no more be nurse', the farmer flees to the field, only to discover his wife kissing John 'behind the barley-mow', a turn of events which reinforces the bawdy implications of his opening insistence that the two of them must 'plow' together.

Whilst these accidents are clearly signalled as products of the churlish husband's incompetence, they also suggest the frustrations of women's work, as does the moment in *A Midsummer Night's Dream* when Titania's fairy demands of Puck:

> *are not you he*
> *That frights the maidens of the villagery;*
> *Skim milk, and sometimes labour in the quern*
> *And bootless make the breathless housewife churn;*
> *And sometime make the drink to bear no barm ...?*[36]

In a scene which stages the popular culture of fairies and spirits for a city audience, Puck's tricks expose varied attitudes to the women's work of dairying, flour milling and brewing. Wendy Wall argues that the fairy's recognition 'Those that Hobgoblin call you and sweet Puck, / You do their work, and they shall have good luck' (2.1.41–2) demonstrates that popular legend was used to reinforce the work patterns and values of the middling sort,

---

[33] Nicholas Udall, *[Ralph Roister-Doister] What creature is in health, eyther yong or olde* (London: H. Denham for T. Hacket?, 1566?), sig. B3v–B4v.

[34] 'Ballad of a Tyrannical Husband', ed. Eve Salisbury, *TEAMS Middle English Texts*, http://www.lib.rochester.edu/camelot/teams/thfrm.htm. The ballad is extant in one fifteenth-century miscellany, and discussed in Helena Graham, '"A woman's work...": Labour and Gender in the Late Medieval Countryside', in P.J.P. Goldberg ed., *Woman Is a Worthy Wight: Women in English Society, c. 1200–1500* (Wolfeboro Falls, NH: Alan Sutton, 1992), pp. 126–48.

[35] *A new song call'd The churlish husband* (London?, 1770?).

[36] William Shakespeare, *A Midsummer Night's Dream*, ed. Peter Holland (Oxford: Oxford World's Classics, 2008), 2.1.34–9.

imaginatively rewarding discreet and obedient service.[37] Mary Ellen Lamb further suggests that references to fairy lore functioned as a 'weapon of the weak', allowing the dispossessed to displace their ill fortune onto wilful sprites.[38] Puck's practical jokes, however, also stage the unpredictable difficulty of domestic chores, and the apparently malevolent agency which might disrupt complex processes. Yet in his insistence that his tricks lead finally to laughter as 'the whole choir ... / ...waxen in their mirth, and neeze, and swear / A merrier hour was never wasted there' (2.1.55–7), as well as his invocation of 'the wisest aunt telling the saddest tale' (2.1.51–2), Puck attests to the sociability of domestic work, and the extent to which women's labour constructed a social and domestic space for gossip, shared experience and household merriment. At the same time, his suggestion that this is 'wasted' time again threatens to render women's work invisible. Whilst the 'churlish husband' tradition highlights the demands of women's household work, the early modern stage frequently effaced the skill required to negotiate difficult tasks.

The lewd undercurrent of *The churlish husband* reminds us of the popular equation of women's work with sexual activity, concisely articulated in the double meaning of 'travail' as 'bodily or mental labour or toil' and 'the labour and pain of child-birth'.[39] The two meanings were linked through the story of the Fall, understood to have introduced the necessity not only of hard but of gendered work: a division reproduced in the popular proverb 'When Adam delved and Eve span / Who was then the gentleman?'[40] Women's work as sellers was linked to promiscuity in the popular imagination, a depiction that, to modern readers, reveals their vulnerability to sexual abuse.[41] Powell warned parents against the 'pretty way of breeding young Maides an Exchange shop, or St. *Martins le grand*', suggesting the danger of illegitimate pregnancy through his coy assertion that 'many of them get such a foolish Crick with carrying the Bandbox under their Apron to Gentlemens Chambers, that in the end it is hard to distinguish whether it be their belly or their bandbox makes such a goodly show'.[42] In its cheerful invocation of sexual incontinence, Powell's commentary, like the bawdy ballads, renders invisible the realities of an insecure market for women's work, and the economic necessity which compelled some women to work as prostitutes. In February 1625, for example, Mary Hall, a spinster, accused Jane Bankes of having sold Hall's maidenhead twice, and the maidenhead of another woman, Jane Waters, five times.[43]

The Countrey peoples Felicity hints at the bawdy possibilities of co-labour in an agricultural context:

> ... *those Lads and Lasses*
> *were all together that day,*

---

[37] Wendy Wall, *Staging Domesticity: Household Work and English Identity in Early Modern Drama* (Cambridge: Cambridge University Press, 2002), p. 110

[38] Mary Ellen Lamb, *The Popular Culture of Shakespeare, Spenser, and Jonson* (London: Routledge, 2006), p. 33.

[39] *OED* 'travail' *n.* Defs. 2, 4.

[40] See Albert Friedman, '"When Adam Delved...": Contexts of an Historic Proverb', in Larry Benson ed., *The Learned and the Lewd: Studies in Chaucer and Medieval Literature* (Cambridge, MA: Harvard University Press, 1974), pp. 213–30.

[41] See Laura Gowing, *Common Bodies: Women, Touch and Power in Seventeenth-Century England* (New Haven: Yale University Press, 2003), esp. pp. 60–65, and '"The Freedom of the Streets": Women and Social Space, 1560–1640', in Paul Griffiths and Mark Jenner eds, *Londinopolis, c. 1500–c.1750: Essays in the Cultural and Social History of Early Modern London* (Manchester: Manchester University Press, 2000), pp. 130–52.

[42] Powell, *Tom of all Trades*, sig. G3v.

[43] 'The Information of Mary Hall, Westminster Sessions Roll, 23rd February 1625', in Helen Ostovich and Elizabeth Sauer eds, *Reading Early Modern Women: An Anthology of Texts in Manuscript and Print, 1500–1700* (London: Routledge, 2004), p. 41.

> *In that same gallant Meddow,*
> *a making of the Hay.*[44]

Within the rural economy, women engaged in the varied tasks of husbandry, including dairying, harvesting and gleaning. In the late seventeenth century, Sarah Fell kept accounts recording payments to Pegg Didgson for a variety of jobs undertaken at Swarthmoor Hall in Cumbria, including 'filling manure, scaling manure, washing, harrowing, and dressing meadows', 'setting and dressing 5 daywork of peats', 'swingling, washing, and rinsing', 'and washing rinsing, rubbing, and scalding mole hills'.[45] Despite the fact that their rigorous work makes 'the pretty Maidens brows ... drop a pace with sweat', the possibility of 'ill businesse' is displaced on to the ballad's metropolitan audience, consumers of a bucolic fantasy of women's agricultural work. The young men simply wipe the maidens' brows, and steal a kiss, leaving the speaker wishing: 'Would every one in London were, / as pure in Deed and Thought'. It is striking, however, that the ballad, whilst registering the physical demands of the women's employment, situates haymaking less as back-breaking work than as a 'gallant' fiction of innocent cross-sex sociability.

In its self-identification as 'a Song for Maids to Sing', *A womans work* separates the carefree virgin from her married acquaintance, and even – as the final stanza's injunction to 'make the use of the time you may' suggests – her future self, reminding us that 'while gender is an integral category to understanding patriarchy, marital status was just as crucial in the early modern era'.[46] Yet in its confidence that marriage is the destiny of maids, the ballad may be seen to respond obliquely to an economic situation in which around a third, and in some areas up to a half, of women were unmarried, and many singlewomen undertook the tasks of housewifery as part of the work of domestic employment. Powell famously recommended that 'in stead of reading Sir *Philip Sidneys Arcadia*', young women should 'read the grounds of good huswifery' and 'In stead of Song and Musicke, let them learne Cookery and Laundrie'. If a mother 'be a good Huswife, and Religiously disposed', Powell suggests she may be allowed to bring up one daughter, but recommends placing the others in service 'in the house of some good Merchant, or Citizen' or 'some Lawyer, some Iudge, or well reported Iustice' where 'she may learne what belongs to her improvement, for *Sempstrie*, for Confectionary, and all requisits of Huswifery'.[47]

In her study of domestic employment in Shakespeare's plays, Michelle Dowd notes that 'women were expected to work as servants not in order to gain occupational training per se ... but in order to learn the domestic skills that they would need as wives and to delay their marriages until they were economically and socially prepared for them'. Arguing that dramatic texts are not transparent representations of the conditions either for or of women's labour in this period, Dowd reminds us that narratives 'perform an important social function by offering reassuring fantasies, posing potential solutions, and managing perceived dangers'.[48] *The knitters jobb* charts the trajectory from work to marriage: a 'Lovely Las [sic]', who is skilled in 'Carding, Spinning, Knitting yarn', initially prefers her spinning

---

[44] *The Countrey peoples Felicity*. The ballad exists in a number of different forms, but the dynamic of innocent heterosocial labour remains a constant.

[45] *The Account Book of Sarah Fell of Swarthmoor Hall*, ed. Norman Penney (Cambridge: Cambridge University Press, 1920), cited in Crawford and Gowing eds, *Women's Worlds*, pp. 83–5.

[46] Froide, *Never Married*, p. 7.

[47] Powell, *Tom of all Trades*, sig. G3r.

[48] Dowd, *Women's Work*, pp. 23, 10. Dowd argues that the sudden rise of Shakespeare's maidservants offers a reassuring fiction 'that women in service will secure good ends' at the same time as it 'eliminates the threat of the sexually unruly female servant', p. 30. On women in service, see also Anne Laurence, *Women in England 1500–1760: A Social History* (London: Phoenix Giant, 1996), pp. 134–5.

wheel to the revolutions of matrimony.[49] Whilst this ballad suggests the attractions of a skilled textile worker, pursued by 'many Suitors', in a way that directly links work and matrimonial success, *A womans work* draws a vivid distinction between 'you merry Girls that hear this Ditty' and the tautological 'married Wives', rendering invisible both the uncertainty of the latter position, and the working lives of unmarried women, popularly understood to prepare them for marital labour.

The paratexts of *A womans work* complicate the version of female experience put forward by its verbal contents, meaning that the broadside presents not a unified category of 'woman's work' but a series of possible identifications and labours. The recycled woodcuts depict, on the left, a woman who is clearly not confined to the household. Her plaintive posture invokes either the pathetic subject position of the male-authored, female-voiced complaint or popular narratives of female criminality, whilst the facing man suggests a ballad of courtship: a prelude to, rather than recounting of, the activity of 'the Beds making' invoked by the title of the ballad's tune.[50] On the right, we see Queen Elizabeth. The male figure who faces her appears appropriately less confident than his counterpart, with his gaze lowered, and sword hanging down behind his legs. Elizabeth's elaborate costume scarcely suggests her familiarity with the work of cooking porridge or changing linen, let alone breastfeeding, whilst the lack of a printed frame around this single woodcut offers a material fantasy of unbounded freedom.

The evident disjunction between the station of the speaker and that of the Queen serves to remind us of the displacement of certain forms of work from elite women to their more humble counterparts. Wetnursing, in particular, allowed married women to combine income-generating activity with their own domestic commitments, at the same time that the presence of lower-status women in the nurseries of the great served as another point of contact between the aristocracy and the world of popular culture encapsulated in ballads and old wives' tales.[51] In 1581, the translator William Lowth reminded readers that no less an authority than Plato 'seemeth verie diligently to admonish Nurses, that they sing not to their babes and yong infants everie trifling tale, rusticke ryme, baudie Ballet, and olde wives fabled fansies, lest from their cradles it shall fortune, that they be nouseled in folly, and frought with corrupt conditions'.[52]

In *Shakespeare's Domestic Economies*, Natasha Korda suggests a gradual transformation, in which the housewife's role shifted from domestic producer to consumer.[53] The distinctive costumes of the ballad's pictured women hint at a female identity rooted in consumption and display, rather than production and use, reminding us that the housewife 'adorns' her head with 'dressings' each morning, though this work is temporally elided, invoked only in the context of cleaning and fire-building that she must undertake 'before' she works upon her own appearance. Her concern with dress locates the ballad in the context of neighbourly contact and scrutiny; she is aware that 'how my self I do bestow / ... all my Neighbours well do know', a formulation used here to proclaim the speaker's credit, but which also reminds us of the visibility and permeability of the early modern household.[54] The ballad's

---

[49]   *The knitters jobb* (London: for P. Brooksby, [1672–96]).

[50]   The ballad's 'delicate Northern Tune, A womans work is never done, Or, The Beds making' encourages audiences to situate this as a bawdy tale. On the significance of ballad tunes see Christopher Marsh, *Music and Society in Early Modern England* (Cambridge: Cambridge University Press, 2010), ch. 6.

[51]   See Lamb, *Popular Culture*, pp. 49–52.

[52]   Barthélemy Batt, *The Christian mans closet* (London: Thomas Dawson and Gregory Seton, 1581), sig. O2r.

[53]   Natasha Korda, *Shakespeare's Domestic Economies: Gender and Property in Early Modern England* (Philadelphia: University of Pennsylvania Press, 2002), pp. 33–8.

[54]   See Gowing, *Domestic Dangers*, esp. ch. 1.

illustrations at once stage women as purchasers, particularly in the case of the splendidly dressed Elizabeth, and position them as objects for consumption, aspirational examples of the complexity of women's costumes (though by 1660 Elizabeth, like her fashions, must have been a peculiarly dated revenant). Korda's most recent book, however, complicates the division between production and consumption, as she draws attention to the gendered labour which went into making the desirable ruffs, cuffs and linens evident in the ballad woodcuts, as well as, in elite and theatrical contexts, the work of 'dressing' or 'tiring' involved in helping an aristocrat or actor into an elaborate costume.[55] The images of clothing which establish women as potential or actual consumers thus also record women's labour in specific textile activities, and remind us that the 'woman's work' of knitting, spinning, laundering and sewing contributed materially both to the well-being of the household and to the consumer goods to which those same women were popularly imagined to aspire.

Women sellers emerged as both agents and objects of popular culture in the *Cries of London*, a series of engravings depicting hawkers. In one seventeenth-century example, women make up 22 of the 37 criers pictured, selling goods from buttons to 'good sasages', toasting irons to blue starch (central to women's work in the cleaning and re-forming of ruffs and cuffs) and shoes to purses (Figure 11.3). Many of the women sell food, from damsons to 'any maydes', a term for young skate, but one which inevitably connects women's sales-work to their sexual availability, particularly when the central verse of the engraving, attributed to the bellman on his evening rounds, encourages 'Mayds in your smocks. Loocke

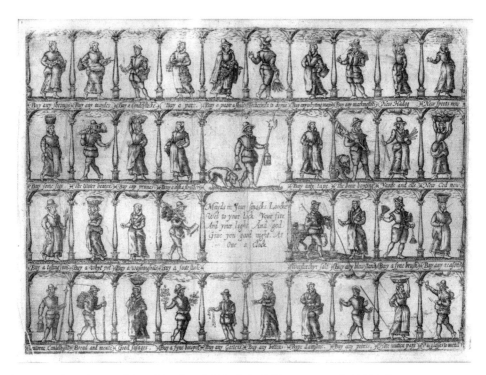

Figure 11.3   Anon., *Cries of London,* C17th. British Museum 1843, 0311.279.
© Trustees of the British Museum.

---

[55]   Korda, *Labors Lost*, esp. ch. 3.

Buy any Wax or Wafers.
Cire d'Espagne, et oublies.
Ostie e cera spagnâ.

Figure 11.4   After Marcellus Laroon II, 'Buy any Wax or Wafers', from *The Cryes of the City of London Drawne after the Life* (London: Pierce Tempest, 1688). British Museum 1972, U.370.11. © Trustees of the British Museum.

/ Wel to your lock'.[56] By the mid-seventeenth century women mercuries were well known as distributors of cheap print and polemical pamphlets, and women also sold the 'wax and wafers', and the ink, crucial to writing (Figure 11.4). Women's voices echoed in the streets of early modern London, whilst their work as street-hawkers was both represented in, and central to the circulation and production of, popular print and song.[57]

Some women also sold ballads. The earliest extant copy of *A woman's work* was printed for John Andrews in around 1660, yet the text had an earlier history. On 1 June 1629, a group of six booksellers, known collectively as the 'ballad partners', went to Stationers' Hall in London to record their acquisition of 'All the estate that the widow Trundle had in the Copies following'. The ballad partners registered their right to print six books, 24 ballads, including 'A womans workes never done', and 'all other Booke[s] and Ballades. that belonged of Right to the said Marg. Trundle'.[58] Margery Trundle, widow of the bookseller, John, whose texts were the subject of frequent satire for their sensational contents, specialised in cheap books and ballads.[59] Trundle's shop, near the Hospital gate in Smithfield, was at the centre of the market for cheap print, close to one of the major routes out of London, so that chapmen and women could stock up on her wares as they left the city each spring.

Trundle was a prominent agent of popular culture, but she was also its subject, starring in a sales ballad in which the singer assures the prospective purchaser: 'Heer's no sussex serpent to fright you here in my Bundle, / nor was it ever printed for the widow Trundle'.[60] Trundle's emergence as an early – perhaps the first – owner of the rights to print and sell *A womans work is never done*, and the probability that her name appeared at the foot of the ballad sheet in its first incarnation establishes her as a ghostly paratextual figure, haunting – and disrupting – the text's careful enclosure of women's work within the household. The public and dispersed nature of Trundle's business, as of her textual representation as a bookseller, stands in stark contrast to the claustrophobic ballad text. What we are offered, if we restore Trundle's imprint to the broadside sheet, is a marked disjunction between one discourse of confined, domestic feminine labour, and another of the mobile, popular commitments of a woman print worker. Where the ballad already articulates a distinction between maid and wife, Margery Trundle's inclusion as an epitext introduces a third possibility: the relative economic and topographical freedoms afforded to the widow who succeeded to her husband's business.

The journeys of ballads, as they circulated within and beyond London, remind us of women's work as sellers of ballad texts, of the materials to make ballads, and of the commodities that lubricated their recitation and reception. Women worked as ale-wives and tavern hostesses in sites of popular sociability at which ballads might be reproduced orally by customers and sellers, or textually, pasted to walls or laid on tables.[61] In *The Sorrowful*

---

[56]   *Cries of London*, with bellman at centre, seventeenth century, reproduced in Korda, *Labors Lost*, p. 152. See also Karen Beall, *Cries and Itinerant Trades: A Bibliography* (Hamburg: Hauswedell, 1975), and Sean Shesgreen, '"The Manner of Crying Things in London": Style, Authorship, Chalcography, and History', *Huntington Library Quarterly* 59 (1996), 404–63, and *Images of the Outcast: the Urban Poor in the Cries of London* (New Brunswick: Rutgers University Press, 2002).

[57]   On criers as part of the soundscape see Smith, *Acoustic World*, pp. 63–70.

[58]   Edward Arber, *A Transcript of the Registers of the Company of Stationers of London, 1554–1640 A.D.* (4 vols, London, 1875–94; rpt New York: Peter Smith, 1950), IV. p. 213.

[59]   See Gerald D. Johnson, 'John Trundle and the Book Trade 1603–1626', *Studies in Bibliography* 39 (1986), 177–99. On women in the book trades, see Helen Smith, *Grossly Material Things: Women and Book Production in Early Modern England* (Oxford: Oxford University Press, 2012), esp. chs 3 and 4.

[60]   'Will You Buy a New Merry Booke'. The text does not survive as a broadside but is reproduced in John Hilton's collection *Catch that catch can, or, A choice collection of catches, rounds & canons for 3 or 4 voyces* (London: for John Benson and John Playford, 1652), sig. F1v–F2r.

[61]   Judith M. Bennett argues that women were gradually excluded from tavern-keeping and brewing across the sixteenth and seventeenth centuries. At the same time, Bennett suggests, the texts of popular culture displaced 'public anxieties about the drink trade from all brewers to women alone, and

Complaint of Conscience and Plain-Dealing, the anonymous speaker establishes millers, usurers, tailors and hostesses as the archetypal villains of a mercantile economy, suggesting that ale-women engaged in sharp accounting ('two pots for one they will commonly score'), served snacks to 'tempt and allure men to tarry all day' and flirted ('Ah then how the Hostis will simper and sneer') in order to improve trade.[62] *The kind beleeving hostess*, in contrast, suggests that women in the drinks trades should be wary of the deceits of their customers. The speaker boasts that he will be revenged on an ale-wife by leaving his substantial debts unpaid, a promise that might stand, at least in part, as a consolatory fantasy for hard-up tavern habitués. A similar scene is staged in *I Henry IV*, when Mistress Quickly takes Falstaff to law to recover the debt ('a hundred mark') which he owes her. Despite the Lord Chief Justice's command that the debt must be paid, by the end of the scene Falstaff has persuaded Quickly to withdraw her suit and lend him an additional ten pounds.[63]

Shakespeare's dramatic elaboration of a popular ballad theme, emblematic of 'the topos of the overly credulous female creditor',[64] illuminates something of the complex relationship between the public theatre and the texts and traditions of popular culture. Numerous ballads and other texts invoke women's work as part of their dramatic or narrative arc, or foreground the particularity of women's labours, hinting – often obliquely – at the possibility of a popular culture *of* woman's work. These texts tread an uneasy line between making explicit the difficulties of women's labour, and rendering invisible the real skill and judgement of its performance. Brought into conversation with the archival evidence of women's employment, these popular fantasies of gendered work (or fantasies of what 'popular' work might look like), remind us that women's work was richly varied in its modes, possibilities and remunerations. At the same time, they insist that, in innumerable ways, female labour not only provided the content *for* but forged the products and practices *of* popular culture across a range of domains.

Select Bibliography

Bennett, Judith M., *Ale, Beer, and Brewsters in England: Women's Work in a Changing World, 1300–1600*. Oxford: Oxford University Press, 1996.

Clark, Alice, *Working Life of Women in the Seventeenth Century*, 3rd ed., ed. and with an introduction by Amy Louise Erickson. London: Routledge, 1992.

Crawford, Patricia, and Laura Gowing eds, *Women's Worlds in Seventeenth-Century England: A Sourcebook*. London: Routledge, 2000.

Dowd, Michelle, *Women's Work in Early Modern English Literature and Culture*. London: Palgrave Macmillan, 2009.

Dowd, Michelle, and Natasha Korda eds, *Working Subjects in Early Modern English Drama*. Aldershot: Ashgate, 2011.

Erickson, Amy Louise, *Women and Property in Early Modern England*. London: Routledge, 1993.

Froide, Amy, *Never Married: Singlewomen in Early Modern England*. Oxford: Oxford University Press, 2005.

---

particularly the figure of the bad hostess'. *Ale, Beer, and Brewsters in England: Women's Work in a Changing World, 1300–1600* (Oxford: Oxford University Press, 1996), p. 12. On ballads in taverns, see Tessa Watt, *Cheap Print and Popular Piety, 1550–1640* (Cambridge: Cambridge University Press, 1991), ch. 5.

[62]   *The sorrowful complaint of conscience and plain-dealing* (London: for J. Deacon, [1684–85]).

[63]   William Shakespeare, *King Henry IV, Part I*, ed. A.R. Humphreys (New York: Routledge, The Arden Shakespeare, 1996), 2.1.30–1, 112–15, 156.

[64]   Korda, *Labors Lost*, p. 64.

Korda, Natasha, *Shakespeare's Domestic Economies: Gender and Property in Early Modern England*. Philadelphia: University of Pennsylvania Press, 2002.

Korda, Natasha, *Labors Lost: Women's Work and the Early Modern English Stage*. Philadelphia: University of Pennsylvania Press, 2011.

Prior, Mary ed., *Women in English Society 1500–1800*. London: Methuen, 1985.

Rapapport, Steve, *Worlds within Worlds: Structures of Life in Sixteenth-Century London*. Cambridge: Cambridge University Press, 1989.

Smith, Bruce, *The Acoustic World of Early Modern England: Attending to the O-Factor*. Chicago: Chicago University Press, 1999.

Smith, Helen, *Grossly Material Things: Women and Book Production in Early Modern England*. Oxford: Oxford University Press, 2012.

Wall, Wendy, *Staging Domesticity: Household Work and English Identity in Early Modern Drama*. Cambridge: Cambridge University Press, 2002.

Würzbach, Natascha, *The Rise of the English Street Ballad, 1550–1650*, trans. Gayna Walls. Cambridge: Cambridge University Press, 1990.

Crime

Duncan Salkeld

Stories of crime have always caught the popular imagination. As today, early modern readers liked to have their impressions of illegality borne out by eye-catching headlines on title pages accompanied by attention-grabbing illustrations. Robert Greene's *Disputation between a Hee Conny-catcher, and a Shee Conny-catcher* (1592) carries a frontispiece wood-cut of a man with the face of a 'cony' or rabbit being met by a tall and strikingly attired weasel-headed woman – evidently a dupe or gull about to be cozened by a high-class prostitute. A 1633 edition of the 1592 play *Arden of Faversham*, printed by Elizabeth Allde, depicts on its title page verso an especially vivid scene, with villains Black Will and Shakebag just about to murder Alice's Arden's husband during a game of 'tables' or backgammon. The same image appears on a broadsheet ballad of the story produced that year by a different printer. A 1616 imprint of Marlowe's *Dr. Faustus*, from the shop of John Wright, famously portrays the doctor standing in his conjuring circle and raising Mephistophilis from hell, as sensational an image as any printer might wish for. A pathetic example comes from a deluded piece of literature called *Witches Apprehended, Examyned and Executed* ... (1613) which carries on its title page an image of the principal alleged felon being ducked for sorcery in a mill-pond. This work pretended to expose the 'severall and damnable practices of Mother Sutton' and her daughter Mary lately executed at Bedford. Mother and Mary Sutton were of course entirely innocent, but had such records been kept, they would have figured in local crime statistics. The point reminds us that many 'guilty' verdicts were likely to have been travesties since sin, prejudice and crime were often conflated, and confessions easily forced.

Contemporary accounts of early modern crime are invaluable for the detail they reveal of popular life in England at the time. They tell of incidents at specific times in specific places, and from them we learn much about people's associations, routines, preferences and belongings. Although it is not mentioned in his *ODNB* entry, we know that Shakespeare's fellow-actor Richard Burbage kept at his remote and rural Shoreditch home a number of expensive items, including a 'darinxe' [dornix] carpet, a hunting gun ('fowling peece'), a substantial number of pewter pots, several aprons, smocks, bands, cuffs, handkerchiefs, and various pieces of linen.[1] We learn this only because he was robbed of them in 1615 by Henry Elliott and Thomas Pierson who broke 'burglariously' into his home in Holywell at midnight one night. His brother Cuthbert had been robbed the same evening. Arrested and charged, Pierson pleaded 'benefit of clergy' (see below), was branded and released. Elliott's

---

[1] I am grateful to my colleague Dr Danae Tankard for pointing out that 'Darinxe' is likely to have been a variant of 'dornix' (*OED*: 'A silk, worsted, woollen, or partly woollen fabric, used for hangings, carpets, vestments, etc. Obs'). A 1558 inventory for Cardinal Pole's estate lists 'A carpet of Darinx'. The National Archives, *State Papers Domestic*, 12/1 no. 10, II. The item may have been an arras or hanging and not a floor carpet. See Mary Edmond's entry for Burbage in *Oxford Dictionary of National Biography*.

wife stood 'Not Guilty' and was acquitted. Elliott himself said nothing. Remaining mute, he was condemned to death by a particularly cruel means, the 'peine fort et dure', better known as 'pressing to death'.[2] This sentence, carried out in 'the pressing yard of Newgate', ordered the gradual crushing of the accused by heavy weights and must have made a quick hanging seem almost desirable by comparison.[3] Five years earlier, in 1611, a Henry Elliott had been caught burgling another house, and on that occasion successfully pleaded 'Not Guilty'.[4] In 1615, he (if it was the same person) was not so lucky.

Among a number of increasingly specialised studies of early modern crime to have appeared in recent years, two works stand out as useful starting points.[5] The first of these is J.A. Sharpe's *Crime in Early Modern England 1550–1750* (1984), an important book that surveys the prior field of scholarship, provides essential definitions and covers both metropolitan and rural documentary sources. Sharpe identified a broad similarity in the patterns of serious crime from the late middle ages to the early modern period, a predominance of property offences, most of them thefts, few but regular indictments for homicide, a near absence of prosecutions of rape or arson and a marked decline in prosecutions over the period.[6] These indications, he observed, do not sit easily with leftist arguments about the transition from feudalism to capitalism, the emergence of a class structure and the expansion of property and empire. In 1991, Ian Archer's influential study *The Pursuit of Stability* presented a detailed analysis of ways in which ruling elites, the ward and parish structure, livery company associations and a social policy directed towards poor relief all contributed to a prevailing – if fragile – sense of orderliness in early modern London. As Archer noted, London's 'social fabric was highly flammable, but it failed to ignite'.[7] City aldermen assumed such 'immense discretionary jurisdiction' that crime in the metropolis was kept by and large under control.[8] Popular grievances were not ignored, though serious tensions caused by immigration, rising prices and crop failures constantly simmered near the surface. Penal institutions like the sessions houses, Newgate gaol, Bridewell Hospital and a variety of local lock-ups gave the City sufficient deterrent against an overwhelming level of criminal activity. Yet the *perceived* threat of crime was at all times keenly felt. More recently, studies of early modern crime have focused on issues of gender, the practice of policy-making, cases of defamation and the roles of particular courts or institutions.[9] Historians have sought to

---

[2]   J.C. Jeaffreson ed., *Middlesex County Sessions Records 1603–1625* (London: GLC, 1974), ii. 108–9. Elliott's sentence was routine: those who stood mute could expect it.

[3]   See Anon., *The life and death of Griffin Flood informer ...* (London, 1623), C4[r].

[4]   Ibid., p. 60.

[5]   Also helpful, or of interest, are J.S. Cockburn ed., *Crime in England, 1550–1800* (Princeton: Princeton University Press, 1977); Joan Kent, *The English Village Constable, 1580–1642: A Social and Administrative Study* (Oxford: Oxford University Press, 1986); Paul Griffiths, A. Fox and Steve Hindle eds, *The Experience of Authority in Early Modern England* (Basingstoke: Palgrave Macmillan, 1996); Garthine Walker, 'Rereading Rape and Sexual Violence in Early Modern England', *Gender and History* 10:1 (1998), 1–25; David Cressy, *Agnes Bowker's Cat: Travesties and Transgressions in Tudor and Stuart England* (Oxford: Oxford University Press, 2000); Simon Devereaux and Paul Griffiths eds, *Penal Practice and Culture, 1500–1900: Punishing the English* (Basingstoke: Palgrave Macmillan, 2004).

[6]   J.A. Sharpe, *Crime in Early Modern England 1550–1750* (Harlow: Longman, 1984), p. 170.

[7]   Ian Archer, *The Pursuit of Stability: Social Relations in Elizabethan London* (Cambridge: Cambridge University Press, 1991), p. 257.

[8]   Ibid., p. 258.

[9]   See, for example, Jenny Kermode and Garthine Walker eds, *Women, Crime and the Courts in Early Modern England* (London: UCL Press, 1994); David Dean, *Law-Making and Society in Late Elizabethan England: The Parliament of England, 1584–1601* (Cambridge: Cambridge University Press, 1996); Laura Gowing, *Domestic Dangers: Women, Words, and Sex in Early Modern London* (Oxford: Oxford University Press, 1998); and Paul Griffiths, *Lost Londons: Change, Crime and Control in the Capital City 1550–1660* (Cambridge: Cambridge University Press, 2008).

re-focus the debate: Garthine Walker and Jenny Kermode have suggested that the shift of focus from crisis to stability needs reassessment via a drive 'to rebuild historical explanation'; and Paul Griffiths has lately asserted, 'Make no mistake, London cannot be called stable on any day covered by this book.'[10] Social instability, however, is likely to remain a relative matter.

By the end of the sixteenth century England had a fairly long-established set of legal processes. Courts of Assize, overseen by circuit judges, formed the main bodies for prosecuting provincial criminality but a variety of other tribunals also managed the day to day business of communities. In rural areas, manorial courts heard land disputes and courts leet handled complaints about highways, boundaries, water-courses, pasture and rights of way, all essential aspects of local administration. Low-level criminality was dealt with by 'hundred courts' (forerunners to today's county courts) and also by petty sessions convened across the country to support the work of the quarter sessions which met, as the name suggests, at Epiphany (January), Easter (April), St Thomas (July) and Michaelmas (October). Ecclesiastical courts or 'courts spiritual' dealt mainly with moral or religious infringements and matrimonial matters. As Martin Ingram has suggested, local communities could often manage their own affairs on the basis of 'a powerful ideal of communal harmony and consensus'.[11] But in cities, especially London with its constant influx of visitors and strangers from the shires and abroad, that solidarity was less assured. To impose order, London had a range of powerful prosecutory bodies. The Star Chamber, essentially the Privy Council sitting as a court, tried cases of riot or fraud but could also confront the power of the landed gentry or 'overmighty' noblemen. Across the river on the east side of Borough High Street, Southwark, the King's Bench dealt not only with riots and disputes but also pleas from the middling sort anxious to pursue a case beyond the sessions. Like the Marshalsea and White Lyon, also located in Southwark, the King's Bench could detain prisoners for extended periods of time.[12] Overseeing all these bodies, the lord mayor remained London's most powerful legal figure: he headed the court of common council and the court of aldermen which appointed the City's most senior magistrate, the London Recorder.

The most serious crimes involved insurrection, treason or seditious speech. Edmund Campion, the Jesuit missionary, was sentenced in 1581 to be hanged, cut down while alive, his 'privy parts' cut off, his entrails emptied out and burnt as he watched, finally beheaded and his limbs distributed to 'be disposed of at her Majesty's pleasure'. In the event, he was probably dead before the real butchery began.[13] A similarly gruesome fate awaited William Garton, seminary priest of Rheims, convicted of treason in September 1588. John Lockwood, another Catholic priest, was likewise condemned in 1610 but accorded a reprieve, the sentence alone having presumably made enough of a point. Instances of seditious speech deemed less serious or inflammatory might be corrected at the pillory.[14] In 1610, Katheren

---

[10]   Kermode and Walker, *Women, Crime and the Courts*, p. 1; Griffiths, *Lost Londons*, p. 433.

[11]   Martin Ingram, *Church Courts, Sex and Marriage in England 1570–1640* (Cambridge: Cambridge University Press, 1987), p. 30.

[12]   For these prisons, see John Stow, *A Survey of London*, ed. C.L. Kingsford (Oxford: Clarendon Press, 1908, 1971), ii. pp. 53, 59, 60–2. See further London Metropolitan Archives (LMA), P92/Geo Item 139, St George, the Martyr, Southwark, composite register for burials of prisoners from the 'White Lyon' (27 and 29 December 1608). Many towns, wards and parishes had small lock-ups known as 'the cage', from which prisoners sometimes escaped: see BCB 3.83ʳ (Arthur Coggens, 3 November 1576); 4.50ʳ (Anne Handburye, 29 November 1598); 4.97ʳ (Anne Flood, 23 July 1599). Stratford-upon-Avon's 'cage' was situated on the corner of Bridge Street and High Street, where now stands a vendor of soothing bathroom products. See Robert Bearman, *Stratford-upon-Avon: A History of Its Streets and Buildings* (Stratford-upon-Avon: Hendon, 1988), pp. 15–16.

[13]   Richard Simpson, *Edmund Campion, A Biography* (London: John Hodges, 1896), pp. 436, 454.

[14]   For Garton, see Jeaffreson, *Middlesex County Sessions*, i. pp. 180; for Lockwood, see ii. pp. 62–3, 204–7; for punishment of seditious speech by pillory, see i. p. 195.

Atkinson had publicly wished a plague upon 'all Scottes that ever came to England' but was merely bound over to keep the peace.[15] The crime of counterfeiting money was taken very seriously and given the severest punishment. Thomas Boswell and Bartholomew Wilkins clipped and filed some of the king's coin for which they were condemned to be executed as traitors.[16] Executions did not always go well. Michael Bankes, held in the King's Bench for an unstated offence, was 'executed & did revive againe & was in the old Vestry at the last, and then he was carried back & was executed againe'.[17] The sessions give no indication that any woman was ever hanged, drawn and quartered, and so Shakespeare's depiction of the mutilated Lavinia in *Titus Andronicus* is likely to have proved especially sensational and shocking in its own time.

Theft was a constant problem, and apprehended thieves, both male and female, would usually hang. As Burbage's case showed, portable household objects were commonly stolen, including plate and linen, but also rings, chains, bracelets, coin, spoons and gilt or silver goblets. In 1615, Henry Pyke, of Cow Cross near Clerkenwell, managed to steal what amounted to virtually an entire bookseller's stock from the premises of one John Drawater.[18] The volumes included 26 'gramers' [grammars], 10 'virgills', 24 'Esop's Fables', 'one book called Castilian Dialogues', three books called 'The Practice of Piety', five with the title 'Delightes wth closett', one edition of 'A Historie Bible', three books of 'Sutton on the Sacramente' and two editions of 'To Learn to live'.[19] The Host of the George tavern in *The Merry Devil of Edmonton* (1608), performed 'sundry times' by the King's Men at the Globe, makes reference to his 'Castilian Dialogues', and the title may lie obscurely behind Sir Toby Belch's quip 'Castilian vulgo' in *Twelfth Night*.[20] 'Delightes wth closett' seems to have been Sir Hugh Platt's '*Delightes for ladies, to adorne their persons, tables, closets, and distillatories. With, bewties, banquets, perfumes and waters. Read, practise, and censure* (1600), printed by Peter Short, a marvellous mix of gastronomic, aromatic and cosmetic advices extolling, among other things, the virtues of boiled lark or sparrow and remedies for the 'Ytch'. The three volumes of *The Practice of Piety*, by Lewis Bayly, seem to have been a first edition (now lost) since the only surviving imprint of this title belongs to 1616, newly 'Amplified by the author' and printed by Robert Allott.[21] It was not only portable household property that was stolen but horses, cattle and sheep too. On 10 September 1594, the sessions heard a case brought by the Lord Chamberlain:

> *Thomas Welde late of Edmonton co. Midd. yoman stole a tambe [sic] stagge of red colour worth ten shillings, with a bell worth two pence and a leather collar attached to the neck of the same stag, of the goods and chattels of the Most Noble Henry Lord Hunesdon, Lord Chamberlain of the Queen's Household.*[22]

Shakespeare, who had been a Chamberlain's player for about four months by this time, may perhaps have been reminded of his own poaching activities, if there is any truth in Nicholas

---

[15] Jeaffreson, *Middlesex County Sessions*, ii. p. 55.

[16] Ibid., p. 57. Thomas Marshall and Roger Newton faced hanging and butchery at Tyburn in 1607 for 'counterfeiting' money (ibid., p. 13), and it is likely that the Stratford cutler Robert Evans, father of prostitute Elizabeth Evans, would have met a similar fate. See 'The Case of Elizabeth Evans', *Notes and Queries* 50:1 (2003), 60–61.

[17] LMA, P92/Geo Item 139, St George, the Martyr, Southwark, composite register (28 June 1610).

[18] This Drawater may have been servant to the Earl of Oxford. See Essex Record Office D/DPr/180, 260, 262.

[19] Jeaffreson, *Middlesex County Sessions*, ii. p. 109.

[20] See Anon., *The Merry Devil of Edmonton* (sig. C[v]), and *Twelfth Night*, 'Castiliano vulgo' (1.3.39).

[21] The books evidently did not originate from a single printer's shop.

[22] Jeaffreson, *Middlesex County Sessions*, i. p. 223.

Rowe's story that he stole deer from Sir Thomas Lucy of Charlecote near Stratford and fled to London because of it.[23] Most thieves brought before the sessions courts were sentenced to hang. Stage thefts, such as Cocledemoy's filching of pewter pots from Mulligrub's tavern in *The Dutch Courtesan* (1604), or the disguised Follywit's robbing of his father, Sir Bounteous Progress, in *A Mad World My Masters* (1608), may have been felonies writ comically large for the purposes of entertaining an audience, but beyond the theatre walls they were taken very seriously indeed. It was Shakespeare who depicted the bleak consequences of such (relatively minor) offences, in *Henry V*, where Bardolph is dismally strung up for stealing a pix.

If theft was a daily problem in the city, so too was violent assault. Because most men carried rapiers and daggers, quarrels could very quickly prove fatal. There were many instances where a sudden disagreement rapidly escalated into mortal wounding, usually by sword or bill. The literate could win reprieve, however, by pleading 'benefit of clergy'. This process was known routinely as 'asking the book' or reading one's 'neck verse'. If the accused managed to read the first verse of Psalm 51 to the court, they might escape with a less severe punishment like branding. Records of such pleas ran in Latin: 'Po se cul [puts himself guilty] or cognoscit indictamentum [He confesses the indictment]; catalla nulla; petit librum; legit ut clericus [has no chattels; asks for the book; reads like a clerk].' In desperation, many illiterate defendants would ask the book, fail to read, and be summarily hanged. In 1564, a coroner's inquest heard that Ralph Houghton had fatally wounded Hugh Lewys with a dagger in his left side. The clerk's note is almost casual: Houghton 'asks for the book, does not read like a clerk: – Therefore, let him be hung.'[24] Two years earlier, Thomas Hewys, accused of slaying Lewis Howell 'by giving him with a dagger a mortal blow on his breast' pleaded that the affray had been 'forced upon him' and that he had acted in self-defence. If it was a dilatory plea, it worked, for Hewys's case was held back and he was returned to gaol.[25] In such cases, Justices of the Peace or a jury had to decide whether the incident amounted to murder, manslaughter or self-defence, and with very imperfect powers of detection the precise facts could often remain murky. The Admiral's man Richard Allen, formerly one of the 'Quenes players' and (like the majority of London's actors at the time) a resident of St Saviour's parish, Southwark, was fatally wounded in a dispute at a tavern reminiscent of another more notable killing. As after Marlowe's death, the full story was probably withheld:

> *Margarett Ellice wiefe of Edmond Ellice saieth that she knoweth one Richard Allen a Player but she never saw him but once and then they supte togeather in Tower streete where there was a fallinge out about paying the Recconinge And the said Allen was hurte there ys ordered to be delivered upon sureties for hir & her husbandes appearance at the next Courte of Aldermen.*[26]

The Ellices did not appear at the next aldermen's court.[27]

On other occasions, the court felt it had sufficient information to make a judgment. When Richard Blunt set upon John Tarlton, who was reported to have been 'in God's and the Queen's peace', with a rapier and dagger, John retreated but found himself hemmed in by a ditch. Being pursued, he turned, drew his own rapier and ran Blunt through the eye. The event was witnessed by a 'multitude of persons there' and Tarlton was granted a verdict of

---

23   René Weis, *Shakespeare Revealed: A Biography* (London: John Murray, 2005), pp. 70–71.
24   Ibid., p. 52.
25   Ibid., p. 41.
26   Bridewell Court Minute Book (hereafter BCB) 4.270ᵛ (31 October 1601).
27   Allen's killing is likely to have been felt by Philip Henslowe. He had lost his star dramatists Marlowe and Kyd, and would later acknowledge his great loss after Jonson's killing of Gabriel Spencer (see note 29).

self-defence.[28] Ben Jonson's quarrel with Admiral's actor Gabriel Spencer became infamous. Jonson was arraigned before a jury at the Old Bailey in October 1598 after fatally wounding Spencer in Hoggesden Fields in Shoreditch. Like Tarlton, Spencer was reported to have been 'in God's and the Queen's peace' when he was set upon. Philip Henslowe wrote to his son-in-law, Edward Alleyne, of his alarm at Spencer's killing, and he seems to have regarded Jonson as culpable.[29] Jonson himself much later insisted to friends that the attack had been a duel initiated by Spencer, and he could point for support to Spencer's slaying of John Feake in a similar quarrel almost two years earlier.[30] Had he genuinely believed himself innocent, Jonson could have put himself 'Not Guilty' and pleaded self-defence, but in any event, he must have known he was unlikely to hang. A memorandum attached to his case reads as follows: 'Cogn' Indictament petit librum legit ut Cl'icus sign' cum lra T Et del' iuxta formam statut' [confesses the indictment, asks the book, reads like a Clerk, is marked with the letter 'T' and is delivered according to the form of the statute].[31] The T-brand stood for 'Tyburn', the site of London's fearful triangular gallows near what is now Marble Arch.

Individual cases like Jonson's may prove compelling, but they can tell us little about patterns of crime, unless offences are tracked in greater numbers and across several years. It would be worth knowing, for example, if there was a crime explosion. Were there 'new' crimes, or new ways of dealing with crime that emerged? Which crimes were most or least common? How successful were processes of detection or apprehension, and how did they work? Are there signs of an increase or decline in crime statistics for the period, and what might that mean? What do instances of crime tell us about popular culture more generally? Records for London perhaps give a more detailed picture than those for the shires but serious obstacles confront the interpretation of data. Statistics for crime in the early modern period are shot through with inadequacies: an unquantifiable number of crimes went unrecorded, and all kinds of local factors or conditions were likely to have affected the figures, including the specific location of the sessions houses. But these difficulties do not mean that no census of early crime can be of significance. The second volume of *Middlesex County Records*, edited by J.C. Jeaffreson, includes a statistical count of felonies for each regnal year from 3 Edward VI (January 1549) to 22 James I (March 1625).[32] These figures are based on selected indictments transcribed from an estimated total of some 30,000 documents, including Newgate Gaol Delivery Rolls, General Sessions of Peace Rolls, Special Sessions of 'Oyer et Terminer' Rolls and Inquest or Composite Rolls. Given the great number of manuscript sources, the hearings they preserve are disproportionately few. Courts met infrequently and considered only a small handful of cases each month. The subsequently published transcriptions were, therefore, themselves only a very limited sample drawn from a range of documents. Water damage, mice, humidity and carelessness had over the centuries ensured that any dream of a complete account of early modern crime must remain a mirage. Numbers of published prosecutions certainly do not equate with numbers of crimes committed: consequently, any inferences drawn from the published sessions must be interpreted with great caution. Those cases do, however, point to evident trends.[33]

---

[28]   Jeaffreson, *Middlesex County Sessions*, i. pp. 104–5 (12 March 1577).

[29]   Ibid., i. pp. xxxviii–xlii, 249; R. Foakes ed., *Henslowe's Diary* (Cambridge: Cambridge University Press, 2002), p. 286.

[30]   Jeaffreson, *Middlesex County Sessions*, i. p. xxxix; see also Ian Donaldson's *ODNB* entry for Jonson.

[31]   Jeaffreson, *Middlesex County Sessions*, i. pp. xxxviii–xxxix. For a valuable discussion of early modern court punishments, see Martin Ingram, 'Shame and Pain: Themes and Variations in Tudor Punishments', in Devereaux and Griffiths eds, *Penal Practice and Culture*, pp. 36–62.

[32]   Jeaffreson, *Middlesex County Sessions*, ii. pp. 239–314.

[33]   Jeaffreson's work may now be somewhat stricken in years but Sharpe repeatedly notes its value, *Crime in Early Modern England*, pp. 9, 56.

Jeaffreson's figures highlight some striking fluctuations: he notes just two indictments for burglary in 19 Elizabeth (Nov 1576–7) but 11 the following year; similarly, he gives two for 24 Elizabeth (Nov 1581–2), but 27 for 42 Elizabeth (Nov 1599–1600). It is difficult to ascertain the precise reasons behind these variations. A drop to seven in 1603 may be due partly to the terrible outbreak of plague that summer.[34] Horse thefts seem also to have varied: six in 1580–1, and 20 the next year.[35] Prosecutions for relatively minor infringements such as keeping dung in a public space (or dropping it into a neighbour's well), selling meat in Lent, encroaching on a highway, forced entry or disseizure, gaming, trespass and harbouring ill-disposed or suspected persons, were infrequent. Jeaffreson notes that from 20 Elizabeth (1577–8) some juries began to find those accused of grand larceny (a charge incurring death, branding or mutilation) guilty merely of petty larceny, deserving the whip only. Under Edward and Mary, the Middlesex sessions dealt with neighbourhood issues of theft, dispute and matters of public order. Midway through Elizabeth's reign, a new crime of recusancy, or 'not coming to church', was invented, an offence that incurred a fine of up to 20 pounds. The crime of recusancy arose in response to threats posed by Douai seminarians, the Northern Rebellion, the 1570 excommunication, the St Bartholomew's Day Massacre and especially the setting foot on English soil of Campion and Persons in 1580–81. The first note of recusancy in the Middlesex sessions occurs on 18 March 1581. After this date, suspected recusants were regularly cited in the sessions rolls, and those apprehended began to appear in prisoner lists for the Wood Street Compter, Marshalsea, Clink and Fleet prisons.[36]

The sessions figures show that serious crimes like murder and rape rarely came to court. Jeaffreson records just five indictments for murder in the whole of Mary's reign: by 1604, that figure had risen only moderately to about five per year. Hanging rates varied little throughout the latter half of the sixteenth century: again, Jeaffreson notes 63 Edwardian capital sentences, under Mary 83, and 78 in the first four years of Elizabeth. They seem to have peaked under James at 76 for the single year of 1616. These are figures for just one court, but they also indicate that many more males than females were hanged, a ratio generally of around 10:1. Sessions indictments for witchcraft and rape were sparse, beginning in 1574 and 1578 respectively. The number of murder and rape cases rose only slightly from 1558–1625, averaging little more than two per year. Such statistics do not mean, of course, that these crimes were not happening.

A table representing 800 indictments from the sessions points up some of these trends (see Table 12.1). In the period 1549–55, thefts accounted for 54 per cent of all cases. This percentage broadly held for the period 1559–66 (55 per cent), declined through Elizabeth's reign to a low of 18 per cent in 1590–93, but rose to 21 per cent for the years 1593–7. By 1607–9, that figure had gone up to 25 per cent, still nearly half the numbers in the reigns of Edward and Mary. When these totals are separated into thefts involving clothing, money and plate, cattle and horses, again all figures show a marked decline over the years 1549–1609. Prosecutions of assaults and murders also reduce. There may be several factors behind this downward trend: economic or demographic changes, better governance and policing in the metropolis or perhaps the devastating effects of plague. But there is one development that Jeaffreson's numbers do not show, and that is the regular use of recognisances and sureties

---

[34]   Jeaffreson, *Middlesex County Sessions*, ii. pp. 261–2. Plague broke out in late June and began to subside only the following January.

[35]   It should be noted that these numbers exceed those in the count Jeaffreson published (ibid., pp. 264-5). For verifiable figures based on his transcriptions, see Table 1.

[36]   Jeaffreson, *Middlesex County Sessions*, i. pp. 122–3. See J.E. Neale, *Elizabeth and Her Parliaments 1559–1581* (London: Jonathan Cape, 1953), pp. 378–406. I am grateful to Dr Paul Quinn for his comments on the context of recusancy. For prisoner lists, see Publications of the Catholic Record Society Vol. XXII, *Miscellanea XII* (London, Leeds: J. Whitehead, 1921), pp. 128–31.

Table 12.1   Crimes in the Middlesex County Sessions 1549–1609*

Years	1549–55	1559–66	1566–73	1573–8	1590–93	1593–7	1603–7	1607–9
Pages	i 1–23	i 34–57	i 58–80	i 89–115	i 189–213	i 213–35	ii 1–31	ii 31–56
Sample	100	100	100	100	100	100	100	100
Thefts	54	55	48	30	18	21	21	25
of clothing	18	13	6	7	3	4	6	10
of cattle	6	4	3	1	1	1	3	0
of horses	13	4	3	1	2	3	1	0
of coin	12	8	3	4	3	5	5	4
Assaults	24	9	11	11	21	25	8	5
Murder	5	5	4	7	4	1	3	0
Sex crime	1	2	0	2	2	0	1	1
Infanticide	0	1	0	1	2	2	0	0
Suicide	1	3	0	0	0	0	0	0
Riot	5	4	4	0	1	1	0	3
Sedition	1	0	0	0	2	0	1	3
Recusancy	0	0	0	0	9	7	17	12
Witchcraft	0	0	0	1	2	1	2	0
Bound	0	0	1	22	21	29	33	31

*Note: Years are given in New Style dating. Page numbers are keyed to volumes 1 and 2 of the *Middlesex County Sessions Records*, edited by J.C. Jeaffreson. Numbers refer to specific instances of prosecution or cases heard. Coin includes theft of precious metals such as gold or silver objects. Murder includes charges of attempted murder. Sex crime includes instances of rape and running a bawdy house. Riot includes unlawful assembly, encroachment and disseizure. Sedition refers mainly to subversive speech. Bound refers to persons placed under conditions of a recognisance.

after 1569.[37] These were orders that bound the accused to appear at the next court, prove themselves good neighbours, keep the peace, refrain from illicit activity or depart the city, all under penalty of a fine. Friends or associates would undertake to see these conditions met, and those accused understood the gallows usually awaited repeat offenders. The order of recognisances became routine. Placing someone under an obligation to act as the court ordered on pain of a fine proved an efficient and cost-effective use of time and resources, especially for less serious misdemeanours. It was an innovative strategy for the 1570s and it worked. Bonds of this kind could be replicated throughout the devolved structures of government associated with gilds and companies and so prevent many cases reaching the sessions or assizes. Similarly effective was an extraordinary, new institution, a 'house of correction' situated in a former royal palace just west of the filthy River Fleet and facing the Thames: London's Bridewell Hospital, awarded its charter in 1553.

Bridewell Hospital had been built as a palace in 1522 by Wolsey, used as an ambassadorial residence, and then granted by Edward VI to the City in 1553 as an institution for 'setting on work' the destitute, idle and vagrant. However charitable the City's initial ambitions might have been, Bridewell quickly evolved into an Elizabethan gulag at the very heart of which stood a whipping-post. Dreadful as must have been, Bridewell had no power to execute criminals and an arrested thief stood a far better chance of survival there than at the sessions, or on remand in Newgate where prisoners regularly died of 'pining sickness' or 'Divine Visitation'. Bridewell's regime was harsh and in protest several prisoners refused or spoiled their work. Some in desperation tried to escape or commit suicide. But the hospital could also keep prisoners long term, its spacious rooms readily adapted to house staff or accommodate prisoners at work spinning, beating hemp for rope or making nails or bricks.[38] Constructed around two courtyards, Bridewell featured a magnificent stairway leading to an imposing Great Hall where the court room was situated. The bench met on Wednesdays and Saturdays and assumed extensive powers of arrest and custody. Runaways, pickpockets, nightwalkers, adulterers and vagrants were brought in by deputies, constables or beadles who trawled London's lanes armed with staves and warrants, in pursuit of parish information. Bridewell's extant hearings begin in 1559 with fairly sporadic cases numbering around 20 per month. By 1579, its work had become routine, processing 154 cases in August alone. Throughout the 1570s, it engaged in intelligence gathering, acting on witness statements to assess just how extensive criminal associations really were in and beyond the City. By 1600, the court could regularly process around 100 items of business each month, often herding large groups of vagrants ('masterless' men, women and children) through its doors and seeing them 'well-whipped' and delivered with passports.[39]

Bridewell took upon itself the task of regulating sexual conduct throughout the City and its environs. It frequently punished women made pregnant out of wedlock, many of whom had been promised marriage by a now absent male. Shakespeare dramatised precisely this kind of distress in *Measure for Measure*. Some women abandoned their infants: there were many Perditas in early modern England. As today, children were vulnerable to abuse, a fact

---

[37] Jeaffreson, *Middlesex County Sessions*, i. p. 65 (26 May 1569).

[38] The Bridewell court books show 'arts-masters' repeatedly petitioning for rooms or chambers, especially after a tenant's dismissal or decease.

[39] The growth in monthly items of business dealt with by the Bridewell court usefully illustrates the hospital's development as an institution of public order. Bridewell cases per month are: May 1559, 17; September 1561, 41; October 1574, 59; May 1577, 86; August 1579, 154; September 1601, 87; July 1605, 99. In March and October 1596, John Wolfe was paid by the Bridgemasters for printing 2,000 and 1,000 passports for those leaving the borough. See LMA, Repertories of the Court of Aldermen, 23, 539v and 585v.

Shakespeare and Wilkins illustrated in *Pericles*. Bridewell's court books hold some pitiful details of cruelty and exploitation: Joan Weekes,

> *a little girle of x. or xi. yeres olde saithe that one Roberte Adames alias vynegar Assauted [sic] hir to Ravishe hir three or fower tymes, but especiallie on this daye three weekes he forced hir and had the use of hir bodie, And at the doinge thereof he helde a knife in his hande & threatened hir that yf she either tolde or cried he wolde sticke hir.*[40]

Eleven-year-old Elizabeth Guy was repeatedly raped in a ditch by Robert Archer over two days: 'she poshed him awaie & cried when he was doing of it but he wolde not awaie or leve her'. The court detained Archer, set him to hard labour and released the girl to her mother 'to be cured & holpe of the said grief'.[41] Women carrying a child through illicit sex would sometimes be whipped, or if near their term given a conditional bail. On 19 July 1603, Patience Painter, 'an harlot great with childe', named Robert Weedon a 'chopper of bones' in Turnagain Lane as the father. Despite being '14 weeks gone', she was whipped before being released.[42]

Other less traumatic cases seem to convey an element of bedroom farce. Servingman Thomas Clarke told the court how he had espied Mistress Joan Quiney visiting the bedroom of a Master Farmer. Clarke 'harde Master Farmor give a great puffe, and with the same the bedde gave a greate cracke, fie saieth she how you sweate, marrie saieth he I always do so when I am in the countrie'.[43] On 10 November 1576, Richard Wright, a cobbler, confessed that:

> *he did attempt to have had thuse of the body of widowe Bakers. And he had her by the geare in her owne house wth her consent And at another tyme the said Bakers wyfe came and satt in his lapp and kyssed hym wth her hand aboute his neck & his wief came & toke them & knocked there hedds together.*[44]

Memorably, as though proud of her achievement, Helen Rowse stood before the Bridewell magistrates on 12 July 1600 to confess that she had cut 'the haer of her secretes & did give the same to her guestes to drincke for tobacco [and] also hath divers tymes held upp her clothes in the presence of her guestes & shewed them her secretes they commending of the same'. Alice Miller, the prison matron, confirmed the 'cuttinge awaie the haier'.[45] Such instances remind that tragedy and comedy did not just belong in playhouses. They lend an effect of proximity to the occasion, of incidents happening at very specific moments of time and place, and a sense of how life was lived, endured and risked from day to day.

Drawing to a close, it should be noted that historical records of early modern crime and their literary representations align in different ways or to varying degrees. Instances of crime may, for example, highlight just how estranged from each other the literary and the historical can sometimes be. The tale of Long Meg of Westminster, for example, became very popular, mentioned in tracts, pamphlets and plays, from the punningly pseudo-Lutheran Martin Marprelate's *Theses Martinianae* (1589) to works by Dekker, Nathan Field, Ben Jonson and Thomas Heywood in the early seventeenth century. A work entitled *The Life of Long*

---

[40]   BCB 2. 128[r] (6 July 1575).
[41]   BCB 3.49[r-v] (14 July 1576).
[42]   BCB 4.397[r].
[43]   BCB 2.196[v] (21 December 1575). Joan was possibly kinswoman to Shakespeare's Stratford associates Richard and Thomas Quiney who had London connections. Farmer's quip anticipates Hamlet's 'country matters' (*Hamlet*, 3.2.111), perhaps a joke circulating among 'private friends'.
[44]   BCB 3.86[r] (10 November 1576).
[45]   BCB 4.173[r] (12 July 1600).

Meg of Westminster was registered in 1590, and Henslowe took 'iii^{li} ix s' at the Rose for a performance of 'longe mege of westmester' on 14 February 1594.[46] A 1635 prose pamphlet, which might have echoed the play, bears the full title *The life of Long Meg of Westminster containing the mad merry prankes shee played in her life time, not onely in performing sundry quarrels with diuers ruffians about London: but also how valiantly she behaued her selfe in the warres of Bolloingne.* Its address to the reader explains that it has been composed 'to please your fantasies', like the stories of Robin Hood or Bevis of Southampton, and that it concerns a woman 'of late memory, and well-beloved, spoken on of all and known of many'.[47] This short picaresque tale comprises 18 episodes illustrating how she beat a carrier, fought off a vicar and thieves, made merry with John Skelton and Will Somers, met Sir Thomas More, took on the French in combat at Boulogne, won a duel, eventually married and out-did local tradesmen upon her return to England. By the end of the story, she has become a folk-hero, a woman to be celebrated for her pranks and displays of courage.

This 'Long Meg' seems to have been largely a literary invention, an entertaining figure who (physically) stands out and ends up winning the admiration of all, but there was also a life behind the myth. On 25 February 1560/1, 'Johanne Hower' was noted to have been 'sondry tymes occupied in the house of one Barnes alias Longe Megge in long wolstable next the waterside wch house is a common bawdy howse wherin she affirmeth to be these harlottes Elizabeth Horspole Luce, and Besse'.[48] This entry locates the historical Long Meg quite precisely.[49] Bernard Capp first brought these details of the real Long Meg to light. On 13 May 1561, one of Long Meg's maidservants, Elizabeth Giles, was detained, and her compatriot Elizabeth Lethermore accused of having been 'abused in the house of Long Meg' by 'one Ratclyff inhabiting at the King's hed in Chepsyd'.[50] Meg in fact turned up at Bridewell voluntarily:

> *Margaret Barnes otherwise called Long Megg came into this house the xvii of May 1561 for that she was accused to be a common bawde and desired to come to make her purgacion [clear her name] But when she came, the matter was so vehemently insisted against her that she could not denye the same, and so departed with shame because she was befor promysed to to go and come safely.*[51]

Two days later, Elynor Colyer was brought in by warrant from the Dean of Westminster for being a 'common resorter to Long Megges at Westmynster'. Colyer confessed that Meg ran 'a very vile house' and that there one 'M. M.' had abused her twice 'contra naturem' [anally], and also Elizabeth Giles in like manner. The actuality of Meg's life seems to have been rather less merry and heroic than the later outlandish pamphlets about her would suggest. Literary and historical documents about Meg diverge in their social purposes on almost every point other than her name and place of residence, Westminster. Capp observes that the posthumous series of picaresque tales about her reflects a 'plausible' tradition.

---

[46]   Foakes, *Henslowe's Diary*, p. 27.

[47]   A3^r.

[48]   BCB 1 121^r.

[49]   Stow tells us the Woolstaple was situated close to the 'high tower, or gate, which entereth the palace court' at Westminster. He also notes that Henry VI had six wool-houses in the staple of Westminster. Stow, *A Survey of London*, ii. pp. 102, 104, 375, 378. Kingsford adds, 'The Long Staple extended from the south end of Canon Row to King Street' (p. 375). Long Meg's house 'next the waterside' is shown as adjoining Westminster Stairs in Adrian Proctor and Robert Taylor eds, *The A-Z of Elizabethan London* (Lympne Castle, Kent: Harry Margary, 1979), Plate 16.

[50]   BCB 1.134^v. See Bernard Capp, 'Long Meg of Westminster: A Mystery Solved', *Notes and Queries* 243 [NS, 45], 3 (September 1998) pp. 302–4.

[51]   BCB 1.135^v.

He may well be right, but it is also evident that popular fiction about Long Meg departed significantly from the history that lay chronologically behind it.

We come, then, to a last example where, by contrast, the real and fictive seem to coincide more nearly. On Saturday 20 January 1598/9, Katherine Cuffe was brought into Bridewell by the Marshall, being suspected of an illicit relationship with Ambrose Jasper. She confessed to have given birth to a boy some three months past and that Jasper, 'Master Cook' of the Inner Temple, had been its father. Jasper had urged her 'to come in boyes apparrell for that he would not have her come in her owne apparrell least that she should be espyed'. Dressed as a boy, she smuggled herself into the Inner Temple and waited for him in his chamber, having already sent word of her arrival by the porter. Jasper's man arrived at the chamber where she gave him 'a little golde ringe' as a 'token' for his master. Both porter and servant corroborated this version of events, adding that Cuffe had appeared in 'A doblett & hose and A cloke and A hatt'. It was not an especially effective disguise for Jasper's man knew all along 'it was Katherine Cuffe in A boyes apparrell that gave him that gold ringe'.[52]

Jasper thereafter disappeared. Summonses were issued against him.[53] In May, the Bridewell governors sought the lord chief justice's advice as to whether Jasper should be arraigned before the court of aldermen or whether they should 'leave the same to his Honors discrecion'. By the end of August, Jasper had still not appeared and it was decided he should be tried at the Guildhall. Then at the end of October, the Bridewell governors responded with some alarm to an action he had launched against alderman Christopher Hodsdon in the Court of Common Pleas, complaining of his wrongful imprisonment and 'molestacon'.[54] The case had rumbled on throughout 1599, and must have caused a stir among lawyers at the Inner and Middle Temples. In February 1601/2, Inns member John Manningham recorded that he had seen a performance of *Twelfth Night* 'at our feast' (Candlemas), noting the device for tricking Malvolio as particularly impressive. He recognised that Shakespeare's play was similar to an Italian play called *Gl'Ingannati* ('The Deceived', published in Venice in 1537):

> Febr: 1601/
> 2/. at our feast wee had a play called ~~mid~~ Twelue night or what you will /.// much like the commedy of errors / or Menechmi in plautus / but most like and neere to that in Italian called Inganni a good practise in it to make the steward beleeue his Lady widdowe was in Loue wth him by counterfayting a lett^r / as from his Lady in generall tearmes / telling him what shee liked best in him / and prescribing his gesture in smiling his apparraile / etc /. And then when he came to practise, making him beleeue they tooke him to be mad.[55]

Shakespeare took the motif of Viola's disguise in 'boyes apparrell' from precursor stories, including *Gl'Inganni* and Barnabe Riche's tale of Apolonius and Silla in his *Riche his Farewell to Militarie Profession* (1581). It seems he took the names of Viola and Olivia, and the giving of a ring from Emanuel Forde's *The Famous History of Parismus* (1598). Yet these aspects of his composition chimed perfectly with a little local difficulty at the Temple in 1599. The Middle and Inner Temples were (and are) situated beside each other, and members would join together for Christmas revels and performances, as they did for the 'night of errors' at Gray's Inn on 28 December 1594. When Prospero makes his valedictory speech about the

---

[52]   BCB 4. 61^{r-v}.

[53]   BCB 4.67^r, 71^r.

[54]   BCB 4.82^v, 119^r. The Bridewell governors noted they would spend whatever it took to fight the case.

[55]   Cited from William Shakespeare, *Twelfth Night*, ed. J.M. Lothian and T.W. Craik (London: Methuen, 1975), p. xxvi.

revels being ended, he refers to 'The clowd-capt Towres, the gorgeous Pallaces / The solemne Temples, the great Globe itself', ceremonial or theatrical spaces in and around London. The Temples were not, it seems, always so solemn. Writing *Twelfth Night*, Shakespeare may have guessed that when the actor playing Olivia tells Malvolio, 'he left this ring behind him, / Would I or not; tell him I'll none of it' (1.5.291–2), he would be touching a lately topical, theatrical and ridiculous nerve.

Select Bibliography

Cockburn, J.S. ed., Crime in England, 1550–1800. Princeton: Princeton University Press, 1977.

Cressy, David, *Agnes Bowker's Cat: Travesties and Transgressions in Tudor and Stuart England*. Oxford: Oxford University Press, 2000.

Dean, David, *Law-Making and Society in Late Elizabethan England: The Parliament of England, 1584–1601*. Cambridge: Cambridge University Press, 1996.

Devereaux, Simon, and Paul Griffiths eds, *Penal Practice and Culture, 1500–1900: Punishing the English*. Basingstoke: Palgrave Macmillan, 2004.

Gowing, Laura, *Domestic Dangers: Women, Words, and Sex in Early Modern London*. Oxford: Oxford University Press, 1998.

Griffiths, Paul, *Lost Londons: Change, Crime and Control in the Capital City 1550–1660*. Cambridge: Cambridge University Press, 2008.

Griffiths, Paul, A. Fox and Steve Hindle eds, *The Experience of Authority in Early Modern England*. Basingstoke: Palgrave Macmillan, 1996.

Ingram, Martin, *Church Courts, Sex and Marriage in England 1570–1640*. Cambridge: Cambridge University Press, 1987.

Jeaffreson, J.C. ed., *Middlesex County Sessions Records 1603–1625*. London: GLC, 1974.

Kent, Joan, *The English Village Constable, 1580–1642: A Social and Administrative Study*. Oxford: Oxford University Press, 1986.

Kermode, Jenny, and Garthine Walker eds, *Women, Crime and the Courts in Early Modern England*. London: UCL Press, 1994.

Sharpe, J. A., *Crime in Early Modern England 1550–1750*. Harlow: Longman, 1984.

Popular Xenophobia

Matthew Birchwood and Matthew Dimmock

Calais was to blame for making England a new Sodom or Gomorrah, argued the clergyman and geographer William Harrison in his *Description of England* (1587). Its acquisition from the French by Edward III began a process of English degeneration that started with 'trade in divers countries' but soon the English 'began to wax idle … and thereupon not only left off their former painfulness and frugality but in like sort gave themselves to live in excess and vanity'. Worse, this process was accelerated by those 'strangers' dwelling in the realm who, 'perceiving our sluggishness and espying that this idleness of ours might redound to their great profit, forthwith employed their endeavors to bring in the supply of such things as we lacked continually from foreign countries, which yet more augmented our idleness'.[1] The celebration and idealisation of an earlier 'glorious isolation' from the Continent; the denigration of the role of 'strangers' in the realm: in many respects, Harrison's vision of contemporary England seems not only familiar but to confirm a 'legendary English xenophobia'.[2]

There is certainly an antipathy in Harrison's work that appears to bear out Laura Hunt Yungblut's thesis that late sixteenth-century England witnessed a 'rising tide of anti-alien expressions' that stemmed from 'xenophobic preconceptions and misconceptions' and was concentrated in (but not exclusive to) the lower classes.[3] Harrison is not so easily characterised as a xenophobe, however. His primary target is not 'strangers' but his own debased countrymen. Bewitched by fashions from abroad – 'the Spanish guise … the French toys … the High Almain fashion … the Turkish manner … the Morisco gowns, the Barbarian sleeves' – the English have no national identity left, and are defined only by their ability to ape others.[4] There is an underlying antipathy for those products associated with the outside world that pollute the English, which might feasibly be extended to that world and its inhabitants. Yet this again does not bear scrutiny. Harrison never loses sight of English volition, nor does he express any hatred for the non-English; rather he laments the monstrous mixing, inconstancy and displacement that a world increasingly interconnected by trade and goods generates. For him, 'we have neglected our own good gifts of God growing here at home' and have 'every trifle and toy in admiration that is brought hither from far countries'.[5]

As Harrison's account and several recent studies have shown, xenophobia is a deeply problematic term when applied to the early modern period. Numerous petitions,

---

1   William Harrison, *The Description of England: The Classic Contemporary Account of Tudor Social Life* [1587], ed. Georges William Edelen (New York: The Folger Library and Dover Publications, 1994), p. 263.

2   Laura Hunt Yungblut, *Strangers Settled Here amongst Us: Policies, Perceptions and the Presence of Aliens in Early Modern England* (London: Routledge, 1996), p. 115.

3   Ibid., pp. 40–41.

4   Harrison, *The Description of England*, pp. 145–6.

5   Ibid., p. 263.

proclamations and plays suggest that strong antipathy towards those perceived to be foreigners both in the capital and in the wider realm was a recognisable feature of early modern society. However, the English are just as often castigated for their love of all things unfamiliar, so this antipathy was far from being a consistent or even prevailing state of affairs. As a concept xenophobia (an early twentieth-century coinage in English) is furthermore difficult to place in early modern England. A document like the 'lewde and vyle ticket or placarde set upon some post in London' in early 1593, recorded in John Strype's *Annals of the Reformation*, might suggest a popular and widespread hatred for 'strangers':

> Doth not the world see that you beastly brutes the Belgians, or rather drunken drones and faint-hearted Flemings, and you fraudulent father Frenchmen, by your cowardly flight from your own natural countries, have abandoned the same into the hands of your proud cowardly enemies; and have, by a feigned hypocrisy and counterfeit show of religion, placed yourselves here in a most fertile soil, under a most gracious and merciful prince, who hath been contented, to the great prejudice of her natural subjects, to suffer you to live here, in better case and freedom than her own people.[6]

The anonymous libeller draws upon national caricature to castigate a specific group, the large number of Protestant refugees fleeing Spanish persecution in the Low Countries who came into England in the 1580s and 1590s. The categorisation that this entails is a polemic version of the vision of the peoples of the world circulated by cosmographers – each defined according to a specific and innate set of observable characteristics – and this is more important to the invective than undifferentiated hatred. The libel seeks to define the 'natural' English apart from those immigrants whom, it suggests, belong elsewhere, in their own 'natural countries' and naturally subject to their own princes. Although it initially appears straightforwardly xenophobic, it is an expression and definition of national identity and is similar to Harrison's account.

English attitudes to 'strangers' could vary considerably depending on context and even the most extreme did not necessarily gain popular support. Strype's libel was the product of a very specific set of circumstances in early 1593 – failed harvests, rapid inflation, demobbed troops in large numbers in London – and, despite its incendiary potential, the document failed to incite violence.[7] Perhaps more revealing are the responses recorded from those that came into contact with the Inuit captives returned to England from Martin Frobisher's ill-fated voyages in search of the North-West passage in 1576 and 1577. From the first voyage Frobisher returned one man and his kayak, from the second a man, a woman and her child. All would die in England, prey either to diseases to which the Inuit had no immunity or the injuries sustained in their capture.[8] The language in which they are described is remarkably varied, suggesting that the English had no single, established vocabulary in which to delineate such encounters, and that different contexts required different lexical registers. The primary account of the second voyage was written by the geographer and mariner George Best. He describes the Inuit as 'strange infidels', as 'savage and brutish' and as 'canibales', and assumes they are 'a kinde of Tartar' but with 'the same couloure & complexio[n] as all

---

[6]   John Strype, *The Annals of the Reformation and Establishment of Religion* (Oxford: Clarendon, 1824) vol. 4, pp. 234–5.

[7]   See P. Clark ed., *The European Crisis of the 1590s: Essays in Comparative History* (London: Allen & Unwin, 1985) and Matthew Dimmock, 'Guns and Gawds: Elizabethan England's Infidel Trade', in Jyotsna Singh ed., *A Companion to the Global Renaissance: English Literature and Culture in the Era of Expansion* (Oxford: Blackwell, 2009), pp. 207–22.

[8]   Neil Cheshire, Tony Waldron, Alison Quinn and David Quinn, 'Frobisher's Eskimos in England', *Archivaria* 10 (Summer 1980), 23–50.

the *Americans* are, which dwell under the Equinoticall line'.[9] Michael Lok, a major funder of the expedition, describes them as 'tawney Moores', whilst William Adams, the Mayor of Bristol, notes only that 'they were savage people and fed only upon raw flesh'.[10] Such accounts alternate between reliance on an Heroditan trope of savagery and an attempt to place and to categorise in terms of the known. The large crowds of onlookers drawn by the spectacle of the Inuit had a slightly different reaction: this 'strange man and his bote ... was such a wonder unto the whole city [of London] and to the rest of the realm that heard of it'.[11]

Wonder, defined by Jonathan Sell as that 'psychosomatic response most frequently regarded as symptomatic of an encounter with the new', is a common response in early modern England to certain kinds of difference.[12] It is a reaction that reflects the English addiction to foreign novelty skewered by Harrison, and – like Harrison's account – does not necessarily preclude xenophobia, but does suggest a complex and multifaceted attitude to the outside world. It is also a reaction repeatedly associated with the popular and the spectacular. When, in *The Tempest*, Trinculo comes across Caliban sheltering from a storm, his thoughts immediately turn to the profit he might make were he to ship this 'monster' home, 'and had but this fish painted, not a holiday-fool there but would give a piece of silver'. There 'would this monster make a man; any strange beast there makes a man. When they will not give a doit to relieve a lame beggar, they will lay out ten to see a dead Indian' (2.2.25–30). The indication that such figures needed to be advertised – 'painted on a pole' (*Macbeth* 5.8.26) – suggests they were not simply lucrative novelties but also prodigies, encouraging the observer 'to praise God, who hath not made him such'.[13] Such images might also generate interest and support for further voyages: many were commissioned of Frobisher's Inuit, including a sculpture 'caste in waxe', and they circulated right across Europe.[14]

Each of these examples suggest how difficult it is to simplify a tangle of shifting commercial, religious, polemical and personal motivations into xenophobia, particularly in a post-Reformation environment where languages of difference were profoundly unstable. Not only did attitudes vary dramatically within and between specific social groups but shifting notions of race, religious identity and nationhood all serve to further complicate the picture. Contemporary terminology also points towards some important distinctions from the modern concept of xenophobia. As well as signifying simply hostility to foreigners, early modern sources are at least as likely to refer to 'aliens' or 'strangers' (even 'immigraunts') as identifiable groups distinct from but co-existent with the majority populace. Othello occupies precisely this ambivalent position as a North African Moor of Venice, the 'extravagant and wheeling stranger' (1.1.134–5). In court, Shylock is reminded that he is an

---

[9]   George Best, *A true discourse of the late voyages of discouerie, for finding of a passage to Cathaya, by the Northwest, vnder the conduct of Martin Frobisher* (London: Henry Bynnyman, 1578), II p. 50; III p. 3; III p. 61.

[10]   Michael Lok quoted in Michael Leroy Oberg, *Dominion & Civility: English Imperialism & Native America, 1585–1685* (Ithaca, NY: Cornell University Press, 1999), p. 23; William Adams, *Adams's Chronicle of Bristol* (Bristol: J. Arrowsmith, 1910), p. 20.

[11]   Michael Lok quoted in Wendell H. Oswalt, *Eskimos and Explorers* (Novato: Chandler & Sharp, 1979), p. 27.

[12]   Jonathan P.A. Sell, *Rhetoric and Wonder in English Travel Writing, 1560–1613* (Aldershot: Ashgate, 2006), p. 3.

[13]   Alexander Ross, 'A Needful Caveat, or Admonition, for Them Who Desire to Know What Use May Be Made of, or If There Be Danger in Reading the *Alcoran*', [unpaginated] appended to the anonymous translation *The Alcoran of Mahomet* (London, 1649).

[14]   William C. Sturtevant and David B. Quinn, 'This New Prey: Eskimos in Europe in 1567, 1576, and 1577', in Christian F. Feest ed., *Indians & Europe: An Interdisciplinary Collection of Essays* (Aachen: Alano Verlag, 1989), pp. 61–140, at p. 75.

'alien' and therefore subject to specific conditions under the 'laws of Venice' (*The Merchant of Venice*, 4.1.349). Recurrent legislative attempts to address the issue of aliens or strangers in the realm all point towards the perennial currency of the problem for the English authorities.

Precedents and Paradigms

One notorious public insurrection incited by the issue lived long in the popular imagination. On the so-called 'Evil May Day' of 1517, a mob of apprentices and other disaffected citizens rampaged through the streets of London, targeting foreign denizens of the city, apparently incited by the inflammatory rhetoric of John Lincoln, a disgruntled 'broker' who had earlier seized the opportunity presented by the traditional Easter sermons and petitioned a preacher at St Paul's Cross to air his grievances towards those 'alyens and straungers [who] eate the bread from the poore fatherless children, and take the liuynge from all artificers, and the entercourse from all merchauntes, wherby pouertie is so muche encreased'.[15] According to Edward Hall, the chief chronicler of this episode, the mob ignored the entreaties of the mayor, aldermen and Sir Thomas More, then undersheriff of the city, and ransacked St Martin's, an affluent district of the city known for its foreign inhabitants. When the riot abated, the authorities took swift and decisive control. Lincoln along with 300 other insurrectionists was arrested; public disorder directed against foreign interests was adjudged to be tantamount to treason since 'the kyng had amitie with all Christen prynces'.[16] A very public display of the state's displeasure ensued with the construction of gallows and pyres in prominent sites around the city. On 7 May, the ringleaders were hauled to Cheapside to suffer the customary hanging, drawing and quartering reserved for treasonable criminals. Hall recounts that, in the event, Lincoln repeated his protest at 'the mischief that is ensued in this realm by straungers' and suffered his full sentence.[17] With the noose around the necks of the other prisoners, word dramatically arrived of the king's clemency and the sentence was commuted. Within a week, the remainder of the protestors, some 400 citizens symbolically bound and haltered, were brought before the King and Cardinal at Westminster Hall in what seems to have been a carefully stage-managed act of public admonishment, not only of the rioters themselves but of the mayoral and civic authorities who were also now in the dock. Following the King's general pardon, the prisoners rejoice, throwing their halters in the air in a scene of jubilant reconciliation. In Hall's rendition, there was 'many a good praier said for the kyng, and the citezens toke more hede to their seruantes'.[18] Thus, an inflagration of civil disobedience fuelled by divisive rhetoric is reconstrued as the occasion for a salving display of royal munificence.

Despite the show of reconciliation, those same tensions between populace, city and crown would continue to put strain on political relations throughout the Tudor reign. The threat of so-called 'anti-alien' riots resurfaced again in Elizabeth's reign, in 1588, 1593 and 1595. As before, royal authorities reacted with a mixture of concession and repression. A year of economic hardship, 1595 seems to have been a particularly turbulent year in the city culminating in a summer of discontent. Following a series of protests concerning rising food prices at Southwark and an incident of civil disobedience at Tower Street, five apprentices

---

[15]   Edward Hall, *The union of the two noble and illustre families of Lancastre and Yorke* (London, 1548), p. lxi.

[16]   Ibid., p. lxiii.

[17]   Ibid., p. lxiii.

[18]   Ibid., p. lxiii.

were arraigned at Guildhall before the Earl of Essex and city dignitaries. The charge again was that of treason and each was hanged, drawn and quartered on Tower Hill.[19] Ordinances of curfew designed to pre-empt further trouble demonstrate the extent of official disquiet towards what Peter Burke has termed a 'blue-apron culture'.[20]

Whilst annals and ordinances give one aspect of the official response to the challenge of foreigners within, it is the drama which provides some of the richest and most nuanced indications of popular attitudes towards difference. Characteristically, theatre was uniquely apt and able to respond to contemporary events. Anthony Munday's collaborative play, *The Book of Sir Thomas More*, jointly authored by a number of playwrights including Shakespeare, dramatised More's reputed part in the earlier Evil May Day riots with daring currency. As annotations to the manuscript reveal, the Master of the Revels was not prepared to countenance a direct representation of civil disobedience, commanding the authors to 'Leave out the insurrection wholly and the cause thereof' and to substitute merely 'a report afterwards of his good service done ... upon a mutiny against the Lombards only by a short report and not otherwise at your own perils'.[21] However, the episode in which More mollifies the mob (that ascribed to Shakespeare's hand) offers a challenge to, rather than incitement of, what might be termed popular xenophobia. Cautioning the rioters that the most lenient punishment to be expected from the king would be banishment, More turns the tables and shifts the perspective to that of the Englishman as 'stranger':

> *Whither would you go?*
> *What country, by the nature of your error,*
> *Should give you harbour? Go you to France or Flanders,*
> *To any German province, Spain or Portugal –*
> *Nay, anywhere that not adheres to England –*
> *Why, you must needs be strangers ... What would you think*
> *To be thus used? This is the strangers' case,*
> *And this your mountanish inhumanity. (6.141–56)*[22]

Such a basic and profound insight – that foreignness is essentially relative – distinguishes the drama from contemporary libels and polemic and is a natural if sometimes unintended consequence of the inherent polyphony of early modern theatre.[23] If a prerequisite of xenophobia is the facile classification of 'others' on the grounds of nationality, ethnicity, religion or any other mark of difference, then the drama tends to complicate the perspective. At the crescendo of More's speech and final epithet, there is also the suggestion of a yet further degree of difference which supersedes all others and underlines the 'inhumanity' of the mob. Karl Wentersdorf in particular has argued that the perplexing word which appears as 'momtanish' in the *More* manuscript ought more properly to be read as 'mahometanish' rather than 'mountanish', an intriguing possibility which would sharpen the edge of

---

[19]   Andrew Tretiak, '*The Merchant of Venice* and the "Alien" Question', *The Review of English Studies* 5:20 (1929), 402–9.

[20]   Peter Burke, 'Popular Culture in Seventeenth-Century London', in Barry Reay ed., *Popular Culture in Seventeenth-Century England* (London: Routledge, 1985), p. 32.

[21]   Quoted in William Shakespeare, *The Book of Sir Thomas More: The Arden Shakespeare*, ed. John Jowett (London: Methuen Drama, 2011), p. 139.

[22]   All references to this play are taken from Anthony Munday *et al.*, *Sir Thomas More*, ed. Vittorio Gabrielli and Giorgio Melchiori (Manchester: Manchester University Press, 2002).

[23]   For an amplification of this argument with specific relation to 'Turk' drama see Linda McJannet, *The Sultan Speaks: Dialogue in English Plays and Histories about the Ottoman Turks* (New York: Palgrave Macmillan, 2006).

More's rhetoric yet further.[24] Certainly, the characterisation of non-Christian, Muslim peoples as being beyond the pale of 'humanyty' is a familiar discursive strategy of early modern treatments of Islam, and continues themes present in some of the earliest Christian writings on the subject.[25]

As has been noted, the latter decades of Elizabeth's reign saw a rapid growth in the population of immigrant residents and workers from the Continent, particularly in London. As Jacob Selwood observes, 'The metropolis was home not just to people from throughout the British Isles but to a significant population of French and Dutch immigrants. A 1593 survey counted 7,113 strangers in the City and its suburbs, part of a wider metropolitan population of almost 200,000.'[26] A striking example of one dramatic response to this contemporary phenomenon is to be found in Thomas Dekker's *The Shoemaker's Holiday* (1599) although the precise significance of this portrayal is still critically contested. As part of a ruse to avoid the war in France and pursue a forbidden romance with the daughter of the Lord Mayor (a mere citizen), an English nobleman Rowland Lacy dons the disguise of a Dutch shoemaker. Posing as an itinerant craftsmen seeking work, Rowland Lacy enters in a scene of typical comic gusto, singing a drinking song in Dutch: 'Der was een bore van Gelderland, / Frolick sie byen; He was als dronck he could niet stand...' [There was a boor from Gelderland/Merry they be / He was so drunk he could not stand...] (iv. 52–4). 'Hans' is an obvious national caricature, speaking in a presumably exaggerated accent and singing of the fabled drunkenness of his kinsmen. The first response of the English workers is not to disparage the funny-sounding foreigner or to confront him as an economic migrant, a threat to their precarious livelihoods but to persuade their master to hire him as a 'brother of the Gentle Craft' (iv. 58–9). To some extent, the shoemakers' welcome is simply part and parcel of the liberating comic exuberance of the play, presenting a fantasy of the transformative powers of 'mirth' and camaraderie. Hans is taken on by the master Simon Eyre and becomes instrumental in the master shoemaker's rise to the lord mayoralty. However, critics have deliberated the wider significance of a prominent Dutch character, positively incorporated into the social world of London and its suburbs so vividly evoked by Dekker. On one hand, the shoemaker's instant acceptance can seem to suggest the international fraternity of the workers, cutting across and transcending local or national loyalties and identities. On the other, the whole thing is a show and Lacy's true noble (and English) identity must perforce be revealed at the play's denouement; there is after all no actual Dutchman represented in the play at all.[27] Impossible though it is to guess the reaction of a contemporary audience to this refraction of Dutch national identity, it is plausible to suppose that religious affiliation would have played a part in deciphering the Lacy/Hans character. The Dutch occupied a particularly conflicted place in the English imagination throughout the period as both co-religionists and economic rivals. As fellow Protestants facing a common enemy in Catholic Spain, the Dutch might expect English sympathy but as maritime traders increasingly competing for the same markets, sporadic hostility would develop into outright enmity and warfare in the succeeding century.

As well as perceptions of foreignness shaped by real encounter and competition with immigrant populations within, the fear of global forces without powerfully informed

---

[24]   See Karl P. Wentersdorf, 'On "Momtanish Inhumanity" in *Sir Thomas More*', *Studies in Philology* 103:2 (2006), 178–85.

[25]   John Tolan, *Saracens: Islam in the Medieval European Imagination* (New York: Columbia, 2002).

[26]   Jacob Selwood, *Diversity and Difference in Early Modern London* (Aldershot: Ashgate, 2010), p. 2.

[27]   For an example of the former interpretation see David Scott Kastan, 'Workshop and/as Playhouse: Comedy and Commerce in *The Shoemaker's Holiday*', *Studies in Philology* 84:3 (1987), 324–7. For the latter, see Andrew Fleck, 'Marking Difference and National Identity in Dekker's *The Shoemaker's Holiday*', *Studies in English Literature 1500–1900* 46 (2006), 349–70.

popular discourse. As ever, the diplomatic manoeuvres and oscillating allegiances of the elite could be a spur to popular anxiety, particularly in matters of religion. For the latter decades of Elizabeth's reign, the Spanish threat had constituted the most evident source of resentment towards foreigners. Upon his accession, James rapidly reversed foreign policy, negotiating peace with Spain at the Somerset House conference of 1604. However, popular mistrust of Spanish influence proved resilient as is attested by the widespread reaction to the breakdown of the proposed marriage alliance between the Stuart heir prince Charles and the Infanta Maria known as 'the Spanish Match' in 1623. Despite royal proclamations intended to curb public censure, torrents of libels appeared in opposition to the proposed alliance and relief at its subsequent failure. A former chaplain to James I produced one of the most notorious satires of the proposed scheme. Thomas Scott's *Vox Populi* published in 1624 purported to narrate the report of the prominent Spanish diplomat charged with negotiating the alliance given upon his return home. Although fabricated, the imagined testimony of 'Gondomar' (Don Diego Sarmiento, Count Gondomar, ambassador to London) gibes the English for their fawning, 'hence are strangers the most admired and entertayned amongst them, and if of quality preferred many times to place and preferment before the English'. Designed to pique Protestant sensibilities, the unctuous narrator boasts of 'the great and gracious respect I found, and fauors I receiued from his Maiesty of Great *Brittaine*' as well as visits from 'some of the best ranke, or received some present or other, from Catholic Gentlemen, or their Ladyes, (so welcome was the very thought of the Spanish match unto them)'.[28] Both representing and fuelling popular feeling, the influence of Scott's pamphlet is reflected in Thomas Middleton's play *A Game at Chess* (1624). In the short term, the failure of the match and Charles' humiliation seems to have rallied public opinion around the young prince and hardened attitudes towards the nefarious Spanish. Nevertheless, the notion that the court was susceptible to the influence of insidious foreign – and popish – interests would continue to dog the Stuart regime.

Charles' second choice, Henrietta Maria of France, hardly assuaged public opinion and suspicion that the marriage entailed a tacit alliance with the French king against the Protestant Huguenot cause on the Continent proved to be perfectly founded. Increasingly at odds with his parliament on matters of taxation and foreign policy, the second Stuart king moved instinctively towards autocracy, finally proroguing parliament in 1629. The subsequent prolonged period of 'Personal Rule' (1629–40) only served to reinforce the popular idea that traditional English liberty had been curtailed by foreign influences. As tension between two factions of the political classes came to breaking point, so the mobilisation of popular opinion became critical in the war of words which followed. With the outbreak of real hostilities in 1642, civic authorities moved quickly to expose the machinations of the royalist party. A widely publicised treatise alerted Londoners to the 'Discovery of a great and wicked conspiracy against this Kingdom in generall, and the City of *London* in particular'.[29] The 'discovery' entailed the interception of a letter from the Hague purportedly designed for Edward Nicholas, Secretary of State to Charles I. The conspiracy outlined played to the worst fears of the citizenry, namely that foreign armies might be mustered to fight in the king's cause and 'what great preparations of money, men and arms, there is now made in *Holland*, *France*, and *Denmark* to assist the Kings Majesty in *England*'. Harnessing the popular media of press and sermon, Parliament ordered that 'this Letter be

---

[28] Thomas Scott, *The second part of Vox populi, or Gondomar appearing in the likenes of Matchiauell in a Spanish parliament wherein are discouered his treacherous & subtile practises to the ruine as well of England, as the Netherlandes faithfully transtated [sic] out of the Spanish coppie by a well-willer to England and Holland* (London, 1624).

[29] Baron George Goring, *The Discovery of a great and wicked conspiracie* (London, 1642).

forthwith printed and published, and read in all Parish Churches within the City of *London* and the Suburbs thereof, by the Parsons, Vicars, or Curates of the same'.[30] The Lord Mayor's recorded response makes clear the terms in which such a prospect might be popularly viewed and exploited:

> *Whereas certain Letters from forrain parts and severall places of the Kingdom have been intercepted, and brought unto the Parliament, discovering the desperate designes and plots of Papists and other ill affected, in collecting great sums of money and providing many thousands of men and Arms, for the ruine of our Religion and Kingdom.*

In order to meet the real and present danger of those Popish insurgents, London's parishioners would be enjoined to raise 'a sum of 30000 l ... by Tuesday in the afternoon, and all such as shall lend any money ... shall be repayed their moneys so lent out, of the first moneys that shall be collected upon the said Ordinance'. The responsibility for raising these war bonds was to be devolved upon local agents, so 'that the Church wardens of every Parish cause an assembly of the Parishioners tomorrow after Sermon [to] raise a proportionable summe, and that upon Munday next, at three of the clock the Church-wardens appear at Guildhall before the said Committee, to give an account of what moneys they have raised'.[31] Although an array of foreign powers of all religious stripes might be imagined as poised to invade, in crisis and in order to raise hard cash it seems that only one bogeyman need be invoked: Catholicism.

To some extent, the religio-political crisis of the mid-century inevitably entailed a redrawing of the existing parameters of what might be termed xenophobia. The use of foreign mercenaries on both sides provided propagandistic opportunities to assert the essential 'outlandishness' of the enemy forces. The very term 'cavalier' as a derogatory nickname for the royalists coined early in the conflict derived part of its pejorative charge from its French etymology, a corruption of *chevalier*. Moreover, as recent historiography has shown, the role of the three kingdoms in the struggle between king and parliament intensified regional identities and hardened longstanding enmities between the English and their near neighbours.[32] The uprising of the Catholic nobility in Ireland in 1641 fuelled fears that the Irish rebels were in league with the English king. Reports of the insurrection circulated in England were designed to outrage popular Protestant opinion and further emphasised the un-Christian behaviour of the rebels. *The Rebels Turkish Tyranny* (1641) described in lurid detail the conduct of the insurgents,

> *Shewing how cruelly they put them to the Sword, ravished religious women, and put their Children upon red hot Spits before their parents eyes; throw them in the fire ... cut off their eares, and nose, put out their eyes, cut off their armes, and legges, broyle them at the fire, cut out their tongues, and thrust hot Irons down their throats, drown them, dash out their brains, and such like cruelty not heard amongst Christians.*[33]

Meanwhile, for the opposite cause, traditional hostility towards the Scots might equally be invoked as in a broadside ballad of 1640 which paints the covenanters as double-dealers who 'under the colour of religion' rebel 'against their native Prince'. The ballad opens with

---

[30] Ibid., title page.
[31] All quotations relating to the Lord Mayor come from the appended document at sig. A.4v.
[32] See Mark Stoyle, *Soldiers and Strangers: An Ethnic History of the English Civil War* (New Haven: Yale University Press, 2005).
[33] Tristram Whetcombe, *The Rebels Turkish Tyranny* (London, 1641).

an appeal to English national pride, placing the conflict in a long line of Anglo-Scottish clashes: 'If ever England had occasion / Her ancient honour to defend / Then let her now make preparation, / Unto an honourable end: / The factious Scot / is very hot, / His ancient spleene is ne'er forget / He long hath been about this plot' and ends with hope 'to tame in time this saucy Iacke'.[34] By 1642, however, such an appeal to a single and coherent English identity seemed increasingly futile as loyalty to centralised authority splintered under the implosive pressure of civil war. This radical devolution of authority meant that the language of anti-alien enmity might apply not only to the Irish 'rebel' and 'factious' Scot but to the neighbouring English county, town or village. Beyond the intense press activity of the metropolis, sermons provide an important source of provincial discourse of the war. Published in 1642 'by order of the committee of the House of Commons' but originally delivered at Great Yarmouth, John Brinsley's sermon tellingly turns to the old figure of the 'stranger' in order to represent the newly invigorated threat. Whilst England is conventionally imagined as Israel, factious tribes within are made analogous to 'Strangers; I mean strangers, and Enemies to our Religion: Such as though they be amongst us; yet they are not of us, *Papists*, and persons Popishly affected.'[35] As well as waging the battle for hearts and minds, Brinsley's elaborate parallel is also an attempt to construe meaning from the chaotic state of identity and allegiance produced by civil war, a meaning authorised by Scripture but also underwritten by the communal appeal to xenophobic mistrust.

With the Restoration came the promise of a new monarch sensitive to the sensibilities of his Protestant nation, offering 'liberty to tender consciences' whilst reasserting the salving authority of a national Church. In the event, the new consensus was at best fragile and resentment of foreign influences upon the court and nation continued to characterise populist politics. This was perfectly illustrated by an early crisis to beset the new Stuart regime. When, in the late summer of 1666, a devastating fire swept through the heart of London, many citizens immediately suspected a terrorist attack. Both Dutch and French operatives were naturally seen as potential culprits and, as the city burned, denizen strangers of all kinds were subject to the violent retribution of dispossessed Londoners. The findings of a Parliamentary 'special committee' set up to assuage public outrage and 'inquire into the late dreadful burning of the city of London' heard from a host of witnesses all testifying to existence of a foreign conspiracy to attack the capital.[36] As the reported statements show, however, the true character or motives of the alleged assailants were far from consistent. A conversation is reported in the '*Greyhound* in *St. Martins*' with 'one Fitz Harris an Irish Papist' darkly alluding to 'a sad Desolation' in London.[37] A 'Papist of *Ilford*' (Mrs Yazly) has been overheard predicting that 'next Thursday will be the hottest day that ever was in England'.[38] Along the way there are Jesuits in disguise and 'Walloon[s] ... with an instrument like a dark Lanthorn ... filled with Gun-powder'.[39] According to the affidavit of three artisans, a suspicious young foreigner was apprehended and subsequently interrogated. Upon being taken aside and warned that telling the truth was the 'only way to save his Life', he openly

[34]   Martin Parker, *A true subjects wish For the happy successe of our Royall Army preparing to resist the factious rebellion of those insolent covenanters (against the sacred Majesty, of our gracious and loving king Charles) in Scotland. To the tune of, O How now Mars, &c.* (London, 1640).

[35]   John Brinsley, *The healing of Israels breaches. Wherein is set forth Israels disease. Cure. Physitian. Danger. All paralleld with, and applyed to the present times. As they were delivered in six sermons at the weekly lecture in the church of Great Yarmouth. By John Brinsly minister of the Word, and pastor of Somerleiton an adjacent village. Published by order of a committee of the House of Commons* (London, 1642).

[36]   *A True and Faithful Account of the Several informations exhibited to the honourable committee appointed by the Parliament to inquire into the late dreadful burning of the city of London* (London, 1667).

[37]   Ibid., p. 6.

[38]   Ibid., p. 6.

[39]   Ibid., p. 9.

confessed that 'there were Three hundred Frenchmen that were in a Plot or Conspiracy to fire the City'. This document gives an indication of the xenophobic hysteria whipped up in the aftermath of the fire. Equally significant, however, are several hints that Londoners are being deprived of their right to extract natural justice against the perpetrators. At first, a Frenchman who had been taken 'in Shoe-Lane ... firing a House there with Fire-ball' is described as being taken into the custody of the 'Life-Guard' (a cohort under the command of James) but 'what became of the *Frenchman* [the witness] knoweth not'. Later, a Constable apprehends a Frenchman firing a house and, *en route* to the magistrate is intercepted by 'His Royal Highness the Duke of York' who 'took him into his costedy'. Again, the upshot is troublingly uncertain and 'he was heard of no more'.[40] This published account was not the officially countenanced version of events, however. According to royal authorities, the fire was an accident and the matter closed. By way of protest, the publication of *A True and Faithful Account* testifies to the powerful popular belief that London had been attacked by malevolent foreign interests with friends in high places.

Contested Positions

In a 2005 essay Nigel Goose asked whether xenophobia in Elizabethan and early Stuart England was 'an epithet too far'.[41] Pointing to the substantial divergence of scholarly opinion on this issue, he cites Laura Hunt Yungblut, Lien Luu, Christopher Hibbert and Simon Schama as all endorsing a dominant English xenophobia, and Ian Archer, Stephen Rappaport and Joe Ward (amongst others) as authorities with 'serious reservations about categorizing Londoners as xenophobic'.[42] Goose marshals a considerable volume of material to demonstrate two points: firstly, that xenophobia is inconsistently used and difficult to define when applied to the early modern period; and secondly, that the England encountered by those immigrants that arrived between the mid-sixteenth and mid-seventeenth centuries should not be characterised as consistently or dominantly xenophobic – instead Goose sees this period as 'a veritable oasis of tolerance between the more violent prejudice of the medieval period and the arrogant self-confidence that, in some quarters at least, accompanied the rise of English nationalism in the eighteenth century'.[43]

Of these two, Goose's first point is particularly persuasive. The *OED* identifies xenophobia to be etymologically derived from a combination of a form of the Greek ξένος – a word that can mean guest, stranger, foreigner or in its adjectival form foreign or strange – and φόβ-ος, the Greek word for fear. The definition of xenophobia that the *OED* provides, however, is 'a deep antipathy to strangers', whereas other dictionaries suggest a deeper hostility by employing the word hatred.[44] Goose's argument is that xenophobia must be more than mere antipathy, and that its meaning has become further clouded by confusion with other factors such as politico-religious or economic rivalries and/or racism. In this context it perhaps makes better sense to return to the etymological root and define xenophobia not as a hatred or even deep antipathy to foreigners, but rather to *foreignness*. Although this modification is subtle, it crucially prevents the specificity of the object of hatred, and instead insists upon a

---

40   The Frenchmen section appears in ibid., pp. 13–14.
41   Nigel Goose, '"Xenophobia" in Elizabethan and Early Stuart England: An Epithet Too Far?', in Nigel Goose and Lien Luu eds, *Immigrants in Tudor and Early Stuart England* (Brighton: Sussex Academic Press, 2005), pp. 110–35.
42   Ibid., pp. 110–11.
43   Ibid., p. 129.
44   Ibid., pp. 111–12.

general hatred for what is foreign or strange since – as Goose asserts – xenophobia 'is not a *selective* attitude'.[45]

The examples we have discussed in this chapter so far appear to demonstrate xenophobia's opposite – that English men and women were fairly selective in their hatreds. The Evil May Day at the start of the sixteenth century is a possible exception – Goose calls it 'the last throw of the medieval dice' – but its later dramatisation on the later sixteenth-century stage whilst libels called for violence against immigrants who in different contexts might be co-religionists as well as economic rivals, and only a few years before a celebrated Inuit had canoed on the Thames, suggests a rich and revealing inconsistency in English attitudes to strangers.[46] The prevailing anti-papist attitude that is initially focused on the Spanish, but later in the seventeenth century might be also applied to the French, is perhaps closer to xenophobia, but is rather a hatred for foreignness in the form of non-Protestant religion, rather than simply foreigners, a deep antipathy to religious difference that may come closer to the ways in which popular conceptions of others worked in practice. It is notable that Peter Burke avoided the word xenophobia in his *Popular Culture in Early Modern Europe*, although his description of popular attitudes to outsiders comes very close: 'Hatred of outsiders was so common [in early modern Europe] as to make one wonder whether most ordinary people were not what psychologists sometimes call "authoritarian personalities", combining submissiveness to authority with aggressiveness towards people outside their group.'[47]

A concluding example illustrates the difficulties in identifying popular xenophobia in this period, and draws upon each of the paradigms outlined above. Roughly contemporary with the writing of *The Book of Sir Thomas More* and the product of the same economic deprivations and cultural tensions that generated Strype's 'beastly Belgians' libel, but also explicitly referencing the London theatre and anti-papal sentiments, the 'Dutch Church Libel' was pinned to the door of one of the churches used by London's immigrant communities on 4 May 1593. The last of a slew of similar libels, the discovery of this 'lewd and malicious' document prompted swift action by the authorities, 'to strengthen their hand, to control the apprentices through their masters and to placate those who felt aggrieved, culminating in the arrest of "several young men", some of whom were put in the stocks, carted and whipped as an example to other would-be trouble-makers'.[48]

The libel's 53 lines of rhymed verse begin in typically inflammatory vein, addressing London's immigrants directly:

> *Ye strangers y* doe inhabite in this lande*
> *Note this same writing doe it vnderstand*
> *Conceit it well for savegard of your lyves*
> *Your goods, your children, & your dearest wiues*
> *Your Machiavellian Marchant spoyles the state,*
>   *Your vsery doth leave vs all for deade*
> *Your Artifex, & craftesman works our fate,*
> *And like the Jewes, you eate vs vp as bread*
> *The Marchant doth ingross all kinde of wares*
>   *Forestall's the markets, whereso 'ere he goes*

---

[45] Ibid., p. 112, emphasis in original.

[46] Ibid., p. 129.

[47] Peter Burke, *Popular Culture in Early Modern Europe* (Aldershot: Ashgate [revised reprint], 1994), p. 169.

[48] Quoted in Arthur Freeman, 'Marlowe, Kyd and the Dutch Church Libel', *English Literary Renaissance* 3 (1973), 44–52; Goose, '"Xenophobia"', p. 120.

> *Sends forth his wares, by Pedlers to the faires,*
> *Retayle's at home, & with his horrible showes:*   *Vndoeth thowsands*[49]

The anonymous author goes on to detail a litany of perceived crimes and to accuse these strangers of 'living far better than at native home' whilst the English 'dye like dogges in Fraunce & Belgia' for them.[50] The libeller certainly intends to portray himself as a mouthpiece for popular discontent – and this libel, alongside the tense circumstances of early 1593, is regularly used in both scholarly and more populist contexts to affirm a fundamental English xenophobia. But can the libel be so straightforwardly identified as popular xenophobia?

The extract quoted above does appear to react indiscriminately against strangers, in eight lines developing an identification of those strangers with mercantilism and popular conceptions of Machiavellianism into an assertion of their Jew-like qualities. In this associative strategy all strangers become merchants, and all stranger-merchants are usurers defined by their own greed. Bringing the demonised phantom of the murderous, cannibalistic usurer-Jew of the popular imagination into play draws upon older mythologies of difference (the Jews had been officially expelled from England in 1290 and would not be publicly readmitted until 1655) in order to deny the sameness of London's Protestant migrants/refugees with their English hosts.[51] The same strategy is employed with a more recently demonised opponent – with 'Spanish gold' all these strangers 'are infected', making them third-columnist enemies within. Thus far this would appear to confirm popular xenophobia – various opprobrious associations are bound together to create an undifferentiated foreignness that is used as a justification for violence and the assertion of 'native' economic rights.

The popular character of the libel would appear to be affirmed in its final lines – a curious combination of the expression of loyalty to the crown and an attack on the nobility:

> *And with y* *gould our Nobles wink at feats*
> *Nobles said I? nay men to be reiected,*
> *Upstarts yt enioy the noblest seates*
> *That wound their Countries brest, for lucres sake*
> *And wrong our gracious Queene & Subiects good*
> *By letting strangers make our harts to ake*
> *For which our swords are whet, to shedd their blood*
> *And for a truth let it be vnderstoode/ Fly, Flye, & never returne.*
> *per. Tam-berlaine*[52]

Here the English nobles are chastised for traitorous corruption, for advocating the cause of the 'strangers' for personal gain. It is notable that the libel again does not differentiate, choosing not to identify specific noblemen known to favour the cause of the Dutch and French migrants such as the Cecils and other members of the Privy Council – although it might be assumed that the constituency addressed here would have known who was specifically implied in such accusations.[53] This too suggests the libel was a manifestation

---

[49]   Freeman, 'Marlowe, Kyd and the Dutch Church Libel', pp. 45–6.
[50]   Ibid., p. 46.
[51]   See James Shapiro, *Shakespeare and the Jews* (New York: Columbia University Press, 1996).
[52]   Freeman, 'Marlowe, Kyd and the Dutch Church Libel', p. 46.
[53]   On those members of the Privy Council known to be favourable (and less so) towards England's Protestant immigrant communities, see Yungblut, *Strangers Settled Here amongst Us*; Lien Bich Luu, *Immigrants and the Industries of London, 1500–1700* (Aldershot: Ashgate, 2005); Bernard Cottret, *The Huguenots in England: Immigration and Settlement c.1550–1700* (Cambridge: Cambridge University Press, 1991).

of popular xenophobia, pitting 'good' subjects against a debased nobility, whilst focusing a sense of national identity on a conspicuous pledge of loyalty to its embodiment: 'our gracious' monarch.

Before accepting that this libel embodies and confirms an early modern English popular xenophobia there are some elements that warrant further consideration and should prompt pause for thought. The signature is a curiosity. It is by no means certain that this otherwise anonymous libeller would have appreciated the irony in his attacking 'strangers' under the persona of a Scythian warlord – but his decision to adopt this pseudonym suggests a complex imaginative engagement. Tamburlaine, as refracted through Christopher Marlowe's plays of the same name, may have been unproblematically assimilable to this belligerent expression of a martial Englishness; as the scourge of God on the London stage, perhaps celebrity had disassociated this mid-Asian conqueror from his ethnic and religious origins. This argument would suggest he had become some kind of honorary Englishman and a legitimate model for emulation or use as a rhetorical mouthpiece.[54] Alternatively, the libeller may have used the name Tamburlaine fully aware of his foreignness, intending the name to indicate an unvanquished warrior whose reputation was for epic destruction and an utter disregard for conventional hierarchies. Either way – and the two positions are not necessarily exclusive – signing the libel 'Tamburlaine' challenges any easy assertions of xenophobia.

The waters are further muddied by a closer examination of the nature of the grievances expressed in the libel, which are consistently economic. Whilst the libeller does use the opprobrious associations of both the Jew and the Spanish to accentuate the immigrants' strangeness, this strategy is used to support the primary argument concerning displacement. These communities are attacked in this document in order to highlight particular – albeit regularly resurfacing – complaints about specific economic practices. They are made different because they are not 'natural born' subjects, but the purpose of the libel is not to attack them for their foreignness, but rather to make them seem excessively foreign in order to activate archetypes associated with rapacious greed, lending money at interest, removing quality English wares from the realm and bringing trash in return; driving up rents, and so on. These are anxieties associated with the new machinery of credit and increasingly globalised markets, not with specific national, religious or ethnic groups, despite appearances to the contrary. Furthermore, the 'popular' character of this document is difficult to determine. The libeller may have sought to speak on behalf of a popular voice, and the various references to Marlowe's highly popular drama would seem to endorse this. However, these and other references were encoded – like other libels from the same period – to be understood not by everyone, but by apprentices, as the specificity of the punishments meted out by the authorities indicates. There may have been fears on the part of the authorities that libels such as these had the potential to provoke a conflagration like Evil May Day nearly a century earlier – a model to which many libellers deliberately referred – but circumstances in 1593 were distinctly different from those in 1517, and there is no record of any resulting violence. This libeller's choice of language with which to chastise resident aliens reflects the complex associations and implications of the language used in so many ostensibly popular documents dealing with the same topic in the late sixteenth and seventeenth centuries. It is a language of unstable referents, elisions and contradictions, one too easily simplified. So if there is popular xenophobia in this document, and in this period, then it is – as the various examples we have included demonstrate – necessarily compromised and qualified.

---

[54] Richard Levin, 'The Contemporary Perception of Marlowe's *Tamburlaine*', *Medieval and Renaissance Drama in England* 1 (1984), 51–70; Rick Bowers, 'Tamburlaine Engraved, 1623–1677', *Huntington Library Quarterly* 59 (1997), 542–9 and 'Tamburlaine at Ludlow', *Notes & Queries* 45:3 (1998), 361–3.

Select Bibliography

Clark, P. ed., *The European Crisis of the 1590s: Essays in Comparative History*. London: Allen & Unwin, 1985.

Cottret, Bernard, *The Hugenots in England: Immigration and Settlement c.1550–1700*. Cambridge: Cambridge University Press, 1991.

Goose, Nigel, and Lien Luu eds, *Immigrants in Tudor and Early Stuart England*. Brighton: Sussex Academic Press, 2005.

Luu, Lien Bich, *Immigrants and the Industries of London, 1500–1700*. Aldershot: Ashgate, 2005.

McJannet, Linda, *The Sultan Speaks: Dialogue in English Plays and Histories about the Ottoman Turks*. New York: Palgrave Macmillan, 2006.

Oberg, Michael Leroy, *Dominion & Civility: English Imperialism & Native America, 1585–1685*. Ithaca, NY: Cornell University Press, 1999.

Sell, Jonathan P.A., *Rhetoric and Wonder in English Travel Writing, 1560–1613*. Aldershot: Ashgate, 2006.

Selwood, Jacob, *Diversity and Difference in Early Modern London*. Aldershot: Ashgate, 2010.

Shapiro, James, *Shakespeare and the Jews*. New York: Columbia University Press, 1996.

Singh, Jyotsna ed., *A Companion to the Global Renaissance: English Literature and Culture in the Era of Expansion*. Oxford: Blackwell, 2009.

Stoyle, Mark, *Soldiers and Strangers: An Ethnic History of the English Civil War*. New Haven: Yale University Press, 2005.

Tolan, John, *Saracens: Islam in the Medieval European Imagination*. New York: Columbia, 2002.

Yungblut, Laura Hunt, *Strangers Settled Here amongst Us: Policies, Perceptions and the Presence of Aliens in Early Modern England*. London: Routledge, 1996.

Games

Joachim Frenk

The human activity of playing games can be traced back to prehistoric times, and scholars from various disciplines have concluded that the gaming urge is part of the *conditio humana*, in the sense that it has its roots in the social aspect of human beings – 'game' probably derives from an old Germanic word that means 'participation, communion' (OED). In 1938, Johan Huizinga, one of the founding figures of modern games studies, famously claimed that the activity of playing even exceeds the human: 'Play is older than culture, for culture, however inadequately defined, always presupposes human society, and animals have not waited for man to teach them their playing.'[1] Still, human gaming practices can and must be historicised to see how the activity of playing specific games was shaped by and shaped a particular culture at a particular time. As an integral element of early modern popular culture, games were a highly productive and contested part of the cultural fabric. In some cases the rules and playing procedures of early modern games have been lost, so that we know that certain games existed but have no hermeneutic access to them any more – always presupposing that we can identify them as games in the first place.

Ever since Ludwig Wittgenstein, in his *Philosophical Investigations*, dealt with the question of how games can be defined, theoreticians have sought to define what games are in order to overcome Wittgenstein's argument that the diversity of human activities that are commonly listed under the term 'game' is almost impossible to unify under one definition.[2] Games have been interesting for structuralists because they can be functionally described within a given set of rules, and they have been interesting from the perspective of semiotics because of the set of different meanings they play with. Definitions have proliferated,[3] but most games theorists seem to agree on the following points: games have rules, often specific gaming tools, and they demand particular knowledge and skills. It seems to be one widely accepted characteristic feature of games that they are, at least initially, pursued for their own sake, without any ulterior motive or view to producing something other than the gaming experience itself. As performative acts, games delineate specific spaces and specific time frames that are distinct from the spatial and temporal orders of everyday, ordinary

---

[1]   Johan Huizinga, *Homo ludens: A Study of the Play-Element in Culture* (Boston: Beacon Press, 1955), p. 1. Huizinga's definition of culture itself as an elaborate game stretches the definition of what games are to the utmost and thus eliminates a dichotomy that is constitutive for this companion.

[2]   See Ludwig Wittgenstein, *Philosophical Investigations*. The German text, with an English translation by G.E.M. Anscombe, P.M.S. Hacker and Joachim Schulte (rev. 4th ed., Chichester: Wiley Blackwell, 2009), pp. 37e–38e and *passim*.

[3]   In one of the most influential studies, Roger Caillois assumes four 'main rubrics' which correspond to four different roles of play: competition (*agon*), chance (*alea*), simulation (*mimicry*) and vertigo (*ilinx*). See *Man, Play and Games*, trans. Meyer Barash (Champaign: University of Illinois Press, 2001), pp. 12–26.

Figure 14.1   Pieter Breugel the Elder's *Children's Games* (1560).
By permission of the Kunsthistorisches Museum, Vienna.

life. However, this supposedly self-centred, non-instrumental character of the immediate gaming experience cannot be applied to the wider cultural frameworks games are and were part of. In their contexts, early modern games were inscribed with a plethora of different meanings. They were played by all strata of society, and they often had intricate social, political and symbolic functions.

Four examples may serve to illustrate the enormous variety of early modern games: in his *Gargantua and Pantagruel* (1532–52), François Rabelais lists more than 200 games his excessive hero Gargantua played in his youth. In his list, which by its sheer length indicates that games were indeed ubiquitous in early modern culture, Rabelais deems it sufficient to give only the names of the games; his contemporaries would obviously have known how most of them were to be played. The second example is from the visual arts. In his painting *Children's Games* (1560; Figure 14.1), Pieter Bruegel the Elder depicts more than 80 games played by children in an imaginary cityscape. The panoramic view of the playing children undoubtedly gestures towards a Christian interpretation of the painting: in the eyes of God, adults and their worldly pursuits are like children obliviously playing inconsequential games. Yet as so often in his art, in addition to the edifying Christian moral, Breugel also provides us with a finely observed survey of games as they were actually played in the sixteenth century, and his painting is imbued with an abundance of activities and material detail.

Just as Breugel's children signify more than the games they are playing, which each of the suggestive individual scenes underlines, early modern games were by no means culturally located in a semiotic void. This is also true for early modern playhouses, which can be regarded as ludic locations par excellence. Staged plays were closely associated with games: '"Game" and "play," "gamehouse" and "playhouse" seem to have been used interchangeably well into the sixteenth century.'[4] The pro- and antitheatrical debates of the age were similar to the general debates about which games should be lawful and which should not. From this vantage point, it is not hard to see why 46 different games are mentioned in Shakespeare's works, some of which can be subdivided into more specific games.[5] Shakespeare uses these games in diverse contexts on many different levels of meaning. One of the most comprehensive English lists of games is to be found in the fourth satire of Samuel Rowlands's *The Letting of Hvmovrs Blood in the Head-Vaine* (1600):

> *Man, I dare challenge thee to throwe the sledge,*
> *To iumpe or leape ouer a ditch or hedge,*
> *To wrastle, play at stooleball, or to runne,*
> *To pitch the barre, or to shoote off a gunne:*
> *To play at loggets, nine holes, or ten pinnes,*
> *To trie it out at foot-ball by the shinnes;*
> *At Ticktacke, Irish, Noddie, Maw, and Ruffe:*
> *At hot-cockles, leap-frogge, or blindman-buffe:*
> *To drinke halfe pots, or deale at the whole canne:*
> *To play at base, or pen-and Ynk-horne sir Ihan [John]:*
> *To daunce the Morris, play at barly-breake:*
> *At all exploytes a man can thinke or speake:*
> *At shoue-groate, venter poynt, or crosse and pile.*
> *At beshrow him that's last at yonder style,*
> *At leaping ore a Midsommer bon-fier,*
> *Or at the drawing Dun out of the myer [...].*[6]

The early modern games listed, depicted and mentioned in all of these sources can be subdivided into categories that are still widely recognised today, for instance into games of chance, games of skill, outdoor games (sports are a large part of this group) and indoor games like dice games, board games and card games. The early modern positions of these games, the cultural connotations and practices attached to them, were often considerably different from those of the games' successors we know – in spite of all attempts at reviving early modern games, it is due to this cultural difference that we cannot play these games in the same way they were played in the sixteenth and seventeenth centuries. One important factor in the changes of gaming practices from the middle ages to the early modern age was the increasing regulation of time, evidenced for instance by the rising importance of clocks and pocket watches that indicates a more technological understanding and instrumentalising use of time and the introduction of the Georgian calendar in 1582 (which the British adopted only in 1752). Modernity created new chronological demands, for instance the need for more regular labour.[7] Games that took their own time would damage the discipline and the availability of the labour force. Gaming activities thus became markers of the distinction between a public / professional time and a private time. The same can be said about gaming spaces: although they were defined in distinction from the spaces of everyday life, they

---

[4]   Louis Montrose, *The Purpose of Playing: Shakespeare and the Cultural Politics of the Elizabethan Theatre* (Chicago: The University of Chicago Press, 1996), p. 19.

[5]   See Paul G. Brewster, *Games and Sports in Shakespeare* (Helsinki: Suomalainen Tiedeakatemia, 1959).

[6]   Samuel Rowlands, *The Letting of Hvmovrs Blood in the Head-Vaine. With a new Morissco, daunced by seauen* Satyres, *vpon the bottome of* Dioginis Tubbe (London, 1600). *The Complete Works of Samuel Rowlands 1598–1628* (n.p.: The Hunterian Club, 1880), vol. 1, pp. 61–85, at pp. 64–5.

[7]   See Gerhard Dohrn-van Rossum, *History of the Hour: Clocks and Modern Temporal Orders*, trans. Thomas Dunlap (Chicago: The University of Chicago Press, 1996).

followed the overarching spatial changes of the age, for instance the changes of public and private, open and closed spaces and the introduction of new spaces – the bear-baiting arena and the Globe playhouse on the southern bank of the Thames as well as the Royal Exchange and the Banqueting Hall illustrate this point.

At the upper end of the social scale, the cultural elites all over Europe were eagerly playing all kinds of games, and they were debating which games should be socially acceptable or indeed necessary for the education of a courtier. One of the most influential early modern conduct books in England, Baldassare Castiglione's *Il cortegiano* (1528), first translated into English in 1561, begins with a group of men and women at the Urbino court of Guidobaldo da Montefeltro who debate which game to choose for the evening they are spending together. After a number of suggestions, they agree that they will 'take in hand to shape in woordes a good Courtyer', whose emerging 'profile' is thus itself the result of a game.[8] Like Castiglione's, other early modern conduct books also insisted that games, in the sense of outdoor sports, were useful and indeed indispensable for the education of gentlemen-courtiers. In *The Boke named The Gouernour* (1531), Sir Thomas Elyot argues:

> *All thoughe I haue hitherto aduaunced the commendation of lernyng, specially in gentil men, yet it is to be considered that continuall studie without some maner of exercise, shortly exhausteth the spirites vitall, and hyndereth naturall decoction and digestion, wherby mannes body is the soner corrupted and brought in to diuerse sickenessis, and finallye the life is therby made shorter: where contrayrye wise by exercise, [...] the helthe of man is preserued, and his strength increased.*[9]

In seven chapters, Elyot then discusses the games and sports best suited for young gentlemen in detail; his extended discussion amounts to 'the first English defense of sport as a functional social phenomenon'.[10] Elyot insists, in an extended excursion, that dancing is a noble occupation that suffers from an 'effeminising' prejudice, and that it should be held in higher esteem in England. Indeed, early modern gaming activities, like their modern successors, were clearly gendered. The focus of most conduct books was firmly on the gentlemen courtiers, and 'writers [...] favoured games in gendered terms, exemplified by [Margaret] Cavendish's insistence on the "Masculine" sports proper to a gentleman and Lawrence Humphrey's defense of "stouter and manlier" sports like "whirling, leaping, casting the darte, wrestling, [and] running" as "more commendable" for his male readers.'[11] Dancing, playing an instrument and other less physical and competitive activities were considered more suitable for women. But it seems that these strict genderings may not have been binding; in *The Book of the Courtier*, Lord Cesare Gonzaga denies that gender differences actually apply in outdoor activities: 'And in my time I have seene woman playe at tenise, practise feates of armes, ride, hunt, and do (in a maner) all the exercises beeside, that a gentilman can do.'[12]

---

[8]   Baldassare Castiglione, *The Book of the Courtier*, trans. Sir Thomas Hoby, introd. Sir Walter Raleigh, ed. W.E. Henley (London: David Nutt, 1900 [1561]), pp. 34–42, at p. 42.

[9]   Sir Thomas Elyot, *The Boke named The Gouernour*, ed. Henry Herbert Stephen Croft (London: Kegan Paul, Trench & Co., 1883 [1531]), p. 169.

[10]   Gregory M. Colón Semenza, *Sport, Politics, and Literature in the English Renaissance* (Cranbury, NJ: Associated University Presses, 2003), p. 31.

[11]   Katherine R. Larson, '"Certein Childplayes Remembred by the Fayre Ladies": Girls and Their Games', in Naomi J. Miller and Naomi Yavneh eds, *Gender and Early Modern Constructions of Childhood* (Farnham: Ashgate, 2011), p. 70. Larson quotes Margaret Cavendish, Duchess of Newcastle, *The Worlds Olio* (1655), p. 63 and Lawrence Humphrey, *The Nobles or of Nobilitye* (1563), sigs v.iiii.r–v.

[12]   Castiglione, *The Book of the Courtier*, p. 220.

The catalogue of respectable gaming activities became more and more established in the course of the sixteenth century. Roger Ascham (who, in 1545, had published the archery treatise *Toxophilus*) repeats and extends Elyot's list of gentlemanly physical activities in *The Schoolmaster* (1570):

> *Therefore, to ride comely; to run fair at the tilt or ring; to play at all weapons; to shoot fair in bow or surely in gun; to vault lustily; to run, to leap, to wrestle, to swim; to dance comely; to sing, and play of instruments cunningly; to hawk, to hunt, to play at tennis, and all pastimes generally, which be joined with labour, used in open place, and on the daylight containing either some fit exercise for war, or some pleasant pastime for peace, be not only comely and decent, but also very necessary, for a courtly gentleman to use.*[13]

As in Ascham's list, tennis often appears in early modern lists of respectable games. Tennis (the early modern version is often called real tennis to distinguish this indoor game from the sport we know today) reached England in the fifteenth century from the Continent. There was a belief in England that tennis came from France, and the name of the game probably derives from the French 'tenez': 'hold / take / receive' (the ball).[14] After initially being penalised under Henry VII, tennis soon became popular, even highly fashionable: the enthusiastic Henry VIII had a tennis coach and sought to excel in this sport like in all others. From his reign onwards, tennis was respectable enough to serve for an illustrating simile in George Puttenham's scholarly *Arte of English Poesie* (1589). Puttenham derives the English name 'rebound' of the rhetorical figure *atanaclasis* from tennis and enlarges on the analogy:

> *Ye haue another figure which by his nature we may call the Rebound, alluding to the tennis ball which being smitten with the racket reboundes backe againe, and where the last figure before played with two wordes somewhat like, this playeth with one word written all alike but carrying diuers sences as thus. The maide that soone married is, soone marred is.*[15]

Shakespeare's Pericles compares himself to a tennis ball being tossed about on the sea, 'that vast tennis-court' (*Pericles*, sc. 5, 96).[16] The best-known tennis reference in Shakespeare is in the histories, when the French Dauphin sends Henry V tennis balls to mock him. Henry takes up the challenge:

> *When we have matched our rackets to these balls,*
> *We will in France, by God's grace, play a set*
> *Shall strike his father's crown into the hazard.*
> *Tell him he hath made a match with such a wrangler*
> *That all the courts of France will be disturbed*
> *With chases. (H V, 1.2.261–6)*

---

[13]   Roger Ascham, *The Schoolmaster* (London: Cassell and Company, 1909), pp. 62–3.

[14]   See A. Forbes Sieveking, 'Games', in C.T. Onions ed., *Shakespeare's England: An Account of the Life & Manners of His Age* (2 vols, Oxford: Clarendon Press, 1917), vol. 2, pp. 451–83, at p. 459. Sieveking also offers a good, if by now necessarily incomplete bibliography of early modern and later literature on early modern games.

[15]   George Puttenham, *The Arte of English Poesie*, ed. Edward Arber (London: n. p., 1869 [1589]), p. 210.

[16]   All references to Shakespeare's works are quoted from Stephen Greenblatt, Walter Cohen, Jean E. Howard and Katharine Eisaman Maus eds, *The Norton Shakespeare: Based on the Oxford Edition* (2nd ed., New York: Norton, 2008).

Henry's metaphorically charged response shows that he, respectively the stage figure's creator, knows the rules of real tennis well. The hazard mentioned by Henry has a meaning relating specifically to real tennis:

> In the inner wall [of the indoor tennis court] are openings, called hazards, such as the trou, or hole near the floor, and later, galleries. The chase is the second impact on the floor (or in a gallery) of a ball which the opponent has failed or declined to return; its value is determined by the nearness of the point of impact to the end wall. A chase does not count to either player until the players have changed sides. A player wins a chase, on sides being changed, if he can cause his ball to rebound nearer the wall than the ball did in the chase for which he is playing.[17]

Henry rhetorically integrates tennis into the early modern power play. The imagery operates on several levels, but it is all about winning: Hazard was also the name of a popular dice game in which large sums were lost and won; the meaning added is that the Dauphin unnecessarily enters into a hazardous and extremely costly game of chance when he provokes Henry.[18] The whole of France will not be able to return Henry's serve, which will make the 'crown' perish, both the regal token and the coin. The mentioned 'courts of France' are the rulers' and the legal courts Henry threatens, but they are also its tennis courts. Henry's 'chases' oscillate between the semantic fields of tennis and of military pursuits.

The Tudor courtiers modelled their courtly gestures of gaming pursuits and themselves according to recommendations like those of Elyot and Ascham. After the untimely death of the much admired courtier Sir Philip Sidney in 1584, Edmund Spenser praised the fellow poet in his pastoral elegy 'Astrophel' (1595) as follows:

> In wrestling nimble, and renning swift,
> In shooting steddie, and in swimming strong:
> Well made to strike, to throw, to leape, to lift,
> And all the sports that shepheards are emong.
> In euery one he vanquisht euery one,
> He vanquisht all, and vanquisht was of none. (ll. 73–8)[19]

His extraordinary physical abilities are among the distinguishing features of the model courtier Sidney, and he demonstrates them in respectable and fashionable courtly sports.

In *Basilicon Doron* (1599), both a treatise on government and a conduct book James VI of Scotland wrote for his son and heir apparent Henry, the royal author's selection of gaming activities is less precise than Ascham's above, but on the whole James follows Ascham's and Elyot's advice. James recommended that Henry should exert himself 'in such honest games or pastimes, as may further abilitie and maintaine health' – he particularly recommended hunting – and cautioned him not to forget 'that these games are but ordained for you, in enabling you for your office'.[20] James foregrounds the educational character of the royal games. Hunting was traditionally a favourite pastime of the nobility, and of the royal

---

[17]   Forbes Sieveking, 'Games', pp. 461–2.
[18]   The play on the associations of 'hazard' pervades the play. On the eve of the battle of Agincourt, Rambures asks: 'Who will go to hazard with me for twenty prisoners?' The Constable replies: 'You must first go yourself to hazard, ere you have them' (*H V*, 3.7.79–81).
[19]   Edmund Spenser, 'Astrophel', in *The Shorter Poems*, ed. Richard A. McCabe (Harmondsworth: Penguin, 1999), pp. 372–84, at p. 376.
[20]   King James VI and I, *Basilicon Doron: Political Writings*, ed. Johann P. Sommerville (Cambridge: Cambridge University Press, 1994) pp. 1–61, at pp. 55–6.

household in particular. The athletic Henry VIII 'hunted, jousted, played tennis, wrestled, could throw a twelve-foot spear many yards, defeated all comers with his heavy, two-handled sword in mock combats, and could draw a bow with greater strength than any man in England'.[21] His daughter Elizabeth, like her father a patron of regally acceptable outdoor sports, was a skilled archer and huntress. In the courtly mythologising she encouraged, she was praised as an early modern Diana, the goddess of the hunt. In her 'games' of political self-fashioning, Elizabeth also played with empowering gender roles.

Especially for the common people, games and the spirit of play were often associated with the holidays and festivals that structured the year: 'family festivals, like weddings; community festivals, like the feast of a patron saint of a town or parish [...]; annual festivals involving most Europeans, like Easter, May Day, Midsummer, the Twelve Days of Christmas, New Year, and the Epiphany; and finally, Carnival'.[22] It is imperative to note that these festive games, as fixed elements of the respective rituals, were often characterised by a high degree of violence, often in the form of ritual group violence. Both the violence unleashed during these games and its ultimate, sometimes difficult containment were socially important functions of early modern festive life. Ballgames were notorious for the violence that went along with them; the manner in which they were played often resembled armed conflicts. Football, which in various forms has long been globally popular in different cultures at different times, was played in Europe from the middle ages. Its early form, which had almost no rules, is also called mob football. Football was one of the most violent kinds of early modern ball games. The rules of the individual games varied according to local custom; there were especially violent forms that sometimes took the best part of a day or longer and resembled miniature wars of attrition, like for instance the ballgame between the parishes of Saint Peter's and All Saints in Derby. Both teams tried to somehow get the ball into their opponents' goal on the other side of town – by all means, as Julius Ruff explains:

> *If the defense of the opposing team was tenacious, all sorts of stratagems might be employed. On several occasions players emptied the woodshavings that filled the ball, concealing it under their clothing [...]. And on one occasion a player carried the ball through a sewer under the town. Such play caused numerous injuries, property damage, and occasional deaths. [...] In some locales strange and violent rites were added to games.[23]*

The fact that football players regularly died while playing the game shows how different early modern gaming activities were and to what a large extent they were subsequently pacified in the civilising process. The organised violence that was associated with the games at the same time shows how close some games were to military activities. As Thomas Fuller was to argue in 1642: 'tilting and fencing is war without anger; and manly sports are the grammar of military performance. But above all, shooting is a noble recreation, and a half liberal art.'[24] Until the end of the sixteenth century, archery was not only a favourite pastime of many, it was also of great military importance (and, with a view to for instance the battle of Agincourt, a source of national pride). It was a gaming activity whose pursuit was always encouraged by the authorities. Both Edward III in 1349 and James II of Scotland in 1457 privileged archery over other sports which they banned, most important among them

---

[21]   Alison Weir, *Henry VIII: King and Court* (London: Vintage, 2008), p. 106.
[22]   Peter Burke, *Popular Culture in Early Modern Europe* (3rd ed., Farnham: Ashgate, 2009), p. 255.
[23]   Julius R. Ruff, *Violence in Early Modern Europe 1500–1800* (Cambridge: Cambridge University Press, 2001), pp. 169–70.
[24]   Thomas Fuller, 'Of Recreations', in *The Holy and Profane States* (Cambridge, MA: Hilliard and Brown, 1841 [1642]), pp. 192–7, 195. See also Forbes Sieveking, 'Games', p. 454.

football, so that these other sports no longer interfered with archery practice. It is somewhat ironic that it was during the reign of Elizabeth I, who fashioned herself after Diana, that the military importance of the bow as a weapon of war sharply decreased. In 1595, a few years after the musket had proven effective in the defeat of the Armada, the bow was abandoned in favour of the musket.[25] Afterwards, the cultural position of archery changed as it became a skill sport of little or no military use.

Football was considered an un-gentlemanly game of the lower classes. In *King Lear*, Kent responds to Oswald's remark that he will not be struck by Lear: 'Nor tripped neither, you base foot-ball player' (1.4.73–4) – and follows his insult by tripping up Oswald's heels. Kent literally beats Oswald at 'his own game'; the mention of football is immediately followed by an act of (in this case, mild) violence associated with the game. According to the general image of football, it is clear that the nobleman treats the disrespectful commoner like he deserves to be treated. At the same time, the rules of football, like those of other popular and unruly outdoor games, came to be more systematised in the early seventeenth century.

Ball games were notorious for serious disturbances of the public order. Like many other popular outdoor games, football was regularly banned in England, for instance in 1349, 1363, 1541 and 1617.[26] The repeated attempts of the authorities, even the authority of the monarch, at banning popular games were largely unsuccessful. For instance, both the 'Statute of Artificers of 1563 and the Poor Law of 1597 referred to idleness, drunkenness, and unlawful games as "lewd practices and conditions of life", and the laws construed these as interfering with agricultural and industrial production.'[27] The most famous early modern edict on games is often referred to as the *Book of Sports*. It was first issued by James I in 1617, and its title is actually *A Declaration of Sports*. While it first referred only to Lancashire, its reissue in 1618 pertained to the whole of England. The declaration was a rebuttal of the Puritans' attempts at prohibiting all activities they considered ungodly. It lists those games and sports that were allowed on Sundays and holidays and some that were explicitly not. James's declarations were then extended by Charles I in 1633. Like his father, Charles also lined with the common people's predilection for Sunday sports while seeking to make sure they attended the services of the Anglican church before they went to play:

> *for our good people's lawful recreation, our pleasure likewise is, that after the end of divine service our good people be not disturbed, letted or discouraged from any lawful recreation, such as dancing, either men or women; archery for men, leaping, vaulting, or any other such harmless recreation, nor from having of May-games, Whitsun-ales, and Morris-dances; and the setting up of May-poles and other sports therewith used: so as the same be had in due and convenient time, without impediment or neglect of divine service: and that women shall have leave to carry rushes to the church for the decorating of it, according to their old custom; but withal we do here account still as prohibited all unlawful games to be used upon Sundays only, as bear and bull-baitings, interludes and at all times in the meaner sort of people by law prohibited, bowling.[28]*

One of the most popular early modern lawn games among all classes, bowling was a threat to the public order because it was played in the proliferating public spaces (e.g. next to taverns)

---

[25] See Andrew Leibs, *Sports and Games of the Renaissance* (Westport: Greenwood Press, 2004), p. xv.

[26] Ibid., pp. 67–8, and see Derek Baker, *England in the Later Middle Ages* (Rochester, NY: Boydell & Brewer, 1995 [1968]), pp. 186–7.

[27] Gerald Handel, *Social Welfare in Western Society* (New Brunswick: Transaction Publishers, 2009 [1982]), p. 99.

[28] Charles I, *The Declaration of Sports* (1633). http://www.constitution.org/eng/conpur017.htm (accessed 7 January 2014).

as well as in private spaces that were difficult to control, and it took up a lot of unproductive time. In 1511 Henry VIII 'banned the games for all but the wealthy [...] Apparently the game distracted "Bowyers, Fletchers, Stringers, and Arrowhead makers" from their military duties.'[29] Bowling is also linked by anecdote to England's greatest military victory in the sixteenth century, the defeat of the Armada in 1588. Allegedly Sir Francis Drake was playing bowls on Plymouth Hoe when he heard that the Spanish fleet was approaching, and he insisted there was still enough time to finish the game before beating the Spaniards (he allegedly lost the game, his defeat on the green contrasting with the sea battle he won). The anecdote is not traceable to any eye witnesses but its wide currency highlights the popularity of bowling as a leisurely activity.

Indoor games were as popular as outdoor games, and they were more frequently, albeit not exclusively, played in winter. In his *Anatomy of Melancholy* (1621), Robert Burton lists indoor games that could be played in the dark season and would help fight melancholy:

> *The ordinary recreations which we have in winter, and in most solitary times busy our minds with, are cards, tables and dice, shovelboard, chess-play, the philosopher's game, small trunks, shuttlecock, billiards, music, masks, singing, dancing, Yule-games, frolics, jests, riddles, catches, purposes, questions and commands, merry tales of errant knights, queens, lovers, lords, ladies, giants, dwarfs, thieves, cheaters, witches, fairies, goblins, friars, &c.*[30]

Certainly, indoor games also varied widely in their cultural prestige, and they could also be subdivided into lawful and unlawful games, even though the definitions shifted. Chess was considered one of the most respectable board games. Having been introduced into Europe in the high middle ages via Italy and Spain, chess continued to evolve during the early modern period. It was a metaphorical enactment of war that turned the 'art of war' into an intellectual exercise whose outcome excluded chance – which appealed to the political elites. In comparison with the gaming tools needed for most other games (even 'tables', i.e. backgammon), chess boards and pieces were expensive to produce, and their possession was a sign of wealth.[31] On the other hand, chess did not have a gambling element, so it was played for its own sake, not for any possible material gain. One of the greatest stage successes and theatrical scandals of the early seventeenth century, Thomas Middleton's *A Game at Chess* (1624), uses the figures and the rules of chess in detail; for example, the play opens with the standard opening 'Queen's Gambit Declined', acted out as an attempt to seduce the White Queen's Pawn. The detailed chess allegory was easily decoded by the theatre audiences that flocked to the Globe theatre to see the play: the characters bear the names of chess figures (the White King and the Black King etc.) which for the theatre audience were easy to translate as members of the British (white) and Spanish (black) political establishments negotiating the marriage of Prince Charles, the heir apparent, to the Infanta Maria. Chess is not only the pivotal vehicle of the game/play allegory, then, it is also 'an alienation device: the most important political events of recent months and years

---

[29]   Leibs, *Sports and Games of the Renaissance*, p. 74.

[30]   Robert Burton [Democritus Junior], *The Anatomy of Melancholy. What is is, with all the kinds, causes, symptoms, prognostics & several cures of it* (1621), The Second Partition, 'Memb. IV. Exercise recitified of Body and Mind', n. p. http://www.gutenberg.org/files/10800/10800-h/ampart2.html (accessed 7 January 2014).

[31]   Ulrike Krampl notes that the emerging games industry, which for instance produced gaming utensils and established the infrastructure of lotteries, became a factor in the early modern economic field. 'Spiele', in Friedrich Jäger ed., *Enzyklopädie der Neuzeit* (16 vols, Stuttgart: Metzler, 2005–12), vol. 12, pp. 337–42, at p. 338.

were translated into a series of moves in a game'.[32] The white side triumphs when the White Knight (Prince Charles) tempts the Black Knight (the Conde de Gondomar, a former Spanish ambassador to London) into confessing how corruptedly ambitious and lecherous the black side is. An indoor game becomes the metaphorical centre of a play that stages its politics in an open playhouse.

At the other end of the indoor games' scale of respectability were dice games and card games, the most popular games of chance. The most popular form of gambling, dicing games were at the same time frequently pronounced unlawful, but no amount of preaching or banning diminished their popularity. The condemnations of dicing had a legitimacy problem because it was well known, and confirmed by court gossip and numerous popular legends, that the upper echelons of society also gambled at dice. In his *Survey of London*, John Stow reports that Sir Miles Partridge diced with Henry VIII; Sir Miles 'did set an hundred pound vpon a cast at dice'[33] against the bell tower of a London chapel, and he won the tower from the king. At the other end of the social scale, Falstaff, the carnivalesque representative of the low life in Shakespeare's histories, avers: 'I was as virtuously given as a gentleman need to be: virtuous enough, swore little; diced not – above seven times a week' (*1 H IV*, 3.3.12–14). The moralising public discourse connected dice games with a high amount of trickery and fraud. The falseness of dice in general and of 'dicer's oaths' was proverbial, and a whole genre of texts reaped profit from the interest in dicing by warning against and discussing the latest tricks. Examples are *A Manifest Detection of the Most Vyle and Detestable Use of Dice Play* (1532), attributed to one Gilbert Walker, John Northbrooke's *A Treatise against Dicing, Dancing, Plays, and Interludes* (c. 1577) and Thomas Dekker's *The Belman of London: Bringing to light the most notorious Villanies that are now practiced in the Kingdome* (1608). In great detail, these texts list many dicing tricks, for instance numerous kinds of false dice and how they are manipulated by sleight of hand. In his abovementioned archery treatise *Toxophilus*, Roger Ascham sought to list the pros and cons of 'vnlawfull games and namely cardes and dise' by comparing them to the lawful game of archery.[34] It is somewhat ironic – and betrays some self-irony on Ascham's part – that he lived and died a comparatively poor man because of his love of dicing and cockfighting.

The cultural practices relating to card games were largely the same as those pertaining to dice games. Although some 'harmless' card games existed, the unlawful gambling card games drew the most attention and were played at all social levels. Instead of discussing a number of card games, I will discuss a case study to show how deeply involved in the fabric of early modern England this card game was. The case study is a card game called primero. It came to England at the beginning of the sixteenth century, from Italy ('primiera') or Spain ('primera') and perhaps via France ('prime'; Rabelais included it in his gargantuan list), and it remained arguably the most popular card game for the next hundred years, under all Tudor rulers, which changed slowly under the Stuarts – the favourite card game of James I was called 'maw', and it was more trump-oriented than primero.

Primero is one of the forerunners of modern poker; it is about having the highest possible hand or bluffing the other players into thinking that one has it. A gambling game in which high sums were staked, primero 'was among the first favourites with royalty and other persons of distinction'[35] but was at the same time also played by other people who

---

[32]   Gary Taylor, 'A Game at Chesse: An Early Form', in Thomas Middleton, *The Collected Works*, ed. Gary Taylor and John Lavagnino (Oxford: Clarendon Press, 2007) pp. 1773–9, at p. 1775.

[33]   John Stow, *A Survey of London* (1603), ed. Charles Lethbridge Kingsford (2 vols, Oxford: Clarendon Press, 1908), vol. 1, p. 330.

[34]   Roger Ascham, *Toxophilus* (1545) and Joseph Addison, *Criticism on Milton's 'Paradise Lost'* (1711–12), ed. Edward Arber (London: Murray & Son, 1868), pp. 23 and 49–57.

[35]   Forbes Sieveking, 'Games', p. 472.

could not afford it, of all social classes. Again, the fallen knight Falstaff gives us a hint at its contagious and ruinous nature: 'I never prospered since I forswore myself at primero' (*Merry Wives*, 4.5.82–3). Queen Elizabeth seems to have excelled at primero, yet the lavish praise of her godson Sir John Harington is certainly exaggerated:

> *For, if her Majestie would play at Primero in that proportion of her estate as I have seen some of her mean subiects in theyr poor callinges, she showld play a dukedom at a rest, and a barrony stake, and then I know none able to hold play with her.*[36]

In its actual performance, primero certainly had an element of Machiavellian manipulation, and Harington seems to underline Elizabeth's absolute mastery in her courtly power play.

A card game of chance that was also a gambling game in which high sums of money could be won would quickly evoke numerous tricksters seeking to exploit the new market. Very shortly after the arrival of the game in England, the London trickster scene located at the court and in the city operated a great number of tricks for cheating at primero. The author of *A Manifest Detection* lists primero among the most corrupted games:

> *Primero, now as it hath most use in court, so is there most deceit in it: some play upon the prick; some pinch the cards privily with their nails; some turn up the corners; some mark them with fine spots of ink. One fine trick brought in a Spaniard: a finer than this invented an Italian, and won much money with it by our doctors, and yet, at the last, they were both overreached by new sleights devised here at home.*[37]

In addition to being a socially prestigious but potentially ruinous game (and probably owing part of its success at the court to the risk of ruin it involved), primero became the subject of the discourse on the folly of gambling and of social pretensions. In a mock conduct book for a would-be city gentleman, *The Gull's Hornbook* (1609), Thomas Dekker's narrator counsels his reader to accept losses at primero quietly: 'whether you be at primero, or hazard, you shall sit as patiently, though you lose a whole half-year's exhibition, as a disarmed gentleman does when he's in the unmerciful fingers of sergeants'. The game can also be rhetorically flaunted to show that one is hobnobbing with the primero-playing nobility: 'All the way as you pass, especially being approached near some of the gates, talk of none but lords, and such ladies with whom you have played at primero.'[38] Open to all kinds of manipulation, primero came to be used as a metaphor of the unregulated game of social mobility in early modern England.

Dekker's satire is echoed in Ben Jonson's *Every Man Out of His Humour* (first performed 1599). Here, the jester and sponger Carlo counsels the naive but rich Sogliardo, who wants to become a gentleman at all costs:

> *First, to be an accomplished gentleman, that is, a gentleman of the time, you must give o'er housekeeping in the country and live altogether in the city amongst gallants [...] learn to play at primero and passage; and, ever when you lose, ha' two or three peculiar oaths to swear by, that no man else swears. (1.2.33–41)*[39]

---

[36]   Sir John Harington, *A Treatise on Playe. Nugae Antiquae* (3 vols, London: J. Dodsley, 1779), vol. 1, pp. 154–208, at p. 178.
[37]   Gilbert Walker [?], *A Manifest Detection of the Most Vyle and Detestable Use of Dice Play*, ed. J. O. Halliwell (London: The Percy Society, 1850 [1532?]), p. 33.
[38]   Thomas Dekker, *The Gull's Hornbook* (1609), ed. R.B. McKerrow (London: De La More Press, 1904), pp. 46 and 65.
[39]   Ben Jonson, *Every Man Out of His Humour*, ed. Randall Martin, in David Bevington, Martin Butler and Ian Donaldson eds, *The Cambridge Edition of the Works of Ben Jonson* (7 vols, Cambridge:

Jonson often used primero as a kind of shorthand for conspicuous and almost institutionalised fraud, particularly in his city comedies, the theatrical genre that would directly address the modern sociotopes in which the gambling logic of primero could be metonymically applied. Thomas Middleton even names one of the characters of his city comedy *Your Five Gallants* (1608)[40] – a 'bawd-gallant', that is, a pimp – Primero. Right in the first scene Frip, the 'broker-gallant', asks Primero to 'Make me perfect in that trick that got you so much at primero' (1.1.144–5). The amoral city gallants are fashioned by the fashionable and corrupting card game.

In Jonson's great trickster play *The Alchemist*, primero plays a primary role as a marker of a well-known kind of cozening that ironically comes to seem honest in comparison with the monumental deceits of the two virtuoso tricksters of the play, Subtle and Face. Surly cannot see how his friend Sir Epicure Mammon can so easily be deceived by the purported saintly alchemist and his assistant:

> SURLY *Heart! can it be,*
> *An this be your elixir,*
> *Your lapis mineralis, and your lunary,*
> *Give me your honest trick yet at primero,*
> *Or gleek. (2.3.281–4)*[41]

Later in the play, the pseudo-alchemist Subtle hilariously recommends to the fool Dapper a sure way to get rich: Dapper should keep 'The gallant'st company and the best games [...] Gleek and primero' (5.2.45–7). *The Alchemist* even alludes to details of the game. When Face stages a fake temper tantrum against Subtle to make the clueless Dapper part with his money as soon as possible, he refers to primero once more:

> '*Slight, I bring you*
> *No cheating Clim-o'-the-Cloughs or Claribels*
> *That look as big as five-and-fifty and flush. (1.2.45–7)*

According to Face, Dapper possesses the moral integrity that is a prerequisite for anybody who wants to consult an alchemist; the undeserving others are likened to a hand in primero. While there is an element of seeming and being involved in Face's phrasing, the connotation is that anybody who has to do with primero has an element of deceit about him. The Cambridge editors annotate 'five-and-fifty and flush': 'In the card game primero, a flush of a complete sequence in one suit (ace, five, six, seven) was worth 55 points (= 1 + 3 x [5 + 6 + 7)] and was unbeatable.' The detailed reference to the best hand in primero indicates that Jonson relied on the largest part of his audience to be familiar with the rules of primero. The details of the card game became signifiers in an urban communication milieu, and the ludic element was transferred from the game itself to the game of language, in which Jonson played an excellent hand and which was another game of power.

The last words on early modern games in England will be Sir John Harington's, who, in *A Treatise on Playe*, describes a courtly idler whose day is filled with playing games and watching others playing. What becomes almost palpable here is a life of play that is full of

---

Cambridge University Press, 2012), vol. 1, pp. 233–428.

[40] Ralph Alan Cohen and John Jowett, 'Your Five Gallants', in Thomas Middleton, *The Collected Works*, ed. Gary Taylor and John Lavagnino (Oxford: Clarendon Press, 2007), p. 594: 'The 1608 quarto edition printed by George Eld [was] the only version of the text available until 232 years later.'

[41] Ben Jonson, *The Alchemist*, ed. Peter Holland and William Sherman, in Bevington et al. eds, *The Cambridge Edition of the Works of Ben Jonson*, vol. 3, pp. 541–710. Gleek was another popular gambling card game.

sensuality, of physical pleasure – the belly, the arms, the motion, the warmth. Harington articulates a pleasure of gaming that is conspicuously lacking in many other texts that seek to bring early modern games under control. His account, dismissive as it is on the surface, once more throws into relief what a prominent part of everyday popular culture games were, and the moralising ending of his description is clearly at odds with the keen interest in all kinds of games that so obviously pervades it:

> Lett us but morally and civilly (as I may say) lay before vs an exampell of some one, of which there is to great choyse, that spendes his whole life in play: as thus, for example, in the morninge, perhapps, at chesse, and after his belly is full then at cardes; and, when his sperites was dull at that, then for some exercyse of his armes at dyce, and, being weary thearof, for a little motion of his body, to tennis; and, having warmd him at that, then, to coole himselfe a little, play at tables; and being disquieted in his paciens for ouerseeing synk and quater, or missing two or three fowle blotts, then to an enterlude, and so (as one well compared yt) lyke to a mill-horse, treddinge always in the same stepps, bee ever as far from a worthy and a wise man as the circle ys from the center.[42]

Select Bibliography

Brewster, Paul G., *Games and Sports in Shakespeare*. Helsinki: Suomalainen Tiedeakatemia, 1959.

Caillois, Roger, *Man, Play and Games*, trans. Meyer Barash. Champaign: University of Illinois Press, 2001.

Clopper, Lawrence M., *Drama, Play, and Game: English Festive Culture in the Medieval and Early Modern Period*. Chicago: University of Chicago Press, 2001.

Colón Semenza, Gregory M., *Sport, Politics, and Literature in the English Renaissance*. Cranbury, NJ: Associated University Presses, 2003.

Crane, Mark, Richard Raiswell and Margaret Reeves eds, *Shell Games: Studies in Scams, Frauds, and Deceits (1300–1650)*. Toronto: Centre for Reformation and Renaissance Studies, 2004.

Egri, Peter, *Modern Games with Renaissance Forms: From Leonardo and Shakespeare to Warhol and Stoppard*. Budapest: Akadémiai Kiadó, 1996.

Forbes Sieveking, A., 'Games', in C.T. Onions ed., *Shakespeare's England: An Account of the Life & Manners of His Age*. 2 vols. Oxford: Clarendon Press, 1917, vol. 2, pp. 451–83.

Handel, Gerald, *Social Welfare in Western Society*. New Brunswick: Transaction Publishers, 2009; first published 1982.

Huizinga, Johan, *Homo ludens: A Study of the Play-Element in Culture*. Boston: Beacon Press, 1955.

Larson, Katherine R., '"Certein Childplayes Remembred by the Fayre Ladies": Girls and Their Games', in Naomi J. Miller and Naomi Yavneh eds, *Gender and Early Modern Constructions of Childhood*. Farnham: Ashgate, 2011, pp. 67–82.

Leibs, Andrew, *Sports and Games of the Renaissance*. Westport: Greenwood Press, 2004.

Mäyrä, Frans, *An Introduction to Game Studies: Games in Culture*. Los Angeles: Sage Publications, 2008.

McClelland, John, and Brian Merrilees eds, *Sport and Culture in Early Modern Europe*. Toronto: Centre for Reformation and Renaissance Studies, 2009.

Ruff, Julius R., *Violence in Early Modern Europe 1500–1800*. Cambridge: Cambridge University Press, 2001.

---

[42] Harington, *A Treatise on Playe*, pp. 168–9.

Cultures of Mending

Abigail Shinn

A Needle (though it be but small and slender)
Yet it is both a maker and a mender[1]

In John Taylor's needlework pattern book *The Needles Excellency* (1631), the water poet appends a poem, 'The prayse of the Needle', which equates domestic labour with the weapons of war: 'It is a Taylors Iavelin, or his Launce / And for my Countries quiet, I should like, / That woman-kinde should vse no other Pike' (A1ʳ). The woman at work on her '*crosse-stitch*' and '*Raisd-worke*' (A2ʳ) is wielding the arms of her sex, the needle with its sharp point a diminutive cousin to the battle-ready 'Launce' or 'Pike'. A correspondence reinforced by the title page's image of a woman representing 'Industrie' who holds her needle aloft (Figure 15.1), its sharp point echoed by the sword carried by a retreating male figure in the background. Given that the tools of needlework, whether the needle or the pin, had the capacity to deliver injury in the form of prickings, this militaristic analogy seems apt, even if it does figure the woman who wields the needle as a weak counterpart to the soldier, making it clear that she is destined to serve only on a domestic front.

Recent critical work on early modern needlework has explored how Taylor's analogy may be more fitting than is immediately apparent, arguing that women who plied the needle exercised political, religious and social agency. On the one hand this was achieved through the production of items which incorporated encoded meanings and formed part of the gift economy or served as objects of display. On the other hand, the communal activity of sewing provided a meeting place for women and the opportunity for conversation and the exchange of information under the guise of virtuous labour. As Peter Stallybrass and Ann Rosalind Jones have argued, for elite needlewomen 'thread and cloth were materials through which they could record and commemorate their participation not in reclusive domestic activity but in the larger public world'.[2] Susan Frye has paid particular attention to the 'political textualities' of needlewomen such as Elizabeth Tudor, Mary Stuart and Bess of Hardwick.[3] Frye's work frames the needle as a tool which successfully operates as a weapon, but, much like Taylor's pattern book, which was ostensibly aimed at women of leisure and incorporated a series of sonnets addressed to 'Honourable' ladies, such as Elizabeth I and

I extend my thanks to the following for references and suggestions, Claire Canavan, Helen Smith, Mark Jenner, Brian Cummings, Catherine Richardson, Susan Vincent, Mary Brooks and Maria Heywood.

[1]   John Taylor, *The Needles Excellency* (4th ed., London, 1640), sig. A1ᵛ. The title page claims that this is the 12th edition but only four editions are listed in the ESTC between 1631 and 1640.

[2]   Ann Rosalind Jones and Peter Stallybrass, *Renaissance Clothing and the Materials of Memory* (Cambridge: Cambridge University Press, 2000), p. 134.

[3]   Susan Frye, *Pens and Needles: Women's Textualities in Early Modern England* (Philadelphia: University of Pennsylvania Press, 2010), p. 30. Frye's work builds on Rozsika Parker's reading of needlework and female agency in *The Subversive Stitch: Embroidery and the Makings of the Feminine* (London: I. B. Tauris, 1984) and identifies the needle as an 'unstable signifier' with important associations with the pen, p. 16.

Figure 15.1   John Taylor, *The Needles Excellency* (4th ed., London, 1640).
                 © The British Library Board. C.31.h.30 (frontispiece).

Mary, Countess of Pembroke (A3ʳ-A3ᵛ), she focuses on the needlework of women from the upper echelons of English society.[4] These women had the time and skill to produce fancy work which advertised their wealth and status, often taking the form of images and emblems which testified to the needlewoman's piety and education or operated as a 'family livery' which declared a family's loyalty to a particular leader or faction.[5]

What happens, however, when rather than being used to embellish fabrics with costly silks, the needle is wielded by women (and men) undertaking the necessary work of mending, darning and patching? Often referred to as 'botching', a term which in the sixteenth century meant to repair with skill as well as to patch a garment clumsily, mending was the indispensible foundation upon which all needlework was based. In order to explore the ways in which the everyday task of closing gaps, rents, tears and breaches in cloth, and the tools of mending, specifically needles, were figured in popular culture, this chapter will examine the labour of mending through a reading of the early Tudor comedy *Gammer Gurton's Needle* (1550s–1560s), a play whose action revolves around a lost needle and a pair of torn breeches.

---

    [4]   For a discussion of Taylor's intended readership for his pattern book see Bernard Capp, *The World of John Taylor the Water Poet 1578–1653* (Oxford: Oxford University Press, 1994), p. 96; Jones and Stallybrass note that Taylor's representations of elite women may be designed to appeal to the social aspirations of middle-ranking women. *Renaissance Clothing and the Materials of Memory*, p. 137.

    [5]   Jones and Stallybrass, *Renaissance Clothing and the Materials of Memory*, p. 162.

Locating the Popular

> As Gammer Gurton, with manye a wyde styche,
> Sat pesynge and patching of Hodg her man's briche,
> By chance or misfortune as shee her geare tost
> In Hodge lether bryches her needle shee lost.[6]

The difficulty of locating popular culture, given that its remains are frequently ephemeral and therefore elusive, is a familiar problem for researchers looking to find evidence of non-elite needlework practices. In general, clothing belonging to the lower orders, with the exception of shoes, does not survive from the sixteenth and seventeenth centuries.[7] Cloth which was darned and patched, doubtless on more than one occasion, through necessity, was unlikely to survive unless the item was of great value. The action of mending can be found mentioned in household manuals (to which I will return later) as a necessary skill required of the good housewife, but evidence for the wider cultural practices and beliefs attached to mending is often hard to discern. It is this absence which has prompted my use of *Gammer Gurton's Needle*, an early Tudor comedy penned by Mr S (commonly identified as William Stevenson, fellow of Christ's College, 1551–4 and again from 1559–61) as a source for attitudes towards the tools and labour of mending.[8]

Gammer Gurton's Needle, as is made readily apparent by the play's title, centres on a lost needle belonging to Gammer Gurton. Startled when she sees her cat Gyb in the milk pan Gammer tosses aside the pair of breeches she is mending for her servant Hodge, inadvertently losing her needle in the process. The uproar that this causes to the household, which resounds with both Gammer's and Hodge's lamentations, is compounded when Diccon the Bedlam (associated with St Mary Bethlehem, the London hospital for the insane) uses this as an excuse for some Machiavellian trickery. He persuades Hodge that he has seen the devil – prompting Hodge to shit his breeches – and tells Dame Chat the alewife that Gammer Gurton believes she has stolen her cock, resulting in a fight between the two women as Gammer Gurton mistakenly believes that Dame Chat has stolen the needle. It is not until the Bayly is called in and insists that Diccon swear an oath on Hodge's breeches that the needle is found: as Diccon claps Hodge on the backside, the needle pricks him in the buttocks.

Gammer Gurton was performed at Christ's College Cambridge in the 1550s or 1560s and was later printed in an edition by Thomas Colwell in 1575. The first printed vernacular English comedy it has clear classical antecedents in Terence and Plautus and the printed edition self-consciously echoes the bibliographic format of classical plays.[9] Kent Cartwright has argued that 'its characters suggest English updates of Roman stereotypes' and its university setting has prompted Douglas Duncan to read its use of the vernacular as a moment of 'holiday

---

[6] William Stevenson, 'Gammer Gurton's Nedle', in William Tydman ed., *Four Tudor Comedies* (London: Penguin Books, 1984), 'prologue', ll. 1–4, p. 217. All further references are from this edition.

[7] Margaret Spufford, *The Great Reclothing of Rural England: Petty Chapmen and Their Wares in the Seventeenth Century* (London: Hambledon Press, 1984), p. 130.

[8] On the dating of *Gammer Gurton's Needle* see Frederick S. Boas, *University Drama in the Tudor Age* (Oxford: Oxford University Press, 1914), pp. 80–88; Philip Dust and William D. Wolf, 'Recent Studies in Early Tudor Drama: *Gorboduc, Ralph Roister Doister, Gammer Gurton's Needle*, and *Cambises*', *English Literary Renaissance* 8:1 (1978), 107–10.

[9] R.W. Ingram, '*Gammer Gurton's Needle*: Comedy Not Quite of the Lowest Order', *Studies in English Literature* 7:2 (1967), 257–68, at p. 259; Wendy Wall, *Staging Domesticity: Household Work and English Identity in Early Modern England* (Cambridge: Cambridge University Press, 2002), p. 85; Douglas Duncan, 'Gammer Gurton's Needle and the Concept of Humanist Parody', *Studies in English Literature* 27:2 (1987), 177–96, at p. 181; *Gammer Gurton* was also the first English play to put a cat on stage, see Bruce Boehrer, 'Gammer Gurton's Cat of Sorrows', *English Literary Renaissance* 39:2 (2009), 267–89, at p. 267.

indecorum, more intent on upsetting the dignity of the curriculum than on furthering the development of native drama'.[10] Frank Ardolino has identified *Gammer Gurton* as 'an early Reformation play deliberately disguised as a coarse vernacular comedy that was intended to promote Protestant English community through correct reading' while Lorna Hutson has conversely argued that the play has continuities with pre-Reformation penitential or sacramental theatre.[11] My use of *Gammer Gurton*, a University play which, as Andrew Hiscock notes, 'constitute[s] an elite reading of popular culture prepared specifically for public consumption', therefore raises one of the central problems for the study of popular culture in the early modern period: can we use elite forms of cultural production as a way of locating the popular?[12]

Gammer Gurton's first audience, comprised of university students and staff, is a far cry from the apprentices and hawkers who made up the groundlings in the playhouses and potentially corresponds to Peter Burke's elite minority who participated in both the 'great' and 'little' traditions:

> [T]he crucial cultural difference in early modern Europe ... was that between the majority, for whom popular culture was the only culture, and the minority, who had access to the great tradition but participated in the little tradition as a second culture. They were amphibious, bi-cultural, and also bilingual.[13]

Mr S and his audience certainly occupy an 'amphibious, bi-cultural' and 'bilingual' position as is evidenced both by the Latin culture of the university and *Gammer Gurton*'s identification as the first English vernacular comedy, and it is the play's straddling of different cultural locations that I hope to exploit here as a means of entry to the otherwise inscrutable popular culture of mending. Rather than reading *Gammer Gurton* solely as, in the words of David M. Bevington, 'a college-man's indulgent laugh at unlearned country folk', I will use the play as an elite source which can illuminate attitudes towards an otherwise frequently overlooked everyday object, the needle, and the task which it performs.[14] While the play offers up a dramatic reconstruction of a domestic environment which is first and foremost designed to provoke laughter from an elite audience, its central fixation on mending nonetheless allows us to trace evidence for cultural objects and practices which would have been familiar to the majority of early modern men and women but which are all too often missing from the historical record.

---

[10] Kent Cartwright, *Theatre and Humanism: English Drama in the Sixteenth Century* (Cambridge: Cambridge University Press, 1999), p. 77; Duncan, 'Gammer Gurton's Needle and the Concept of Humanist Parody', p. 178.

[11] Frank Ardolino, 'Misperception and Protestant Reading in *Gammer Gurton's Needle*', *Studies in English Literature* 50:1 (2010), 17–34, at p. 19; Lorna Hutson, 'Theatre', in Brian Cummings and James Simpson eds, *Cultural Reformations: Medieval and Renaissance in Literary History* (Oxford: Oxford University Press, 2010), pp. 227–8.

[12] Andrew Hiscock, '"Hear My Tale or Kiss My Tail": The *Old Wife's Tale*, *Gammer Gurton's Needle*, and the Popular Culture of Tudor Comedy', in Mike Pincombe and Cathy Shrank eds, *The Oxford Handbook of Tudor Literature 1485–1603* (Oxford: Oxford University Press, 2009), p. 737.

[13] Peter Burke, *Popular Culture in Early Modern Europe* (Aldershot: Ashgate, 2006; 1st ed. 1978), p. 28; Garret Sullivan and Linda Woodbridge point out that the sixteenth century saw the first attempts to classify and thereby construct popular culture, a process which *Gammer Gurton* with its parody of village life and ale-house culture arguably corresponds to, 'Popular Culture in Print', in Arthur F. Kinney ed., *The Cambridge Companion to English Literature, 1500–1600* (Cambridge: Cambridge University Press, 2000), pp. 268–9.

[14] David M. Bevington, *From Mankind to Marlowe: Growth of Structure in the Popular Drama of Tudor England* (Cambridge, MA: Harvard University Press, 1962), p. 33.

Who Mends and Why?

Trying to identify the individuals, like Gammer Gurton, who mended garments both in the home and as part of an informal economy dominated by women, is difficult due to the low status and payment for such work.[15] Susan Cahn argues that women's work on the periphery of the textile trade was indicative of the versatility of domestic skills which could be transferred from the home to the marketplace, but that these skills were neither prestigious nor profitable.[16] This valuation is reflected in a metaphor employed by the Bishop of Durham James Pilkington in order to criticise priests who cannot teach: 'A Tayler that is not cunninge to make a gowne, maye mende hose … but an vnable priest to teach, is good to nothinge in that kynde of lyfe or ministerye.'[17] The lower status and profit afforded to mending in comparison to making garments was reflected in a grievance voiced at the Merchant Taylor's common council in 1518. Complaining that foreign workers licensed solely as 'botchers', as menders of clothing, were in fact making new apparel, the tailors argued they were suffering 'great loss, hurt and damage'.[18] As a trade botchers were clearly distinguished from tailors and the register of the freemen of York from the Elizabethan period identifies numerous 'bochers' alongside tailors, drapers and 'pynner[s]'.[19]

A further distinction was also made between remodelling garments, a job which required a certain amount of skill, and the labour of mending. When examining high status clothing Janet Arnold mentions that while it was common practice for tailors to remodel Queen Elizabeth's clothing, for example removing and replacing stained linings, the Queen's laundry woman, Elizabeth Smith, appears to have undertaken minor repairs.[20] Another source for paid-for mending was the London playhouses. The theatres made a huge investment in costumes, many of which were items of clothing which were 'translated' for the stage and required frequent alteration and mending.[21] Two needles were found at excavations at the Rose theatre, one by the first stage, and may have been used by tiremen acting as wardrobe keepers who made repairs. One of these tiremen, John Rossel is listed as receiving payment for mending garments in Henslowe's diary.[22] Natasha Korda hypothesises that the women who collected the penny entry fee to the playhouses, known as gatherers, may also have been responsible for mending the player's costumes.[23]

Within the domestic sphere of the household it is clear that mending was considered to be one of the many tasks undertaken by the good housewife. Although it is likely that many men – particularly single men away from the household – also undertook mending. In a letter written by the 16-year-old Paul Behaim, to his mother while studying in Leipzig

---

[15]   Natasha Korda, *Labours Lost: Women's Work and the Early Modern English Stage* (Philadelphia: University of Pennsylvania Press, 2011), p. 20.

[16]   Susan Cahn, *Industry of Devotion: The Transformation of Women's Work in England, 1500–1660* (New York: Columbia University Press, 1987), pp. 55–6.

[17]   James Pilkington, *Aggeus and Abdias* (London, 1562), sig. D8[r].

[18]   Quoted in Steve Rappaport, *Worlds within Worlds: Structures of Life in Sixteenth-Century London* (Cambridge: Cambridge University Press, 1989), p. 43.

[19]   Francis Collins ed., 'Admissions to the Freedom of York: 21–45 Elizabeth I (1578–1603)', *Register of the Freemen of the City of York: Vol. 2: 1559–1759* (1900), pp. 21–48. http://www.british-history.ac.uk/report.aspx?compid=50499 (accessed 18 January 2013).

[20]   Janet Arnold ed., *Queen Elizabeth's Wardrobe Unlock'd: The Inventories of the Wardrobe of Robes Prepared in July 1600* (Leeds: Maney, 1988), p. 233.

[21]   Korda, *Labours Lost*, p. 44; for references to the cost of mending costumes see Jones and Stallybrass, *Renaissance Clothing and the Materials of Memory*, p. 178.

[22]   Julian Bowsher and Pat Miller, *The Rose and the Globe: Playhouses of Shakespeare's Bankside, Southwark Excavations 1988–90* (London: Museum of London Archaeology Service, 2009), p. 139, for catalogue entry see p. 213.

[23]   Korda, *Labours Lost*, p. 47.

in 1573 Paul argues that he needs more money for his clothes as he is such a poor mender: 'but what kind of mending is this', he lamented, 'if one mends something today it is torn tomorrow and afterwards one walks around with hose which are just lots of patches'.[24] When giving evidence in a marriage dispute in 1655 David Thomas, a 'husbandman' recounted a conversation with one Humphrey Vale: 'at which time the said Vale sate at his door without, having a needle and thrid and a leather thimble in his hand, and as he believes was about to mend his breeches', indicating that men were as familiar with the tools and practice of mending as women.[25]

Nonetheless, the task of mending was frequently represented as a labour equated with feminine virtue and a necessary component of the female-dominated domestic sphere. Echoing Taylor's use of militaristic imagery in the *Needles Excellencie* Thomas Tusser in *A hundreth good pointes of husbandry* (1570) includes injunctions to the effect that the housewife must undertake mending to defend her household:

> *Peece hole to defende, 85*
>
> *Good semesters be sowing of fine pretie knackes,*
> *good huswiues be mending and peecing their sackes.*
>
> *Thinges tymely amende. 86*
>
> *Though making & mending be huswifely wayes,*
> *yet mending in tyme is the huswife to prayse.*
>
> *Buy newe as ye may. 87*
>
> *Though Ladyes may rend and by new ery day,*
> *good huswifes must mende & by newe as they may.*[26]

Tusser equates mending with good household economy on the part of those women who cannot afford to 'by new ery day', a foregrounding of thriftiness which criticises the wastefulness of the upper classes and locates feminine virtue in necessary stitchery.[27] Mending of this sort would doubtless have been undertaken on the behalf of family members, but domestic labour could also be used to reinforce social bonds within the wider household, bonds which were frequently formed by economies of exchange rather than familiar relationships. This is a process reflected in *Gammer Gurton* as Gammer is mending breeches belonging to her servant Hodge when she misplaces her needle.

The moment when Gammer loses her needle is described in detail by another servant attached to her household, her maidservant Tyb:

> *My Gammer sat her downe on her pes, and bad me reach thy breeches,*
> *And by and by, a vengeance in it, or she had take two stitches*

---

24 Quoted in Ulinka Rublack, *Dressing Up: Cultural Identity in Renaissance Europe* (Oxford: Oxford University Press, 2010), p. 217.

25 Shropshire Archives, Answers to Interrogatories 894/221 [n.d.].

26 Thomas Tusser, *A hundreth good pointes of husbandry* (3rd ed., London, 1570), sig. I1ᵛ–12ʳ.

27 Lena Cowen Orlin argues that needlework was used by women to make female virtue visible in 'Three Ways to Be Invisible in the Renaissance: Sex, Reputation and Stitchery', in Patricia Fumerton and Simon Hunt eds, *Renaissance Culture and the Everyday* (Philadelphia: University of Pennsylvania Press, 1999), p. 185.

To clap a clout upon thin ars, by chaunce asyde she leares,
And Gyb our cat in the milke pan she spied over head and eares! (I, iii, 118–20)

Sitting on her 'pes' or cushion, sewing in the company of her maidservant, Gammer is the picture of the good housewife, albeit one who attacks her task with a 'vengeance', until Gyb disturbs her. The loss of the needle fractures this domestic scene in more ways than one, as Tusser notes that the good housewife must not only mend, but also know where all her household stuff can be located: 'Lose nothing I say / Cal quarterly seruants to court and to lete, / write euery Couerlet, Blanket and Shete' (I2ʳ). Gammer, in losing her needle, is not only unable to continue the necessary and virtuous task of mending, but demonstrates that she cannot hold on to her household stuff and is therefore an unsatisfactory housewife.[28] As Hodge laments upon learning of the needle's loss: 'Now a vengeance light on al the sort that better shold have kept it: / The cat, the house, and Tib our maid that better shold have swept it!' (I, iii, 127–8).

Hodge's outrage that his breeches cannot be mended is unsurprising given the high cost of cloth during the period and it would have been common practice for people to avoid unnecessary expenditure on new items by maintaining clothing for as long as possible.[29] The prohibitive cost of acquiring new apparel would consequently result in patched and darned clothes, a process accompanied by anxieties about the relationship between clothing and social status. While, as I have previously noted, there is little material evidence for the clothing of people from the lower social orders in the early modern period, Margaret Spufford has examined probate inventories in order to glean information about expenditure on clothing for minors. She concludes that whereas it was more common for the well off to use expensive fabrics and trimmings for children's clothes, there was a huge range in costs for the same fabrics, and amongst the 'common sort' while 'there *were* hierarchies of display in clothing … they were not strictly determined'.[30] Nonetheless, clothing in the early modern period, as Stallybrass and Jones note, formed 'a world of social relations put upon the wearer's body'.[31] Clothing might also, as Will Fisher has argued when examining handkerchiefs and codpieces, possess a 'prosthetic' facility which served to construct a materialised sexed identity.[32] One aspect of the relationship between clothing and identity formation was the

---

28   Wall, *Staging Domesticity*, p. 67; Lena Cowen Orlin, *Private Matters and Public Culture in Post Reformation England* (Ithaca, NY: Cornell University Press, 1994), p. 50; for a discussion of how the housewife's knowledge of her domain and the maintenance of its contents were cited as essential skills in household manuals see Catherine Richardson, *Domestic Life and Domestic Tragedy in Early Modern England: The Material Life of the Household* (Manchester: Manchester University Press, 2006), pp. 46–7.

29   Margaret Spufford, 'The Cost of Apparel in Seventeenth-Century England, and the Accuracy of Gregory King', *Economic History Review* 53:4 (2000), 677–705 at pp. 679–80; Jones and Stallybrass, *Renaissance Clothing*, pp. 178–9; there was a huge market in second hand clothing which is particularly well documented for the eighteenth and nineteenth centuries and clothing was also a common pledge in pawnshops, see John Styles, 'Clothing the North: The Supply of Non-Élite Clothing in the Eighteenth-Century North of England', *Textile History* 25:2 (1994), 139–66; Alison Toplis, 'A Stolen Garment or a Reasonable Purchase? The Male Consumer and the Illicit Second-Hand Clothing Market in the First Half of the Nineteenth Century', in Jon Stobart and Ilja Van Damme eds, *Modernity and the Second-Hand Trade: European Consumption Cultures and Practices, 1700–1900* (Basingstoke: Palgrave, 2010), p. 57.

30   Margaret Spufford, 'Fabric for Seventeenth-Century Children and Adolescents' Clothes', *Textile History* 34:1 (2003), 47–63, at p. 57, emphasis in original.

31   Jones and Stallybrass, *Renaissance Clothing*, p. 3.

32   Will Fisher, *Materializing Gender in Early Modern Literature and Culture* (Cambridge: Cambridge University Press, 2006), p. 17; Tim Reinke-Williams discusses how women in early modern London used clothing to enhance their social standing in 'Women's Clothes and Female Honour in Early Modern London', *Continuity and Change* 26:1 (2011), 69–88, at p. 70.

inevitable association of poorly or repeatedly mended clothing with poverty.[33] For example, the physician William Bullein describes a carter or labourer as a 'barberous vplandish Ienking with torne hose, and clouted bootes, foule shurt, and thredbare bonet' and in a sermon *exhorting to pitie the poore* (1573) Henry Bedel reminded his congregation that 'The pride of apparel maketh vs forget the patched poore', directly associating the patching up of threadbare clothing with poverty.[34] It is perhaps understandable in the light of this that Hodge's torn breeches cause him most distress in *Gammer Gurton* when he realises that he will have to go courting while wearing inferior clothing:

> DICCON: *Why, is there any special cause thou takest hearat such sorow?*
>
> HODGE: *Kirstian Clack, Tom Simson's maid, bi the*
> *Masse, coms hether tomorrow;*
> *Channot able to say betweene us what may hap;*
> *She smiled on me the last Sonday when ich put of*
> *my cap. (II, i, 340–4)*

The correlation between ragged clothing and low social status was reflected in a collection of verses by the satirist Samuel Rowlands, *Doctor Merry-man: Or, Nothing but Mirth* (1607). In one poem about a pawnbroker, credit is extended to a man with 'His fashion new' and 'His neck inviron'd with a double Ruffe' rather than 'A Countrey fellow plaine in Russet clad', 'His sleeves at hand button'd with two good pins', only for the pawnbroker to discover that he has been tricked by the fashionable man's 'trappings' and to vow 'That silken Knaves should cozen him no more'.[35] The pawnbroker's mistake, based upon a misreading of his client's attire, is echoed in another poem in Rowlands' collection about a prostitute who prides herself on wearing 'Silkes' while boasting that she empties the purses of men so that they have to pawn their own clothing: 'Some goe to Houns-ditch with their Cloathes / To pawne for Money lending … / Others passe ragged vp and downe, / All tattar'd, rent, and torne; / But being in that scuruie case, / Their companies I scorne' (C4ʳ). Despite the moral of Rowlands' satirical verses being that fine clothing hides a multitude of sins, their comedy hinges on the recognition that people were commonly judged by their outward apparel.

If clothing provides the means by which early moderns extrapolated information about the status of the wearer, and torn clothing was equated with lowly status and poverty, then the needle becomes the guarantor of social position. If you can mend your clothes then you can retain your place within the community; if, like Hodge, you lose your needle and with it the ability to maintain sartorial standards, then you risk slipping down the social scale. In *Gammer Gurton* the villagers frequently lament the poor state of their clothing, indicating that it is not only Hodge who suffers from the ignominy of torn garments. Gammer's maid Tyb bemoans how her servile status is evidenced through her tattered clothing: 'Cham worse then mad, by the Masse, to be at this staye; / Cham chyd, cham blamd, and beaton all thoures on the daye; / Lamed and hunger storved, pricked up all in jagges [tattered clothes],

---

[33]   On clothing as a sign of social position and the relationship between poverty and nakedness see Linda Woodbridge, *Vagrancy, Homelessness, and English Renaissance Literature* (Chicago: Chicago University Press, 2001), p. 197; Susan Vincent discusses how the removal or damaging of clothing could be used as a punishment and to indicate the shamefulness of the wearer in *Dressing the Elite: Clothing in Early Modern England* (Oxford: Oxford University Press, 2003), pp. 100–103.

[34]   William Bullein, *Bulleins bulwarke of defence against all sicknesse, soarenesse, and vvoundes that doe dayly assaulte mankinde* (2nd ed., London, 1579), sig. bbb 3ᵛ; Henry Bedel, *A sermon exhorting to pitie the poore* (London: John Awdely, 1573), sig. B4ᵛ.

[35]   Samuel Rowlands, *Doctor Merry-man: Or, Nothing but Mirth* (3rd ed., London, 1616), sig. A4ᵛ.

/ Having no patch to hyde my backe, save a few rotten ragges!', (Act 1, scene iii, 93–6). Tyb's association of her physical state, 'Lamed and hunger storved', with the condition of her clothing reminds us that tatters and rags provided little protection from the cold. The needle was therefore an essential item for those who could not afford to buy new apparel as it extends the life of both clothing and the wearer, who would otherwise feel the brunt of the elements and risk sickness.

In Dame Chat's ale-house drinkers sing about beer providing the warmth which their poor clothing cannot supply, implying that they have spent what little money they have on beer rather than on new clothes:

> [SINGERS from the ale-house (off stage)]:
> Backe and syde go bare, go bare;
> Boothe foote and hande go colde:
> But bellye, God sende thee good ale ynoughe,
> Whether it be newe or olde.
>
> I cannot eate, but lytle meate,
> My stomacke is not good:
> But sure I thinke that I can drynke
> With him that weares a hood.
> Though I go bare, take ye no care,
> I am nothinge a-colde:
> I stuffe my skyn so full within,
> Of jolly good ale and olde. (II, i, 237–48)

Alcohol in the belly gives a temporary heat which allows the drinker to sit in company with 'him that weares a hood', providing an atmosphere of warmth and conviviality which breaks down social barriers as long as the revellers have enough money for ale. This is a sentiment echoed by Diccon when upon hearing the song he exclaims: 'Well done, be Gog's malt, well songe and well sayde! / Come on, Mother Chat, as thou art true mayde, / One fresh pot of ale let's see to make an ende / Agaynst his colde wether my naked armes to defende' (II, i, 280–3). In *Gammer Gurton* the loss of a needle, the tool which can mend tatters in clothing and cover the 'backe and side' which is open to the elements, can have serious consequences. Not only is Hodge at risk of losing his social standing, but he is also in danger of catching cold or worse. Consequently, not only can 'a missing needle … become the occasion for a complete breakdown of social relations', as Wendy Wall has argued, but, for the lack of this essential and everyday tool, bodies are left exposed to the worst of the weather.[36]

When Gammer Gurton and Dame Chat fall into a fight at the climax of the play they exchange insults which potentially allude to a further need for the lost needle. Gammer calls Chat a 'bawdie bitche' (III, iii, 625), Chat responds with an exclamation of 'A bag and a wallet!' which is probably from the refrain to 'turn to a bag and a wallet' meaning to become a beggar. Gammer retorts with 'A carte for a callet!', calling Chat a whore as prostitutes were often whipped at the tail of a cart. This violent exchange of words includes Chat's exclamations that she will 'patche thy coate' (629) and 'drab, I shall dresse thee!' (633). While both these statements mean to 'do over', they potentially reference how Chat's

---

[36] Wall, *Staging Domesticity*, p. 63; Ninya Mikhaila and Jane Malcolm-Davies note that in the sixteenth century people needed to wrap up warm as it was colder by two degrees celsius than today. *The Tudor Tailor: Techniques and Patterns for Making Historically Accurate Period Clothing* (London: Batsford, 2006), pp. 11–12.

attack on Gammer will damage her clothing. As the two women assault each other it is probable that much of the comedy will result from the tearing of fabric and the damaging of headpieces and ruffs (the removal and/or damage of headpieces, particularly those of married women, was associated with returning the wearer to single status or equating her with a whore), a cacophony of ripping seams which means that by the end of the play all the characters will feasibly look much alike: mud-bespattered and in rags.[37] The disorder and misrule occasioned by the loss of the needle and Diccon's machinations therefore physically manifests itself in torn clothing which cannot now be mended, a reminder of the needle's intrinsic value as a tool.

The labour of mending was an important component of both the informal and domestic economies, a measure of the housewife's virtue and a necessary skill which cemented relationships between dependants and protected the body from being socially ostracised and battered by the elements. In contrast to the elite practices of fancy work and embroidery, mending was an everyday chore which was so ubiquitous that it could be easily overlooked. By placing the needle and the action of mending at the heart of the play, even if it is done for the purpose of elite comedy, *Gammer Gurton* successfully reminds us of the central importance of such quotidian tasks, and the tools which make them possible, to the lives of early modern men and women.

What Is a Needle?

As the villagers in *Gammer Gurton* know all too well mending is a task which is rendered impossible without a needle, but beyond its immediate function as a sewing implement the needle also has a long cultural history. In the Christian tradition it is associated both with the first clothing in the Garden of Eden and with the impossibility of passing an animal through its eye. In the book of Genesis, when Adam and Eve first hide their nakedness, the needle is not invoked, and yet numerous early modern references to the first man and woman sewing nevertheless ensure that its presence is always implied.[38] The Worshipful Company of Needlemakers, incorporated in 1656, understandably assumed that a needle must have been present in the Garden of Eden and their arms bears an image of Adam and Eve. The needle can therefore be identified as the first tool wielded by mankind after the Fall, a sign both for man's degenerate state and for the application of worldly knowledge and human artifice. These biblical antecedents for Gammer's needle were not lost on Mr S, and Hodge can be read as a figure for Adam as he rises out of the earth and searches for a needle in order to hide his nakedness.[39]

The needle is also commonly employed as a pun for male genitalia. The persistent phallic imagery associated with the needle in *Gammer Gurton*, where it is referred to as both a 'cock' and an 'eel', is reinforced when Gammer Gurton bemoans its loss in the manner of a woman lamenting the loss of sexual pleasure: 'My fayre longe straight neele, that was myne onely treasure – / The first day of my sorrow is, and last end of my pleasure!' (I. iv. 135–6). For Gail

---

[37] Reinke-Williams, 'Women's Clothes and Female Honour', p. 82; Cartwright, *Theatre and Humanism*, p. 95.

[38] In the 1560 Geneva Bible Adam and Eve sew 'breeches' out of fig leaves to cover their nakedness while in the King James Version they sew 'aprons'. Lloyd E. Berry ed., *The Geneva Bible: A Facsimile of the 1560 Edition* (Peabody, MA: Hendrickson Publishers, 2007), Genesis 3:6–7, sig. A2ʳ; Robert Carroll and Stephen Prickett eds, *The Bible: Authorized King James Version with Apocrypha* (Oxford: Oxford University Press, 1997), Genesis 3:6–7, p. 3.

[39] Duncan, 'Gammer Gurton's Needle and the Concept of Humanist Parody', p. 180.

Kern Paster the needle in *Gammer Gurton* thus stands as 'a floating signifier' and a 'talisman of gender difference'.[40] Wendy Wall also reads the needle as a loaded metaphor, a 'female economic dildo' which 'makes visible the erotic complexity of domestic relations' and recalls the pleasure and pain associated with the educational birch rod.[41]

Critical work on the role of the needle in *Gammer Gurton* has therefore frequently identified it as an object which stands for something else, a thing which is always more than the sum of its parts. In contrast, I would like to concentrate on the needle as a needle: a ubiquitous object which both makes and mends, but in the confines of the early modern household, an object which is primarily wielded in order to darn, patch and sew together gaps and tears in clothing. In looking to the object in order to explore the interconnectedness of people and things in the early modern popular consciousness I am following a critical thread outlined by Margreta de Grazia, Peter Stallybrass and Maureen Quilligan. In a reading of the relationship between subject and object which resonates particularly strongly with the image of the needle as maker (and even as mender, as to mend is in many ways to re-make), they argue: 'What we have to gain from interrelating the object and subject in the Renaissance is a sense of how objects have a hold on subjects as well as subjects on objects. We need to understand those reciprocal makings and unmaking.'[42]

The social makings and unmakings for which the needle stands as a talisman in *Gammer Gurton*, are perhaps only comprehensible when we establish contemporary and popular attitudes to the needle as a thing, as a component of the ubiquitous 'household stuff' which formed the everyday world of domestic labour.[43] But, it is important to remember that in *Gammer Gurton* the needle is absent for most of the drama, it is a misplaced object which leaves behind a resonant gap in the body of the play, as well as in the seat of Hodge's breeches. This gap allows us to read the needle as a tool which has failed and Julian Yates, following Bruno Latour, has persuasively argued that when tools fail or break it leads to a disruption in their 'prosthetic function' as an extension of the user, forcing 'a conversion or turning back toward things'.[44] Using Yates' focus on the failed tool as the means by which we can 'move through the binary logic of the subject and object … into the world of things' I will propose a reading of the needle in *Gammer Gurton* as an object-out-of-place whose loss reinforces not only the necessity of the task it performs (mending) but its status as a *thing* with a complex position within the Tudor economy.[45]

---

[40]   Gail Kern Paster, *The Body Embarrassed: Drama and the Disciplines of Shame in Early Modern Europe* (Ithaca, NY: Cornell University Press, 1993), p. 118; on Gammer Gurton's love of the needle as an echo of a *Chanson de regret* in which an old woman regrets the instrument of her former pleasures see Duncan, 'Gammer Gurton's Needle and the Concept of Humanist Parody', p. 180.

[41]   Wall, *Staging Domesticity*, p. 70, p. 84.

[42]   Margreta de Grazia, Maureen Quilligan and Peter Stallybrass, 'Introduction', in Margreta de Grazia, Maureen Quilligan and Peter Stallybrass eds, *Subject and Object in Renaissance Literature* (Cambridge: Cambridge University Press, 1996), pp. 11–12.

[43]   Natasha Korda points out that the term 'household stuff' was coined in the sixteenth century and that during the early modern period the parameters of the household were defined as much by material objects as by people. *Shakespeare's Domestic Economies: Gender and Property in Early Modern England* (Philadelphia: University of Pennsylvania Press, 2002), p. 1; Tara Hamling and Catherine Richardson, 'Introduction', in Tara Hamling and Catherine Richardson eds, *Everyday Objects: Medieval and Early Modern Material Culture and its Meanings* (Farnham: Ashgate, 2010), p. 13; Patricia Fumerton outlines the importance of the interconnectedness between familiar objects and collective meanings in 'Introduction: A New New Historicism', in Patricia Fumerton and Simon Hunt eds, *Renaissance Culture and the Everyday* (Philadelphia: University of Pennsylvania Press, 1999), p. 5.

[44]   Julian Yates, *Error Misuse Failure: Object Lessons from the English Renaissance* (Minneapolis: University of Minnesota Press, 2003), pp. 26–7.

[45]   Ibid., p. 27.

In *Gammer Gurton*, when Hodge laments Gammer's loss of her needle to Diccon, Diccon mistakenly thinks he is referring to an 'eel', prompting Hodge to exclaim: 'Tush, tush, her neele, her neele, her neele, man; 'tys neyther flesh nor fysh! / A lytle thing with an hole in the end, as bright as any syller, / Small, longe, sharpe at the poynt, and straight as any pyller' (II, i, 321–3). Hodge's description of the needle as a long, sharp object with a hole in the end, plus Diccon's mistaken belief that Hodge is talking about an eel, has obvious phallic connotations. However, Hodge's outburst also succeeds in distinguishing the needle from both the pin and the bodkin, one recognised by a flattened head, the other by an elongated eye and a blunt end. As well as being used when tailoring and mending, pins were commonly employed to hold together clothing, particularly when attaching collars, ruffs and stomachers.[46] In elite dressing pins were used in vast numbers, as is evidenced by Queen Elizabeth ordering over 100,000 pins of different types in one six-month period in 1565, but they were also used as makeshift fastenings by those who could not afford buttons.[47] Outside of clothing practices, pins were used by secretaries and other fastidious writers to 'prick out' lines in the margin of a page to ensure that handwriting remained in straight lines.[48] The bodkin, which was typically much larger than both the pin and the needle, was designed for threading ribbons, cords and laces and personalised bodkins were also worn as hair decorations. Some bodkins included an ear-scoop at one end to collect earwax which was then used to seal the cut ends of thread to prevent them from unravelling.[49] It is the needle's attempts to permanently join cloth together, rather than temporarily bonding or modifying already completed items of clothing, which ultimately distinguishes it from both the pin or the bodkin. As John Taylor noted, it was both 'a maker and a mender' (A1[v]) and crucial for the construction and maintenance of clothing.

The fuss engendered by the needle's loss in *Gammer Gurton*, while the source of much of the comedy in the play, is also potentially indicative of the needle's relative value as a indispensable tool and the tendency of critics to dismiss the needle as a mere trifle, albeit a trifle with multiple registers and meanings, has masked the various economic, political and social tensions surrounding the production and dissemination of needles in Tudor England.[50] Needle making did not become an established industry in England until the arrival of Flemish refugees mid-way through the sixteenth century.[51] This is thought to have been due

---

[46]   Mary Carolyn Beaudry, *Findings: The Material Culture of Needlework and Sewing* (New Haven: Yale University Press, 2006), pp. 13–14; Tanya Cooper with Jane Eade, 'Thimbles and Pins, late 1500s and early 1600s' in *Elizabeth I and her People*, Tanya Cooper with Janes Eade, eds. (London: National Portrait Gallery Publications, 2013), p. 168.

[47]   Arnold, *Queen Elizabeth's Wardrobe Unlock'd*, p. 218; on the large number of pins used for elite dressing see Korda, *Labours Lost*, p. 39; on the use of pins by the poor see Beaudry, *Findings*, p. 13 and C. Willett Cunnington and Phillis Cunnington, *Handbook of English Costume in the Seventeenth Century* (London: Faber, 1955), p. 17, p. 52, p. 54; on the pin as an essential everyday object which modifies ideas of physical proximity see Jenny Tiramani, 'Pins and Aglets', in Hamling and Richardson eds., *Everyday Objects*, pp. 85–9.

[48]   Andrew Hadfield has pointed out that this is one of the meanings behind the 'multivalent pun' on 'pricking' from the line 'The gentle knight was pricking on the plaine' which opens Edmund Spenser's *Faerie Queene*. *Edmund Spenser: A Life* (Oxford: Oxford University Press, 2012), pp. 209–10. To make a pinprick in the margin of a book was also a means of highlighting a particular passage if the reader was without a pen or lacked the necessary writing skills, Heidi Brayman Hackel, *Reading Material in Early Modern England: Print, Gender, and Literacy* (Cambridge: Cambridge University Press, 2005), p. 62.

[49]   Beaudry, *Findings*, p. 66.

[50]   Duncan associates the needle in *Gammer Gurton* with the humanist interest in *nugae*, small things attended to with wit and seriousness by the skilful rhetorician. 'Gammer Gurton's Needle and the Concept of Humanist Parody', p. 180.

[51]   S.R.H. Jones, 'The Development of Needle Manufacturing in the West Midlands before 1750', *Economic History Review* 31:3 (1978), 354–68, at p. 355.

to problems with steel production, the metal that most needles were made of after 1500.[52] Until the establishment of larger scale production, a shift marked by the incorporation of the Worshipful Company of Needlemakers in 1656, the bulk of needles were imported from the Continent.[53] A copper alloy needle and two iron needles dating from 1500–50 were excavated at riverside sites in Southwark and have been identified as imported objects.[54] In Thomas Smith's *A Discourse of the Common Weal of this Realm of England* (1549) needles were listed amongst 'merchandise that we bye beyonde the seas'.[55] Pin production worked on similar lines, with the majority of pins being imported from France.[56] Despite the introduction of the 1563 *Acte for the avoiding of dyvers forreyne wares made by handye craftsmen beyonde the seas* which prohibited the import of foreign manufactured goods, including pins, the pinmakers and needlemakers of London petitioned in 1597 for the act to be enforced, claiming that £40,000 worth of pins and needles were illegally imported every year.[57] In light of the needle's status as a foreign import Curtis Perry has read *Gammer Gurton* as a parody of reformist literature attacking a rising commodity culture and identified the needle as 'a commodity fetish' which threatens the economic and domestic stability of England.[58] While this fits with Gammer Gurton's seemingly exaggerated attachment to the tool which she names her 'treasure' (I, iv, 134), this reading of the needle as a 'fetish' disguises the value attached to an object which was not manufactured in large numbers in England and yet was an indispensible tool of household economy.

While needles were not particularly expensive they were more costly than pins and as only a single needle was required at any one moment (although needle types would have varied depending upon the nature of the fabric being sewn) they were almost certainly owned in far smaller numbers.[59] This may explain Elizabeth Isham's recollection in her diary that when she was eight years old she had been so worried about her mother's reaction when she lost her needle that she prayed to God for help: 'I wel remember my praying unto thee to avoyde my mothers displeasure, even for my nedle when I had lost it.'[60] While the smallness of the needle indicates Elizabeth's piety in praying for its return, nonetheless, its loss is worthy of notice and potentially reflects the difficulty and cost involved in replacing such items. An inventory of the goods owned by the fletcher and needlemaker Thomas Ospringe who died in Canterbury in 1598, lists alongside an 'old wheel to point needles', '300 needles'

---

[52]   Beaudry, *Findings*, p. 44.

[53]   Joan Thirsk notes that while the output of England's rural industries was able to replace some imported goods by the latter half of the sixteenth century, needles were not amongst them. *Economic Policy and Projects: The Development of a Consumer Society in Early Modern England* (Oxford: Oxford University Press, 1978), pp. 121–2.

[54]   Geoff Egan, *Material Culture in London in an Age of Transition: Tudor and Stuart Finds c1450–c1700 from Excavations at Riverside Sites in Southwark* (London: London Archaeological Services, 2005), for catalogue entry see p. 130 and needles as imported commodities see pp. 12–13.

[55]   Elizabeth Lamond ed., *A Discourse of the Common Weal of this Realm of England* (Cambridge: Cambridge University Press, 1954), p. 16; Thirsk, *Economic Policy and Projects*, p. 14.

[56]   The early history of the pinners' craft in England can be found in Barbara Megson ed., *The Pinners' and Wiresellers' Book 1462–1511* (London: London Record Society, 2009).

[57]   The act does not list needles but does include 'Pynnes', 'Blades' and 'Pointes' and refers to the impoverishment of 'Poyntmakers'. R.H. Tawney and Eileen Power eds, *Tudor Economic Documents* (London: Longmans, 1951), vol. 1, pp. 126–7; for the pinmakers and needlemakers petition see T.S. Willan ed., *A Tudor Book of Rates* (Manchester: Manchester University Press, 1962), p. li.

[58]   Curtis Perry, 'Commodity and Commonwealth in *Gammer Gurton's Needle*', *Studies in English Literature* 42:2 (2002), 217–34, at p. 221.

[59]   Beaudry, *Findings*, p. 44. Beaudry also notes that needles rarely make it into the archaeological record and that finds are often fragmentary.

[60]   Elizabeth Isham, *The Perdita Project: Elizabeth Isham's Lives*. http://web.warwick.ac.uk/english/perdita/Isham/bor_p3v.htm (accessed 3 July 2013).

valued at 18d.[61] An inventory of the goods belonging to a Great Yarmouth chapman, John Uttinge, from 1628, lists what must have been a large number of 'pins and Needles' at 3s.[62] In the *The Rates of the Custome house* (1582) the custom rate attached to 'Needles the dosen thousand' is 'xxs'.[63] As Tudor books of rates were concerned less with rates of duty than with the value of goods this tells us that needles were imported in bulk and individually afforded a small value (by this calculation five needles would be valued at 2 pence or 0.4 pence per needle), although importantly the 1582 book of rates quoted here was a re-issue of the 1558 edition and therefore its valuations did not take into account inflation in the intervening years.[64] As a comparison the custom rate attached to another everyday object, the iron pot, is listed at 'x s' 'the dosen', the same value ascribed to a 'groce' of 'spectacles'.[65] As an essential item needles were therefore relatively affordable, but as they could not be fashioned easily, were inevitably lost given their size, and frequently broke, they also had to be regularly replaced, ensuring that there was always a steady market. The indispensable nature of the needle, and its position as a tool which cannot be easily manufactured, or approximated in foreign materials, is indicated by its inclusion in Lewis Hughes's list of essential items required by Englishmen planning on settling in Bermuda. In *A Letter Sent into England from the Summer Islands* (1615), alongside 'candlesticks', 'spades' and 'soap' appear 'needles', 'thread' and 'scissors'.[66]

For those English men and women who lived in the provinces, like the villagers in *Gammer Gurton*, distinguished by their use of nonce words and West Country dialect, needles would also have been relatively hard to come by.[67] Outside of urban centres haberdashery items would often have to be purchased from itinerant tradesmen. Those tradesmen who travelled on foot, known as 'packmen', would have carried a comparatively large number of haberdashery items, given their low weight in contrast to the fabric which was the peddler's usual stock in trade.[68] This meant that the purchasing of needles was not only a recurring cost carried by households, but that their acquisition could also be dependent upon the unpredictable movements of wandering tradesmen. The fact that no effort is made by Gammer or Hodge to replace the missing needle in *Gammer Gurton*, Hodge instead resorts to holding his breeches together by using a thong and awl borrowed from Sym Glover (III, i), may accurately reflect the difficulty of acquiring haberdashery items in the countryside as well as an inevitable reluctance to incur further cost for an object which has been mislaid rather than broken.[69]

By the end of *Gammer Gurton* the needle appears to have been entirely subsumed by the social discord resulting from its loss. Hodge demands of Dame Chat 'Geve my Gammer again her washical thou stole away in thy lap!' (5, ii, 1061). In becoming a 'whats-it-called',

---

[61]   Inventory of Thomas Ospringe of Canterbury, d.1598, CKS PRC 10.26.125.

[62]   The inventory of Uttinge's goods is reproduced by Margaret Spufford in *The Great Reclothing of Rural England*, p. 185.

[63]   Willan, *A Tudor Book of Rates*, p. 42.

[64]   Ibid., p. xix, p. xliii.

[65]   Ibid., p. 35, p. 57.

[66]   Louis B. Wright ed., *The Elizabethans' America: A Collection of Early Reports by Englishmen on the New World* (Cambridge, MA: Harvard University Press, 1965), p. 204, quoted in Thirsk, *Economic Policy and Projects*, pp. 50–51.

[67]   On *Gammer Gurton*'s use of regional dialect and archaisms see Boas, *University Drama in the Tudor Age*, p. 79; Ardolino, 'Misperception and Protestant Reading', p. 30; Andrew Hiscock notes that there was an expectation during the Tudor period that low born characters would be identified by a West Country dialect in '"Hear My Tale or Kiss My Tail"', p. 742.

[68]   Spufford, *The Great Reclothing of Rural England*, p. 21, p. 90.

[69]   An awl was used to pierce holes in leather and would have been an essential tool for a glovemaker.

in contrast to Hodge's earlier detailed description directed at Diccon in Act II, the needle becomes an implied presence comparable to the silent tool wielded by Adam and Eve. This is compounded when Hodge is pricked in the buttocks by the lost needle only to cry out 'He thrust me in the buttocke with a bodkin or a pin!' (5, ii, 1240), rather than successfully identifying the source of his pricking as the needle. The irony of the needle's unnamed status at this point affords the audience another moment of comedy, but the silence of the object also indicates that its importance and omnipresence has been established to the point of rendering its naming superfluous. Critical responses to *Gammer Gurton* which have fixated on the needle as a sign for something else, rather than affording the tool and the labour which it performs equal footing with the talismanic and metaphorical properties which it represents, have perhaps allowed this silence to extend too far and in doing so overlooked the importance of such everyday objects and tasks to our understanding of both Tudor drama and early modern popular culture.

Select Bibliography

Ardolino, Frank, 'Misperception and Protestant Reading in *Gammer Gurton's Needle*', *Studies in English Literature* 50:1 (2010), 17–34.

Beaudry, Mary Carolyn, *Findings: The Material Culture of Needlework and Sewing*. New Haven: Yale University Press, 2006.

Cahn, Susan, *Industry of Devotion: The Transformation of Women's Work in England, 1500–1660*. New York: Columbia University Press, 1987.

Duncan, Douglas, 'Gammer Gurton's Needle and the Concept of Humanist Parody', *Studies in English Literature* 27:2 (1987), 177–96.

Egan, Geoff, *Material Culture in London in an Age of Transition: Tudor and Stuart Finds c1450–c1700 from Excavations at Riverside Sites in Southwark*. London: London Archaeological Services, 2005.

Frye, Susan, *Pens and Needles: Women's Textualities in Early Modern England*. Philadelphia: University of Pennsylvania Press, 2010.

Fumerton, Patricia, and Simon Hunt eds, *Renaissance Culture and the Everyday*. Philadelphia: University of Pennsylvania Press, 1999.

Hamling, Tara, and Catherine Richardson eds, *Everyday Objects: Medieval and Early Modern Material Culture and Its Meanings*. Farnham: Ashgate, 2010.

Hiscock, Andrew, '"Hear My Tale or Kiss My Tail": *The Old Wife's Tale, Gammer Gurton's Needle*, and the Popular Culture of Tudor Comedy', in Mike Pincombe and Cathy Shrank eds, *The Oxford Handbook of Tudor Literature 1485–1603*. Oxford: Oxford University Press, 2009, pp. 733–48.

Hutson, Lorna, 'Theatre', in Brian Cummings and James Simpson eds, *Cultural Reformations: Medieval and Renaissance in Literary History*. Oxford: Oxford University, 2010, pp. 227–46.

Jones, Ann Rosalind, and Peter Stallybrass, *Renaissance Clothing and the Materials of Memory*. Cambridge: Cambridge University Press, 2000.

Kern Paster, Gail, *The Body Embarrassed: Drama and the Disciplines of Shame in Early Modern Europe*. Ithaca, NY: Cornell University Press, 1993.

Korda, Natasha, *Labours Lost: Women's Work and the Early Modern English Stage*. Philadelphia: University of Pennsylvania Press, 2011.

Orlin, Lena Cowen, *Private Matters and Public Culture in Post Reformation England*. Ithaca, NY: Cornell University Press, 1994.

Perry, Curtis, 'Commodity and Commonwealth in *Gammer Gurton's Needle'*, *Studies in English Literature* 42:2 (2002), 217–34.

Reinke-Williams, Tim, 'Women's Clothes and Female Honour in Early Modern London', *Continuity and Change* 26:1 (2011), 69–88.

Richardson, Catherine, *Domestic Life and Domestic Tragedy in Early Modern England: The Material Life of the Household*. Manchester: Manchester University Press, 2006.

Spufford, Margaret, *The Great Reclothing of Rural England: Petty Chapmen and Their Wares in the Seventeenth Century*. London: Hambledon, 1984.

Spufford, Margaret, 'The Cost of Apparel in Seventeenth-Century England, and the Accuracy of Gregory King', *Economic History Review* 53:4 (2000), 677–705.

Woodbridge, Linda, *Vagrancy, Homelessness, and English Renaissance Literature*. Chicago: Chicago University Press, 2001.

Yates, Julian, *Error Misuse Failure: Object Lessons from the English Renaissance*. Minneapolis: University of Minnesota Press, 2003.

PART III
The Experience of the World

Politics

Andrew Hadfield

Popular notions of politics underwent a seismic shift in the early modern period. In the early 1500s political understanding could not be separated from religious belief and was conceived primarily in terms of symbols of allegiance – most significantly the banner of the five wounds of Christ that accompanied the major revolt, The Pilgrimage of Grace (1536–7).[1] By the time of the Civil War (1640s) literacy levels had undoubtedly improved and so had the technology that enabled pamphlets to be printed quickly and in significant numbers leading to a vast explosion in printed material.[2] Politics was still inextricably linked to religion and it was invariably conceived in terms of images, but it was also clear that a developed public sphere was now emerging that would lead to more modern conceptions of political culture.[3] Milton argued in *Areopagitica* (1644) that public life and civil society could not function without the freedom of the press, an argument that would have made little sense in 1500.[4]

There were continuities as well. In pre-democratic times the key issues were the character and powers of the monarch and the role of his or her inner circle of advisers. People asked whether kings and queens were legitimate and whether they were good. The contested claims to the throne that formed the basic justification for the series of conflicts known as the Wars of the Roses between the houses of Lancaster and York demonstrate how important such claims were and how they were necessary in order to persuade a sceptical populace. Issues of legitimacy were then intertwined with questions of whether the monarch was able to govern well, subjects closely linked in people's minds. The sixteenth century was no different even though it was dominated by one dynasty, the Tudors. As it became increasingly clear that Elizabeth would be the last Tudor after the failure of the Alençon match in 1580, opposition to her rule centred on the claims of Catholics that she was a usurper and a tyrant, alongside an ever more frantic search for a successor who would satisfy all parties. Eventually and not without some anxiety and opposition, James VI of Scotland managed to combine Tudor and Stuart claims mirroring the achievement of the Tudors in uniting the houses of York and Lancaster over a century earlier.

---

[1] Eric Ives, *The Reformation Experience: Living through the Turbulent 16th. Century* (Oxford: Lion, 2012), p. 155.

[2] John Barnard and Maureen Bell, 'Appendix 1: Statistical Tables', in John Barnard and D.F. McKenzie, with the assistance of Maureen Bell eds, *The Cambridge History of the Book in Britain, Volume IV, 1557–1695* (Cambridge: Cambridge University Press, 2002), pp. 779–93, at p. 783.

[3] Jürgen Habermas, *The Structural Transformation of the Public Sphere: An Inquiry into a Category of Bourgeois Society* (Cambridge: Polity, 1989).

[4] Joad Raymond, 'The Development of the Book Trade in Britain', in Joad Raymond ed., *The Oxford History of Popular Print Culture: Volume 1, Cheap Print in Britain and Ireland to 1660* (Oxford: Oxford University Press, 2011), pp. 59–75, at p. 72.

Subjects were always keen to ask the vexed and problematic question: when was it legitimate to depose a monarch? The only monarch in early modern England who suffered this fate was Charles I, although all rulers had to face a determined opposition that was prepared to take arms against them. Charles may well have been unlucky but he certainly provoked his enemies in parliament and helped to crystallise and harden opposition into a concerted rebel army. But one interpretation of the English Civil War is that the issues that caused it could have led to widespread conflict long before Charles became king.[5] In an era in which there were few constitutional checks and balances and the vast majority of the population existed outside the accepted political process such explosions of violence were a constant danger. Debate would invariably concentrate on individual figures who would be lavishly praised as potential saviours of the realm such as Robert Devereux, 2nd Earl of Essex; or, more often, become targets for widespread ire, notably Mary I; Robert Dudley, 1st Earl of Leicester; Mary Stuart (Mary Queen of Scots); William Cecil, Lord Burghley; and Charles I. Political debate could never be easily separated from personalities.

In an age when far more people were illiterate than literate the most potent forms of disseminating political arguments had to be oral. As everyone had to attend church they would have had to listen to sermons delivered by the local parish priest. After the Reformation the authorities recognised the power that they had to influence a wider public opinion in support of the theological revolution they had inaugurated. Plans for a book of homilies were first floated by Archbishop Cranmer in 1539 as a means of ensuring that the diverse clergy were forced into a basic form of orthodoxy. Nothing came of this until a few years later when collection was printed for clergy to read in order to ensure that the new Protestant orthodoxy would be disseminated and enforced throughout the church. In 1571 a larger book of 21 homilies was produced designed to enforce a more all-encompassing social message alongside a more strictly theological one. There were now homilies dealing with 'Contention and Brawling', 'Whoredom and Uncleanness' and 'An Exhortation concerning good order, and obedience to Rulers, and magistrates', as well as ones that dealt with the nature of Christian faith, love and charity and other more obviously religious themes.

The last entry in the 1571 version was the most overtly political: 'An Homily against Disobedience and Wilful Rebellion', written in response to the Northern Rebellion of 1569–70. This was probably the most dangerous crisis of the first half of Elizabeth's reign when a significant section of the Catholic aristocracy in the north rebelled in an attempt to depose Elizabeth and place Mary Stuart on the throne.[6] The Homily, which would have been a political statement familiar to virtually everyone living in late sixteenth-century England, makes it clear that there can never be any armed opposition to a monarch, God's deputy on earth. The second part of the homily concludes:

> There be many and divers … examples of the obedience to princes, even such as be evil, in the New Testament, to the utter confusion of disobedient and rebellious people; but this one may be an eternal example, which the Son of God, and so the Lord of all, Jesus Christ hath given to us his Christians and servants, and such as may serve for all, to teach us to obey princes, through strangers, wicked, and wrongful, when God for our sins shall place such over us. Whereby it followeth unavoidably, that such as do disobey or rebel against their own natural gracious sovereigns, howsoever they call themselves, or be named of others, yet are they indeed no true Christians, but worse than Jews, worse than heathens, and such as shall never enjoy the kingdom of

---

[5]   John Morrill, *The Nature of the English Revolution* (Harlow: Longman, 1993).
[6]   K.J. Kesselring, *The Northern Rebellion of 1569: Faith, Politics, and Protest in Elizabethan England* (Basingstoke: Palgrave, 2007).

heaven, which Christ by his obedience purchased for true Christians, being obedient to him the King of all kings, and to their prince, whom he hath placed over them: the which kingdom, the peculiar place of all such obedient subjects, I beseech God our heavenly Father[.][7]

The extent of this vehement attack – which continues throughout the long homily – points to an underlying anxiety. There were regular rebellions through the early modern period and, in the end, a bloody civil war broke out.[8] The crown was right to assume that in a pre-democratic world opposition could easily become violent and that the expression of ideas critical of the status quo had to be carefully policed. This problem undoubtedly helped cause the rebellion of Robert Devereux, 2nd Earl of Essex, who was executed for treason in 1601. Essex, anxious about the succession, wanted to take action to ensure the accession of James VI of Scotland, and in the process clearly strayed beyond what was acceptable in his behaviour towards the queen and in the correspondence that he burned as Essex House was besieged.[9] Even a figure as exalted as Essex had no means of expressing his criticism of the government once avenues of counselling the monarch had failed.

As Ethan Shagan has pointed out a study of popular politics reveals that opposition to government policies during the reign of Henry VIII was far more widespread and fundamental than has usually been realised. It has generally been assumed that the Pilgrimage of Grace was a protest at the imposition of the Reformation on a recalcitrant northern population who were nostalgic for the traditional ways of the late medieval church. But the evidence indicates that the rebellion 'must be conceptualised within a considerably more complex and multivariate system, where reactions to the government-sponsored Reformation were determined not only by theology but by interpretations of the royal supremacy, political temperament and economic circumstances'.[10] In short, the Pilgrimage was the focus for a cluster of popular grievances which were concentrated on one particular goal. The rebel leaders sought to establish their own system of government that was a direct critique of the brutal policies of the Tudor regime. A number of rebels failed to respect the policies established by their leaders and started to loot the countryside around Hull. They were quickly apprehended and were told that they should prepare themselves for execution. However, they were not executed but ritually punished and then banished. For Shagan this indicates that the Pilgrims had established an alternative state, fulfilling 'the basic role of magistrates in preserving good order'. As this did not involve bloodshed we witness 'the epitome of civil justice, performed not by the king, who had temporarily abdicated his role, but within the rebel host.'[11]

Shagan's analysis suggests that beneath the surface of many forms of opposition was an articulate desire for a more widespread system of justice and political representation and responsibility. The same point is made in Mark Goldie's argument that early modern England was an unacknowledged republic, full of provincial officeholders who took their political roles very seriously and who played a vital role in making the political fabric of the country function. On the one hand there was the aristocratic republicanism that flourished

---

[7]   'An Homily against Disobedience and Wilful Rebellion', in *Certain Sermons Appointed by the Queen's Majesty to be declared and read by all parsons, vicars and curates, every Sunday and Holiday in their churches* (1574) (Cambridge: Parker Society, 1850), pp. 551–601.

[8]   Anthony Fletcher, *Tudor Rebellions* (Harlow: Longman, 1983).

[9]   Alexandra Gajda, *The Earl of Essex and Late Elizabethan Political Culture* (Oxford: Oxford University Press, 2012), ch. 4.

[10]   Ethan Shagan, *Popular Politics and the English Reformation* (Cambridge: Cambridge University Press, 2003), p. 127.

[11]   Ibid., p. 97.

in the Sidney circle, fuelled by the resentment of men who were excluded from the inner circles of political power. On the other there were those who actually ran the country and who were able to take part in its infrastructure in ways that more socially advantaged compatriots found more problematic.[12] Political culture was reflected and shadowed across the class divide. Moreover, as Andy Wood has argued, we need to be adept at reading between the lines: 'the biases, absences, repetitions and contradictions within the record can be as revealing as any more straightforward statement'.[13]

Of course, it is important to record what was actually produced as an expression of popular political protest. The banner of the five wounds of Christ was designed to unite the rebels under one religious symbol and so unify the different rebellions in Lincolnshire, which had broken out first in October 1536, and the ones that had followed in Yorkshire, Durham, Northumberland, Cumberland, Westmorland, Lancashire and Cheshire. The rebel leaders had no desire to challenge Henry's right to rule England – although a number of the rebels did have radical aims – and were keen to limit their protest to demands that they thought had a chance of succeeding and which might prick the conscience of a king whom they believed was really on their side and simply misled by the ubiquitous 'evil counsellors' who were continually threatening the basic contract between crown and people. The principal demands were the return of papal power to England; the end of Thomas Cromwell's baleful influence; the dissolution of the monasteries to be halted; the advent of a new parliament to pass new laws to alleviate poverty in the north; Mary to be restored as heir to the throne; and the punishment of the commissioners and others responsible for the attack on religious foundations. The aim was to keep the rebellion within the boundaries of popular protest in the middle ages when it had been – in theory, at least – more feasible to criticise the actions of the monarch, notably in the political philosophy of Marsilius of Padua.[14] After the Reformation with the much heavier emphasis in many political theories on the sacred nature of the monarch, especially in countries like England which had monarchical-led religious reform, this was a vain hope, as events proved.[15] Ballads that accompanied the Pilgrimage suggest a more aggressive political culture than the stated aims of the leaders, supporting the claims of Ethan Shagan and Andy Wood:

> *Alack! Alack!*
> *For the church sake*
> *Poor commons wake,*
> *And no marvel!*

> *For clear it is*
> *The decay of this,*
> *How the poor shall miss*
> *No tongue can tell.*[16]

The restoration of the traditional church is closely connected to the care for the poor in the mind of this and other writers and it was indeed true that the dissolution of the monasteries

---

[12]   Mark Goldie, 'The Unacknowledged Republic: Officeholding in Early Modern England,' in Tim Harris ed., *The Politics of the Excluded, c.1500–1850* (Basingstoke: Palgrave, 2001), pp. 153–94.

[13]   Andy Wood, '"Poore Men Woll Speke One Daye": Plebeian Languages of Deference and Defiance in England, c.1520–1640', in Harris ed., *Politics of the Excluded*, pp. 67–98, at p. 82.

[14]   Janet Coleman, *A History of Political Thought* (2 vols, Oxford: Blackwell, 2000), vol. 2, ch. 4.

[15]   Franklin Le Van Baumer, *The Early Tudor Theory of Kingship* (New Haven: Yale University Press, 1940).

[16]   Cited in John Guy, *Tudor England* (Oxford: Oxford University Press, 1988), pp. 149–50.

removed the key defence of the needy and destitute, who had good reason to be worried by the events set in train during the Reformation.[17]

The church, as this ballad illustrates, featured significantly in a medieval and early modern political discourse centred on the issue of poverty, which looked backwards and forwards. There was a widespread belief that it was the duty of the church to protect and nurture the poor and that the failure to do so was a sign of a lapse from the proper ideals of Christian society. This notion was widely represented in literature and – to a lesser extent – art and it is easy to see how writers in particular chose to concentrate on such a powerful image as the honest shepherd or ploughman. The General Prologue to Chaucer's *Canterbury Tales* appears to exonerate the humble ploughman and the parson as upstanding figures, who are spiritual 'brothers', amid an extensive rogues' gallery of the self-interested. The parson is described as 'riche' of 'hooly thought and werk', who gives as much as he can to 'his povre parisshens aboute / Of his offryng and eke of his substaunce'.[18] The ploughman is his counterpart in the field, being 'A trewe swynker [worker] and a good… / Lyvynge in pees and parfit charitee' (531–2). They anchor the estates satire in the real value of preaching and pastoral care, allied to real, productive work.[19] More radical was William Langland's representation of the condition of England in *Piers Plowman*, written at about the same time, a work that was to have a major influence on English political discourse in the next 200 years. Langland's work describes the painful and exhausting search of the narrator for the ideal figure of the proper Christian ploughman, an inconclusive journey which leaves him unsure whether an integration of social and Christian ideals can take place on earth or whether the poor will have to wait for their reward in heaven. Whatever the intention of Langland's much revised poem it provided an oppositional image of the good Christian man who is ignored by a corrupt and self-interested society, one that was often used as a rallying cry by rebels eager to oppose a government indifferent to their needs.

It is a sign of the potency of the myth of *Piers Plowman* that it entered political discourse as soon as it was written, and that it played a significant role in the Peasants' Revolt of 1381. A contemporary chronicler even thought that Piers Plowman was the name of one of the leaders of the revolt.[20] This was just the start of a long history. The radical Protestant writer and editor Robert Crowley (1517–88) published an edition of *Piers Plowman* in 1550, which clearly signalled his unhappiness at the state of contemporary England. Andy Wood points out how significant Crowley's edition was in linking Langland's poem to the ideas of contemporary radical thinkers eager to challenge what they saw as the indifference of the Edwardian regime to the deserving poor:

> *The clearest connection between the commonwealth writers [writers eager to establish a more just and integrated society, who were critical of market forces] and late medieval radical Christian thought was to be found in Robert Crowley's edition of Langland's Piers Plowman, in which Christ appears 'in pore man's apparayle'. In the climax of Crowley's version of Langland, Piers Plowman himself appears as Christ:*

---

[17] Christopher Dyer, *Standards of Living in the Later Middle Ages: Social Change in England, c.1200–1520* (Cambridge: Cambridge University Press, 1989), ch. 9.

[18] Geoffrey Chaucer, *The Riverside Chaucer*, ed. Larry D. Benson (Oxford: Oxford University Press, 1987), fragment A, lines 479, 488–9. All subsequent references to this edition in parentheses in the text.

[19] Jill Mann, *Chaucer and Medieval Estates Satire: The Literature of Social Classes and the General Prologue to* The Canterbury Tales (Cambridge: Cambridge University Press, 1973).

[20] Rodney Hilton, *Bond Men Made Free: Medieval Peasant Movements and the English Rising of 1381* (London: Routledge, 1988, rpt of 1973), p. 178.

> 'painted all bloodye and came in with a crosse before the commune people, and right
> lyke in all lymes to our lorde Jesus'.[21]

Writers eager to combat social ills frequently turned to the ploughman figure as a representation of Christ, in conscious imitation of Langland.

The image of the good ploughman was, in essence, a conservative as well as a radical reaction to fears that the world was moving too fast and furiously away from the ideal of the good Christian society. It was a potent image that could exist both in the popular political imagination and as an imagined ideal of a popular political stance, propagated by an intellectual elite who wished to reach out to a wider public. Thomas Churchyard (c. 1520–1604), who was to enjoy a long and varied career as a writer, produced an imitation of Langland as his first significant poem, perhaps out of political conviction, perhaps because Langland had become such a popular cultural force. 'Dauy Dycars Dreame' is based on a minor character in *Piers Plowman*, Davy Diker, a poor itinerant labourer, who is exactly the sort of vulnerable creature that society needs to protect or he will starve to death. The late middle ages witnessed a period of land improvement as a large number of ditches and dykes were built to improve drainage and so increase crop yield, an agricultural process that became even more important in the sixteenth century as the East Anglian fens were drained.[22] Churchyard, who was from East Anglia, was clearly writing from personal experience and was reminding his readers of the significance of labourers like Davy, who had done so much to help them achieve prosperity and who did not deserve to be neglected.

The poem itself fits into a long tradition of working-class Utopian visions, concentrating on an Apocalyptic moment when all pain and labour has ceased to torment the lowest strata of society:

> When faith in frendes beare fruit, and folysh fancyes fade,
> & crafty catchers cum to nought, & hate gret love hath made
> Whan fraid flieth far from towne, & lewterers [loiterers] leave the fielde,
> And rude shall runne a rightfull race, and all men be well wude [mad?]:
> Wehngropers after gayne, shall carpe for comen welth,
> And wyly workers shall disdayne, to fugge [fight] and lyve by stelth:
> When wisdome walks a loft, and folly syts full low,
> And virtue vanquish pampered vice, and greate begins to grow.
> When Justice ioynes to truth, and law lookes not to meede [gain, reward]
> & bribes help not to build fair bowres, nor gifts gret glotons feede…
> When dete no sergeant dreeds, and cowrtiers credit keepe,
> And might melles not with merchandise, nor lords shall sell no sheepe:
> Whe[n] lucre lasts not long, and hurd great heapes doth hate,
> And euery wight is contente, to walke in his estate,
> And truth doth tread ye strets and liers lurke in den,
> And Rex doth raigne and rule the ro[a]st, and weedes out wicked men:
> Then balefull barnes [children] be blythe, that here in England wonne [live],
> Your strife shal steynte I undertake, your dreadful daies are done.[23]

---

[21]   Andy Wood, *The 1549 Rebellions and the Making of Early Modern England* (Cambridge: Cambridge University Press, 2007), pp. 32–3.

[22]   Joan Thirsk, 'The Farming Regions of England', in Joan Thirsk ed., *The Agrarian History of England and Wales: IV, 1500–1640* (Cambridge: Cambridge University Press, 1967), pp. 1–112, at pp. 38–41.

[23]   Thomas Churchyard, *Davy Dycars Dreame* (London, 1552), lines 1–10, 21–8.

The poem imagines the dream of an illiterate labourer who longs for a just and fair society in which everything can be taken at face value.[24] Not only can friends be trusted and the schemes of the devious come to nothing, but truth and justice operate without those charged to administer them being corrupted by bribes. It is further worth noting the standard political charges made in the poem: the king rules without falling prey to evil counsellors; there is no point in hoarding wealth as it is better to put it to use (alluding to the parable of the three servants, Matthew 25:14–30); and masters do not sell their sheep. Sheep were the mainstay of the English economy in this period, a fact signalled in Raphael Hythloday's complaint that they were devouring men as enclosure made ever more land available for the rich to profit from large estates, and so reducing the common land available to the poor. Churchyard's reference was especially pointed and undoubtedly alludes to the chaos caused by the introduction of a sheep tax in 1549, an act designed to help the poor but which actually benefited the rich after amendments were made.[25]

'Davy Dykers Dream' is part of a long European literary tradition that can be dated back to the middle ages. The most famous representation is undoubtedly Pieter Bruegel the elder's 'The Land of Cockaigne' (1567), which represents a series of prostrate figures lying underneath a tree to which a table laden with food has been attached. In the background a roast pig with a carving knife in its side squeals, 'Eat me! Eat me!'[26] The important point of this fantasy is that it combines the two most significant elements of the life of the hungry poor: a wish to be served abundant food and a desire to be released from the burdens of tedious and painful work. Churchyard's poem bears a distinct resemblance to the English medieval poem, 'The Land of Cockaigne', probably written in the fourteenth century in Ireland, which has an identical vision of a mythical land or time of a comfortable and just society:

> There is many a sweet sight,
> All is day, there is no night,
> There is no quarrelling nor strife,
> There no death, but endless life;
> There no lack of food or cloth,
> There no man or woman wroth,
> There no serpent, wolf or fox,
> Horse or nag or cow or ox,
> Neither sheep nor swine nor goat,
> Nor creeping groom, I'd have you note,
> Neither stallion there nor stud.
> Other things you'll find are good.
> In bed or garment or in house,
> There's neither flea nor fly nor louse.
> Neither thunder, sleet nor hail,
> No vile worm nor any snail,
> Never a storm, not rain nor wind,

---

[24]   For analysis see Scott Lucas, 'Diggon Davie and Davy Dicar: Edmund Spenser, Thomas Churchyard, and the Poetics of Public Protest', *Spenser Studies* 16 (2002), 151–65 (which includes a transcription of the poem); Andrew Hadfield, 'Foresters, Ploughmen, and Shepherds: Versions of Tudor Pastoral', in Mike Pincombe and Cathy Shrank eds, *The Oxford Handbook of Tudor Literature, 1485–1603* (Oxford: Oxford University Press, 2009), pp. 537–54.

[25]   Joan Thirsk, 'Enclosing and Engrossing', in Thirsk ed., *Agrarian History*, pp. 200–55, at pp. 221–3; Thomas More, *Utopia*, ed. Raymond Guess and Quentin Skinner (Cambridge: Cambridge University Press, 1989), pp. 18–21.

[26]   Walter S. Gibson, *Bruegel* (London: Thames and Hudson, 1977), pp. 178–9.

> There's no man or woman blind,
> All is sporting, joy and glee,
> Lucky the man that there may be.[27]

Again, animals are significant in the poem, the speaker imagining a life without the drudgery of caring for them, as are physical comfort and the absence of conflict. In popular culture radical political vision was inseparable from fantasy.

The significance of literature in establishing the nature of popular political culture cannot be underestimated. As most people were excluded from the political process, they had to find means for political debate outside what historians have regarded as regular channels.[28] The stories that appeared in a variety of literary texts often had a political resonance, not as direct allegories of political events, but more often as useful ways of thinking about a particular issue or problem. There is now a wealth of literary analysis that shows how such major works as Sir Philip Sidney's *Arcadia* or Edmund Spenser's *The Faerie Queene* reflected on the political situation in the 1580s and 1590s and directed readers towards relevant debates.[29] The principal way in which such political thought reached a wider audience was through the commercial theatre, which developed rapidly after its inception in the 1560s until it became a key feature of London life, as well as life in provincial towns when companies went on tour.[30] Andrew Gurr estimates that between 15,000 and 25,000 people went to the theatre every week from the time when the first commercial theatres opened until they were closed down by the Commonwealth government in 1642. The population in that period grew from *c.* 200,000 to *c.* 400,000 out of a total population of about 4 million. This means that about 8–10 per cent of the capital's population were attending plays in this period, an astonishing number which testifies to the potent influence of this new form of entertainment.[31] And more were seeing plays on tour.

Plays were a common means of disseminating popular political ideas, as has long been recognised.[32] The first English tragedy, *Gorboduc, or Ferrex and Porrex* (1561), was performed at court but it is clear that its timely message of the national chaos that could be caused by the failure of a monarch to marry and secure the succession had a much wider impact and that William Haughton's lost play, *Ferrex and Porrex* (1600) was an adaptation for a wider audience near the end of Elizabeth's reign.[33] Discussion of the succession was forbidden and the MP, Peter Wentworth, was imprisoned for raising the issue as a matter of wider public concern in the House of Commons in the 1590s.[34] It was hardly surprising, therefore, that so many literary works – in particular, plays – found it easy to interest an audience with stories

---

[27]   Cited (and modernised) in A.L. Morton, *The English Utopia* (London: Lawrence & Wishart, 1978, rpt of 1952), p. 280.

[28]   A useful overview of these is provided in David Loades, *Power in Tudor England* (Basingstoke: Macmillan, 1997).

[29]   Blair Worden, *The Sound of Virtue: Philip Sidney's Arcadia and Elizabethan Politics* (New Haven: Yale University Press, 1996); Paul Suttie, 'Spenser's Political Pragmatism', *Studies in Philology* 95 (1998), 56–76.

[30]   Andrew Gurr, *Playgoing in Shakespeare's London* (Cambridge: Cambridge University Press, 1987); Andrew Gurr, *The Shakespearean Playing Companies* (Cambridge: Cambridge University Press, 1996), ch. 2.

[31]   Andrew Gurr, *The Shakespearean Stage* (3rd ed., Cambridge: Cambridge University Press, 1999), p. 213.

[32]   David Bevington, *Tudor Drama and Politics: A Critical Approach to Topical Meaning* (Cambridge, MA: Harvard University Press, 1968).

[33]   Thomas Sackville and Thomas Norton, *Gorboduc, Or Ferrex and Porrex*, ed. Irby B. Cauthen (London: Arnold, 1970); Gurr, *Shakespearean Playing Companies*, p. 241.

[34]   J.E. Neale, 'Peter Wentworth', in E.B. Fryde and Edward Miller eds, *Historical Studies of the English Parliament: Vol. 2, 1399 to 1603* (Cambridge: Cambridge University Press, 1970), pp. 246–95.

that cast light on current affairs. Elizabeth herself recognised this when she complained that she was represented as Richard II, the last monarch to be formally deposed, and that versions were performed throughout the streets and in private houses.[35]

Plays cannot, of course, be reduced to topical political messages. But it is obvious that there was a significant appetite among playgoers for works that had political resonances, which raises a host of questions. Were companies and playwrights putting forward serious ideas designed to persuade their audiences much as court plays and masques sought to counsel a monarch into taking the right course of action?[36] Or were they simply reacting to commercial pressures and producing what an audience would have thought was interesting? Probably, inevitably, the truth must be that both processes were taking place at the same time. The topical nature of drama varied in its focus and purpose and is not always easy to recover. John Webster's *The Duchess of Malfi* (1612–3) seems to have a plot that makes a series of allusions to the fate of Arbella Stuart (1575–1615), imprisoned by James I as a rival after a foolhardy plan to marry William Seymour, who also had a claim to the throne.[37] It is hard to tell whether the play is a robust – and therefore quite dangerous – defence of Arbella's actions, or whether it is simply alluding to an interesting and newsworthy event. In the play the Duchess makes a moving speech as she woos Antonio, her steward, the chief servant in the household, explaining why she has to make the first move:

> *Now she pays it!*
> *The misery of us that are born great –*
> *We are forc'd to woo, because none dare woo us;*
> *And as a tyrant doubles with his words,*
> *And fearfully equivocates, so we*
> *Are forc'd to express our violent passions*
> *In riddles and in dreams, and leave the path*
> *Of simple virtue, which was never made*
> *To seem the thing it is not. Go, go brag*
> *You have left me heartless – mine is in your bosom:*
> *I hope 'twill multiply love there. You do tremble:*
> *Make not your heart so dead a piece of flesh*
> *To fear more than to love me: sir, be confident –*
> *What is 't distracts you? This is flesh and blood, sir;*
> *'Tis not the figure cut in alabaster*
> *Kneels at my husband's tomb. Awake, awake, man!*
> *I do here put off all vain ceremony,*
> *And only do appear to you a young widow*
> *That claims you for her husband, and like a widow,*
> *I use but half a blush in't.*[38]

This fascinating speech raises a host of questions about how dramatic speeches with political resonances might further our understanding of popular political culture. Politics

---

[35]   Andrew Hadfield, *Shakespeare and Renaissance Politics* (London: Thomson, 2003), p. 16; Marie Axton, *The Queen's Two Bodies: Drama and the Elizabethan Succession* (London: Royal Historical Society, 1977).

[36]   Greg Walker, *Plays of Persuasion: Drama and Politics at the Court of Henry VIII* (Cambridge: Cambridge University Press, 1991); Greg Walker, *The Politics of Performance in Early Renaissance Drama* (Cambridge: Cambridge University Press, 1998).

[37]   Sarah Jayne Steen ed., *The Letters of Lady Arbella Stuart* (Oxford: Oxford University Press, 1994).

[38]   John Webster, *The Duchess of Malfi*, ed. John Russell Brown (Manchester: Manchester University Press, 1974), Act 1, scene 1, lines 440–59.

was, as everyone knew, personal and centred on personalities, how they behaved, who they married and the nature of their children. The Duchess duly marries Antonio and every indication is given that their union is a happy one; that is until her deranged and warped brothers intervene to thwart it. More usually the marriage of a wealthy widow to a servant was viewed with suspicion and was the subject of robust comedy, as it is in *Twelfth Night* when Malvolio is goaded into wooing his mistress, Olivia. But it is difficult for us to work out how we should read the speech. The Duchess's desire for a private life seems reasonable enough to us. Read one way what we witness is a tragedy of state, as J. W. Lever argued, the destruction of the identity and security of a virtuous individual by the brutal forces ranged against her.[39] But the play might also be read to suggest that the Duchess is culpable, a powerful woman living in a corrupt state who puts her own happiness first over that of the people she governs and so pays a terrible price.[40] Did an audience feel a natural sympathy with the restricted life of their superiors, recognising the limitations that were placed on their own lives, as most people married for property and the sake of family alliances in early modern England, not love?[41] Or did they see yet another aristocrat who failed to fulfil her duty to the state and society? It is hard to tell.

The lines about equivocation are especially powerful and topical. The Duchess claims that she is forced by circumstances – the rule of tyranny – to disguise what she really means. We are brought back to the central question of early modern political thought, when was it possible to depose a tyrant? Should one retreat into private life and let events take their course until there is a turn for the better? Or, as another play put it, 'take arm against a sea of troubles, / And by opposing end them'?[42] The use of the word 'equivocation' would surely have reminded the audience of a time when a group of dedicated rebels tried to do just that. One of the key players in the Gunpowder Plot was the Jesuit Father Garnett, who famously defended the right of Catholics to equivocate in order to defend themselves and to bring about the desired end of Protestant tyranny. Garnett's scandalous defence was represented in the speech of the porter in *Macbeth*: 'Faith, here's an equivocator, that could swear in both the scales against either scale, who committed treason enough for God's sake, yet could not equivocate to Heaven.'[43] In using the word 'equivocate' the Duchess was undoubtedly reminding a theatre-going public of the Gunpowder Plot and its aftermath, and perhaps the safest reading of her words is that she is reminding the audience just how dangerous it was to actually oppose anyone considered a tyrant, which is how the plotters thought of James as a Protestant monarch.[44] But if the play does represent the Duchess as Arbella Stuart then perhaps there is some substance to the accusation that James could certainly behave in a tyrannical manner. As Sara Jayne Steen argues, audience reactions to political problems, then as now, were probably mixed, suggesting that we can identify issues and questions but should be wary of assuming that we can easily determine the answer:

> *some playgoers probably entered Blackfriars prepared to judge the Duchess of Malfi's marriage harshly and find in her punishment a lesson for ladies: others would have*

---

[39]   J.W. Lever, *The Tragedy of State* (London: Methuen, 1971).

[40]   Frank Whigham, *Seizures of the Will in Early Modern English Drama* (Cambridge: Cambridge University Press, 1996), ch. 4.

[41]   Ralph A. Houlbrooke, *The English Family, 1450–1700* (Harlow: Longman, 1984), ch. 4.

[42]   William Shakespeare, *Hamlet*, ed. G.R. Hibbard (Oxford: Oxford University Press, 1987), Act 3, scene 1, lines 60–61.

[43]   William Shakespeare, *Macbeth*, ed. Nicholas Brooke (Oxford: Oxford University Press, 1990), Act 2, scene 3, lines 8–10.

[44]   Antonia Fraser, *The Gunpowder Plot: Terror & Faith in 1605* (London: Weidenfeld and Nicolson, 1996), pp. 104–6.

been ready to cheer the marriage and her heroism; and most would have been inclined to pity her, for 'all may be attributed to the great love she had for the person she had chosen to be her husband'.[45]

Popular political discourse in drama could range from the intensely serious to the gossipy. In the 1590s Shakespeare was involved in the production of eight plays on English history that charted the contested succession and the bloody Civil Wars that ravaged England in the fifteenth century before the Tudors assumed control.[46] These surely had a political significance, showing what might happen if the succession question was not resolved before Elizabeth's death, especially if we further consider that two more plays had plots based on assassinations (*Julius Caesar* and *Hamlet*), and that under the new king who wished to unite the kingdoms Shakespeare turned his attention to Britain rather than England. Ben Jonson's political work was far more obviously satirical in design than Shakespeare's. His first play, *The Isle of Dogs*, written with Thomas Nashe, disappearing forever undoubtedly because it represented a number of prominent courtiers as fawning hounds (Elizabeth kept her dogs on the island in the Thames). Jonson was imprisoned and later enjoyed great success at court, but he still had an appetite for satirical attacks on the monarch.[47] In *Eastward Ho!* (printed in 1605), written with George Chapman and John Marston, a tale of absurd city rogues, the writers aggressively lampooned the new king and his desire to promote his favourites. A group of adventurers led by a drunk captain, Seagull, imagine that they are on their way to a life of wealth in the New World only to land on the Isles of Dogs, a conspicuous allusion to the banned play. In the tavern before they sail Seagull explains to the others why the Americas are such a desirable place to live:

> *Scapethrift: And is it a pleasant country withal?*
>
> *Seagull: As ever the sun shined on: temperate and full of all sorts of excellent viands. Wild boar is as common there as our tamest bacon is here, venison as mutton. And then you shall live freely there, without sergeants, or courtiers, or lawyers, or intelligenciers; only a few industrious Scots, perhaps, who indeed are dispersed over the face of the whole earth. But as for them, there are no greater friends to Englishmen and England, when they are out on't, in the world than they are. And for my part, I would a hundred thousand of 'em were there, for we are all one countrymen now, ye know, and we should find ten times more comfort of them than we do here.*[48]

This is a piece of harsh, witty satire, aimed at the common perception that James had brought too many Scots with him to court and over-promoted most.[49] The comment is cast in terms of the popular discourse of a fabled place in which the cares and troubles of everyday life melt away, the myth of the land of Cockaigne: here, the New World. The joke is that even in that Utopia, when every other hated figure has disappeared – policemen, lawyer, courtiers, spies

[45] Sara Jayne Steen, 'The Crime of Marriage: Arbella Stuart and the Duchess of Malfi', *The Sixteenth-Century Journal* 22 (1991), 61–76, at p. 76.

[46] For further discussion, see Andrew Hadfield, *Shakespeare and Republicanism* (Cambridge: Cambridge University Press, 2005), ch. 3.

[47] Ian Donaldson, *Ben Jonson: A Life* (Oxford: Oxford University Press, 2011), pp. 111–22.

[48] George Chapman, Ben Jonson and John Marston, *Eastward Ho!*, ed. Suzanne Gossett and W. David Kay, in Ben Jonson, *The Cambridge Edition of the Complete Works of Ben Jonson*, ed. David Bevington, Martin Butler and Ian Donaldson (7 vols, Cambridge: Cambridge University Press, 2012), vol. 2, pp. 529–640: Act 3, scene 3, lines 26–35.

[49] Roger Lockyer, *James VI & I* (Harlow: Longman, 1998), pp. 59–60, 165–6.

(Jonson is partly making a joke about his own brushes with the law) the Scots still remain eager to get more than their fair share of the wonderful provisions on offer, spreading themselves throughout the world in search of gain. The comment about the integration of English and Scots is obviously ironic: if the two nations were so seamlessly integrated as Seagull suggests then he would not even notice who was who or draw attention to the two nationalities. The satire is at once playing to the gallery of popular prejudice, and a serious comment on the ubiquity of political corruption and its impact on the lives of the population.

Popular politics started to develop much more seriously after James' death in 1625 and the accession of his son, Charles I. Historians disagree about Charles, many seeing him as a foolish and stubborn ruler who lost touch with the people through his autocratic tendencies, while others argue that he was a principled man who was misunderstood, now as then.[50] However, all agree that, whatever Charles' personal merits, his rule was seen as disastrous, oppressive and misguided by a wider public and that he failed to promote a series of policies that could unite the disparate peoples and kingdoms he governed. Perhaps the task would have been beyond even the most gifted of monarchs and that his father had left him with too many problems to solve. He was also the victim of a developing civil society that contained more educated people than the kingdom that Henry VIII governed, many eager to see their own version of Christianity tolerated, promoted or triumph over all others.[51]

The advent of the Civil War saw all restrictions lifted from the printing presses and a wealth of popular political material appeared as each faction – Presbyterians, Levellers, Diggers, Royalists, Anabaptists, Quakers – produced their own works. A central control disappeared from the political world. During the reigns of Elizabeth and James there were, on average, some 15–35 titles of religious controversy published each year; by the 1640s this had mushroomed to 20–50 titles per month.[52] As Tom Corns has pointed out, political language could still be rudimentary, and debate often concentrated on personalities and moral issues rather than political principles, theories and issues:

> As the decade [the 1640s] progresses, debate is widened by more fundamental discussion of what the state is for, how it is to serve its citizens, what the rights and powers may be and what indeed is the contract between government and the governed. By the 1650s something approaching a mature republican theoretical position may be identified. Moreover, in the Levellers, England had its first modern political party, indeed, a party that probably more closely resembled the popular movements of the nineteenth and twentieth centuries than the Whigs and Tories of the late Stuart and early Hanoverian period.[53]

Political life in England had developed as elections to parliament were now more widely and genuinely contested. Until the English Revolution local figures of substance could rely on the support of people they regarded as their clients. But by the 1640s a more literate, property-owning electorate – still a relatively small section of the population – with very different political and religious ideas voted for candidates of opposed views.[54] It finally

---

[50] Kevin Sharpe, *The Personal Rule of Charles I* (New Haven: Yale University Press, 1992); Richard Cust, *Charles I: A Political Life* (Harlow: Longman, 2005).

[51] David Cressy, *England on Edge: Crisis and Revolution, 1640–1642* (Oxford: Oxford University Press, 2006); Nigel Smith, *Literature & Revolution in England, 1640–1660* (New Haven: Yale University Press, 1994).

[52] Thomas N. Corns, *A History of Seventeenth-Century Literature* (Oxford: Blackwell, 2012), p. 295.

[53] Ibid., p. 296.

[54] Derek Hirst, *The Representative of the People? Voters and Voting in England under the Early Stuarts* (Cambridge: Cambridge University Press, 1975).

mattered what people thought. Alongside the growth of political representation there developed a concomitant interest in newspapers and news books, a sign of intellectual and technological changes that made a concern with current affairs feasible and desirable beyond the political elite.[55]

The Levellers' political ideals were disseminated in a frequently revised pamphlet, later reprinted as a broadsheet, *An Agreement of the People for a Firme and Present Peace, upon Grounds of Common-Right and Freedome* (1647). This work laid out the basic principles of government that the Levellers believed were fundamental to the establishment of a fair and just society and which were necessary to end years of bitter conflict. The Levellers sought to establish agreement on basic human rights and to protect the individual from the encroaching power of the state, a reversal of the fundamental premise of Royalist treatises from the early 1500s onwards which assumed that the object of politics was to persuade or force the people to pledge obedience to their protector, the monarch. They were determined, having won the war to win the peace too and to move into a new, more harmonious political era:

> We do now hold our selves bound in mutual duty to each other, to take the best care
> we can for the future, to avoid both the danger of returning into a slavish condition,
> and the chargable remedy of another war: for as it cannot be imagined that so many of
> our Country-men would have opposed us in this quarrel, if they had understood their
> owne good, so may we safely promise to our selves, that when our Common Rights
> and liberties shall be cleared, their endeavours will be disappointed that seek to make
> themselves our Masters[.][56]

The pamphlet tries to sweep away the assumption that society must be divided into the governors and the governed, concentrating instead on a language of common rights and liberties for all, as well as a hope that the last war can be put aside as swords are transformed into ploughshares. There is also the hope that because the principles outlined here seem so obvious and reasonable to the author that all foolish opposition will just melt away, a familiar trope of idealistic political discourse, which is repeated later: 'every true English man that loves the peace and freedome of England will concurre with us' (p. 12).

The pamphlet outlines four basic principles. First, that there be equal units 'for the election of their Deputies in Parliament' (p. 2); second, that the current parliament be dissolved in order to inaugurate the new political era in England; that Parliaments should be elected every two years (p. 3); that Parliament is sovereign and has the power to govern the country, in the name of the people, as the power of deputies is 'inferior only to those who chuse them' (p. 3). The *Agreement* further laid out a series of universal rights, most importantly that there should be no restriction on individual religion: 'That matters of Religion, and the ways of Gods Worship, are not at all instructed by us to any humane power, because therein wee cannot remit or exceed a tittle of what our Consciences dictate to be the mind of God, without wilfull sinne' (p. 4).

For the Levellers it was a question of establishing a way forward for the 'Free-born People of England' after 'the King raised warre against you and your Parliament' (p. 7). Originally signed by 10 officers in the New Model Army, the *Agreement* was designed to put an end to the need for war, to replace a political language of power and domination with one of shared rights and principles and to ensure that no particular faction could govern for ever

---

[55] Joad Raymond, *The Invention of the Newspaper: English Newsbooks, 1641–1649* (Oxford: Clarendon Press, 1996).

[56] Anon., *An Agreement of the People for a Firme and Present Peace, upon Grounds of Common-Right and Freedome* (London, 1647), p. 1.

without the will of the people, a sound republican principle. Such political language would have been unthinkable during the Pilgrimage of Grace, an event which looked back to an ideal of a society that looked after and protected people rather than granted them rights and the power to choose who governed them. Popular political language had come a long way.

Select Bibliography

Bevington, David, *Tudor Drama and Politics: A Critical Approach to Topical Meaning*. Cambridge, MA: Harvard University Press, 1968.

Coleman, Janet, *A History of Political Thought*. 2 vols. Oxford: Blackwell, 2000.

Fletcher, Anthony, *Tudor Rebellions*. Harlow: Longman, 1983.

Hadfield, Andrew, *Shakespeare and Renaissance Politics*. London: Thomson, 2003.

Harris, Tim ed., *The Politics of the Excluded, c.1500–1850*. Basingstoke: Palgrave, 2001.

Hilton, Rodney, *Bond Men Made Free: Medieval Peasant Movements and the English Rising of 1381*. London: Routledge, 1988, rpt of 1973.

Hirst, Derek, *The Representative of the People? Voters and Voting in England under the Early Stuarts*. Cambridge: Cambridge University Press, 1975.

Kesselring, K.J., *The Northern Rebellion of 1569: Faith, Politics, and Protest in Elizabethan England*. Basingstoke: Palgrave, 2007.

Loades, David, *Power in Tudor England*. Basingstoke: Macmillan, 1997.

Morton, A.L., *The English Utopia*. London: Lawrence & Wishart, 1978, rpt of 1952.

Shagan, Ethan, *Popular Politics and the English Reformation*. Cambridge: Cambridge University Press, 2003.

Skinner, Quentin, *The Foundations of Early Modern Political Thought*. 2 vols. Cambridge: Cambridge University Press, 1978.

Smith, Nigel, *Literature & Revolution in England, 1640–1660*. New Haven: Yale University Press, 1994.

Wood, Andy, *The 1549 Rebellions and the Making of Early Modern England*. Cambridge: Cambridge University Press, 2007.

Riot and Rebellion

Elizabeth Sauer

On 23 July 1637 the congregation at St Giles's Cathedral rioted in reaction to Charles I's attempt at introducing a new Anglican prayer book in Scotland to enforce religious conformity. The move outraged the Scottish Presbyterians (Covenanters) and also Puritans in England. The same year saw the pillorying of William Prynne, Henry Burton and John Bastwick for 'makinge, contriving, publishinge, divulginge' libelous books, and the arrest of John Lilburne. The future spokesman for the Levellers had attended the public punishment of the Archbishop of Canterbury's latest victims, and months later was himself charged with importing 'scandalous' books from the Continent.[1] Like their Scottish counterparts in 1637, the English who protested against Archbishop William Laud's repressive measures took matters of justice to the streets. Laud, who revised and reissued the Book of Common Prayer, became a target of libellers because of the St Giles riot, the recent Star Chamber proceedings and the alleged rise of the '*Popish* Faction',[2] for which the Archbishop was held responsible. Reviled in the numerous manuscript and printed libels that suddenly appeared, a very agitated Laud excuses an interruption in correspondence with the Earl of Strafford: 'the Truth is, I have been so exercised with Libellings and Star-Chamber Business, and the Consequences which have followed upon them'; 'a little more Quickness in the Government would cure this Itch of Libelling'.[3] But there would be no letup for years. At midnight, reports Laud on 11 May 1640, 'my house at Lambeth was beset with 500 of these rascal routers .... Since [then] I have fortified my house as well as I can; and hope all may be safe.' Still, he complains, 'libels are continually set up in all places of note in the city.'[4] Laud renders the riots and the declamatory writings – the textual revolts – synonymous as he documents his distress about the vexing and menacing nature of both. In some ways, the libels pose a greater threat than the 'routers' or common protesters, who presumably fail to penetrate the fortress; the ubiquitous defamatory literature would in fact help script Laud's 'doom,' as William Prynne would call it in wake of the Archbishop's decollation.[5]

---

[1]   *Calendar of State Papers Domestic, Charles I*, vol. 11 (1637), p. 49; Pauline Gregg, *Free-Born John: The Biography of John Lilburne* (London: George G. Harrup, 1961), pp. 47–51.

[2]   Peter Heylyn, *Cyprianus Anglicus* (London, 1668), p. 359.

[3]   'The Archbishop ... to the Lord Deputy' (28 August 1637), *Earl of Strafforde's Letters and Dispatches*, ed. William Knowler (2 vols, Dublin, 1740), vol. 2, p. 99.

[4]   William Laud, *The History of the Troubles and Trial of ... William Laud*, vol. 3 (1853), *The Works of ... William Laud*, ed. W. Scott and J. Bliss (7 vols, Oxford: J. H. Parker, 1847–60), pp. 235–36.

[5]   William Prynne, *Canterburies Doome. or The First Part of a Compleat History of The Commitment, Charge, Tryall, Condemnation, Execution of WILLIAM LAUD Late Arch-Bishop of Canterbury* (London, 1646).

This essay considers the category of popular culture in relation to riots – a term derived from the Old French *riote* or debate – and it reviews protest literature that accompanied the risings. Riots and protests and, correspondingly, textual revolts are (though in no unqualified manner) important expressions of the popular interests, conservative and radical. Acts of resistance – political, legal, religious – regularly intersected. Sociological models offer frameworks and discourses for conceptualising resistance and protest. In social theory, the 'repertoire of contention' refers to the set of various performances and tools available to a protest movement or demonstration in a given time frame.[6] Actions and instruments that belong to common repertoires of contention include public meetings, elections, rallies, demonstrations, petitioning, strikes and pamphleteering. The public disorders surveyed in this essay include and are accompanied by printed pamphlets and petitions, which asserted the right of the marginalised to influence authorities, and of which religious dissenters were the most active framers, as highlighted in the second half of this chapter.

As well as reviewing concepts of 'the popular', this essay examines methodologies for constructing a history of popular culture. A consideration of the relationship of riots, protest, and 'paper-conflicts' provides a partial corrective to a traditional historiography that restricts rioting to extra-textual events. The examples of rioting in this essay, which range from street rioting to anti-enclosure rioting to army mutinies, can productively be situated in relation to other forms of protest, including those reliant on print as a mode of communication and resistance. The printed protests take various forms that serve as mediums through which social order is represented and undermined. The genres of social protest include ballads, libels, news, manifestoes, declarations, appeals and petitions.[7] Through the paper wars, people on both sides of the Civil War engaged in symbolic behaviour, using cultural codes to assert their identities, provoke or ridicule their enemies and in general register writing as a form of protest and mass participation. The circulation of petitions in particular ,often preceded crowd action, including rioting, which is here examined as a social, philosophical and textual practice. Finally this essay also comments on whether and how protests are connected to the rise of a politically motivated populace in the Civil War and to the historiographical debate about the nature of the English rebellion / revolution.

Paper-Conflicts

Thomas May's history of the causes of civil war connects paper protests with military conflicts and violence: 'those Paper-contestations became a fatall Prologue to that bloudy, and unnaturall War, which afterward ensued'; 'For now the fatal time was come, when those long and tedious Paper-conflicts of Declarations, Petitions and Proclamations, were turned into actuall and bloody Wars.'[8] The pamphlet literature was the product of the new print technology in the seventeenth century, whose development corresponded with an ideology of common liberties, a rise in literacy rates and the emergence of an increasingly litigious climate. The press's extraordinary output rose from 625 titles in 1639 to three

---

[6] See the essays in David A. Snow, Sarah A. Soule and Hanspeter Kriesi eds, *The Blackwell Companion to Social Movements* (Oxford: Blackwell, 2004).

[7] Jason C. Scott, *Weapons of the Weak: Everyday Forms of Peasant Resistance* (New Haven: Yale University Press, 1985); Adam Fox, *Oral and Literate Culture in England, 1500–1700* (Oxford: Oxford University Press, 2000).

[8] Thomas May, *The History of the Parliament of England which began November the third, MDCXL* (London, 1647), 2:20; 2:96.

times the number by 1641 and to over 3,666 the next year.[9] The collapse of pre-publication censorship following the opening of the Long Parliament in November 1640 and the subsequent abolition of the Court of Star Chamber in August 1641 helped account for the surge in publications. The Civil War era also witnessed the eruption of 'contestative' modes of reading[10] as impassioned readers perused and annotated texts for polemical and political rather than just aesthetic purposes. Further, developments in print culture and distribution at this time increased the availability for the middle and upper classes to what became a shared body of writings. Recent scholarship on early readerships and interpretive communities registers the tenuousness of commonly drawn distinctions between a popular culture concerned with local affairs and a high culture engaged in national affairs. Such categories shifted in the heterogeneous society of the early modern era. In a cultural and material context, the boundaries of the communities that audiences and readers inhabited were in a constant state of flux. Literary communities both generated and reflected public opinion, which became a formidable force in politics.[11] Popular consciousness in turn splintered into polarised views, thus dismantling the notion of a single unified 'public opinion'. The result was the emergence of 'inchoate public opinions' that redefined the terms of authority.[12] The intense interest in becoming informed corresponded with the wider representation of the voices in the writings of the day. Developments in print and political engagement can be characterised as 'popular' because they allowed for communication to new audiences through an appeal to visual, aural and textual literacies.[13] In such works as satirical poems, dialogues, controversialist literature, libels and petitions, we also discover how print and information networks could heighten resistance to political and religious power structures and to dominant ideologies.

The production and distribution of Civil War newsbooks and pamphlets, whose numbers, as previously mentioned, surged during this period, facilitated the interpenetration of the local and the national. Through print, public opinion was invoked, courted and promoted, thus also establishing agendas for social policy and political practice. Building on the theories of Roger Chartier who interrogated assumptions about linking specific audiences on the social scale with specific cultural forms of expression, Tessa Watt outlines the challenges of establishing the readerships of cheap print during the time. Given that the gentry and middles classes were as likely to purchase chapbooks, broadsides, newsbooks and ballads, audiences should be judged as variegated rather than definable, as 'inclusive rather than exclusive', Watt observes.[14] Additionally cheap print possessed a performative

---

[9]   John Barnard, D.F. McKenzie and Maureen Bell eds, *The Cambridge History of the Book in Britain, Vol. 4, 1557–1695* (Cambridge: Cambridge University Press, 2002), chs 1, 2 and 26, (esp. pp. 557–67), and appendix 1, from which these figures are taken.

[10]   Kevin Sharpe and Steven N. Zwicker eds, *Reading, Society and Politics in Early Modern England* (Cambridge: Cambridge University Press, 2003), p. 301; Jonathan Barry, 'Literacy and Literature in Popular Culture: Reading and Writing in Historical Perspective', in Tim Harris ed., *Popular Culture in England, c. 1500–1850* (New York: St Martin's Press, 1995), pp. 69–94.

[11]   Peter Lake, 'Agency and Appropriation at the Foot of the Gallows: Catholics (and Puritans) Confront (and Constitute) the English State', in Peter Lake and Michael Questier eds, *The Anti-Christ's Lewd Hat: Protestants, Papists and Players in Post-Reformation England* (New Haven: Yale University Press, 2002), p. 262.

[12]   Terence Kilburn and Anthony Milton, 'The Public Context of the Trial and Execution of Strafford', in J.F. Merritt ed., *The Political World of Thomas Wentworth, Earl of Strafford, 1621–1641* (Cambridge: Cambridge University Press, 1996), p. 231.

[13]   See also Joad Raymond, 'Introduction', in Joad Raymond ed., *The Oxford History of Popular Print Culture, Vol. 1: Cheap Print in Britain and Ireland to 1660* (Oxford: Oxford University Press, 2011), p. 7.

[14]   Tessa Watt, *Cheap Print and Popular Piety, 1550–1640* (Cambridge: Cambridge University Press, 1991), p. 3. On this point, Watt cites Roger Chartier's *The Cultural Uses of Print in Early Modern France*, trans. Lydia C. Cochrane (Princeton: Princeton University Press, 1987) and Chartier's *Cultural*

function and conditioned different kinds of interpretive practices. Pamphlets in particular could generate collectivities and fuel dissent. Often commenting on events as they were happening, pamphlets also helped determine how history would be documented. For that reason, they need to be considered in conjunction with their history of production, circulation and reception.[15]

As speech acts, petitions, which were the products of 'a mass-participation activity',[16] register the intersection between popular politics and textual revolts. The common practice of *printing* petitions[17] helped galvanise popular support. Examples of these printed appeals at the time range from the Root and Branch petition of 1640 to the anti-monopoly petitions of tradespeople, and to the political petitions that lobbied for redress for injustices in the affairs of state. Dorset MP Lord George Digby protested in response to the relentless petitioning of the early 1640s, stating that 'no man of judgement, that will thinke it fit for a Parliament, under a Monarchie, to give countenance to irregular, and tumultuous assemblies of people, bee it for never so good an end'.[18] Yet that same year, 1641, saw the printing of several hundred petitions. Among them was one received by the Commons on 24 April and signed by 20,000 Londoners, who called for Strafford's death. The petition included the signature of John Lilburne, who would emerge as a key performer and author of popular protests in the mid-seventeenth century. Prior to Strafford's execution, riots also erupted outside the Queen's apartments in Whitehall (8–9 May) in response to suspicions about conspiracies between her courtiers and a Catholic army prepared to fight English Protestants, allegedly at Strafford's instigation.[19]

How much can protest literature, including notably petitions, actually teach about the subject of 'popular culture', a category that is itself difficult to conceptualise in an early modern context? Historical research on this topic is complicated by the fact that accounts of campaigns in printed pamphlets and newsbooks are coloured by propagandist purposes and that petitions, despite their claims, often do not express popular sentiments; indeed they mask as much as they illuminate public opinion.[20] Early modern petitions also raise questions about political partisanship and religious affiliation, and even unsettle claims about popular support. Petitioners at this time, for example, included Catholics, the Earl of Strafford and the imprisoned bishops, who issued *The Petition and Protestation of Twelve Bishops*.[21]

History: Between Practices and Representations, trans. Lydia C. Cochrane (Cambridge: Cambridge University Press, 1988).

[15]   See Nigel Smith, *Literature and Revolution in England 1640–1660* (New Haven: Yale University Press, 1994); Sharon Achinstein, *Milton and the Revolutionary Reader* (Princeton: Princeton University Press, 1994); Michael Mendle, *Henry Parker and the English Civil War* (Cambridge: Cambridge University Press, 1995); Joad Raymond, *The Invention of the Newspaper: English Newsbooks, 1641–1649* (Oxford: Clarendon Press, 1996); Alexandra Halasz, *The Marketplace of Print Pamphlets and the Public Sphere in Early Modern England* (Cambridge: Cambridge University Press, 1997). In the marketplace of print, average publication lengths became shorter and anything over a sheet or two (8–16 pages in quarto format) became harder to place. Nicholas Von Maltzahn, 'John Milton: The Later Life (1641–1674)', in Nicholas McDowell and Nigel Smith eds, *Oxford Handbook of Milton* (Oxford: Oxford University Press, 2009), p. 34.

[16]   Thomas Cogswell, 'Parliament and the Press', in Raymond ed., Vol. 1, *The Oxford History of Popular Print Culture*, p. 316.

[17]   Anthony Fletcher, *The Outbreak of the English Civil War* (London: E. Arnold, 1981), p. 198.

[18]   See *The Third Speech of the Lord George Digby to the House of Commons concerning bishops and the citie petition the 9th of Febr. 1640* ([London,] 1641), p. 8.

[19]   Robin Clifton, 'The Popular Fear of Catholics during the English Revolution', in Paul Slack ed., *Rebellion, Popular Protest and the Social Order in Early Modern England* (Cambridge: Cambridge University Press, 1984), p. 134.

[20]   David Underdown, *Revel, Riot and Rebellion: Popular Politics and Culture in England 1603–1660* (Oxford: Clarendon Press, 1985), pp. 231.

[21]   *The Petition and Protestation of Twelve Bishops, for which they were accused of High Treason* (printed for T. Bankes, 1641); Thomas Cogswell, 'Parliament and the Press', p. 315.

Petitioning was frequently intended to promote conservative values or restore traditional forms of order that included the return of the king to power, the reinstatement of church government and the dismantling of the army. For pro-parliamentary authorities in the Civil War era, the issuing or publishing of these otherwise conservative demands was tantamount to insurrection: 'divers who have been in Armes against Parliament … have upon a specious pretence of Petitioning the Parliament … drawne together great multitudes of People in a riotous and warlike manner'. The petitioning that plagued other counties like Kent, Surrey and Sussex now threatened civic order in Southampton, whose officials called upon all citizens to prevent disorders and lawlessness by 'forbear[ing] all Tumultuous meetings, whether upon pretence of reading, setting hands too [sic], promoting any such Petitions, or upon any other pretences whatsoever'.[22]

The validity of claims expressed in many pamphlets and petitions about the identity and number of supporters should be viewed sceptically. Still, adds Underdown, many did communicate the consensus of a wide spectrum of local society.[23] Scribner observes that in various cases, not the texts themselves but their circulation and use determined their status as works of popular culture.[24] The reading history and influence of a given text, however, are not always directly proportional to the history of its circulation. Further, the supposition that popular culture has a much larger following than high culture, and that it therefore more accurately reflects the attitudes of the masses has also been queried. Given the prevalent practice of coercion and manipulation in securing signatures, such questioning is justifiable.[25] And yet a cautious and critical approach to extant pamphlets and petitions does makes it possible to talk about the relationship between protests, including riots, and the popular literature that was found scattered in the streets.[26]

Historiographical Debates and Anti-Enclosure Riots

Peter Burke defined culture as a process – 'a system of shared meanings, attitudes and values, and the symbolic forms (performances, artefacts) in which they are expressed or embodied'. Popular culture refers to the culture of ordinary people, those lower on the social scale than the elite, though not necessarily excluding the elite.[27] Expanding the concept further, Natalie Zemon Davis and Sue Wiseman identified popular culture with the mimicking of behaviours and styles labelled 'low' or comic and with widely practised customs, creeds, arts and rituals.[28] Popular culture is dynamic, the product of discontinuity and disequilibrium

---

[22]   *A Declaration of the Committee for the Safetie of the County of Southampton, Sitting at Winton the 9th day of June. 1648* (London, 1648).

[23]   Underdown, *Revel, Riot and Rebellion*, pp. 138–9.

[24]   Bob Scribner, 'Is a History of Popular Culture Possible?', *History of European Ideas* 10:2 (1989), 175–91, at p. 177. On this matter, see also Roger Chartier, *The Cultural Uses of Print in Early Modern France*, pp. 145–264.

[25]   Jonathan Rose, 'Rereading the English Common Reader: A Preface to a History of Audiences', *Journal of the History of Ideas* 53 (1992), 47–70; J.S. Morrill, *Cheshire 1630–1660: County Government and Society during the 'English Revolution'* (Oxford: Clarendon Press, 1974), 31–74; Fletcher, *Outbreak of the English Civil War*, pp. 289–90; David Zaret, *Origins of Democratic Culture: Printing, Petitions, and the Public Sphere in Early-Modern England* (Princeton: Princeton University Press, 2000), p. 235.

[26]   Underdown, *Revel, Riot and Rebellion*, p. viii.

[27]   Peter Burke, *Popular Culture in Early Modern Europe* (1978, 3rd ed., Burlington, VT: Ashgate, 2009), p. xiii.

[28]   Natalie Zemon Davis, 'Towards Mixtures and Margins', *American Historical Review* 97:5 (1992), 1409–16, at p. 1411; Sue Wiseman, '"Popular Culture": A Category for Analysis', in Matthew

through 'inculcation, appropriation, competition, assimilation or rejection of any given set of cultural values or practices'.[29] Recently Burke reaffirmed the validity of the traditional distinction between high and low or popular culture, but has in the process challenged three assumptions: first that the popularity of literary artefacts is determined by use; second, that the 'people' constitute a homogeneous cultural group; and finally, that the distinctions between high and low, and between literate and illiterate remain inviolable.[30]

Corresponding with the historiography on popular culture are developments in the scholarly approach to the history of rioting. Social historians traditionally characterised popular protests and rioting as actions largely detached from interest in political engagement beyond the local level. Buchanan Sharp, for example, insisted that the non-ideological and non-revolutionary, that is, the essentially conservative nature of the riots in the rural areas during the mid-seventeenth century, was more indicative of the forms of resistance at the time than were the actions of 'the tiny minority' who boldly confronted the national government.[31] The hallmark of 1640s riots, according to Sharp, was indifference to the Civil War by protesters who sought only to address their immediate deprivation.[32] As far as enclosure riots were concerned, they did not result in a general rising and in fact only imitated earlier forms of rural protest.

Historians who locate early protests in broad socio-political rather than local contexts have taken a different position on the question of the politics of riots and rebellions. Roger B. Manning, for example, characterised riots as pre-political movements rather than as exercises in participation in the political nation, and yet, as he points out, the rioters' actions displayed some legal proficiency as well as engagement with national affairs.[33] Before the rise of the modern social movement, repertoires of contention, as designated by modern social theory, included food and enclosure riots – the most popular forms of social uprising in the early modern era – which were economic in nature, but also increasingly tied to questions of social, legal and political involvement and partisanship.[34] Partly reliant on the valuable, highly instructive resource of judicial archives, John Walter, in his research on riots – which he designates more appropriately as crowd actions – argues for the 'necessarily political' nature of a popular politics and culture conversant with church, state, and commonwealth discourses.[35] By extension a study of popular uprisings unsettles the restriction of political participation to the realm of high politics. Riots as collective actions were among the numerous forms of protest deployed by the lower orders to challenge authorities at various levels. Also locating rioting in a socio-political history, E.P. Thompson and Natalie Zemon Davis, David Underdown, Charles Tilly and others ascribed to rioters a clear mandate and agenda.[36] Popular 'disorder' had an underlying rational basis and was paradoxically even

---

Dimmock and Andrew Hadfield eds, *Literature and Popular Culture in Early Modern England* (Burlington, VT: Ashgate, 2009), p. 21.

[29]   Scribner, 'Is a History of Popular Culture Possible?', p. 182.

[30]   Peter Burke, 'Popular History', in Raymond ed., Vol. 1, *The Oxford History of Popular Print Culture*, p. 443.

[31]   Buchanan Sharp, *In Contempt of All Authority: Rural Artisans and Riot in the West of England, 1586–1660* (Berkeley and Los Angeles: University of California Press, 1980), p. 8.

[32]   Ibid., p. 249. See Andy Wood, *Riot, Rebellion and Popular Politics in Early Modern England* (New York: Palgrave, 2002), pp. 138–9 for a response that underscores the connections between local and national politics for the rioters.

[33]   Roger B. Manning, *Village Revolts: Social Protest and Popular Disturbances in England, 1509–1640* (Oxford: Clarendon Press, 1988), p. 188.

[34]   Ibid., p. 311.

[35]   John Walter, *Crowds and Popular Politics in Early Modern England* (Manchester: Manchester University Press, 2006), pp. 10–11.

[36]   E.P. Thompson, 'The Moral Economy of the English Crowd in the Eighteenth Century', *Past and Present* 50 (February 1971), 76–136 and Natalie Zemon Davis, 'The Reasons of Misrule' and 'The Rites

motivated by a desire for the restoration of order. These historians studied protests from the perspective of the protesters and they treated disorder as rational collective action, inflected to varying degrees by class consciousness. A richer understanding of anti-enclosure riots of the time requires that they be situated in these larger contexts.[37]

Protests against enclosure and deforestation fuelled uprisings in the sixteenth and seventeenth centuries. In England and Wales, enclosure, which involved the seizure and privatisation of once common land, deprived many of subsistence and sparked revolts. Though much of England had already been enclosed before 1600 and enclosure continued until the early twentieth century, the seventeenth century saw the greatest amount of land being appropriated.[38] When enclosing the commons or fencing and hedging in the land, largely to allow sheep to pasture, early modern landlords claimed occupied lands as unoccupied. Inside the enclosure, the 'reformed' land symbolised the civilised propriety on which an orderly society was based. Since only the landlords needed to be consulted for enclosures to be set up, peasants and labourers lost their common rights and were evicted. As for the 'vagrants' and 'rebels', they were prevented from penetrating the enclosed lands lest they unleashed disorder, thus levelling all distinctions of rank and corrupting the commonwealth. The actual and symbolic significance of the ordering of space, then, involved the expulsion of those beyond the borders of newly defined private property.[39] The connection between the eviction of people from land that they traditionally occupied and the new class of 'masterless men'[40] was established by naturalising the distinctions between those who had a stake in the new economic order and those pushed to the periphery. The Midland Rising in June 1607, the biggest of the anti-enclosure riots in James I's reign, involved over 1,000 people ('levellers' or 'diggers') who sought to level or dig up the enclosures. John Reynolds, a rebel leader, helped ensure the orderliness of the protest. James demanded that the groups disband and he eventually called in the army to repress the protesters. Punishments and executions of leaders followed.

The practice of rioting against enclosures accelerated in the Civil Wars and persisted thereafter.[41] In the 1640s, rioters in Windsor Forest sought to level the land by breaking down the enclosures and laying claim to the woods and the formerly common lands. Legislation to protect and restore the rights of freeholders came in the form of a 'General Order for Possessions, to secure them from Riots and Tumults', which decreed that 'no Inclosure or Possession shall be violently, and in a tumultuous Manner, disturbed or taken away from any Man, which was in Possession the First Day of this Parliament or before, but by due Course and Form of Law'.[42] By the following year, however, it was not only Civil War that erupted but also revolts in the fenlands and forests in the east counties.[43] Like those in the

---

of Violence', in Natalie Zemon Davis, *Society and Culture in Early Modern France* (Stanford: Stanford University Press, 1975), pp. 97–123; 152–87; David Underdown, 'The Problem of Popular Allegiance in the English Civil War', *Transactions of the Royal Historical Society*, 5th ser., 31 (1981), 69–94; Charles Tilly, *The Politics of Collective Violence* (Cambridge: Cambridge University Press, 2003).

[37] Manning, *Village Revolts*, p. 311.

[38] Enclosure peaked in the seventeenth century. J.R. Wordie, 'Chronology of English Enclosure, 1500–1914', *The Economic History Review* 36:4 (1983), 483–505, at p. 494.

[39] Henri Lefebvre, *The Production of Space*, trans. Donald Nicholson-Smith (Oxford: Blackwell, 1991), p. 36.

[40] Early modern London was inundated with 'masterless men', some of whom were 'victims of enclosure'. Christopher Hill, *The World Turned Upside Down: Radical Ideas during the English Revolution* (London: Temple Smith, 1972), p. 16.

[41] Manning, *Village Revolts*, p. 188.

[42] 'Declaration against enclosure riots 13 July 1641', *Journal of the House of Lords: vol. 4: 1629–42* (1767–1830), 311–12. http://www.british-history.ac.uk/report.aspx?compid=35647 (accessed 11 July 2012).

[43] Underdown, *Revel, Riot and Rebellion*, p. 136. Underdown nevertheless concedes the conservatism of the enclosure rioters, p. 137. See also Keith Lindley, *Fenland Riots and the English Revolution* (London:

western forests a decade earlier, the fen riots were risings against courtiers and landlords who deprived the peasants and labourers of their livelihood. Such risings were small-scale but still significant revolts against a gentry that was also involved in the Civil War which engulfed key parts of the country and kingdom.

Riots were often preceded by such measures as mediation and the documentation and publication of grievances.[44] Rioters regularly employed ridicule, reproach, sedition, libels, pamphleteering, petitioning and inversion rituals, as Underdown famously surveyed in a study that situates social protests in the context of geographical regional differences.[45] Enclosure riots displayed 'order within disorder' and, because they were also stage-managed, historians like Steve Hindle distinguish them from rebellions.[46] A discordia concors likewise characterised the movements of the dissenters who publically opposed the enclosing of the land. According to the Diggers, often identified as Levellers, the king, lords and wealthy landowners were the heirs of the Norman Yoke who 'would have all the Commons to themselves'. They thereby upheld 'the Norman Tyranny' over the common people declared Gerrard Winstanley, who served as an author and spokesperson for the Digger movement.[47] The reclaiming of what the Diggers regarded as a common space for the tenants who tilled the land necessitated a struggle against private ownership.

At a time of heightened political tensions, social upheaval, disputes in the New Model Army and widespread starvation, the Diggers in the spring of 1649 occupied St George's Hill, near Weybridge in Surrey, as the first step to cultivating what they designated as common land. The dissenters repossessed enclosed lands 'in the name of the Commons of England, and of all the Nations of the world, it being the righteous freedom of the Creation'.[48] In a declaration of 1649, they stated that 'they intend not to meddle with any mans Propriety, nor to break down any pales or inclosures; but only to meddle with what was common and untilled, and to make it fruitful for the use of man'.[49] Diggers and also Levellers associated pre-enclosure with the Old Testament equivalent of the golden age, the prelapsarian state. In the beginning, writes the anonymous author of the pamphlet *Light shining in Buckinghamshire*, all was held in common until 'man following his own sensualitie became a devourer of the creatures, and an incloser', thus denying the people their birthright. As the subtitle to this tract indicates, enclosure is deemed to be the 'originall cause of all the slavery in the world, but cheifly in England'.[50] Gerrard Winstanley's *Declaration from the Poor Oppressed People of England* (1649) urged that the liberation of England be realised according to the ancient biblical example, so that the nation would 'become a common Treasury to all her children, as every portion of the Land of *Canaan* was the Common livelihood of such

---

Heinemann Educational Books, 1982), pp. 135–60.

[44] Steve Hindle, 'Crime and Popular Protest', in Barry Coward ed., *A Companion to Stuart Britain* (Oxford: Blackwell, 2003), p. 139.

[45] Underdown, *Revel, Riot and Rebellion*.

[46] Hindle, 'Crime and Popular Protest', p. 139.

[47] G.H. Sabine ed., *The Works of Gerrard Winstanley: With an Appendix of Documents Relating to the Digger Movement* (Ithaca, NY: Cornell University Press, 1941), p. 282.

[48] J. Gurney, 'Gerrard Winstanley and the Digger Movement in Walton and Cobham', *Historical Journal* 37 (1994), 788–802. See also Steve Hindle who amassed valuable evidence of the relationship between local early seventeenth-century instances of protest and the popular politics of the radicals in the mid-century. 'Persuasion and Protest in the Caddington Common Enclosure Dispute, 1635–39', *Past and Present* 158 (1998), 37–78, at pp. 76–7.

[49] Bulstrode Whitelocke, *Memorials of the English Affairs, or, An historical account of what passed from the beginning of the reign of King Charles the First, to King Charles the Second his happy restauration* (London, 1682), p. 383v.

[50] See E.C.K. Gonner, *Common Land and Inclosure* (intro. G.E. Mingay, 2nd ed., London: Frank Cass, 1966), pp. 53–5; *Light shining in Buckinghamshire* (London, 1648), *The Works of Gerrard Winstanley*, ed. George H. Sabine (Ithaca, NY: Cornell University Press, 1965), pp. 612, 611.

and such a Tribe, and of every member in that Tribe, without exception, neither hedging in any, nor hedging out'.[51] Certainly the Diggers had connected their local interests to national and historical struggles for justice. Despite harassment by Cromwell's officers and local landlords, the Diggers persisted in their efforts until 1651 when their members dispersed and the movement folded.

Levelling and Textual Revolts

It has become a commonplace, reports Underdown, that in the early seventeenth century, provincial Englishmen generally viewed national politics through the prism of localism. But that does not mean, he adds, that they were detached from the broad questions of constitutional debates.[52] By the time of the English Civil Wars in the mid-century, the Levellers who advanced their own agenda and furthered that of the Diggers, developed a political movement that embraced the cause of popular sovereignty, and that extended suffrage, equality before the law and religious tolerance. Levellers appealed for free trade, religious freedom, constitutional reform and the abolition of tithes and privileges for the upper class, including the House of Lords members. These dissenters rendered their reformist proposals public and sought to extend their reach through their publication as pamphlets.[53] Their efforts at petitioning helped consolidate a social movement concerned about popular politics. That their petitions were condemned and burned by the common hangman (e.g. May 1647) is confirmation of their circulation and impact.[54] The Levellers' response to the burning was the production of more petitions of like nature.[55] Having appealed to the Commons as the 'supreme authority' and refused to recognise the Lords, the Levellers sought to reconstitute authority through a commitment to popular sovereignty and to the representation of the interests of the populace.[56]

In a survey of petitions that appeared at the outbreak of the Civil War, Anthony Fletcher observes that the majority were pro-Parliament (but not anti-monarchist). Many registered a consciousness of the nation's ills and frequently focused on economic hardships. They tended to be more restrained than the Root and Branch petition. What they do not show, according to Fletcher's influential study, is any 'constructive wrestling with the constitutional dilemmas of the moment': the petitioners, whom Fletcher characterises as escapist, sought to smooth over the tensions between king and Parliament without addressing the rift in the relationship between the two parties.[57] The Levellers' petitions are of a different variety altogether: they are interventionist. The propositions advanced by the dissenters became a threat to the

---

[51]   [Winstanley], *A Declaration from the Poor Oppressed People of England, Directed to all that call themselves, or are called Lords of Manors, through this nation; that have begun to cut ... down the woods and trees that grow upon the commons and waste land* (1649), sig. A4r.

[52]   Underdown, *Revel, Riot and Rebellion*, pp. 124–5.

[53]   Joad Raymond, *Pamphlets and Pamphleteering in Early Modern Britain* (Cambridge: Cambridge University Press, 2003), p. 227.

[54]   For the imprisonment of Levellers and the order for the burning of their petitions, see *The Journal of the House of Commons* (London, 1802), 5 (1646–8), 179–80; [William Walwyn], *Gold Tried in the Fire, or The burnt Petitions revived. A preface* (June 1647), sig. A2. Consult Andrew Sharp, Introduction, 'The English Levellers', in Andrew Sharp ed., *The English Levellers* (Cambridge: Cambridge University Press, 1998), pp. xiv; 73–97 for an edition of *Gold Tried*.

[55]   Zaret, *Origins of Democratic Culture*, p. 227.

[56]   Tim Harris, 'The Leveller Legacy', in Michael Mendle ed., *The Putney Debates of 1647: The Army, the Levellers, and the English State* (Cambridge: Cambridge University Press, 2001), p. 235.

[57]   Fletcher, *Outbreak of the English Civil War*, p. 227.

New Model Army, again underscoring the material and political work performed by their paper protestations. As government officials who later intercepted a Leveller petition would claim, 'a Petition may well deserve to be burnt and the Petitioners punished, if the matter be unjust … a Petition is to set forth your grievances, and not to give a rule to the Legislative Power'.[58] Appearing in 1647, *An Agreement of the People* defended liberty of conscience as a God-given right to all people, while denouncing state authority: the 'matters of Religion, and the wayes of Gods Worship, are not at all intrusted to us by any humane power, because therein wee cannot remit or exceed a tittle of what our Consciences dictate to be the mind of God, without wilfull sinne'.[59] The document also condemned conscription and insisted that Parliament itself be held accountable to the law. The imagined readership of *An Agreement* is inclusive insofar as the petition is aimed at the citizens and the officers in the army and even royalist supporters. A moderate version of the more militant *Case of the Army*, the *Agreement* was still intended to secure Cromwell's support.

The first *Agreement* was read and opened for discussion in a meeting of officers and agitators on 29 October 1647 at Putney, where Cromwell chaired the General Council. The Putney debates refer to the meetings of the victors in the first Civil War about the form of government that should be established in England. Among the issues on the table were the franchise and the place of the monarchy and the House of Lords in any settlement. The Army Council convened in late 1648 to participate in debates at Whitehall concerning the new constitution. At this point, the Levellers put forth their proposal for a Representative of the People. The role of the English people became a central issue in these debates, and differences of opinion about this role heightened tensions between Independents like Henry Ireton, who maintained that the franchise be restricted to property holders, and radicals, including John Wildman and Thomas Rainsborough, who demanded wider suffrage.[60] In general, the Levellers' definition of the people was largely reserved for propertied, namely the craftsmen, merchants, artisans and farmers, rather than labourers and wage-earners.[61] The tension in the Levellers' pamphlets between their populist (demotic) and elitist language[62] registered as well in Parliament's own contradictory protestations about its alleged support of the populace.

In the spring of 1649 the Levellers strengthened their campaign against the generals and Council of State, and asserted the rights of soldiers to defy parliamentary commanders and army grandees. Arrested in March 1649 for their role in the publication of *The Second Part of England's New Chains Discovered* (24 March 1649), an attack on Cromwell's Council of State, the four leaders, Lilburne, Walwyn, Prince and Overton, were imprisoned in the Tower. John

---

[58]   'A Declaration of Some Proceedings of Lt. Col. John Lilburn' (1648), in William Haller and Godfrey Smith eds, *Leveller Tracts 1647–1653* (Gloucester, MA: Peter Smith, 1964), p. 118; see Robert Ashton, *Counter-Revolution: The Second Civil War and Its Origins, 1646–8* (New Haven: Yale University Press, 1994), p. 127.

[59]   *An Agreement of the People for a firme and present Peace...* (1647), in Don M. Wolfe ed., *Leveller Manifestoes* (New York: Humanities Press, 1967), p. 227.

[60]   See Henry Noel Brailsford, *The Levellers and the English Revolution* (London: Cresset Press, 1961), ch. 13; G.E. Aylmer ed., *The Levellers in the English Revolution* (Ithaca, NY: Cornell University Press, 1975), pp. 28–33; and especially Ian Gentles, 'The Agreements of the People and Their Political Contexts, 1647–1649', in Mendle ed., *The Putney Debates of 1647*, pp. 148–74.

[61]   Brian Manning, *The English People and the English Revolution, 1640–1649* (London: Heinemann, 1976), p. 279. See Christopher Hill, 'Liberty and Equality: Who Are the People?', in Christopher Hill, *Liberty Against the Law: Some Seventeenth-Century Controversies* (London: Penguin Press, 1996), pp. 242–51. See also Christopher Hill, *Milton and the English Revolution* (New York: Viking Press, 1978), pp. 168–70. Hill quotes statements on the nature of the people expressed by Daniel Taylor, Oliver Cromwell, Colonel John Jones and Thomas Scott. On Winstanley's qualifications of the 'people', see Hill, *The World Turned Upside Down*, p. 135.

[62]   See Wood, *Riot, Rebellion and Popular Politics*, p. 167.

Harris's *Mercurius Militaris* was revived in April 1649, mainly to defend the prisoners and the petitioners who demanded freedom for the prisoners. On 23 April 1649 10,000 women signed a petition, and from 23–25 April, hundreds demonstrated at the House of Commons.[63] The protestors objected to their exclusion from the world of letters and law, and demanded justice from the authorities as they pleaded for the prisoners' release. Women had participated in protests against enclosures earlier in the seventeenth century, since the enclosures affected their livelihood as much as that of their husbands.[64] Now, as prominent, active members of the dissenter movements, women pleaded on Lilburne's behalf. Their 1649 petition was followed by the printing of the 5 May 1649 *Humble Petition of Divers wel-Affected Women*, and later by *To the Supreme Authority ... severall Wives and Children* (1650), *To the Parliament ... the humble Petition of divers afflicted Women* (1653) and *Unto every individual Member of Parliament: The humble Representation of divers afflicted Women-Petitioners*, which protested against Lilburne's 1653 sentence. The petitions at large confirm female political activism and collective resistance. Such evidence compels a reconsideration of the role of women not as marginal or passive members of the sectaries but rather as what Hilary Hinds recognises as 'centrally formative of all aspects of the sectarian phenomenon: their congregational composition, the writings and prophecies produced from within their ranks'.[65]

In April 1649 a mutiny had broken out in the army, in part because of the refusal of some soldiers to participate in what would be a highly popular campaign against the Irish 'rebels', allegedly in revenge for the Rising of 1641. The Leveller Robert Lockyer, a common soldier and one of the ringleaders of the revolt, was singled out by Fairfax to be sentenced to death. Levellers had intervened to defend the rights of disgruntled soldiers who opposed the parliamentary commanders. Lilburne and Overton notified Fairfax that a riot would ensue if the judgement against Lockyer was carried out, but their warning fell on deaf ears. The regiment was quickly suppressed, and Lockyer was court-martialled and executed,[66] resulting in more petitions, demonstrations, and uprisings.

The MP Bulstrode Whitelocke described the ritual procession that took place in the aftermath of the execution of Lockyer on 26 April 1649:

> *About one hundred went before the Corpse, five or six in a file; the Corpse was then brought, with six trumpets sounding a soldier's knell; then the Trooper's horse came, clothed all over in mourning and led by a footman. The corpse was adorned with bundles of Rosemary, one half stained in blood; and the Sword of the deceased along with them. Some thousands followed in rank and file: all had sea-green-and-black Ribbon tied on their hats, and to their breasts: and the women brought up the rear. At the new Churchyard in Westminster, some thousands more of the better sort met them, who thought not fit to march through the City. Many looked on this funeral as an affront to the Parliament and the Army; others called these people Levellers; but they took no notice of any of them.*[67]

---

[63]   *To the Supreme Authority of this Nation, the Commons assembled in Parliament. The Humble Petition of Divers wel-affected Women Inhabiting the Cities of London, Westminster ... In behalf of Lieutenant Col. John Lilburn, Mr. William Walwyn, Mr. Thomas Prince, and Mr. Richard Overton* (London, 1649). *Mercurius Militaris, or the People's Scout*, 23 April 1649, 1 (17–24 April 1649), pp. 13–14.

[64]   Patricia Crawford '"The Poorest She": Women and Citizenship in Early Modern England', in Mendle ed., *The Putney Debates of 1647*, p. 206.

[65]   Hilary Hinds ed. and intro., *'The Cry of a Stone' by Anna Trapnel* (Tempe: Arizona Center for Medieval and Renaissance Studies, 2000), p. xxxi.

[66]   *The Army's Martyr, or A faithful relation of the barbarous and illegall proceedings of the court-martiall at White-Hall upon Mr. Robert Lockier... with a Petition ... to the General* (London, 1649).

[67]   Bulstrode Whitelocke, *Memorials of the English Affairs*, p. 384v.

Supportive of the army and the Leveller cause, *The Moderate* offers a more sympathetic reading of the Levellers and Lockyer than does Whitelocke in his *Memorials of the English Affairs*. The Levellers' 'civilities would not admit any notice to be taken of them', that is, of those who opted not to join in the procession for Lockyer. Further, reports the pro-Leveller *Moderate*, the attendees of Lockyer's funeral observed that the king, who had been executed several months earlier, 'had not half so many mourners to attend his Corps, when interred, as this Trooper'.[68]

In the meantime, public outcries against the imprisonment of the four Leveller leaders in the Tower persisted. Whitelocke cites 'A Petition from ten thousand well affected persons of London, Westminster, Southwark and the Hamletts, in the behalf of Lilburn, Walwyn, Prince and Overton' in which the illegality of the proceedings was decried. Whitelocke does not mention that the petitioners were women, though he reports that their efforts were futile and ineffectual. Thereafter Whitelocke describes the activities in April 1649 of the Diggers (whom he identifies as Levellers) at St Margaret's Hill and St George's Hill. According to the *Memorials of the English Affairs*, the Diggers dug and sowed the land, and threatened 'to pull down Park Pales, and to lay all open' to create common lands.[69] Whitelocke's remarks on the Diggers give way to an account of the third Leveller *Agreement*, which takes up the cause of the 'people' in a major constitutional document.

The collaborate undertaking that constituted *An Agreement of the Free People* (1 May 1649) represents the final form of the Leveller programme in a work of prison literature. Advancing the legal issues debated at Putney and seeking to protect common rights, *An Agreement* revealed the authors' confidence in the judgement of the voting public. Among the Levellers' demands outlined in the 30 articles were annual parliaments and the replacement of the parliamentary court of law with a court of justice so that military power would be checked by civil authority. The Levellers' programme was intended to restore civil liberty, while the act of levelling itself was equated with rioting insofar as parliamentary representatives who caused disturbances or opposed the *Agreement* were designated *levellers*. In their 11 September 1648 petition, the Levellers declared that the Commons of England was to have prevented 'all future Parliaments from abolishing propriety, levelling mens Estats, or making all things common'.[70] In their last *Agreement*, they distance themselves from levelling practices and from 'levell[ing] mens Estates, destroy[ing] Propriety, or mak[ing] all things Common', while also describing any violation of their *Agreement* as riotous. Further, they recommend that anyone found guilty of disrupting elections of parliamentarians should 'incurr the penalty of a Riot'.[71]

Pamphlets and newsbooks of the day frequently cited the *Agreement* of which 20,000 copies were printed. Despite its professions of peace-making and its measured tone, the document was rewritten by the crisis-ridden events that coincided with its appearance and thus greatly impacted its initial reception. The imprisoned Lilburne and Overton continued their protest to Fairfax from the Tower, while William Thompson outlined the grievances of the soldiers in a manifesto, titled *Englands Standard Advanced* (6 May 1649), which included the *Agreement*. Thompson reminds the reader about the subtitle of the *Agreement* as 'a Peace offering', while explaining that his 'annexing' of the document to *Englands Standard Advanced*

---

68   *The Moderate*, 29 April 1649, n. 42 (24 April–1 May 1649), p. 483.

69   Whitelocke, *Memorials of the English Affairs*, pp. 383r, 383v.

70   [William Walwyn], *To the Right Honorable, The Commons of England … The humble Petition of divers wel affected Persons inhabiting the City of London…*, *Leveller Manifestoes*, ed. Wolfe, 288; Maurice Goldsmith, 'Levelling by Sword, Spade and Word: Radical Egalitarianism in the English Revolution', in Colin James, Nalyn Newitt and Stephen Roberts eds, *Politics and People in Revolutionary England: Essays in Honour of Ivan Roots* (Oxford: Blackwell, 1986), p. 74.

71   *An Agreement of the Free People of England*, in Wolfe ed., *Leveller Manifestoes*, p. 409.

confirmed his resolve to see the terms of the Levellers' document enacted.[72] Thompson's textual revolt was following by yet another mutiny and, in reaction, the issuing on 14 May of a new parliamentary act that would see mutineers charged with treason.

Paper protests, notably the *Agreement of the Free People,* were not left unpunished by the Rump. On 12 October, Parliament ordered the prosecution of Lilburne for the treacherous act of having written, published and circulated among the soldiers various pamphlets designed to *'raise force against the present Government, and for the subversion and alteration of it'.*[73] His trial was held before a jury of London citizens upon Lilburne's insistence that the doors of the courtroom be opened to the public. The famous partisan account, *The Triall, of Lieut. Collonell John Lilburne,* which publicised the proceedings widely, draws attention to the crowds in attendance and to the courtroom readings of such tracts as *An impeachment of high Treason against Oliver Cromwell, and his Son in Law* Henry Ireton, *The Preparative to the hue and cry after* Sir Arthur Haslerigge, the *Apprentices Outcry,* and *The legall fundamentall Liberties of the people of England revived.* Most critical was *The Agreement of the People,* which allegedly 'strikes ... at the very root of all Government,'.[74] Acknowledging that writing could incite readers to rebellion, and specifically against the Council of State, Lilburne's accusers unwittingly acknowledged the power of print and petitioning.

Lilburne's popularity and his success at crowd management threatened the court officials, who again cited the seditious nature of the May 1649 *Agreement.* 'Mr. *Lilburn* hath been very free in his writing, in his speaking, in his printing, and it now riseth in judgment against him, and the law must now give him his due', the prosecution declared in judging Lilburne's tract as a provocation to war. 'This Agreement', the prosecution charged, 'shall be the Center, the Banner, and the waved Standard unto which they shall flock.' Throughout the trial, Lilburne continually appealed to the jury, which eventually returned a verdict of not guilty. The people packed in the courtroom reportedly shouted acclamations for half an hour, to the shame of the judges.[75]

Riots and the Revolution

In 'Treason and Rebellion', a study concentrating largely on the sixteenth century, Andrew Hadfield argues that most forms of resistance to authority were justified by recourse to religion.[76] Hadfield's observation applies as well to later social movements: the revolutionary ideas published in the tracts of dissenters, for example, in the oft-quoted words of Acts 17:6, supported 'a world turned upside down'. The biblical and religious bases for protests were tied in the early modern era to socio-political engagement, fuelled by textual production, a key element in the repertoire of contention. Whitelocke discusses the 'slid' into Civil War, triggered by 'Paper Combates, by Declarations, Remonstrances, Protestations, Votes, Messages, Answers and Replies'.[77] His testimony suggests not only that there was greater

---

[72]   *Englands Standard Advanced, a Declaration from M. Will. Thompson and the oppressed People of this nation ...* (6 May 1649), p. 2.
[73]   *The Triall, of Lieut. Collonell John Lilburne .... Being exactly pen'd and taken in short hand, as it was possible to be done in such a croud and noyes ... that so matter of Fact, as it was there declared, might truly come to publick view* (London, 1649), p. 67.
[74]   Ibid., pp. 92ff., 102.
[75]   Ibid., pp. 144, 144, 151.
[76]   Andrew Hadfield, 'Treason and Rebellion', in Donna B. Hamilton ed., *A Concise Companion to English Renaissance Literature* (Oxford: Blackwell, 2006), p. 180.
[77]   Whitelocke, *Memorials of English Affairs,* p. 58.

interest in public representation, but also that there were more opportunities for critical inquiry, intervention, reaction and protestation by a public whose presence was also made known in the marketplace of print. The mention of 'Paper Combates' thus invites a re-evaluation of the concept and constitution of the public sphere and participation therein.

The interaction of literature, writers and the court of public opinion produced a culture of debate and political dissent, and a war of words that accompanied the Civil War. A consideration of the printed protests and of the category of the popular exposes more dramatic tensions and ruptures than revisionists have allowed in constructing a unified picture of seventeenth-century history. Pamphlets and popular literature demonstrate how texts imagine, generate and respond to audiences, which were liberated into critical consciousness and courted by authorities in various spheres. Investigations of the textual revolts that accompanied rioting call for a reassessment of Civil War historiography; indeed a strong case can be made for the war as a 'grand rebellion'. There is equally compelling evidence, however, that the troubled times of the mid-seventeenth century created the conditions for the rise of popular movements – radical and conservative – and for revolts, petitioning, paper-wars and collective protests in ways that the pre-Civil War era of strict censorship could not.[78]

Select Bibliography

Davis, Natalie Zemon, *Society and Culture in Early Modern France*. Stanford: Stanford University Press, 1975.

Dimmock, Matthew, and Andrew Hadfield eds, *Literature and Popular Culture in Early Modern England*. Burlington, VT: Ashgate, 2009.

Goldsmith, Maurice, 'Levelling by Sword, Spade and Word: Radical Egalitarianism in the English Revolution', in Colin James, Nalyn Newitt and Stephen Roberts eds, *Politics and People in Revolutionary England: Essays in Honour of Ivan Roots*. Oxford: Blackwell, 1986, pp. 65–80.

Hadfield, Andrew, 'Treason and Rebellion', in Donna B. Hamilton ed., *A Concise Companion to English Renaissance Literature*. Oxford: Blackwell, 2006, pp. 180–99.

Hill, Christopher, *The World Turned Upside Down: Radical Ideas during the English Revolution*. London: Temple Smith, 1972.

Hindle, Steve, 'Crime and Popular Protest', in Barry Coward ed., *A Companion to Stuart Britain*. Oxford: Blackwell, 2003, pp. 130–47.

Lindley, Keith, *Fenland Riots and the English Revolution*. London: Heinemann Educational Books, 1982.

Manning, Roger B., *Village Revolts: Social Protest and Popular Disturbances in England, 1509–1640*. Oxford: Clarendon Press, 1988.

Morrill, J.S., *Cheshire 1630–1660: County Government and Society during the 'English Revolution'*. Oxford: Clarendon Press, 1974.

Sharp, Buchanan, *In Contempt of All Authority: Rural Artisans and Riot in the West of England, 1586–1660*. Berkeley and Los Angeles: University of California Press, 1980.

Slack, Paul ed., *Rebellion, Popular Protest and the Social Order in Early Modern England*. Cambridge: Cambridge University Press, 1984.

Snow, David A., Sarah A. Soule and Hanspeter Kriesi eds, *The Blackwell Companion to Social Movements*. Oxford: Blackwell, 2004.

---

[78] On this point, see also Wood, *Riot, Rebellion and Popular Politics*, p. 139.

Tilly, Charles, *The Politics of Collective Violence*. Cambridge: Cambridge University Press, 2003.

Underdown, David, *Revel, Riot and Rebellion: Popular Politics and Culture in England 1603–1660*. Oxford: Clarendon Press, 1985.

Walter, John, *Crowds and Popular Politics in Early Modern England*. Manchester: Manchester University Press, 2006.

Wood, Andy, *Riot, Rebellion and Popular Politics in Early Modern England*. New York: Palgrave, 2002.

Time

Neil Rhodes

The first computer to be so called was a calculator for reckoning time, devised in the early eighth century by the Venerable Bede at the Northumbrian monastic outposts of Jarrow and Wearmouth where he spent his entire life. The *computus* was a system for determining the date of Easter, crucial in every sense of the word. Bede's calculations were based on the tables produced in the third century by Dionysius Exiguus, Bishop of Alexandria (and later Pope), and he recorded his method first in a short work, *Liber de temporibus*, written in 703, and then in a longer version called *De Temporum ratione* ('On the reckoning of time') in 725. It was the second of these that was widely influential, and over a hundred copies of Bede's work have been located at libraries throughout Europe.[1] At the start of the early modern period the Dionysius/Bede system was standard, but in time all things must pass, including the method of its own computation, and by the late sixteenth century it became clear that the old calendar was out by 11 days. In 1582 Pope Gregory initiated a new calendar, a move that brought much popular consternation, since those days were suddenly 'lost' as the date jumped forward in order to realign it with the solar year. The new calendar was resisted by Protestant countries and the European year remained unsynchronised until the eighteenth century. When England finally adopted the Gregorian calendar in 1752 it was greeted with perhaps even greater popular protest than it had been elsewhere in Europe nearly two centuries before, since the spread of basic literacy and numeracy meant that ordinary people were now more attuned to the demarcations of calendar time.

Popular opposition to calendar change in the early modern period is quite understandable. Procrastination may be the thief of time, but that is a rather literary and abstract maxim, and the reverse is much easier to grasp: if the year is brought forward by 11 days it is fairly obvious that you will lose 11 days of your life, and life is short enough in the first place – even shorter if you are poor. What this illustrates is the discrepancy in the perception of time between the educated classes and the populace. Official or institutionalised time based on mathematical calculations, whether those of Bede in Jarrow or the Pope in Rome was largely irrelevant to the common man and woman. For example, it is well known that in the early modern period the New Year officially began on 25 March, but this was significant mainly for written records, and as a popular festival New Year was celebrated on 1 January; in Scotland, Hogmanay was always on 31 December. Writing in the early fifteenth century, the poet John Lydgate says that he has tucked himself up in bed against the cold 'whan of Ianuarye/Ther be kalendes of the new yere', while at the end of the sixteenth century Thomas Pie makes clear that the new year was generally understood to be on 'the first day of *Ianuarie*: which we in this realme and other countries doe commonly call new yeares

---

[1]   See Bede, *The Reckoning of Time*, trans. Faith Wallis (Liverpool: Liverpool University Press, 1999); David Ewing Duncan, *The Calendar* (London: Fourth Estate, 1998), p. 121.

day; because the late Astronomers begin their new yeare there: as our yearly Almanackes doe witnesse'.[2] In the 'generall argument' of *The Shepheardes Calender* (1579) Spenser writes that though it is 'stoutely mainteyned with stronge reasons of the learned, that the yeare beginneth in March', he will start with January because 'it fittest according to the simplicitie of commen understanding, to begin with Ianuarie'.[3] Though not itself, of course, a 'popular' calendar, this is wholly in keeping with the poem's affectation of rusticity and commonness.

But however the calendar was organised, for uneducated people time would be marked by the succession of days and nights and the movement of the seasons.[4] The point is obvious, but we need to imagine how very much more closely life was attuned to and determined by the physical facts of sunlight and darkness, summer warmth and winter cold, accompanied by longer and shorter daylight hours. At nighttime the only source of light would be the small, naked flame of a candle – stinking tallow for most people, rather than the more expensive wax. The intensity of the darkness was an image of hell itself, as Thomas Nashe vividly records in *The Terrors of the Night* (a work that may have been a source for some of the night scenes in *Macbeth*):

> God would have made all day and no night, if it had not been to put us in minde,
> there is a Hell as well as a Heaven ... The only peace of minde that the divell hath is
> dispaire, wherefore wee that live in his nightly kingdome of darknes, must needs taste
> some disquiet.[5]

Unlike hell, however, nighttime and winter are not eternal. Hundreds of Elizabethan songs and lyrics reflect the movement of the seasons, celebrating the arrival of spring in terms that may strike the modern reader as banal. But the association of love and springtime in a song such as 'It was a lover and his lass' isn't just a tired literary convention: 'sweet lovers love the spring' because it offers possibilities for sex that are not available in the winter, when people are confined to communal indoor space.[6] The impact of the seasons on every aspect of life is why the two songs at the end of *Love's Labour's Lost* ('When daisies pied and violets blue' and 'When icicles hang by the wall' (5.2.869, 887))[7] represent the most perfect expression of the play's themes of love and death. The intimate relationship between time and the environment in the early modern period meant that for everyone, but especially for ordinary people, the movement of time was a physical experience.

That movement was also demarcated in very much simpler and more immediate ways than those of Bede's *computus*, most obviously by the sound of bells. The first bells were supposed to have been made at the Italian town of Nola in Campania (hence the term

---

[2]   John Lydgate, *The Temple of Glas* (Westminster: William Caxton, 1577?), p. 1; Thomas Pie, *An Hourglasse* (London: John Wolfe, 1597), p. 89.

[3]   Edmund Spenser, *The Shorter Poems*, ed. Richard A. McCabe (London: Penguin, 1999), pp. 33–4.

[4]   For my own account of what constitutes 'popular culture' see the introduction to Stuart Gillespie and Neil Rhodes eds, *Shakespeare and Elizabethan Popular Culture* (London: Arden Shakespeare, 2006), pp. 1–12; but see also the very useful analysis by Tim Harris, 'Problematising Popular Culture', in Tim Harris ed., *Popular Culture in England, c. 1500–1850* (London: Palgrave Macmillan, 1995), pp. 1–27. In the present chapter I use the terms 'common' and 'ordinary' people to refer to the uneducated populace.

[5]   *The Works of Thomas Nashe*, ed. R.B. McKerrow, rev. F.P. Wilson (Oxford: Blackwell, 1958); Ann Pasternak Slater, '*Macbeth* and The Terrors of the Night', *Essays in Criticism* 28 (1978), 112–28; see also the excellent study by A. Roger Ekirch, *At Day's Close: A History of Nighttime* (London: Weidenfeld and Nicholson, 2005).

[6]   'It Was a Lover and His Lass', in Ross W. Duffin, *Shakespeare's Songbook* (New York: W.W. Norton, 2004), pp. 221–3.

[7]   All references to Shakespeare are to Stephen Greenblatt, Walter Cohen, Jean E. Howard and Katharine Eisaman Maus eds, *The Norton Shakespeare: Based on the Oxford Edition* (New York: W.W. Norton, 1997).

'Campanola bells') and they then spread to monasteries. In the middle ages monastery bells tolled the canonical hours of prayer, imprinting church time on the consciousness of the labourer in the fields. Eventually, every parish had its bell, marking the time of church services. At first, the points at which bells were rung were determined by water clocks, but the end of the middle ages saw the coming of the mechanical clock, and with it a huge shift in the popular consciousness of time. The first public clock in England was made by Italians in London and set up in the great Tower of Windsor Castle in 1353. The first public clock in London itself appeared at the Palace of Westminster in the following decade.[8] By the sixteenth century public clocks had become commonplace in small towns throughout England and bells were synchronised accordingly. So time could now be both heard and seen by ordinary people, and though hearing and seeing are also physical experiences, the fact that this had been brought about by man-made devices tended to make time seem more remote and abstract, less part of nature and more the product of officialdom.

From the large mechanical clocks, which represented the public face (and sound) of time to all and sundry, evolved the small, personalised time-keeping device, the watch. The transition was brought about by the invention of the spring drive in the fourteenth century, which made possible the portable domestic clock, and it was then only a matter of time, as it were, before it was realised that a small clock might be worn about the person. Craftsmen in southern Germany were at the forefront of this development, and the first person to make one of these miniature clocks 'carried on the breast or in the purse' was said to be Peter Henlein of Nuremberg.[9] The earliest known dated watch, made of iron, was produced by his contemporary Caspar Werner in 1548. The privatisation of time took it further away from the sphere of popular culture but it was consonant with the new emphasis on the consciousness and experience of the individual that came with Protestantism.

This new sense of time was also associated with a Protestant work ethic that regulated the hours of the day in order to maximise productivity.[10] It was Protestantism, too, that did away with many of the church festivals and holidays, ostensibly because of their pagan associations, but also for economic reasons. The Reformation impacted on people's sense of time in relation both to the order of the day and the order of the year. The first is the realm of the clock, the second the realm of the calendar.

The institutional and popular perceptions of time at the level of the annual cycle do, however, come together in the context of the liturgical year. Determining the dates of the movable feasts of the Church may have been an operation of huge mathematical complexity, but its operations affected everyone. Moreover, the structure of the Church year was superimposed on the older seasonal rituals and festivities, so it represented a 'deep' time that was understood to be part of nature rather than an artificial construct.[11] Deep time is lunar rather than solar, and it is the lunar calendar that determines the various festivals assimilated by the Church. The solar calendar, on the other hand, represented 'official' time. Yet this distinction can be misleading if we start to use it to separate the perception of time

---

[8]   Gerhard Dohrn-van Rossum, *History of the Hour: Clocks and Modern Temporal Orders*, trans. Thomas Dunlap (Chicago: University of Chicago Press, 1996) pp. 131, 135.

[9]   See David S. Landes, *Revolution in Time: Clocks and the Making of the Modern World* (rev. ed., New York: Viking, 2000), pp. 86–7; Kristen Lippincott with Umberto Eco, E.H. Gombrich and others, *The Story of Time* (London: Merrell Holberton, 1999), p. 141.

[10]   On Protestantism and the mechanical clock see William Shakespeare, *The Sonnets and A Lover's Complaint*, ed. John Kerrigan (London: Penguin, 1986), pp. 35–7.

[11]   On the evolution of the pagan calendar to its Christian version see E.K. Chambers, *The Mediaeval Stage* (2 vols, Oxford, 1903), vol. 1, pp. 228–73. For a comparative calendar based on Chambers's work see Glynne Wickham, 'Drama of the Christian Calendar', in *Early English Stages: 1300–1600* (3 vols, London, 1959–72), vol. 3, pp. 23–47; 258–63.

in popular culture from its institutionalised record. The sun shines on all alike and its daily and annual cycles (it was the sun that moved, of course, not the earth) presented the most direct and physically apprehensible experience of the passage of time. The solar calendar is also responsible for the division of the year into two halves, marked by the midwinter and midsummer solstices, an arrangement which was universally understood. The first half of the year, from 23 December to 22 June, was the festive and ritualistic half, containing the 12 days of Christmas, Shrovetide (February/March), Easter (March/April) and Corpus Christi (May/June).[12] The second half of the year was dominated by the demands of labour and other economic activity and had its own festivals, which were linked to the world of work rather than being ritualistic. In the country these were agricultural and included sheep-shearing (late June), rush-bearing (mid-July) and harvest home (late August/early September); in the towns there were the fairs of St Bartholomew (August), St Giles (September), St Luke (October) and in London the Lord Mayor's Show (November). The last is at the furthest remove from deep time, since it marks the beginning and end of a term of office and is therefore purely institutional.

We can see, then, that the lunar and solar calendars intersect in the construction of time as an annual cycle of festivals, with the lunar calendar dominating the first half of the year and the solar calendar the second. In both halves, and whether ritualistic or economic, festivals act as reference points in a world of flux: they are days in the year (movable in the first half and fixed in the second) that could be anticipated and remembered and used to frame events in the life of the individual and the experience of the community. Their function in communal experience finds cultural expression in the popular drama, and while this has been very thoroughly studied, it is worth remembering here that festive form in drama is rooted in the popular calendar and thus in the popular perception of time. The Mystery plays were known from the middle ages to the end of the seventeenth century as the Corpus Christi plays; although not necessarily performed on the day itself, the plays were specifically associated with the feast of Corpus Christi, which moved between 21 May and 24 June, or between Whitsun and Midsummer.[13] These pageants compressed the Bible story, and therefore the whole of history, into the confines of a single day, and in the final scene of the Last Judgement looked forward to the promise of salvation and the end of time itself. In the secular drama the marriage of pagan and Christian ritual is evident in motifs derived from the battles between Carnival and Lent, which inform plays such as the two parts of *Henry IV*. Here, the progress of the Church year towards Easter is figured as a conflict between a time of plenty and a time of abstinence. European carnival is English Shrovetide, and Shrovetide mayhem surfaces from the ritualistic structures of deep time in urban holidays for the working classes. The popular drama, Dekker's *The Shoemaker's Holiday* (1599) commemorates this kind of occasion, though replacing the traditional apprentice boys' riots with a more emollient picture of master–servant harmony. In the other world of work, that of agricultural labour, harvest home was celebrated in dramatic entertainments such as Nashe's *Summer's Last Will and Testament* (1592), even if that play is more elegy than celebration as the summer dies in offering up its bounty.[14] Structured by seasonal change and the feast days of the Church, time was experienced in the popular imagination as a long

---

[12]   On the festive year see François Laroque, *Shakespeare's Festive World: Elizabethan Seasonal Entertainment and the Professional Stage*, trans. Janet Lloyd (Cambridge: Cambridge University Press, 1991), pp. 75–92.

[13]   See Helen Cooper, 'Shakespeare and the Mystery Plays', in Gillespie and Rhodes eds, *Shakespeare and Elizabethan Popular Culture*, pp. 18–41.

[14]   Like many other Elizabethan works, most notably Spenser's *The Shepheardes Calender*, Nashe's play transfers motifs from popular culture into a more elite context. *The Works of Thomas Nashe*, ed. R.B. McKerrow, rev. F.P. Wilson (Oxford: Basil Blackwell, 1958), III, pp. 230–95.

passage of survival, through penury and occasional plenty, ending always in death, but with the promise of something else in the time beyond time.

Festive form gives a social dimension to time. To understand how an individual might have tried to make sense of the passing of time we can turn to a form which literary scholars, at least in English, have been much less ready to study, but which is an indisputable part of the fabric of popular culture. This is the proverb or saying. Although they are obviously communal expressions, since they are part of a shared oral culture, sayings are not *only* communal in the way that festive forms are. The sophisticated modern reader may feel that the proverbial is banal and by its very nature not individualistic, yet in any age it is part of the experience of the individual as he or she journeys through life to discover for themselves the truth of many of these oak-aged nostrums. For that reason it may be arbitrary to assign any group of proverbs to the early modern period, but modern collections do certain reveal clusters in the sixteenth century: 'take time while time comes, lest time will steal away'; 'time and tide stays for no man'; 'time lost we cannot recall'; 'times change and we change with them'.[15] Reflections of this kind crop up again and again in the popular drama and are proffered as folk wisdom of general application, yet each might be understood by individuals as having a personal resonance in their own experience. Such reflections are often admonitory or rueful, but the passage of time was not always represented negatively. The stock of proverb lore was not and could not be consistent and it was recognised that proverbs might contradict each other, as Nicholas Breton's *The Crossing of Proverbs* (1616) demonstrates.[16] In the case of time, while it was universally acknowledged that 'time devours (or "consumes", or "wears out") all things', it was equally agreed that 'time tries all things', that 'time cures (or "heals") all things' and that 'time reveals (or "discloses") all things'. The last saying is the belief that underpins romance, which is one of the most enduringly popular fictional forms in prose, poetry and drama, and the genre in which Shakespeare decided to end up.

Festive form and oral tradition are indisputably popular contexts for the understanding of time in early modern England, but at least one class of printed book also falls into that category, though it came in up-market as well as down-market versions. This is the almanac, which represents the single most important record of how time was packaged, as it were, for sixteenth- and seventeenth-century men and women. In terms of volume the almanac was almost certainly the most popular print publication after the Bible throughout the early modern period. Printed almanacs survive from the late fifteenth century, but they really started to take off as mass-market publications in the second half of the sixteenth century and were published in extraordinary numbers through to about 1700.[17] So popular were they, and the demand so predictable, that the Stationers' Company closely guarded their patent privilege, as it did for bibles. By the early seventeenth century the form of the almanac had become so familiar that parodies appeared, such as Dekker's *The Raven's Almanac* (1609) and

[15]   See M.P. Tilley, *A Dictionary of Proverbs in England in the Sixteenth and Seventeenth Centuries* (Ann Arbor: University of Michigan Press); R.W. Dent, *Proverbial Language in English Drama exclusive of Shakespeare, 1495–1616* (Berkeley and Los Angeles: University of California Press, 1984); Adam Fox, 'Proverbial Wisdom', in *Oral and Literate Culture in England, 1500–1700* (Oxford: Oxford University Press, 2000), pp. 112–72.

[16]   Nicholas Breton, *Crossing of Proverbs: crosse-answers and crosse-humours* (London: John Wright, 1616).

[17]   See especially Bernard Capp, *Astrology and the Popular Press: English Almanacs, 1500–1800* (London: Faber, 1979). The most succinct account of the significance of the almanac within popular culture is Adam Smyth, 'Almanacs and Ideas of Popularity', in Andy Kesson and Emma Smith eds, *The Elizabethan Top Ten* (Farnham: Ashgate, 2013), pp. 125–34.

The Owl's Almanac (1618), which is probably by Middleton.[18] Almanacs are the forerunners of the modern diary, but with an astrological element, so they combine a prognostication with a calendar for the coming year. The almanac formula is essentially a pocket compendium of time with related practical advice on husbandry (when to plant, when to harvest) and communications (tide tables, routes between towns).

Some of the most popular almanacs of the seventeenth century were those produced by Thomas Bretnor and Edward Pond, which were also the models for Dekker and Middleton's parodies. And while these were more down-market publications than the kind of almanac compiled in the Elizabethan period by Leonard and Thomas Digges (both father and son were serious mathematicians), they nevertheless offer their purchasers fairly elaborate systems for the computation of time. Indeed, 'computation' is a standard piece of almanac terminology and by the seventeenth century not something that is offered only to a learned elite. Arthur Hopton, for example, aimed to provide 'a new, easie, and most exact Computation of Time', having 'observed the inconveniences that happened to the vulgar wits, and meane capacities, in the calculation of the expiration of time, by such Rules and Computations as be now extant'.[19] Hopton's system may be simplified, but it still assumes that 'vulgar wits' will want to do their own calculations, which is a far cry from the days of Bede's *computus*, when such knowledge was certainly not accessible to 'meane capacities'. So almanacs offered a set of tools for calculating time organised in a standard formula, which included the 'epact' (the number of days that constitutes the excess of the solar over the lunar year); the 'dominical letter' (the letter used to denote the Sundays in a particular year); and the 'Roman Indiction' (a 15-year cycle instituted by the Emperor Constantine). This was followed by a calendar and the 'four quarters' of the year. And though almanacs all had a standard template, individual almanac-makers sometimes offered special features to distinguish their products: Edward Pond, for example, offered a lecture on how to tell the time by the moon, which is parodied in Middleton's account of the 'moon-clock' in *The Owl's Almanac*.[20]

There was, however, one specific point on which almanacs differed, and this was a point of – quite literally – cosmic proportions. Should the calculations for time be based on a geocentric or heliocentric model of the universe? The first appearance of the Copernican system in an almanac comes as early as 1576, when Thomas Digges revised his father's almanac by substituting a new diagram of the solar system, showing 'that the Earth resteth not in the Center of the whole world, but onely in the center of this our mortall world . . . [and] is caried yearely rounde aboute the sunne'.[21] Such a momentous change in the perception of the world obviously took a long time to sink in, as even a highly learned man such as John Donne was still referring to 'the new philosophy' in 1624.[22] Some almanacs continued to use the old Ptolemaic model after 1576, while others changed to the Copernican system. But even here it is not easy to make a distinction between 'popular' and more up-market kinds of almanac. Thomas Bretnor's almanacs, published in the first two decades

---

[18] Thomas Dekker, *The Ravens Almanacke* (London: Thomas Archer, 1609); Anon., *The Owles Almanacke* (London: Laurence Lisle, 1618).

[19] Arthur Hopton, *A Concordancy of Yeares* (London: Thomas Adams, 1615), sig. A3v.

[20] See *The Owl's Almanac*, ed. Neil Rhodes in Thomas Middleton, *The Collected Works*, ed. Gary Taylor and John Lavagnino (Oxford: Clarendon Press, 2007), p. 1279.

[21] Leonard and Thomas Digges, *A Prognostication Everlasting* (London: Thomas Marsh, 1576), M1r, STC 435.47, image 46.

[22] John Donne, *Devotions upon Emergent Occasions*, ed. Anthony Raspa (New York: Oxford University Press, 1987), p. 111 (Meditation 21).

of the seventeenth century, certainly fall into the 'popular' category, but they adopted the heliocentric model of the universe.[23]

It was also Bretnor's almanacs that provided Middleton with the principal model for his parodic work, *The Owl's Almanac*, which adds another dimension to the perception of time in early modern popular culture. By the seventeenth century print had lodged the main features of the almanac so firmly in popular consciousness that they had become subjects of mockery. The 'computation of time', for example, referred not only to calendar reckoning by the 'epact' and the 'dominical letter' and so forth, but to a timetable of history. This was a sort of countdown of major events from Adam to the present day, which was included by Bretnor and other almanac makers. The Owl's computation begins: 'since the first lie was told is (as I remember) 5565 years: and that was by all computation in Adam's time, but now in these days men and women lie downright'.[24] He follows it up with a record of memorable events such as the first appearance of tobacco and oranges, the death of the old bear, George Stone, and the year that the dancing horse stood on the top of St Paul's. Another feature of the almanac parodied by the Owl is the list of 'good days' and 'bad days' that was an indispensable part of the prognostication for the coming year. Among the Owl's 'good days' are 'Not one whore in all of Westminster' on the first of the month and 'Bob for eels now or never' on the 18th; among the bad days, 'He hunts close, yet has lost his hare' on the 19th and 'My maid is poisoned with a pudding' on the 22nd.[25] Parts of Middleton's satire are extremely funny, and it also offers a fascinating perspective on the way in which popular culture mediates popular perceptions of time. The printed almanac had provided the man or woman in the street with a ready reckoner to plan for the year ahead, but Middleton adds a further layer of sophistication as proverbially styled mock advice mingles with what look like Pooteresque diary entries and knowing reflections on the way of the world.

Popular culture transformed people's understanding of time by providing them with the equipment to chart the progress of their own lives, to anticipate the year to come and remember the time past, in relation to a conveniently packaged, objective structure that could be consulted on a daily basis. The enhanced perception of time framed by the new world of print, and especially by the almanac, left its mark on a wide range of imaginative literature beyond the sophisticated, urban prose satire of a writer such as Thomas Middleton. The literary genre that offers perhaps the most interesting engagement with almanacs and calendars, and also with popular culture in this period, is pastoral. The new Elizabethan poetry announced itself in 1579 with the publication of a pastoral poem constructed as a calendar. Spenser's *The Shephearde's Calender* takes its name from a rudimentary kind of almanac, which in printed form dates back to the very beginning of the sixteenth century. *The Kalendar of the Shyppars* was translated into Scots from a French original and published at Paris in 1503. The 'corrupte englysshe' of this version was then revised and published by Pynson in London three years later.[26] Ten editions of this publication appear at intervals throughout the sixteenth century prior to the printing of Spenser's poem. The original *Kalender* is undoubtedly part of popular culture and contains advice on husbandry, the zodiacal man, which provided the astrological basis for the predictions for the coming year and gloomy reminders that we are all going to die. Spenser's poem, on the other hand, is an elite publication and it plays numerological games with the calendar, as do later poems of Spenser's such as the *Amoretti*, which is constructed to represent the 52 weeks of the year and the *Epithalamion*, which represents the 365 days. But while Spenser's work cannot

---

[23]   Capp, *Astrology and the Popular Press*, pp. 191–2.
[24]   *The Owls Almanac*, pp. 1277–8.
[25]   Ibid., p. 1302.
[26]   *The Kalendar of Shepherdes* (London: Richard Pynson, 1506), STC 22408, image 2.

be regarded as 'popular', it nonetheless advertises its roots in the English countryside and authenticates itself in terms of rusticity and antiquity: the tunes of 'those auncient Poetes', E. K. writes, 'as thinking them fittest for such rusticall rudenesse of shepheards ... bring great grace and, as one would say, auctoritie to the verse'.[27] The calendrical framework of Spenser's pastoral marries high status poetic form with the primitive.

There are other ways in which almanac and pastoral engage in the sixteenth century. The zodiacal man was a hardy perennial of these publications, like the 'computation of time' and the 'good days and bad days'. It takes the form of a diagram showing a human figure and the 12 signs of the zodiac which govern its various parts, with indicator lines connecting the human body to the celestial bodies. It was also the subject of a work that arguably falls a little more clearly into the category of 'popular culture' than anything by Spenser. This is Barnabe Googe's translation of Palingenius's poem, *Zodiacus vitae*. Written in Italy in the 1530s, the poem offers a general survey of knowledge gathered under the 12 astrological signs. When the Catholic Church placed it on the Index of proscribed books it attracted the attention of Protestants and Googe translated the first three books in 1560, extending this to six books in 1561 and completing the translation as *The Zodiacke of Life* in 1565; there were further editions in 1576 and 1588. The full-text English version gives as its remit on the title page 'the whole compasse of the world' and comes with an elaborate index of topics, one of which is 'Stage of mans life'; the passage to which this refers has the marginal gloss in the 1576 edition, 'The theatre or stage of mans life'.[28] There are, of course, many other possible sources for Jaques's speech 'All the world's a stage' in *As You Like It* (and similar comparisons at *The Merchant* 1.1.77–8 and *Lear* 4.6.176–7), but the attraction of this one is that Palingenius was used as a school text in both Latin and English in Shakespeare's youth.[29] This was the Elizabethan Children's Encyclopaedia or a sixteenth-century version of that improving 1960s publication *Look and Learn*. It is also one of the very few known sources to combine the world as stage theme with that of the seven ages of man.[30]

It is fitting that the most famous speech on time in Shakespeare should occur in a pastoral play. (A chorus figure called 'Time' appears in another of his pastoral plays, *The Winter's Tale*.) Though often used as an elite literary genre, pastoral is also an aspect of popular romance, and it offered a fantasy of timelessness to noble and peasant alike in a world that was all too aware that life was short. In pastoral it is always springtime, its inhabitants are always young and the shepherds have time for love because the sheep look after themselves. Jaques's anthology piece, with its *memento mori* message, is only one element in a play that gently satirises the conventions of pastoral by allowing the time-keeping practices of the modern world to invade ever-land. In this play the timelessness of pastoral romance is turned inside out as Rosalind, disguised as the boy Ganymede, insists that she and Orlando woo by the clock. Her initial chat-up line to him sounds well worn to modern ears: 'I pray you what is't o'clock', i.e. 'have you got the time on you', and Orlando replies reasonably enough by saying 'You should ask me what time o'day. There's no clock in the forest' (3.2.274–6). Undeterred, Rosalind demands that he follow a strict time-keeping regime for the rendezvous in which Orlando is to rehearse his love for her. When he pleads a prior dinner engagement with the Duke, he promises 'By two o'clock I will be with thee again' (4.1.154–5), but as the hour arrives, Rosalind is fretting: 'How say you now? Is it

[27] Spenser, *Shorter Poems*, p. 26.

[28] Marcellus Palingenius Stellatus, *The Zodiake of Life*, trans. Barnabie Googe (London: Raufe Newberie, 1576), p. 194, STC 19151, image 107.

[29] See Foster Watson, *The Zodiacus Vitae of Marcellus Palingenius Stellatus: An Old School-Book* (London: Philip Wellby, 1908), p. 73.

[30] See John Erskine Hankins, *Shakespeare's Derived Imagery* (Kansas: University of Kansas Press, 1953), p. 21.

not past two o'clock. And here much Orlando' (4.3.1–2). This all starts to feel more like the pressurised arrangements of urban dating than eternal spring in the greenwood. Besides, we have already seen that there *is* a clock in the forest: not a public clock, but a personal timepiece or 'dial'. The court fool, Touchstone, has evidently come well equipped for his journey into Arden, as Jaques reports:

> And then he drew a dial from his poke,
> And looking on it with lack-lustre eye
> Says very wisely 'It is ten o'clock.'
> 'Thus we may see', quoth he, 'how the world wags.
> 'Tis but an hour since it was nine,
> And after one hour more will be eleven.
> And so from hour to hour we ripe and ripe,
> And then from hour to hour we rot and rot;
> And thereby hangs a tale.' (2.7.20–8)

The new *memento mori* is not a skull, but a watch. In *As You Like It* the routines of modern life have caught up with the pastoral world, and the intimations of mortality that haunt all pastoral are signalled by the moving dial of mechanically ordered time.

Elsewhere in early modern literature we can find examples of the almanac–pastoral mix in which both forms blend into something that is neither one nor the other, yet retains features of both. Nicholas Breton's *Fantasticks* was entered in the Stationers Register in 1604, though it was not actually published until 1626. Breton was part of Spenser's circle, but this is a light piece of popular prose aimed firmly at middle-class taste. What Breton offers is a calendar illustrated with word-pictures, a literary version of the medieval Book of Hours. Each month of the year is given a vignette:

> It is now March, and the Northerne wind dryeth up the Southerne durt ... the Milke-mayd with her best beloved, talke away wearinesse to the Market, and in an honest meaning, kind words do no hurt: the Foot-ball now tryeth the legges of strength, and merry matches continue good fellowship: It is a time of much worke, and tedious to discourse of: but in all I find of it, I thus conclude in it: I hold it the Servant of Nature, and the Schoole-master of Art: the hope of labour, and the Subject of Reason.[31]

Breton's cosy, calendrical panorama of Elizabethan England is the perfect complement to Tillyard's famous 'world picture' with its reassuring vision of an ordered, hierarchical social structure. The smooth passage of the year is followed by a merry progress through the hours of the day:

> It is now the fourth houre, and the Sunne beginnes to send her beames abroad, whose glimmering brightnesse no eye can behold: Now crows the Cocke lustily, and claps his wings for joy of the light, and with his Hennes leaps lightly from his Roust: Now are the Horses at their Chaffe and Provender: the servants at breakfast, the Milk-maid gone to the field, and the spinner at the Wheele: and the Shepheard with his Dog are going toward the Fold: Now the Beggers rousethem out of the Hedges, and begin their morning craft: but if the Constable come, beware the stocks ... I thus conclude of it: I hold it the Messenger of action, and the Watch of Reason.[32]

---

[31] Nicholas Breton, *Fantasticks: serving for a perpetuall prognostication* (London: Francis Williams, 1626), STC 3650, image 8.
[32] Ibid., image 18.

That milk-maid gets everywhere. But then she does have a job to do, which is more than can be said of the beggars, though that does not deter Breton from assimilating them into his fiction of a harmonious timetable in which everyone has a part to play.

Breton's merry England, in which everything happens at its appointed hour and season, is orderly because it is governed by 'Reason'. It is the everyday world, not Arcadia, but the everyday world transformed by 'Reason' into a quasi-Arcadian state of contented bustle. What disrupts all idylls is passion, and through passion time puts on the mask of tragedy. Time is the universal destroyer, which is why Old Father Time is synonymous with Death the mower, reminding us of the biblical warning that all flesh is as grass (1 Peter 1:24), but passion frequently helps to accelerate his operations. Nowhere is this more true than in love tragedy, which is the polar opposite of Arcadian romance.

The most enduringly popular love tragedy from early modern England (as the graffiti on the entirely fictitious Capulet residence in present-day Verona bear witness) is *Romeo and Juliet*, and this is undoubtedly a work in which time is of the essence. The play's chorus tells us that the action will unfold over a bare two hours, and that is generally accepted as the standard running time of performances in the Elizabethan theatre, but nothing else in Shakespeare matches *Romeo and Juliet* for its sense of urgency, cramming the whole of life into 120 minutes of headlong, precipitate emotion. Shakespeare's immediate source for the play, the poem by Arthur Brooke published in 1562, stretches the action over several months, but Shakespeare reduces it to a few days. As Romeo says, after killing Paris at the tomb, it shows us 'a lightning before death' (5.3.90). Romeo's phrase is a proverbial expression, referring to the merry-making of the condemned criminal. We catch this sense earlier in the humour of Mercutio's dying speech. But in a play which is so vividly marked out by its alternations of sunlight and darkness, dusk and dawn, we are more likely to hear an echo of Juliet's premonition that their love is 'Too like the lightning, which doth cease to be/Ere one can say it lightens' (2.1.161–2). And Juliet's 'lightning' is itself echoed in the fragile moment between day and night that the lovers inhabit. They see each other as the dawn, but long for nightfall. Sunrise is life, promise, anticipation – the moment when 'jocund day / Stands tiptoe on the misty mountain tops' (3.5.9–10) – but it is also the moment of parting. In fact, the lovers live almost every minute of the day and night, burning the candle at both ends. Romeo is up before dawn both before and after he meets Juliet, and she sleeps in only when she is feigning death.

This is a play set in an age before the mechanical clock, yet we are aware of time in almost every scene, accelerated or standing still. For Juliet it is '20 year' till she hears back from Romeo the following day about their wedding arrangements; in the morning, three hours become an eternity as she waits from 9 o'clock (the time is precise) for the Nurse to return, and then has to endure her deliberate procrastinations as she holds back the longed-for message. When Paris later tells Capulet that the day is Monday, the older man thinks that Wednesday is too soon for a wedding and suggests Thursday instead: 'Do you like this haste?', he asks his daughter's suitor (3.4.22). But by then Juliet is already married, a 'three-hours wife', as she calls herself on hearing of Tybalt's death from the Nurse (3.2.99). Everything in the play happens at speed. In the short first quarto of 1597 some of the lyrical passages are stripped out (Juliet's part is reduced by 40 per cent), making the action even more rushed and intense. The stage directions in Q1 indicate the pace: in the scene at Friar Laurence's cell we have 'Enter Juliet, somewhat fast, and embraceth Romeo' (scene 9) and a little later, 'Enter Nurse hastily' (scene 14), after Romeo has shinned down a rope-ladder from Juliet's window.[33]

---

[33] *The First Quarto of Romeo and Juliet*, ed. Lukas Erne (Cambridge: Cambridge University Press, 2007), pp. 98, 119.

In the more familiar version of the text, the sublime poetry allows the frenetic pace of the action on occasion to be momentarily suspended, but our experience of time is manipulated in other ways too. For the lovers time is measured in terms of hours, of day or night, but these are framed within the much longer perspectives of the older generation. The Nurse's wonderfully digressive speech in, 'On Lammas Eve at night shall she be fourteen' (1.3.17–48), maps the whole of Juliet's short life onto the old liturgical calendar, as well as taking in memorable events such as the earthquake of 11 years back and reminiscences of her own dead husband. The speech helps to underline the brevity and intensity of the few days that Romeo and Juliet share at the same time as it reminds us that this is also a play about coming of age. For Juliet this moment cannot come too soon. In her most passionate speech, 'Gallop apace, you fiery-footed steeds' (3.2.1–31), she begs the mythical charioteer of the sun to bring it on: 'Come night, come Romeo, come thou day in night'. In contrast, the perspectives of her father's generation seem almost endless: Capulet says to his cousin that it is 25 years 'Come Pentecost' since they last had a masque (1.5.34). This telescoping of time shows us the lives that the young people will never have. Love comes, and death comes, too soon. And not just for the lovers, for by the end of the play all the young men are dead – Mercutio, Tybalt and Paris, as well as Romeo.

The movements of time, in hours or years, radiate through the poetry of the play, while at the level of plot bad timing is at the core of the tragedy. Because Romeo does not receive Father Laurence's message in time, he arrives at the tomb believing Juliet to be dead. The lovers never see each other alive again after their night of consummation, for when Juliet wakes from her drugged sleep Romeo has already killed himself. The happy ending of Nahum Tate's *King Lear* is well known, but for a century and a half the ending of *Romeo and Juliet* was also deemed too painful to stage. From the late seventeenth century audiences were given, first, Otway's radical adaptation, in which the lovers were allowed some last moments together, and then, from 1748 through into the nineteenth century, Garrick's version, which restored most of Shakespeare's text but kept that brief, final reunion.[34] Friar Laurence bears a heavy responsibility for the fate of the lovers, but time's other agent in the play, the Nurse, also has a major part. The expansion of her character is one of Shakespeare's principal additions to the story told in Brooke's poem. Together, these vital subsidiary roles of Nurse and Priest remind us of the brevity of all our lives, the one bringing us into the world and the other seeing us out.

Romeo and Juliet combines clock time and calendar time and compresses them into theatre time. The 'wooden O' reduced the world to the confines of a platform stage, and its 'two hours' traffic' reduced lives to the compass of a short afternoon, bringing with it intimations of mortality. Especially in late season when the light started to fade in the final act.

Select Bibliography

Bede, *The Reckoning of Time*, trans. Faith Wallis. Liverpool: Liverpool University Press, 1999.

Capp, Bernard, *Astrology and the Popular Press: English Almanacs, 1500–1800*. London: Faber, 1979.

Cipolla, Carlo M., *Clocks and Culture: 1300–1700*. London: Collins, 1967.

Dohrn-van Rossum, Gerhard, *History of the Hour: Clocks and Modern Temporal Orders*, trans. Thomas Dunlap. Chicago: University of Chicago Press, 1996.

---

[34] See *Romeo and Juliet*, ed. G. Blakemore Evans (updated edition, Cambridge: Cambridge University Press, 2003), pp. 35–8.

Duncan, David Ewing, *The Calendar*. London: Fourth Estate, 1998.

Ekirch, A. Roger, *At Day's Close: A History of Nighttime*. London: Weidenfeld and Nicholson, 2005.

Kerrigan, John, 'Introduction', in *William Shakespeare: The Sonnets and A Lover's Complaint*. London: Penguin, 1986, pp. 7–74.

Landes, David S., *Revolution in Time: Clocks and the Making of the Modern World*. Rev. ed. New York: Viking, 2000.

Laroque, François, *Shakespeare's Festive World: Elizabethan Seasonal Entertainment and the Professional Stage*, trans. Janet Lloyd. Cambridge: Cambridge University Press, 1991.

Leclerq, Jean, 'Experience and Interpretation of Time in the Early Middle Ages', in John R. Sommerfeldt, Larry Syndergaard and Rozanne E. Elder eds, *Studies in Medieval Culture* 5. Kalamazoo, MI: Medieval Institute, 1975, pp. 137–50.

Le Goff, Jacques, *Time, Work and Culture in the Middle Ages*, trans. Arthur Goldhammer. Chicago: University of Chicago Press, 1980.

Lippincott, Kristen, with Umberto Eco, E.H. Gombrich and others, *The Story of Time*. London: Merrell Holberton, 1999.

Smyth, Adam, 'Almanacs and Ideas of Popularity', in Andy Kesson and Emma Smith eds, *The Elizabethan Top Ten*. Farnham: Ashgate, 2013, pp. 125–34.

Wickham, Glynne, 'Drama of the Christian Calendar', in *Early English Stages: 1300–1600*. 3 vols. London, 1959–72, III, 23–47; 258–63.

Property

Ceri Sullivan

This chapter first suggests why property has recently fascinated commentators on early modern culture, and accounts for why debates then and now largely focus on intangible property. Cash and credit are the principal loci for debates about how value is created, held, transferred or destroyed. The chapter then gives a case study from a seventeenth-century mercantile handbook, showing how virtual property is created. Finally, a survey of recent literary criticism on property is followed by some speculation about what research is likely to develop on the topic.

Why Is There Now a 'New Economic Criticism'?

How did the middling sorts experience having and getting (or, less cheerfully, not doing so)? Part of the answer lies in popular fictional representations of property. Part lies, more intriguingly, in where these fictions were met and how they were responded to. Most interestingly of all, a third part lies in how the fictions, in turn, fed real life with topics, narratives and tropes. The study of popular culture is, above all, dialogic.

What is being called the 'new economics' in early modern literary studies is two-thirds of the way through the three-stage investigation. The first stage focused on popular *literary* representations of property, particularly cash flow in city comedies, and did so mostly in terms of sex and anxiety. Critics in the 1980s and 1990s often referred back to Sigmund Freud's model of the economics of desire, where desire is figured as an energy that is saved then redirected into the pursuit of civilisation – wealth – or (in later readings influenced by Jean Baudrillard and Jean-François Lyotard) magnificently squandered. The two literary stereotypes almost exclusively possessing these readings were the miser/usurer and the gallant: rich (but foolish and impotent) or poor (but witty and virile), respectively. Analyses played brilliant variations on the identification of coin with semen, as productive forces when they are circulated, in a fluid and fertile market.

The second stage in the investigation was *historicist*, considering contemporary economic and legal concepts of ownership and acquisition, from the loftiest notions of a country's balance of trade down to a lone widow's double entry book-keeping. Late 1990s and early 2000s critics extracted topics from an eclectic range of primary material from popular culture other than fiction, such as sermons, account books, prescriptive handbooks for merchants, lawyers or estate stewards, court records, government decisions, diaries and letters. Critics then took these debates back to find how they were handled in an equally eclectic range of popular and elite genres, such as romances, country house poems, citizen and city comedies, chorographies, satires, eulogies, masques, city pageants and domestic tragedies.

Excitingly, however, the third stage of the investigation is now under way: a swivel around towards considering *how fictions are used in the world of real life work*, in having and getting. Following (it has to be said) some way behind theorists of the creative industries today, critics are now asking how workers and owners create narratives, characters and images which allow them to think about and act upon their responsibilities for property. The new economic criticism is beginning to understand what Peter Burke was talking about in 1978 (and before him, Raymond Williams): culture is ordinary. It comprises a whole way of life, expressed by a range of working practices that include, but are not limited to, the high arts.[1] Fictions mould, just as much as express, the way we act in daily life. They are created by everyone, not just a few elite writers. So the hot topic now is not 'property in literature' but 'literature in property'.

To show these approaches in practice, a typical reading by the first group of commentators would look in detail at the libidinal word-play of one piece, say Thomas Middleton's *A Chaste Maid in Cheapside* of 1613. It would discuss how the goldsmith Yellowhammer's money is to be put into circulation by the marriage of his daughter Moll to the profligate knight Sir Walter Whorehound (whose name is pronounced as 'water', and who has already been 'watering' his mistress to good effect, in terms of finance and fertility), while the brother of Moll's suitor, Touchwood, 'waters' the dry Lady Kex, again very profitably. The second group of critics would typically analyse contemporary advice on investment opportunities in offering cash and credit to the careful or the careless, given in texts such as John Browne's *Marchants Avizo* (1589). They would then turn to *Chaste Maid* and note the techniques used by Yellowhammer to distinguish between the two sorts of investment, weighing up external signs of social and financial weightiness, and the specific references made to accounting terms for credit and debit. The third group of critics, however, might look at how a merchant such as Sir Thomas Myddelton, who (with his brother, the king's goldsmith, Sir Hugh Myddelton) in 1613 employed his namesake, the playwright Middleton, to write a pageant to celebrate the financial, logistical, managerial and engineering expertise and effort with which Hugh had brought piped water to London (the *New River* entertainment) and a city pageant to celebrate the election of Sir Thomas as Lord Mayor (*Triumphs of Truth*). Even more to the point, they might investigate the accounts of the New River venture which the Myddeltons drew up for the king (a tiresomely on/off investor, who required ceaseless reassurance about the returns he would get) to show the range of epic tropes they used to persuade him to take the long view. Traders use narratives, on and off stage. These critics would discern the play's credit-creation techniques in the activities of the Myddelton family.

There are three reasons why critics have come enthusiastically (albeit late) to this position: a shift from physical to virtual property in twenty-first-century wealth; a different understanding of where creativity is typically found; and an interest in sustainable governance, where the stake-holder is also an 'owner'.

First, we are starting to see parallels between early modern and current concepts of property as *not* being, primarily, something you can go out and kick. Property is not, now or then, the goods you own but rather the resources you can mobilise for your own purposes. We are increasingly familiar with virtual property, from personal online banking accounts to back-to-back interest-rate swaps to Linden dollars on Second Life. Securitisation, for instance, involves discerning a flow of potential profits, and imagining them as a current asset. A virtual asset is a form which offers many advantages over realty, and in particular, those of portability, imperviousness to changes in the physical environment, a frictionless exchange and a global recognition of its value. It is, moreover, something that can easily be increased by the owner's creativity. However, these advantages are cyclically tempered

---

[1]   R. Williams, *Culture and Society, 1780 to 1950* (London: Chatto and Windus, 1958).

with a sense of the risks involved in putting wealth into virtual products, demonstrated by the ongoing banking crisis which started in September 2008. Specifically, the value of virtual property is based on crediting a narrative about your property. If you and others do not believe – or even suspect – that the asset you hold can be used in its former ways then, in sober fact, it does not have its former value. A Tinkerbell economy takes great narrative energy to maintain, which is why studying and repairing your image, whether it be by using a PR company or checking your individual online footprints, is vital.

The new forms of property created by such postmodern ideas and digital technologies have made critics sensitive, in turn, to the early modern concept of property. They are beginning to understand this as a ladder of increasingly 'virtual' resources, each of which the owner has a right to use. Going up the rungs are land > buildings > movables > cash > credit instruments > annuities, perquisites or reversions (the legal, individualised right to receive a stream of income or belongings in the future, or to take up an official post in the future with its associated remuneration) > customary rights (granted over future actions to a group, rather than an individual, such as a freeman's right to graze sheep on a common) > personal assets (the unearned increment of wealth that is granted by others in response to a sound education, good looks, male gender or higher rank) > family connections and personal acquaintances (who can arrange a meeting with other connections, or give a reference, or suggest a tip, or lend a suit of clothes, or some such consumer durable). Even just being spoken of as having these assets at command allows one to acquire others (Pierre Bourdieu's idea of how social capital is acquired or lent or given or swapped, by those in the know, is a suggestive model in this context). Thus, early modern texts are as touchy as our own about maintaining reputation, honour or credit. A good name in this context is nothing 'personal' (any more than is a well-maintained avatar) in the sense of referring to the person herself – it refers to a widespread belief in that person's ability to access assets.

The second feature which has inspired the new economic criticism is a changed understanding of the nature of creativity. Work in this area has stopped marvelling at how inspiration inexplicably appears in a few lucky or tormented souls, and started to see creativity as a widely shared faculty, expressed in the affairs of everyday life.[2] Managers now are convinced that non-financial capital, especially the creativity and personal engagement of their employees, is key to success. Thus, artistic entrepreneurs are providing training in imagining how colleagues think, in refining business writing styles, in improvisation and in investigating how the metaphors we use in work affect how we work.[3] The company Mythodrama, for instance, run by Richard Olivier, uses leadership stories from Shakespeare, organisation theory and practical theatrical expertise to create transformational experiences in the safe environment of a rehearsal room, for clients ranging from the National Health Service to Standard Chartered Bank, INSEAD to Nokia. Business gurus refer to Teresa Amabile's contention that, in a growing economy society, employees will be driven more by intrinsic motivation than fear of management. Firms must give transformational leadership (where workers are inspired), rather than transactional leadership ('do this or you're out'), if they want to recruit and retain excellent staff. The advice is mirrored in scores of railway-store self-help books for the executive, which urge her to innovate and to breathe new life

---

[2] A. Maslow, 'Creativity in Self-Actualizing People', in A. Rothenberg and C. Hausman eds, *The Creativity Question* (Durham, NC: Duke University Press, 1976), pp. 86–92.

[3] T. Amabile, *Creativity in Context* (Boulder: Westview Press, 1996); B. Jackson, 'Re-engineering the Sense of Self: The Manager and the Management Guru', *Journal of Management Studies* 33:5 (1996), 571–90; J. Henry, *Creativity and Perception in Management* (London: Sage and the Open University, 2001), chs 2, 7 and 9.

into her employees.[4] Conversely, in studies of the creative industries there is an increasing emphasis on how, as Chris Bilton, says, 'creative thinking takes place neither inside the box nor outside the box, but at the edge of the box', depending on managing constraints as much as on waiting for and then harvesting spontaneous ideas.[5] Thus, today's business people and creative artists are mutually interested in each other's modes of operation. Such interest is bubbling back into a reconsideration of early modern notions of wealth and wealth-creation as relying on narrative power. Moreover, it finds no bar in early modern notions of creativity, where writers could work in all sorts of businesses, from money lending, to property speculation, to brick-laying, without surprise or comment, and where, as many critics have noted, theatre and poetry were themselves regarded as business ventures.

Finally, and most recently of all – in part in response to repeated global financial crises – has come a welcome revision of our concept of ownership. Our talk now is not of shareholders but stake-holders, a category which includes owners, employees, management, customers, co-located and other directly affected people, and, even more widely, 'society', present and future, in the shape of responsibility for the environment and for equality. We are, it appears, finally becoming aware of the increased dangers of neo-liberalism in a global market. Classical economics dates the rise of capitalism in Britain to the end of the early modern period. In 1902–3, Max Weber seminally argued that the impetus for this came from a Protestant – or, more specifically, Puritan – drive to convert time to godly use. This drive was enforced by an individualist approach to salvation, intense self-discipline and regular internal accounting for one's actions. Weber argued that Protestantism's focus on the individual produced the hard-working capitalist entrepreneur; success in trade was evidence of election.[6] Sixty years later C.B. Macpherson traced the political and legal systems arising from such a view of the individual as essentially the proprietor of his own person or capacities. Individuals related to each other in an economically rational mode, and prioritised the safeguard of private property.[7] John Brewer and Susan Staves take Macpherson's point into popular culture from the late seventeenth century onward: a particular property regime is the expression of a particular political ideology within which personality is constructed. In the Enlightenment, private ownership (of land in particular) was taken to encourage honest labour and hence high productivity, from which all could benefit. Some 'things', however, were new in form and could resist being owned (for example, slaves, genetic property in the shape of new breeds, literary property), so state-endorsed force, including physical force, could become necessary.[8]

These are dispiritingly familiar concepts from which we, as global citizens, are currently trying to escape. We and our peers in the sixteenth and early seventeenth centuries sit on either side of this hard-edged cusp. Our own struggles to move towards sustainable governance – effectively, to de-secularise the concept of ownership – are inversely paralleled

---

[4] For an instance of such literary self-help, see B.J. Pine and J.H. Gilmore, *The Experience Economy: Work Is Theatre and Every Business a Stage* (Boston: Harvard Business School, 1999).

[5] C. Bilton, *Management and Creativity: From Creative Industries to Creative Management* (Oxford: Blackwell, 2007), pp. 70–74.

[6] M. Weber, *The Protestant Ethic and the Spirit of Capitalism* (1904–1905), trans. T. Parsons (1930; London: Routledge, 1992). Paul Seaver and John Sommerville point out that treatises produced by moderate Anglicans after 1660 were as likely as those by Puritans to praise these qualities, but have the advantage of involving less ratiocination about why a doctrine of faith (and not works) should produce a work ethic. P. Seaver, 'The Puritan Work Ethic Revisited', *Journal of British Studies* 19:2 (1980), 35–53; C.J. Sommerville, 'The Anti-Puritan Work Ethic', *Journal of British Studies* 20:2 (1981), 70–81.

[7] C.B. Macpherson, *The Political Theory of Possessive Individualism: Hobbes to Locke*, intro. F. Cunningham (Oxford: Oxford University Press, 2011).

[8] J. Brewer and S. Staves eds, *Early Modern Conceptions of Property* (London: Routledge, 1995); 'early modern' here largely refers to the eighteenth century.

by early modern struggles to move away from this position. They were (as we are becoming) more familiar with a theology of property which saw stewardship, not ownership, as key. They cited the parable of the talents (Matt 25:14–30) to prove that property is given you by God to do good with, to use, not just to hold. Given that property encompassed even impalpables such as time, specialist knowledge, skills or contacts, it followed that everyone had some social capital to lend or give away. It was especially virtuous to give to risky prospects, such as the poor or ill-connected, from whom no return was sure (on earth, at least). As Craig Muldrew's study of domestic credit-relations shows, the period was more interested in the social benefits of lending, which bound a community together, than in the 'sin' of usury. Debt was a public means of circulating social judgement and its aim was outward, to the community; moral probity maintained, not just was evidenced by, being granted credit.[9] However, since being freehanded with your assets also signals your deep pockets, which in turn increased your personal credit, it could be both godly and prudent to take more of a risk than the finances of the beneficiary might seem to justify at first sight. Moreover, in the case of dire need even involuntary contributions (those filched from you by the starving) might be justified. In short, on the one hand your property was never yours alone, in either moral or social terms, but on the other hand, you could only go ever broke, bankrupt, if you had run through all your rights to everyone else's resources.

All three changes in our own conditions of work – new forms of virtual property, new ideas about where and how creativity emerges and new concepts of stake-holding – are encouraging literary commentators to reconsider the situations investigated by the 1990s/2000s historicist critics.

What the Literary Critics Say

Over the sixteenth and seventeenth centuries, Britain developed a metropolitan market in wool, where products were processed *in situ*, then brought to London for export overseas. At the same time luxuries and novelties flowed in from overseas, in sufficient quantity and range of price to put the possibility of consumption expenditure to the fore for a far greater number of people. Merchants began to make strategic investments in international markets well beyond the Continent, such as the Americas and Asia. The available labour force expanded rapidly, in number and in accessibility due to increased urbanisation. Accumulation, for reinvestment in a business, became a guiding light for entrepreneurs. Political power began more directly to follow economic power, rather than rank. The following section describes the recent and substantial body of research into how late Elizabethan and Jacobean aesthetics grew out of the new modes of value-creation.[10]

First, though come three caveats about the scope of this work. The literary vitality of the five decades between 1580 and 1630, especially in the field of drama, has produced a correspondingly dense and vigorous commentary focused on it. While this effort is laudable in itself and its results can be dazzling, it has had three drawbacks. First, the economic models of 50 years have come to be seen as a synecdoche for the whole of the early modern period. There are far fewer studies of literature that respond, for instance, to the disruption of trade during the Civil War and its resumption under the Commonwealth, or to the effects

---

[9]   C. Muldrew, *The Economy of Obligation: The Culture of Credit and Social Relations in Early Modern England* (New York: St Martin's Press, 1998).

[10]   K. Thomas, *Earthly Necessities: Economic Lives in Early Modern Britain* (New Haven: Yale University Press, 2000) surveys relevant recent research in how shifts in the economy affected daily life.

on the metropolitan market of political union between England and Wales. Second, as noted in the introduction to the chapter, the focus has been largely (though not wholly) on credit-based transactions, not on other forms of acquisition and property-ownership. Third, even now critics tend to deal mainly with dramatic texts (with Shakespeare exerting his usual centripetal drag), though this state of affairs is starting to change, as some commentary moves away from city and citizen comedy to look at other dramatic genres, and some even turns to poetry and prose.

At present, there are three main divisions in the new economic criticism. Much the largest are the two groups engaged by the risks and opportunities of trade in general and of credit in particular; the third, smaller, group deals with literature as a property in itself.

Those who discern more risk than reward in holding and creating property usually refer to Jean-Christophe Agnew's study. Agnew was one of the first in the field to look beyond usury as the standard trope for all economic relations, and to give a role to theatre audiences as consumers of fictions.[11] He argues that the period saw the idea of the market shift: from being a place of ceremonialised exchange between individuals to being a placeless and impersonal state of constant exchange. Theatre could give a protean shape to this fearsome formlessness, urging the audience to acts of belief that might make the market meaningful again. Critical work following Agnew is tinged by a similar anxiety – partly because it tends to concentrate on those who buy rather than those who make or sell, in the market – and often refers to macro-economic explanations of the market. In particular, these critics refer to the new model of a national balance of trade, set out in tracts by four early seventeenth-century theorists (Gerard Malynes, Thomas Mun, Edward Misselden and Thomas Milles), which thought a nation's wealth consisted in an established and ever-increasing flow of goods, not a store of physical assets such as gold. Thus, Douglas Bruster proposes that the widening trade of the period saw increased opportunities for consumption; owning more, or more valuable, or more exotic things could make you more of an individual. But then the prospect of losing them, through poor commercial judgement or just plain chance, could make you even more anxious. For Bruster, theatres played on this fear.[12] David Hawkes thinks the period was troubled by the growing distinction between exchange and use value in a cash economy; fetishised commodities appeared in literary tropes of sodomy, alchemy and idolatry.[13] Refreshingly, Hawkes widens the discussion to include poets and prose writers who take up the topic, as well as dramatists. Jonathan Gil Harris analyses macro-economic mercantilist literature, which clarified the concept of the nation as a single economic body. It was a body under threat, however, wincing under the threat of being, in Gil Harris's terms, castrated of its treasure, infected by trade with overseas and tainted by usury.[14] For Linda Woodbridge, revenge tragedy expresses the feeling that the market is fundamentally unfair. The genre's characters harp on about unrewarded merit and unmerited reward, unpunished guilt and underserved punishment, in a metaphorical engagement with the way that regulation of the exchange, of prices, and of wages had failed. Chancers, not the hard-working, were getting rich.[15]

---

[11]   J.-C. Agnew, *Worlds Apart: The Market and the Theater in Anglo-American Thought, 1550–1750* (Cambridge: Cambridge University Press, 1986).

[12]   D. Bruster, *Drama and the Market in the Age of Shakespeare* (Cambridge: Cambridge University Press, 1992).

[13]   D. Hawkes, *Idols of the Marketplace: Idolatry and Commodity Fetishism in English Literature, 1580–1680* (Basingstoke: Palgrave Macmillan, 2001).

[14]   J. Gil Harris, *Sick Economies: Drama, Mercantilism, and Disease in Shakespeare's England* (Philadelphia: Pennsylvania University Press, 2004).

[15]   L. Woodbridge, *English Revenge Drama: Money, Resistance, Equality* (Cambridge: Cambridge University Press, 2010).

Then comes a more optimistic group of critics, who think that given so many people were in business there must have been something enjoyable and useful in it as a career. These critics tend to see agency as being more possible in market conditions, and study business leaders who take control over their working lives rather than those who suffer as personal debtors or consumption purchasers (though the distinction between personal and business debt could be hazy, at a time when the household was the most usual site of production). Theodore Leinwand asks how it feels to be the subject of sustained socio-economic pressures.[16] He points out how lending, borrowing and venturing are described in emotive terms, as exhilarating and exotic, albeit also sometimes labour-intensive and worrying. He draws out the range of economic relations beyond simple usury, appearing in fiction as well as in discussions about the uses of trade. Ceri Sullivan analyses mechanisms for creating trust in the merchant's word, in his books, and in the physical coins he uses. She concentrates on popular print, looking at prescriptive texts which show how to create value, especially commercial handbooks (such as those introducing the new technique of double entry book-keeping as an art of adequation, with safely virtual money), and popular comment on how the market was working in practice.[17] Aaron Kitch thinks the literature of the period tries to promote political stability by linking it to the economic well-being of the citizen.[18] As with Hawkes, Kitch does not limit himself to the drama, as when he analyses epyllia as poems on the management of wealth, or epics as poems on international trade. Valerie Forman, taking a macro-economic approach like Gil Harris, discusses how the economic depression of the 1620s encouraged investors to distinguish between the loss or the illiquidity of how they held property. Investors looked to the long term, finding the nation's wealth in the to and fro of goods registered in the balance of trade, not in any store of physical treasure. The genre of tragi-comedy helped think through the new economic narratives that prompted further overseas ventures, those where loss was eventually turned into profit. Jill Phillips Ingram finds that even self-interest has a social function in fiction, in promoting economic growth through entrepreneurship.[19] Blair Hoxby's study of Milton is original in approach, confining himself to the economic ideas of a single author (and a poet not a dramatist, at that, and one, moreover, who comes later than the 1620s).[20] Hoxby argues that Milton's poems endorse trade which does not coerce either party, for instance by restraints on trade, such as monopolies, or in terms of an unbalance of power between the buyer and seller, as happens in imperial enterprises.

The final group of critics has a self-reflexive line of approach, where the text itself is regarded as a 'thing' which meditates on itself as a 'thing' which has been produced. This is, of course, a well-trodden area in terms of how authors (Ben Jonson is the prime example) thought about originality and plagiarism, how they wanted their work circulated or printed, what sort of patronage they sought and, in the case of dramatists, how they thought of the playing companies in which they held a share. Some literary critics, however, turn around to consider what understanding theatres as businesses does to the concept of getting and holding property. Laura J. Rosenthal discusses how pieces of literature come to be seen

---

[16]   T. Leinwand, *Theater, Finance, and Society in Early Modern England* (Cambridge: Cambridge University Press, 1999).

[17]   C. Sullivan, *The Rhetoric of Credit: Merchants in Early Modern Writing* (London: Associated University Presses, 2002).

[18]   A. Kitch, *Political Economy and the State of Literature in Early Modern England* (Farnham: Ashgate, 2009).

[19]   J. Phillips Ingram, *Idioms of Self-Interest: Credit, Identity, and Property in English Renaissance Literature* (New York: Routledge, 2006).

[20]   B. Hoxby, *Mammon's Music: Literature and Economics in the Age of Milton* (New Haven: Yale University Press, 2002).

as customary, commercial and legal properties, whose owners can be distinguished and, hence, remunerated. This was complicated by the high degree of intertextuality in the fiction of the period, and also by the prevalence of a collaborative mode of composition, especially in drama, where the performance, not the script, was the 'thing' to be rewarded by box-office receipts.[21] David Baker traces career choices made by dramatists after studying the market, in a consumer-led market where plays were just one of the novelties which could be bought, to find out what justifications their authors offered for buying the luxury of entertainment.[22]

When talking about plays on political topics it is a given that what is on stage reflects on what is being done in the centres of power, and may be watched by people who take the handling of the topic back to their own situation, in ways which affect their actions in real life. For instance, it is a truism to say that the sovereign's right to rule is expressed by the theatricality of court procedure, of which court masques are part (indeed, expressed much more forcefully by these performances than by any proclamation). The same is beginning to be true for discussion about early modern texts on property from popular as much as elite culture. Because literary critics now think differently about how value is held, where creativity can be found and whether society has a share in private assets, they reconsider how early modern drama shows how property can be created by literary techniques used in non-fictional, real-life situations.

Case Study: Richard Dafforne's *Merchants Mirrour*

Thus, literary critics are beginning to investigate the tropes in handbooks on estate management or in a suite of ledgers, not for evidence of concepts of ownership which can then be taken back to illuminate canonical fiction, but in themselves, as fictions which structure the handling of property in real life. When Richard Dafforne's *Merchants Mirrour: or, Directions for the Perfect Ordering and Booking of his Accounts* (1635) or his *Apprentices Time-entertainer Accomptantly* (1640) recommend keeping accounts that are transparent, correct, give each creditor and debtor his own and are regularly audited, or when they describe levying interest as an art of adequation which takes into account the opportunity costs of what the money could have done had it not been lent out, then they are revising popular representations of the merchant as usurer, and doing so by the arts of characterisation and narrative of what could have been.

The *Merchants Mirrour* starts with prefatory matter on the importance and history of accounting, then gives a tutorial on how to do it and finally gives extensive and detailed sample books of account, running for six months from 1 January 1634 (new style): an opening inventory or balance of accounts (I1r–v), a 'waste-book' (that is, a day book) which records events as they unfold, day by day (I2r–K1v), a journal to separate the items out of the waste-book and into different accounts (that is, different forms of holding value, K2r–M4r), a 'kalendar' or index to significant accounts in the ledger (N1r–O1r) and the general 'leager' or ledger itself (O1v–R3r), before repeating the sequence with more complex accounts, such as factorage, insurance and accounting for damaged goods (R4r–QQ4v).

Double entry book-keeping was introduced into Britain as a practice, not just an aspiration, after British merchants became aware of how beneficial continental merchants,

---

[21]   L.J. Rosenthal, *Playwrights and Plagiarists in Early Modern England* (Ithaca, NY: Cornell University Press, 1996).

[22]   D. Baker, *On Demand: Writing for the Market in Early Modern England* (Stanford: Stanford University Press, 2010).

particularly in the Netherlands, found it. Until about the end of the sixteenth century, accounts were generally more or less complex systems of tallies. A trader gauged the value of his property by a stock-take, a review of the ad hoc notes he had made of who owed what to him or vice versa, and a count of his cash. Profit or loss was simply the difference between what this totalled and what the total was the last time he did so. By the late seventeenth century, however, double entry had become the rule, not the exception.

The technique has four aims, the four 'Cs'. It cleaves the property and actions of the business from that of the owner of the business. It captures in writing all events happening to that property, moment by moment. It classifies these events in terms of translation of value, from tangible to intangible, or back, as value is created, exchanged, or lost. It clarifies where the business owned property held by another, or vice versa.

Double entry's basic mechanism is simple: every time property changes form, then the old form is reduced and the new form is increased. So, for instance, making a loan increases the value of the business's debts and decreases the value of the business's cash account (in shorthand, debit debtors, credit cash). Value which is put into the business at its inception by its owners is called capital, and is a debt the business owes its owners (that is, debit cash, credit capital). Value which is created by the business increases the assets and that debt to the owners (debit, say, cash, credit capital). More complex double entry allows the accountant to trace exactly how that value has been created, through a profit and loss account.

Dafforne opens with a wide-ranging invitation to British merchants trading across the world, especially to the Americans, the East Indies and the Levant, to consider their activities as a vocation, acting as good and faithful servants of God's property which has been lent to them (Matt. 25:21–3). But he then reproves them for failing to follow the Low Countries in supporting the study of double entry. A commendatory epistle follows, on how accounting is 'a rule of equality, that restoreth to one just as much as it taketh from another, without partiality' (a5v). A short treatise on the antiquity of accounting suggests (improbably) that it has a genealogy which would impress any humanist: begun in the Rome of Julius Caesar, and furnishing turns of thought and phrase which suffuse Cicero's speech defending Roscius (A1r). A caveat comes next, about the difficulty of achieving equivalence across cultures with different weights, measures and currencies.

The training section which prefaces the sample ledgers stresses the duty of good stewardship once more, where all property is held from the 'All-giver', and praises the 'exquisite' knowledge of accounts, which can only be gained by someone who is endlessly patient, diligent and careful. The ledger, into which all subsidiary accounts feed, is the perfect – exact, true – mirror of his estate for the owner of the business (B2v), unlike all other forms of account.

Dafforne, citing the proverb, 'that which is written, remaineth' (B3v), stresses the importance of entering into the waste-book (the property's boundary, the dividing line between 'them' and 'us') every transaction: 'even as it is truely acted ... entered immediately upon the action of the thing acted ... entered in plaine sincerity as it is acted ... parcells [items] entred close under each other as they were acted, without leaving of any empty paper' (B3v). This mode – what will become realism – appears too in the list of details which must be given of each transaction in the waste-book: parties to it, date, place, quantity and quality, values and additional circumstances or conditions. The journal formalises this realist narrative, and gives it a different cast, as it separates the transaction recorded in the waste-book, into its component headings or accounts. These become, in Dafforne's terminology, stern characters which demand their due. For instance, when cash is received, Dafforne explains that cash is debited:

> *because Cash (having received my mony into it) is obliged to restore it againe at my*
> *pleasure: for Cash representeth (to mee) a man to whom I (only on confidence) have*
> *put my mony into his keeping, the which by reason is obliged to render it backe, or, to*
> *give mee an account what is become of it. (C1r)*

Here, the owner of the cash is even assessing his own account, to see whether it inspires him with 'confidence', that is, has credit-worthiness. The owner's property has become a co-partner in the deal. For Dafforne, all accounts are ultimately in the debt of their creditor 'Stock' (that is, capital), whose body they supply (C2r).

Dafforne goes on to give the 15 basic rules of accounting, and then gives 22 pages of virtuoso question-and-answers between two scholars of the art. For instance, the demand 'Receits of mony, 1. Remitted unto us: booking the same without an account of time, and Ready-mony' provokes a quick 'Cash, or Bancke debitor to A.A. His account currant', answered by 'Suppose the Bill is not yet due to be received?', and then by 'The Acceptor Debitor to A.A., his account currant: and being received, Cash or Banke, Debtor to the Acceptor.' The tone of the conversation is not that of a Bartleby: its interlocutors are precise, confident, rapid and expert.

When Dafforne produces the sample account books, the drama increases. His two waste-books give 361 transactions, to be journalled and eventually balanced up in a trial balance at the period end. The world's commodities – sack, pepper, sugar, figs – are received, valued and classified by this written control centre. The business man is shown to be able to master the risk and disorder of the real, messy, contingent world of trade. For instance, on 30 June, parcel (that is, item) number 88 records that: 'Jack Pudding writeth me from London, that shipper John Clason, saling upon a sand, was forced somewhat to disburden his ship, casting (among other Goods) 100 Frailes of my Figs overboard, producing, at £2 per peece — 200.' Parcel 89 is able to record that later, 'he advertiseth mee, that 6 peeces of my Cambrix-cloth insured the 7 present, are likewise cast away, my receipt for them at £40 per peece, produceth — 240'. By parcel 97 more news comes about the wreck. 'Jaques Jolyt hath Letters from Lisbourne, wherein is mentioned that the [other] 88 peeces of Cambrix-cloth, by me the 23 June insured, are wholly lost, the ship being rent, and broken upon a Rocke, so that hee renouncing the same, surrendreth her to mee, the insured summe was — 3300.' By parcel 98, the story takes another turn:

> *Shipper Jacob Jacobson, of Marken, being at that time in the Fleet next to Randoll*
> *Ruyve, cast forth his boat immediately, and daved Radol, with his people; so that by*
> *his great industry hee (amongst some other goods) recovered the Cambrix, and sould*
> *them there for Ready-mony at £36 the peece; the said proceeds than he sent to Jacques*
> *Jolyt, being — 3168.*

The journal duly and formally credits and debits its way through the intricacies of the story as recorded by the waste-book, taking charge of these dizzying turns of event.

Dafforne's *Merchants Mirrour* shows how the art of accounting uses an aesthetic which, in literature, we would recognise as realist. It peoples its books with credit-worthy accounts, which record – in due form – the messy drama of the real world. The merchant broods over the reports made by his servants, these books. He is able to act because he has an exact and careful representation of an estate which is ever changing. His books are his principal means of knowing what property he has, in what form and where. They are also, in turn, the evidence he proffers to others, to get them to believe in his estate. In some ways, they are his greatest asset.

What Next, for Early Modern Research into Property?

The next step for modern debates on early modern notions of what value is will be to move outside the narrow focus on the cash and credit economy. There are some signs that literary critics are also getting interested in a long-running debate elsewhere about the importance of material forms. Sociologists and anthropologists such as Roland Barthes, Arjun Appadurai and Daniel Miller are leading the way in thinking about the 'street-level' consequences of seeing objects as signs of how a society operates and what concerns it.[23] Miller, who gives an incisive and witty overview of the principles and developments in this area of research, points out that taxonomies of popular everyday 'stuff' – objects disregarded as trivial – are important precisely because of stuff's very humility, as a key unchallenged mechanism of ideology. Objects have a primitive association to emotions and basic orientations towards the world. They are powerful in moderating the way we get on together. They are also, in the view of sociologists, as useful as what people say, in letting us understand what they think matters – indeed, some sociologists would go so far as to say that there is no subject prior to the process of objectification.

Early modern studies have begun to turn towards physical property. The most widely circulated unit of popular culture, the coin, is studied by David Landreth, who argues that it was seen more as part of a political than an economic discourse.[24] Carrying the prince's stamp, coins flew up and down ranks, as well as between social equals, making their exchangers into peers for the nonce. In literature, coinage has the power to impose its will on events, so authors (here including pamphleteers and poets) are worried about those who fetishise it or waste it. Stephen Deng points out that, when coins appear in drama, they facilitate discussion about how a nation state is formed by the relations between the monarch, the central administration, natural law and local custom.[25]

Then from cash to movables: Natasha Korda, for instance, investigates what fictions concentrate on material objects, in an age of consumer durables, to express political and affective relationships in a household.[26] Using things to keep women in their place is a regular topos of popular literature – as is the sly revenge which a woman, in her domestic kingdom, could take. Korda, with Michelle M. Dowd, also edited a collection on popular representations of the workmen who produced all this lovely 'stuff'. These literary figures show a mixture of desire for, and irritation over, goods produced by migrants or imported commodities.[27] Book history is a particularly vibrant subdivision of the study of portable and virtual property: how the different physical elements of a book (initiating manuscript, paper, print, collation, binding) are produced and why these methods were chosen over others, how stored, how catalogued, how circulated (sold or bequeathed or lent or lost

---

[23]   Roland Barthes, *Mythologies* (1957), selected and trans. A. Lavers (London: Cape, 1972); Arjun Appadurai ed., *The Social Life of Things: Commodities in Social Perspective* (Cambridge: Cambridge University Press, 1986); Daniel Miller, *Stuff* (Cambridge: Polity Press, 2010); Daniel Miller ed., *Material Cultures: Why Some Things Matter* (London: UCL Press, 1998).

[24]   D. Landreth, *The Face of Mammon: The Matter of Money in English Renaissance Literature* (Oxford: Oxford University Press, 2012).

[25]   S. Deng, *Coinage and State Formation in Early Modern English Literature* (Basingstoke: Palgrave Macmillan, 2011).

[26]   N. Korda, *Shakespeare's Domestic Economies: Gender and Property in Early Modern England* (Philadelphia: Pennsylvania University Press, 2002). Amy L. Erikson uses non-fictional sources to show how women tended to inherit equally with their brothers (within a gender division of realty and personalty), but that coverture still made care over marriage settlements sensible. *Women and Property in Early Modern England* (London: Routledge, 1993).

[27]   M.M. Dowd and N. Korda eds, *Working Subjects in Early Modern English Drama* (Farnham: Ashgate, 2011).

or thrown away), how read, how indexed or annotated, how copied out of, how doodled upon, what objects are left in them (from spectacles to biscuit crumbs) and so on. Far from being a dull complement to their exciting contents, what the physical book says about social relations intrigues early modern textual historians such as Joad Raymond, James Daybell and Adam Smyth, whether it be a massive tome, a pamphlet or a notebook.[28]

Finally, from personalty to realty. Richard Burt and John M. Archer edit a collection which is interested in how the enclosure of land and modes of bodily containment are mutually troped in literature, in order to express the opportunities and risks arising from seeing land as a personally owned capital asset, that is to be enclosed and intensively farmed, rather than as a commonly used asset, that is held in common.[29] Garrett A. Sullivan brings together contemporary techniques of surveying, estate management and road-building to investigate what social relations were expressed by popular literary depictions of land.[30] Land sales peaked in 1610. Tenantry became less a matter of fealty to the land's owner, and land-holding less a matter of stewardship, as land came to be seen as an asset, owned outright, which could be mapped, divided, sold on and so translated into other commodities.

Today's general readers are fond of books with a monosyllabic common noun for a title (*Salt, Cod, Drugs, Chavs* and the like). Museum trustees now are equally fond of exhibitions with a narrative link-in, such as the British Museum's A History of the World in 100 Objects (where its director, Neil MacGregor, told radio listeners about the social history surrounding the production and collection of an individual item, building up a sense of how things relate to other things, in social ways), or the Museum's Shakespeare: Staging the World (where early modern London is explored as a world-city, through common objects, referred to in Shakespeare's plays, which are in the Museum's collection). Paying attention to the material is not at the cost of attending to the social, for our senses of ourselves and of other selves are expressed in the way we handle property.

In conclusion, it seems likely that these two trends – a renewed understanding of virtual assets in the early modern period, and a fascination with the sociology of small-scale, barely noticed 'stuff' – will provide the most fruitful research into early modern property, in the next few years.

Select Bibliography

Agnew, J.-C., *Worlds Apart: The Market and the Theater in Anglo-American Thought, 1550–1750*. Cambridge: Cambridge University Press, 1986.
Brewer, J., and S. Staves eds, *Early Modern Conceptions of Property*. London: Routledge, 1995.
Burt, R., and J.M. Archer eds, *Enclosure Acts: Sexuality, Property, and Culture in Early Modern England*. Ithaca, NY: Cornell University Press, 1994.
Dowd, M.M., and N. Korda eds, *Working Subjects in Early Modern English Drama*. Farnham: Ashgate, 2011.

---

[28] Joad Raymond, *Pamphlets and Pamphleteering in Early Modern Britain* (Cambridge: Cambridge University Press, 2003); James Daybell ed., *Material Readings of Early Modern Culture: Texts and Social Practices, 1580–1730* (Basingstoke: Palgrave Macmillan, 2010); Adam Smyth, *'Profit and Delight': Printed Miscellanies in England, 1640–1682* (Detroit: Wayne State University Press, 2004).

[29] R. Burt and J.M. Archer eds, *Enclosure Acts: Sexuality, Property, and Culture in Early Modern England* (Ithaca, NY: Cornell University Press, 1994).

[30] G.A. Sullivan, *The Drama of Landscape: Land, Property, and Social Relations on the Early Modern Stage* (Stanford: Stanford University Press, 1998).

Hawkes, D., *Idols of the Marketplace: Idolatry and Commodity Fetishism in English Literature, 1580–1680*. Basingstoke: Palgrave Macmillan, 2001.

Hoxby, B., *Mammon's Music: Literature and Economics in the Age of Milton*. New Haven: Yale University Press, 2002.

Ingram, J. Phillips, *Idioms of Self-Interest: Credit, Identity, and Property in English Renaissance Literature*. New York: Routledge, 2006.

Kitch, A., *Political Economy and the State of Literature in Early Modern England*. Farnham: Ashgate, 2009.

Korda, N., *Shakespeare's Domestic Economies: Gender and Property in Early Modern England*. Philadelphia: Pennsylvania University Press, 2002.

Leinwand, T., *Theater, Finance, and Society in Early Modern England*. Cambridge: Cambridge University Press, 1999.

Miller, D. ed., *Material Cultures: Why Some Things Matter*. London: UCL Press, 1998.

Muldrew, C., *The Economy of Obligation: The Culture of Credit and Social Relations in Early Modern England*. New York: St Martin's Press, 1998.

Sullivan, C., *The Rhetoric of Credit: Merchants in Early Modern Writing*. London: Associated University Presses, 2002.

Sullivan, G.A., *The Drama of Landscape: Land, Property, and Social Relations on the Early Modern Stage*. Stanford: Stanford University Press, 1998.

Thomas, K., *Earthly Necessities: Economic Lives in Early Modern Britain*. New Haven: Yale University Press, 2000.

Popular Medicine

Margaret Healy

In 1602, Frances Herring, Fellow of the prestigious London College of Physicians, remonstrated:

> If a man have a scruple in Conscience, hee will not repaire unto an Hedge Priest … for resolution, but to some Learned, godly, and Judiciall divine. If a suit in Lawe, he will not resort to a Husbandman or Artificer, for Counsell and Direction, but to a skilful, well-studied and approved Lawyer: And yet (such is the extreme folly and madnesse of many Men), that in case of Health and Life (things most pretious) they think every Tinker, Bankerupt, or wandering fugitive, who has over-runne his creditors, forsaken his Trade, and seeketh to live (like a Droan without any Calling) a sufficient and compleat Physition, to advise, counsel, and direct them.[1]

Employing a lexicon of pronounced binaries, Herring's tract evokes a picture of the early modern medical marketplace in which the services of the professional, university-educated, 'compleat' and 'True Physition' were continuously passed over in favour of 'Counterfeit Mountebanks': a motley line-up of dubious types including criminals, debtors, the unemployed and – according to his tract's suggestive title – exotic foreigners (hence 'Orient Colours'). By the early seventeenth century such complaints were familiar: in 1566 the eminent physician John Securis railed in print against the 'unlearned surgeons, meddling empirics, and "presumptuous" women' who offended his sense of proper medical order and in 1565 the surgeon John Hall lamented the way 'true' practitioners had to compete against 'smiths, cutlers, carters … and a great rabble of women'.[2] Dedicating his tract to the Lord Chief Justice, Sir John Popham, Herring was ostensibly seeking judicial help to save sick people from their own 'folly and madnesse' by restricting medical practice to professionals; in reality, as revisionist historiography has compellingly argued, Herring and his colleagues in the College of Physicians and Barber Surgeon's Hall were waging war against unlicensed practitioners, with the aim of increasing their share of a lucrative commercial sphere.[3] It was

---

[1] Frances Herring, *Anatomyse of the True Physition, and the Counterfeit Mountebank, Wherein both of them, are graphically described and set out in the Right and Orient Colours* (London, 1602), sig. A3r.

[2] John Securis, *A Detection and Querimonie of the Daily Enormities and Abuses Committed in Physic* (London, 1566), and John Hall, *A Most Excellent and Learned Woorke of Chirurgerie* (London, 1565), sig. 3r–v; both cited in Deborah E. Harkness, 'A View from the Streets: Women and Medical Work in Elizabethan London', *Bulletin of Medical History* 82:1 (2008), 52–85, at pp. 53–4.

[3] See Harkness, 'A View from the Streets' and Mary Elizabeth Fissell, 'Introduction: Women, Health, and Healing in Early Modern Europe', pp. 1–17; both part of the important collection of essays in *Bulletin of Medical History* 82:1 (2008). See also, Charles Webster, 'William Harvey and the Crisis of Medicine', in Jerome J. Bylebyl ed., *William Harvey and His Age* (Baltimore: Johns Hopkins, 1978), pp. 1–28; Andrew Wear, *Knowledge and Practice in English Medicine, 1550–1680* (Cambridge: Cambridge University Press, 2000), p. 58.

a tough challenge; recent scholarship has revealed that licensed physicians, surgeons and apothecaries were, indeed, probably vastly outnumbered by a wide range of other health care workers. In an important study of community health work in London between 1560 and 1610, Deborah Harkness has identified just over 1,400 men and women who did medical work 'including apothecaries, midwives, carers for the sick in hospitals and private settings, surgeons and physicians'. She calculates that 70 per cent of these were unlicensed, and approximately 30 per cent of the unlicensed practitioners were women.[4]

The activities of that 70 per cent are the central concern of this chapter on popular medicine which seeks to achieve two ends: first, to look beyond the hostile rhetoric and professional jealousies of medical men such as Herring, Securis and Hall – those who inhabited the privileged spaces of the College of Physicians and Barber Surgeons Hall – and to peer instead into the homes, streets and marketplaces of London and beyond, in order to gain a more balanced picture of the most prevalent medical providers and their practices. Who were these intriguing 'presumptuous women', 'meddling empirics', 'mountebanks' and 'orient' types and what were they selling? Secondly, by surveying the range and matter of the commonest medical publications, this study aims to uncover the most popular sixteenth- and seventeenth-century beliefs – 'those with the greatest cultural permeation or purchase' – about the body, its illnesses and cures.[5]

Medical Choices

We begin in the home of the Reverend Ralph Josselin: where did this man of the 'middling sort' turn when his family and servants were unwell? Strikingly, as Mary Lindemann describes, Josselin's journal records illness 762 times but he only mentions seeking help from outside the family circle on 21 occasions.[6] Margaret Pelling has demonstrated how at times of illness the first place people turned to was the household where women's presence, knowledge and skills were focused.[7] As for the majority of early modern families, then, diagnosis and treatment took place in Josselin's home with his wife, Jane, providing the necessary medicines and nursing care. She concocted common herbal remedies such as hyssop syrup herself and occasionally bought preparations from an apothecary or purchased brand-label medicines such as Tabor's Pills and Daffy's Elixir. Ralph and Jane sometimes sought advice from neighbours, from a nearby gentlewoman and assistance from two local female bonesetters. The Josselins called upon a physician on just four occasions: once when a child was dying; once when Ralph suffered a bout of ague; and twice for Ralph

---

[4]   Harkness, 'A View from the Streets', p. 58. See also, Margaret Pelling, *The Common Lot: Sickness, Medical Occupations and the Urban Poor in Early Modern England* (London: Longman, 1998); Mary Elizabeth Fissell, *Patients, Power and the Poor in Eighteenth-Century Bristol* (Cambridge: Cambridge University Press, 1991).

[5]   See Sue Wiseman, '"Popular Culture": A Category for Analysis?', in Matthew Dimmock and Andrew Hadfield eds, *Literature and Popular Culture in Early Modern England* (Farnham: Ashgate, 2009), p. 21.

[6]   *The Diary of Ralph Josselin, 1616–1683*, cited in Mary Lindemann, *Medicine and Society in Early Modern Europe* (Cambridge: Cambridge University Press, 2010), pp. 246–7; see also Alan Macfarlane, *The Family Life of Ralph Josselin, a Seventeenth-Century Clergyman: An Essay in Historical Anthropology* (Cambridge: Cambridge University Press, 1970).

[7]   Margaret Pelling, 'Thoroughly Resented: Older Women and the Medical Role in Early Modern London', in Lynette Hunter and Sarah Hutton eds, *Women and Science, 1500–1700: Mothers and Sisters of the Royal Society* (Stroud: Sutton Publishing, 1997), pp. 63–88, at p. 70. See also Lucinda Beier, *Sufferers and Healers: The Experience of Illness in Seventeenth-Century England* (London: Routledge, 1987).

in his terminal illness.[8] Since the primary cause of illness was always God's displeasure, and healing came from him too via His 'instruments', we should not forget that prayers and the avoidance of sin were integral to both prevention of sickness and the recovery of health for a godly family such as Josselin's.

The journal's mention of seeking help from a 'gentlewoman' is interesting: in recent years, much has been uncovered about the extensive medical activities of charitable gentlewomen who might resemble the one consulted by the Josselins.[9] As Linda Pollock, Lynette Hunter and Elaine Leong have illuminated, many of these women were renowned for practising fashionable 'kitchin physick', distilling herbal and mineral remedies in large quantities to supply family, friends and the local neighbourhood.[10] Elizabeth Grey, Countess of Kent, appears, for example, to have built up an impressive recipe collection that was published posthumously in *A Choice Manual of Rare and Select secrets in Physick and surgery* (1653).[11] Lady Grace Mildmay was particularly renowned for her knowledge in 'physicke and surgerie' – she had apparently received instruction in this at home – and her journal between 1570 and 1617 suggests she carried out a wide range of medical activities in her neighbourhood as part of her godly, religious duty.[12]

To turn now to a less devout household, Samuel Pepys' diary provides a salutary window onto the sorry and painful business of living with chronic illness – in his case kidney stones. The 'magic bullet' cures that we expect from medicine today simply did not exist – patients were rarely cured and frequently had to manage a life-time of chronic discomfort and disability. Many, too, likely had their suffering increased by iatrogenic illnesses inflicted on them through harmful medical interventions and poisonous drugs.[13] Pepys' diary entries find him periodically crying, roaring, trembling and performing all kinds of bodily contortions during his attacks of excruciating pain caused by stones.[14] He did, however, endure lesser suffering with considerable fortitude: for example, on 3 and 4 June 1664, suffering 'constant akeing' in his back, which he had experienced for six days, he criss-crossed London travelling from his home, to his office, to the exchange, to Whitehall, to St James, engaging in a cramped schedule of business meetings and social gatherings.[15] He was obsessively anxious about 'catching' cold, or overheating, and actively avoided horseback when his 'old pains' were bad. Understandably, his favourite self-medication seems to have been good, mature wine. He kept his bowels loose by self-dosing with unpleasant preparations like Cassia and Turpentine but he swore by something else too – a 'Hares foot' worn against

---

[8] See Lindemann, *Medicine and Society*, p. 247.

[9] See, for example, the many excellent essays in Hunter and Hutton, *Women, Science and Medicine 1500–1700*. See also Wear, *Knowledge and Practice*, pp. 50–5.

[10] See Elaine Leong, 'Making Medicines in the Early Modern Household', *Bulletin of Medical History* 82:1 (2008), 145–68.

[11] See Lynette Hunter, 'Women and Domestic Medicine: Lady Experimenters, 1570–1620', in Hunter and Hutton eds, *Women Science and Medicine*, pp. 89–107, at pp. 89–90, 103–4.

[12] Linda Pollock, *With Faith and Physic: The Life of a Tudor Gentlewoman Lady Grace Mildmay 1552–1620* (London: Collins and Brown, 1993), pp. 66, 146; Margaret P. Hannay, '"How I These Studies Prize": The Countess of Pembroke and Elizabethan Science', in Hunter and Hutton eds, *Women, Science and Medicine*, pp. 108–21, at p. 110; William Kerwin, '"Where Have You Gone, Margaret Kennix?": Seeking the Tradition of Healing Women in English Renaissance Drama', in Lillian R. Furst ed., *Women Healers and Physicians: Climbing a Long Hill* (Kentucky: University Press of Kentucky, 1997), pp. 93–113, at p. 111, n. 10.

[13] Fissell, 'Introduction: Women, Health, and Healing', p. 14.

[14] See, for example, 11 October 1661, vol. 2, p. 194; 2 August 1662, vol. 3, p. 153; 14 May 1664, vol. 5, p. 150 in Robert Latham and William Matthews eds, *The Diary of Samuel Pepys: A New and Complete Transcription* (10 vols, London: G. Bell and Sons, 1970–2).

[15] Discussed in Margaret Healy, 'A Most Troublesome and Dangerous Ailment: Encounters with the Stone in Early Modern Europe', *Journal de la Renaissance* 3 (2005), 207–16, at p. 210.

the body to ward off wind and colic.[16] Supernatural and other placebo effects and 'doing something' in the face of discomfort should not be dismissed – these were undoubtedly important psychological props. In 1662 he felt 'exceedingly full of blood' and called upon a surgeon to let his blood; he regularly consulted physicians, too, whose prime prescriptions for his condition were 'glisters' (enemas). As a young man, in 1658, Pepys had chosen to have a life-threatening kidney stone surgically removed; he selected a surgeon from St Thomas' and Bart's hospital and he survived this radical and dangerous procedure that was frequently fatal, declaring himself fully recovered after 35 days.[17] However, it appears that his old wound had never really healed: when he died in 1703 an autopsy revealed that his left kidney was a mass, full of stones, adhering to his back and that his old wound, bladder and gut were all septic.[18]

Against this picture of chronic infection in the lower regions throughout his adult life, it is, perhaps, not surprising that Pepys and his wife were afflicted by infertility. For this, as Mary Lindemann describes, he sought advice from friends and gathered a range of harmless but ineffective suggestions in the form of 'old wives' tales'. These included, not hugging his wife too hard; not eating late; drinking sage juice and herbal ale with sugar; keeping his stomach warm and his back cool; wearing cool Holland-drawers and asking his wife not to go too 'straitlaced'.[19] When his eyes failed in 1668 he consulted a famous eye specialist who prescribed a laxative and an eye drop. A year later (spring 1669) the situation was no better and his haberdasher recommended treatment by 'the mistress of the house, an oldish woman in a hat'. The latter bathed and dressed his eyes and made them smart 'most horribly'. His vision worsened and a month later he had to stop writing his journal.[20]

As we have seen, Pepys' sources of advice and medical choices ranged widely, involving self-medication, supernatural, folkloric and dietary measures, surgical procedures, apothecary's drugs, professional physic, treatment from an eye specialist and at least one local healer or cunning-woman. Pepys was of the middling sort, but would the choices of an aristocrat in extremis be so wide-ranging, or more confined to expensive, elite practitioners? The case of the 35-year-old Earl of Derby's final illness in 1594 is fairly well documented and might provide some insights into this question. As Judith Bonzol describes, when the Fifth Earl's frightening symptoms of vomiting blood, jaundice, weight-loss and distressing hiccups gave rise for concern, his physicians – who lived some distance away – were summoned to his bedside.[21] However, in the interval before they arrived, the Earl had self-medicated with a 'glister' followed by an oral laxative of rhubarb and manna; he was also consuming rare drugs containing 'Bezar's stone' and 'Unicorn's Horn' (probably ground bone) – thought to be antidotes against poison. Two surgeons were on hand and when he ceased to pass urine they attempted – unsuccessfully – to catheterise him and drain his bladder. When the physicians eventually arrived, they found the Earl being treated by a 'homely woman', 'straining herbs in a pot and chanting … blessings' – a local cunning-woman.[22] It would seem, then, that the Earl did employ the services of at least one unlicensed, neighbourhood healer. Cunning-folk, wise-women and white witches, root-wives and herbalists probably existed in every village and were plentiful in towns. They had special knowledge of local plants which could

---

[16]   Ibid., p. 214.
[17]   See Pepys' biography by Claire Tomalin, *Samuel Pepys: The Unequalled Self* (Penguin: Viking, 2002), pp. 61–5.
[18]   Ibid., p. 38.
[19]   See Lindemann, *Medicine and Society*, p. 245.
[20]   Ibid., p. 246.
[21]   For a detailed account see, Judith Bonzol, 'The Death of the Fifth Earl of Derby: Cunning Folk and Medicine in Early Modern England', *Renaissance and Reformation* 33:4 (2010), 73–100, at pp. 77–9.
[22]   Ibid., p. 79.

be brewed into herbal remedies or concocted into salves and lotions to be smeared onto bruises, sore gums, blisters and wounds.[23] As folk healers, some went beyond traditional herbal remedies and employed astrology and/or magic, or religious incantation too.

Early modern drama is revealing of the range of activities and specialist practices popularly associated with such local healers. Thomas Heywood's cunning-woman of *The Wise-woman of Hogsdon* (quarto 1638) maps out London on the basis of her fellow practitioners' specialisms:

> You have heard of Mother Nottingham, who for her time, was prettily well skill'd in casting of Waters: and after her, Mother Bombye; and then there is one Hatfield in Pepper-Alley, hee doth prettie well for a thing that's lost. There's another in Coleharbour, that's skill'd in the Planets. Mother Sturton in Goulden-lane, is for Fore-speaking: Mother Phillips of the Banke-side, for the weakenesse of the backe: and then there's a very reverent Matron on Clarkenwell-Green, good at many things: Mistris Mary on the Banke-side, is for recting a Figure: and one (what doe you call her) in Westminster, that practiseth the Booke and the Key, and the Sive and the Sheares: and all doe well, according to their talent.[24]

Hogsdon's own wise-woman is presented as a cunning entrepreneur who diagnoses diseases by inspecting flasks of urine; additionally, she reads palms, tells fortunes, treats madness, as well as engaging in a range of more questionable practices (3.1, p. 310). She boasts:

> Let mee see how many Trades have I to live by: First, I am a Wise-woman, and a Fortune-teller, and under that I deale in Physicke and Fore-speaking, in Palmistry, and recovering of things lost. Next, I undertake to cure Madd folks. Then I keepe Gentlewoman Lodgers, to furnish such Chambers as I let out by the night: Then I am provided for bringing young Wenches to bed; and for a need, you see I can play the Match-maker. (3.1, p. 310)

The cunning-woman of John Lyly's, *A Pleasant Conceited Comedie called Mother Bombie* (printed 1594),[25] is rather more strange and intriguing. 'Fowle' and 'olde' (2.3.l.97, p. 191) – a 'beldam' (3.1, p. 195) – she is hailed as a good woman but also as a witch; significantly, she quickly corrects her clientele, insisting that she is not a witch but rather an honest, cunning-woman. Among her skills are those of expounding dreams and telling fortunes by reading hands and peering into eyes. There is an oracular, mysterious quality to her riddling pronouncements. Mishap, misconception and mistaken identity are resolved through Mother Bombie's interventions and the community's harmony is engineered by her riddling utterances. Crucially, she does not deceive and she does not do harm; in fact she is presented as a gifted social healer.[26]

Cunning-women's outlandish and superstitious activities could easily be dismissed today as the ineffectual stuff of comedy; however, they do appear to have been key players in the real medical economy and the interventions of such healers probably did no more

---

[23] Lindemann, *Medicine and Society*, p. 259. See also Owen Davies, *Popular Magic: Cunning-Folk in English History* (London: Hambledon Continuum, 2007).
[24] Thomas Heywood, *The Dramatic Works of Thomas Heywood*, ed. R.H. Shepherd (6 vols, 1874; New York: Russell and Russell, 1964), vol. 5, Act 2, scene 1, pp. 292–3. No line numbers given.
[25] John Lyly, *The Complete Works of John Lyly*, ed. R. Warwick Bond (Oxford: Clarendon Press, 1942).
[26] See William Kerwin, *Beyond the Body: The Boundaries of Medicine and English Renaissance Drama* (Amherst: University of Massachusetts Press, 2005), pp. 62–96; and '"Where Have You Gone Margaret Kennix?"', pp. 99–101.

harm, and potentially just as much good, as those of licensed physicians. Many of their practices (reading flasks of urine, casting horoscopes, interpreting dreams) appear to have overlapped with those of the 'professionals', and there is, after all, little evidence that learned medicine was helpful beyond its placebo effects; its bizarre and intrusive regimes of purging, inducing vomits, sweating and bleeding were painful and dangerous, even causing diseases and death. Indeed, the commercially successful empiric Simon Forman railed against learned physicians virtually accusing them of homicide: 'For they wold mak the pisse & excrement of the bodi to be greter then the bodie yt cam from … And they thrive therafter for wher they cuer on[e] they hurte 20, and where they helpe on[e] they kill 20.'[27] Meanwhile, Francis Bacon reflected that 'empirics and old women are more happy many times in their cures than learned physicians, because they are more exact and religious in holding to the composition and confection of tried medicines'.[28] Undoubtedly, folk healing based on tried and tested experience and practised by skilled practitioners might well have been a safer choice than consulting an expensive academic physician. This could help to explain why traditional healers like the renowned Margaret Kennix were sometimes protected (not always successfully) from the onslaughts of the College of Physicians by Queen Elizabeth's intervention.

In 1581 Francis Walsingham, the queen's secretary of state, addressed this letter to the college:

> *Whereas heretofore by her Majesties commandment upon the pitiful complaint of Margaret Kennix I wrote unto Dr. Symondes of your College and fellowship of Phisitions within the City, signifying how that it was her Highness pleasure that the poore woman should be permitted by you quietly to practise and minister to the curing of diseases and woundes, by the means of certain Simples, in the applying wherof it seemeth God hath geven her an especial knowledge, to the benefit of the poorer sort and chiefly for the better maintenance of her impotent husband and charge of Family, who wholy depend on the exercise of her skill: Forasmuch as now I am enformed, she is restrained either by you … contrary to her Majesties pleasure, to practise any longer said manner of mynistring of Simples … I shall therefore desire you forthwith to take order amongst yourselves for the readmitting of her into the quiet exercise of her small Talent …*[29]

Kennix's special 'talent', notably her God-given knowledge of 'simples' and her ability to cure wounds thereby, are reminiscent of another, rather more reputable and authoritative stage healer than the wise-women encountered above: the 'empiric' (unlicensed healer), Helena, in Shakespeare's *All's Well That Ends Well.* Her goodness and simplicity are stressed, she works by 'inspired merit' using tried and tested medicinal receipts and she is successful in curing the king's 'past-cure malady' – his fistula – when the combined efforts of the 'congregated College' of 'learned doctors' have failed.[30] It is significant that early modern drama often foregrounds the woman healer as socially marginalised yet possessing an oracular nature and heightened spiritual and curative powers. As William Kerwin observes,

---

[27] Cited in Lauren Kassell, *Medicine and Magic in Elizabethan London: Simon Forman, Astrologer, Alchemist, and Physician* (Oxford: Clarendon Press, 2005), p. 119.

[28] Francis Bacon, *De Augmentis Scientiarum* (1623), in *The Works of Francis Bacon*, trans. and ed. James Spedding, Robert Ellis and Douglas Heath (15 vols, London, 1858), vol. 4, p. 388.

[29] *Annals of the College of Physicians.* Manuscript, Royal College of Physicians, London, 6; cited in Kerwin, *Beyond the Body*, p. 81.

[30] William Shakespeare, *All's Well That Ends Well: The Complete Works: Compact Edition*, ed. Stanley Wells and Gary Taylor (Oxford: Clarendon Press, 1988), Act 2, Scene 2, ll. 148, 114–23.

'she' (the stage healer) frequently refutes the attacks on women practitioners – she is not malevolent and she is often highly skilful.[31] Such representations are a healthy antidote to the slurs and aspersions cast upon them in the physicians' and surgeons' polemics.

In the early modern period, the relationship between performance and healing was particularly intimate: with a wide range of healing options to choose from, patients would certainly have been inclined to spend their pennies on those practitioners who were most effective at convincing of their authority and the efficacy of their 'cures' and products. Acting a convincing part was also crucial to securing placebo effects – patients had to be persuaded to believe in their healer. While learned physicians harnessed professional mystique by advertising their university credentials, using Latin, strutting about their consulting rooms and environs in special gowns inspecting flasks of urine ritualistically, Europe's army of itinerant practitioners, including mountebanks, charlatans, quacks, tooth-drawers, bone-setters, oculists and lithotomists, were renowned for their – sometimes very sophisticated – marketplace theatre.

Distinct lines between mountebanks, charlatans and quacksalvers are difficult to draw, however, M.A. Katritsky suggests that, 'broadly speaking, mountebanks are itinerant performers who sell medical products and services, charlatans are itinerant performers who sell medical products and services, and quacksalvers are sellers of medical products and services who may or may not be itinerant or perform in public'.[32] As Katritsky describes, stage quacks have an interesting history: they first appear in Latin mystery plays preserved in twelfth- and thirteenth-century manuscripts, emerging occasionally as dominant, 'extremely popular', non-biblical characters in Easter mystery plays. The German religious stage developed particularly extensive quack scenes and, interestingly, in the fifteenth-century Erlau Easter play, Medicus introduces himself as 'a skilled master of noble birth from Asia'. He claims to have brought the troupe's medicines from 'Milan, Flanders and Arabia'.[33] The association of Medicus and his drugs with exotic locations appears to heighten their desirability and imagined efficacy, increasing the value and earning power of both his services and his wares. We might pause to reflect, here, on Herring's anxiety about 'Orient Colours' expressed in the title of his tract, and the way these are associated with 'counterfeit' physicians: claiming exotic connections seems to have been a regular feature of later mountebank theatre which incorporated foreign rhetoric and costumes with 'a strong Eastern flavour' – a clever ruse designed to heighten takings.[34] Quack theatre was also one of the earliest venues where the curious might encounter female performers for the first time. As Katritsky foregrounds, in the Erlau play, Medica, the quack's wife, comically interrupts the action, requesting that her medical skills, too, be enumerated; while she apparently offered marriage guidance, counselling and a women's clinic, her husband performed surgery.[35] That quack and mountebank theatre made people laugh and was often combined with music and dance was important for two reasons: the latter were widely considered to have therapeutic powers and comic engagement attracted larger audiences. Katritsky explains that there were other aspects of mountebank performance which sound compelling and significant:

> Central to the theatrical activities of many quacks was a class of performative
> routines ultimately intended not simply to attract and divert potential customers,
> or even to showcase the merits of their skills and patent medicines, but as powerful

---

[31] Kerwin, '"Where Have you Gone, Margaret Kennix?"', p. 100.
[32] M.A. Katritsky, *Women, Medicine and Theatre, 1500–1750: Literary Mountebanks and Performing Quacks* (Aldershot: Ashgate, 2007), p. 5.
[33] Ibid., pp. 37, 40.
[34] Ibid., p. 81.
[35] Ibid., p. 40.

> demonstrations, by natural or supernatural means, of the quack's personal authority
> over death. It encompassed onstage medical procedures, reports of wondrous
> happenings or other news items, or the staging of dangerous or magical routines
> ranging from sleight of hand or playing with live snakes to decapitations or even
> human flight.[36]

It would appear that powerful stage enactments of authority over death (reminiscent of shamanistic activities) could be highly lucrative; medicine and performance were certainly closely intertwined in early modern times.

Margaret Cavendish's *Sociable Letters* reveal that she was captivated by an Italian Mountebank group during her sojourn in Antwerp, returning every day to watch them perform:

> Here coming an Italian Mountebank, who had with him several persons to Dance, and
> Act upon the open Stage, also one which did Act the part of a Fool, and that all to draw
> a Company of People together, to hear him tell the Virtues, or rather Lies of his Drugs,
> Cures, and Skill, and to Intice, or Perswade them to Buy ... I saw this Fool Act his
> part so well, that many of the People bought more Drugs for the Fool's sake, than for
> the Apocryphal Physician's, which was the Mountebank.[37]

Cavendish was particularly riveted by the troupe's actresses and disappointed when the company disappeared from the city. She speculates:

> some said, the Physitians through Envy to the Mountebank, Bribed them out; the
> truth is, they had Reason, for the Mountebank was then so much in request, as most
> of the people made him their Doctor, and Jaen Potage (for so the Fool was named) was
> their Apothecary.[38]

The envious polemic of Dr Frances Herring encountered at the outset of this chapter, suggests that the situation in seventeenth-century London was probably very similar; indeed, Sir Francis Bacon's words confirm that physicians were not a popular medical choice – 'men ... will often preferre a Montabanke or Witch before a learned Phisitian'.[39]

The Body in Common

It would be easy to assume a sharp dichotomy separating the 'true' understanding about the body held by early modern university-trained physicians from the presumed ignorance and erroneous beliefs of unqualified healers and the general populace. In fact until the 1970s, the history of early modern medicine focused, almost exclusively, on the academic men who practised learned medicine and their management of diseases; however, the 1970s experienced a surge of interest in recovering and studying alternative forms of healing – 'popular' medicine, as it was labelled at the time. In the first decades of this research, unorthodox,

---

[36]   Ibid., p. 87.
[37]   Margaret Cavendish, *CCXI Sociable Letters* (London: William Wilson, 1664), pp. 405–6.
[38]   Ibid., pp. 407–8.
[39]   Francis Bacon, *The Two Bookes of Francis Bacon. Of the Proficience and Advancement of Learning, Divine and Humane* (London: Henry Tomes, 1605), II, f.3v.

unlicensed, empirics, quacks, mountebanks, cunning-folk and white witches sat largely on the superstitious, supernatural, 'low' side of the imagined fence, while educated, licensed practitioners who were assumed to practise a more scientific, secular, therapeutically sound form of physic, occupied the orthodox, 'elite' side of the fence. The divisive, vitriolic attacks against unlicensed practitioners readily accessed in the archives of the Royal College of Physicians and the Barber Surgeons' Hall encouraged historians to think in these terms. However, as Mary Lindemann reflects, there is now widespread agreement among medical historians that rigid binaries were a misrepresentation: 'It became clear that such dichotomies were flawed and that the overlap of "popular" and "elite" – or rather the presence of a broad substratum of common beliefs about health, illness, and therapeutics that most members of the society shared – best characterized early modern medicine.'[40] An examination of the cheaper end of the medical print market will help to illuminate these 'common beliefs'.

The sixteenth century witnessed a vast outpouring of relatively inexpensive quarto publications in the vernacular that might best be described as self-help guides to maintaining the body in health. Sir Thomas Elyot announced that his treatise or medical regimen, *The Castel of Helth* (London, 1539), dealt with, 'the Conservation of the body of mankynde, within the limitation of helth, which (as Galene sayth) is the state of the body, wherin we be neyther greved with peyne, nor lette from doing our necessary busynesse' (f.1r). His was a ground-breaking and highly influential text, which essentially pedalled the same Galenic, humoral model of the body that was taught in all the universities of early modern Europe. Academic medicine *c.* 1500 relied solely on book-learning: it was static knowledge gained largely from ancient Greek and Roman texts; there was no experimental element and it was not scientific in the modern sense of the term. The Galenic paradigm basically imagined the body as a large container of seething fluids called humours, which were made from the food and drink people consumed, and which had a nasty habit of increasing to the point of 'repletion' and excess, leading to 'corruption' and subsequent sickness (f.8r). Humoral balance was also affected by changes in the external environment – strong winds and rain, or periods of drought, could, for example, impact on the internal bodily environment.[41] Air that stank and was 'corrupted' by putrid things like unburied carcasses and stagnant water was thought to produce 'miasmas' – airborne poisons – which could be breathed in and give rise to diseases such as plague (Elyot, f.12r).[42] Bodies that were not in humoral homeostasis were prone to contracting such infections. The planets, too, influenced health and sickness; man and the universe were thus closely intertwined. From ancient times, through the early modern period and beyond, this was the dominant medical model of the body and it is probably how most people – lay and learned – imagined themselves.[43]

The literate could refine and extend their knowledge of the humoral body by reading texts such as Elyot's where they would learn that the four humours were blood, phlegm, black bile and yellow bile and these each had 'qualities' of heat/cold and dryness/moisture; the predominance of particular qualities determined one's 'complexion' or personality type.[44] Elyot's *Castel* provides a list of characteristics of each complexion. Thus the 'colerike' complexion is 'hote and drie' with a lean and lofty body; black or dark auburn, curly hair; a face as red as fire; a high voice; and the 'colerike' temperament is associated with little sleep; dreams about fire, fighting or anger; and a sharp wit (f.2v). In order to maintain health, the

---

[40]   Lindemann, *Medicine and Society*, pp. 1–17, at p. 16; Wear, *Knowledge and Practice*, pp. 28–9; Fissell, 'Introduction: Women, Health and Healing'.

[41]   Margaret Healy, *Fictions of Disease in Early Modern England: Bodies, Plagues and Politics* (Basingstoke: Palgrave, 2001), pp. 18–28; Wear, *Knowledge and Practice*, pp. 37–40.

[42]   Healy, *Fictions of Disease*, pp. 35–7.

[43]   Lindemann, *Medicine and Society*, p. 17.

[44]   Sir Thomas Elyot, *The Castel of Helth* (London, 1539), f.2r–3r. All citations are to this edition.

individual needed to identify his complexion – choleric, sanguine, melancholy, phlegmatic – from such lists and adjust his 'regimen', or habits and self-government, to suit his particular 'complexion' (f.2r–3r). 'Proper regimen' meant assiduously attending to the six 'non-naturals': namely, air quality; sleep and waking; food and drink; rest and exercise; excretion and retention; and the passions, including sex and the emotions (f.3r). Exercising temperance, with the restraint of all excesses, was the key to maintaining health. If the body became over-full it required some assistance: the diet had to be adjusted and the bodily container could be vented, and balance restored, by enemas, by taking purgatives and emetics, and by blood-letting (usually undertaken by a surgeon or other healer). Such notions about the body and its care were also transmitted orally and were widely accepted; they 'informed not only medical theories but more popular conceptions of health and illness as well'.[45] By the early seventeenth century, however, the humoral body had a powerful rival in the form of an alchemical-religious medical model introduced by the Swiss-German physician, Paracelsus, a century earlier. This encouraged a view of the body and the universe (the two were even more closely intertwined in this model), as a vast chemical distillery overseen by God, the divine alchemist. From the mid-seventeenth century a more mechanistic body-type – man as machine – also competed for attention. However, the dominant idea of the body throughout the early modern period was undoubtedly the age-old one – that of a seething sack of fluids prone to overfilling.[46]

In the sixteenth and seventeenth centuries, astrology and astronomy had a strong presence in medical theory (both Galenic and Paracelsian) and popularised versions of these ideas were disseminated to broad and heterogeneous audiences through the millions of almanacs that poured off the presses. In the 1660s one in three families bought an almanac yearly.[47] Many of these contained an image of a 'zodiacal man' which illustrated how each part of the body was governed by an astrological sign.[48] The four humours of the body were influenced by the planets and the signs of the zodiac and restoring the body to humoral equilibrium inevitably required some knowledge of the state of the heavens at different times of the year. Moon-lore and knowledge of eclipses were particularly important. A purge or phlebotomy administered at the wrong time could produce a negative outcome so almanacs supplied simple advice on the best times to be bled or receive a purge or emetic: 'Now art thou bid by gentle May/ Purge, vomit, bath and bleed.'[49] Additionally, they carried prognostications about the weather for the coming year, prevalent diseases and disastrous events like plagues, earthquakes, the deaths of high-ranking persons and civil unrest. Plagues could be caused by God's 'instruments' – the stars operating through divine permission. Almanacs also contained medical notes and advertised proprietary remedies such as 'Bateman's famous spirit of scurvy grass', as well as data on gardening and farming.[50] Astrological medicine was not considered marginal or confined to back alleys; many prominent members of the College of Physicians were practising astrologers and it was particularly fashionable in European court circles.[51]

Just as individuals like Pepys and Josselin employed several different forms of medical help simultaneously or sequentially, so there appears to have been relatively little cognitive

---

[45]   Lindemann, *Medicine and Society*, p. 14.

[46]   Ibid., pp. 16, 19.

[47]   Bernard Capp, *Astrology and the Popular Press: English Almanacs 1500–1800* (London: Faber and Faber, 1979), p. 23. See also Louise Hill Curth, *English Almanacs, Astrology and Popular Medicine, 1550–1700* (Manchester: Manchester University Press, 2007).

[48]   Capp, *Astrology*, pp. 204–5; Lindemann, *Medicine and Society*, pp. 28–9.

[49]   Capp, *Astrology*, p. 35; Wear, *Knowledge and Practice*, p. 381.

[50]   Capp, *Astrology*, p. 205.

[51]   Lindemann, *Medicine and Society*, pp. 251–2.

discomfort about the close association between supernatural/religious and naturalistic medical explanations and cures. While ancient Hippocratic medicine had largely excluded the supernatural from its theories of the origins of disease, from the inception of Christianity, religion demanded a key role in medical explanations.[52] Divine displeasure on account of collective human sin was thus the prime explanation for plague visitations; however, secondary causes – the mechanisms whereby God's punishment reached its victims – could be both supernatural and naturalistic. Evil angels, the stars, miasmic air and contagion were the favoured delivery agents listed in the vast number of plague pamphlets that poured off the presses during epidemics.[53] In 1603–4 alone, 28 books on plague were printed, circulating such beliefs.[54] The physician and playwright Thomas Lodge railed in his treatise:

> *This sicknesse of the Plague is commonly engendered of an infection of the aire, altered with a venomous vapour ... this dangerous and deadly infirmitie is produced and planted in us, which Almightie God as the rodde of his rigor and justice and for the amendment of our sinnes sendeth downe upon us. (sig. B2v)*[55]

Lodge foregrounded 'contagion' – 'an evil qualitie in a bodie, communicated unto an other by touch' (sig. B2v) – as an important mechanism for plague transmission and advocated fleeing from 'the conversation of those that are infected' (sig. L3r); indeed, most treatises urged readers to call upon God for help and then to get as far away as they could from the infected place.

God sent disease, but he played a key role in healing too. A remedy for fever taken from a manuscript written in Latin by the highly educated medieval nun trained in humoral medicine, Hildegard of Bingen, is illuminating of the important role of incantation in holy healing:

> *But when the person has a fever, take the fruit of the beech when it first ripens and mix it together in pure water, that is in spring water, and say these words: 'Through the holy girdle of the holy incarnation by which God became man, grow weak, you fever and you feverish conditions, and weaken your coldness and heat in this person N.'; and then give this water to the person to drink; you shall provide it for five days, and if the person has a quotidian or quartan fever, he will be delivered from them quickly, or God does not wish to free him.*[56]

It is likely that early modern 'white witches' regularly used such methods in which superstition overlapped with religion, and it is easy to understand how they could be accused by their detractors of darker practices. Other forms of religious healing included the use of relics, exorcism, the laying on of hands, supplications to saints and blessings.

Judging by the popularity throughout the medieval and early modern periods of a book enticingly called *The Book of Secrets of Albertus Magnus*, magical cures were very commonly employed. The first English edition was published in 1550 and from then until 1637 it went

---

[52]   Healy, *Fictions of Disease*, p. 19.
[53]   Ibid., pp. 23–69.
[54]   Paul Slack, *The Impact of Plague in Tudor and Stuart England* (1985; Oxford: Clarendon Press, 1990), pp. 23–4.
[55]   Thomas Lodge, *A Treatise of the Plague* (London, 1603). All citations are to this edition.
[56]   Jacques-Paul Migne, *Patrologia Latina*, tom. 197, *S. Hildegardis abbatissae Opera Omnia* (1855; Paris: Migne, 1882), p. 197: 1235C; trans. and cited in Debra L. Stoudt, 'Medieval German Women and the Power of Healing', in Lilian R. Furst ed., *Women Healers and Physicians: Climbing a Long Hill* (Kentucky: The University Press of Kentucky, 1997), pp. 13–42, 23–4.

through nine editions.[57] Writing on books of secrets in this period, Louis B. Wright concluded that these texts were eagerly consumed by middle-class readers who were hungry for information about pseudo-science.[58] They often suggest that their information comes from reputable sources like Aristotle and Pliny or, as in this case, Albertus Magnus. Magnus' *Secrets* reads as an anthology of superstitious lore, explaining the 'virtues' or marvellous properties of beasts, stones and herbs. The address is engagingly personal and practical; for example: 'If thou wilt overcome beasts, and interpret or expound all dreams and prophesy of things to come. Take the stone which is called *Amandinus*. It is of divers colours …' (p. 32). The following intriguing description is of a particularly efficacious herb, Verbena or Vervain:

> *The seventh is the herb of the planet Venus, and is called Peristerion, of some Hierobotane, id est Herba columbaria, and Verbena, Vervain. The root of this herb put upon the neck healeth the swine pox, impostumes behind the ears, and botches of the neck, and such as can not keep their water. It healeth also cuts, and swelling of the tewel, or fundament, proceeding of an inflammation which growth in the fundament; and the haemorrhoids. If the juice of it be drunken with honey and water sodden, it dissolveth those things which are in the lungs or lights. And it maketh a good breath, for it saveth an keepeth the lungs and the lights. It is also of great strengthin venereal pastimes, that is, the act of generation. If any man put it in his house or vineyard, or in the ground, he shall have abundantly revenues, or yearly profits; moreover the root of it is good to all them will plant vineyards or trees. And infants bearing it shall be very apt to learn, and loving learning, and they shall be glad and joyous. It is also profitable, being put in purgations, and it putteth aback devils.*
>
> *Yet this is to be marked, that these herbs be gathered from the twenty-third day of the moon until the thirtieth day, beginning the gathering of them from the sign Mercurius, by the space of a whole hour, and in gathering make mention of the passion or grief, and the name of the thing for the which thou dost gather it. (pp. 22–4)*

As well as curing incontinence and a spectrum of infections, Verbena heals cuts and haemorrhoids, lung diseases, solves bad breath and improves sexual potency and conception rates. Additionally, it can make you rich and your children happy and more apt to learn. It is useful as a laxative ('in purgations'); and in the same manner that it helps to expel faeces it can eject devils. However, the herb must be gathered with an eye to moon-lore and under the astrological sign, Mercury, within an hour, during which time you must talk aloud, naming the reason why you are gathering the herb. Ritual and performance are thus crucial to maximising Verbena's 'virtues'.

To modern readers, this may seem like nothing more than laughable 'hocus pocus', akin to the homely, ludicrous 'old-wives'' remedies advocated by the middle-class citizen's wife in Beaumont and Fletcher's, *The Knight of the Burning Pestle*:

> *Faith and those chilblains are a foul trouble; mistress Merriethought, when your youth comes home, let him rub all the soles of his feet, and the heels, with a mouse skin, or if none of your people can catch a mouse, when he goes to bed, let him roll his feet in*

---

[57] Michael R. Best and Frank H. Brightman eds, *The Book of Secrets of Albertus Magnus: of the Virtues of Herbs, Stones and Certain Beasts* (Oxford: Clarendon Press, 1973), Introduction, p. xii. All citations are to this edition.

[58] Louis B. Wright, *Middle-Class Culture in Elizabethan England* (Cornell: Cornell University Press, 1935), p. 562.

the warm embers, and I warrant you he shall be well, and you make him put his fingers between his toes and smell to them, it's very sovereign for his head if he be costive.[59]

This is certainly humorous; however, we should not underestimate the value of taking action and doing something, and of placebo effects, at a time when there were no true medical 'cures'. Magnus' *Secrets* alerts us to another widespread practice known as sympathetic magic in which herbs, minerals and animals that resembled – in terms of shape, colour, texture – something about the affliction, were thought to have curative virtues. For example, 'the stone which is called Chalzia' and 'hath the figure of hail and the colour and hardness of the Diamond', would, on account of its coldness (resembling hail), cool the heat of anger and lust (pp. 44–5). In a similar way, red plants would be used to treat bloody discharges and spotted and scaly plants to cure skin infections, while maidenhair tackled baldness.[60] Amulets worn on the body were imagined to harness sympathetic powers to enhance health or counter disease. There was also a notion of transference: if you rubbed a cut onion on a wart and then left the onion to rot, the wart would shrivel along with the onion.[61]

By the 1640s books of magical secrets were clearly losing a certain currency (the last English edition was published in 1637) and texts such as *Gerard's Herbal* (1597) were gaining ground. It is informative to compare Gerard's description 'Of Vervaine' to the one above. *Gerard's Herbal* supplies a detailed, technical description of the plant with an accurate picture. It tells the reader where to find it, the month it flowers, its Latin and English names, and proceeds to 'the Vertues':

> *Of Vervaine:*
> *It is reported to be a singular force against the Tertian and Quartaine fevers: but you must observe mother Bombies rules, to take just as many knots or sprigs, and no more, lest it fall out so that it do you no good, if you catch no harme by it. Many odde old wives fables are written of Vervaine tending to witchcraft and sorcery, which you may reade elsewhere, for I am not willing to trouble your eares with reporting such trifles, as honest eares abhorre to heare.*
>
> *Most of the later Physitions do give the juice or decoction hereof to them that have the plague: but these men are deceived … they looke for some truth from the father of falsehood … for it is reported, that the divill did reveale it as a secret and divine medicine.*[62]

This text is clearly determined to separate itself from superstitious herbals such as books of secrets 'tending to witchcraft and sorcery' and peddling 'odde old wives fables'; the sort of thing 'honest eares abhorre'. However, it advocates 'mother Bombie's rules'; that is, cunning-woman's lore about gathering Vervaine, and it takes a curious swipe at 'Physitions' who use the herb to treat plague. It suggests that such physicians have taken the devil's advice – they are practising Satanic physic which they have sought from 'the father of falsehood': by implication, they are in league with the devil. In *Gerard's Herbal* religious belief has replaced magical lore and even as it presents itself as more objective and quasi-scientific, it confirms its belief in a supernatural environment troubled by the foul workings of the devil.

---

[59]   Beaumont and Fletcher, *The Dramatic Works of Beaumont and Fletcher*, ed. Fredson Bowers (Cambridge: Cambridge University Press, 1966), Act 3, Scene 3, ll. 188–95.

[60]   Lindemann, *Medicine and Society*, p. 26.

[61]   Ibid., p. 26.

[62]   John Gerard, *Gerard's Herbal: The History of Plants*, ed. Marcus Woodward (London: Senate, Studio Editions, 1994), pp. 161–2.

To conclude, then, in early modern Europe, medical care began in the home and neighbourhood and the majority of healers were thus women. From time-to-time families sought the services of a variety of mostly unlicensed practitioners ranging from herbalists and cunning-women to quacks and mountebanks; professional physicians were not the popular choice even in well-to-do households. There was a broad stratum of shared cultural beliefs about health, illness and cures, which incorporated both supernatural and naturalistic ideas, and which traversed high and low, learned and lay social domains; this was popular medicine.

Select Bibliography

Beier, Lucinda, *Sufferers and Healers: The Experience of Illness in Seventeenth-Century England*. London: Routledge, 1987.

Davies, Owen, *Popular Magic: Cunning-Folk in English History*. London: Hambledon Continuum, 2007.

Fissell, Mary Elizabeth, *Patients, Power and the Poor in Eighteenth-Century Bristol*. Cambridge: Cambridge University Press, 1991.

Furst, Lillian R. ed., *Women Healers and Physicians: Climbing a Long Hill*. Kentucky: University Press of Kentucky, 1997.

Harkness, Deborah E., 'A View from the Streets: Women and Medical Work in Elizabethan London', *Bulletin of Medical History* 82:1 (2008), 52–85.

Healy, Margaret, *Fictions of Disease in Early Modern England: Bodies, Plagues and Politics*. Basingstoke: Palgrave, 2001.

Hunter, Lynette, and Sarah Hutton eds, *Women and Science, 1500–1700: Mothers and Sisters of the Royal Society*. Stroud: Sutton Publishing, 1997.

Kassell, Lauren, *Medicine and Magic in Elizabethan London: Simon Forman, Astrologer, Alchemist, and Physician*. Oxford: Clarendon Press, 2005.

Katritsky, M.A., *Women, Medicine and Theatre, 1500–1750: Literary Mountebanks and Performing Quacks*. Aldershot: Ashgate, 2007.

Kerwin, William, *Beyond the Body: The Boundaries of Medicine and English Renaissance Drama*. Amherst: University of Massachusetts Press, 2005.

Leong, Elaine, 'Making Medicines in the Early Modern Household', *Bulletin of Medical History* 82:1 (2008), 145–68.

Lindemann, Mary, *Medicine and Society in Early Modern Europe*. Cambridge: Cambridge University Press, 2010.

Pelling, Margaret, *The Common Lot: Sickness, Medical Occupations and the Urban Poor in Early Modern England*. London: Longman, 1998.

Wear, Andrew, *Knowledge and Practice in English Medicine, 1550–1680*. Cambridge: Cambridge University Press, 2000.

Superstition and Witchcraft

Simon Davies

When in the autumn of 1589 first one and then the rest of their daughters fell into strange fits and trances, Robert and Elizabeth Throckmorton, newly resident at Warboys in Huntingdonshire, at first refused to countenance witchcraft as an explanation. That the girls might be bewitched was the suggestion of the first physician they consulted; they got a second opinion. When this physician too was unable to explain the fits, a lengthy process was initiated which would end in the execution for witchcraft of John and Alice Samuel, and their daughter Agnes, in late December 1592.[1] Lord of the manor Sir Henry Cromwell, recipient of the Samuels' forfeited goods, used the money to institute a yearly sermon against witchcraft in Huntington.[2] Two hundred years later the sermons were still being given; only now 'the antiquated subject of Witchcraft' was seen as part of 'the gloomy gothic mansion of superstition', maintained only by 'the odious and mischievous powers of bigotry and ignorance'.[3]

The narrative may seem a comfortable one to the modern reader, and we may be inclined to agree with that assessment of the nature of witchcraft belief: a gloomy superstition borne of ignorance that we have long since thrown off. The reality is more complex, and recent research in this area has revealed levels of complexity and detail as never before. This standard narrative (which, as we can see, is a very old one) misrepresents not only early modern belief in witchcraft but also the debate around superstition itself during the early modern period, which went to the heart of the definition of religion itself. Both the latter and the views quoted above, however, which saw popular belief as borne of ignorance, are layers of interference that need to be passed through if we are to attempt to understand what witchcraft and magic meant for the majority of early modern people.

The traditional definition of witchcraft is the ability possessed by certain individuals to cause harm through magical or supernatural means, a process known in medieval and early modern Europe as *maleficium*.[4] This idea forms the basis for witchcraft beliefs wherever they

---

[1] *The most strange and admirable discouerie of the three Witches of Warboys* (London: for Thomas Man & John Winnington, 1593), sig. B1ʳ, B1ᵛ–B2ʳ, P2ᵛ–P4ʳ. For a modern account of the case see Philip C. Almond, *The Witches of Warboys: An Extraordinary Story of Sorcery, Sadism and Satanic Possession* (London: I.B. Tauris, 2008).

[2] Cuthbert Bede, 'The Witches of Warboys and the Huntingdon Sermon against Witchcraft', *Notes and Queries* 12 (1879), 70–71.

[3] M.J. Naylor, *The Inantity [sic] and Mischief of Vulgar Superstitions* (Cambridge: B. Flower for J. Deighton & W.H. Lunn, 1795), pp. i–ii.

[4] The historiography of witchcraft is large. Good places to begin include: James Sharpe, *Instruments of Darkness: Witchcraft in England 1550–1750* (London: Penguin, 1997); P.G. Maxwell-Stuart, *Witchcraft in Europe and the New World, 1400–1800* (Basingstoke: Palgrave, 2001); Robin Briggs, *Witches and Neighbours: The Social and Cultural Context of European Witchcraft* (2nd ed., Oxford: Blackwell, 2002); Richard M. Golden ed., *Encyclopedia of Witchcraft: The Western Tradition* (4 vols, Santa Barbara: ABC-CLIO, 2006);

have arisen in the world (which, at one time or another, is most of it).[5] The specific forms taken by the means, the source of power, the effects, the motivation and the strength of the beliefs, however, may differ greatly from place to place and over time. In the scholarly discourse of late medieval and early modern Europe, the source of this power was some form of contract with the Devil; many commentators made this contract the sole basis for their definition of witchcraft. Accusations and trials, however, overwhelmingly revolved around specific acts of *maleficium*, because it was this that the majority of lay people were interested in. 'What witchcraft *meant* to most ordinary people', writes Stuart Clark, 'was that it caused misfortune, not that it led to devil-worship. What was important was the harm it could do to themselves, their livelihoods and their families and communities.'[6] Popular beliefs about witchcraft were centred around the harm that witches caused.

In England, witchcraft was not a felony under common law until 1542. Prior to that it would have been prosecuted in the church courts; records are scarce and there are few known prosecutions. The 1542 statute was repealed under Edward VI and witchcraft was not brought back to the statute books until 1563. This 'Act against Conjurations, Enchantments and Witchcrafts' decreed imprisonment and the pillory for a first offence that did not cause death; death was the penalty for causing death and for repeat offenders. The Act also proscribed non-harmful magic such as divining for treasure and love magic. The 1563 Act was replaced by a revised Act in 1604: this added emphasis on consulting and interacting with evil spirits (where the 1563 Act had only specified conjuring them), and an extra passage on necromancy, for both of which the penalty was death. It also decreed death on the second offence for those practising love magic, and other ostensibly beneficent magic.[7] As a felony rather than a religious crime, the death penalty in England for witchcraft was hanging, unlike in Scotland and most of the rest of Europe, where witches were burnt at the stake. Relative to many other areas, England was an area of low conviction rates: 'Current estimates indicate that no more than 500 people were executed as witches in England, and the number may actually have been much lower.'[8] The majority of cases brought to trial in England ended in the acquittal of the accused.[9] Witchcraft was always a contested category, and however strong an individual's belief in it, such a belief did not rule out an equally strong belief in the highest possible standards of proof.

Brian P. Levack, *The Witch-Hunt in Early Modern Europe* (3rd ed., Harlow: Pearson Education, 2006); Brian P. Levack ed., *The Oxford Handbook of Witchcraft in Early Modern Europe and Colonial America* (Oxford: Oxford University Press, 2013). For useful overviews of the historiography, see Jonathan Barry and Owen Davies eds, *Palgrave Advances in Witchcraft Historiography* (Basingstoke: Palgrave Macmillan, 2007); Malcolm Gaskill, 'The Pursuit of Reality: Recent Research into the History of Witchcraft', *The Historical Journal* 51:4 (2008), 1069–88; Jacqueline Van Gent, 'Current Trends in Historical Witchcraft Studies', *Journal of Religious History* 35:4 (2011), 601–13.

[5]   See Wolfgang Behringer, *Witches and Witch-Hunts: A Global History* (Cambridge: Polity Press, 2004), p. 3.

[6]   Stuart Clark, 'Popular Magic', in Bengt Ankarloo and Stuart Clark eds, *The Athlone History of Witchcraft and Magic in Europe – Vol. 4: The Period of the Witch Trials* (London: The Athlone Press, 2002), p. 114.

[7]   James Sharpe, 'England', in Golden ed., *Encyclopedia of Witchcraft*. On the 1563 Act see also Norman Jones, 'Defining Superstitions: Treasonous Catholics and the Act against Witchcraft of 1563', in Charles Carlton ed., *State, Sovereigns & Society in Early Modern England* (Stroud: Sutton Publishing, 1998), pp. 187–203; on the 1604 Act see Jo Bath and John Newton eds, *Witchcraft and the Act of 1604* (Leiden: Brill, 2008). For the texts of the laws see Marion Gibson, *Witchcraft and Society in England and America, 1550–1750* (London: Continuum, 2003). For a detailed study of English legal procedure in relation to witchcraft, see Orna Alyagon Darr, *Marks of an Absolute Witch: Evidentiary Dilemmas in Early Modern England* (Farnham: Ashgate, 2011).

[8]   Sharpe, 'England', in Golden ed., *Encyclopedia of Witchcraft*, p. 411.

[9]   See Sharpe, *Instruments*, ch. 4.

There was only one major witch-hunt in England, and it was nothing compared to the great sixteenth- and early seventeenth-century panics on the European mainland. In East Anglia in 1645–7 'Witchfinder General' Matthew Hopkins and his colleague John Stearne were at the forefront of a movement which saw over a hundred people executed as witches. Before Hopkins – who was only in his late 20s – died, probably of consumption, in 1647, the witchfinders' activities were already under attack and their witch-hunt had effectively been halted by mounting doubts concerning their methods.[10] While in the short term the East Anglian witch-hunt re-ignited the witchcraft debate in print and elsewhere, it seems likely that in the long term it contributed to the spread of doubt concerning the evidence required to secure a conviction for witchcraft.[11] Previously, the largest single trial had occurred in Lancashire in 1612, at which 12 people were executed.[12] Usually trials were much smaller affairs, with only a handful of people tried.

Older witchcraft historiography posited England as significantly different from continental Europe in its witchcraft beliefs, the latter having its wild mountain-top sabbats and orgiastic devil-worship. This model was based, on the continental side, on limited study of a few major episodes of witch-hunting and their accompanying demonological treatises, generally in Germany and France, which were not representative of wider belief. It is now recognised that the traditionally claimed distinction between English and continental witchcraft is rather a distinction between endemic concern over *maleficium* at the local level and accompanying small-scale trials, originating within communities; and the large-scale witch-panics and accompanying witch-hunts (often but by no means always driven from 'above'; that is, not at the local level, and originating in scholarly rather than popular belief), which were rare anywhere in Europe. The focus on *maleficium* in English accusations and trials is typical of Europe more generally, and originates from popular beliefs about witchcraft, and from specific fears about material harm. The East Anglian witch-hunt is more akin to the larger, top-down witch-hunts of the old 'continental' model – although it remains true that it and others like it on the Continent would not have been possible without widespread popular support.[13] In fact there was an enormous diversity of patterns for the witch figure across medieval and early modern Europe, varying according to the intellectual traditions and folkloric histories of the place and time under consideration; a fertile area of scholarship in recent years has been close examinations of the beliefs of a particular region.[14] As Malcolm Gaskill writes, 'Historians now tend to see England as one of many

---

[10]   The best account is Malcolm Gaskill, *Witchfinders: A Seventeenth-Century English Tragedy* (London: John Murray, 2005). For a fascinating study of witchcraft in the popular press in the immediate build-up to the East Anglian trials, see Mark Stoyle, *The Black Legend of Prince Rupert's Dog: Witchcraft and Propaganda during the English Civil War* (Exeter: University of Exeter Press, 2011).

[11]   See Malcolm Gaskill, 'Witchcraft and Evidence in Early Modern England', *Past and Present* 198 (2008), 33–70.

[12]   See Robert Poole ed., *The Lancashire Witches: Histories and Stories* (Manchester: Manchester University Press, 2002); Philip C. Almond, *The Lancashire Witches: A Chronicle of Sorcery and Death on Pendle Hill* (London: I. B. Tauris, 2012).

[13]   See Robin Briggs, '"Many Reasons Why": Witchcraft and the Problem of Multiple Explanation', in Jonathan Barry, Marianne Hester and Gareth Roberts eds, *Witchcraft in Early Modern Europe: Studies in Culture and Belief* (Cambridge: Cambridge University Press, 1996), pp. 53–4.

[14]   Examples include: Éva Pócs, *Between the Living and the Dead: A Perspective on Witches and Seers in the Early Modern Age*, trans. Szilvia Rédey and Michael Webb (Budapest: Central European University Press, 1999); Alison Rowlands, *Witchcraft Narratives in Germany: Rothenburg, 1561–1652* (Manchester: Manchester University Press, 2003); Wolfgang Behringer, *Witchcraft Persecutions in Bavaria: Popular Magic, Religious Zealotry and Reason of State in Early Modern Europe* (Cambridge: Cambridge University Press, 2003); Robin Briggs, *The Witches of Lorraine* (Oxford: Oxford University Press, 2007); Julian Goodacre, Lauren Martin and Joyce Miller, *Witchcraft and Belief in Early Modern Scotland* (Basingstoke: Palgrave Macmillan, 2007); Michael Ostling, *Between the Devil and the Host: Imagining Witchcraft in Early*

European variants rather than an exception to a uniform pattern.'[15] An enormous variety of social conflicts and disputes could lie behind witchcraft accusations, and 'witchcraft' itself could manifest itself in a similar variety of forms. 'There is no such thing as a "typical" witchcraft case', writes Robin Briggs, 'although the vast majority do conform to a limited range of patterns.' Witchcraft accusations should be seen as 'a mosaic of small overlapping narratives', rather than forced into a single uniform model.[16]

One aspect of English popular witchcraft belief which does appear to have been almost unique to England – although this has not been satisfactorily explained – is the belief that witches kept an animal familiar. Ursula Kemp, for example, one of a large number of people tried as witches at St Osyth in Essex in 1582, reportedly confessed to having two cats, a toad and a lamb as familiars. The cats 'were to punishe and kill vnto death' while the toad and lamb 'were to punishe with lamenes, and other diseases of bodyly harme, and also to destroy cattell'.[17] Another St Osyth suspect confessed to having two familiars, one 'blacke like a Dogge' and the other 'red like a Lion'.[18] Familiars owned by suspected witches from Lincolnshire and Leicestershire in 1618 included a crow, a kitten and a mole.[19] The latter two were given to one Ellen Greene by another witch tried at the same assize; when she first came into possession of them, so the report goes, in a relatively typical narrative, they drank her blood:

> After they had suckt her, shee sent the Kitlin to a Baker ... whose name shee remembers not, who had called her Witch & stricken her; and bad her said spirit goe and bewitch him to death: the Moldiwarpe shee then bad go to Anne Dawse ... and bewitch her to death, because she had called this examinate witch, whore, jade, &c. and within one fortnight after they both dyed.[20]

The interrogation techniques of Matthew Hopkins turned up some even more bizarre examples, including 'a fat Spaniel without any legs at all' and a greyhound with the face of an ox that, when spoken to, 'immediately transformed himselfe into the shape of a child of foure yeeres old without a head, and gave halfe a dozen turnes about the house, and vanished at the doore'.[21] Familiars were often said to drink blood from their owners, and thus the belief in familiars was assimilated into much wider beliefs about the witches' mark, left by the Devil to seal the compact. Familiars drank blood from a teat or similar, which thus became a form of witches' mark; suspected witches were often stripped and searched

---

Modern Poland (Oxford: Oxford University Press, 2011); Laura P. Stokes, *Demons of Urban Reform: Early European Witch Trials and Criminal Justice, 1430–1530* (Basingstoke: Palgrave Macmillan, 2011); Wanda Wyporska, *Witchcraft in Early Modern Poland, 1500–1800* (Basingstoke: Palgrave Macmillan, 2013).

[15]   Malcolm Gaskill, *Crime and Mentalities in Early Modern England* (Cambridge: Cambridge University Press, 2000), p. 35. See also Bengt Ankarloo and Gustav Henningsen eds, *Early Modern European Witchcraft: Centres and Peripheries* (Oxford: Oxford University Press, 1990).

[16]   Briggs, '"Many Reasons Why"', in Barry et al. eds, *Witchcraft in Early Modern Europe*, pp. 54, 63. See also Malcolm Gaskill, 'Witchcraft in Early Modern Kent: Stereotypes and the Background to Accusations', in Barry et al. eds, *Witchcraft in Early Modern Europe*, pp. 257–87.

[17]   W.W., *A true and iust Recorde, of the Information, Examination and Confession of all the Witches, taken at S. Oses in the countie of Essex* (London: Thomas Dawson, 1582), sig. A8ʳ. For an excellent study of the construction of news pamphlets featuring witchcraft, such as this one, see Marion Gibson, *Reading Witchcraft: Stories of Early English Witches* (London: Routledge, 1999).

[18]   W.W., *A true and iust Recorde*, sig. B7ʳ.

[19]   *The Wonderful Discoverie Of The Witchcrafts of Margaret and Phillip Flower* (London: George Elde for John Barnes, 1619), sig. D4ᵛ, F1ᵛ. On this case see M. Honeybone, *Wicked Practise & Sorcerye: The Belvoir Witchcraft Case of 1619* (Buckingham: Baron Books, 2008).

[20]   *Wonderful Discoverie*, sig. F2ʳ.

[21]   Matthew Hopkins, *The Discovery of Witches* (London: for Richard Royston, 1647), p. 2.

in order to discover such marks. Thus popular belief in the familiar was accommodated within the diabolic discourse of scholarly demonology; familiars were simply labelled devils. The precise chronology and time-scale of the interactions between traditional belief and folklore on the one hand, and learned demonological theory on the other, are murky; it is likely that there was traffic in both directions, over a long period of time.[22] The diabolical nature of the familiar, for example, had been an aspect of the belief since the earliest known early modern trials.[23]

On average around 75 per cent of accused witches were women, and of those a majority were married; this is in line with wider European averages, though the statistics vary greatly over time and place, within England as much as between England and other areas.[24] There has been a tendency to overstate the gender imbalance in attempts to explain the rise of the witch-trials: while undoubtedly an issue, more significant are the intricate complexities of social relationships and the myriad factors that could affect their breakdown at any one time.[25] 'Witches tended to be women; but primarily witches were people whose conduct breached customary rules about neighbourliness – a breach which men as much as women were liable to commit.'[26] This aspect of the stereotype was certainly not imposed from 'above'; it was a longstanding element of traditional belief whose origins lay centuries in the past. As was the case throughout Europe, English writers on witchcraft simply were not interested in the predominance of women in witchcraft accusations, and gave it little consideration; many of them wrote about witches using the male pronoun.[27] Recent research has widened the gender question to look at the oft-neglected male witch, and to consider issues surrounding masculinity in relation to witchcraft.[28]

Witchcraft accusations within English communities were not limited by social class; although accused witches were more likely to be poor, it was not unheard of for those from wealthier backgrounds to be accused of the crime. But accusations were not made on the basis of class; witchcraft accusations were more likely to arise 'between closely matched rivals, rather than between those at opposite ends of the spectrum of wealth and power'.[29] The direct causes of witchcraft accusations were usually local disputes, often based around conflict over resources or the disruption of expected social relations. As Malcolm Gaskill writes, witchcraft accusations 'were the product of interpersonal conflicts rather than crazes sucking in scapegoats – conflicts which had many causes and took many forms'.[30] For

---

[22] On familiars see James Sharpe, 'The Witch's Familiar in Elizabethan England', in G.W. Bernard and Steven J. Gunn eds, *Authority and Consent in Tudor England: Essays presented to C.S.L. Davies* (Aldershot: Ashgate, 2002), pp. 219–32; James A. Sherpell, 'Guardian Spirits or Demonic Pets: The Concept of the Witch's Familiar in Early Modern England, 1530–1712', in Angela N.H. Creager and William Chester Jordan eds, *The Animal/Human Boundary: Historical Perspectives* (Rochester, NY: University of Rochester Press, 2002), pp. 157–92; Darr, *Marks of an Absolute Witch*, ch. 6.

[23] See Sharpe, *Instruments*, pp. 71–5, 82–5.

[24] Gaskill, *Crime and Mentalities*, pp. 48–9; Briggs, *Witches and Neighbours*, p. 6.

[25] For some clear-sighted discussion of the issues, see Robin Briggs, 'Women as Victims? Witches, Judges, and the Community', *French History* 5:4 (1991), 438–50; James Sharpe, 'Witchcraft and Women in Seventeenth-Century England: Some Northern Evidence', *Continuity and Change* 6:2 (1991), 179–99.

[26] Gaskill, *Crime and Mentalities*, p. 78.

[27] See Stuart Clark, 'The "Gendering" of Witchcraft in French Demonology: Misogyny or Polarity?', *French History* 5:4 (1991), 426–37; Clark's analysis also applies to English demonology. See also Stuart Clark, *Thinking with Demons: The Idea of Witchcraft in Early Modern Europe* (Oxford: Oxford University Press, 1997), ch. 8.

[28] Rolf Schulte, *Man as Witch: Male Witches in Central Europe*, trans. Linda Froome-Döring (Basingstoke: Palgrave Macmillan, 2009); Alison Rowlands ed., *Witchcraft and Masculinities in Early Modern Europe* (Basingstoke: Palgrave Macmillan, 2009).

[29] Briggs, *Witches and Neighbours*, p. 264.

[30] Gaskill, *Crime and Mentalities*, pp. 54–5.

witchcraft accusations to come to a trial it took 'a peculiar concatenation of circumstances: the contingent functions of institutions, officers and law codes from above, reacting with the beliefs, fears and customs of the lower orders. This peculiarity also explains why at many times and in many places there were no witch-trials.'[31] The traditional image of community-wide persecutions of deviant figures who became scapegoats for wider problems is not borne out by the evidence. Witchcraft accusations were often disputed and were more likely to be the result of specific interpersonal conflicts than collective hysteria.[32]

Elizabeth Bennett, for example, one of those tried at St Osyth, was accused of bewitching her neighbours to death because they had fallen out; her neighbours called her 'oftentimes olde trot and olde witche, and did banne and curse' her and her livestock.[33] The Lancashire witch-hunt of 1612 was precipitated by an encounter between a pedlar and young woman, Alizon Device, who was begging; accounts differ, the pedlar either refusing to sell or refusing to give some pins to Alizon, who subsequently, the report goes, bewitched him 'so that his bodie wasted and consumed'.[34] In 1621 Elizabeth Sawyer was accused (though she denied it) of bewitching Anne Ratcliffe to death because the latter 'did strike a Sow of hers in her sight, for licking vp a little Soape where shee had laid it'.[35] Such examples show a combination of very specific, yet petty, altercations, against a backdrop of mutual resentment, often revolving around scarce resources, that had usually simmered under the surface for long periods of time. They are typical examples of popular belief about how witchcraft functioned – the focus is on *maleficium* rather than diabolism.

That, when brought to trial, suspects were often said to have had bad reputations going back many years has much to tell us about the everyday experience of witchcraft in early modern English communities. Joan Cunny, for instance, tried at Chelmsford in Essex in 1589, confessed 'that she hath hurt diuers persons within this sixteene or twenty yeeres, but how many she now knoweth not'.[36] Agnes Browne, one of those tried for witchcraft at Northampton in 1612, was said to have been 'many yeares before shee died both hated, and feared among her neighbours: Beeing long suspected in the Towne where she dwelt of that crime, which afterwards proued true.'[37] It was reported of Elizabeth Sowtherns, also known as Demdike, one of the more notorious of the Lancashire witches (also tried in 1612), that she 'had been a Witch for fiftie yeares'. Thomas Potts, the authors of the pamphlet, commented: 'What shee committed in her time, no man knowes.'[38] 'A Great, and long suspicion' was held of Elizabeth Sawyer before proceedings were finally moved against her.[39]

As such examples demonstrate, recourse to law was far from a first resort. Often communities would attempt to deal with witchcraft without external help, either by simply placating the 'witch', or through extra-legal methods and folk remedies, the latter often via the assistance of white witches (discussed below). That this was the case indicates a degree of tolerance towards suspicious characters that only flared up into an official accusation when the circumstances were right or during periods of particular tension.[40] 'Witches were people

---

[31]   Gaskill, 'Witchcraft and Evidence', p. 34.
[32]   See Gaskill, *Crime and Mentalities*, p. 50.
[33]   W.W., *A true and iust Recorde*, sig. B6ʳ–C1ᵛ, at B6ᵛ.
[34]   Thomas Potts, *The Wonderfvll Discoverie Of Witches In The Covntie Of Lancaster* (London: William Stansby for John Barnes, 1613), sig. R3ʳ. See Almond, *The Lancashire Witches*, pp. 1–3.
[35]   Henry Goodcole, *The wonderfull discouerie of Elizabeth Savvyer a Witch, late of Edmonton* (London: Augustine Mathewes for William Butler, 1621), sig. B2ʳ.
[36]   *The Apprehension and confession of three notorious Witches* (London: Edward Allde, 1589), sig. A3ᵛ.
[37]   *The Witches Of Northamptonshire* (London: Thomas Purfoot for Arthur Johnson, 1612), sig. B2ʳ.
[38]   Potts, *Wonderfvll Discoverie*, sig. B1ᵛ.
[39]   Goodcole, *The wonderfull discouerie of Elizabeth Savvyer*, sig. A4ʳ.
[40]   See Briggs, *Witches and Neighbours*, conclusion.

you lived with, however unhappily, until they goaded someone past endurance.'[41] This is also key to understanding why, when neighbourly conflict arose, witchcraft was turned to as an explanation in some situations, but not others. As Barry Reay has convincingly suggested, 'those accused of witchcraft when neighbourly relations were breached ... were not chosen randomly'. 'They were those who had cultivated a reputation of witchcraft as a means of survival, who were linked to such people by blood or household ties, or who actually thought that they practised the art of black or white witchcraft.'[42] There were good reasons to believe certain people were witches, and it was these people who were targeted when events moved in that direction. But in general, witchcraft was only one of many available explanations for misfortune – if there was no connection with someone who had a reputation for witchcraft, it may never have been countenanced as an explanation (as in the Warboys case, where the Throckmortons protested that witchcraft was unlikely as they were 'but newly come to the towne to inhabite'[43]). Witchcraft suspects were not plucked out at random as a result of ignorance, but on the basis of what in the circumstances seemed a reasonable explanation: 'Notorious defamation', as Cambridge cleric William Perkins put it; that is, 'a common report of the greater sort of people, with whome the partie suspected dwelleth, that he or she is a Witch'.[44] Some people may have cultivated such a reputation; it is not unlikely that in many cases they believed in their powers. Witchcraft was not an explanation clutched at when others failed, but a deep-rooted belief held throughout society, by both accusers and accused.

There was another type of witch in operation during the period that definitely cultivated reputations for magical power: the white witches, also known as cunning folk, wise men/women, wizards or good witches. They offered services such as healing (of both humans and livestock), diagnosing and curing bewitchment, finding lost or stolen goods, divining for buried treasure, love magic, and a range of other beneficial magical services, and they appear to have been widespread throughout the period (and indeed beyond).[45] Owen Davies suggests that there were likely to have been several thousand cunning folk in England at any one time. They were found throughout the country, but were probably concentrated in towns and cities; they were predominantly male.[46] An idea of the prevalence of white witches in London can be gained from a list provided by John Melton in an anti-astrological

---

[41]   Ibid., p. 344.

[42]   Barry Reay, *Popular Cultures in England 1550–1750* (London: Longman, 1998), p. 130.

[43]   *Witches of Warboys*, sig. B2ʳ.

[44]   William Perkins, *A Discovrse Of The Damned Art of Witchcraft* (Cambridge: Cantrell Legge, 1608), p. 201.

[45]   The best study of cunning folk is Owen Davies, *Popular Magic: Cunning-Folk in English History* (London: Hambledon Continuum, 2007); see also Kirsteen Macpherson Bardell, 'Beyond Pendle: The "Lost" Lancashire Witches', in Poole ed., *The Lancashire Witches*; Sharpe, *Instruments*, pp. 66–70; Leland L. Estes, 'Good Witches, Wise Men, Astrologers, and Scientists: William Perkins and the Limits of the European Witch-Hunts', in Allen G. Debus and Ingrid Merkel eds, *Hermeticism and the Renaissance: Intellectual History and the Occult in EM Europe* (London and Toronto: Associated University Presses, 1988). On the wider European context, see Willem de Blécourt, 'Witch Doctors, Soothsayers and Priests: On Cunning Folk in European Historiography and Tradition', *Social History* 19:3 (1994), 285–303. The work of Keith Thomas was pioneering in this area, and remains valuable; see *Religion and the Decline of Magic: Studies in Popular Belief in Sixteenth- and Seventeenth-Century England* (London: Weidenfeld & Nicolson, 1971), ch. 8. Two studies of individual cunning men are Lauren Kassell, *Medicine and Magic in Elizabethan London: Simon Forman: Astrologer, Alchemist, & Physician* (Oxford: Oxford University Press, 2005); Alec Ryrie, *The Sorcerer's Tale: Faith and Fraud in Tudor England* (Oxford: Oxford University Press, 2008).

[46]   Davies, *Popular Magic*, pp. 68–9. On numbers of cunning folk see also Emma Wilby, *Cunning Folk and Familiar Spirits: Shamanistic Visionary Traditions in Early Modern British Witchcraft and Magic* (Brighton: Sussex Academic Press, 2005), p. 28.

tract which, although written for polemical purposes, is clearly intended to provide a recognisable picture: Melton lists 'the cunning Man on the *Bank side*, Mother *Broughton* in *Chicke-Lane*, yong Master *Oliue* in *Turneboke-street*, the shag-hair'd Wizard in *Pepper-Alley*, the Chirurgion with the Bag-pipe Cheeke, Doctor *Fore-man* at *Lambeth* ... and many such Impostors' – at least one of these can be identified as astrologer-physician Simon Forman.[47]

Sometimes the remedies of white witches could be what we would now term perfectly natural: as in the case of 'one Herring', who when consulted by a woman suffering 'straung aches in her bones' prescribed 'a little lynnen bagge of the breadth of a groate, full of small thinges like seedes, and willed her to put the same where her payne was most ... after a while ... she recouered, and was well'.[48] This was reported while the client was being tried as a witch, but the visit to a cunning man had no apparent relevance to the trial. Other practices fit more closely with our definition of magic. Norfolk clergyman Alexander Roberts reported a bewitched woman whose father visited 'a Wisard' for help; the latter offered the following advice:

> To make a cake with flower from the Bakers, & to mix the same instead of other liquor, with her own water, and bake it on the harth, wherof the one halfe was to be applyed and laid to the region of the heart, the other halfe to the back directly opposit; & further, gaue a box of ointment like triacle, which must be spread vpon that cake, and a powder to be cast vpon the same, and certaine words written in a paper, to be layd on likewise with the other[.]

Roberts complained that the practice was 'in no way iustifiable, and argued but a small measure of religion, and the knowledge of God'; nevertheless he also reported its effectiveness.[49] Joan Peterson, 'the witch of Wapping', worked as a cunning woman; among other things, she was reported to be able to identify the person responsible for bewitching a local woman's cow by boiling its urine and showing the face of 'the woman ... suspected to have bewitched it' in the bubbles.[50]

For the clerics who published treatises on witchcraft – scholarly works aimed at instructing readers in the correct responses, both spiritual and legal, to suspected witchcraft – such figures were not only wicked, they were *more* wicked than harmful witches. The '*Blesser or good Witch* (as we terme her)', declared Midlands clergyman Thomas Cooper, 'is farre more dangerous then the *Badde* or *hurting Witch*'.[51] Where the popular view (that is, the view of most lay people) focused on the ends to which magic was used, and condemned or made use of it accordingly, these pastor demonologists focused on the Satanic origin of magical power. If it was not divinely sanctioned, they argued, there was only one other place from which it could have come. While black witches merely harmed the body, therefore, white witches harmed the soul, because they seduced their customers away from God to the Devil – all the while appearing to do good. The traditional image might be of clerics

---

[47] John Melton, *Astrologaster, Or, The Figvre-Caster* (London: Bernard Alsop for Edward Blackmore, 1620), p. 21. On Forman, see Kassell, *Medicine and Magic*. An interesting fictional parallel to Melton's list is provided in Thomas Heywood's play about a cunning woman, *The Wise-Woman of Hogsdon* (written/performed *c.* 1604, printed 1638), see Act 2 scene 1.

[48] W.W., *A true and iust Recorde*, sig. C2r–v.

[49] Alexander Roberts, *A Treatise of Witchcraft* (London: Nicholas Okes for Samuel Man, 1616), pp. 52–4.

[50] *The Witch of Wapping* (London: for Th. Spring, 1652), p. 4.

[51] Thomas Cooper, *The Mystery Of Witch-craft* (London: Nicholas Okes, 1617), p. 232. See also Perkins, *Discovrse*, p. 174; John Gaule, *Select Cases of Conscience Touching VVitches and VVitchcrafts* (London: William Wilson for Richard Clutterbuck, 1646), pp. 30–31.

and demonologists whipping up the masses to greater fury in their witch-hunts; in fact the majority of those who wrote about witchcraft in England complained about the zeal with which the common people sought out witches to blame for their misfortunes, and argued for greater rigour and higher standards of proof when convicting them. Where they *did* call for more trials and executions was for white witches. As Perkins explained,

> though the Witch were in many respects profitable, and did no hurt, but procured much good; yet because he hath renounced God his king and gouernour, and hath bound himselfe by other lawes to the seruice of the enemie of God, and his Church, death is his portion iustly assigned him by God; he may not liue.[52]

Indeed, even those who visited white witches, it was argued, should feel the full force of the law.[53] This was nothing new – scholarly and clerical writers had been condemning popular magical practitioners, their clients and other 'superstitious' practices for centuries.[54] For Protestant reformers, such practices were an insult to providence: misfortune came directly from God, either as punishment for sin or as a trial for the elect, therefore seeking for help to get rid of it from charms, rituals, spirits, saints, magical professionals or anything else was blasphemous and idolatrous. English demonologies persistently stressed that the only true preventative and curative measures for witchcraft were, on the personal level, a godly life and, on the societal level, the maintenance of a learned, preaching ministry.[55] In this respect, therefore, the clerical theorists of witchcraft saw it as just one symptom of much wider problems, problems of true belief, for which the solution was widespread godly social reform. Both the ongoing existence and the polemical fervour of the attempt testifies to the gulf between this definition of witchcraft and the state of belief on the ground.

If the complaints of clerics are anything to go by – and indeed on this their descriptions of popular behaviour are corroborated by other evidence – despite its illegality there was little popular concern over making use of white witches, and much utilisation of their services. As we have seen, the activities of cunning folk were covered by the anti-magic statutes just as prominently as harmful magic; but few white witches were brought to trial during the period, and very few indeed for white magic alone. Cunning folk were usually brought to court when they were said to have also dabbled in harmful magic, although there is little evidence to suggest they were particularly prone to accusations of black witchcraft.[56] 'Charming is in as great request as Physicke, and Charmers more sought vnto then Physicians in time of neede', complained Perkins.[57] Physicians were expensive and remote during the period, and their success rate was not high. Nicholas Culpeper, himself a physician, commented on 'the medicines of the Colledge of Physicians that are so dear and

---

[52] Perkins, *Discovrse*, pp. 184–5; see also pp. 255–6.
[53] E.g. Roberts, *Treatise*, pp. 79–80; Stuart Clark, 'Protestant Demonology: Sin, Superstition, and Society (*c*.1520–*c*.1630)', in Henningsen and Ankarloo eds, *Early Modern European Witchcraft*, p. 77.
[54] See Euan Cameron, *Enchanted Europe: Superstition, Reason, and Religion, 1250–1750* (Oxford: Oxford University Press, 2010); Helen Parish and William G. Naphy eds, *Religion and Superstition in Reformation Europe* (Manchester: Manchester University Press, 2002); Alan Knight and S.A. Knight eds, *The Religion of Fools? Superstition Past and Present* (Oxford: Oxford University Press, 2008); Michael D. Bailey, *Magic and Superstition in Europe: A Concise History from Antiquity to the Present* (Plymouth: Rowman & Littlefield, 2007).
[55] E.g. Henry Holland, *A Treatise Against VVitchcraft* (Cambridge: John Legate, 1590), sig. H2ᵛ, I1ʳ; Perkins, *Discovrse*, p. 229; Cooper, *Mystery*, sig. A5ʳ⁻ᵛ; Richard Bernard, *A Gvide To Grand-Ivry Men* (London: Felix Kingston for Edward Blackmore, 1627), pp. 184–7.
[56] See Davies, *Popular Magic*, ch. 1, on cunning folk in the courts during the period.
[57] Perkins, *Discovrse*, p. 153.

scarce to finde'.[58] Most lay people saw white witches as a legitimate alternative, and must have obtained relief from them. Even physicians could recommend consulting cunning folk, having as they did generally clear ideas about where natural diseases ended and supernatural afflictions began.[59]

Beneficial magic was not just used by professionals; there was also a vast range of magical and quasi-magical practices used by ordinary folk on a regular basis. Such practices included the wearing of magical amulets, heeding omens and prophecies, sympathetic magic, avoiding or performing specific activities at specific times, spoken or written charms; used either to gain beneficial effects or to avoid malignant ones.[60] At the end of the seventeenth century, for example, John Aubrey recalled: 'I remember at Bristow (when I was a boy) it was a common fashion for the woemen, to get a Tooth out of a Sckull in the Church-yard: which they wore as a preservative against the Tooth-ach.'[61] Reginald Scot, though he did it for polemical purposes, included many examples of such magic in his sceptical treatise *The discouerie of witchcraft* (1584).[62] This sort of magic is difficult to trace; it was certainly rarely if ever prosecuted. While to some extent certain practices may have had links with old Catholic rituals, in fact popular magic had been condemned just as vociferously by Catholic writers before the Reformation as it was by Protestant writers afterwards.[63] It has been suggested that Protestantism drove people to magic by removing so much ritual from ecclesiastical orthodoxy, but this view is now being challenged. Not only did the Catholic clergy worry about popular superstition just as much as the Protestants did, Protestantism itself inspired a whole range of new forms of popular ritual and 'superstition'.[64]

Pertinent examples of popular 'magic' are the various methods of discovering witches or removing the effects of witchcraft which appear to have been widely practised. Famous among these is the ordeal known as swimming, which involved binding a suspected witch's hands and feet before throwing the suspect in water; if they floated they were guilty, if they sank they were innocent. There are two common misconceptions about the practice: first, it is often confused with use of the ducking stool, used not for witches but scolds (and otherwise troublesome women), and which was punitive rather than a method of determining guilt;[65] second, that people tried in this manner had to drown in order to prove their innocence – they were pulled out before this could happen (although being dunked in a river can hardly have been beneficial for the health of those experiencing it). The swimming ordeal was used, for example, in Bedfordshire in 1613 at the instigation of 'a Gentleman ... forth of the North', who provides instructions on how to carry it out and adds, 'I haue seene it often tried in

---

[58]   Nicholas Culpeper, *The English Physician Or An Astrologo-physical Discourse of the vulgar Herbs of this Nation* (London: William Bentley, 1652), p. 10.

[59]   See James Sharpe, *The Bewitching of Anne Gunter* (London: Profile Books, 1999), pp. 7, 46.

[60]   On beneficent magic and other rituals see Stephen Wilson, *The Magical Universe – Everyday Ritual and Magic in Pre-Modern Europe* (London: Hambledon, 2000); Edward Bever, *The Realities of Witchcraft and Popular Magic in Early Modern Europe: Culture, Cognition, and Everyday Life* (Basingstoke: Palgrave Macmillan, 2008), ch. 7.

[61]   John Aubrey, *Three Prose Works*, ed. John Buchanan-Brown (Fontwell: Centaur Press, 1972), p. 229.

[62]   R. Scot, *The discouerie of witchcraft* (London: Henry Denham for William Brome, 1584), esp. book 12. On Scot, see Philip C. Almond, *England's First Demonologist: Reginald Scot & 'The Discoverie of Witchcraft'* (London: I. B. Tauris, 2011).

[63]   See above, n. 54.

[64]   See Robert W. Scribner, 'The Reformation, Popular Magic, and the "Disenchantment of the World"', *The Journal of Interdisciplinary History* 23:3 (1993), 475–94; David J. Collins, 'Magic in the Middle Ages: History and Historiography', *History Compass* 9:5 (2011), 410–22.

[65]   On the ducking, or cucking stool, see Lynda E. Boose, 'Scolding Brides and Bridling Scolds: Taming the Woman's Unruly Member', *Shakespeare Quarterly* 42:2 (1991), 179–213.

the North countrey'.[66] James I had commended the practice in his treatise on witchcraft, explaining that 'the water shall refuse to receiue them in her bosome, that haue shaken off them the sacred Water of Baptisme'.[67] Matthew Hopkins would cite James' support for the practice in his justification of his own use of it; he claimed that only those found with the Devil's mark floated, although he protested that it 'was never brought in against any of them at their tryals as any evidence'.[68] Most authors of treatises on witchcraft thoroughly condemned the practice.[69]

Other measures of counteracting witchcraft or detecting its instigators included scratching the suspected witch, burning thatch from the suspected witch's house or, in the case of bewitched livestock, burning one of the livestock so afflicted. In 1579, for example, following a recommendation from a cunning man, an ostler scratched the witch he suspected to have bewitched him, 'that he made the blood come after, & presently his paine went awaie'.[70] Thatch from the cottage of Elizabeth Sawyer was burnt to try her guilt – the author of the pamphlet report of her trial, while condemning the practice as 'an old ridiculous custome', nevertheless notes its efficacy.[71] A pamphlet of 1579 reports of one Robert Lathburie that after sending away one Mother Staunton when she came begging, 'his Hogges fell sicke and died, to the number of twentie, and in the ende he burned one, whereby as he thinketh, he saued the reste'.[72] Anne Stiles, victim of an alleged possession in 1653, claimed in one of her lucid periods: 'if any thing at the present would give me ease, it must bee the burning of the Witches Cat and Dog, for then I know and am sure that the Devill will leave me, and goe and torment the Witch'. Eyewitness and author of the pamphlet report Edmund Bower admonishes her, writing that 'it was but a fancy, and a cure of the Devils own suggestions, and not a lawfull cure'.[73] Such examples make clear the likelihood that many cases of suspected witchcraft were dealt with within communities, never making it to court – communities had their own methods of dealing with bewitchment. The clerical view condemned such practices as out-and-out witchcraft themselves.[74]

However, we should not necessarily follow the clerics' lead, and condemn such practices, and the much wider sphere of popular magic of which they were a part, as 'superstitious' or necessarily opposed to 'right' religion. Although the theologians would not have agreed, for many if not most people during the period such activities, along with belief in ghosts, fairies and a wide range of spirits, were not seen as incompatible with Christianity.[75] Just because

---

[66]   *Witches Apprehended, Examined and Executed, for notable villanies by them committed both by Land and Water* (London: [William Stansby?] for Edward Marchant, 1613), sig. C2^r–C3^r. The pamphlet includes a woodcut illustration of the practice.

[67]   James I, *Daemonologie* (London: Arnold Hatfield for Robert Waldegrave, 1603), p. 80 (misnumbered 64). James' dialogue was first published in Edinburgh in 1597.

[68]   Hopkins, *The Discovery of Witches*, p. 6.

[69]   E.g. Perkins, *Discovrse*, pp. 206–7; John Cotta, *The Triall Of Witch-craft* (London: George Purslowe for Samuel Rand, 1616), ch. 14.

[70]   *A Rehearsall both straung and true* (London: [J. Kingston] for Edward White, 1579), sig. B2^r

[71]   Goodcole, *The wonderfull discouerie of Elizabeth Savvyer*, sig. A4^{r-v}.

[72]   *A Detection of damnable driftes, practized by three VVitches arraigned at Chelmisforde in Essex* (London: [John Kingston] for Edward White, 1579), sig. B1^r. William Drage lists a number of similar practices, *Daimonomageia* (London: J. Dover, 1665), p. 21.

[73]   Edmund Bower, *Doctor Lamb Revived, Or, VVitchcraft condemn'd in Anne Bodenham* (London: T[homas] W[ilson?] for Richard Best & John Place, 1653), p. 19.

[74]   E.g. George Gifford, *A Dialogve concerning Witches and Witchcraftes* (London: John Windet for Toby Cooke and Mihil Hart, 1593), sig. G1^r; Perkins, *Discovrse*, pp. 152, 206–7; Gaule, *Select Cases of Conscience*, pp. 75–7.

[75]   On ghosts, see John Newton ed., *Early Modern Ghosts* (Durham: Centre for Seventeenth Century Studies, 2002); Peter Marshall, *Beliefs and the Dead in Reformation England* (Oxford: Oxford University Press, 2002), ch. 6; P.G. Maxwell-Stuart, *Ghosts: A History of Phantoms, Ghouls, and Other Spirits of*

in the terms of the clerics aspects of popular belief may have been considered superstitious does not mean we should not think of them as equally devout as those beliefs prescribed by the Church (although on the other hand we should not presume devotion if we cannot find evidence for it). So often labelled part of the history of superstition, popular magic should really be considered part of the history of Christianity itself – when one considers that these beliefs were quite probably held by a majority of early modern Christians. Those beliefs of the learned theologians which have come down to us historically as 'right' religion were in the minority. The boundary between religion and magic was less starkly drawn for the majority during the period.[76] Rather than popular superstition, it would be fairer simply to think of these practices as popular religion.

The last person was executed as witch in England in 1685, and the witchcraft statute was repealed in 1736; the law that replaced it made magical imposture a crime.[77] The older view, as hinted at at the outset of this chapter, is of such beliefs and practices fading from view across the seventeenth century, and being all but gone by the time of the repeal of the witchcraft Act. But a great deal of critical work is currently revising this narrative. Ian Bostridge has shown that belief in witchcraft represented religious and political orthodoxy in the decades after the Restoration. Witchcraft, as an 'other', in both a religious and social sense, was a useful tool in developing ideas of social consensus and Christian fellowship, part of attempts to unify society after the shattering years of the Civil War and Protectorate. The decline, in intellectual circles at least, came when this vision ceased to be a plausible one, and the debate became linked to factional political causes.[78] The process was not one of inevitable growing consensus, however, but of multiple complex debates.[79] Ultimately it seems that it was a decline in confidence in the ability to secure a conviction for witchcraft, because of the questionable nature of the evidence involved, and hence a decline in and then cessation of convictions for witchcraft, which led to a decline in the belief, rather than the other way round.[80] No convictions made the crime easier to disbelieve, because doing so no longer led to worrying questions about the judicial process itself.

The repeal of the witchcraft Act was by no means the end of popular belief in witchcraft, however, and much current scholarship looks beyond the typical chronological boundaries of work in this field, set by the beginning and end of the witch-trials. Such research challenges the older model which has the Enlightenment sweeping away the cobwebs of superstition.[81] Popular belief in witchcraft remained robust long after the intellectual debate

---

the Dead (Stroud: Tempus, 2006); Owen Davies, *The Haunted: A Social History of Ghosts* (New York: Palgrave Macmillan, 2007); Jane P. Davidson, *Early Modern Supernatural: The Dark Side of European Culture, 1400–1700* (Santa Barbara: Praeger, 2012), ch. 5. On fairies, see Diane Purkiss, *Troublesome Things: A History of Fairies and Fairy Stories* (London: Allen Lane, 2000); Peter Marshall, 'Protestants and Fairies in Early Modern England', in C. Scott Dixon, Dagmar Freist and Mark Greengrass eds, *Living with Religious Diversity in Early-Modern Europe* (Farnham: Ashgate, 2009), pp. 139–60; Peter Marshall, 'Ann Jeffries and the Fairies: Folk Belief and the War on Scepticism in Later Stuart England', in Angela McShane and Garthine Walker eds, *The Extraordinary and the Everyday in Early Modern England: Essays in Celebration of the Work of Bernard Capp* (Basingstoke: Palgrave Macmillan, 2010), pp. 127–41. On both see also Thomas, *Religion and the Decline of Magic*, ch. 19.

[76]   See Sharpe, *Instruments*, p. 70; Wilson, *The Magical Universe*, pp. xxv–xxvi.

[77]   For the text of the Act, see Gibson, *Witchcraft and Society*.

[78]   Ian Bostridge, *Witchcraft and Its Transformations c.1650–c.1750* (Oxford: Clarendon Press, 1997).

[79]   For a recent analysis of a particularly important debate, see Julie A. Davies, 'Poisonous Vapours: Joseph Glanvill's Science of Witchcraft', *Intellectual History Review* 22:2 (2012), 163–79.

[80]   Gaskill, 'Witchcraft and Evidence'.

[81]   See Sharpe, *Instruments*, conclusion; Bostridge, *Witchcraft and Its Transformations*; Owen Davies, *Witchcraft, Magic and Culture 1736–1951* (Manchester: Manchester University Press, 1999); Owen Davies and Willem de Blécourt eds, *Beyond the Witch Trials: Witchcraft and Magic in Enlightenment Europe* (Manchester: Manchester University Press, 2004); Willem de Blécourt and Owen Davies eds,

had died away; people were being 'swum' as black witches into the nineteenth century; and white witches were plying their trade into the twentieth.

Early modern witchcraft is being uncovered as an ever more complex set of beliefs and practices than early research based only on specific areas and select trial records suggested. It was also a more mundane phenomenon than traditionally conceptualised: magic was a part of everyday life for most people; one of a number of possible explanations for when things went wrong, and at other times a source of help. The terms themselves, 'witches' and 'witchcraft', are contingent; both were used differently by different people and at different times; they could refer to an enormous variety of different practices. Current trends in witchcraft studies tend towards greater contextualisation of belief in witchcraft as just one element of much wider systems of belief and thought, with a concomitant focus on everyday manifestations of the belief, rather than periods of intense persecution which, current consensus suggests, were exceptional rather than the norm. Fruitful future study will no doubt come from further situating English witchcraft in its context, not only at the level of learned scholarship but in more detail at the level of popular belief. A more thorough contextualisation of witchcraft within wider discourses of what was once considered popular superstition is just one example of where this might occur.

Select Bibliography

Ankarloo, B., and S. Clark eds, *The Athlone History of Witchcraft and Magic in Europe – Vol. 4: The Period of the Witch Trials*. London: The Athlone Press, 2002.

Ankarloo, B., and G. Henningsen eds, *Early Modern European Witchcraft: Centres and Peripheries*. Oxford: Oxford University Press, 1990.

Bailey, M.D., *Magic and Superstition in Europe: A Concise History from Antiquity to the Present*. Plymouth: Rowman & Littlefield, 2007.

Barry, J., and O. Davies eds, *Palgrave Advances in Witchcraft Historiography*. Basingstoke: Palgrave Macmillan, 2007.

Barry, J., M. Hester and G. Roberts eds, *Witchcraft in Early Modern Europe: Studies in Culture and Belief*. Cambridge: Cambridge University Press, 1996.

Behringer, W., *Witches and Witch-Hunts: A Global History*. Cambridge: Polity Press, 2004.

Bever, E., *The Realities of Witchcraft and Popular Magic in Early Modern Europe: Culture, Cognition, and Everyday Life*. Basingstoke: Palgrave Macmillan, 2008.

Bostridge, I., *Witchcraft and Its Transformations c.1650–c.1750*. Oxford: Clarendon Press, 1997.

Briggs, R., *Witches and Neighbours: The Social and Cultural Context of European Witchcraft*. 2nd ed. Oxford: Blackwell, 2002.

Cameron, E., *Enchanted Europe: Superstition, Reason, and Religion, 1250–1750*. Oxford: Oxford University Press, 2010.

Clark, S., *Thinking with Demons: The Idea of Witchcraft in Early Modern Europe*. Oxford: Oxford University Press, 1997.

Darr, O.A., *Marks of an Absolute Witch: Evidentiary Dilemmas in Early Modern England*. Farnham: Ashgate, 2011.

Davies, O., *Witchcraft, Magic and Culture 1736–1951*. Manchester: Manchester University Press, 1999.

Witchcraft Continued: Popular Magic in Modern Europe (Manchester: Manchester University Press, 2004); Jonathan Barry, *Witchcraft and Demonology in South-West England, 1640–1789* (Basingstoke: Palgrave Macmillan, 2011).

Davies, O., *Popular Magic: Cunning-Folk in English History*. London: Hambledon Continuum, 2007.

Davies, O., and W. de Blécourt eds, *Beyond the Witch Trials: Witchcraft and Magic in Enlightenment Europe*. Manchester: Manchester University Press, 2004.

Gibson, M., *Reading Witchcraft: Stories of Early English Witches*. London: Routledge, 1999.

Golden, R.M. ed., *Encyclopedia of Witchcraft: The Western Tradition*. 4 vols. Santa Barbara: ABC-CLIO, 2006.

Knight, A., and S.A. Knight eds, *The Religion of Fools? Superstition Past and Present*. Oxford: Oxford University Press, 2008.

Levack, B.P., *The Witch-Hunt in Early Modern Europe*. 3rd ed. Harlow: Pearson Education, 2006.

Levack, B.P. ed., *The Oxford Handbook of Witchcraft in Early Modern Europe and Colonial America*. Oxford: Oxford University Press, 2013.

Maxwell-Stuart, P.G., *Witchcraft in Europe and the New World, 1400–1800*. Basingstoke: Palgrave, 2001.

Parish, H., and W.G. Naphy eds, *Religion and Superstition in Reformation Europe*. Manchester: Manchester University Press, 2002.

Sharpe, J., *Instruments of Darkness: Witchcraft in England 1550–1750*. London: Penguin, 1997.

Wilson, S., *The Magical Universe: Everyday Ritual and Magic in Pre-Modern Europe*. London: Hambledon, 2000.

Military Culture

Rory Rapple

In bustling London in 1609 an exclamation of *Pardonnez moi, je vous en prie* may have sounded a marvellously genteel note in the midst of the noisy chaos of urban life, but when the composer Thomas Ravenscroft used a rough phonetic approximation of this phrase – *Pardona moy ie vous an pree* – in one of his *Freemens songs for three voices* he seems to have had something other than courtesy in mind.[1] He put the words in the mouths of three demobilised military men, one treble, one tenor and one bass, and made them declaim: 'Wee be Souldiers three, / *Pardona moy ie vous an pree*, / Lately come forth of the low country, / with neuer a penny of mony.' In this context, the cosmopolitan phrase, so mannered in the abstract, became more menacing. The soldiers' apparent courtesy cannot hide their assertiveness, their appetite and their poverty. And when they demand that their fellow drinkers toast them – 'And he that will not pledge me this / *Pardona moy ie vous an pree*: / Payes for the shot what euer it is, / with neuer a penny of mony' – it is clear that they are threatening to exact an on-the-spot fine on all who resist their charm. Ravenscroft's ditty not only summons up a common scenario – the unsettling effect caused by an aggressive group, galvanised by drink and a sense of entitlement – but also gestures to the elusive and imponderable nature of early modern 'popular culture'.

As was the case with his more famous song *Three blinde mice*, the subject matter of *Wee be Souldiers three* probably made little difference to its reception. The song would have been transmitted to men and women not only in print but also orally – sung in the kitchen, the tavern and on street corners.[2] The reasons the early modern public bought Ravenscroft's *Deuteromelia* (1609) were manifold. Some may have been interested in the quality of his part-writing, others wanted to use it with friends or family, still others for musical instruction and some, no doubt, bought it on a whim or as a present for someone else. Can the complexities of human motivation and taste, especially in the past, really be categorised? Resisting the temptation to needlessly mystify, we should not be surprised that current historiographical consensus accepts that 'popular culture' in this period was socially fluid, marked by a lively interchange between oral and written forms of communication and expression.[3] Although the idea that firm divisions existed between 'elite' and 'popular' spheres of 'popular culture' has been in many ways abandoned, English social historians have posited the thesis that the shared 'common culture' that had existed at the beginning of the sixteenth century had become increasingly polarised over the following three centuries. While the relative

---

[1] T. Ravenscroft, *Deuteromelia: or the seconde part of Musicks melodie, or melodius musicke of pleasant roundelays; K. H. mirth, or freemens songs. And such delightful catches* (London, 1609), sig. B2v–B3r.

[2] Tessa Watt, *Cheap Print and Popular Piety, 1550–1640* (Cambridge: Cambridge University Press, 1991), ch. 1.

[3] A. Fox, 'Rumour, News and Popular Political Opinion in Elizabethan and Early Stuart England', *The Historical Journal* 40:3 (1997), 597–620.

downgrading of retrospectively imposed categories of social stratification can be liberating for scholars it does not mean that the challenges of reconstructing, analysing or measuring early modern 'popular culture' have been made any easier.

Theory can, perhaps, help us to get a grasp on the immensity of the question, creating a methodology by which the matter can be parsed: Peter Burke has suggested the potential usefulness of Bourdieu's arsenal of categories: *habitus*, field, symbolic production and social and cultural capital in our attempts to get at the pith of the matter of early modern cultural expression.[4] One can understand why. It is clear that the term 'popular culture' is not nuanced enough to do all the work historians have on occasions asked of it. Tim Harris has suggested that the utility of the concept is limited; it is a blunt instrument incapable of assessing the antagonisms between social stratification, religious doctrines, regional identity or political commitment.[5] We are also enjoined to be suspicious of the materials we extrapolate our findings from. The late lamented Bob Scribner cautioned that printed works could be false friends being less the direct testament of the masses but rather 'forms of downward mediation by educational or literate elites': if the study of popular culture were to deliver up its fruits, he argued, they would be found in uncovering the 'inherent tensions' between 'hegemonic' values, 'dominant' values and 'subordinate' values.[6] Certainly, the effect the wares of early modern 'popular culture' exerted on society may not have been as counter-hegemonic as once fondly thought. Tessa Watt has put forward the persuasive thesis that the availability of cheap printed works between 1550 and 1640 likely enhanced the homogeneity of attitudes throughout England, reinforcing existing opinions rather than challenging them.[7] But then again, the *poésie sur la page*, what remains in print, need not have been the *poésie dans la rue*, the unrecorded and perhaps unrecordable fashions and trends of the people, and it is almost impossible to say categorically how they might have diverged.

This chapter does not seek to resolve these theoretical and methodological matters. Dealing with a category of political culture that relates to a specific profession and the matters attached to it, it ends up being much more conservative. My aim is to provide a survey of some attempts to merchandise martial culture using the printed word over the sixteenth and early seventeenth century drawing on both primary and secondary works. I also intend to address and evaluate in some way the range of cultural expression about matters to do with war, soldiering and related topics during this period. Of course, because we are relying on the survival of written material to take the measure of opinion during the early modern period we can only access a fragment of what 'popular military culture' might have meant at that time, or what civilians' perception of the martial might have been. Whatever intimations of an oral tradition we have can only really be measured from sources like early printed books, State Papers, Court reports or other manuscript materials. Thankfully, there is no shortage of printed works with martial themes or military settings, or even works by soldier-authors, dating from the period between the battles of Bosworth and Sedgemoor. This material runs the gamut of genres, including, memoirs of military service, patriotic exhortations, apologies for the soldiers' profession, technical treatises on any of the many varied aspects of soldiering, accounts of battles and campaigns – domestic and foreign, ballads, as well as love-stories, picaresque accounts of quests, journeys from rags to riches, satires, comedies and tragedies.

---

[4]   U.P. Burke, 'Afterword', in M. Dimmock and A. Hadfield eds, *Literature and Popular Culture in Early Modern England* (Farnham: Ashgate, 2009) pp. 209–13.

[5]   Tim Harris, 'Problematizing Popular Culture', in Tim Harris ed., *Popular Culture in England, 1500–1850* (Basingstoke: Macmillan, 1995), pp. 1–27.

[6]   R.W. Scribner, 'Is a History of Popular Culture Possible?', *History of European Ideas* 10:2 (1989), 175–91, esp. pp. 177, 186.

[7]   Watt, *Cheap Print*, p. 330.

But before we move through a selection of the cultural riches of the early modern period, it is worth pausing, if only to remember that the unease expressed by Ravenscroft's *Wee be Souldiers three* had long been perennial. Before the late nineteenth century and the phonograph cylinder the only means of recording music was to write it down using some form of notation, and in Western Europe the vast majority of music so recorded had long been liturgical or semi-liturgical. Yet even in this genre (which we are often disposed to consider rarefied because of the circumstances in which it is encountered today) late medieval foreboding about the swaggering sense of entitlement exuded by martial men has left a significant legacy to the ear. No one is entirely sure what use the fifteenth-century melody *l'homme armé* was first put to – maybe it was a tune used initially to accompany forced recruiting, or, perhaps, it was a musical means of signalling protest against the pressing of resources and men by ravaging soldiers – but its subsequent use as the cantus firmus in over 40 mass cycles between the middle of the fifteenth and the end of the seventeenth century from the English Channel to Naples speaks for itself.[8] The original lyrics to *l'homme armé* warned the listener to fear the 'armed man' and don 'a coat of mail' as a precaution when he came. Yet during the fifteenth and sixteenth centuries people of all classes knelt before their God to the accompaniment of variations on this rather simple theme. Dufay's and La Rue's settings of the melody for masses are startling examples of how this popular song about the ravages of war spread far and wide. Settings by Obrecht, Josquin (two versions), Guerrero, Morales and even Palestrina survive. It is as if Elgar had composed a mass setting made up of variations on the theme of *It's a long way to Tipperary*. It is perhaps significant that the oldest surviving setting of *l'homme armé* we have is probably from the hand of the English priest-composer Robert Morton (*fl.* 1457–79), whose highly successful career in the Burgundian court chapel demonstrates how deeply England had been integrated into continental European affairs, an integration brought about by martial endeavour, spoil and conquest.[9] Here we have a potent example of the meeting of cultures, high and low, in the expression and adaptation of a martial theme.

Although England, unlike France, for much of this period had no standing army and relied on occasional recruitment by means of feudal array and enterprising captains to pursue its war aims, we should not be surprised that almost all aspects of English life were capable of being tagged with a martial theme. Storytellers had long found that a military backdrop could make any activity, any tale, any scenario appear more compelling, seasoning the mundane with urgency. Shakespeare's works – dramas intended for a socially mixed audience – illustrate this very well. Charles Edelman has demonstrated the extent to which the playwright's works were peppered with technical military vocabulary, from 'alarums' to 'palisades'.[10] This lexicon was obviously not alien to Shakespeare and not entirely incomprehensible to his audience – although we should be cautious on that score as much of that jargon may have been deployed to set the ambience in much the same way as high-sounding incoherent scientific and technological vocabulary might be employed in bad science fiction. Be that as it may, it cannot be denied that the array of martial settings Shakespeare brought to the stage was staggering, ranging from the Siege of Troy (emulating Chaucer) through Rome's civil convulsions onto the Wars of the Roses, but never contemporary England. And when it came to sketching martial characters, on one hand he

---

[8]   David Fallows, 'L'homme armé', in *Grove Music Online. Oxford Music Online* (Oxford University Press); Alison Latham, 'Homme armé, L'', in *The Oxford Companion to Music. Oxford Music Online.* Oxford University Press.

[9]   David Fallows, 'Morton, Robert (*fl.* 1457–1479)', in *Oxford Dictionary of National Biography* (Oxford: Oxford University Press, 2004). Morton's setting was secular not religious.

[10]   C. Edelman, *Shakespeare's Military Language: A Dictionary* (London: Athone, 2000).

could render with precision the patrician distain of the aristocratic officer Coriolanus, while on the other hand proffer his audience a vulgarian like Falstaff: both stock martial types.

Falstaff, in particular, epitomised the tarnish that grubby humanity brought to Chivalry's lustre. It is easy to imagine being intimidated by his shameless *pardonnez moi je vous en prie*. Falstaff's chivalric posing falls aside to reveal absurdity and self-interest. He stands as the emblematic early modern captain: unreliable, dishonest and dutiless. Nevertheless, Sir John's popularity with his audience shows that the mockery of this disparity between chivalric aspiration and reality bore some mark of verisimilitude for many people. Shakespeare's depiction of his corrupt mustering of substandard troops in Henry IV Part II, Act III, Scene 2, shows sharp satirical instincts at work. In one fell swoop Shakespeare mocks both the military profession and all early modern magistracy. His was but one response to omnipresent concerns about moral degeneracy, administrative corruption and social violence. We will return to the way martial themes threw the relationship between appetite and discipline into relief later in this essay. For now, it is enough to note that this tension conditioned attitudes to the martial profession throughout England's social hierarchy, co-existing with, and sometimes tempering, the allure of patriotism, prowess and glory. It is to the vexed question of how vainglorious patriotism could sit with the jarring reality of England's place in the military world that we now turn.

England's Martial Legacy

Sixteenth-century England lived under the shadow of a triumphant past. Once upon a time, during the fourteenth and fifteenth centuries, success had bred success. As a result the martial profession had been glamorous, at once a lure for aspirational and materialistic souls: soldiering had been a spectacular means to a lucrative end. The reminder that soldiering could provide windfalls was everywhere to be seen. When John Leland, the Tudor antiquary, wandered the highways of England in the late 1530s and early 1540s he was repeatedly informed that much of England's built environment had been erected *ex spoliis nobilium bello Gallico captorum.*[11] As K.B. McFarlane demonstrated, the real Sir John Fastolf, and many like him, had invested their proceeds from the spoils won during the French wars in magnificent ways which had a considerable impact on their environment and culture. In the early fifteenth century martial endeavour could enable a man to rise from being a mere esquire to become a knight of the garter and finally a baron of France.[12] The proceeds that the real Fastolf garnered from spoil and ransoms had facilitated the acquisition of estates in both England and France, and in turn had allowed him to project the proper image of gentility. He acted as patron for a circle of *littérateurs* translating de Pisan and composing works like *The Boke of Noblesse* articulating a moral vision that melded Roman virtues with chivalric endeavour.[13]

Upward mobility secured through winning favour and fortune on military campaign remained a common hope; once one's prowess had caught the monarch's eye the finer things

---

[11] K.B. McFarlane, 'The Investment of Sir John Fastolf's Profits of War', *Transactions of the Royal Historical Society*, 5th series, 7 (1957), 91–116.

[12] Ibid., p. 104.

[13] J. Hughes, 'Stephen Scrope and the Circle of Sir John Fastolf: Moral and Intellectual Outlooks', in C. Harper-Bill and R. Harvey eds, *Medieval Knighthood, 4* (Woodbridge: Boydell Press, 1990), pp. 109–46; K.B. McFarlane, 'William Worcester, a Preliminary Survey', in *England in the Fifteenth Century: Collected Essays* (London: Hambledon Press, 1981), pp. 199–225.

in life might follow. In Castiglione's *Il cortegiano*, the author had Federico Fregoso advise ambitious readers that if they found themselves on the battlefield it would be shrewd to

> *worke the matter wisely in separating himself from the multitude, and undertake his notable and bold feates which he hath to do with as little company as he can, and in the sighte of noble men that be of most estimation in the campe, and especially in the presence and (if it were possible) before the very eyes of his king.*[14]

Those entranced by the prospect of rewards from fighting ranged from the younger sons of gentry left to fend for themselves by primogeniture – for example, Sir Peter Carew (1514–75) whose enterprising wandering led him to fight at the battle of Pavia – to others, from yeoman to peasant, who felt restless enough to take a gamble on a new life: for example, Sydenham Poyntz (1607–60?) who left his apprenticeship, a 'life … [he] deemed little better than a dog's life and base', to go to the wars.[15] Even in Leland's time, however, lasting fortunes were more likely to be made from royal grants of monastic lands or leases in reversion rather than the battlefield.

The truth was that England's one-time martial glory proved difficult for Tudor and Stuart society to digest, let alone emulate. The brutal successes of Edward of Woodstock and Henry V in France, inspiring as they may have been, found no real echo during the sixteenth and seventeenth centuries despite the best efforts of Henry VIII, the second earl of Essex and the duke of Buckingham. Furthermore, in the sixteenth century, the ever-present genealogical crisis occasioned by the Tudors' lack of fecundity meant the horror of the Wars of the Roses remained potent and threatening examples of what could happen. Furthermore, the rise of confessional conflict cut across old dynastic and aristocratic loyalties and identifications changing the complexion of European martial activity, and indeed wonted ideas of Chivalry. This process of readjustment was necessarily combined with acclimatisation to the loss of all former English territories in France. But while the English could continue to feel phantom pains for their lost territories, the French retained customary ways of thinking about their erstwhile opponents. The perception that the English were a hardened bloodthirsty crew endured: Montaigne, for instance, continued to conjure up Froissartian images of the Black Prince, hard-hearted in the face of the wailing women and children of Limoges, and stories of English aristocrats, each covering their left eye until they had undergone the rite of passage of spilling French blood.[16] But, then again, he was a Gascon.

England's Battle-Roll

In England, by contrast, jingoistic attempts to recapitulate old glories fell flat. Henry VIII's expensive 'vanity' campaigns in France (1515–21, 1522–5, 1543–6) brought diminishing returns: Boulogne was sold back to the French only six years after annexation; Mary I's efforts to harness England to global Habsburg aims led to the loss of Calais; Elizabeth's piecemeal actions in the Low Countries and northern France, growing more sustained from the mid-1580s until her death were, despite their subsequent glorification as Protestant crusades,

---

[14] *The courtyer of Count Baldesser*, trans. T. Hoby (London, 1561), sig. Mi.r–Mi.v.

[15] J. Hooker, alias Vowell, 'Life of Sir Peter Carew', in *Calendar of Carew MSS preserved at Lambeth* (London, 1867), pp. lxvii–cxviii; *Relation of Sydenham Poyntz 1624–1636*, ed. A.T.S. Goodrick, *Camden Society Third Series Vol. XIV* (1908), p. 45.

[16] Montaigne, *The Complete Essays*, trans. and ed. M. Screech (London: Allen Lane, 1991), pp. 3, 782, see also p. 286.

defensive and were entered into because no alternative seemed possible; the limpness of uninspiring efforts to intervene in Cleves-Jülich (1610) and the Palatinate (1624) during James I's reign, were amplified by Charles I's lacklustre engagements with Spain (1625) and France (1627), each of which brought cumulative public disillusionment and protest from a political estate that demanded the impossibly glorious from foreign policy, but refused to fund it. Within decades Charles I's ignominious first and second Bishops' Wars (1639/40) were followed devastatingly by the 'Great Rebellion' or Civil War, which turned England's martial endeavours inward, resulting in the creation of an unprecedentedly self-aware, empowered, confessionalised and politicised martial caste. This new martial self-confidence, however, was not necessarily matched by international success. The most stirring martial performance on the international scene during that later period was, perhaps, the conduct of English troops under Sir William Lockhart's command at the battle of the Dunes during the siege of Dunkirk (1658), a display of prowess that would not be emulated again until the intervention of Williamite English troops in the European Nine Years' War.

Proximate theatres of war brought more assured success. England continued to project itself onto its northern and western hinterlands. English actions against Scotland brought devastating wins for Henry VIII at Flodden (1513) and Solway Moss (1542), pyrrhic victories at Pinkie (1547) and Leith (1559) (under Edward VI and Elizabeth I respectively), humiliating defeat with destabilising consequences for Charles I during the aforementioned Bishops' Wars. Scotland's military might had been bolstered by the experience of mercenaries who had served under Gustavus Adolphus and other Protestant leaders in the Thirty Years' War, but England's military dominance reasserted itself unexpectedly through Cromwell's 'providential' victory at Dunbar (1650). England's interaction with Ireland followed a different pattern. Under the Tudors a normatively small English army, augmented by many Irish-born troops, took upon itself the defence and gradual aggrandisement of governmental control there. The garrison's fragmentation around the sister-kingdom under the lax stewardship of English captains led to their parasitic integration into indigenous politics. Major rebellions in 1569 and 1579–83 brought short-term increases in troop numbers. Matters came to a head in the last decade of Elizabeth's reign, which was dogged by the profoundly destabilising 'Nine Years' War' which emptied Elizabeth's coffers. The rebellion was eventually broken by the decisive Crown victory at Kinsale in 1601. A rough 'pacification' followed, after which Jacobean Ireland presented an altogether more placid environment until the rebellion of 1641 which inaugurated a horrible decade of violence made bitter by confessional enmity, landlust and fear of expropriation.[17] This ended in the brutal suppression of the native population and its army in 1649 and 1650 by the New Model Army.[18] So, to sum up, the period witnessed relative withdrawal from continental Europe, but saw the rise of unassailable English hegemony in Great Britain and Ireland.

Alongside this undoubted archipelagic domination came a significant record of maritime endeavour. The lustre of England's naval record during the Elizabethan period was perhaps over-burnished by seventeenth-century public opinion. The early Stuarts' attempts to revisit these successes – especially Buckingham's pitiful failure in 1625 to repeat the storied Elizabethan raids on Cadiz of 1587 and 1596 – fell far short of expectations. Robert Blake's blockade of 1656 was much more successful and his sterling performances against the Dutch and the Spanish were the best promise of a better day to come.[19] It was clear by the early

---

[17]   R.J. Hunter ed., 'Men and Arms': The Ulster Settlers, c. 1630 (Belfast: Ulster Historical Foundation, 2012).

[18]   P. Lenihan, Consolidating Conquest (London: Longman, 2007), pp. 127–46.

[19]   M. Fissel, 'English Amphibious Warfare, 1587–1656', in D. Trim and M. Fissel eds, Amphibious Warfare 1000–1700: Commerce, State Formation and European Expansion (Brill: Leiden, 2005), pp. 242–50, 253–5.

seventeenth century, however, that the popular view of England's place in international affairs had fused with a hardened Protestantism and had fettered the realm's military options internationally. It was now the accepted view that England was indelibly Protestant and her natural enemies were Catholic Spain and the Papacy. But the public attitude to soldiers and their officers never ceased to be complex.

Shifting Views of the Martial Man

Prior to the sixteenth century the prevailing opinion about war and soldiering in England seems to have been largely suffused with the glamour of chivalry and knighthood. This made a significant impact on early English printing. In the 1480s, works to do with knighthood like Ramon Llull's *book of the ordre of chivalry or knyghthode* (1484), Malory's *Le Morte d'arthur* (1485) and de Pisan's *boke of the fayt of armes and of chivalry* (1489) were a staple of Caxton's output. Nevertheless, a number of intellectual trends contrived to challenge the chivalric worldview those titles espoused, and they soon percolated into the public sphere. Competing accounts of the virtues arose which were antagonistic to the chivalric ethos. The hope of erecting and defending a Christian commonwealth prevailed over the pessimistic Augustinian worldview that had obtained hitherto in influential educated circles. Consequently, greater priority was placed on the skills required to be a good participating citizen in a *res publica*. Italian humanism's fetishisation of the Stoicism of the Roman Republic valorised not only Cicero's destruction of Catiline, but also his antagonism with Julius Caesar, the epitome of charismatic military leadership. Civic republican thinkers were also renowned for their tirades against those who fought for money because of their vested interest in sabotaging peace. Any bright grammar-school boy in England, once he had learnt enough Latin and had been brought into contact with works like Cicero's letters or *De Officiis*, had the wherewithal to imbibe some of this ethos of civil engagement in the affairs of the *res publica*.

But, north of the Alps, a more pietistic influence was also in play. Here the idea of a universal call to holiness was becoming increasingly fashionable in the fifteenth and early sixteenth centuries. It was commonly believed that all the people of God – nobleman, knight and esquire, bishop, monk and priest, merchant, yeoman and bondsman – irrespective of their discrete professions should emulate Christ's meekness and mildness in the same way. This sat awkwardly with the wonted emphasis on magnificence, prowess and pre-eminence that characterised the chivalric programme. Desiderius Erasmus, who insisted on personal and institutional reform along rational lines, became the most erudite and influential ambassador for the assumptions that fuelled this new moral understanding. Erasmus was not merely a fierce critic of war, arguing that it was fundamentally irrational and therefore contrary to human nature, but also castigated the pretensions of the chivalric code. His *Querela Pacis*, an intense meditation on the infernal character of war, was a bestseller, being reprinted 20 times between 1517 and 1529 alone. According to Erasmus, the most significant obstacle to the successful attainment of education and holiness was the horror and chaos of war. In this light, soldiers, tainted by their association with war and the appetites it unleashed, could be seen, not as Christian professionals, but as profoundly anti-Christian, even bestial.[20] Erasmus went so far as to suggest that men of war should be refused a Christian burial. In his, much republished, lengthy treatment of the adage *Dulce bellum inexpertis*, he proposed that society had unrealistically glamorised warfare, ignoring its horror: 'it is the

---

[20] Desiderius Erasmus, *Collected Works of Erasmus, Vol. 27*, trans. B. Radice, ed. A.H.T. Levi (Toronto: University of Toronto Press, 1986), pp. 289–322.

cause of contempt for duty, disregard for law, readiness to dare any sort of crime. It is the source of the huge teeming flood we have of mercenaries, robbers, despoilers of churches and assassins'.[21] Kings and princes rather than inciting the people to acts of violence, should restrain their inhumane urges. But it was not merely the fetishised status of the man-at-arms that came under attack during this period. The Protestant Reformation levelled a radical challenge to the sacramental character of the Catholic priesthood. Following Henry VIII's break from Rome many who had been, or were being, trained up as priests, found new opportunities opening up before them in the service of kings, new opportunities that, once they had renounced mandatory celibacy, meant that they could themselves inaugurate successful dynasties based on royal largess. Furthermore, in England these *clercs manqués* were the very men who would set the intellectual tone during the period of Edward VI's reign and later take up the mainstay of state administration during the first two decades of Elizabeth I's reign.

Even though Henry VIII's appreciation of humanistic education and his growing commitment to overturning 'spiritually sterile' monasticism seemed, in some quarters, to signal his assent to some type of Erasmian or reformed programme, his warlike proclivities meant that the pursuit of pacifism for civic or salvific reasons would never find great favour during his reign.[22] Over the next century, it could be argued, those who strove for an ever greater reformation of England's church, state and society, having closed the monasteries sought to make a monastery of the whole world. After Henry's death, thinkers formed by 'commonwealth' thought and Ciceronian political thinking came to greater prominence in public affairs, not least the future pivotal Elizabethan state servants Sir William Cecil and Sir Thomas Smith.[23] While Smith briefly served as Secretary of State under Edward VI and again between 1573 and 1576, Cecil, later Baron Burghley, was undoubtedly the most influential figure in Elizabethan government, serving as Secretary of State from 1558 to 1571 and Lord Treasurer from 1572 until his death in 1598.[24] These Cambridge trained intellectuals found it difficult to accept at face value the great store military professionals placed in their own intrinsic value. Afterwards even in times of acute crisis Burghley never seems to have quite shaken off the anti-militaristic prejudices garnered from Erasmian and civic republican critiques of soldiers and soldiering, even though his eldest son (not his pet Robert) Thomas cut a somewhat martial figure. Thomas's own third son, Edward, became in his turn perhaps the most prominent early Jacobean soldier.

While there was always a place for patriotic appreciation of soldiers' service to the commonwealth during times of war, it was during periods where England was not formally at war that anxiety about the place of the martial man in society resurfaced with a vengeance, not least during the period between Elizabeth's intervention at Newhaven in 1563 and Leicester's expedition to the Netherlands in 1584. It was at these times that the category of martial man seemed somewhat anomalous and even dangerous.[25] Society had to cope with

---

[21] Desiderius Erasmus, *Collected Works of Erasmus, Vol. 35*, trans. D.L. Drysdall, ed. J.N. Grant (Toronto: University of Toronto Press, 2005), p. 322.

[22] For the confluence of humanist formation and an Henrician foreign policy agenda see R. Moryson, *An exhortation to styrre all Englyshe men to the defence of theyr countreys* (London, 1539).

[23] W.S. Hudson, *The Cambridge Connection* (Durham, North Carolina: Duke University Press, 1980), pp. 18–20, 26–30, 36–56; S. Alford, 'Reassessing William Cecil in the 1560s', in J. Guy ed., *The Tudor Monarchy* (London: Arnold, 1997), pp. 233–53; R. Ascham, *English Works of Roger Ascham: Toxophilus, report of the affaires and state of Germany, and The Scholemaster*, ed. W.A. Wright (Cambridge: Cambridge University Press, 1904), p. 231.

[24] S. Alford, *Burghley: William Cecil at the Court of Elizabeth I* (New Haven: Yale University Press, 2011).

[25] R. Rapple, *Martial Power and Elizabethan Political Culture: Military Men in England and Ireland, 1558–1594* (Cambridge: Cambridge University Press, 2008), pp. 19–50.

demobilised or unemployed soldiers. On stage Falstaff might amuse, but if he arrived in your street he could rape your daughter, pilfer your coin and ransack your house. As Sir Thomas Smith put it in his anatomy of the English commonwealth *De Republica Anglorum*: 'where men of war, Captains and soldiers be plentiful ... when they have no external wars wherewith to occupy their busy heads and hands accustomed to fight and quarrel [they] must needs seek quarrel and combats amongst themselves'.[26] Cecil was pithier when he stated: 'Soldiers in peace are like chimneys in summer.'[27] Other magistrates even believed that the state's own trained bands, established in 1573 – supposedly the epitome of civic republican engagement – were dangerous. In Herefordshire, for instance, a local worthy feared that the adult males mustered for the local militia 'being once trained and made meet for the martial service [would] afterwards be unruly and doe their Masters little work and small service'.[28] In short, arming the hoi polloi eroded deference.

The Garrison Writes Back

In spite of the *regnum Cecilianum*'s wariness of the martial profession London's printing presses continued to publish works with a martial theme. It is obvious a market existed for these titles, and while it is impossible to reconstruct with precision what the anticipated demographic for individual military works may have been, the range of works and authors of a martial character indicate that it had diverse tastes. It is hard to conceive that many people enjoyed the narcissistic meanderings of the peripatetic soldier Thomas Churchyard. Nevertheless he was certainly prolific: over 50 works of his were published appearing from 1552 until his death in 1604.[29] He specialised in two genres in particular. The first of these were jeremiads about the 'Tragical', 'unhappy' or 'hapless' nature of his life. In these works Churchyard, when not mired in self-pity would sharply blame the effeminate times he lived in for his misfortunes. The lingering moral turpitude in the body politic and the dominance of 'clerks', he argued, had frustrated not only all his efforts at advancement but also those of valiant soldiers just like him. He was not alone in pursuing this theme. Works by other soldier-authors, like Barnaby Rich and Geoffrey Gates, expressed impatience with the status quo quite as splenetically as Churchyard did.

The second genre that became Churchyard's *métier* was detailed accounts of the picaresque exploits of individual martial men. These accounts featured a kaleidoscope of, often forgotten, English captains such as Sir William Drury, Nicholas Malby, Captain Ward and Captain Shute, fighting in foreign theatres from Edinburgh to Malta, Leith to Metz. It is not clear what the utility or appeal of these works was. While their subject matter might be conceived of as stirring *per se*, Churchyard's execution of the tales was often poor and almost impenetrably prosopographical. Was Churchyard's *oeuvre* conceived as a means of creating martial celebrity during a period of official recusal from war by erecting a monument over the prowess of neglected English martial men, a boost in their reputation that might lead to greater public regard and, perhaps, royal or aristocratic patronage?

---

[26] T. Smith, *De Republica Anglorum*, ed. Mary Dewar (Cambridge: Cambridge University Press, 1982), p. 126.

[27] L.B. Wright, *Advice to a Son: Precepts of Lord Burghley, Sir Walter Raleigh, and Francis Osborne* (Ithaca, NY: Cornell University Press, 1962), p. 11.

[28] Quoted in L. Boynton, *The Elizabethan Militia 1558–1638* (Toronto: Toronto University Press, 1967), p. 91.

[29] Raphael Lyne, 'Churchyard, Thomas (1523?–1604)', in *Oxford Dictionary of National Biography* (Oxford: Oxford University Press, 2004); online ed., May 2006; Rapple, *Martial Power*, p. 73.

Churchyard seemed to signal this himself when he wrote that: 'if at large [he] touched some of [the captains'] noble exploites … [he] should make a greate volume of the same, and so seeme to write a Chronicle, that meanes but to treate of a fewe passages, for the passyng of the tyme, and the pleasuryng of [his] freendes'.[30] We see many of the same impulses and instincts at work elsewhere, for instance in William Blandie's dialogue *The castle, or picture of policy* (1581) where Geoffrey Gates, in between pursuing his favoured hobby of disparaging lawyers, lionises obscure captains, like Captain Corn and Captain Carey, who had served under John Norris in Friesland the previous year.[31]

Did out-of-work Elizabethan captains have the means to purchase these works? When it came to a 30-page quarto like *The castle* there should have been no problem, but more voluminous publications like *Churchyardes Chippes* (first published in 1575 and republished in 1578) and *Churchyardes Choise* (otherwise known as *A generall rehearsal of warres*) cannot have been inexpensive, and probably sold for about 1s 6d.[32] An unbound copy of *Chippes* coming in at 110 leaves may have cost about as much as one-and-a-half day's pay for a skilled workman in London (many of Barnaby Rich's works would have cost the same) while a behemoth of a publication like *Choise* (246 leaves) may have cost more. Perhaps they were purchased by the officers mentioned in the text, who then sponsored their reading aloud to a wider martial audience; in any case, such a price was not easily within the reach of the rank and file and would have required some sacrifices for a financially honest captain (if such a thing existed) although perhaps not for one on the take.[33] Churchyard's blow-by-blow accounts of military encounters accrued from eye-witness accounts may well have been a grittier, more authentic account of European warfare than, say, John Polemon's 1578 *All the famous battels that haue bene fought in our age throughout the worlde*, an anthology of European battles accrued and translated from continental authors such as Guicciardini and Natalis Comes. More Paul Kennedy than Andy McNab, Polemon's book, at almost 350 pages long, seems to have been pitched at a wealthy, erudite audience who took an interest in military history in their free time. It is culturally significant that no Hakluyt-type figure emerged in late Tudor England, offering a single majestic vision of English martial endeavour filling the undeniable gap between the messiness of Churchyard and the erudite reportage of Polemon. In different ways the service that both authors rendered may have provided some of the type of information that consumers in the seventeenth century sought in corantos purveying news from continental Europe, especially matters related to the Thirty Years' War, such as the *German History* or the *Swedish Intelligencer*.

As generation followed generation, the soldiers who had served in the campaigns of Henry VIII, Edward VI and Philip and Mary came to be replaced by men who came of age under Elizabeth. Unlike their predecessors these men were born into a world where the

---

[30] Rapple, *Martial Power*, pp. 86–91.

[31] W. Blandie, *The castle, or picture of pollicy shewing forth most liuely, the face, body and partes of a commonwealth, the duety quality, profession of a perfect and absolute souldiar, the martiall feates encounters and skirmishes lately done by our English nation, vnder the conduct of the most noble and famous Gentleman M. Iohn Noris Generall of the Army of the states in Friseland. The names of many worthy and famous gentlemen which liue and haue this present yeare. 1580. ended theyr liues in that land most honorably. Handled in manner of a dialogue betwixt Gefferay Gate, and William Blandy, souldiars. Anno 1581* (London, 1581), p. 23.

[32] Thanks to Elizabeth Evenden for her assistance in estimating a plausible price for this work and for pointing me in the direction of H.R. Plomer, 'Some Elizabethan Book Sales', *The Library*, series 3, 7:28 (1916), 318–29.

[33] For a sustained treatment of the erratic and corrupt mechanisms by which Elizabethan soldiers were paid see C.G. Cruickshank, *Elizabeth's Army* (Oxford: Oxford University Press, 1966), pp. 143–56. Captains did well by defrauding both their Queen and their soldiers. Philip Sidney's entertainment for the year of 1585 was meant to be 8d per diem, his Lieutenant's 4d per diem and his Surgeon's 20d per diem.

faith by law established, although not reformed enough for all tastes, was unambiguously Protestant. In this new world the old dynastic wars between Habsburg and Valois had been replaced by confessional conflict – civil war in France and insurrection in the Low Countries. The maelstrom that was engulfing northern Europe looked set to arrive on the beaches of England bringing atrocities and chaos like that recounted by George Gascoigne in his eyewitness account *The spoyle of Antwerpe* (1576).[34] These wars may have provided opportunities for employment for those motivated by conscience, but they also provided a revenue stream for men-at-arms who needed some work. Englishmen had thrown themselves into the fight against the King of Spain and the Pope in France and the Netherlands as volunteers in the early 1570s, but subsequently, from 1585 to 1603, with England and Spain officially at war (although no formal declaration was ever made) mobilisation was near total. The sectarian view of England's place in the world stuck in the public imagination, and the period from the Armada to the Twelve Year Truce in the Netherlands provided the model for international relations which much public opinion into the future believed to be the higher form of foreign policy. Blandie's *castle* with its treatment of Sir John Norris's exploits shows early intimations of this switch in focus from exploits in relatively non-confessionalised theatres of warfare, such as made up the most part of Churchyard's, to the sectarian crusades of the late sixteenth century. Significantly, the two greatest memoirs of English engagement in the Netherlands, Sir Roger Williams's *The Actions of the Lowe Countries* and Sir Francis Vere's *Commentaries* were published posthumously: Williams's in 1618, just three years before the ending of the Twelve Years' Truce and Vere's much later in 1657 at the height of the Protectorate's Anglo-Spanish War by Cambridge University Press. Vere's work, however, had long circulated widely in manuscript form.[35]

The increased opportunities for employment provided by greater engagement in French and Dutch wars did not satisfy every soldier however. Barnaby Rich's *martial conference ... betweene two soldiers* published in 1598, retained the spleen of his earlier works even though the international context had entirely altered. In spite of the persistent allure of martial matters now Rich managed to maintain the pose of the spurned retainer. The old enmity between knight and clerk that he had rehearsed in his earlier works, however, was now replaced by contention between two types of captain: the poor man of prowess, bloodied and bruised, versus the inexperienced, profiteering *parvenu* who had received a commission by means of corruption merely to make money. So Rich pitted Captain Skill, a veteran of France and the Low Countries against Captain Pill, a hoity toity officer, who had only ever brandished a sword 'in Finsbury fields'. The most telling criticism that Rich laid against the new military dispensation was that inexperienced captains – the 'gallant gentlemen' – were prodigal with the lives of their soldiers, raw men whom, he argued, they opportunistically 'sent to butchery', often for no better reason than to collect their dead pays.[36] War, like peace, had its own complaints.

Nevertheless in the popular mind, England had found its place in the global world order. The fusion of patriotism, anti-popery and warlike rhetoric burgeoned following the end of

---

[34]   G. Gascoigne, *The spoyle of Antwerpe. Faithfully reported, by a true Englishman, who was present at the same. Nouem. 1576. Seene and allowed* (London, 1576). This was republished in London in 1602 as *A larum for London, or The siedge of Antwerpe VVith the ventrous actes and valorous deeds of the lame soldier. As it hath been playde by the right Honorable the Lord Chamberlaine his Seruants.*

[35]   D.J.B. Trim, 'Vere, Sir Francis (1560/61–1609)', in *Oxford Dictionary of National Biography* (Oxford: Oxford University Press, 2004); online ed., January 2008.

[36]   B. Rich, *A martial conference pleasantly discoursed betweene two souldiers, the one Captaine Skil, trained vp in the French and Low Country seruices, the other Captaine Pill, only practised in Finsburie fields in the modern warres of the renowmed Duke of Shordich and the mightie Prince Arthur / newly translated out of Essex into English by Barnabe Rich* (London, 1598), sig. Diiir.

Elizabeth's Anglo-Spanish war and the accession of James VI and I. This heady cocktail was a product that was easy to market.[37] As D.R. Lawrence has demonstrated, between 1603 and 1645, almost 100 discrete titles related to military matters were published. Some, like William Barriffe's *Military Discipline: Or, The Yong Artillery Man* (first published 1635) were reprinted numerous times over span of decades.[38] The market for these works seems obvious. The wars that had lasted from 1585 to 1603 resulted in a great proportion of the male population having had military experience. According to David Trim, between 1585 and 1603 up to 108,625 were fighting for Queen and country on one front or other, a further 8,900 more had been mustered during the mass mobilisation of 1588. *Pace* Burghley, winter had returned and chimneys were once more getting use. This must have had a momentous impact on the orientation of English culture. In spite of the Treaty of London of 1604, as Trim has argued, the ideal of militant Protestant solidarity endured and many members of England's political elite remained active sympathisers with the Protestant internationalist cause. Recruiting for the Dutch army continued discreetly. According to Trim, 'On average there were almost 5,000 English mercenaries in Dutch pay each year from 1604 to 1610 inclusive.'[39] The potential market for materials about soldiering and war had greatly increased.

The court of James's eldest son, Prince Henry, was renowned for its fetishisation of the Protestantised chivalric ethos which sought to emulate the example of Philip Sidney and Robert Devereux, second earl of Essex.[40] The outpourings of grief that accompanied the prince's death in 1612 demonstrated the public sense of loss at the passing of what he had represented, a resilient militaristic Protestant future.[41] After the early 1620s, however, the Protestant foreign policy vaunted in the first half of James's reign was put to one side to be replaced by the irenic realpolitik that the King pursued in international relations, a vision that allowed for dynastic marriage alliances across the confessional divide.[42] James's reluctance to wade into the Palatinate to face down the Habsburgs on behalf of Frederick, his son-in-law signalled a tension between Protestant internationalist aspirations and prudent foreign policy. In the 1620s and 1630s Englishmen were aware of the horrors that were being perpetrated in Germany from works like *Lacrymae Germaniae: or, The Teares of Germany...* (1638) and *The Warnings of Germany: By Wonderfull Signes and Strange Prodigies Seen in Divers Parts of that Countrye between the Yeare 1618 and 1638* (1638) or cheaper news-sheets.[43] Most of this literature was anti-imperialist and larded with anti-popish rhetoric. Nevertheless, it is worth recalling that some Englishmen sought to make their fortune from serving in the armies of Catholic powers, some of them were even Catholic.[44]

---

[37] Watt, *Cheap Print*, pp. 158–9.

[38] D.R. Lawrence, *The Complete Soldier: Military Books and Military Culture in Early Stuart England 1603–1645* (Brill: Leiden, 2009) pp. 376–92, on Barriffe, see pp. 221–9.

[39] D.J.B. Trim, 'Calvinist Internationalism and the Shaping of Jacobean Foreign Policy', in Timothy Wilks ed., *Prince Henry Revived: Image and Exemplarity in Early Modern England* (London: Paul Holberton, 2007), pp. 239–58.

[40] R. Strong, *Henry Prince of Wales and England's Lost Renaissance* (London: Thames and Hudson, 1986), pp. 169–70.

[41] A good example is G. Wither, *Prince Henries obsequies or Mournefull elegies vpon his death vvith a supposed inter-locution betweene the ghost of Prince Henrie and Great Brittaine* (1612). See also G. McNamara, '"Grief Was as Clothes to Their Backs": Prince Henry's Funeral Viewed from the Wardrobe', in Wilks ed., *Prince Henry Revived*, pp. 259–79. For the works with a military theme dedicated to Prince Henry, see Lawrence, *The Complete Soldier*, p. 111.

[42] Trim, 'Calvinist Internationalism', pp. 250–53.

[43] B. Donagan, 'Halcyon Days and the Literature of War: England's Military Education before 1642', *Past and Present* 147:1 (1995), 65–100. See also Lawrence, *The Complete Soldier*, pp. 81–2.

[44] B. Donagan, *War in England 1642–1649* (Oxford: Oxford University Press, 2008), pp. 42–3.

New Discipline

In this fraught international climate attentiveness to the apparatus of military mobilisation at home was deemed a matter of urgency. As Barbara Donagan has demonstrated, although England's proper territory was never breached throughout the 'halcyon' period before the Civil War, the culture of the kingdom was becoming more and more militarised. The Armada experience of 1588 provided a plausible idea of what a threat to English national territory might look like and what the imperative to defend it would entail. War in the Netherlands had necessitated changes in technical military training so troops could come to grips with changes in technology. Training manuals became more and more popular during this period, despite the repealing of the militia law from 1604 to 1612, which meant that annual musters took place in few counties during that period.[45] The most lofty intellectual milieux advocated new forms of mobilisation, deployment and discipline as intently as military captains did. Reconstructing classical infrastructure and discipline had been a lively intellectual pursuit in northern Europe since Guillaume Budé had turned his attention to Roman coinage in his *De Asse*, and works by Frontinus and Vegetius, in particular, were pored over to glean relevant data about military matters from the classical masters. Particularly influential in this respect was Justus Lipsius, probably the most renowned intellectual of his day, who pondered the need to face up to the technical and logistical challenges posed by modern warfare in books five and six of his 1589 *Politicorum libri sex* (*Six Books of Politics*). Lipsius understood that, now more than ever, war required the skilful management of plentiful resources. Echoing Erasmus he posited that the biggest challenge which military commanders were forced to face was their raw material: their soldiers. Armies, he argued with great candour, were normally populated by the criminal classes. Training and drilling was vital in order to maintain control over them. The best model of discipline to follow was that proffered by the Romans. Any nation, once they had received the right instruction, could be moulded into effective soldiers. Lipsius advocated rigid adherence to clear rules for camps and garrisons and the incorporation of a regime of positive and negative incentives to bolster good behaviour.[46]

Intimations of this new discipline and rigour in martial matters had already been discernible in Blandie's *castle* in 1581 where some attempt was made to anatomise the command structure of the English forces in the Netherlands. A year later Thomas Styward's *The pathway to martial discipline … devided into three books* (1582) had produced a handbook which purported to give the 'order and use of the Spaniards in their martiall affaires'.[47] Later in the same decade the title of Barnaby Rich's 1587 effort, *A path-way to military practise: containing offices, lawes, disciplines and orders to be observed in an army, with sundry stratagems very beneficiall for young gentlemen, or any other that is desirous to have knowledge in martiall exercises* summed up almost all the ingredients sought after during this technical turn in military literature. Sir Roger Williams's *A briefe discourse of warre … with his opinion concerning some parts of the martiall discipline*, seemed somehow more authoritative not only because it was an assessment based explicitly on his personal experience fighting with both the Spanish and the Dutch, but also because Williams was renowned as a man of prowess. Leonard and Thomas Digges's treatise *Stratioticos* first published in 1579, republished in 1590

---

[45]   Lawrence, *The Complete Soldier*, p. 89. For an example of gentry opposition to the expense of mustering when the practice was revived in 1613 see T. Cogswell, *Home Divisions: Aristocracy, the State and Provincial Conflict* (Manchester: Manchester University Press, 1998), p. 111.

[46]   J. Lipsius, *Politica: Six Books of Politics or Political Instruction*, ed. and trans. Jan Waszink (Assen: Royal Van Gorcum, 2004), V, pp. 535–663.

[47]   A copy was later owned by Sir John Gell the Parliamentarian officer, see Donagan, *War in England*, pp. 144–5.

(with the last chapter reworked with annotations in 1624 and 1628 by Robert Norton as *Of the art of great artillery*), was much more technical focusing more on the hard mathematical requirements of 'modern militare discipline' and 'the rules and aequations algebraicall and arte of numbers cossicall ... requisite for the profession of a soldiour'.[48]

In the early seventeenth century most Drill Manuals published in England were based on the instructions devised by the Stadtholder Maurice of Nassau in his *Wapenhandelinghe van roers musquetten ende spiessen* first published in The Hague in 1607. English soldiers first came into contact with them while serving alongside Dutch forces against the Spanish, but they were domesticated by certain militia groups at home, most notable the London Artillery Company.[49] Maurician images of troop formations based on engravings of Jacob de Gheyn were commonly disseminated. De Gheyn's *Exercise of Armes* (1608), with a dedication to Prince Henry, was imported from The Hague in a format designed precisely for the English market.[50] English derivatives were frequently to be seen on the market, for example Clement Edmondes's *Maner of our modern training* (1600), Edward Panton's *A Table of the Art Military* (1614), John Bingham's classically influenced and widely acclaimed *Tacticks of Aelian: Or art of embattalling and army*, John Weymouth's *Low-Countrie training* (1617), and Gervase Markham's single sheet primer *A Schoole for young souldiers* (1615 and 1616) *inter alia*. In 1623, the Privy Council mandated the publication of England's first official manual for the trained bands, *Instructions for Musters and Armes*, which would be republished in 1625, 1631 and the summer of 1642.[51] But despite the existence of an English codification, foreign models remained marketable: for example *The Swedish Discipline, Religious, Civile and Military* (1632), the articles followed by the army of that 'New Starr of the North' Gustavus Adolphus, and the lavishly illustrated *The Principles of the Art Militarie; Practised in the Warres of the United Netherlands* (1637) by Henry Hexham. Hexham praised the Elizabethan tradition of fighting in the Netherlands, a tradition of which he had personal experience having been Sir Francis Vere's page in the early years of the century. His *Principles* was reprinted in 1642 and having recused himself from the Civil War he produced another book on discipline, in The Hague in 1643, which maintained, given how the English war was being conducted, that Dutch military discipline was still far superior.[52]

Ballads

The populace did not need to spend serious money to encounter military themes or soldier authors. Broadside ballads reflect to some degree more plebeian English feeling about the

---

[48]   L. Digges, *An arithmeticall militare treatise, named Stratioticos compendiously teaching the science of nu[m]bers, as vvell in fractions as integers, and so much of the rules and aequations algebraicall and arte of numbers cossicall, as are requisite for the profession of a soldiour. Together with the moderne militare discipline, offices, lawes and dueties in euery wel gouerned campe and armie to be obserued: long since atte[m]pted by Leonard Digges Gentleman, augmented, digested, and lately finished, by Thomas Digges, his sonne* (London, 1579).

[49]   For the London Artillery Company in Jacobean times see Donagan, *War in England*, pp. 56–7; Lawrence, *The Complete Soldier*, pp. 216–23.

[50]   For a full treatment of the famous depiction in Drayton's *Poly-olbion* of Prince Henry in a De Gheyn pose see T. Wilks, 'The Pike Charged: Henry as Militant Prince', in Wilks ed., *Prince Henry Revived*, pp. 180–211.

[51]   Lawrence, *The Complete Soldier*, pp. 135–94.

[52]   Ibid., pp. 185–94. A.F. Pollard, 'Hexham, Henry (*fl.* 1601–1650)', rev. M.R. Glozier, in *Oxford Dictionary of National Biography* (Oxford: Oxford University Press, 2004). For Gustavus Adolphus's glamour in England see Donagan, *War in England*, pp. 36, 45.

threat of war that emanated from the Continent.[53] As early as 1570 Thomas Bette's ballad *Against rebellious and false rumours* peeked disapprovingly into affairs in France and expressed particular worry about the way that the status of soldiers in that country was rising. Bette associated the prominence of men-at-arms with tyranny, expressing the anxieties of many about standing armies and what they could do to the liberties of the people.[54] Yet not all enlisted men were equally demonised. Thomas Ravenscroft's companion piece to *Wee be Souldiers three* entitled: *We bee three poore Mariners*, praises sailors and disparages soldiers: 'We care not for those martiall men, / that doe our states disdaine: / But we care for those Marchant men, / which doe our states maintaine.' This growing respect for the maritime calling as a constructive pursuit was not uncommon and can be seen, further augmented, in the 1630 ballad sheet: *Saylors for my money. A new Dity composed in the praise of Saylors and Sea affaires, briefly shewing the nature of so worthy a calling, and effects of their industry.*[55]

Old-fashioned militaristic patriotic prejudice also thrived in cheap print. For instance, the 1612 ballad *Saint Georges commendation to all Souldiers: or, S. Georges Alarum to all that professe Martiall discipline, with a memoriall of the Worthies, who have been borne so high on the winges of Fame for their brave adventures, as they cannot be buried in the pit of oblivion* displays the plaiting together of Protestantism, the martial, and national chauvinism. Perhaps soldiers who had fought in the Netherlands or at Jülich were meant to find its message energising. After reciting a list of renowned military figures from the biblical, classical, chivalric pantheons the author even found space to disparage the Irish and the Catholic cult of saints: 'Saint Patricke of Ireland, which was saint Georges boy, / and seven yeeres he kept his Horse, that then stole him away: / For which filthy fact, as slaves they doe remaine / Saint George, Saint George the Dragon he hath slaine.'[56] Simple patriotism and nostalgia for former glories remained a favourite theme as in, *A new Ballad, intituled, The Battell of Agen-Court, in France, betweene the English-men and Frenchmen*; and a favourite air for many ballads during this period remained *King Henries going to Bulloign.*[57] But there also was some passive-aggressive acknowledgement of England's martial shame to be found in the cheap print market as well. Following the humiliating failure of Buckingham's Île de Ré expedition of 1627, the common frustration of English Protestants was expressed in *Rochell her yielding to the obedience of the French King.* Here guilt and anxiety were given free reign through the contemplation of the sorry fate of the Huguenots: 'About twelve thousand soules / perished by hunger / While many needlesse bowles / in England were ill-spent.' The shame was enduring and the warning stark: as late at 1645 a pamphlet entitled *Malignants remember Rochell* could be subtitled *A warning to the Protestants of England.*[58]

Gallants, to Bohemia or, let us to the warres againe..., probably published around 1620, celebrated the opportunities for fame and fortune that the first stirs of the Thirty Years' War offered English soldiers. According to its author, these new stirs would give Englishmen the chance to emulate a catalogue of heroes – much the same list that Hexham would extol in 1637 – 'Essex , Cumberland and Drake', John Norris, the Veres, Philip Sidney, Willoughby, Humphrey Gilbert, John Hawkins and Frobisher. Already an Elizabethan cast had categorically eclipsed Arthurian and Plantagenet worthies. Nevertheless, it was hoped

---

[53] Watts, *Cheap Print*, pp. 11–38, 81–127.

[54] T. Bette, *A nevve ballade intituled, Agaynst rebellious and false rumours To the nevve tune of the Blacke Almaine, vpon Scissillia* (1570).

[55] *Saylors for my money a new ditty composed in the praise of saylors and sea affaires briefly shewing the nature of so worthy a calling and effects of their industry to the tune of The joviall cobler / [by] M.P.*

[56] Early English Broadside Ballad Archive (EEBA) ID: 20041, Pepys 1.87.

[57] *A New ballad, intituled, The battell of Agen-Court, in France, betweene the English-men and Frenchmen to the tune of, When flying fame* (c. 1615).

[58] *Rochell her yielding to the obedience of the French King*, EBBA ID: 20282 Pepys 1.96–7.

that the current stock of soldiers would hold fast: 'It never shall of us be said, / that English Captaines stood afraide: / Or such adventures would refraine, / Then let us to the warres againe.' It is difficult to say for sure what the intended use or audience for these ballads were. Angela McShane's exhaustive researches on seventeenth-century broadside ballads have led her to argue that ballads with military themes 'were written for and about ordinary soldiers and sailors' and show that the 'rank and file expected career progression; identified with a military culture and cause; and sought employment in the army as a rational and alternative choice of trade'. This certainly holds fast for the period from the Restoration on, but, as McShane points out, while 200 to 300 military ballads were published in London between 1639 and 1695, very few survive from before that time.[59] Yet D.R. Lawrence's research indicates the survivals from other genres dealing with military themes from the earlier period are significant.

But, in time, the distracted times came to England. Looking back over the period prior to the outbreak of England's Civil War for reasons why all hell broke loose, some chose to believe that the conflict had a superlunary cause and could have been predicted. James Howell's *The True Informer, who … discovereth unto the world the chiefe causes of the sad distempers of Great Brittany and Ireland* (1643) suggested that the chaos in England had been presaged by the comet of 1618 'which seem'd to looke directly to these North-west islands, in which posture it spent it self'.[60] Howell's output was dedicated to the attempt, from a royalist perspective, to carve out a moderate position in the midst of intensifying religious and political polarisation. In the maw of civil conflict, godly ballads on martial themes were becoming more common, one example would be William Starbuck's *spirituall song of comfort or incouragement to the souldiers that now are gone forth in the cause of Christ*, with its woodcuts of the earls of Essex and Warwick, John Pym and William Waller, each looking quite as impressive a Protestant military leader as Gustavus Adolphus.[61]

The religious complexion of the conflict was very apparent in print. The aforementioned *True Informer* contained a letter supposedly written by Sergeant Major Robert Kirle, to a Friend at Windsor. Kirle, having returned from serving in the Swedish and Dutch army enlisted in Parliament's army initially, but then changed his mind. A committed Protestant he nonetheless complained at the religious discord that had seized his regiment – 'some liked the chaplain of the regiment another thought his corporall preached better; some had so much of the spirit they wanted courage, and when they should fight, thought it better to pray'.[62] The religious formation that Parliament desired for its army can be seen in *The Souldiers Pocket Bible* of 1643, published by Giles Calvert; a robust statement of orthodox Presbyterian faith. Given its imprimatur by Edmund Calamy, Parliament's licenser for books of divinity, it consisted of verses excerpted (and occasionally abridged) from the Geneva Bible. The material was organised under headings that admonished the reader: 'A soldier must not do wickedly', 'A soldier must pray before he go to fight', 'A soldier must love his enemies, as they are his enemies, and hate them as they are God's enemies' and 'Soldiers, and all of us must consider that though God's people have the worst yet it cometh of the Lord'. The aim of the verses chosen was to convince the soldier of the rectitude of the cause for which he was fighting without getting too politically specific, to allay despair and doubt

---

[59]   A. McShane, 'Recruiting Citizens for Soldiers in Seventeenth-Century English Ballads', *Journal of Early Modern History* 15 (2011), 105–37, esp. pp. 108, 137.

[60]   J. Howell, *The trve informer who in the following discovrse or colloqvie discovereth unto the vvorld the chiefe causes of the sa[l]d distempers in Great Britanny and Ireland / deduced from their originals ; and also a letter writ by Serjeant-Major Kirle to a friend at VVinsor* (1643), p. 3.

[61]   W. Starbuck, *A spirituall song of comfort or incouragement to the souldiers that now are gone forth in the cause of Christ, Printed in the yeere wherein Antichrist is falling* (1644).

[62]   Howell, *The trve informer*, p. 39.

occasioned by adversity and defeat, and to enjoin the offering up of the credit for victory and its benefits to God, its author. All of which was designed to 'be also useful for any Christian to meditate upon, now in this miserable time of war'.[63]

The 1645 *Souldiers Catechisme: composed for the parliaments Army* by Robert Ram, Minister of Spalding, Lincolnshire, aspired to be more politically detailed, speaking to a particular context. The answer, for instance that Ram suggested, to the question: What side are you of, and for whom do you fight? Was:

> *I am for the King and Parliament; or, in plainer terms, 1, I fight to recover the King out of the hands of a Popish Malignant Company ... 2, I fight for the Laws and Liberties of my Country ... 3, I fight for the preservation of our Parliament ... 4, I fight in the defence and maintenance of the true Protestant Religion.*

The work in particular disparaged those who wished to remain neutral in the conflict and levelled opprobrium at those 'Protestants, of all degrees, [who] join with our Popish enemies'. It asserted that the proper war aims were 'the pulling down of Babylon', 'suppression of an Antichristian Prelacy'; 'the advancement of Christ's kingdom' and 'the preservation and continuing of the Gospel'. True to Ram's Presbyterian aims, the Catechism attributed Parliamentarian successes to God's pleasure at the National Covenant.[64]

Ram's Catechism went through a number of editions. It must have been its success that inspired Thomas Swadlin, a royalist clergyman, to produce a parody edition in 1645. Swadlin's subversive version, at first glance the eighth printing of the Catechism, not only mocked the Scriptural inaccuracies in the original, but mimicked its question and answer format to comic effect. For instance, the replies Swadlin gave to the question 'What is it that moves you to take up Armes and to engage your selfe in this Civill Warre?' included 'The ill will I bear to my Country'; 'The general forwardness of Anabaptists, Brownists, Antinomians, and Independents'; and 'The consent and provocations of all Scottish Ministers'. Swadlin's brazen satirical presentation of what he believed to be the essence of the ruinous, treacherous and evil ideology of the Parliamentarian army was designed to raise a laugh, but also to infiltrate itself into the hands of those who believed themselves to be picking up Ram's original to infuriate them, or give them food for thought.[65]

The Civil war brought with it many 'full relations' of the military events, although the royalists' inability to take London meant that the Parliamentarians initially stole the march on them when it came to printed propaganda. Charles Carlton, using Edgehill as an example, has shown how reports of battles in the early years of the Civil War were haphazard and inaccurate, although the quality of reportage improved as the conflict wore on. Attempts were made to provide overviews of the war so far, for example *A Briefe relation of ... what His Most Gracious Majesties commanders hath done in England* (1644) a royalist tract printed in Waterford and imported into England. Atrocity literature, once the staple of accounts of continental warfare, also became widespread, each side attempting to blacken the name of the other in order to deprive it of public support with titles like *An Exact Relation of the Bloody and Barbarous massacre at Bolton by an Eyewitness* (1644) tarring the Parliamentarians and *A True Relation of Prince Rupert's Barbarous Cruelty against the Town of Birmingham* (1643)

---

63   R.T. Fallon ed., *The Christian Soldier: Religious Tracts Published for Soldiers on Both Sides during and after the English Civil Wars, 1642–1648* (Tempe: Arizona Center for Medieval and Renaissance Studies, 2003), p. 7.

64   Fallon, *The Christian Soldier*, pp. 44–56.

65   Richard Bagwell, 'Ram, Thomas (1564–1634)', rev. Alan Ford, in *Oxford Dictionary of National Biography* (Oxford: Oxford University Press, 2004); Glenn Burgess, 'Swadlin, Thomas (1599/1600–1670)', in *Oxford Dictionary of National Biography* (Oxford: Oxford University Press, 2004).

or *A perfect declaration of the barbarous and cruell practises committed by Prince Robert* (*sic*) (1642) levelling accusations against the royalists. Rupert's supposed savagery was a regular theme in the Parliamentarian Press, while *An elegie on the death of Sir Charls Lucas and Sir George Lucas* commemorated General Fairfax's and Henry Ireton's reviled execution of the 'Twins of Valour' Sir Charles Lucas and Sir George Lisle.[66] Alongside these countless partisan accounts about sieges and pitched battles, came works alluding to the impact of the depredations carried out by armies forced to find free quarter and support themselves in the field. The New Model Army – 'no mere mercenary Army' – an entity brought into existence to defeat Parliament's enemies refused to disband at the assembly's request in 1647. By early 1649 English military men had purged Parliament of its enemies and had brought about the execution of the king, effecting a hitherto unimaginable seismic change in England's ancient constitution. Led by plebeian commanders and espousing radical religious and political opinions this political force seemed to go far beyond the fulfilment of every negative opinion voiced by the earlier Erasmians or Italian humanists on the dangers of martial men. Given the squeamishness that the Elizabethan architect of Protestant England Baron Burghley manifested about the inherent vices of soldiers it is somewhat ironic that from 1655 to 1657 11 military commanders ruled the morals of the country as Major Generals stamping out licentiousness.[67] But the military were in an unassailable ascendancy: after the death of Oliver Cromwell, the epitome of the military dictator who attempted between 1649 and 1658 again and again to put England back together, the toing and froing of the unfolding political and constitutional situation up to the Restoration of Charles II was determined by armed men. Essentially, in the first two-thirds of the seventeenth century the English went from being keen consumers of military culture to being consumed by it themselves.

Select Bibliography

Boynton, L., *The Elizabethan Militia 1558–1638*. Toronto: Toronto University Press, 1967.

Carlton, C., *Going to the Wars: The Experience of the British Civil Wars, 1638–1651*. London: Routledge, 2002.

Cruickshank, C.G., *Elizabeth's Army*. Oxford: Oxford University Press, 1966.

Donagan, B., 'Halcyon Days and the Literature of War: England's Military Education before 1642', *Past and Present* 147:1 (1995), 65–100.

Donagan, B., *War in England 1642–1649*. Oxford: Oxford University Press, 2008.

Durston, C., *Cromwell's Major-Generals: Godly Government during the English Revolution*. Manchester: Manchester University Press, 2001.

Fallon, R.T. ed., *The Christian Soldier: Religious Tracts Published for Soldiers on Both Sides during and after the English Civil Wars, 1642–1648*. Tempe: Arizona Center for Medieval and Renaissance Studies, 2003.

Fissel, M., 'English Amphibious Warfare, 1587–1656', in D. Trim and M. Fissel eds, *Amphibious Warfare 1000–1700: Commerce, State Formation and European Expansion*. Brill: Leiden, 2005, pp. 242–55.

Hunter, R.J. ed., 'Men and Arms': The Ulster Settlers, c. 1630*. Belfast: Ulster Historical Foundation, 2012.

---

[66] Charles Carlton, *Going to the Wars: The Experience of the British Civil Wars 1638–1651* (London: Routledge, 2002), pp. 171–3, 188.

[67] C. Durston, *Cromwell's Major-Generals: Godly Government during the English Revolution* (Manchester: Manchester University Press, 2001), pp. 154–86.

Lawrence, D.R., *The Complete Soldier: Military Books and Military Culture in Early Stuart England 1603–1645*. Brill: Leiden, 2009.

Lenihan, P., *Consolidating Conquest*. London: Longman, 2007.

McShane, A., 'Recruiting Citizens for Soldiers in Seventeenth-Century English Ballads', *Journal of Early Modern History* 15 (2011), 105–37.

Rapple, R., *Martial Power and Elizabethan Political Culture: Military Men in England and Ireland, 1558–1594*. Cambridge: Cambridge University Press, 2009.

London and Urban Popular Culture

Lawrence Manley

Popular Culture and Urban Culture

The concept of popular culture is enriched and complicated when considered in the context of early modern London. The rapid development of the metropolis in the period 1500–1700 was profoundly transformative of almost every aspect of English life. It is perhaps not surprising, then, that Peter Burke, a pioneering scholar of popular culture in the early modern period, significantly altered his concepts, definitions and approach to popular culture when he came to write specifically about London. In *Popular Culture in Early Modern Europe* (1978), a wide-ranging study extending into the nineteenth century covering areas 'from Norway to Sicily, from Ireland to the Urals', Burke first developed a number of ideas still influential in the study of popular culture.[1] The most important of these, based on the anthropologist Robert Redfield's contrast between 'the "great tradition" of the educated few and the "little tradition" of the rest',[2] was Burke's 'residual' theory of popular culture, which identified popular culture as belonging to the vast majority of non-noble and non-clerical commoners. In line with this distinction, Burke also contrasted the traditional forms in which popular culture was embodied, by way of participation and performance, with the modern textual forms through which popular culture was recorded and mediated.[3] He offered important refinements and qualifications to these distinctions, noting, for example, that 'there were many popular cultures or varieties of popular culture' and explaining that the two cultural traditions did not fully correspond to 'the two main social groups, the elite and common people' because the elite 'were amphibious, bi-cultural' and 'participated in the little tradition as a second culture'.[4] Nevertheless, Burke's account of popular culture was governed by a number of strong binarisms – his division of traditional early modern society into 'the elite and common people', his narrative about alteration of traditional popular culture by its textual dissemination (an initial flowering, but inflected by modernising forces like secularisation and the political development of the populace), and his conclusions about the eventual withdrawal of the elite from participation in popular culture.

But in 'Popular Culture in Seventeenth-Century London' (1985), where Burke turned in more detail to the special case of London, he significantly modified this bipolar approach. While contrasting, as he had in his earlier study, the participatory 'culture which came from the people' with the mediated 'culture which was intended for the people', Burke explained

---

[1]   Peter Burke, *Popular Culture in Early Modern Europe* (New York: New York University Press, 1978), p. xii.
[2]   Ibid., p. 24.
[3]   Ibid., p. 65. See also Stuart Gillespie and Neil Rhodes, 'Shakespeare and Elizabethan Popular Culture', in *Shakespeare and Elizabethan Popular Culture* (London: Arden Shakespeare, 2006), p. 1.
[4]   Burke, *Popular Culture*, p. 28.

that the culture of seventeenth-century London was 'something in between, or more exactly, a whole spectrum of artifacts and performances with a greater or less degree of participation from below or imposition from above'.[5] If Burke continued to polarise by speaking of 'interaction between the two cultures, learned and popular' or by dividing his essay between the 'traditional popular culture' reflected in London's 'calendar festivals' and the professionalisation of popular culture in entertainment and print, his primary focus on what he called the 'unusual environment' of early modern London led him to stress a number of factors specific to the city – its role as capital and centre of the printing trade, the development of its service economy and the high degree of social interaction it entailed, its high rates of literacy, population growth and in-migration – which made for exceptional fluidity in the cultural sphere. Burke's consideration of London, in other words, contributed to a key turn in the study of early modern popular culture and to the development of more recent interpretations which stress 'diversity and multiplicity' and concentrate on 'differentiated uses and plural appropriation of the same goods, the same ideas, and the same actions'.[6]

In keeping with this approach, the pages that follow take up both forms of popular culture distinguished by Burke – the performative practices associated with London's calendrical rituals and public celebrations and, more briefly, the textual mediation of popular culture in print and professional entertainment – with a view to underlining the elements of diversity and multiplicity inherent in each. Beginning with an account of London's traditional popular festivities as mediated by the chronicler and antiquarian John Stow in *The Survey of London* (1598), I suggest that inside Stow's intended narrative, which anticipates modern 'bipolar' stories in contrasting traditional popular rituals with the modern, textualised, elitist innovations and commercialised entertainments that replaced them, there is a counter-narrative showing that in sixteenth-century London the performance of public rituals and festive observances was already marked not only by the social polyvalence inherent to all such rituals themselves but also by the particular social complexities of sixteenth-century London life. Having examined, in this counter-narrative, the reciprocal influences of behaviour and writing, popular and elite purposes, I turn briefly to some 'mediated' varieties of popular literature and entertainment, where, in keeping with the nature of urban life, the inter-orientation of social perspectives helped to define the multiple uses and meanings of popular culture. To put the 'urban culture' of early modern London in the analytical foreground is not to dismantle or diminish the value of the concept of 'popular culture' but to see how popular culture signified and functioned in the myriad contexts of urban life.

'In Those Days': Narrating the History of London's Popular Culture

To emphasise the customary and ritualised nature of London life, Stow began his *Survey of London* (1598) with a commentary based on lengthy quotations taken from William Fitzstephen's *Descriptio nobilissimae ciuitatis Londoniae*, an account of twelfth-century London that formed part of Fitzstephen's biography of the City's most important saint, Thomas à Becket. In chapters on 'orders and Customes' and the 'Sports and pastimes

---

[5]   Peter Burke, 'Popular Culture in Seventeenth-Century London', in Barry Reay ed., *Popular Culture in Seventeenth-Century England* (London: Croom Helm, 1985), p. 32.

[6]   Barry Reay, *Popular Culture in England, 1550–1750* (London: Longman, 1998), p. 198 and p. 200, quoting Roger Chartier, *The Cultural Uses of Print in Early Modern France* (Princeton: Princeton University Press, 1987), p. 6.

of old time vsed in this Citie', Stow assembled something like a calendar of the popular practices associated with the traditional festive year: the sports and games enjoyed 'euery yeare ... at Shrouestuesday' to mark the beginning of Lent, the 'holy playes' performed at Whitsuntide and Corpus Christi, the winter holidays marked by 'Boares prepared for brawne' and 'fine and subtle disuisinges, Maskes and Mummeries'.[7] Citing Fitzstephen's praise for the culture of London – 'I doe not thinke that there is any Citie, wherein are better customs, in frequenting the Churches, in seruing God, in keeping holy days, in giuing almes, in entertaining straungers, in solemnisizing Marriages, in furnishing banquets, celebrating funerals, and burying dead bodies' (1:80) – Stow explained that his purpose in quoting Fitzstephen on 'the estate of things in his time' was to establish an historical contrast, so that 'by conference' with the present, 'the alteration' of London's customary, ritualised social life 'will easily appeare' (1:81).

To Fitzstephen's account of the past, the elderly Stow (b. 1524/5) added numerous memories of his own. He recalled, for example, the 'Lords of Misrule' who served the Lord Mayor and Sheriffs, 'beginning their rule on Alhollon Eue', and continuing their reign 'till the morrow after the Feast of the Purification, comonlie called Candlemas day' (1:97). Nearly every one of Stow's memories of the festive past is soured by some notice of its discontinuation under the Tudor regime. While it was the custom that 'in the moneth of May, the Citizens of London of all estates, lightly in euery Parish, or sometimes in two or three parishes ioyning together, and did fetch in maypoles, ... with Morice daunters, and other deuices for pastime all the day long, and towards the euening they had stage playes, and Bonefiers in the streets', this custom, following the 1517 May Day 'insurrection of youths against Aliens' was not 'so freely vsed as afore' (1:99). Stow recalled with particular bitterness that the great parish maypole of St Andrew Undershaft in Aldgate ward, once 'higher than the Church steeple' and then hung in an alleyway of the parish after 1517, was finally destroyed in the reforming reign of Edward VI, when a zealous preacher, claiming 'this shaft was made an Idoll', persuaded the neighbours to saw it in pieces and burn it (1:144). Stow observed with equal bitterness the decline of the 'the feast of S. Bartholomew the Apostle', when the London Skinners had once held their play at Clerkenwell and when wrestling and long-bow matches were held before the Lord Mayor, Aldermen, and Sheriffs:

> *What should I speake of this ancient dayly exercises in the long bow by Citizens of the Citie, now almost cleane left off and forsaken? I ouerpass it: for by the meane of closing in the common grounds, our Archers for want of roome to shoote abroad, creepe into bowling Allies, and ordinary dicing houses, nearer home, where they have roome enough to hazard their money an vnlawfull games: and there I leaue them to take their pleasures. (1:104)*

For the Catholic Stow, nostalgic for the past, it appeared that the traditional forms of celebration among the people of London were being displaced by the pursuit of religious reform, the development of modern commerce and the withdrawal of Londoners from a common public life into diversified private interests and pleasures. The many customary practices of the past, recorded in Fitzstephen and verified by his own research and personal memory, 'do plainely proue', said Stow, 'that in those days, the inhabitants & repayrers to this Citie of what estate soeuer, spirituall or temporall, hauing houses here, liued together in good amity with the citizens, euery man obseruing the customes & orders of the Citty' (1:84). The implication could not be plainer: the 'spirituall and temporall' authorities of the

---

[7]   John Stow, *A Survey of London* [1598], ed. Charles Lethbridge Kingsford (2 vols, 1908; rpt Oxford: Clarendon Press, 1971), vol. 1, pp. 92–7. References in the text are to this edition.

modern day, having withdrawn themselves from 'good amity' with the people of London, had abandoned the customary past and imposed new order from above.

For Stow, no festival offered a more disturbing example of this pattern than the transformation of the traditional Midsummer Watch, suppressed during his lifetime. Though city watches had 'laborious' aspects linked to the functions of policing imposed by the authorities, Stow's interest clearly lay in the popular nature of 'our pleasures and pastimes in watching by night':

> In the moneths of Iune, and Iuly, on the Vigiles of festiuall days, and on the same festiuall days in the Euenings ... there were visually made Bonefiers in the streets, euery man bestowing wood or labour towards them: the wealthier sort also before their doors near to the said Bonefiers, would set out Tables ... whereunto they would inuite their neighbours and passengers also to sit, and bee merrie with them in great familiaritie, praysing God for his benefites bestowed upon them. (1:101)

The 'good amitie' of these neighbourhood feasts was accompanied by a huge public display during the standing and marching watches held 'on the Vigil of Saint Iohn the Baptist [24 June], and on Saint *Peter* and *Paule* the Apostles [28 June]', when 'euery mans door' was adorned with green birch, fennel, lily garlands and 'lampes of glasse, with oyle burning in them all the night', while a massive procession of London's officials and guildsmen 'passed through the principal streets' of the city along the long-accustomed ceremonial route. Included were 'diuers pageants' and 'Morris dancers': the Lord Mayor 'had besides his Giant, three Pageants', while 'each of the Sheriffes had besides their Giantes but two Pageantes, ech their Morris Dance' (1:102–3).

Coming at the summer solstice and marking the end of the series of major religious feasts extending from Christmas and New Year through Easter, Whitsuntide and Corpus Christi, the Midsummer Watch also inaugurated the secular half of the ceremonial year.[8] London's shrieval election and the confirmation of the Chamberlain, Clerk and chief Sergeant, coinciding with the feasts of John the Baptist and Saints Peter and Paul, began the series of civic events that annually created a new City government – the swearing-in of the Sheriffs on Michaelmas eve, the Michaelmas mayoralty election, and the installation of the new Lord Mayor on the feast of Saints Simon and Jude (29 October) and its morrow. This round of secular events, lasting from June through the end of October, left the new City government in place just in time for it to preside over the semester of religious feasts that began with All Saints on 1 November and then proceeded through Advent, Christmas, New Year's and Lent to Easter and Whitsuntide. Sitting astride the juncture of religious and civic seasons, and enacting a transition between them, the Midsummer Watch combined civic with liturgical observance, policing and secular authority with religious symbolism. Pageants associated with the Watch included religious subject-matter, both biblical figures (such as Jesse, Solomon and Christ's Disputation) and saints (such as Our Lady and St Elizabeth, the Assumption or the local London saint, Thomas à Beckett).[9]

Stow's account of London's traditional Midsummer festivities – and of the 'good amitie amongst neighbores that, being before at controuersie, were there ... reconciled, and made of bitter enemies, louing friends' (1:101) – reads like a textbook example for modern accounts of life in traditional societies. Held in the public space of the streets, involving all

---

[8] On the idea of the ceremonial year, see Mervyn James, 'Ritrual, Drama, and the Social Body in the Late Medieval English Town', *Past and Present* 98 (1983), 3–29.

[9] Jean Robertson and D.J. Gordon eds, *A Calendar of Dramatic Records in the Books of the Livery Companies of London* (Oxford: Malone Society, 1954), pp. xx–xxii.

the social strata of the community, effecting a key transition in communal life and sharing with other rituals the property of quasi-liturgical invariance, the Midsummer festival, as Stow describes it, suspended everyday norms in the sort of anti-structural condition which the anthropologist Victor Turner describes as 'liminality'; it produced what Turner calls 'communitas', a condition of solidarity expressing the deepest and most basic values of the collectivity.[10]

In his account of the discontinuation of the Watch, however, Stow proves to be less a simple source of information about the way that traditional festivals and ceremonial practices organised communal space and time than a key originator of modern narratives about the displacement and transformation of such practices by the political and cultural innovations of the early modern period. 'This Midsommer Watch', Stow explained, 'was thus accustomed yearely, time out of mind, vntill the yeare 1539. the 31. of Henry the 8.', when it was suppressed by royal edict and replaced with a purely military muster. The royal order suppressing the Watch cited the ceremony's excessive costs and the more pressing need for military preparedness in the face of the threat of Catholic invasion, but Stow explained the matter differently. He claimed that it was actually 'the great charges of the Cittizens for the furniture of this vnusuall Muster' imposed by the king that led to the abolition of 'the marching watch prouided for'. The Watch, 'once being laid aside, was not raysed againe till the yeare 1548' (1: 103), when there was a brief attempt to revive it before it was suppressed again in 1549, for reasons to be explained below. Stow was prudently silent on the actual reasons for the suppression of the traditional watch in 1539 – the government's concern over large public assemblies in the wake of the 1536–7 Pilgrimage of Grace and its enforcement of 1538 Injunctions against traditional religious imagery (including the image of the London Saint Thomas à Becket). But there is no mistaking the story Stow meant to tell, a story in which liturgically invariant popular festivals, observed 'time out of mind', were suppressed and replaced from the top down by the modern improvisations of the elite, the Tudor state and the Protestant reformers who were shaping it. Though he was a humble and exceptionally long-lived London tradesman, Stow was also a prodigious autodidact, skilful archivist and subtle polemicist, a Catholic writer whose loyal conformity to the Protestant state religion of his time was balanced by attachment to the Catholic past and by disaffection towards the unprecedented changes in the social, political and economic life of early modern London. Stow's narrative thus anticipates modern scholarly claims about the suppression of popular religious culture by the state-sponsored reformation as well as more general claims about the opposition popular vs. elite culture, practice vs. textuality, ritual vs. commerce.

There is, on the one hand, some support for Stow's narrative in the history of popular London ceremonies, as there also is for Peter Burke's account of early modern popular culture. The discontinuation of the festivities at Midsummer, for example, coincided quite precisely with an escalation in the importance of the purely civic inauguration of the Lord Mayor on the feast of saints Simon and Jude, 29 October. Unlike the Midsummer pageants, those associated with the emerging Lord Mayor's Inaugural Show, sponsored by the guild of the mayor elect, were secular in nature and made use of scripted texts, speeches commissioned at first to local humanists like Nicholas Grimald and the schoolmaster Richard Mulcaster and eventually to leading popular theatre playwrights like George Peele, Anthony Munday, Thomas Dekker and Thomas Middleton. The newfound programmatic eloquence of the Inaugural Show bespeaks a quest for influence and prestige on the part of London's elite magistracy and leading companies of the city. The first Inaugural Show

---

[10]   Victor Turner, 'Liminal to Liminoid in Play, Flow, and Ritual: An Essay in Comparative Symbology', in *From Ritual to Theater: The Human Seriousness of Play* (New York: Performing Arts Journal Publications, 1982), p. 44.

known to have made use of speeches as well as pageants dates from 1541, just after the pageants and processions of the Midsummer Watch began to be suppressed, and the final attempt of a single Catholic alderman to restore the discontinued Watch[11] occurred during the mayoralty of Sir Thomas Roe (1568–9), a staunch Protestant whose inauguration was celebrated in a pageant text written by the learned Mulcaster, first headmaster of the newly founded (1561) Merchant Taylors' School. Mulcaster's speeches – the second earliest such speeches to survive – have St John the Baptist proclaiming the advent of a new and godly order wherein the preaching of the word is bestowed upon the City by the Queen and heard by the Lord Mayor:

> God save oʳ quene oʳ maiden Prince
>   whom he hathe sett in place,
> That Iohn maye preache, yᵗ Roe maye heare
>   The gyftes of heavenly grace
>
> The Courte forbad Iohn ones to speake,
>   A mayden made the meene,
> The Courte nowe biddes Iohn Baptist preache,
>   Vnder our mayden Quene.[12]

In replacing the older Midsummer festivities and in shifting the ceremonial focus from the people and their traditional observances to the prestige of civic hierarchy and the promulgation of its ideological innovations, the emergence of the scripted Inaugural Show might seem to exemplify a series of transitions, from popular pastime to politicised ceremony, from commensality to hierarchy, from the embodied forms of traditional wisdom to their re-inscription as political indoctrination. This transformation of London's ritual life also coincided, in the 1560s and 1570s, with the suppression of the amateur religious cycle plays traditionally performed in communities throughout England and with the nearly simultaneous development of the first purpose-built professional theatres in London.[13] Stow curtly dismissed these modern 'publike places' erected 'of late time in place of' those older 'holy playes' and 'representations of miracles' rehearsed by Fitzstephen or the eight-day performance of 'of matter from the creation of the world' by the London Skinners in Smithfield (1:92–3). Contemptuous of the theatricalised script for the inaugural pageant of the Fishmongers in 1590, and probably of a related public theatre play on *The Life and Death of Jack Straw* (1593), Stow dismissed the Fishmongers as 'men ignorant of their Antiquities' and overly reliant upon a 'fabulous booke' for their account of William Walworth, Fishmonger and Lord Mayor during the 1381 Peasants' Rebellion (1:215). For Stow, the replacement of older London rituals by 'fabulous' theatrical novelties like these belonged with numerous other developments – the transformation of 'open pastimes' into 'worser practices within doores' (1:95), the 'closing in of the common grounds', the creation of commercial establishments like 'bowling Allies, and ordinarie dicing houses' (1:104), the decline of communal participation, the polarisation of society, and the rise of commerce. In all of them, Stow saw popular culture drifting from its sources in tradition.

---

[11] See Lawrence Manley, 'Civic Drama', in Arthur F. Kinney ed., *A Companion to Renaissance Drama* (Oxford: Blackwell, 2002), pp. 294–313.

[12] Jean Robertson and D.J. Gordon eds, *A Calendar of Dramatic Records in the Books of the Livery Companies of London* (Oxford: Mlone Society, 1954), p. 49.

[13] See Harold C. Gardiner, *Mysteries' End: An Investigation of the Last Days of the Medieval Religious Stage* (New Haven: Yale University Press, 1946); Louis Montrose, *The Purpose of Playing: Shakespeare and the Cultural Politics of the Elizabethan Theatre* (Chicago: University of Chicago Press, 1996), ch. 1.

It should be noted, though, that in almost every case where Stow describes a decline of customary holiday, the decline can actually be linked to some popular disturbance on the occasion or to the influence of popular opinion which was itself laying claim to roots in tradition. The decline of May Day began 'by meane of an insurrection of youths against Aliens' in 1517, an apprentice riot of a sort which was actually typical of London's youth community on Shrove Tuesdays and May Days and often reflective of 'the moral economy of the London community'.[14] The parishioners and tenants who sawed up and burned the maypole of St Andrew Undershaft had first assembled for a sermon at Paul's Cross, one of the city's most prominent outdoor pulpits and, along with the pulpit at St Mary Spital (where notable sermons were preached during Easter week), an important venue for holiday sermons. Preaching, like clowning, belonged to an old tradition of oral performance, and Stow clearly saw the clownish element in the performance of this curate who, seeing idolatry in the naming of St Andrew Undershaft for a maypole, 'persawded that the names of Churches might bee altered, ... that the names of the days in the weeke might be changed, the fish days to be kept any days, expect Friday and Saturday, and the Lent any time, saue only betwixt Shrouetide and Easter' (1:144). The Pilgrimage of Grace, which contributed to the decline of London Midsummer assemblies and to the rise of military musters, began as a popular uprising with the shoemaker Nichols Melton and his fellow parishioners of Louth, Lincolnshire, who, like Stow himself, were attached to the trappings of traditional devotion and resentful of religious reform. The re-suppression of the London Midsummer watch in 1549, just a year after attempts to revive it in 1548, followed close on the heels of popular risings in south-west England, and it coincided (in June 1549) with Kett's rebellion, a rising which began at 'a publike plaie kept and Wimondham ... which plaie had beene accustomed yearlie to be kept in that town'. Kett's followers were said to invoke popular sentiment by associating themselves with 'The countrie gnuffes, Hob, Dick and Hick / with clubs and clowted shoone.'[15]

If the old ceremonies were disrupted by popular risings and sentiments, the new ones found ample popular support. For example, the crown-imposed military musters that replaced the Midsummer Watch spawned newly popular activities that continued, in updated form, the archery displays formerly used at Bartholomew-tide.[16] Similarly, the new Inaugural Show, while scripted to extol London's elite, put on display the whole *cursus honorum* of civic officeholding in a processional form which, extending from the humblest apprenticeship through all the echelons of guild life and citizenship, held open the fullest prospect of participation in City life. Written by popular playwrights, performed by celebrity actors and making use of elaborate spectacle, the shows were a beloved adjunct to the popular stage, an institution which itself provided 'an adaptable occasion to defend the common people's perspective'.[17]

This is not just to say that Stow's writing about non-literate popular culture – and other writing like it – is inevitably distorting (though it is), or that Stow, as a writer with a

---

[14] Paul Seaver, 'Apprentice Riots in Early Modern London', in Joseph P. Ward ed., *Violence, Politics, and Gender in Early Modern England* (New York: Palgrave Macmillan, 2008), p. 32; see also Steven R. Smith, 'The London Apprentices as Seventeenth-Century Adolescents', *Past and Present* 61 (1973), 149–61.

[15] Raphael Holinshed, *The Third volume of Chronicles* (1586), fols 1028, 1038; cf. Anthony Fletcher, *Tudor Rebellions* (1968; 3rd ed., London: Longman, 1983), p. 59.

[16] See, for example, *A learned and True Assertion* (1582), sigs A4v–B; Richard Robinson, *The Auncient Order, Societie, and Unitie Laudable, of Prince Arthure ... with a Threefold Assertion friendly in fauour and furtherance of English Archery at this day* (1583), Epistle Dedicatory; Richard Niccols, *Londons Artillery: Briefly Containing the noble practice of that worthie Societie* (1616), pp. 97–101.

[17] Diana E. Henderson, 'From Popular Entertainment to Literature', in Robert Shaughnessy ed., *The Cambridge Companion to Shakespeare and Popular Culture* (Cambridge: Cambridge University Press, 2007), p. 17.

sophisticated intellectual commitment, is religiously partisan in his assessments of popular culture (though he is). It is also to say that early modern representations of popular culture in its traditional, communal form, read carefully, can introduce us to the genuine complications and contradictions to be found within the pastimes and observances themselves. On the one hand, the observances Stow describes were a performative way of regulating the communal life, and the commensality and amity he extols as their effects actually promoted control of London by church and civic authorities. As Victor Turner explains, 'the *communitas* values' associated with ceremony and festivity, expressing the solidarity of the collective group, are 'put into the service of normativeness'. Communal festivals tend to 'set people up'; that is, they 'elevate those of low status before returning them to their permanent humbleness'.[18]

But on the other hand, much of the disruptive modern novelty and social turmoil that Stow associates with the decline of communal spirit was equally an inherent element and product of celebrations in London. Peter Burke draws an implicit contrast between the two when he speaks of popular participation in 'happenings which, if not entirely unplanned, were rather more spontaneous and rather less carefully scripted than the Lord Mayor's Shows'.[19] Yet a description of the 1617 Inaugural Show by the Venetian ambassador to London shows that the popular tumult manifest in spontaneous (and presumably political) 'happenings' was also inherent to formal public celebration:

> On looking into the street we saw a surging mass of people, moving in search of some resting place which a fresh mass of sightseers grouped higgledy piggledy rendered impossible. It was a fine medley: there were old men in their dotage; insolent youths and boys, especially the apprentices alluded to; painted wenches and women of the lower classes carrying their children, all anxious to see the show ... the insolence of the mob is extreme. They cling behind the coaches and should the coachman use his whip, they jump down and pelt him with mud. In this way we saw them bedaub the smart livery of one coachman, who was obliged to put up with it. In these great uproars no sword is ever unsheathed, everything ends in kicks, fisticuffs and muddy faces.[20]

Busino's description, like Stow's account of apprentice rioting on May Day 1517, demonstrates that communal celebration could sometimes include the expression of popular sentiment in the form of political resistance. 'Though not entirely separable from festive practices', this form of popular culture, as Annabel Patterson explains, 'had manifestly non-recreational functions, ... the purposive development of a "popular voice," a self-conscious speaking from below.'[21] The elements of popular performance, mimicry, folk symbolism, song, dance that were part of the ludic permissiveness of festivals allowed for the expression of popular sentiment, criticism of the status quo and the airing of conflicts and controversy within the limits of play and imaginative hypothesis. But as Turner explains, 'the key *communitas* values' promoted by festive events generated common 'metaphors and symbols' which could in turn 'fractionate into sets and arrays of cultural values', thereby creating 'the latent system of political alternatives from which novelties ... arise'.[22] In other words, while promoting solidarity, the practices of festivity could also – very in much keeping with other aspects of urban life – generate multiple understandings of the same event and lead eventually to innovation, differentiation, social variety and outright contestation. Drawing upon the ludic

---

[18]   Turner, 'Liminal to Liminoid', in *From Ritual to Theater*, pp. 45, 25.

[19]   Burke, 'Popular Culture in Seventeenth-Century London', p. 46.

[20]   Allen B. Hines ed., *Calendar of State Papers Relating to English Affairs in the Venetian Archive, Volume 15: 1617–1619* (1909), p. 60.

[21]   Annabel Patterson, *Shakespeare and the Popular Voice* (Oxford: Basil Blackwell, 1989), p. 34.

[22]   Turner, *From Ritual to Theater*, p. 50.

permissions of festive practice, the idea – and sometimes the embodied reality – of popular expression and political dissent was a familiar part of London life. As Brian Manning notes, there were, in support of a variety of causes and grievances, 'at least 96 insurrections, riots and unlawful assemblies in London between 1517 and 1640'.[23]

As published in countless 'complaints', 'supplications', 'petitions', 'homilies' and satires, such popular expression was represented as the authentic voice of the disempowered majority of the 'poor commons', the vast majority of labourers, yeomen and townsmen who belonged neither to the clergy nor the gentry and nobility. In some instances it mostly was – as, for example, in Thomas Deloney's pamphlets and ballads on the grievances of weavers and the shortages of corn in the 1590s,[24] or in some of the political writings of the English Revolution. In other cases, as in the use of the humble persona of Piers Plowman by the protestant clergyman Robert Crowley, or in the adaptation of popular clowning and vernacular expression in the puritan-authored pamphlets attributed to Martin Marprelate, or in the low-vernacular Civil War journalism of Richard Crouch,[25] popular rhetoric and attitudes were mobilised in support of established authority. In publications, as in Stow's account of festivity in London, popular expression cannot be wholly disentangled from the sophisticated written medium that recorded it, nor can it easily be characterised as exclusively traditional or modern, conservative or innovative in its effects. Just as that is perhaps the deeper lesson to be drawn from Stow's narrative about popular festivity in London it is the lesson to be drawn from the popular literature of London as well.

Popular London Literature and the Urbanising Process

Capital of the nation, seat of the royal administration and legal system, centre of trade, engine of economic growth and metropolis of perhaps 200,000 people by 1600, nearing two-thirds of a million by 1700, London was a remarkably diverse and dynamic community. The traditional core of 'the City', the municipality proper, was an established citizenry of craftsmen, retailers and wholesale traders, a high proportion of them literate, who belonged to the City's guilds and leading livery companies. Expansion of international markets elevated some members of this body into a mercantile and political elite, but a majority remained in non-liveried yeoman or journeyman status in their trades; they belonged to what was called 'the middling sort'. The city harboured a large 'youth culture', including a corps of apprentices linked to the guild system and a multitude of domestic servants, male and female, recruited from the often distant countryside. A growing population of casual labourers, petty producers, hawkers, transients and paupers frequented the expanding suburbs outside the city walls. Legal proceedings, business, the marriage market and developing luxury and leisure industries attracted landed gentry to the Westminster and the Strand. It is estimated that in 1590 one-eighth of the English people became Londoners at some point in their lifetimes.[26] They were, said one contemporary, 'by birth for the most part

---

[23]   Brian Manning, *Village Revolts: Social Protest and Popular Disturbances in England, 1509–1640* (Oxford: Clarendon Press, 1988), p. 187.

[24]   See Alexandra Halasz, *The Marketplace of Print: Pamphlets and the Public Sphere in Early Modern London* (Cambridge: Cambridge University Press, 1997), pp. 118–25.

[25]   See David Underdown, '*The Man in the Moon*: Loyalty and Libel in Popular Politics, 1640–1660', in *A Freeborn People: Politics and the Nation in Seventeenth-Century England* (Oxford: Clarendon Press, 1996), pp. 90–111.

[26]   Roger Finlay, *Population and Metropolis: The Demography of London 1580–1650* (Cambridge: Cambridge University Press, 1981), p. 9.

of all countries' of the realm.[27] Coming from such varied backgrounds and representing so many social ranks, the people of early modern London participated in a complex 'urbanising process', a process of adaptation whereby evolving moral and behavioural technologies – working alongside economic and infrastructural developments – organised and equipped the population for cohabitation and co-operation on a massive scale.[28] As essential elements in this process, popular reading and entertainment shaped, and were shaped by, London's manifold possibilities for exchange and combination.

As essential to these possibilities as the growth of London itself was the technology and marketplace of print. The exclusive right of publishers belonging to the London company of Stationers to own and reproduce intellectual 'copy' helped to put into circulation as purchasable commodities perspectives and experiences drawn from, and addressed to, much of what transpired in the urban environment – its streets and places of assembly, its courtrooms, stages, scaffolds, churches, taverns, alehouses and close-packed lodgings. To the extent that London's emerging market for print and popular entertainment 'marked off a new and specialized sense of "culture" as a sphere of activity governed by commerce and distinguished from the practical, moral, and religious imperatives of communal life',[29] it provoked resistance from the elite custodians of those older communal spheres. Clergymen, for example, inveighed against the busy booksellers' stalls in Paternoster Row as a 'confused world of trumpery' where 'every stationers shop, stal, & almost every post, gives knowledge of a new toy'.[30] Many varieties of popular print were condemned in their attacks on 'ballads, books of love, and idle discourses and histories', 'wanton Pamphlets and Promiscuous love-bookes', 'libels, invectives and Satyres', the works of 'Pamphletters and ballad-Writers', of 'Poets, Pipers, and suche peeuishe cattel'.[31] Even while such inventories were meant to characterise a single commercialised popular culture opposed to that of the traditional elite, they actually reveal a marketplace rooted in diversification and variety.

London clergymen objected even more vociferously to the several purpose-built public playhouses – The Theatre (1576), The Curtain (1577), the Rose (1587), the Globe (1599) and The Fortune (1600) that, like several City inns, hosted plays. While protesting the lurid subject-matter of plays, preachers perceived the challenge to their own authority by the new entertainment market: 'God onely gave authority of publique instruction and correction but to two sorts of men: to his Ecclesiastical Ministers and temporal Magistrates. He never instituted a third authority of Players.'[32] Noting, moreover, that 'play is like a sink in a town', clergy and other anti-theatricalists objected to the illicit social mixing of the theatres, the 'unclean assemblies' where 'all sorts, young and old', drawn by 'common minstrels' whose popular trade was in 'masks, vaunting, tumbling, dancing of jigs, galliards, morrises, hobby-horses', formed socially heterogeneous crowds who brought 'the whole Common-weale into disorder'.[33] Their fears were echoed by those of secular authorities, who saw in the

---

[27]   *An Apologie of the Cittie of London*, in Stow, *Survey*, vol. 2, p. 207.
[28]   See Jan de Vries, *European Urbanization, 1500–1800* (Cambridge, MA: Harvard University Press, 1984), p. 14.
[29]   Michael D. Bristol, 'Theater and Popular Culture', in John D. Cox and David Scott Kastan eds, *A New History of English Drama* (New York: Columbia University Press, 1997), p. 244.
[30]   Hugh Holland, *Continued Inquisition*, quoted in Hyder Rollins, 'The Black-Letter Broadside Ballad', *PMLA* 34 (1919), 258–339, at p. 323; Henry Crosse, *Vertues Common-Wealth* (1603), sig. P.
[31]   William Perkins, *A Direction for the Government of the Tongue according to God's Word* (1593), p. 88; Crosse, *Vertues Common-Wealth*, sig. N8; William Vaughn, *The Spirit of Detraction* (1611), sigs. O4, P; Stephen Gosson, *The schoole of abuse* (1579), p. 9.
[32]   I.G., *A Refutation of the Apology for Actors* (1615), pp. 57–8.
[33]   Crosse, *Vertues Common-wealth*, sig. Q1; Philip Stubbes, *The Anatomie of Abuses* (1583), p. 6; Stephen Gosson, *Playes confuted in fiue actions* (1582), sigs E1, G6v; Anthony Munday, *A second and third blast of retrait from plaies and theaters* (1580), p. 44.

popularity of the playhouses 'dailie occasion of the idle riotous and dissolute livinge of great numbers of people, that leavinge all such honest and painfull Course of life, as they should followe, do meete and assemble there … to mispend their time'.[34]

Similar objections to popular writing and theatre can be found among writers themselves, including educated humanists and aristocratic amateurs. William Webbe, for example, contrasted the amateur productions of courtly poets, meant for the 'priuate recreation … of Ladies and young Gentlemen, or idle Courtiers', to 'the uncountable rabble of rhyming ballad-makers', while George Puttenham spoke slightingly of 'small and popular musics sung by these *cantabanqui* [i.e., ballad-sellers] upon benches and barrels' heads' and 'old romances or historical rhymes, made purposely for the recreation of the common people at Christmas dinners and bride-ales, and in taverns and alehouses and such other places of base resort'.[35] Sir Philip Sidney, adhering to the canon of classical literature and discrediting commercial motives, expressed disdain both for the 'mongrel' indecorum of 'mingling kings and clowns' on the popular stage and for the professional writing of 'seruile wits … who think it inough, if they can be rewarded of the Printer'.[36] The laureate ambitions of the poet Ben Jonson, placing him in ambivalent relation to his own career as an actor and popular playwright, led him to say that 'Shakespeare wanted art'.[37] Yet even as such statements purport to distinguish between elite and popular tastes, they also betray an underlying inter-orientation, as writers from a range of social backgrounds and working in different forms, all sought to define their ambitions with reference to, and even by way of, the varieties of popular expression.

It is less useful, therefore, to think of London literature in bipolar terms than to think of it in terms of a spectrum. At the end of the spectrum of closest to traditional popular culture was the broadsheet ballad, printed on the same single sheet that served for civic proclamations and church edicts, selling for less than a penny on average, and sharing the oral and performative features of popular pastimes. Sometimes linked specifically with performers like William Elderton, clowns like Richard Tarlton and William Kemp, and singing ballad-sellers like Stephen Peele or the tavern-keeper Martin Parker, the ballad mediated ludic performance to the wider urban environment, where 'print was everywhere present, posted, exhibited, cried in the streets, and highly visible'.[38] In one respect the printing of ballads divorced them from their musical and social contexts, making them widely available to a varied audience; but on the other hand, printed form was re-deployed in a variety of popular performative settings. Puttenham's 'small and popular musics' were 'sung by these *catabanqui*,' performed 'by blind harpers or such like tavern minstrels', or sung at popular recreations 'in carols and rounds'.[39] The hybridity of orality and print in the ballad form is nicely reflected in the fact that texts were normally printed as 'sung to the tune' of songs omitted from the broadsheet itself, so that both oral transmission of the tune and musical performance were required to fully activate the text. Quickly adapted

---

[34]   Privy Council order 22 June 1600, in E.K. Chambers, *The Elizabethan Stage* (4 vols, Oxford: Clarendon Press, 1923), vol. 4, pp. 330–1.

[35]   William Webbe, *A Discourse of English Poetrie* (1586), in G. Gregory Smith ed., *Elizabethan Critical Essays* (2 vols, 1904; rpt Oxford: Oxford University Press, 1971), vol. 1, p. 246; George Puttenham, *The Art of English Poesy*, ed. Frank Whigham and Wayne A. Rebhorn (Ithaca, NY: Cornell University Press, 2007), p. 173.

[36]   *An Apology for Poetry*, ed. Geoffrey Shepherd (1967; rpt Manchester University Press, 1973), pp. 135, 132.

[37]   *Conversations with William Drummond of Hawthornden* in *Ben Jonson: The Complete Poems*, ed. George Parfitt (New Haven: Yale University Press, 1975), p. 462.

[38]   Roger Chartier, *The Cultural Uses of Print*, in Tessa Watt, *Cheap Print and Popular Piety, 1550–1640* (Cambridge: Cambridge University Press, 1991), pp. 5–6.

[39]   Whigham and Rebhorn, *The Art of English Poesy*, p. 173.

to communicating information, entertainment, protest, advice and instruction – a range of matters that Thomas Middleton termed 'fashions, fictions, felonies, fooleries'[40] – broadsheet publication took up the sorts of news, scandals and calamities that did not exclude audiences for social or religious reasons or, given the low cost of the broadsheet and the possibility for oral transmission, economic reasons either.[41] Bringing the immediacy of oral life into the public realm of print, it prepared the way for public discussion in such pamphlet wars as the Marprelate debate, the feminist polemics of the early seventeenth century and the outpouring of political printing that, during the puritan revolution, transformed London into what John Milton called 'the mansion house of liberty'.

Essential to the development of these later forms of popular print were the Elizabethan playwrights and polemicists, many of them university educated, who worked in the medium of cheap pamphlet publication. Varying in length and format, and costing from twopence to sixpence, the popular pamphlet accommodated writing on numerous subjects, from works of piety, pedagogy and self-improvement to current news and polemic.[42] But in the hands of professionals like the university-educated Thomas Nashe and Robert Greene, who wrote from the literary-social margins of the burgeoning metropolis, the pamphlet became a medium for an innovative style of seriocomic prose that contaminated the learned styles of prose with the colloquial idiom of tavern, marketplace and theatre. Such adaptation, in the case of Nashe's colloquial satires on politics and religion or Greene's immensely popular cony-catching pamphlets, has been described as an 'appropriation' in which popular activities and forms were not just re-purposed but literally 'constructed' in the course of being designed for, and produced and consumed by, the literate elite.[43] In such formulations, where 'popular culture' is understood only as the elite product of such appropriation, the concept is reduced to a mere 'social sign, to refer to a simulacrum existing in early modern social imaginaries created from cultural materials assembled from lower status groups'.[44]

But appropriation can also be described in terms of reciprocation and mutual shaping, including a 'continual reciprocal exchange between oral, scribal, and print culture'[45] and ongoing adjustments across a spectrum of expressive possibilities. Thus the inflection of elite forms by popular language and experience, in the case of Nashe and Greene, could be answered, in turn, by the downmarket adaptation of their work in the pamphlet fictions and fantasias of Thomas Dekker, Samuel Rowlands, Richard Johnson and countless others. The same could be said of the novels of the balladeer and weaver Thomas Deloney, who, adapting the elevated decorum of chivalric romance to a more inclusive social vision and a broader popular readership, made heroes of the 'honest men' – clothiers and shoemakers – whose 'memorable liues' were 'omitted by Stow, Hollinshedd, Grafton, Hal, froysart … and

---

[40]   Thomas Middleton, *The World Tost at Tennis* (1620), in *Works*, ed. A.H. Bullen (rpt, New York: AMS press, 1962), vol. 7, p. 154.

[41]   Natascha Würzbach, *The Rise of the English Street Ballad, 1550–1650*, trans. Gayna Walls (Cambridge: Cambridge University Press, 1990), pp. 17, 25–6, 64–74; Frederick O. Waage, 'Social Themes in the Urban Broadsides of Renaissance England', *Journal of Popular Culture* 11 (1977), 730–42.

[42]   Sandra Clark, *The Elizabethan Pamphleteers: Popular Moralistic Pamphlets, 1580–1640* (Rutherford, NJ: Fairleigh Dickinson University Press, 1983), pp. 17–39.

[43]   See Garrett Sullivan and Linda Woodbridge, 'Popular Culture in Print', in Arthur F. Kinney ed., *The Cambridge Companion to English Literature, 1500–1600* (Cambridge: Cambridge University Press, 1999), p. 269.

[44]   Mary Ellen Lamb, *The Popular Culture of Shakespeare, Spenser, and Jonson* (London: Routledge, 2006), p. 2.

[45]   Mark Jenner, 'London', in Joad Raymond ed., *The Oxford History of Popular Print Culture: Volume 1* (Oxford: Oxford University Press, 2011), p. 296.

all the rest of those wel deseruing writers'.[46] Social inter-orientation was certainly the hallmark of the London theatrical world, whose different venues and repertories – from the upscale indoor private theatres, to leading public theatres like the Globe and the Rose, to downscale ventures like the Hope and the Red Bull – accommodated a variety of audiences and tastes, none entirely homogeneous, and none isolated from the others.

For example (to select a small handful of London city comedies that depict the complexities of the social life and culture of early modern London), Thomas Dekker's *The Shoemaker's Holiday* (1599), Francis Beaumont's *The Knight of the Burning Pestle* (1607), Thomas Middleton's *A Chaste Maid in Cheapside* (1613) and Ben Jonson's *Bartholomew Fair* (1614) all take up the matter and formal properties of the traditional holiday observances extolled by Stow – Shrove Tuesday (Dekker), Lent (Middleton), May Day (Beaumont), Bartholomew-tide (Jonson) – even while they also show these observances to be, like theatre itself, contaminated and enlivened by the commercialising, reforming, secularising and socially diversifying influences lamented by Stow. Social differentiation is reflected to a considerable degree in the backgrounds of the playwrights themselves – Dekker was a popular writer of obscure origin, possibly Dutch; Middleton, the son of a London tiler-become-gentleman, left Oxford without a degree; Beaumont, descended from prominent Leicestershire gentry, was an Oxford graduate and Inns of Court resident, while Jonson was a fatherless Londoner 'brought up poorly' but educated at the elite Westminster grammar school. Some of these playwrights (Dekker and Middleton) tended to write (in John Danby's terms) 'down' Fortune's hill, to audiences comprising lower status groups, while others (Beaumont and Jonson) tended (or at least aspired) to write 'up' the hill, to those more privileged.[47] Moreover, their London comedies were performed by different acting companies at different theatre venues for different combinations of Londoners. *The Shoemaker's Holiday*, one of the last plays to be performed by Lord Admiral's Men at the ageing Rose theatre, belonged to one of the two greatest public theatre companies of the 1590s (both of whom also regularly performed at Court), and despite its focus on London shoemakers, it depended for its full affect on conscious dialogue with Shakespeare's *Henry V*, a property of the rival Lord Chamberlain's Men. *The Knight of the Burning Pestle* was probably performed by the Children of the Queen's Revels at one of the elite indoor private theatres, either the Blackfriars or the Whitefriars. *A Chaste Maid in Cheapside* was performed at the ageing downmarket Swan Theatre by The Lady Elizabeth's Men (a company formed from former boy actors who had once played the elite private theatres) and supplemented by boys recruited from the recently failed Queen's Revels Company. This same hybrid company, after performing *Bartholomew Fair* at the Hope Theatre, a dual-purpose bear-baiting ring that was among London's least savoury theatre venues, took the play to Court the very next day for performance before King James I on the old feast of All Souls, the feast which began the winter holiday season.

Comedy in all of these plays turns on the central question of what Londoners share and what, across various divides, they understand of each other; it depends, in other words, on theatre's orchestration of possibilities of exchange and combination across the social, economic, cultural and geographical boundaries in the early modern metropolis. Boundaries and divisions of all kinds drive the antagonisms and predatory intrigues of these plays. In *The Shoemaker's Holiday*, love affairs thwarted by class antagonisms pitting aristocracy against London citizenry and London craftsmen against gentry finally end in triumph, aided by the ascendancy of Simon Eyre, a legendary shoemaker become Lord Mayor, and by the ludic permissions of comedy – both of them symbolised in the traditional pancake feast of Shrove Tuesday. A London Grocer and his wife and apprentice, out of place in a fashionable theatre

---

[46]   Thomas Deloney, *Kemps nine daies wonder* (1600), sig. D3v.
[47]   John Danby, *Poets on Fortune's Hill* (London: Faber and Faber, 1952), p. 16.

catering to gentry, precipitate a battle of genres and outlooks in *The Knight of the Burning Pestle*, where a clever erotic intrigue, driven by economic motives, collides hilariously with old-fashioned citizen tastes for pageants and chivalry. Starring as the hero in a travesty of popular romance, the Grocer's apprentice is crowned as Lord of the May and leads the London militia in a preposterous muster to Mile End, even while the wily apprentice Jasper Merrythought rises from his coffin to claim the daughter of the wealthy merchant Venturewell. Middleton's *A Chaste Maid in Cheapside* becomes a theatrical counterpart to Breughel's *Battle between Carnival and Lent*, as the grotesque pursuit of flesh in all its forms – from mutton disguised as a baby to the pursuit of offspring through self-cuckoldry – adapts to modern London economy the traditional religious symbolism of Lent and Eastertide, including the apparent resurrection of the dead in a clever coffin trick. Jonson, appropriating the traditional Smithfield fair held Bartholomew-tide, and orchestrating a variety of comic encounters, produces a microcosm of London's intersecting cultures and communities. In all of these cases, popular holidays and festivals of the sort celebrated by Stow combine with modern commerce and transformative social interchange, even as the theatre itself adapts traditional practices to the enterprise of popular entertainment. In keeping with Steven Mullaney's view that London's theatres provided a place for 'the rehearsal of cultures',[48] the social diversity of the theatres, where popular culture combined with commerce, enabled the cultures of London to speak to each other.

By the early to mid-seventeenth century, as cultivation of the pleasures of elite 'Town' life among the urbanising gentry was taking form in self-validating classical genres like the epigram, ode and epistle, and when the development of picturesque genres like the prose character and the droll were reducing popular urban life to a quaint spectacle for elite consumption, there were conspicuous signs of the withdrawal of elite from popular culture that Peter Burke has described.[49] Yet even here, where the shaping of elite values entailed the open cultivation of 'distastes, disgusts provoked by horror of visceral intolerance ... of the tastes of others',[50] the popular tastes, habits and perceptions of common Londoners remained indisputably vital in dialogue with those around them. In a metropolis like early modern London, where economic growth and social development were tied to ever-increasing diversification and specialisation, even the 'effecting of distances' *from* the popular – what might appear immediately as a withdrawal or disassociation – was 'in reality of the elemental forms of socialization',[51] the structuring of differences in a complex urban society. In the urbanising process, which involves so many kinds of 'interaction between the cultural worlds of the educated and the humbler ranks of society', popular culture was a vital but always mobile component.[52]

---

[48]   Steven Mullaney, *The Place of the Stage: License, Play, and Power in Renaissance England* (Chicago: University of Chicago Press, 1988), pp. 69–75.

[49]   See Lawrence Manley, *Literature and Culture in Early Modern London* (Cambridge: Cambridge University Press, 1995), ch. 9.

[50]   Pierre Bourdieu, *Distinction: A Social Critique of the Judgment of Taste*, trans. Richard Nice (Cambridge, MA: Harvard University Press, 1984), p. 50.

[51]   Georg Simmel, 'The Metropolis and Mental Life', in Richard Sennett ed., *Classic Essays on the Culture of Cities* (Englewood Cliffs, NJ: Prentice-Hall, 1969), p. 53.

[52]   Tim Harris, 'Problematising Popular Culture', in *Popular Culture in England, c. 1500–1850* (New York: St Martin's Press, 1995), p. 5.

Select Bibliography

Archer, Ian, *The Pursuit of Stability: Social Relations in Elizabethan London*. Cambridge: Cambridge University Press, 1991.

Bailey, Amanda, and Roze Hentschell, *Masculinity and the Metropolis of Vice*. London: Palgrave Macmillan, 2010.

Beier, A.L., and R. Finlay eds, *London 1500–1700: The Making of the Metropolis*. London: Longman, 1986.

Bristol, Michael, *Carnival and Theater: Plebeian Culture and the Structure of Authority in Renaissance England*. London: Routledge, 1989.

Bucholz, Robert O., and Joseph P. Ward, *London: A Social and Cultural History, 1550–1750*. Cambridge: Cambridge University Press, 2012.

Clark, Sandra, *The Elizabethan Pamphleteers: Popular Moralistic Pamphlets, 1580–1640*. Rutherford, NJ: Fairleigh Dickinson University Press, 1983.

Dillon, Janette, *Theatre, Court, and City, 1595–1610: Drama and Social Space in London*. Cambridge: Cambridge University Press, 2000.

Fumerton, Patricia, *Unsettled: The Culture of Mobility and the Working Poor in Early Modern England*. Chicago: University of Chicago Press, 2006.

Fumerton, Patricia, and Anita Guerrini eds, *Ballads and Broadsides in Britain, 1500–1800*. Farnham, Surrey: Ashgate, 2010.

Griffths, Paul, and Mark S.R. Jenner, *Londinopolis: Essays in the Cultural and Social History of Early Modern London*. Manchester: Manchester University Press, 2000.

Hadfield, Andrew, and Matthew Dimmock eds, *Literature and Popular Culture in Early Modern England*. Farnham, Surrey: Ashgate, 2009.

Halasz, Alexandra, *The Marketplace of Print: Pamphlets and the Public Sphere in Early Modern England*. Cambridge: Cambridge University Press, 1997.

Howard, Jean, *Theater of a City: The Places of London Comedy, 1598–1642*. Philadelphia: University of Pennsylvania Press, 2007.

Lake, Peter, and Michael A. Questier, *The Anti-Christ's Lewd Hat: Protestants, Papists and Players in Post-Reformation England*. New Haven: Yale University Press, 2002.

Manley, Lawrence, *Literature and Culture in Early Modern London*. Cambridge: Cambridge University Press, 1995.

Mardock, James D., *Our Scene Is London: Ben Jonson's City and the Space of the Author*. London: Routledge, 2007.

Munro, Ian, *The Figure of the Crowd in Early Modern London: The City and Its Double*. London: Palgrave Macmillan, 2005.

Newman, Karen, *Cultural Capitals: Early Modern London and Paris*. Princeton: Princeton University Press, 2007.

Raymond, Joad, *Pamphlets and Pamphleteering in Early Modern Britain*. Cambridge: Cambridge University Press, 2006.

Spufford, Margaret, *Small Books and Pleasant Histories: Popular Fiction and Its Readership in Seventeenth-Century England*. Cambridge: Cambridge University Press, 1981.

Twyning, John, *London Dispossessed: Literature and Social Space in the Early Modern City*. London: Palgrave Macmillan, 1997.

Wright, Louis B., *Middle-Class Culture in Elizabethan England*. Chapel Hill: University of North Carolina Press, 1935.

Würzback, Natascha, *The Rise of the English Street Balled, 1550–1650*, trans. Gayna Walls. Cambridge: Cambridge University Press, 1990.

371

Index

All page references for illustrations are in bold.

Act for the Advancement of True Religion 124
*Act for the avoiding of dyvers forreyne wares made by
   handye craftsmen beyonde the seas* 247
Act to Restrain Abuses of Players 20
Agnew, Jean-Christophe 300
alabaster overmantel Burton Agnes Hall, 179, **180**;
   see also plasterwork overmantel
alchemy 318
alcohol 157, 243; *see also* food and drink
Alençon match 253
Allen, Richard 197
Allanson, Elizabeth 21
allegorical designs **91**
almanacs 287–90, 318
Allde, Elizabeth 193
Amadis de Gaule 31
Americas 263
animals 259–60
Andrews, John 190
Anglo, Sydney 46
Appadurai, Arjun 305
Archer, Ian 194
Archer, Jane 47
Archer, John Michael 168, 179, 306
Ardolino, Frank 238
Aristotle 320
Armada 349
Arnold, Janet 239
Ascham, Roger 225, 226, 230
atrocity literature 353–4
Aubrey, John 332

Bacon, Francis 106–7, 314
Bagot Anthony 134
Bailey, Joanne 23
Baker, David 302
Bakhtin, Mikhail 47, 166
Balam, Jone 68
Baldwin, T.W. 104

Bale, John 119
ballads 5, 36, 39, 64, 143, 177–8, 182–91, 214–15,
   256, 350–54, 367; *see also* myth and legend
   and *A woman's work is never done*
ballad-sellers 190–91
Barber, C.L. 43
Barnfield, Richard 144
Barker, William 149
Barrington Court, Somerset 95
Barthes, Roland 305
Bartholomew Fair 157, 175
Baudrillard, Jean 295
Baxandall, Michael 77
Baxter, Richard 35
Bayly, Lewis 196
Bayman, Anna 64
Beaumont, Francis 31, 39–40, 320–21, 369
Becket, Thomas 358, 360–61
Beckwith, Sarah 127–8
Bede, Venerable 283–4
Bedel, Henry 242
beer, *see* food and drink
Behaim, Paul 239–40
Béhar, Pierre 47
Bellany, Alastair 53, 55
Ben-Amos, Ilana 34–5
Bennett, Ronan 22
Bergeron, David 47
Bermuda 175
Bess of Hardwick 1, 235
Best, George 208
Beverley Fair 157
Bevington, David M. 238
Bevis of Hampton 59
bible
   Geneva Bible 63, 64, 352
   Bishop's Bible 63
Biblia Pauperum 94
Bilton, Chris 298

black letter 63–4
Blewett family pew **97**; *see also* Bluett family
    detail from Blewett family pew **97**
Bluett family 95–7
Boleyn, Anne 3, 83
Bolles, George 48
Bonas, Elizabeth 149–50, 154, 157, 159
Bonas, Matthew 157
Bonas, William 149–50, 154, 156–7, 159
book-keeping 302–4
Book of Hours 94
Book of Sports 228
botching, *see* mending
Boudier, Pierre 338
Bowyer, Robert 17
Branton, Isabel 156
Brathwait, Richard 183
Braudel, Fernand 2
Bray, Alan 144
Breton, Nicholas 287, 291–2
Brenner, Robert 164, 171
Brewer, John 298
Bridewell Hospital 194, 201, 203–4
Bridget of Sweden 71
Bridgen, Susan 123
Brinsley, John 215
Bruegel, Pieter (the Elder) 3, 222, **222**, 259, 370
Bruster, Douglas 300
Bucket, Rowland 48
Buckingham, Duke of 27, 51
Budé, Gulliaume 349
Bullein, William 242
Bullokar, John 107
Bunyan, John 35
Burbage, Richard 193
Burdas, Elizabeth 157–8
Burke, Peter 1, 15, 20, 41, 47, 104–5, 117, 124–5,
    137, 177, 211, 238, 271–2, 338, 357–8, 361,
    370
Burnett, Mark 31, 39
Burt, Richard 306
Burton, Robert 39, 229
Bush, Douglas 104
Busino, Orazio 49–50
Butler, Samuel 113
Byrd, William 4

Cahn, Susan 239
calendars 285–6
Calthorpe, Elizabeth 81
Calvert, George 54
Cambridge 21
Camden, William 112, 116
Campion, Edmund 195
The Canterbury Tales 40

Capp, Bernard 203–4
cast-iron fireback 92–4, **93**; *see also* Lenard fire-back
Castiglione, Baldassare 224, 341
Carleton, Mary 34
Cartari, Vincenzo 108
Cartwright, Kent 237
carved exterior of Bishop Lloyd's House, Chester
    98, 99–100 ; *see also* Lloyd, George
    detail of carved exterior of Bishop Lloyd's
        House **99**
Catherine of Siena 71
Catholic, Catholicism, 253–4, 262, 270, 290, 332,
    343, 359, 361
Cavendish, Margaret 316
Caxton, William 106–8, 343; *see also The Golden*
    Legend and *Morte Darthur*
Cecil, William 334, 354
censorship 280
Certeau, Michel de 14, 155–6
Challoner, Jacob 48
chapbooks 59–60
Chapman, George 39, 263
charity 158
Charles I 254, 264, 267, 342, 354
Charles, Prince 51, 54
Chartier, Roger 5, 269
Chastleton House 81
Chaucer, Geoffrey 120, 257, 339
Chaytor, Miranda 23, 25
Chester, Robert 107–8
children 180
    Children of the Revels 31
Christ's College, Cambridge 237
Christian of Denmark 45
Churchyard, Thomas 258–9, 345–6
Cicero 343
city comedies 369
City of London 52
City Waits 49
Civil Wars 253–4, 263–6, 268, 273–5, 334, 349–50,
    353
Clare of Assisi 71
Clark, Emma 149–51
Clark, Stuart 324
Clarke, William 19
Clarke, Sir William 62
Clint, Edward 149–51, 157–8
clocks 285
Clopper, Lawrence 43
Cockaigne, Land of 259–60, 263
Cockeram, Henry 107
Coleman, Joyce 15
Collinson, Patrick 76, 83, 126
cony-catching pamphlets 170
colonialism, *see* work and xenophobia

Colwell, Thomas 237
commonplace books 62
Commons, House of 260, 275, 277
Commons Journal 16–17
conduct books 224
Conti, Natale 108
Cooper, Katerin 68–9
Cooper, Thomas 108–9
Cotgrave, John 38
Court of Chivalry 79
courtship, sex and marriage 133–47
    clandestine weddings 139–40
    conflict 140
    masturbation 146
    number of marriages 139
    privacy 135
    prostitution 143–4
    sexuality 141–5
    verbal contract 138
    wedding ceremony 139–40
Coventry 44
Cressy, David 44, 51, 52, 54–6, 61, 137–44
Cromwell, Oliver 276, 354
Cromwell, Thomas 256
Cries of London 188–90, **188**
crime 193–205
    child abuse 202
    Courts of Assize 195
    murder 199
    punishment 195–8
        prison 201
    rape 199
    statistics 198–201
    theft 193–4, 196–7
        horse theft 199
        poaching 196–7
    violent assault 197–8
    witchcraft 199
Crimes in the Middlesex County Sessions
    1549–1609 199, **200**
Crossman, Samuel 37
Crouch, Nathaniel 37
Crowley, Robert 257
The Cryes of the City of London Drawne after the Life
    189, 190
Culpepper, Nicholas 331–2
Cummings, Brian 124, 126
cunning-women 313–14

The Dacre Beasts (London, Victoria and Albert
    Museum) 80–81, **80**
Dacre, Lord Thomas 80
Dafforne, Richard 302–4
Danby, John 369
Davies, Owen 329

Daybell, James 306
Deane, Roger 149
Davidson, Clifford 44
Davis, Leonard 71
Davis, Natalie Zemon 271–2
Dee, John 62
Dekker, Thomas 170, 174, 179, 202, 212, 230, 231,
    286, 287–8, 361, 368, 369
Delony, Thomas 113, 365, 368
Deng, Stephen 305
Denham, Henry, device and imprint from John
    King, *Lectures upon Jonas* **90**; *see also*
    King, John
Denning, James 149
Derrida, Jacques 14
D'Ewes, Simonds 53, 55
Devereux, Robert *see* Essex, second Earl of,
Dickens, A.G. 120–21
diet, *see* food and drink
Digby, George 270
Diggers 274–5, 278
Digges, Leonard and Thomas 288, 349
Dimmock, Matthew 43, 48
Dobranski, Stephen 62
Dolan, Frances E. 140–41, 145
Donaghan, Barbara 349
Donne, John 13, 126, 136, 288
Dowd, Michelle 186, 305
Drake, Sir Francis 229
Draper's Company 112
drink, *see* food and drink
Drunkenness 50
Duffy, Eamon 121–2, 127
Duncan, Douglas 237–8
Dutch Church Libel 217–19
Dutch wars 347–50

East India Company 158
economics 295–9
Eden, John 157
Edward VI 324, 342
Egerton, John 62
Eisenstein, Elizabeth 121, 124
Elector Palatine 45
Elias, Norbert 161
Eliot, T.S. 1
Elizabeth I 1, 2, 83–4, 95, 112, 115, 187–8, 228,
    235, 239, 263, 314, 342, 359
Elizabeth, Princess 45
Elizabeth Tudor 235
Ellinghausen, Laurie 173
Elton, G.R. 120–21
Elyot, Sir Thomas 224, 226, 317–18
enclosure 172, 273–5,
equivocation 262

Erasmus, Desiderius 13, 103–5, 108, 111, 123–4,
    126, 343–4
Erickson, Amy Louise 181
Essex, Second Earl of, 255, 348
Euhemerus 111
Evett, David 168
Evil May Day 217, 219

Farrington, John 160
feminist polemic 368
Ferguson, Margaret 61
Ferne, John 33
Festivals 43–57, 287, 360–61
    allegory 44
    critical approaches 46–8
    festival in action 48–56
    genre 43–6
    materiality 54
    print 45
    ritual year 44
    royal entries 45
    street pageantry 47, 360–61
Field, Nathan 202
Finchingfield 18
Fire of London 215–16
Fisher, Will 241
Flandrin, Jean-Louis 153
Fletcher, Anthony 36, 275
Fletcher, John 320–21
Fliegen, Eve 65–8, 71–2
Fogel, Robert 155
food and drink 149–62, 318
    beer 154
    calories 155
    cook-books 151
    famine 150
    food riots 154
    herring 149–51, 162
    historiography 151–2
    hunger 155
    legal testimony 152
    place and space 155–60
    political economy 153–5
        British imperialism 153
        European trade 153–4
    poor relief 154
    sociability 150
    taste 161–2
    tobacco 157
The Forge at Much Hadham 95
Forman, Simon 314, 329–30
Forman, Valerie 301
Fortune Theatre 49; *see also* playhouses
Foucault, Michel 141, 167
Fox, Adam 61

Foxe, John 72, 120, 124
Freud, Sigmund 295
*The Friers Chronicle: Or, The True Legend of Priests
    and Monkes Lives* 108
Frobisher, Martin 208
Fruiterers' Company 90
Frye, Susan 235
Fuller, Thomas 180, 227
funeral monuments 79

Galen 317–18
Games 221–33
    bowling 228–9
    chess 229–30
    definitions and history 221–3
    football 227–8
    hazard 226
    holidays 227
    hunting 226–7
    Primero 230–32
    social hierarchy 224
    space 223–4
    tennis 225–6
    time 223
Gammer Gurton's Needle 6, 236–49
Garrioch, David 88
Garton, William 195
Gascoigne, George 173, 347
Gaskill, Malcolm 20, 325–7
gender, *see also* work and mending
Geoffrey of Monmouth 112
Georgian calendar 223
Gerard's Herbal 321
Gillespie, Stuart 177
Ginzberg, Carlo 126
Giraldi, Lilio Gregorio 108
Globe Theatre 196, 205, 229; *see also* playhouses
Goade, Thomas 108
Goose, Nigel 216–17
Gosson, Stephen 179
Glibery, William 18
The Golden Legend 105, 108, 117; *see also* Caxton
Goldie, Mark 255
Goldring, Elizabeth 47
Googe, Barnabe 290
Gorboduc 260–61
Gordon, Andrew 88, 91–2
Gowing, Laura 20–21, 23
Grafton, Anthony 62
Grazia, Margreta de 245
Great Yarmouth 248
Green, Ian 124–5
Greene, Robert 170, 193, 368
Greenblatt, Stephen 15, 128, 166
Gregorian calendar 283

Griffiths, Paul 21–2, 31, 56
Grimald, Nicholas 361
Grimm brothers 5
Grocer's Company 48–50
Grotius, Hugo 13
Gunpowder Plot 262
Gurr, Andrew 260
Gustavus, Adophus 352
Guy of Warwick 59

haberdashery, *see* mending
Hadfield, Andrew 43, 48, 279
Haigh, Christopher 122
Hakewill, George 65
Hale, Sir Matthew 24
Hall, Edward 210
Hall, Lesley 143
Halpern, Richard 170
Halstead 18
Hamling, Tara 179
Harkins, Matthew 32
Harkness, Deborah 310
Harper, Sir William 112
Harrington, Sir John 231, 232–3
Harris, Jonathan Gil 300–301
Harris, Tim 338
Harrison, Peter 67
Harrison, Stephen 45
Harrison, William 15, 170, 207, 209
Harvard House, Stratford upon Avon 86
Harvey, Gabriel 62
Hatfield House 2
Hathway, Richard 114
Haughton, William 260
Hawkes, David 301
Hawkins, Francis 37
Head, Richard 39
Helgerson, Richard 173
Henderson, Frances 19
Henry VIII 3, 225, 227, 255, 264, 341, 344
Henry, Prince 45, 348
Henslowe, Philip 114, 239, 198, 202
herring, *see* food and drink
Herring, Francis 309, 316
Hexter, J.H. 17
Heywood, Thomas 39, 110–11, 113, 202, 313
The high and mighty Prince Charles…his happy returne, and hearty welcome 51
Hildegard of Bingen 319
Hindle, Steve 26–7, 56, 274
Hinds, Hillary 277
Hippocrates 319
Hiscock, Andrew 238
Hobbes, Thomas 13–14
Hocus Pocus Junior 38

Hodgson, Edward 149, 152
Hoefnagel, Joris 2–4
Hogarth, William 90–91
Holcombe Rogus, Devon 95
holidays 363
Holland, Philemon 105
Holinshed, Raphael 167
Holme, Randle, 87–9, **89**
homilies, Elizabethan 254–5
Hopkins, Matthew 325–6, 333
Hoskins, Anne 20
hospitality 80, 158; *see also* visual culture
Houlbrooke, Ralph 133–4, 139
House of Commons 16, 27
Hoxby, Blair 301
Hubbersted, Rowland 20–21
Hughes, Lewis 248
Huizinga, Johan 221
humours 317–18 *see also* Galen
Hunter, Barbara 21
hunting, *see* games
Huss, Jan 120
Hutson, Lorna 238, 179
Hutton, Sir Richard 35

Inns of Court 46
Ingram, Jill Philips 301
Ingram, Martin 195
Isham, Elizabeth 247

James IV and I 55–6, 253, 255, 261, 226, 228, 333, 342, 348, 369
James, William 125
James of Vitry 71
Jardine, Lisa 62
Jeaffreson, J.C. 198–201
Jolles, Sir John 112
Jones, Ann Rosalind 235, 241
Jones, Walter 81–3
Jonson, Ben 34, 39, 51, 136, 157, 175, 198, 202, 231–2, 263, 301, 367, 369, 370
Josselin, Ralph 310–11, 318
Joyce, Patrick 179
Julian of Norwich 71
Junius, Franciscus 64

Kastan, David Scott 166
Katritsky, M.A. 315–16
Kempe, Margery 71
Kennix, Margaret 314
Kermode, Jenny 195
Kerridge, Eric 164–5
Kerwin, William 314
Keyser, Peter 106
King, Gregory 163–4, 169

King, John 90; *see also* Denham, Henry
King's Bench 195–6
King's Men 196
Kingsley-Smith, Jane 108
Kipling, Gordon 47
Kirkman, Francis 34, 39
Kitch, Aaron 301
Knights, L.C. 164
Korda, Natasha 239, 187–8, 305
Kyle, Chris 17

labour, *see* work
Lake, Peter 127–8
Lamb, Mary Ellen 185
Lambeth Palace 120
The Lamentable Tragedy of Locrine 114–15
Lancashire, Anne 43
Landreth, David 305
Langland, William 257–8
Laqueur, Thomas 141
Laslett, Peter 165, 168
Latour, Bruno 245
Laud, Archbishop William 51, 267
Lawrence, D.R. 348, 352
Leinwand, Theodore 301
Leland, John 107, 112, 340
Lenard fireback 92–4; *see also* cast-iron fireback
Lenard, Richard 92–4; *see also* cast-iron fireback
        and Lenard fireback
Lenton, Francis 33–4, 40
Levant Company 154, 158
Levellers 264–6, 274–9
Lever, J.W. 262
libels 54–5
Lilburne, John 267, 270, 276–7
Lilham, Jane 21
Linche, Richard 108
Lindemann, Mary 310, 312, 317
Lipsius, Justus 349
literacy 4; *see also* reading and writing
        bible 61
Llewellyn, Nigel 79
Lloyd, George 99; *see also* carved exterior of
        Bishop Lloyd House
Llwyd, Humphrey 112
Lodge, Thomas 319
Lollards 122
London 357–71
Long Meg of Westminster 202–4
Lord Mayor's Show 47–50, 112, 158, 361, 364
Lowth, William 187
Lucy, Sir Thomas 197
Luther 126
Lydgate, John 283–4
Lyly, John 313

Lynch, Kathleen 126–7
Lyotard, Jean-Francois 295

MacGregor, Neil 306
Macpherson, C.B. 298
McFarlane, K.B. 340
McLuhan, Marshall 14
McRae, Andrew 53, 55
McShane, Angela 352
Magnus, Albertus 319–21
Maguire, Laurie 19
Maltby, Judith 124
Malton, Robert 149, 152
Manning, Brian 365
Manning, Roger 272
Marlowe, Christopher 144, 193, 197, 219
Marprelate Tracts 18, 62, 202, 365, 368
marriage, *see* courtship, sex and marriage
Marshall, Stephen 18
Marston, John 39, 263
Marvell, Andrew 159–60
Marx 171
Mary I 341
Mary, Countess of Pembroke 236
Mary Queen of Scots 1, 113, 235, 254
May Day 210–11, 363–4, 369
May, Thomas 268
medicine 309–22
Meisel, Perry 1
mending 235–50
        bodkins 246
        clothing and status 242–4
        cost of apparel 241
        historical record 237
        needles 238, 244–9
        needles, supply of 248
        pins 246, 247
Merchant Taylors' Company 91, 173, 239
Meurs 65
Middleton, Thomas 48–56, 183, 213, 229–30, 232,
        288–9, 296, 361, 368, 369–70
Midland Rising 273
Midsummer Watch 44
migrants 171; *see also* xenophobia
military culture 337–55
Miller, Daniel 305
Milton, John 116, 126, 141, 253, 301, 368
Mitchell, W.J.T. 91–2
More, Thomas 123, 126
Morineau, Michel 155
Morral, Andrew 95
Morrill, John 17, 19
Morte Darthur 107
Morton, Robert 339
Mulcaster, Richard 361–2

Muldrew, Craig 155, 174, 299
Mullaney, Steven 370
Mulryne, J.R. 47–8
Munday, Anthony 115, 211, 361
myth and legend 103–29
    definition 105–8
    drama 105, 109
    grammar schools 103–4
    King Arthur 112–15
        ballads 113; *see also* ballads
        pageants 115
        plays 114–15
    pageants 111–12

Nantwich 26
Nashe, Thomas 263, 284, 286, 368
Naworth Castle 81
needlework, *see* mending and textiles
Nelthorpe, Edmond 159–60
Newcomb, Lori Humphrey 60
Newgate Gaol 194, 201
Nicholas, Edward 213
Nichols, John 46
Nicholson, Ellen 20
Nonsuch Palace 2
Norman Yoke 274
Norden, John 172
Northern Rebellion 254
    rebellion 199
Norton, Benjamin 50
Norwich 44, 112
Norwood, Richard 35

Old Bailey 24
The Old Merchant's House, Great Yarmouth
    84–6
Ong, Walter 14–15
oral culture 287–8, 367
Orlin, Lena Cowen 181
Ospringe, Thomas 247–8
Ovid 33–4, 103–5, 110, 143

Packwood House 86
Palmer, Mary 159
Palmerin of England 31
pamphlets 313, 366
Paracelsis 318
Parker, Sir Henry 81
parliament 275, 352
Partridge, John 151
Patterson, Annabel 364
Paster, Gail Kern 244–5
pawnbroker 242
Peacey, Jason 59
Peacham, Henry 81, 83

pedlars 158
Peele, George 361
Pelling, Margaret 310
Pepys, Samuel 62, 311–12, 318
performers 367
Perry, Curtis 247
Pettegree, Andrew 62
Phelips, Sir Edward 81
Phelips, Sir Robert 16
Physicians and Barber-Surgeons, College of
    309–10, 317, 318
Piers the Plowman 4, 120, 365
Pilgrimage of Grace 253, 255–6, 266, 361, 363
Pilkington, James 239
The Pinder of Wakefield 39
plague 318–19
plasterwork overmantel, Barrington Court 95, **96**;
    see also alabaster overmantel Burton
    Agnes Hall
plasterwork overmantel, Harvard House **86**
plasterwork overmantel, Packwood House 86–7,
    87
plasterwork overmantel, St Nicholas Priory **84**
Platt, Hugh 196
playhouses 39, 239, 222–3, 366–7, 369; *see also*
    Fortune Theatre, Rose Theatre and
    Globe Theatre
Plautus 237
Pliny 320
poor relief, *see* food and drink
pornography 145
Porter, Roy 143
Powell, Thomas 182
Plutarch 105
political culture 4
politics 253–66
Portsmouth 51
Powell, Vavasour 35
Pratt, Millicent 158
Proceedings in Parliament 17
property 295–307
prostitutes 242; *see also* courtship, sex and
    marriage
Protestants, Protestantism, 262, 343, 348, 361
proverbs 287
Prynne, William 267
Purchas, Samuel 107
purse, embroidered with heraldic shields 81, **82**;
    see also visual culture
Putney debates 19
Puttenham, George 225, 367

Quakers 158
Questier, Michael 123, 128
Quilligan, Maureen 245

Rabelais, François 222, 230
Rainborough, Colonel Thomas 19–20
Rampley, Matthew 78
Raymond, Joad 59–60, 306
Ravenscroft, Thomas 6, 337
reading and writing 59–73
    eyewitnesses 67
    fasting maidens 65–72
    hagiography 71–2
    hybridity 60, 66–8
    literacy 61–2; see also literacy
    material history 59
    politics 68
    popular print 62–4
Reames, Sherry 106
Reay, Barry 329
Red Bull Theatre 110, 117; see also Fortune
    Theatre and playhouses
Reformation 256–7, 285, 332, 344
religious belief 119–29
    conversion 125
    historiography 119–23
    literary sources 126–7
        spiritual autobiography 126–7
    print 123–5
    theatre 128
Rich, Barnaby 345–7, 349
The Return from Parnassus, Part Two 104
Reynolds, John 65
riot and rebellion 267–81
Rhodes, Neil 177
Riche, Barnaby 204
Robbins, Bruce 167–8
Robins, Thomas 69–72
Rochester, Alice 21
Rocke, Michael 144
Rogers, Thomas 86
roman type 64
Rose Theatre 203; see also playhouses
Rosenthal, Laura J. 301–2
Rossel, John 239
Rowe, Nicholas 196–7
Rowlands, Samuel 242, 223
Rowley, William 114
Ruff, Julius 227
Rutter, Tom 163
Ryder, Sir Dudley 24
Ryrie, Alec 122

Sabean, David 28
St Bartholomew's Day Massacre 199
St John's College, Cambridge 104
St Margaret in Tivetshall 83
St Mary's Church 4
St Nicholas Priory in Exeter 84

St Paul's School 103
Sawyer, Elizabeth 328, 333
Scots, Scotland 263–4
Saunders, J.W. 172–3
Scot, Reginald 332
Scott, James 26
Scott, Thomas 56, 213
Scribner, Robert 25–7, 338
Scudéry, Madeleine de 70
Sell, Jonathan 209
Selwood, Jacob 212
servants, see work
sex 185, 318; see also courtship, sex and marriage
Shagan, Ethan 122–3, 255–6
Shakespeare, William 33, 109–10, 133–6, 139–40,
    144–5, 173, 175, 183, 184–5, 186, 191, 193,
    196–7, 201, 204–5, 209–10, 211, 225–6,
    230, 262–3, 284, 290–93, 314, 339–40
Sharp, Buchanon 272
Sharpe, J.A. 194
Shell, Alison 128
Shepard, Alexandra 21, 41
Sherman, William 62
Shewring, Margaret 47
Shirley, Sir Thomas 79–81
Shrove Tuesday riots 32, 38, 369
Sibbes, Richard 35
Sidney, Philip, 260 173, 186, 226, 348, 367
Simpson, James 127
Simpson, Eizabeth 158
Smith, Adam 174
Smith, Bruce 182
Smith, Elizabeth 239
Smith, George 85
Smith, John 86
Smith, Captain John 175
Smith, Margaret 86
Smith, Ralph 86
Smith, Steven 35–6
Smith, Sir Thomas 156, 169, 247, 344–5
Smuts, R. Malcolm 47
Smyth, Adam 306
Snell, Esther 24
Spanish match 213
Speculum Humanae Salvationis 94
speech acts 13–29
    ballad-singing 15
    bible 13
    civil conversation 13–14
    gossip 27
    law courts 20–25
    parliament 16–17
    public shaming 21
    sermons 17–19
    shorthand 19–20

Spenser, Edmund 126, 226, 260, 289–90
Sports and Pastimes: Or, Sport for the City and
    Pastime for the Country 37–8
Spufford, Margaret 36, 63
Stallybrass, Peter, 47, 235, 241, 245
Star Chamber, court of, 267, 269
Stationers' Company 287
Staves, Susan 298
Steen, Sara Jane 262
Statute of Artificers 167, 169–70
Stevenson, William 237
Stone, Lawrence 25, 136–9, 143, 145, 165
Stourbridge fair 157
Strafford, Thomas 270
Stow, John 230, 358–65, 370
Stretton, Jane 65
Strong, Roy 46
Stuart, Arbella 261
Strype, John 208
Sullivan, Ceri 301
Sullivan, Garrett A. 306
sumptuary laws 80
Swathmoor Hall 186
Syme, Holger 23

Tadmor, Naomi 156
Tallis, Thomas, 4
taste, *see* food and drink
Taverner, Thomas 4
Tawney, R.H. 164–5
Taylor, John 52–4, 235–6, **236**, 240, 246
Taylor, Martha 65, 69–72
Terence 237
textiles, 179, 183–4, 188; *see also* mending
theatre, public 260–64
Thomas, David 240
Thomas, Keith, 113
Thomason, George 62
Thompson, E.P. 166–7, 272
Tilley, Charles 272
time 283–94
Tittler, Robert 92
tobacco, *see* food and drink
Tomson, Laurence 64
Tower of London 4
Traub, Valerie 144
Trim, David 348
Trowlop, John 158
Trumbull, William 53
Trundle, Margery 190
Turner, Richard 33, 37
Tusser, Thomas 240–41
Tyndale, William 119, 123, 126
tyrant, tyranny 262

Underdown, David 272, 274
utopia, utopias 263
Udall, Nicholas 183
Uttinge, John 248

vagrants 170
Vale, Humphrey 240
visual culture 75–101
   heraldry 78–100
     biblical imagery 94–100
     chimney pieces 81–3
     firebacks 92–4
     heraldic sculpture 80–81
     hospitality 80; *see also* hospitality
     ornament 78
     purse 81
     royal arms 83–8
     trade signs 88–91
Virginia Company 175
Voragine, Jacobus de 105–6
Vries, Jan de 153

Walker, Garthine 23, 25, 195
Walker, John 28
Wall, Wendy 243, 245, 184
Walsham, Alexandra 122, 127
Walsingham, Francis 314
Walter, John 272
Wanley, Nathaniel 65
Ward, Samuel 17
Warren, Austin 5
Wars of the Roses 253, 339, 341
Watermen's Company 54
Watson, Thomas 158
Watt, Tessa 4, 63, 123, 125–6, 128, 269, 338
Wantanabe-O'Kelly, Helen 47
Webbe, William 367
Weber, Max 127, 298
Webster, John 173, 261
Wellek, René 5
Wells-Cole, Anthony 78
Wentworth, Peter 260
Wentersdorf, Karl 211–12
Westminster Abbey 107
Whewell, William 14
White, Allon 47
Whitelock, Bulstrode, 277, 279
Whiting, Robert 123
Wilde, Henry 48
Williams, Raymond 296
Williamson, Elizabeth 128
Wilson, Margery 158
Wilson, Thomas 19
Winchester Grammar School 104

Winstanley, William 65
Wiseman, Susan 271
witchcraft 323–36
Withington, Richard 46
Wittgenstein, Lugwig 221
A woman's work is never done 177–8, **178**, 182, 184;
    see also ballads
Womersley, David 128
Wood, Andy 27–8, 256–7
Wood, Anthony 62
Wood, Ellen 164
Woodbridge, Linda 170, 300
Woolf, Daniel 15
Woolley, John 53
work 163–76
    citizens 168–9
    class 165
    colonialism 162, 165–6, 174–5
    gendered labour 177–92; *see also* gender and
        textiles
        ale-wives 190–91
        wetnursing 187
        woman sellers 188
    intellectual labour 163–4
    labour history 163–7
    professional authors 172–4
    rural labour 171–2
    servants 168
    unemployment 164
    urban labour 167–72
Worshipful Company of Needlemakers 244, 247;
    see also mending

Wright, John 193
Wrightson, Keith 56
Wyatt, Thomas 126
Wycherley, William 35
Wycliffites 120
Xenophobia 207–20
    anti-alien riots 210
    anti-Catholicism 214–15
    French 207
    immigration 212–13
    Inuits 208–9
    Protestant refugees 208
    Scottish 214

Yates, Julian 245
York 149–50, 157
Young, G.M. 28
Youth Culture 31–42, 365–6
    romance fiction 31–2
    textual representation 32–6
    popular texts 36–40
    misrule 38–9
    tavern 39
    popular culture 40–41
Youths Tragedy 37
Youth's Treasury, or, A Store-House of Wit and
    Mirth 37
Youths Warning-Piece 37

Zemon Davis, Natalie 6, 22, 38–9
Zodiac, Signs of 318
Zurcher, Amelia 70